KEYS TO
BETTER
COLLEGE
READING

The Other Books in the Townsend Press Reading Series:

GROUNDWORK FOR COLLEGE READING
TEN STEPS TO BUILDING COLLEGE READING SKILLS, FORM A
TEN STEPS TO BUILDING COLLEGE READING SKILLS, FORM B
TEN STEPS TO IMPROVING COLLEGE READING SKILLS
TEN STEPS TO ADVANCING COLLEGE READING SKILLS
IMPROVING READING COMPREHENSION SKILLS

Books in the Townsend Press Vocabulary Series:

GROUNDWORK FOR A BETTER VOCABULARY
BUILDING VOCABULARY SKILLS
IMPROVING VOCABULARY SKILLS
ADVANCING VOCABULARY SKILLS
BUILDING VOCABULARY SKILLS, SHORT VERSION
IMPROVING VOCABULARY SKILLS, SHORT VERSION
ADVANCING VOCABULARY SKILLS, SHORT VERSION

Supplements Available for Most Books:

Instructor's Edition
Instructor's Manual, Test Bank and Computer Guide
Set of Computer Disks (Apple, IBM, or Macintosh)

KEYS TO BETTER COLLEGE READING

Carol H. Bader
MIDDLE TENNESSEE STATE UNIVERSITY

Harley F. Anton
MIDDLE TENNESSEE STATE UNIVERSITY

TOWNSEND PRESS   Marlton, NJ 08053

For our parents

Send book orders and requests for desk copies or supplements to:

Townsend Press
1038 Industrial Drive
Berlin, New Jersey 08009

For even faster service, call us at our toll-free number:
1-800-772-6410

Or FAX your request to:
1-609-753-0649

ISBN 0-944210-65-1

Contents

PART II
Intermediate Readings   127

PART III
Longer Readings   335

PART IV
Making Reading a Habit   561

Preface to the Instructor

One needs to read to become a skilled reader. That is the central principle of *Keys to Better College Reading*. The book emphasizes reading itself because many students taking a college reading course have done little reading in their lives. They are unpracticed readers who have never gotten into the habit of regular reading.

Perhaps they grew up in homes where a television set dominated the household, and there was little in the way of books or reading matter. Perhaps they got off to a bad start in reading courses in school and then never seemed to catch up. Most of all, perhaps there was never a point in their lives when they discovered the pleasure of reading for its own sake. They never learned what it is like to be caught up in the excitement and joy of the special world that reading can provide. As a result of these or other reasons, reading became an artificial and unpleasant activity rather than a natural and easy one.

For people who are not good readers, there is one main key to becoming a better reader. That key, startlingly simple as it might sound, is to do a great deal of reading. The truth of the matter is that **reading is like any other skill. The more one practices, the better one gets.** The latest reading research supports this point of view. In *The Power of Reading: Insights from the Research* (Libraries Unlimited, Inc., 1993), Stephen Krashen surveys an extensive number of studies, many of them recent, and concludes that reading itself is the "way that we become good readers." The primary goal of this book, then, is to provide students with abundant reading practice.

Towards this end, many of the forty selections in the book are of intermediate or longer length. Included are entire chapters from a few popular books and several long, highly readable pieces from magazines. The intermediate selections appear in Part II of the book. They are arranged on five levels of difficulty, with five selections written on Level A, the easiest level; five selections on Level B, a slightly more difficult level; and so on through the five selections in Level E, the most difficult level. The long selections appear in Part III, and these selections, for the most part, are arranged in order of increasing difficulty.

A special effort has been made to provide truly interesting readings—ones that will catch students up in a writer's experience. As teachers, we know what it is like to read for pleasure. All of us have been drawn into the magic of worlds that authors can create. We want our students to experience some of that magic. If they are touched by it, reading can be transformed into something other than the classroom drudgery that it may have been in the past. More importantly, if they experience some of that magic, they may themselves go on to develop the habit of reading.

Reading for its own sake has long been an integral part of our reading program at Middle Tennessee State University. We inform entering students that they must read four or more books to pass the reading course in which they have been placed. In addition, we tie the number of pages read into the grade they want to earn:

1200 pages to be eligible for a C;
1800 pages to be eligible for a B;
2400 pages to be eligible for an A.

Upon learning so much reading is expected, students often react as if we have just detonated a bomb in the classroom. Many of them have not read a single book in the past year. Now they are expected to read four or more books—in addition to doing the work required in the reading comprehension skills part of the course! But after the shock wears off, students do what they need to do. By the end of the semester, there are seldom students who complain that we have made them do too much reading. They realize that all the reading has helped them become more practiced and assured readers. In some cases, they have cultivated a habit that stands a fair chance of being part of the rest of their lives.

In addition to abundant practice, there are other keys to becoming a successful reader. These keys are the six essential reading comprehension skills that we present in Part I of the book:

- Recognizing vocabulary in context;
- Locating main ideas;
- Understanding supporting details;
- Identifying transitions;
- Making inferences;
- Outlining and summarizing.

Each reading in the book is followed by work in these six key comprehension skills. (As explained on page 3, there are ten comprehension questions for each selection. Space is provided in the "Reading Performance Chart" on the inside back cover so that students can enter their scores for these questions.) Students, then, become better readers through a balanced approach of abundant reading and regular skills practice. We also provide a series of discussion questions so that teachers can involve students in a variety of reading and critical thinking skills. Suggested answers to these discussion questions appear in the *Instructor's Manual and Test Bank*—a supplement that is free to teachers adopting the book. The supplement also includes a general answer key, added skill mastery tests, and notes to the instructor.

The last part of the book, Part IV, "Making Reading a Habit," is short but crucial. Students learn that the key to better reading is *regular* reading. They are reminded that the power of reading is in their hands and must be the result of their personal decision to succeed. They learn as well a series of steps to becoming a regular reader. Finally, students are provided with a list of suggested books along with brief descriptions of the books.

This list will also be published separately by Townsend Press as part of a booklet titled "Becoming a Better Reader." The booklet, available at no charge, will be updated and added to regularly. You are invited to share with us any books that you have found to be well received by students, or that you otherwise believe will be good candidates for an ongoing reading list. Send your ideas to the Book List Editor, Townsend Press, Pavilions at Greentree—408, Marlton, NJ 08053. The books you recommend will be read, and if they are added to the ongoing list, your contribution will be acknowledged.

Acknowledgments

Our thanks go to the staff at Townsend Press who worked very closely with us on this long-developing project: John Langan, Carole Mohr, Janet M. Goldstein, Amy K. Fisher, Beth Johnson Ruth, Dot Carroll, and Elaine J. Lessig. We also wish to acknowledge Jerry Otey of St. Philip's College and R. Kent Smith of the University of Maine for preliminary work on some of the reading selections. On a personal note, our gratitude goes to our parents, Hugh and Virginia Hopper and Milton and Mary Anton. We thank them for their belief in education, their moral encouragement, their financial support, and their faith in our abilities.

Carol H. Bader
Harley F. Anton

Becoming a
Better Reader

Chances are that you are not as good a reader as you should be to do well in college. If so, it's not surprising. You live in a culture where people watch an average of *over seven hours of television every day!* All that passive viewing does not allow much time for reading. Reading is a skill that must be actively practiced. The simple fact is that people who do not read very often are not likely to be strong readers.

Another reason for not reading much is that you may have a lot of responsibilities. You may be going to school and working at the same time, and you may have many family duties as well. Given a hectic schedule, you're not going to have much opportunity to read. When you have free time, you may be exhausted and find it easier to turn on the TV than to open up a book.

A third reason for not reading is that our public school system may have soured you on it. One government study after another has said that our schools have not done a good job of turning people on to the rewards of reading. If you had to read a lot of uninteresting and irrelevant material in grade and high school, you may have decided (mistakenly) that reading in general is not for you.

These reasons may help explain why you are not in the habit of regular reading. For people who are unpracticed readers, there is one overall key to becoming a better reader. That key, simple as it may sound, is to do a great deal of reading. The truth of the matter is that **reading is like any other skill. The more you practice, the better you get.** The primary goal of this book, then, is to provide you with a great deal of practice in reading.

To do so, *Keys To Better College Reading* contains a number of high-interest reading selections. To begin with, in Part I of the book there are six mostly short readings. Here, for example, is what two of the readings are about:

- A newspaper editor tells about her anger after being deceived by a con man.
- A young man describes a conflict with his father: he wants to play football after school; his father wants him to attend special classes.

In Part II of the book, there are twenty-five selections, many of them of intermediate length. Here are descriptions of several of the readings:

- A student is at the bottom of his class in school and going nowhere. Then something happens that helps him move to the top of his class and eventually go on to become a world-famous neurosurgeon.
- A young woman disguises herself as an old woman to see how the elderly are treated in our society.
- A boy has a weak bladder, and his abusive stepmother forbids him the use of the bathroom at night. He wonders how he is going to survive.

In Part III of the book, there are nine longer readings. Here are examples of some of these longer selections:

- The famous entertainer Sammy Davis, Jr., describes an ugly racial incident that made him determined to become a star.
- In a series of inspiring personal essays, college students of the '90s detail the challenges they faced in getting to college and how they overcame them.
- A lonely man goes on a hike in the mountains, meets an unusual dog, and then senses that someone, or something, is following them.

Part IV of the book then describes steps you can take to do more reading on your own and includes a list of suggested books to read as well.

A special effort has been made to provide *engaging* readings—ones that will truly catch you up in a writer's experience. One of the joys of life is to be drawn into the magic of a world that an author can create. When this happens, reading is transformed into something other than the classroom drudgery that it may have been in the past. More importantly, if you experience some of that magic, you may be encouraged to develop the habit of reading and make it a part of your life.

In addition to abundant practice in reading, there are other keys to becoming a successful reader. These keys are the six essential reading comprehension skills presented in Part I of the book. The skills include the following:

- Recognizing vocabulary in context;
- Locating main ideas;
- Understanding supporting details;
- Identifying transitions;
- Making inferences;
- Outlining and summarizing.

The skills have immediate and practical value: they can help you perform better and more quickly—giving you an edge for success—in all of your college courses. Each reading in the book is followed by work in these key comprehension skills. The objective is to make you a better reader through a balanced approach of abundant reading and regular skills practice.

A NOTE ON HOW TO PROCEED

Here is a suggested way of using this book.

1   Read the explanations and examples in Chapter 1 of Part I until you feel you understand the ideas presented. Then carefully work through the practice in the chapter. Next, check your answers with the "Limited Answer Key" that starts on page 573.

For your own sake, don't just copy in the answers without trying to do the practice! The only way to learn a skill is to practice it first and *then* use the answer key to give yourself feedback. Also, take whatever time is needed to figure out just why you got some answers wrong. By using the answer key to help teach yourself the skills, you will prepare yourself for the mastery tests that come next.

2   Do the three mastery tests that follow the chapter. The third mastery test in each chapter is made up of a reading followed by comprehension questions. Read each selection once just for the sake of enjoying it. Then reread it for the sake of practicing your comprehension skills.

3   Keep track of your progress. Enter your scores for the mastery tests in the "Reading Performance Chart" on the inside back cover. Continue entering your scores as you answer comprehension questions in the other parts of the text. (There are ten questions for each reading selection.) The scores will help you measure your performance as you work through the book.

4   Go on then to Chapter 2 and the other chapters. After covering Part I, you will be ready to read the mostly intermediate selections in Part II and then the longer selections in Part III.

5   Finally, make it your goal to obtain and read one or more of the books excerpted in Parts II and III. Each book you read will be a major step down the road to becoming a regular reader.

A FINAL THOUGHT

To motivate yourself, keep in mind that regular reading is a habit with important rewards.

1   Research has shown that frequent reading improves vocabulary, spelling, and reading speed and comprehension, as well as grammar and writing style. All of these language and thinking abilities develop in an almost painless way for the person who becomes a habitual reader.

2   Regular reading will increase your chances for job success. Increasingly in today's world, jobs involve the processing of information. More than ever, words are the tools of our trades. The better your command of words, the more success you are likely to have. And nothing will give you a command of words like regular reading.

3   Reading can enlarge your mind and your heart. Books and other printed matter allow us to enter minds unlike our own and to learn about the ideas of other people. Knowing what other people think about important matters can help us decide what we ourselves think. Also, knowing what other people think provides information we can use to advance our lives and our careers.

   Reading also frees us from the narrow confines of our own experience. People who read a lot find themselves saying, "That's exactly how I feel" or "I know this character" or "How could this author know so much about my life?" Through reading we connect with others and realize our shared humanity. We become less lonely as we share the common experiences, emotions, and thoughts that make us human. We grow more sympathetic and understanding because we realize that others are like us. We are enlarged and enriched.

In summary, regular reading, especially in the form of books, can be a source of enormous power. If you want that power in your life, it is yours to have. Regular reading can change your life.

Part I

KEY COMPREHENSION SKILLS

1

Vocabulary in Context

If you were asked to define the words *futile*, *erode*, and *versatile*, you might have some difficulty. On the other hand, chances are you could come up with quite accurate definitions if you saw these words in the following sentences:

> My boss is so stubborn that once she has made a decision, it is *futile* to try to change her mind.

> As water *eroded* the topsoil, the rocks below became more and more visible.

> Joan is the most *versatile* person I know. She draws cartoons, plays piano, does gymnastics, and is a math whiz.

Now see if you can choose the meaning of each word based on the way each is used above. Circle the letter of the meaning you think is correct.

Definition of *futile*:

a. helpful   b. useless   c. wise

Definition of *eroded*:

a. avoided   b. held together   c. wore away

Definition of *versatile*:

a. musical   b. many-sided   c. strong

The sentences' *context*—the words surrounding the unfamiliar words—provides clues to each word's meaning. Thus you may have guessed that *futile* means "useless," *eroded* means "wore away," and *versatile* means "many-sided."

Using context clues to understand new words will help you in a few important ways:

1   It will save you time when reading: you won't have to stop to look up words in the dictionary. (Of course, you won't always be able to understand a word from its context. You should always have a dictionary nearby to look up key words you cannot understand from context.)

2   It will improve your understanding of what you read because you will know more of the words.

3   It will expand your vocabulary. When you see a word more than once in context and guess its meaning, the chances increase that it will become part of your working vocabulary.

CHECK YOUR UNDERSTANDING

Try to figure out the meaning of each word in *italic* type in the following sentences. Circle the letter of what you think is the meaning of each word. Then read the answers and explanations that follow.

1. There is something in a spider's thread that makes bugs *adhere* when they touch the web.

   a. move away   b. stick   c. let go

2. When I applied for financial aid, I had to *disclose* my annual income. But it embarrassed me to reveal this information.

   a. make known   b. earn   c. hide

3. Lucy likes *urban* living because she grew up in a large town, but Arturo grew up on a farm and prefers country life.

   a. country   b. city   c. quiet

4. All religions have their *rituals*, such as lighting candles on a holiday or saying a blessing over food.

   a. holidays   b. foods   c. ceremonies

5 . No one knows the name of the *anonymous* donor who helped open the homeless shelter.

a. large   b. financial   c. unidentified

Explanations

1. Context provides clues that can help you figure out the meaning of a new word. In sentence 1, the general meaning of the sentence plus your own experience with spider's webs probably told you that *adhere* means "stick."

   If you're not sure about the meaning of a new word, it may help to ask yourself a key question about the context. In this case, for example, you might have asked yourself, "What might the thread in a spider's web do to a bug?"

2. Item 2 provides another type of context clue—a synonym of the new word. Synonyms are words that mean the same, or almost the same, as another word. In item 2, the synonym for *disclose* is "reveal." Noticing the synonym helps you conclude that *disclose*, like *reveal*, means "make known"—I had to make known my annual income.

3. Just as a synonym can be helpful, so can an antonym—a word that means the opposite of another word. By contrasting urban living with its opposite, country life, sentence 3 suggests the meaning of *urban*: "city."

4. Another common context clue is one or more examples of a new word. In sentence 4, two examples are given for the word *rituals*: 1) lighting candles on a holiday and 2) saying a blessing over food. The examples are both ceremonies, so you know that *rituals* must mean "ceremonies."

5. The general meaning of sentence 5 suggests that *anonymous* means "unidentified"—the donor whose name no one knows is unidentified.

Now that you see how a word's context can suggest its meaning, try figuring out some more meanings in the following practice.

➤ *Practice*

Using context clues to help you, circle the letter of the best definition for the italicized word in each sentence.

1. I am so *inept* at sewing that once when I was trying to hem a skirt, I ended up stitching it to the pants I was wearing.

   a. skilled   b. clumsy   c. willing

2. The smallest thing, like seeing a rainbow or finding a colorful rock, can make a child *ecstatic*.

   a. joyful   b. worried   c. sleepy

3. Since you went for a bike ride on Super Bowl Sunday, I *inferred* you were not a football fan.

   a. forgot   b. regretted   c. concluded

4. Because Gina likes to send postcards, she *compiled* a list of her friends' addresses before she went on vacation.

   a. mailed   b. gathered   c. gave away

5. If someone with a hatchet demands your wallet, it is safer to *comply* than to resist.

   a. fight   b. do as asked   c. yell

6. My neighbor doesn't think it is *appropriate* for children to call adults by their first names.

   a. proper   b. sportsmanlike   c. dangerous

7. Sometimes *overt* racism is easier to deal with than the hidden kind. You can better fight what is out in the open.

   a. legal   b. secret   c. obvious

8. I don't believe that our tax laws should benefit the *affluent* more than the poor or the middle class.

   a. needy   b. voters   c. wealthy

9. Because Carla is an *advocate* of free speech, she printed the birth control article in our school newspaper.

   a. disbeliever   b. enemy   c. supporter

10. I am *skeptical* about the articles on TV stars and flying saucers in supermarket newspapers. My brother, however, believes every word he reads in those papers.

    a. accepting   b. doubtful   c. educated

SCORE: Number right (_____) x 10 = _____ %

A STUDY HINT

You don't always have to use context clues or the dictionary to find definitions. Textbook authors usually give definitions of important terms. Here are three short excerpts from college texts. In each case, the term to be defined is set off in **boldface** type or *italic* type, and the definition then usually follows.

Excerpt from a psychology textbook:

Many children of normal intelligence have great difficulty learning how to read, write, or work with numbers. Often thought of as "underachievers," such children are said to have a *learning disability*, a disorder that interferes in some way with school achievement. The problem is common, affecting as many as 30 percent of all school children.

Excerpt from a business textbook:

The changing work force has changed lifestyles and needs. No wonder many workers have found **flextime** a desirable option. Instead of working the standard nine-to-five day, five days a week, they choose their own hours within certain limits. For instance, a company may stipulate that everyone has to be at work between 10:00 a.m. and 2:00 p.m., but workers may arrive or depart whenever they want as long as they work a total of eight hours.

Excerpt from a sociology textbook:

Some older people respond to the fact of aging with *disengagement*—a retreat from relationships, organizations, and society. This behavior is considered normal and even satisfying for the individual because withdrawal brings a release from social pressures to compete and conform.

By using *italic* or **boldface** type, textbook authors are signaling to you that these terms are important to learn. Indeed, the first major step you should take to understand a textbook chapter is to mark off definitions and any examples in the text. Then write down those definitions and, if available, an example that makes the definition clear to you. Your focus on definitions and examples will help as you reread a chapter and work to increase your understanding of its content.

Name _____

Section _____ Date_____

VOCABULARY IN CONTEXT: Mastery Test 1

Using context clues for help, circle the letter of the best meaning for the italicized word in each sentence.

1. When I'm nervous, I'm *liable* to laugh. Once I giggled in church when the woman in front of me fainted.

   a. unlikely   b. afraid   c. likely

2. Many cars are stolen while owners are in them, so it is *prudent* to drive with all your doors locked.

   a. wise   b. difficult   c. ignorant

3. Winning the Nobel Prize can make a little-known scientist into a *notable* world figure.

   a. rejected   b. famous   c. unknown

4. Some things are *inevitable,* such as taxes, death, and TV reruns.

   a. unavoidable   b. impossible   c. welcome

5. When the mugger said to me, "Give me your purse or I'll kill you," I didn't like either *option.*

   a. choice   b. person   c. opinion

6. Although his friends think he is *miserly,* Brad insists that thirty cents is too much to pay for a pack of gum.

   a. stingy   b. friendly   c. wise

7. Don't *equate* all homework with busywork. Homework can often increase one's understanding of a subject.

   a. consider to be equal   b. separate   c. reward

8. Using sign language, chimpanzees can *convey* such ideas as "candy sweet" and "gimme hug."

   a. forget   b. communicate   c. write

9. To *initiate* a conversation with someone, it's not necessary to be clever. Say something simple, like "It's a beautiful day" or "Hello."

   a. continue   b. avoid   c. begin

10. Chocolate was *lethal* for my cousin Harry. He was killed by a car while rushing across the street to a candy store.

    a. fattening   b. harmless   c. deadly

SCORE: Number right (_____) x 10 = _____%

Name _____

Section _____ Date_____

VOCABULARY IN CONTEXT: Mastery Test 2

Using context clues for help, circle the letter of the best meaning for the italicized word in each sentence.

1. Clutching his chest, Marcos complained of *acute* pains near his heart.

    a. sharp   b. pleasant   c. mild

2. Most Hollywood movies have a happy ending: good *prevails* over evil.

    a. loses   b. understands   c. wins out

3. Good weather is *vital* to the successful launching of a spaceship.

    a. harmful   b. necessary   c. not related

4. The little boy likes to *savor* chocolate bars by allowing each square to melt on his tongue.

    a. hide   b. gather   c. enjoy

5. The letter stating I had won $500 was *deceptive*—I had to buy a boat to claim my prize.

    a. truthful   b. misleading   c. friendly

6. To make sidewalks *accessible* to people in wheelchairs, ramps must be built at all corners.

    a. interesting   b. inexpensive   c. easy to enter

7. If you can't decide on a career, you might wish to take a test that reveals which *vocations* you're suited for.

    a. travels   b. occupations   c. hobbies

8. After trying for ten minutes, the new army recruit had to *concede* that he had no idea how to lace up his boots.

    a. admit   b. pretend   c. suggest

9. If the drugstore manager wishes to sell more of a particular product, he has it put in a *prominent* place on the shelves.

   a. hidden   b. reasonable   c. very noticeable

10. An advantage of having so many ethnic groups in the U.S. is that we enjoy a wonderful *diversity* of music, traditions, and foods.

   a. absence   b. variety   c. sameness

SCORE: Number right (_____) x 10 = _____ %

Name _____

Section _____ Date_____

VOCABULARY IN CONTEXT: Mastery Test 3

Here is a chance to apply the skill of understanding vocabulary in context to an article. If you have ever been cheated by someone, you may understand better than most the feelings that motivated the author to write her essay. After reading it, answer the vocabulary questions that follow.

Words to Watch

Following are some words in the reading that do not have strong context support. Each word is followed by the number of the paragraph in which it appears and its meaning there. These words are indicated in the story by a small circle (°).

> *acute* (1): severe, extreme
> *skeptical* (9): doubting
> *scrounged* (10): searched
> *scurried* (12): rushed
> *deceit* (21): dishonesty
> *fraud* (23): trickery, cheating
> *cynical* (24): believing that people are motivated only by selfishness

---

ONE LESS SUCKER LIVES

Jeanne R. Smith

1   The thing that struck me most about him was his acute° discomfort.

2   He approached the door of the newspaper office timidly, walked in and stood on the threshold as if uncertain about the kinds of creatures he would face inside.

3   He wore regular work clothes. There was nothing extraordinarily distinguishing about him. He just looked nervous and uncomfortable.

4   He'd never done anything like this in his life, he told me as he timidly neared my desk.

He didn't even know how to go about it . . . but if I would just   5
bear with him, maybe he could get his story out.

He was just so embarrassed.   6

He was a driver for the Arnold Baking Company, he said. His   7
truck had broken down up the highway, filled with his day's
delivery of breadstuffs. He'd gladly give our office staff a few
loaves of our favorite bread if only someone could lend him eight
dollars to catch a bus back to his company to get a substitute truck.

Oh, this was just so embarrassing.   8

Seeing what might have been a slightly skeptical° look on my   9
face, he produced a wad of credit and identification cards. One in
particular, an Arnold ID card, had his picture on it. He was who he
said he was. And he really did need help.

He just sat there looking woebegone while I pondered whether   10
or not to help my fellow man in distress and seemed overjoyed
when I pulled out my wallet, scrounged° out the eight bucks and
handed it to him.

He was so grateful. After all, this had been so embarrassing.   11

He scurried° out the door, promising English muffins as a   12
thank you when he returned before our office closed at five.

I never saw him again.   13

In fact, when I called the Arnold Baking Company the next   14
day to inquire about their poor driver with all the truck trouble, I
found that they never heard of him.

Indeed, someone from Arnold's called back to warn me that   15
this same man had pulled the same scam on someone in Cherry Hill
. . . the same story . . . the same ID cards . . . the same eight bucks.

Everyone ribbed me about being too trusting. I got kind advice   16
from the local police department when I reported the flim-flam so
others could be alerted to the perpetrator's method.

But no one taught me as valuable a lesson as the con artist   17
himself. And, thanks to him, someday, some person who is really in
need will find a deaf ear when he or she approaches me for help. At
least when it comes to money, anyway.

That's really very sad.   18

We were brought up to believe in the virtue of helping one's   19
neighbor. One of the greatest commandments given by the Almighty
involves the way we should treat each other.

Just try it.   20

After the incident, I pondered what it was about the whole   21 thing that really stuck in my craw. Was it the money? Or was it the lie? . . . the deceit°? . . . the con?

It really wasn't the money. Had the guy come into the office, 22 poured out his heart about being out of work, with sick kids and nowhere else to turn, I probably would have given him the money to help out. At least before yesterday I might have.

It was the lie . . . the deliberate resort to fraud° to cheat me out 23 of money that is as important to me as to him that really angers me.

It's probably true that there's a sucker born every minute. But 24 yesterday, one sucker died. And a wiser, more cynical° person emerged. 25

There's the pity of it all.

Vocabulary Questions

1. The word *timidly* in "He approached the door of the newspaper office timidly, walked in and stood on the threshold as if uncertain about the kinds of creatures he would face inside. . . . He just looked nervous and uncomfortable" (paragraphs 2–3) means
   - a. confidently.
   - b. shyly.
   - c. loudly.
   - d. on schedule.

2. The word *wad* in "Seeing what might have been a slightly skeptical look on my face, he produced a wad of credit and identification cards" (paragraph 9) means
   - a. story.
   - b. large amount.
   - c. lack.
   - d. photograph.

3. The word *woebegone* in "Oh, this was just so embarrassing. . . . He just sat there looking woebegone while I pondered whether or not to help my fellow man . . . and seemed overjoyed when I pulled out my wallet " (paragraphs 8 and 10) means
   - a. pleased.
   - b. healthy.
   - c. unhappy.
   - d. confident.

4. The word *pondered* in "he just sat there looking woebegone while I pondered whether or not to help my fellow man" (paragraph 10) means
   - a. considered.
   - b. remembered.
   - c. forgot.
   - d. knew.

5. The word *scam* in "Indeed, someone from Arnold's called back to warn me that this same man had pulled the same scam on someone in Cherry Hill . . . the same story . . . the same ID cards . . . the same eight bucks" (paragraph 15) means
   a. practical joke.
   b. anger.
   c. agreement.
   d. dishonest scheme.

6. The word *flim-flam* in "I got kind advice from the local police department when I reported the flim-flam so others could be alerted to the perpetrator's method" (paragraph 16) means
   a. truck trouble.
   b. embarrassment.
   c. cheating.
   d. credit cards.

7. The words *perpetrator's method* in "I got kind advice from the local police department when I reported the flim-flam so others could be alerted to the perpetrator's method" (paragraph 16) mean
   a. method of the person who committed the crime.
   b. method of a beginner.
   c. method of a citizen.
   d. method of the local police department.

8. The phrase *stuck in my craw* in "After the incident, I pondered what it was about the whole thing that really stuck in my craw. Was it the money? Or was it the lie?" (paragraph 21) means
   a. delighted me.
   b. destroyed me.
   c. informed me.
   d. troubled me.

9. The words *resort to* in "It was the lie . . . the deliberate resort to fraud to cheat me out of money that is as important to me as to him that really angers me" (paragraph 23) mean
   a. avoiding of.
   b. use of.
   c. hiding of.
   d. knowledge of.

10. The word *emerged* in "It's probably true that there's a sucker born every minute. But yesterday, one sucker died. And a wiser, more cynical person emerged" (paragraph 24) means
    a. disappeared.
    b. took advantage.
    c. died.
    d. appeared.

SCORE: Number right (_____) x 10 = _____ %

2

Main Ideas

More than any other skill, the ability to recognize the main idea is a key to better reading. The basic question you should ask about any selection that you read is, "What is the main point the author is trying to make?" The answer will be the main idea. The rest of the selection will be made up of supporting details for that main idea.

The purpose of this and the following chapter is to give you a solid sense of these two chief parts of any selection:

- The *main idea*—the main point of the selection;

- The *supporting details*—the specific ideas that explain and support the main idea.

THE TOPIC SENTENCE

Authors often clearly state the main idea of a paragraph in a single sentence called the *topic sentence*. The topic sentence is often a brief summary of the paragraph. It is a general statement that includes all or most of the details of the passage.

To better understand how to find an author's main point, read the paragraph below. Try to find the topic sentence. Test the sentence you choose by asking, "Is this statement supported by all or most of the other material in the paragraph?" Write the number of the sentence you choose in the space provided, and then read the explanation that follows.

¹There are two strong influences on the content of dreams. ²One influence is the time of your dream. ³When you are closest to waking, your dreams are apt to be about recent events. ⁴In the middle of the night, however, your dreams are more likely to involve childhood or past events. ⁵The other influence on the content of dreams is presleep conditions. ⁶In one study, subjects who had six hours of active exercise before sleep tended to have dreams with little physical activity. ⁷The researcher concluded that dream content may offset waking experiences to some extent. ⁸Other research supports that conclusion. ⁹For instance, subjects who had experienced a day of social isolation had dreams with a great amount of social interaction. ¹⁰Also, subjects who had been water-deprived dreamed of drinking.

Topic sentence: _____

Sentences 2–10 each give specific details; each one is too narrow to cover all of the other details. Sentence 1, however, is about dream content in general. You may have suspected it was the topic sentence when you began reading the paragraph. If so, you should have checked yourself by asking, "Does the other material in the paragraph support the idea that dream content is related to a number of different factors?" In fact, the rest of the paragraph *does* discuss factors that are associated with dream content:

1) The time of the dream (close to waking or in the middle of the night);

2) Presleep conditions (active exercise, social isolation, and water-deprivation).

Therefore sentence 1 is the topic sentence—it is a general statement that covers all of the specific details of the paragraph.

Check Your Understanding

Topic sentences may appear at the beginning of a paragraph (as in the paragraph about dream content), within the paragraph, or at the very end of a paragraph. Try to find the topic sentences in the following three paragraphs. (One topic sentence is at the beginning of the paragraph, one is within the paragraph, and one is at the end of the paragraph.) After reading each passage, write the number of the sentence that you think expresses the main idea—in other words, the sentence that states the main point of the paragraph. Then read the explanations that follow.

1.   ¹If you are like most people, you feel that writing is not one of your talents and there's nothing you can do about it. ²The truth is that some common sense tips can help you become a better writer. ³First of all, write often. ⁴Like other crafts, writing improves with practice. ⁵Also, organize your material with an outline. ⁶An outline will provide you with a good guideline without limiting you, as you can change it at any time. ⁷Don't try to use overly fancy language; say what you mean simply and clearly. ⁸Finally, tighten your writing—nothing improves writing more than eliminating unnecessary words.

Topic sentence: _____

2.   ¹Working at an all-night gas station was depressing. ²The job involved sitting in a lighted glass box (roughly 6' x 6' x 6'), an island of light in a darkness that extended in all directions. ³I worked the "graveyard shift," which was 11 p.m. to 6 a.m. ⁴It was especially dismal from 3 a.m. to 5 a.m. because it was during that time that I sat numbly in my broken chair thinking to myself, "I am one of the few people within a thirty-mile radius who is still awake." ⁵The highway was gloomily still in those hours, except for the occasional bread and newspaper truck that would roll silently by.

Topic sentence: _____

3.   ¹A dermatologist brought together sixty-five young people who were prone to acne. ²Every day for four weeks, he fed each of them either a super-chocolate bar, containing ten times the chocolate of an ordinary candy bar, or a look-alike candy bar that tasted like chocolate but contained none. ³None of the subjects knew whether or not they were eating real chocolate. ⁴Halfway through the experiment, the dermatologist switched bars on the subjects. ⁵The subjects' acne was not affected by including chocolate in their diets. ⁶The dermatologist's experiment shows that chocolate is not to blame for complexion problems.

Topic sentence: _____

Explanations

1. Most of paragraph 1 is made up of tips for becoming a better writer. Sentences 3–8 present the specific tips. But sentence 2 makes the general statement that "some common sense tips can help you become a better writer." Therefore sentence 2 is the topic sentence— it provides the main idea of sentences 3–8. Sentence 1 is an

introductory statement meant to arouse the reader's interest. (If sentence 1 were the topic sentence, then the rest of the paragraph would have to be about feeling that writing is not one of your talents.)

Sentences that come before the topic sentence in a paragraph may serve other purposes as well, including providing background or relating the main idea to the previous paragraph.

2. In paragraph 2, sentence 1 makes the summary statement that "Working at an all-night gas station was depressing." Sentences 2–5 provide specific details to illustrate that general statement. Therefore sentence 1 is the topic sentence.

3. When the topic sentence is at the end of a paragraph, the previous sentences build up to the main idea. That is the case with paragraph 3. Sentences 1–5 each provide one part of the dermatologist's experiment; none of those sentences is general enough to be the main point. For example, the first sentence states only that the dermatologist brought the young people together. It does not refer at all to the experiment. But sentence 6 is general enough to cover all of the other sentences—it mentions the dermatologist, his experiment, and what the experiment proved. Therefore sentence 6 is the topic sentence.

IMPLIED MAIN IDEAS

Sometimes a selection lacks a topic sentence, but that does not mean it lacks a main idea. You must figure out what that implied main idea is by deciding upon the point of all the details. For example, read the following paragraph.

One way that pigs show their intelligence is through curiosity. If you put something in their pens, such as a key chain, they'll sniff and poke at it to find out what it is. Also, hog farmers have noted that if a pig finds an escape hole in the pasture fence one summer and then is put in the barn for the winter, he'll head right over to the hole when he's back in the pasture next spring. One farmer said he had a terrible time with one sow who learned how to use her snout to open the gate latch when it wasn't completely fastened. "She'd be checking it out every half hour to see if we'd slipped up, which we sometimes did," he said. More evidence for a pig's intelligence is the fact that they are more subject to psychological stress than other farm animals. They get bored and distressed when they're confined and there's nothing to do. In fact, like people, they can develop ulcers from a hostile environment.

You can see that no sentence in the paragraph is general enough to cover all of the others. The first sentence, for example, is about "one way that pigs show their intelligence," yet the paragraph is about other ways as well. We can decide on the main idea by considering all the details and asking, "What is the primary point made by all or most of the details?" or "What general statement would summarize or include all the details of the paragraph?" In this case, every detail of the paragraph illustrates the intelligence of pigs. Therefore we can conclude that the author's main point is that pigs are intelligent creatures. Although this point is not directly stated, it is a broad enough summary to cover all the details in the paragraph—it is the implied main idea.

Check Your Understanding

Now read the paragraph below, and see if you can pick out which of the four statements that follow it expresses the implied main idea. Circle the letter of the statement you choose, and then read the explanation that follows.

Newspapers are usually thrown out after a day. Magazines, however, may stay around the house or office for weeks or months. In addition, they may be passed from person to person. Therefore the ads in them have a better chance of being read and remembered. Magazines also allow for colorful photography and artwork. They provide a way for advertisers to create a quality image with ads. Furthermore, many magazines now publish a range of editions aimed at specific areas and groups, instead of a single national edition. For example, *Time* magazine publishes 357 different editions worldwide. They include special editions for doctors, educators, and college students.

    a. Magazine ads have a better chance of being read and remembered than newspaper ads.
    b. Magazines allow advertisers to reach specific market segments.
    c. All advertisers should place ads in magazines.
    d. Magazines have some important advantages for advertisers.

The first point of the paragraph is that magazine ads have a better chance of being read and remembered than newspaper ads. If that were the main idea, then the rest of the passage would go on to give details about how well magazine ads are read and remembered. Instead, the paragraph goes on to provide several other advantages of magazines to advertisers. So answer *a* is too narrow to be the main idea.

Answer *b* is also too narrow to be the main idea—it also covers only one advantage of magazines to advertisers.

Answer *c* is incorrect because the details of the paragraph do not include any judgment about what advertisers should do.

Answer *d* is a correct statement of the main idea. The "important advantages for advertisers" mentioned in answer *d* is a general reference to the three specific advantages listed in the paragraph:

1) Magazine ads have a better chance of being read and remembered than newspaper ads.

2) Magazine photography and artwork are important for advertisers that want to create a quality image with attractive ads.

3) Various magazine editions allow advertisers to reach many different markets.

THE CENTRAL POINT

In longer selections made up of many paragraphs, such as articles or textbook chapters, the overall main idea is often called the *central point*. The central point may be directly stated by the author or implied. For example, in the reading on page 17, the central point is that the author's experience with the con artist has made her less trustful of her fellow human beings. The selections in this text will give you practice in finding the central point, as well as in finding the main ideas of paragraphs and groups of paragraphs within a reading.

➤*Practice*

A. Topic sentences appear at different locations in the following six paragraphs. Identify each topic sentence by writing its sentence number in the space provided. Test your answer by asking, "Does all or most of the material in the paragraph support this idea?"

1. ¹Congratulations, your tire is as flat as the road, you're supposed to be at an important meeting in an hour, and there's no help to be found anywhere. ²What should you do? ³You can change your own tire by following several safe, effective steps. ⁴First, park on level ground away from traffic, put the car gear in park, and put on the emergency brake. ⁵Next, lock the wheels at the opposite end from the flattened tire to prevent the car from rolling. ⁶Then take out the spare tire and the jack and take off the hub cap. ⁷Jack the flat tire up

at least two or three inches above the ground, remove the lug nuts, and put them inside the hub cap, where you won't lose them. [8]Then pull off the flat tire, and put on the spare tire. [9]Replace the lug nuts, but don't tighten them all the way. [10]Jack down the car most of the way, and then finish tightening the lug nuts. [11]Finally, lower the car all the way, clean yourself up, and continue on your way.

Topic sentence: _____

2. [1]Elderly people are often the victims of discrimination. [2]Those who were once attractive, active, and powerful may no longer be so. [3]They must live on restricted incomes that are further restricted by inflation. [4]They must face health problems and death. [5]Some elderly, especially the poor and those in many nursing homes, live lives of desperation and hopelessness. [6]Being old can be a very difficult stage in life for individuals.

Topic sentence: _____

3. [1]Don't cut up raw chicken and then use the same knife to chop vegetables. [2]Wash it first. [3]Otherwise, if the chicken had disease-causing bacteria on it, you would have just passed it on to your salad greens. [4]Likewise, after preparing raw meat or poultry, always scrub your hands, utensils, and cutting board thoroughly with soap and hot water. [5]Cleanliness in the kitchen can help you keep your family well.

Topic sentence: _____

4. [1]Memory can be both strengthened and weakened with drug use. [2]Much of the research in this area has been on alcohol. [3]Overall, the results show that alcohol weakens the ability to remember new information. [4]It has little effect, however, on how one remembers data already stored in long-term memory. [5]But heavy use of alcohol may result in significant memory loss. [6]Research on marijuana shows that drug also weakens memory. [7]Subjects who had smoked marijuana could recall items for a brief period, but they forgot more and more of the information over time. [8]In contrast, some drugs have been shown to strengthen memory. [9]For example, there is a hormone that improves memory if given to a subject right after a learning session.

Topic sentence: _____

5. ¹Services have more and more become a vital part of our economy for various reasons. ²First, improvements in manufacturing have made it possible for fewer people to turn out more goods. ³Therefore more people are freed to open restaurants, practice law, write songs, and the like. ⁴Also, there is a growing trend for firms to take over services that companies once performed themselves. ⁵Instead of having its own legal staff, for example, a company might hire a law firm. ⁶In addition, foreign producers with access to cheap labor have taken over much of the world's manufacturing. ⁷This has furthered the shift to services in the U.S. ⁸Also, computers are responsible for many services. ⁹Recent studies suggest that fully half of the nation's economic activity now consists of computer services.

Topic sentence: _____

6. ¹Counterfeiters of U.S. money tend to be skillful artists. ²Expert engravings of paper money can fool all but the trained eye. ³Illegal engravings have been so expert that the U.S. Treasury has tried to make counterfeiting more difficult. ⁴In 1991, the Treasury began putting polyester security threads into the nation's hundred-dollar bills. ⁵Color photocopiers, often used by counterfeiters, can't copy the narrow threads. ⁶In addition, the Treasury is putting tiny "microprinting" on its new dollars. ⁷The letters, only five one-thousandth of an inch tall, are too tiny for a photocopier to reproduce.

Topic sentence: _____

B. The following four paragraphs have implied main ideas, and each is followed by four sentences. In each case, circle the letter of the sentence that best expresses the implied main idea.

Remember to consider carefully all of the details and ask yourself, "What is the primary point made by all or most of the details?" or "What general statement would summarize the details of the paragraph?" Then test your answer by asking, "Does all or most of the material in the paragraph support this idea?"

7. To make your clothes last longer, avoid using the dryer. Over time, the heat will fade colors and weaken fabrics. Instead, hang your clothing to dry inside the house in cold weather and outside (but away from direct sunlight, which can also fade colors) when it's warm. Also, don't use bleach more than absolutely necessary.

Bleach contains strong chemicals that can weaken fibers. Never store knitted clothes on hangers—they can stretch out of shape. Instead, keep them folded in a drawer. Finally, get rid of stains promptly—if you let them set, they are much harder, if not impossible, to remove.

The implied main idea is:

a. Most people don't know how to make their clothes last longer.
b. There are several ways to make your clothes last longer.
c. Dryers and bleach are bad for your clothes.
d. There are several reasons to avoid using your dryer.

8. Piano students often learn the sentence "Every Good Boy Does Fine." The first letter of each word represents the lines in the treble clef staff. They also learn the word FACE, whose letters represent the spaces in the treble clef staff. Likewise, in a spelling lesson, students are taught the rhyme "*I* before *E* except after *C*, or when sounded like *A* as in *neighbor* or *weigh*." People often work out similar tricks to help them remember their phone numbers or other important information.

The implied main idea is:

a. "Every Good Boy Does Fine" helps piano students learn the lines of the treble clef staff.
b. A certain rhyme can help students remember when to use "ie" and "ei" in words.
c. Rhymes and jingles can help people remember various types of information.
d. Rhymes and jingles can help people remember all of the musical notes.

9. Tick bites can cause a serious illness called Lyme disease. To protect yourself from Lyme disease, say the experts, stay on cleared trails and avoid thick vegetation—because ticks live in wooded and grassy areas. Also, on nature walks, wear long-sleeved shirts and long pants to limit the amount of exposed skin. For the same reason, you should wear high boots and tuck your pant legs into your socks. Keep in mind that light-colored clothing makes ticks easier to spot. Use the repellent DEET on your skin and clothing. And most importantly, caution the experts, examine your body for ticks each time you return from any place where you may be exposed to them.

The implied main idea is:

a. Lyme disease, a serious illness, is caused by tick bites.
b. According to experts, you can protect yourself from Lyme disease in several ways.
c. Because ticks live in wooded and grassy areas, the experts recommend staying on cleared trails and away from thick vegetation.
d. According to experts, the most important precaution to take against Lyme disease is to examine your body for ticks when you return from any place where you may be exposed to them.

10. Every ten seconds a home or business somewhere is broken into, according to police reports. To learn about discouraging theft, some researchers went to the experts. Who were these experts? They were six hundred inmates around the country doing time for armed robbery, burglary, and auto theft. It seems anything that slows a thief down is useful. Half of the inmates said there are so many unlocked houses that if it took more than two minutes to get in a house, they'd move on to an easier target. Surprisingly, lights, police patrols, fencing, and bars on windows were rated almost ineffective. Neighborhood watches and someone in the home were seen as only moderately useful. Rating highest in deterring break-ins were security systems linked to police stations, electronic window sensors, and closed-circuit TV. But what would most career criminals choose to protect their own property if they could use only one method? A large dog!

The implied main idea is:

a. Criminals have something to offer to society.
b. Our jails are filled with inmates imprisoned for armed robbery, burglary, and auto theft.
c. Security systems linked to police stations are among the best devices for discouraging theft.
d. Researchers learned how effective some methods of home protection are by going to the experts—inmates imprisoned for stealing.

SCORE: Number right (_____) x 10 = _____ %

Name _____

Section _____ Date_____

MAIN IDEAS: Mastery Test 1

Topic sentences appear at different locations in the following five paragraphs. Identify each topic sentence by writing its sentence number in the space provided. Test your answer by asking, "Does all or most of the material in the paragraph support this idea?"

1. ¹Many people keep guns in their homes for protection. ²Actually, though, a gun in your home is likely to make you less safe, not safer. ³For one thing, more people are killed by gun accidents than by murder. ⁴Also, most murders are committed by family members or friends of the victim. ⁵A gun in the house can sometimes turn a family quarrel into a deadly tragedy.

   Topic sentence: _____

2. ¹Going to a reunion can be stressful, but doing some physical and mental preparations can help you survive the reunion. ²Of course, staying home is the ultimate way to avoid reunion stress. ³Otherwise, scan your yearbook so you won't be caught off guard by your feelings. ⁴Realize that everyone changes and some classmates may not know who you are. ⁵Remember to avoid judgments and be honest about yourself. ⁶Understand that close ties made in school are hard to keep. ⁷Finally, recognize that it's not unusual to feel sad once the reunion is over.

   Topic sentence: _____

3. ¹The set of cooking knives is offered at an unbeatable price. ²You hurry to the department store. ³There, the sympathetic clerk tells you he is so sorry, but he's all sold out. ⁴But, he adds, the quality of the knives wasn't that good, anyway. ⁵If you want a real value, he suggests that you purchase this set. ⁶True, it costs more, but the knives are certainly worth the extra money. ⁷So you buy the more expensive knife set. ⁸Later, you notice that the super-low-priced set of knives you had originally wanted is still being advertised. ⁹The store ran an illegal operation, a bait-and-switch: you were "baited" with an inexpensive item, then "switched" to something more expensive.

   Topic sentence: _____

4. ¹Support for the "right to die" is increasing. ²In 1973, most Americans agreed with the following: It is wrong "to give a patient who is terminally ill, with no cure in sight, the right to tell the patient's doctor to put the patient out of his or her misery." ³By 1985, in response to the same question, a solid majority now said it was right to give a patient his or her choice in the matter. ⁴Since 1985, the number of people supporting the "right to die" has continued to grow.

Topic sentence: _____

5. ¹Most computer terminals emit a high-pitched tone that can produce stress-related symptoms. ²Research shows it can affect the nervous system, producing headaches, irritability and even increased blood pressure. ³To lessen the effect of the computer tone, follow three procedures. ⁴First, do not put your face close to your computer while working on it. ⁵If you find that for comfortable viewing, you must keep your face closer than one and a half feet from the screen, it may mean that you need your vision corrected—consult an eye-care professional about this. ⁶Second, turn the computer off when it's not in use. ⁷Many people routinely keep their computer "idling." ⁸Third, you can try wearing special high-frequency earplugs, which are generally available at drugstores. ⁹These will filter the tone, but allow you to hear conversation.

Topic sentence: _____

Name _____

Section _____ Date_____

MAIN IDEAS: Mastery Test 2

The following paragraphs have implied main ideas, and each is followed by four sentences. In each case, circle the letter of the sentence that best expresses the implied main idea.

1. Housework is the first thing to fall by the wayside in the time-pressured lives of professional women. In a survey by *Family Circle* magazine, over 80 per cent of full-time working women said the only way they could balance job, home, and family was to sacrifice high cleaning standards. The next thing to get put on the back burner was sex. Almost 75 percent said that by the end of the day, they or their spouses were too tired for anything but TV. Fifty per cent reported that friends and social occasions were third in line to get squeezed off the calendar.

   The implied main idea is:

   a. According to a *Family Circle* survey, full-time working women have to cut back on several customary activities.
   b. Women who work full-time say they must sacrifice high cleaning standards.
   c. According to a *Family Circle* survey, full-time working women would be better off if they took on part-time jobs instead.
   d. Half of all full-time working women report that working full-time has meant less time for getting together with friends.

2. Newspapers had been carrying reports on the famine in Ethiopia for months. Although stories described how people were starving, there was little response from the public. All that changed in October, 1984 when NBC-TV showed a five-minute report on the famine. As soon as the pictures of starving children were shown, the network switchboard lit up. This was the beginning of a huge worldwide effort to send aid to Ethiopia. Similarly, the television coverage of the Vietnam War contributed to the growing anti-war movement.

   The implied main idea is:

   a. The first network TV report on the Ethiopian famine was shown in October, 1984.
   b. People who read newspaper reports are not moved by them.

    c. Pictures can be more powerful than words alone in moving people to action.

    d. TV viewers are more interested in international news than in local news.

3. Patients should always be aware of a prescription drug's possible side effects. Unexpected side effects, such as nausea or dizziness, can be frightening and even dangerous. The consumer should ask, too, if he can take the medication along with other drugs he is using. Some combinations of drugs can be lethal. Finally, medication should always be stored in its own labeled bottle, never transferred to another. Accidental mix-ups of drugs can have tragic results.

The implied main idea is:

    a. Consumers may use drugs carelessly.

    b. Drugs can be dangerous.

    c. There are several guidelines for taking prescription medications safely.

    d. To avoid tragic mix-ups, medications should always be stored in their own labeled bottles.

4. It is widely believed that the institutions of marriage and the family are less stable today than ever before. It is true that divorce is very common these days. However, the divorce rate has been rising and falling for years. It was nearly as high during the 1920s as it is now. And while divorce creates many single-parent households today, the same was true about death in earlier times. So many parents died early during the eighteenth and nineteenth centuries that most children spent at least part of their early lives growing up in single-parent households.

The implied main idea is:

    a. The institutions of marriage and the family are unstable today.

    b. Divorce is very common now, and it was also common during the 1920s.

    c. The institutions of marriage and family are no less stable today than at other times.

    d. Divorce and death have been responsible for creating many single-family homes.

SCORE: Number right (_____) x 25 = _____ %

Name _____

Section _____ Date_____

MAIN IDEAS: Mastery Test 3

How does the family life of your youth compare with your family life now? Read the following essay to see how your own experience compares with the changes in family life in America.

This essay also provides the chance to apply your understanding of main ideas to a full-length piece. After reading it, answer the questions on the central point and main ideas that follow. There are also vocabulary questions to help you continue practicing the skill of understanding vocabulary in context.

Words to Watch

Following are some words in the reading that do not have strong context support. Each word is followed by the number of the paragraph in which it appears and its meaning there. These words are indicated in the selection by a small circle (°).

leisurely (3): done without rushing
self-reliance (8): independence

AMERICAN FAMILY LIFE:
THE CHANGING PICTURE

Donna Barron

It's another evening in an American household.   1

The door swings open at 5:30 sharp. "Hi, honey! I'm home!"   2
In walks dear old Dad, hungry and tired after a long day at the office. He is greeted by Mom in her apron, three happy children, and the aroma of a delicious pot roast.

After a leisurely° meal together, Mom does the dishes. That,   3
after all, is part of her job. The whole family then moves to the living room. There they spend the evening playing Scrabble or watching TV.

Then everyone is off to bed. And the next morning they wake   4
up to the sounds and smells of Mom preparing pancakes and sausage for breakfast.

What? You say that doesn't sound like life in your house? 5
Well, you're not alone. In fact, you're probably in the majority.

A few years ago, the above household might have been typical. 6
You can still visit such a home—on television. Just watch reruns of
old situation comedies. *Leave It to Beaver,* for example, shows
Mom doing housework in pearls and high heels. Dad keeps his suit
and tie on all weekend. But the families that operate like Beaver
Cleaver's are fewer and fewer. They're disappearing because three
parts of our lives have changed. These are the way we work, the
way we eat, and the way we entertain ourselves. Becoming aware of
the effects of those changes may help us improve family life.

Let's look first at the changes in the way we work. Today the 7
words "Hi, honey! I'm home!" might not be spoken by dear old
Dad. Dear old Mom is just as likely to be saying them. A generation
ago, most households could get by on one paycheck—Dad's. Mom
stayed home, at least until the children started school. But today,
over half the mothers with young children go to work. Even a
greater percentage of mothers of older children are in the work
force. And the number of single-parent homes has mushroomed in
the last thirty years.

These changes in work have affected children as well as 8
parents. When only Dad went out to work, children came home
from school to Mom. (In TV situation comedies, they came home to
Mom and home-baked cookies.) Today, we'll find them at an after-
school program or a neighbor's house. Or they may come home to
no one at all. In every community, children are caring for
themselves until their parents return from work. Are these children
missing out on an important part of childhood? Or are they
developing a healthy sense of self-reliance°? These are questions
that Mrs. Cleaver never had to deal with.

In addition, Dad—and now Mom—are often gone from home 9
longer than ever. Not too long ago, most men worked close to home.
The office or factory was just downtown. Dad often walked to work
or hitched a ride with a friendly neighbor. But no more.

Today's working men and women are commuters. They travel 10
distances to work that would have made their parents gasp.
Commutes of forty-five minutes or an hour are common. Workers
travel on buses, subways, and crowded highways. Many leave their
suburban homes at dawn and don't return until dark. No running
home for lunch in the 1990s.

And speaking of lunch, there's been a second big change in   11
American family life. If both parents are away from home for long
hours, who's whipping up those delicious meals in the kitchen? The
answer, more and more, is nobody.

These days, few people have time to shop for and prepare   12
"home-style" meals. The Cleavers were used to dinners of pot roast
or chicken. Potatoes, salad, and vegetables went with the main
course, with pie or cake for dessert. But this kind of meal takes
several hours to fix. People can't spend hours in the kitchen if they
get home at 5:30.

So what does the working family eat? They choose meals that   13
are easy to prepare or are already prepared. Fast food, take-out, and
heat-n-serve dishes make up much of the modern American diet.
Dad may arrive home with a bag of Big Macs and shakes. Mom
may phone out for Chinese food or ask the local pizza parlor to
deliver. And more and more people rely on microwaves to thaw
frozen food in minutes.

One consequence of these quickly prepared meals is that   14
families spend less time dining together. It's hard to make single
servings on aluminum trays special. And classic fast foods, like
hamburgers and fries, are meant to be eaten on the run, not slowly
enjoyed at the dinner table. The '90s family no longer shares the
evening meal. As a result, it no longer shares the day's news . . . or
the feeling of togetherness.

Finally, what about after dinner? Is the family evening at least   15
something the Cleavers could relate to?

Not a chance.   16

We don't even have to look outside the home to see the   17
changes. The modern American family entertains itself in ways the
Cleavers would never have dreamed of.

Thirty years ago, families gathered around a radio each   18
evening. Later, television took over. Most families had just one set,
which they watched together. Today, television and computers bring
a dizzying array of entertainments into the home. Cable television
provides everything from aerobics classes to Shakespeare. VCRs
expand the choices even more. If there's nothing good on network
TV or cable, the video store offers the best and worst of Hollywood:
recent movies, cartoons, "adult" films, exercise programs, travel,
sports, how-to tapes. Computer games, which make us part of the
action, also provide excitement. Players can compete in the

Olympics, search out aliens, or wipe out entire civilizations on their little screens.

With all these choices, it makes sense to own more than one   19
television set. The two-or-more-TV family used to be rare.
Nowadays, Dad might want to rent an action movie when Mom's
cable shopping service is on. Or Junior is playing a let's-blow-up-
Saturn video game while Sis wants to see the Cosby show. Why not
invest in several sets? Then each family member can enjoy himself
or herself in peace.

What's wrong with this picture of today's family?   20

Only this. Today's Cleavers spend their evenings in front of   21
their separate TV screens. Then they go to bed. The next morning,
they rush off to their separate jobs (work and school). They come
home at separate times. They eat separately. Finally, they return to
their separate TV screens for another evening's entertainment.
During all of these times, when do they talk to each other or even
see each other? When are they a family?

Certain realities of modern life cannot change. One is the need,   22
in most families, for both parents to bring home a paycheck.
Another is the distance many of us must travel to work or to school.
But must everything change? And must we lose the family structure
in the process?

No one is suggesting that we go back to the 1950s. The   23
Cleaver household was a fantasy even then, not reality. But we
might borrow one important lesson from the Cleavers. It is that
family life is just as important as work or play. If we agree, we'll
find ways of spending more time together. We'll find things to
share. And then there will be something *right* with the picture.

Reading Comprehension Questions

Vocabulary in Context

1. The word *operate* in "the families that operate like Beaver
   Cleaver's are fewer and fewer" (paragraph 6) means
   a. dress.
   b. perform surgery.
   c. function.
   d. eat.

2. The word *mushroomed* in "the number of single-parent homes has mushroomed in the last thirty years" (paragraph 7) means
   a. fallen.
   b. grown rapidly.
   c. behaved.
   d. returned.

3. The word *consequence* in "One consequence of these quickly prepared meals is that families spend less time dining together" (paragraph 14) means
   a. delay.
   b. advantage.
   c. result.
   d. example.

4. The word *array* in "Today, television and computers bring a dizzying array of entertainments into the home" (paragraph 18) means
   a. purpose.
   b. loss.
   c. topic.
   d. collection.

5. The word *fantasy* in "The Cleaver household was a fantasy even then, not reality" (paragraph 23) means
   a. very true idea.
   b. unrealistic fiction.
   c. danger.
   d. pleasure.

Central Point

6. Which sentence best expresses the central point of the selection?
   a. Three important changes in America have made a significant impact on family life, which must be restrengthened.
   b. Many children take care of themselves while their parents are at work.
   c. American families have many new ways to entertain themselves.
   d. Because of recent changes in family life, it is harder for American families to spend time together in the evening after dinner.

Main Ideas

7. Which sentence best expresses the main idea of paragraph 7?
   a. Households used to be able to get by on one paycheck.
   b. Mothers used to stay home and care for their young children.
   c. There has been a great increase in the number of single-parent homes.
   d. More mothers of young and even older children are in the American work force today than in the fifties.

8. Which sentence best expresses the main idea of paragraphs 9 and 10?
   a. Most men used to work close to home.
   b. Today, working people don't go home for lunch.
   c. Work is very different today than it was in the fifties in many ways.
   d. Today, parents are gone from home longer than ever because of long commutes.

9. Which sentence best expresses the main idea of paragraphs 11–14?
   a. There's been a change in how Americans eat, which in turn weakens family life.
   b. The Cleavers were used to full-course dinners that took several hours to fix.
   c. Microwaves have made it easier for families to serve quick meals.
   d. The '90s family doesn't share the day's news.

10. Which sentence best expresses the main idea of paragraph 18?
    a. VCRs have greatly improved home entertainment in America.
    b. Over the last thirty years, there has been a great increase in electronic entertainments.
    c. Computer games provide a great deal of excitement.
    d. It wasn't so long ago that the only electronic entertainment in the American home was radio.

SCORE: Number right (_____) x 10 = _____ %

3

Supporting Details

You know from the previous chapter that the main idea is the general statement covering all of the other material in a paragraph—examples, reasons, steps, and other specific details. All of those specific details are also called *supporting details*—they are the information that backs up and explains the main idea. Main ideas and their supporting details are the two basic parts of paragraphs.

MAJOR AND MINOR DETAILS

There are two kinds of supporting details—major and minor. The *major supporting details* are the primary points that support the main idea. Paragraphs often contain minor details as well. While the major details explain and develop the main idea, they, in turn, are expanded upon by the *minor supporting details*.

You've already seen that a paragraph's main idea is more general than its supporting details. Similarly, major supporting details are more general than minor supporting details. An important reading skill is the ability to distinguish the major details from the minor ones.

To get a better idea of the role of major and minor supporting details, look again at a main idea considered in the last chapter:

Main Idea

There are two strong influences on the content of dreams.

This sentence brings to mind the question "What are those two strong influences?" This is where the supporting details come in: they clarify and explain. Below is the same main idea with its two major supporting details:

Main Idea and Major Details

There are two strong influences on the content of dreams. One influence is the time of your dream. The other influence on the content of dreams is presleep conditions.

Now we know what the two strong influences referred to in the main idea are; they are the major details. Often, however, the major details themselves are further explained, and that's where the minor support comes in. A major detail introduces a new point, and the minor details develop that point. Here is the full paragraph, with the main idea **boldfaced** and the two major details in *italics*; the other sentences are minor details.

Main Idea, Major Details, and Minor Details

There are two strong influences on the content of dreams. *One influence is the time of your dream.* When you are closest to waking, your dreams are apt to be about recent events. In the middle of the night, however, your dreams are more likely to involve childhood or past events. *The other influence on the content of dreams is presleep conditions.* In one study, subjects who had six hours of active exercise before sleep tended to have dreams with little physical activity. The researcher concluded that dream content may offset waking experiences to some extent. Other research supports that conclusion. For instance, subjects who had experienced a day of social isolation had dreams with a great amount of social interaction. Also, subjects who had been water-deprived dreamed of drinking.

Authors often use addition words to introduce new points. Examples of addition words are *first, second, one, next, another,* and *finally*. Note that the first major detail in the above paragraph is introduced by the addition word *one*. The second major detail is also introduced with an addition word: *other*.

Check Your Understanding

Now see if you can separate major from minor support in the following paragraph. It begins with a definition; then the second sentence presents the main idea, which has been boldfaced. The passage goes on to give two major details and several minor details. Put a check (✓) in front of the two major details that support the main idea. Note that addition words introduce each major detail.

> Phobias are intense, crippling fears of something in the absence of any real danger. **Phobias can be divided into two categories.** The first is simple phobias—fears of specific situations or objects. The fears of darkness and snakes are examples of simple phobias. Some people are even overly fearful of running water. One woman was so afraid of thunderstorms that she would stay inside whenever the sky became overcast or rain was predicted. Perhaps the most common simple phobia is agoraphobia. This phobia is an extreme fear of being alone or in public places that might be difficult to escape from. Sufferers avoid such things as elevators and crowds, especially in crowded stores or busy streets. Another category of phobias is social phobias. Social phobias are fears connected with the presence of other people. Fear of public speaking is a common social phobia. For some people, even eating in public can cause severe anxiety.

Now see if you correctly checked the two major supporting details. You'll find them after the main idea in the following outline of the paragraph:

Main idea: Phobias (intense, crippling fears in the absence of danger) can be divided into two categories.

Major supporting details:

1. Simple phobias: fears of specific situations or objects
2. Social phobias: fears connected with the presence of other people

Following is a more complete outline, showing the minor details as well.

Main idea: Phobias (intense, crippling fears in the absence of danger) can be divided into two categories.

Major and minor supporting details:

1. Simple phobias: fears of specific situations or objects
   a. Fear of darkness
   b. Fear of snakes
   c. Fear of running water
   d. Fear of thunderstorms
   e. Agoraphobia: an extreme fear of being alone or in public places that might be difficult to escape from

2. Social phobias: fears connected with the presence of other
   people
   a. Fear of public speaking
   b. Fear of eating in public

Notice how the complete outline on phobias goes from the general
to the specific. The more general statements are clarified and developed
by the ideas beneath them. Simple phobias and social phobias support the
more general idea of phobias. Specific examples, in turn, clarify what
simple and social phobias are. At a glance you can see that the major
supporting details introduce new points and that the minor details expand
on those points. The outline, by its very nature, divides the paragraph into
main idea, major supporting details, and minor supporting details.

One excellent way, then, to gain experience in identifying major
supporting details (and the minor details that support them) is to outline a
selection. In doing so, you make clear the relationships between the basic
parts of a passage. Recognizing such relationships is an important part of
effective study.

HOW TO LOCATE MAJOR DETAILS

By now you may see that to locate major details, you must (1) find the
main idea and (2) decide on the points that are *primary support* for that
main idea. Practice these steps by reading the paragraph below. Identify
and underline the main idea. Then ask yourself, "What are the major
points the author uses to back up the main idea?" Finally, fill in the main
idea and major details in the outline that follows. The rest of the details in
the passage will be minor details.

[1]Money is a token of wealth with three main purposes. [2]First,
money is a medium of exchange, a tool for simplifying transactions
between buyers and sellers. [3]With money in your pocket, you can
go to a travel agent and get a ticket. [4]The travel agent can then give
the money to the airline, which uses it to meet expenses. [5]Second,
money also acts as a measure of value. [6]As a result, you don't have
to negotiate the relative worth of dissimilar items every time you
buy something, as you would if you were bartering milk for airline
tickets. [7]The value of the ticket is stated in dollars, and your
resources are measured in the same terms. [8]Because of this common
denominator, you can easily compare your ability to pay with the
price of the item. [9]Third, money serves as a place to store value.
[10]Unlike many goods, it will keep. [11]You can put it in your pocket
until you need it, or you can deposit it in a bank.

Main idea: _____

_____

1._____

_____

2._____

_____

3._____

_____

By the time you finished the paragraph, you may have realized that the first sentence presents the main idea: "Money is a token of wealth with three main purposes." The rest of the paragraph develops that idea by introducing and discussing each of the three purposes. Each major detail is introduced by an addition word: "first," "second," and "third." The first major detail is the first purpose of money, introduced in sentence 2: "First, money is a medium of exchange, a tool for simplifying transactions between buyers and sellers." The next major detail is the second purpose, introduced in sentence 5: "Second, money also acts as a measure of value." The final major detail is given in sentence 9: "Third, money serves as a place to store value." Sentences 2, 5, and 9, then, contain the major supporting details—the three primary points that support the main idea.

Those major details are developed by the rest of the passage, the minor supporting details. Minor details may be important to a thorough understanding, but they can be eliminated without removing the basic meaning of the paragraph. Note how the following version of the paragraph—without the minor details—still makes sense:

> Money is a token of wealth with three main functions. First, money is a medium of exchange, a tool for simplifying transactions between buyers and sellers. Second, money also functions as a measure of value. Third, money serves as a place to store value.

Of course, authors do not always present each major detail in its own sentence. For instance, a sentence may provide a combination of major and minor details. But with practice, you will learn to recognize the points that are primary support for main ideas.

➤ *Practice*

A. Complete the outline of the following paragraph by filling in the four missing major details. Note that the topic sentence of the paragraph is boldfaced.

The United States has one of the highest divorce rates in the world, with more than one million divorces a year. **There are several reasons why divorce is more common today than it was in the past.** One reason is that women are less financially dependent on their husbands. Even with children, they manage to go to school and train for positions in today's job market. With their own income, they are not trapped at home as they were in the past. Another reason for divorce is less opposition. Legally, it is easier to obtain a divorce than was the case with earlier generations. There is less religious opposition as well, and less of a social stigma. Divorced people, who were once the subject of whispers and scandal, are now all around us. A third reason for the increase in divorce is that people expect more from marriage now. They want their mates to enrich their lives, help them develop their potential, and be loving companions and good sexual partners. They are not as willing as their parents were to settle for less. Finally, men and women today are more realistic. If a marriage does not work out, they are more ready to simply accept that fact. Perhaps the marriage is not meant to be, they may decide, and to try to continue it might only damage both of them as well as their children. The talk shows and newspaper and magazine articles are full of stories about people who go on to make new beginnings in their lives. Couples in unhappy marriages are prompted to react in a similar way: better to put a bad experience to an end, and to make a new start in life.

Main idea: There are several reasons why divorce is more common today than it was in the past.

1. _____

2. _____

3. _____

4. _____

B. Recognizing the main idea and its major and minor details helps you organize and make better sense of what you read. To get more practice in this productive method of reading, check (✓) the major details as you read the paragraph below. Then answer the questions that follow. Note that the main idea of the paragraph is boldfaced.

> [1]**Any buying process has five stages.** [2]The first occurs when you become aware that you have a problem that a purchase might solve. [3]This may be as simple as noticing that you have run out of breakfast cereal. [4]However, this realization may be much more complex, as when you decide that you are unhappy with your living room furniture and need to redecorate. [5]In the second stage, you begin your search for alternative solutions, such as various brands of breakfast cereal. [6]You may conduct this search in your own memory ("Which brand was it that I ate last week and enjoyed so much?"), or you may engage in a search by visiting one or more stores to examine the brands they offer. [7]Then, in the third stage of this buying process, you evaluate the alternatives. [8]You weigh one against the other, compare them on various features, and try to decide which alternative will best solve the problem you have recognized. [9]The fourth stage is the actual purchase of the product—the result of your evaluation. [10]After purchase, you use the product and then generally go through the final stage of reevaluating the alternative you have chosen. [11]Was the cereal as good as you remembered? [12]Are you satisfied with your new living room furniture?

5. In general, the major details of the passage are
    a. problems that a purchase might solve.
    b. stages in any buying process.
    c. types of purchases.
    d. the best ways to make a purchase.

6. The first major detail is given in
    a. sentence 1.
    b. sentence 2.
    c. sentence 3.
    d. sentence 4.

7. In general, the minor details of the passage are
    a. reasons.
    b. questions.
    c. examples.

8. Sentences 11 and 12 provide
   a. major details.
   b. minor details.

9. *Fill in the missing word:* The purchase of a product takes place in
   the _____ stage.

10. _____ TRUE OR FALSE? The last stage of the buying process actually
    takes place after the product has been purchased.

SCORE: Number right (_____) x 10 = _____%

Name _____

Section _____ Date_____

SUPPORTING DETAILS: Mastery Test 1

A. (1-6) As you read each of the following passages, mark with a check (✓) the major details. Then complete each outline by filling in the major details. Note that the topic sentence of each paragraph is boldfaced.

Two causes come to mind for the increased stress suffered by today's college students. The first is less family support. In previous years, students could count on two parents to help them through the difficult transition from high school to college. Today, however, with divorce rates at an all-time high, many parents have their own problems to cope with. They are therefore less sympathetic to their children's college pressures. Another source of student stress is financial problems. Tuition costs have risen sharply—in fact, at many schools, tuition is nearly double what it was ten years ago. Low-cost college loans are pretty much a thing of the past. Today, college loans, if available at all, come with near-market interest rates. Many students then wind up working at a part-time job at the same time they're trying to be full-time students. It is no wonder that college students today feel more pressured than students of a generation ago.

Main idea: There are two causes for the increased stress suffered by today's college students.

1._____

2._____

There are several reasons for poor recall. First is negative thinking. Many of us reinforce our lack of recall so often it makes it difficult to remember. For example, how often have you heard "I'm awful with names" or "I can never remember numbers"? All this habit does is to encourage the mind not to even try to remember. Another reason for poor recall is a weak impression. It's very easy to forget something that never made a strong impression on you to begin with. It takes time and attention to make a strong impression. A third reason is interference. It is not a good idea, for example, to try to study geometry immediately after algebra. Your memory will be confused by similar figures and symbols. Finally, lack of training is another common reason for poor recall. There are various proven memory techniques. Go out your way to learn them, and you'll greatly improve your memory.

Main idea: There are several reasons for poor recall.

3._____

4._____

5._____

6._____

B. Answer the questions following the passage. Again, you will find it helpful to check (✓) the major details as you read. Note that the main idea of the passage is boldfaced.

> [1]**Elements of cultures can be divided into two categories.** [2]The first is material culture, which consists of all the physical objects that people make and attach meaning to. [3]Books, clothing, and churches are examples. [4]A compact disk is also part of American material culture. [5]It is a physical object that people in our society have created. [6]We have a shared understanding of its purpose and meaning. [7]In contrast, nonmaterial culture consists of human creations that are not physical. [8]Examples of nonmaterial culture are values and customs. [9]Our beliefs and the languages we speak are also part of our nonmaterial culture.

7. Specifically, the major details of the passage are
    a. 1) a physical object and 2) our shared understanding of its purpose and meaning.
    b. 1) material culture and 2) nonmaterial culture.
    c. 1) people, 2) human creations, and 3) beliefs and languages.
    d. 1) books, 2) clothing, 3) churches, 4) values, 5) beliefs, and 6) customs.

8. One sentence that provides a major detail is
    a. sentence 1.
    b. sentence 3.
    c. sentence 7.
    d. sentence 9.

9. One sentence that provides a minor detail is
   a. sentence 1.
   b. sentence 2.
   c. sentence 4.
   d. sentence 7.

10. According to the passage, material culture consists of
    a. all living things.
    b. human creations that are not physical.
    c. meaningful human creations that are physical.
    d. nonmaterial culture.

SCORE: Number right (_____) x 10 = _____%

SUPPORTING DETAILS: Mastery Test 2

A. (1-7.) Check (✓) the major details as you read the following paragraphs. Then complete the outlines by filling in the major details. Note that the topic sentence of each paragraph is boldfaced.

Often, people shun others who have rashes because they're scared of "catching" them. **However, many rashes are due to common skin conditions that are not infectious.** One example is hives, which appear as red, raised, itchy patches of skin. Hives are often brought on by simple stress, though they can also be allergy-related. The hives themselves are almost never serious or permanent; indeed, hives can clear up in a matter of hours. Another example is eczema, which forms red, scaly, itchy patches on the skin. The causes of eczema are not known, though stress may play a part. However, there are over-the-counter creams that will ease the symptoms. Last, there's psoriasis, which appears as itchy red patches with some white scaling. There are many treatments, which include medications as well as changes in lifestyle, that will soothe this condition.

Main idea: Many rashes are due to common skin conditions that are not infectious.

1. _____

2. _____

3. _____

Traditionally, men preferred to be the sole breadwinners of their families. **Men, however, have discovered several benefits to having a working wife.** First of all, of course, a working wife's income can raise her family's living standards. Also, men with working wives are more free to try changing careers. The woman's income can tide the family over economically during his career change. Third, should a husband lose his job, some of the problems of unemployment are offset by his wife's earnings. Among other things, her earnings provide him with the luxury of search time to locate the best job opportunity. Finally, sharing the burden of earning a living has allowed men to discover the joys of fatherhood. In earlier times, fathers were so busy earning a living they had little chance to know their children.

Main idea: Men have discovered several benefits to having a working wife.

4. _____

5. _____

6. _____

7. _____

B. Answer the questions following the passage. Again, you will find it helpful to check (✓) the major details as you read. Note that the main idea of the passage is boldfaced.

> ¹When school boards purchase texts, they also buy an entire system of instruction. ²**Two publishers of popular math texts promote very different approaches.** ³The Scott, Foresman Company publishes traditional math texts. ⁴Their method allows teachers to decide how much time should be used for lectures and exercises. ⁵The emphasis is on learning concepts while gaining math skills. ⁶Scott, Foresman texts are colorful, filled with graphics, and include long explanations. ⁷The second publisher, John Saxon, promotes a quite different approach. ⁸For Saxon's system, teachers lecture in class for only ten minutes, leaving the rest of the time for exercises. ⁹A great deal of class work is spent on reviewing previous lessons. ¹⁰Saxon's books have short explanations and no pictures.

8. In general, the major details of the passage are
   a. the contrasting approaches of two publishers of math textbooks.
   b. the various ways that school subjects can be taught.
   c. two ways for teachers to lecture in math classes.
   d. ways that textbooks are illustrated.

9. The second major detail is introduced in
   a. sentence 3.
   b. sentence 4.
   c. sentence 7.
   d. sentence 8.

10. _____ TRUE OR FALSE? Students do more exercises for the Scott, Foresman method than for the Saxon method.

SCORE: Number right (_____) x 10 = _____ %

Name _____

Section _____ Date_____

SUPPORTING DETAILS: Mastery Test 3

Job interviews, like final exams, can cause self-doubts and upset stomachs. You may feel that interviews are even worse than finals since you can't prepare for them. In the reading below, however, Marcia Prentergast explains that there is much you can do to get ready for job interviews—and to make yourself stand out from the crowd of other applicants.

This selection also provides the opportunity for you to apply your understanding of supporting details to a full-length reading. To help you reinforce the skills taught in previous chapters, there are also questions on vocabulary in context, central point, and main ideas.

Words to Watch

Following are some words in the reading that do not have strong context support. Each word is followed by the number of the paragraph in which it appears and its meaning there. These words are indicated in the selection by a small circle (°).

personable (1): friendly
conservative (4): customary, traditional
flustered (5): nervously confused
potential (14): possible

WINNING THE JOB INTERVIEW GAME

Marcia Prentergast

Few things in everyday life are dreaded more than going to a   1
job interview. First you have to wait in an outer room, which may
be filled with other people all applying for the same job you want.
You look at them and they look at you. Everyone knows that only
one person is going to get the job. Then you are called into the
interviewer's office, where you have to sit in front of a complete
stranger. You have to try to act cool and personable° while you are
asked all sorts of questions. The questions are highly personal, or

confusing, or both. *"What are your strengths and weaknesses?"* *"Where do you see yourself in five years?"* The interview may take twenty minutes, but it may seem like two hours. Finally, when you're done, you get to go home and wait a week or so to find out if you got the job.

The job-interview "game" may not be much fun, but it is a 2 game you can win if you play it right. The name of the game is standing out of the crowd—in a positive way. If you go to the interview in a Bozo the Clown suit, you may stand out of the crowd, all right, but not in a way that is likely to get you hired.

A few basic hints can help you play the interview game to win: 3

1. Dress like you're in charge. That means wearing business 4 clothing: usually a suit and tie or a conservative° dress or skirt suit. Don't dress casually or sloppily, but don't overdress—remember, you're going to a business meeting, not a social affair. Business attire will impress the interviewer. More than that, it will actually help *you* to feel more businesslike, more in charge. As the old saying goes, the clothes make the man (or woman).

2. Plan to arrive early. This will keep you from getting hurried 5 and flustered°, and also help you avoid the disaster of being late. Give yourself a few minutes to catch your breath and mentally go over your application or résumé.

3. Expect to do some small talk first. Knowing what to expect 6 can put you ahead of the game. When the interviewer calls you in, you will probably spend a minute or so in small talk before getting down to the actual interview questions. This small talk is a good time to make a positive impression, though. Follow the interviewer's lead, and if he or she wants to discuss the weather, let's say, by all means do so for a little bit.

4. Be prepared. Certain questions come up regularly in job 7 interviews. *You should plan for all these questions in advance!* Here are common questions, what they really mean, and how to answer them:

"Tell me about yourself." This question is raised to see how 8 organized you are. If you give a wandering, disjointed answer, the interviewer may put you down as a scatterbrain. You might talk briefly about where you were born and raised, where your family lives now, where you went to school, what jobs you've had, and how you happen to be here now looking for the challenge of a new job. You should have planned and rehearsed your answer, so you

can present this basic information about yourself quickly and smoothly.

This question can also give you a chance to show that you're right for the job. If you're applying for a sales job, for example, you might want to point out that you like being around people.   9

"What are your weaknesses?" This question is asked to put you off your guard, perhaps making you reveal things you might not want to. A good ploy is to admit to a "weakness" that employers might actually like—for example, admit to being a workaholic or a perfectionist.   10

"Why did you leave your last job?" This can be a "killer" question, especially if you were fired, or if you quit because you hated your boss. According to the experts, never badmouth anyone when asked this question. If you were fired, talk about personality conflicts, but without blaming anyone. If you hated your boss, say you quit for some other reason—to find a position with more growth opportunities, for example.   11

"Why did you apply for this job?" This question is really asking how eager an employee you will be. The simple answer might be "I need the money"—but that is not what job interviewers and employers want to hear. They want employees who will work hard and stay with the company. So be honest, but give a suitable response. You might say that this is the sort of work you've always wanted to do, or that you see this company as the kind of place where you would like to create a career.   12

Other typical questions are pure softball—if you're ready. If you are asked, "Are you creative?" or "Are you a leader?" give some examples to show that you are. For instance, you may want to discuss your organizational role in one of your college clubs. Perhaps you helped recruit new members or came up with ideas to increase attendance at events. If you are asked, "What are your greatest strengths?" be ready to talk about your abilities that fit the job. Perhaps you'll mention your ability to learn quickly, your talent for working with others, your skill with organizing time efficiently, or your ability to solve problems.   13

No amount of preparation is ever going to make job interviews your favorite activity. But if you go in well-prepared and with a positive attitude, your potential° employer can't help but think highly of you. And the day will come when you will be the one who wins the job.   14

Reading Comprehension Questions

Vocabulary in Context

1. The word *attire* in "Business attire will impress the interviewer. . . .
   As the old saying goes, the clothes make the man (or woman)"
   (paragraph 4) means
   a. notes.
   b. answers.
   c. clothing.
   d. posture.

2. The word *ploy* in "A good ploy is to admit to a 'weakness' that
   employers might actually like—for example, admit to being a
   workaholic or a perfectionist" (paragraph 10) means
   a. question.
   b. mistake.
   c. approach.
   d. wish.

3. The word *badmouth* in " 'Why did you leave your last job?' . . .
   According to the experts, never badmouth anyone when asked this
   question. If you were fired, talk about personality conflicts, but
   without blaming anyone" (paragraph 11) means
   a. answer.
   b. criticize.
   c. recognize.
   d. imitate.

Central Point and Main Ideas

4. Which statement best expresses the central point of the selection?
   a. Interviewers may ask some difficult and highly personal
      questions.
   b. When going to an interview, dress in business clothing, mentally
      go over your application or résumé, and go in with a positive
      attitude.
   c. There are several things you can do to make yourself stand out in
      a positive way at job interviews.
   d. Employers may ask you why you left your last job.

Supporting Details

5. If you were fired from your last job, the author advises you
   a. to make sure your interviewer realizes how unfair your former
      boss was.

     b. not to blame anyone for the firing during your interview.

     c. not to tell the truth, but to convince the interviewer that you quit.

     d. to tell your interviewer a lot of people were fired by the same boss.

6. According to the author, some advantages of arriving early to an interview are

     a. you will not be flustered or late, and you'll have time to review your application or résumé.

     b. you will have time for small talk with the interviewer.

     c. you will have time to see all the other people applying for the same job.

     d. you will have time to check your appearance and to speak to the interviewer's secretary.

7-10. Complete the following outline of "Winning the Job Interview Game" by filling in the main idea and the missing major and minor details, which are listed below in random order.

Main idea: _____

1. To look like you're in charge, dress in business clothing.

2. _____

3. Expect to do some small talk at the beginning of the interview.

4. Be prepared to answer certain questions that are often asked in job interviews.

     a. _____

     b. What are your weaknesses?

     c. Why did you leave your last job?

     d. Why did you apply for this job?

     e. Are you creative?

     f. Are you a leader?

     g. _____

Items Missing from the Outline

    There are ways to do well at job interviews.

    Plan to arrive at the interview a few minutes early.

    Tell me about yourself.

    What are your greatest strengths?

SCORE: Number right (_____) x 10 = _____%

4

Transitions

I respect my boss. She has a quick temper.

Does the writer respect his boss *because* she has a quick temper? We're not sure because the relationship between the above sentences is unclear. To make it clear, a transition is needed. *Transitions* are words and phrases that show the relationships between ideas. To see how transitions guide us, look at the same two ideas, but this time with a transition:

I respect my boss even though she has a quick temper.

Now we know that the writer likes his boss *despite* her quick temper. The relationship between the two sentences is clear. A transition has bridged the gap from one idea to the other. In Latin, *trans* means "across," and transitions live up to their name—they carry the reader "across" from one thought to another.

There are a number of ways in which transitions connect ideas and show relationships. Here is a list of five major types of transitions:

1 Words that show **addition**
2 Words that show **time**
3 Words that show **contrast**
4 Words that show **illustration**
5 Words that show **cause and effect**

Each of these types of transition is explained in the pages that follow.

1   WORDS THAT SHOW ADDITION

Addition words tell us that an author is presenting two or more ideas in a list of items. These words introduce ideas that are first in a list or ideas that add to items already mentioned. Here are some common addition words:

Addition Words

one	first of all	in addition	furthermore
first	also	next	last of all
second	another	moreover	finally

Note how addition words work in the following sentences:

One of the most common fears is the fear of speaking before a group. *Another* is the fear of heights.

These sentences list two common fears. The first fear is introduced with the addition word *one*. The second is introduced with the word *another.*

Check Your Understanding

To see how addition transitions work, insert an appropriate word or phrase from the above box into each of the following blanks. Then read the explanations.

1. One advantage of taking a train is that it is much less expensive than flying. _____, it lets you see the country as you travel.

2. You can lose weight without going hungry by following a few rules. First of all, eat more carbohydrates. Second, cut way back on fat. _____, exercise more.

3. Telephone sales work is a hard way to earn a living. _____, the calling lists are often out of date. The caller asks to speak to a particular person, only to get the frustrating reply that the person is no longer with the company. _____, many firms do not accept marketing calls; instead, they coldly inform the caller that information must be sent in the mail. _____, many people are just rude, and they refuse to take the call. These setbacks can make it hard for the caller to dial the next number.

Explanations

1. The first sentence in item 1 provides one advantage of taking a train, introduced with the addition word *one*. The second sentence gives an *additional* advantage of train travel. You could have introduced the second advantage with any of these addition transitions: *also, in addition, moreover,* and *furthermore.* For example: "One advantage of taking a train is that it is much less expensive than flying. *Also,* it lets you see the country as you travel."

2. Item 2 lists three ways to lose weight without going hungry. Each of the first two ways is introduced with an addition transition: *first of all* and *second.* The last way can be introduced with various transitions: *also, in addition, moreover, furthermore, last of all,* or *finally.* For instance: "*Last of all,* exercise more."

3. The passage in item 3 lists three ways in which telephone sales work is difficult. Each difficulty can be introduced with an addition transition. Below is one version of the passage, with the addition words in italics. You could have chosen other transitions from the box.

   Telephone sales work is a hard way to earn a living. *First of all,* the calling lists are often out of date. The caller asks to speak to a particular person, only to get the frustrating reply that the person is no longer with the company. *Moreover,* many firms do not accept marketing calls; instead, they coldly inform the caller that information must be sent in the mail. *Finally,* many people are just rude, and they refuse to take the call. These setbacks can make it hard for the caller to dial the next number.

2   WORDS THAT SHOW TIME

Time words tell us *when* something happened in relation to something else. Here are some common time words:

Time Words

first	before	when	previously
next	during	then	at present
often	after	now	soon
as	until	later	

Note what time words accomplish in the following sentences:

> *Previously* I went to college to satisfy my parents. *Now* I go to college to get a better career.

The words *previously* and *now* make clear the relationship between the two ideas: *Before*, the speaker thought of college as something his parents wanted him to do. *At present*, he goes to college for his own purposes.

Check Your Understanding

To get a better idea of how time transitions work, insert an appropriate word or phrase from the box on the previous page into each of the following blanks. Then read the explanations.

1. I floss my teeth _____ I'm in the shower.

2. _____ planting the tomato seeds, dig up the ground and add some fertilizer.

3. To study your textbook more effectively, follow a few helpful steps. _____, preview the reading. This means a quick reading of the first and last paragraphs and of the headings. Previewing will help you understand the selection better once you do begin reading. _____ previewing, you are ready to read—and mark—the selection. _____ you read, mark important parts of the text: definitions ("Def"), useful examples ("Ex"), important lists of items ("1, 2, 3," etc.), and key points (underline). Your _____ step is to write study notes of the selection. By selecting and writing out the important parts of the chapter, you will have already begun to learn them. The last step of this process is to recite the ideas in your notes to yourself. Do so repeatedly, _____ you really know the material.

Explanations

1. The missing time word in the first sentence shows that the speaker flosses *at the same time* that he or she is in the shower: "I floss my teeth *when* I'm in the shower."

2. The missing time word in sentence 2 shows the sequence in which the steps are supposed to be done: "*Before* planting the tomato

seeds, dig up the ground and add some fertilizer."

3. The passage in item 3 presents a series of steps to help you study a textbook more effectively. Transitions help to make the time relationships between these steps clearer. Below is one version of the passage, with the time words in italics. For several of the blanks, you could have chosen other words from the box.

To study your textbook more effectively, follow a few helpful steps. *First,* preview the reading. This means a quick reading of the first and last paragraphs and of the headings. Previewing will help you understand the selection better once you do begin reading. *After* previewing, you are ready to read—and mark—the selection. *As* you read, mark important parts of the text: definitions ("Def"), useful examples ("Ex"), important lists of items ("1, 2, 3," etc.), and key points (underline). Your *next* step is to write study notes of the selection. By selecting and writing out the important parts of the chapter, you will have already begun to learn them. The last step of this process is to recite the ideas in your notes to yourself. Do so repeatedly, *until* you really know the material.

3 WORDS THAT SHOW CONTRAST

Contrast words show that two things *are different* in one or more ways. They also inform us when something is going to *be different* from what we might expect. Here are some common contrast words:

Contrast Words

but	in contrast	on the other hand
however	instead	even though
yet	still	although
despite	unlike	difference

Note how contrast words work in the following sentences:

College students with A averages say they have about three alcoholic drinks a week. *On the other hand,* students with D averages have over ten alcoholic drinks a week.

The words *on the other hand* signal that a contrast of some sort will follow. The sentence contrasts the number of alcoholic drinks of D average students with the number of drinks of A average students.

Check Your Understanding

To get a better idea of how contrast transitions work, insert an appropriate word or phrase from the box on the previous page into each of the following blanks. Then read the explanations.

1. If vegetables are flash-frozen soon after being picked, they keep most of their nutrients. _____, their texture probably won't be equal to that of well-prepared fresh vegetables.

2. _____ the brain represents only 2 percent of the total weight of the human body, it uses 20 percent of the body's total oxygen supply.

3. In India, boys are valued as gifts from God. Girls, _____, are considered at best a disappointment. Centuries of tradition determine that boys be given better treatment throughout life. In their parents' house they are, for instance, fed first so that they get the largest portions and choicest bits of food. In the recent past, strangling newborn girls was not uncommon in rural India. Today, although the outright murder of girl babies may occur less often, female children are done away with in other ways. For instance, a baby girl who falls ill is often left untreated. _____, her family would do anything possible to to get medical care for their male children.

Explanations

1. Item 1 contrasts an advantage of flash-freezing vegetables with a disadvantage. You could have chosen to signal this contrast with any of the following transitions: *however, in contrast,* or *on the other hand.* For example: "If vegetables are flash-frozen soon after being picked, they keep most of their nutrients. *On the other hand*, their texture probably won't be equal to that of well-prepared fresh vegetables."

2. Sentence 2 contrasts the relatively small size of the brain with the larger percentage of oxygen it uses: "*Although* (or *Even though*) the brain represents only 2 percent of the total weight of the human body, it uses 20 percent of the body's total oxygen supply."

3. The passage in item 3 contrasts the ways in which boys and girls are viewed in India. Points of contrast can be signaled with contrast transitions. On the next page is one version of the passage, with the contrast words in italics.

In India, boys are valued as gifts from God. Girls, *on the other hand*, are considered at best a disappointment. Centuries of tradition determine that boys be given better treatment throughout life. In their parents' house they are, for instance, fed first so that they get the largest portions and choicest bits of food. In the recent past, strangling newborn girls was not uncommon in rural India. Today, although the outright murder of girl babies may occur less often, female children are done away with in other ways. For instance, a baby girl who falls ill is often left untreated. *In contrast*, her family would do anything possible to to get medical care for their male children.

4   WORDS THAT SHOW ILLUSTRATION

Illustration words point out that one or more examples are being used to explain a given idea. They tell us that a specific detail is being provided as *an example*. Here are some common illustration words:

Illustration Words

for example	to illustrate	such as
example	illustration	including
for instance	once	

See how an illustration transition works in the following passage:

People might be more likely to recycle if they realized that it takes a long time for some objects to decay. *For instance*, an aluminum can may take several hundred years to decompose.

The first sentence makes a general point about some objects taking a long time to decay. The second statement illustrates that point with the supporting detail about aluminum cans. The example is introduced with the illustration transition *for instance*.

Check Your Understanding

To get a better idea of how illustration transitions work, insert an appropriate word or phrase from the above box into each of the following blanks. Then read the explanations.

1. Our neighbors are cruel to their dog. _____, to keep him from barking, they tape up his mouth.

2. Benjamin Franklin had a great interest in science. _____ he chased a small tornado on horseback to see if he could break up the storm with a whip.

3. Folkways are the customary ways by which the members of a group do things. American folkways, _____, include the expectation that we should bathe frequently. Other _____ of folkways are that we should show up on time for appointments and offer friends or neighbors a ride in our car if we are going in the same direction. We should not use foul language in the classroom. And we should dress nicely when we go to a formal occasion. We view people who violate folkways, especially those who violate a good number of them, as "bad-mannered," "different," and perhaps even "strange." But ordinarily we do not consider them immoral, wicked, or criminal.

Explanations

1. The statement that the neighbors are cruel to their dog is a general point. The specific example in the second sentence makes that general statement more clear. You could have introduced the example with any of the following: *for example, for instance,* or *to illustrate.* ("Our neighbors are cruel to their dog. *For instance*, to keep him from barking, they tape up his mouth.")

2. When an event is used as an example, it is often introduced with the illustration word *once*: "Benjamin Franklin had a great interest in science. *Once* he chased a small tornado on horseback to see if he could break up the storm with a whip."

3. The passage in item 3 defines, illustrates, and explains the term "folkways." Some of the examples are signaled by illustration transitions. Below is one version of the passage, with the illustration words in italics. You might have chosen other transitions from the box.

Folkways are the customary ways by which the members of a group do things. American folkways, *for instance*, include the expectation that we should bathe frequently. Other *examples* of folkways are that we should show up on time for appointments and offer friends or neighbors a ride in our car if we are going in the same direction. We should not use foul language in the classroom. And we should dress nicely when we go to a formal occasion. We view people who violate folkways, especially those who violate a good number of them, as "bad-mannered," "different," and perhaps even "strange." But ordinarily we do not consider them immoral, wicked, or criminal.

5 WORDS THAT SHOW CAUSE AND EFFECT

Cause-and-effect words show that the author is discussing the reason or reasons why something happened. They indicate that one event caused another to happen or that a certain reason is behind some circumstance. Here are some common cause-and-effect words.

Cause-and-Effect Words

because	cause	result	therefore
because of	caused	result in	so
since	effects	reason	thus
leads to	as a result	if . . . then	

Note how a cause-and-effect transition works in this sentence:

The bank alarm didn't ring *because* the burglar had cut the power line.

The word *because* signals that a cause-effect relationship is being discussed. The cause is that the burglar cut the power line. The effect is that the alarm didn't ring.

Check Your Understanding

To get a better idea of how cause-and-effect transitions work, insert an appropriate word or phrase from the above box into each of the following blanks. Then read the explanations.

1. Private mail companies have succeeded _____ U.S. post offices are not always close by and their hours are not always convenient.

2. Almost 60 percent of the student body has come down with the flu; _____, the school has been closed.

3. The depression of the 1930s had powerful _____ on families. It forced many couples to delay marriage. It also led to

a sharp drop in the divorce rate _____ many couples could not afford to keep up separate households. The depression also _____ the birthrate to fall. In addition, unemployment meant a loss of status for many men. By 1933, one quarter of the nation's families had no breadwinner. _____ women sometimes found it easier to find jobs than men, women gained status at that time. The fact that they brought home paychecks strengthened their voice in family decisions.

Explanations

1. The causes in this sentence are that 1) U.S. post offices are not always close by, and 2) their hours are not always convenient. The effect is that private mail companies have succeeded. The missing cause-effect word is *because*: "Private mail companies have succeeded *because* U.S. post offices are not always close by and their hours are not always convenient."

2. In item 2, the two parts of the sentence have a cause-effect relationship. The cause is that 60 percent of the student body came down with the flu. The effect was that the school was closed. You could have filled in the blank with *therefore, thus,* or *as a result.* For example: "Almost 60 percent of the student body has come down with the flu; *as a result*, the school has been closed."

3. The passage in item 3 discusses some effects of circumstances during the Great Depression. The causes and effects are signaled by cause-effect words. Below is one version of the passage, with the cause-effect words in italics. You might have chosen other words from the box.

The depression of the 1930s had powerful *effects* on families. It forced many couples to delay marriage. It also led to a sharp drop in the divorce rate *because* many couples could not afford to keep up separate households. The depression also *caused* the birthrate to fall. In addition, unemployment meant a loss of status for many men. By 1933, one quarter of the nation's families had no breadwinner. *Since* women sometimes found it easier to find jobs than men, women gained status at that time. The fact that they brought home paychecks strengthened their voice in family decisions.

FINAL NOTES ABOUT TRANSITIONS

1. Authors try to present supporting details in a clearly organized way. To do so, they often use transitions as guides both for themselves and for their readers. Noticing transitions will help you understand more quickly the relationships between ideas and will help you take organized study notes on those ideas.

2. Often an entire passage is organized according to one kind of relationship. Such passages have a pattern in which one kind of transition is common. For example, many passages list a series of items. The items listed are often introduced with addition words, such as *first, also,* and *finally.* The pattern of organization of such passages is known as a list of items.

   Many other passages have a time order, in which events are marked by time transitions—*first, next, after,* and so on. Other patterns that are marked by one type of transition are the contrast and the cause-effect patterns.

   Finally, some passages, especially in textbooks, use a definition-and-example pattern of organization: They define a term and illustrate it. The examples are often signaled with illustration words.

➤ *Practice*

A. First, complete each sentence with the appropriate transition. Then underline the kind of transition you have used.

1-2. a. Most students have more study time than they realize. First of all, they could spend less time watching TV. _____, they could cut back a bit on social activities.

   In contrast   As a result   Also

   b. The relationship of the second sentence to the first is one of
   contrast.   addition.   cause and effect.

3-4. a. The seventh-inning stretch takes place before the home team comes to bat. It became popular _____ the number seven is thought to be lucky.

   during   because   even though

   b. The relationship indicated by the transition is one of
   contrast.   addition.   cause and effect.

5-6. a. Chewing gum was first introduced in a flavorless form in 1871. _____ came flavored gum in 1875, and bubble gum a decade after that.

Next   Once   Nevertheless

b. The relationship indicated by the transition is one of
illustration.   contrast.   time.

7-8. a. On the whole, fish do not sleep, but there are a few exceptions. _____, some fish in coral reefs sleep by standing on their tails or leaning on rocks.

In contrast   For example   In addition

b. The relationship of the second sentence to the first is one of
contrast.   addition.   illustration.

9-10. a. Gangster Al Capone ("Scarface") claimed he got the scar on his face fighting in World War I. In reality, _____, he was knifed in a fight over a woman.

soon   therefore   however

b. The relationship between the two sentences is one of
time.   contrast.   cause and effect.

B. Transitions have been removed from each of the following passages and placed above it. Write the missing transitions in the spaces provided. Read each passage carefully to see which word or words logically fit in each answer space.

11-13.   *In addition*   *But*   *First of all*

What makes for a happy marriage? Psychologists have identified some general characteristics that are seen in lasting happy marriages. _____, commitment to marriage appears to be one of the most important conditions. _____, previous general adjustment and ability to maintain good relationships with parents seem to be important factors. Children of happily married couples are more likely to have successful marriages. Although most people do not choose the year they plan to marry, age does make a difference. Marriages by those under 21 are most likely to fail. The most favorable age for successful marriages is 21 to 29 for women, and 24 to 29 for men. (_____ keep in mind that marriage at other ages can be successful. If you are over 29, do not despair; a happy marriage is still possible.)

14-16. *For example* *Unlike* *On the other hand*

     Beliefs about the value of talk differ from one culture to another. Western cultures view talk as desirable and use it for social purposes as well as to perform tasks. Silence has a negative value in these cultures. It is likely to be seen as lack of interest, hostility, anxiety, shyness, or a sign of not getting along. Westerners are uncomfortable with silence, which they find embarrassing and awkward. _____, Asian cultures view talk quite differently. For thousands of years, Asian cultures have discouraged the expressions of thoughts and feelings. _____, here are two revealing Taoist sayings: "In much talk there is great weariness," or "One who speaks does not know; one who knows does not speak." _____ Westerners who are uncomfortable with silence, Japanese and Chinese believe that remaining quiet is the proper state when there is nothing to be said.

17-20. *however* *example* *often* *as a result*

     One series of experiments focused on how chimpanzees solved the problem of reaching a banana placed on the ground just outside their cage. The chimps almost always tried first to reach the food with their hands. They very _____ noisily and actively showed their frustration at their lack of success. After a while, _____, the chimps would start looking at what was lying around the cage, including a stick left there by the experimenters. Sometimes quite suddenly, a chimp would grab the stick, poke it through the bars of the cage, and drag the banana within reach. If the stick was too short but a longer stick was within reach, the chimps quickly learned to retrieve the longer stick and, if necessary, to connect the two sticks together in order to reach the banana. The chimps' reaction is an _____ of insight. Insight is learning that occurs rapidly _____ of understanding all the ingredients of a problem.

SCORE: Number right (_____) x 5 = _____%

Name _____

Section _____ Date_____

TRANSITIONS: Mastery Test 1

A. First, complete each sentence with the appropriate transition word or phrase. Then underline the kind of transition you have used.

1. a. _____ the toothbrush was invented in 1770, people cleaned their teeth by rubbing them with a rag.

   Because   Before   Once

   b. The relationship between the two parts of the sentence is one of
      time.   illustration.   cause and effect.

2. a. _____ punishment is generally either painful or frustrating, it can lead to aggression.

   Although   Since   Until

   b. The relationship indicated by the transition is one of
      time.   cause and effect.   contrast.

3. a. Thomas Jefferson taught his pet mockingbird to sit on his shoulder. He _____ trained the bird to peck food from his lips.

   also   in contrast   therefore

   b. The relationship indicated by the transition is one of
      contrast.   addition.   cause and effect.

4. a. _____ friends are among the strongest influences in your life, it's important to choose them carefully.

   Although   Because   Before

   b. The relationship indicated by the transition is one of
      time.   contrast.   cause and effect.

5. a. Employers are not required to provide pensions. _____, many do so as a way of attracting and keeping good workers.

   In addition   Nevertheless   As a result

   b. The relationship indicated by the transition is one of
      cause and effect.   addition.   contrast.

B. Transitions have been removed from the following passage and placed above it. Write the missing transitions in the spaces provided. Read the passage carefully to see which word or words logically fit in each answer space.

In contrast   differences   including   also   because

There are notable (6) _____ between people with high self-esteem and those with low self-esteem. Researchers have concluded that people with good self-concepts tend to be more accepting of others. They are (7) _____ more accepting of their own failures. However, they fail less, since they tend to be better achievers than people with low self-esteem. High self-esteem is also related to independence and open-mindedness. People with positive self-images will be more willing to accept criticism and suggestions. (8) _____, persons with low self-esteem are sensitive to criticism and blame themselves whenever things go wrong. (9) _____ they lack confidence, they will give in to pressure and can usually be influenced easily. Flattery is sought and others are criticized to boost their own self-images. Several studies have shown that low self-esteem is a factor in various behavior problems, (10) _____ cheating and drug abuse.

Name _____

Section _____ Date_____

TRANSITIONS: Mastery Test 2

A. This part of the test will check your ability to recognize the relationships (signaled by transitions) within and between sentences. Read each passage and answer the questions that follow by circling the letter of the best response.

Passage 1

¹Some people remember high school as the best time of their lives. ²However, some of us remember it only when we're forced to. ³During my high school career I disliked myself thoroughly. ⁴I was too busy regretting I was not part of the "in" crowd; as a result I couldn't notice the good things about myself. ⁵For instance, I was a good English student and was active in music and drama. ⁶But because it was me doing those things, I didn't think they were worth much. ⁷Also, I didn't realize that I was surrounded by wonderful people who were ready and willing to become my friends. ⁸It was only after I got to college that I realized that many of the nicest, smartest, and most interesting people aren't ever part of the "in" crowd. ⁹I then learned to like myself and made many wonderful friends.

1. The relationship between sentences 1 and 2 is one of
   a. addition.   c. illustration.
   b. contrast.   d. time.

2. The relationship between the two parts of sentence 4 is one of
   a. time.   c. cause and effect.
   b. contrast.   d. addition.

3. The relationship of sentence 7 to the few sentences before it is one of
   a. time.   c. contrast.
   b. addition.   d. illustration.

Passage 2

¹Superior students are not always rapid readers, but they read a great deal and with excellent comprehension. ²You don't need a high IQ to read well. ³In fact, 70 percent of all poor readers have an average or above-average IQ. ⁴It's important to be a good reader because you will get 75 percent of all your information from printed material. ⁵A useful guideline is this: If your grades are low, the first

thing to suspect is poor reading skills. ⁶It's not difficult to improve them, provided you seek qualified help. ⁷Once you're satisfied with your reading skills, use them. ⁸Read as much as you can, and also read material with varying levels of difficulty. ⁹It's not enough to read the morning newspaper if you want to be really well read. ¹⁰Read textbooks, nonfiction, bestsellers, and magazines. ¹¹The important thing is to read as much as you can.

4. The relationships between the two parts of sentence 1 is one of
   a. time.
   b. addition.
   c. cause and effect.
   d. contrast.

5. Sentence 4 expresses a relationship of
   a. contrast.
   b. cause and effect.
   c. illustration.
   d. time.

6. The relationship of the second part of sentence 8 to the first part is one of
   a. addition.
   b. time.
   c. contrast.
   d. illustration.

B. Transitions have been removed from the following passage and placed above it. Write the missing transitions in the spaces provided. Read the passage carefully to see which transition logically fits in each answer space.

because   *reasons*   *another*   *for instance*

Various circumstances influence a product's price. There are a couple of (7) _____ for companies to price a product above the market. One reason is that some firms want their products to be seen as high quality. Orville Redenbacher, (8) _____, wants his popcorn to be seen as top quality, so it is generally priced above the market—that is, at prices higher than those of competitors. His choice is appropriate (9) _____ he wants consumers to see a price-quality relationship. (10) _____ reason to decide on a premium price is to appeal to the status-conscious buyer. The expense of owning a Rolls-Royce is part of its appeal.

SCORE: Number right (_____) x 10 = _____ %

Name _____

Section _____ Date_____

TRANSITIONS: Mastery Test 3

What would happen if parents came from a culture that valued different activities than those that their children valued? This is a question that Jim Yoshida faced when he was a high school freshman and his parents opposed his joining the football team. To see how they managed their conflict, read the following selection.

This reading also provides the opportunity for you to apply your understanding of transitions to a full-length piece. To help you continue to strengthen your work on the skills taught in previous chapters, there are also questions on

- vocabulary in context
- central point and main ideas
- supporting details.

Words to Watch

Following are some words in the reading that do not have strong context support. Each word is followed by the number of the paragraph in which it appears and its meaning there. These words are indicated in the selection by a small circle (°).

Japanese school (1): an after-public-school ethnic school
ventured (8): dared to say
varsity (13): the school's main team
transgression (21): sin
momentum (28): force of movement
exhilaration (30): joy
ardent (34): enthusiastic

TWO WORLDS

Jim Yoshida, with Bill Hosokawa

When I was fifteen years old and a freshman in a Seattle high   1
school, I stood 5 feet 7 inches tall and weighed 168 pounds. Many of my friends signed up to try out for the freshman football team. I couldn't because I had to go to Japanese school°.

Still, I figured it wouldn't hurt to watch football practice for a 2
little while. I sat on the sidelines, glancing at my watch frequently to
make sure I would leave in time to get to Japanese school. On the
third day of practice, the freshmen engaged in a scrimmage, and I
couldn't tear myself away. I had played some sandlot football, and I
figured I could do just as well as the freshmen in uniform. Before I
knew it, it was too late to get to Japanese school on time. It didn't
take me long to rationalize that being absent was only a little worse
than being tardy. I decided that I might just as well watch football
practice for the remainder of the day. Before long, nothing seemed
to be more important than playing football with the freshman team.
I approached the coach and told him I wanted to try out.

Coach Heaman looked at my stocky frame. "What's your 3
name?" he asked.

"Jim Yoshida," I replied. 4

He reached into a pocket and pulled out a form. "You have to 5
get your parents' permission," he said. "Take this home and get it
signed. Come down to the locker room after school tomorrow and
check out a uniform."

My heart sank. Here I was being invited to try out for the team, 6
and parental permission—an impossible obstacle—blocked the way.

Full of apprehension, I went home at the normal time. 7
Apparently Mom was unaware of my absence from Japanese
school, and if my sister Betty had noticed, she hadn't said anything.
I knew that Mom could sense when I had something on my mind.
Besides, I wanted to talk to her before Dad came home, so I came
straight to the point.

"Mom," I ventured°, "I want to try out for the football team at 8
school."

After hesitating a moment she replied, "What if you were 9
injured playing football? Besides, what would you do about
Japanese school? I think you had better forget about football."

I knew it was useless to try to change her mind and even more 10
useless to talk to Dad.

Next morning during a study period, I gave myself permission 11
to play football. My hands were clammy when I gave the slip to
Coach Heaman. I was sure he could hear the pounding of my heart
and see the look of guilt that I knew was written on my face. He
failed to notice, however, and routinely filed the permission form
and issued me an ancient, hand-me-down uniform and a pair of ill-
fitting shoes.

I made the team as a running guard. This meant I pulled out of 12
the line and ran interference for the ball carrier. If I did what I was
supposed to do and threw a good block, the ball carrier had a chance
of making a good gain.

At the end of the freshman season, I was one of several 13
freshman players invited to suit up with the varsity. In the season
finale, the varsity° coach let me play half the game.

Meanwhile, for some reason I have never understood, my 14
absence from Japanese school went unnoticed until Betty brought
home her Japanese-school report card right after the football season
ended. Mom and Dad grinned as they examined her record. I knew
what was coming next; Dad turned to me and asked to see my report
card.

"Sir," I said, "I don't have one." 15

His eyebrows shot up. "Why not? Did you lose it?" 16

"No, sir, I haven't been attending Japanese school." 17

He fixed me with a stare that bored right through me. We were 18
at the dinner table, and all of us had hot boiled rice to eat with
cooked meat and vegetables. Steam rose from the bowl in front of
my father, and I could see his temper rising too.

"Explain yourself," Dad ordered. 19

So I told him the whole story, including the way I had signed 20
the form, and his frown grew darker and darker. Mom averted a
very explosive situation by suggesting that the dinner table was not
the place for a scolding. She suggested we finish our dinner and
then talk about the problem.

Sometime during the meal, Dad must have seen the humor of 21
my transgression°. Perhaps he remembered pranks he had pulled as
a boy. I was relieved to see his anger had given way to simply a
serious mood when finally the dishes were cleared away.

First he lectured me about how wrong it was to deceive one's 22
parents, and I had to agree with him. Eventually he got around to
football. "I can understand why you would want to play the game,"
he said. "You should, however, take an interest in a Japanese sport
like judo."

Judo is like wrestling, a sport in which a smaller and weaker 23
person learns to use an opponent's strength to defeat the opponent. I
didn't have much enthusiasm for judo.

Dad was saying, "Judo will give you the discipline you need. 24
You must learn to grow tougher physically, mentally, and morally."

Then I saw a way that I might be able to play football next 25
season. I apologized for what I had done. I was truly sorry. I agreed
to go back to Japanese school and try my best to make up for what I
had missed. I said I would go to judo class—if I could play football
again next year.

The smile that had started to take shape on Dad's face vanished. 26
Then he said, "All right, play football if it's that important to you, but
remember there are things that are important to me too. So go to
Japanese school and try to learn a little about the language; and go to
judo classes and learn a little about discipline." We shook hands.

Several nights later, when I came home from Japanese school, 27
Dad introduced me to a man who was about ten years older than I.
His name was Kenny Kuniyuki; he was an instructor at a judo
school. Dad told me Kenny would be my judo teacher. I liked
Kenny immediately. We had dinner together, and then he drove me
to the judo school.

For the next three weeks, every Monday, Wednesday, and 28
Friday, I went to the school and learned to fall. Falling without
hurting yourself is an art in itself. Gradually I learned to roll to absorb
the impact as I hit the mat and to break the momentum° with my arms
and legs and shoulders before I crashed to the floor. Then Kenny
began on the holds and throws. From seven to nine-thirty I would
practice throwing and being thrown with the other students. After
everyone else had left, Kenny had me stay and practice with him.

I must admit that I thought about quitting, especially on 29
mornings after a particularly strenuous workout. I knew, though,
that if I dropped judo, I could forget about playing football.

Approximately six months after I began judo lessons, 30
everything began to fall into place. I was tough physically; I had
learned, finally, to take the hardest falls without hurting myself; and
I was able to coordinate my skill with my strength. I found a new
exhilaration° and excitement in judo. Judo was as much fun as
football!

Soon I was good enough to skip over all the intermediate 31
steps—yellow, green, brown, and purple—and get a black belt. It
usually takes a student three or four years of hard work to win
black-belt rating. I had done it in a fraction of that time. Mom and
Dad beamed approval.

Dad raised no objection when I turned out for football in the 32
fall of my sophomore year. I had kept my end of the bargain, and he

kept his. I made the team as a running guard and was lucky enough to be an all-city selection even though we didn't win a single game. I still continued practicing my judo after the daily football workouts.

When I returned to school for my junior year, I had 190 muscular pounds on my 5-foot-9½-inch frame. The judo training had given me a better sense of balance, which helped me as a football player. I had no trouble making the team, and at the end of the season, I was again named all-city.   33

By the time my senior year rolled around, both my parents had become ardent° football fans, and they came to watch me play. My new coach shifted me to fullback. I guess the move was a success because even though we still didn't win a game, we scored a touchdown—the first in three years. I was the one who carried the ball over the line! As I picked myself up after scoring, I saw Dad standing just outside the end zone with a big grin on his face. I think the sight of that grin made me the happiest of all!   34

Reading Comprehension Questions

Vocabulary in Context

1. The word *apprehension* in "Here I was being invited to try out for the team, and parental permission—an impossible obstacle—blocked the way. Full of apprehension, I went home at the normal time" (paragraphs 6–7) means
   a. confidence.
   b. uneasiness.
   c. good humor.
   d. hate.

2. The word *averted* in "Mom averted a very explosive situation by suggesting that the dinner table was not the place for scolding. . . . I was relieved to see his anger had given way to simply a serious mood when finally the dishes were cleared away" (paragraphs 20–21) means
   a. prevented.
   b. ignored.
   c. caused.
   d. discussed.

3. The word *intermediate* in "Soon I was good enough to skip over all the intermediate steps—yellow, green, brown, and purple—and get a black belt" (paragraph 31) means
   a. more difficult.
   b. middle.
   c. entertaining.
   d. boring.

Central Point and Main Ideas

4. Which statement best expresses the central point of the selection?
   a. Judo is a Japanese sport in which a weaker person uses his opponent's strength against him.
   b. Students often disagree with their parents about how teenagers should spend their time.
   c. Through compromise, Jim Yoshida and his parents came to benefit from accepting parts of both the Japanese and American cultures.
   d. Young people who wish to do well in football ought to work at judo.

5. Which statement best expresses the main idea of paragraphs 28 to 30?
   a. Falling without hurting yourself is difficult.
   b. The author practiced falling three days a week for the next three weeks.
   c. After six months of difficult judo lessons, Yoshida had made great progress and became as excited about judo as about football.
   d. From seven to nine-thirty each evening, the author would practice throwing and being thrown, first with the students and then with Kenny.

Supporting Details

6. Yoshida's parents first realized that he wasn't attending Japanese school when
   a. they attended a high school football game and saw him playing.
   b. his sister told them that she hadn't been seeing him at Japanese school.
   c. he didn't have a report card from Japanese school to show them.
   d. he asked them to sign a permission slip for Coach Heaman.

7. Jim Yoshida's father allowed Jim to play football his sophomore year if he
   a. grew tougher physically, mentally, and morally.
   b. learned judo and attended Japanese school.
   c. attended summer school to make up for what he had missed in Japanese school.
   d. apologized to his football coach for forging his parents' signatures on the permission slip.

Transitions

8. The second sentence below expresses a relationship of
   a. addition.
   b. time.
   c. cause and effect.
   d. illustration.

   Many of my friends signed up to try out for the freshman football team. I couldn't because I had to go to Japanese school. (Paragraph 1)

9. The relationship of the second sentence below to the first sentence is one of
   a. contrast.
   b. illustration.
   c. addition.
   d. time.

   I was sure he could hear the pounding of my heart and see the look of guilt that I knew was written on my face. He failed to notice, however. . . . (Paragraph 11)

10. Narratives usually benefit from time transitions, which indicate some of the time relationships between the events of the story. Write here three of the time transitions used in paragraph 14:

   _____   _____   _____

SCORE: Number right (_____) x 10 = _____ %

5

Inferences

You have probably heard the expression "to read between the lines." When you "read between the lines," you pick up ideas that are not directly stated. These implied ideas are usually important for a full understanding of what an author means. Discovering the ideas that are not stated directly is called *making inferences*, or *drawing conclusions*.

AN INTRODUCTION TO INFERENCES

You have already practiced making inferences in this book. Do you remember the following sentence from the first chapter?

> There is something in a spider's thread that makes bugs *adhere* when they touch the web.

That sentence does not tell us the meaning of *adhere*. But from the general meaning of the sentence and our experience with spiders, we can infer that *adhere* means "stick." When you guess what words mean by looking carefully at their context, you are making inferences.

You have also already practiced inferences in the chapter on implied main ideas. Implied ideas, by definition, are never stated directly. Instead, you must figure them out by making a reasonable judgment after looking at all the material in a passage. Just as you use evidence in a sentence to infer the meaning of a vocabulary word, so you use supporting details in a passage to infer the main idea.

An *inference*, then, is a logical conclusion or a reasonable guess that is based on the available evidence, and on our own experience and logic as well. In this chapter, you will get more practice in making inferences.

Check Your Understanding 1

Reread the passage about the influences on the content of dreams, and then answer the inference question that follows.

> There are two strong influences on the content of dreams. One influence is the time of your dream. When you are closest to waking, your dreams are apt to be about recent events. In the middle of the night, however, your dreams are more likely to involve childhood or past events. The other influence on the content of dreams is presleep conditions. In one study, subjects who had six hours of active exercise before sleep tended to have dreams with little physical activity. The researcher concluded that dream content may offset waking experiences to some extent. Other research supports that conclusion. For instance, subjects who had experienced a day of social isolation had dreams with a great amount of social interaction. Also, subjects who had been water-deprived dreamed of drinking.

Which of the following inferences is most soundly supported by the evidence in the passage?

a. Some people rarely dream.
b. People don't dream during daytime naps.
c. A student studying for finals will probably dream about studying.
d. People who go to bed hungry probably tend to dream of eating.

Explanations

a. The statement in answer *a* is not supported at all. The passage discusses when and what people dream, not how often.

b. Statement *b* is also unsupported. Just because the passage doesn't discuss daytime sleeping doesn't mean we don't dream then. Your personal experience, in fact, may tell you that people do dream in the daytime.

c. According to the passage, dreams don't mirror presleep conditions—they contrast with them. Therefore a student studying for finals would be *less* likely to dream about studying.

d. Answer *d* is most soundly supported by the passage. Since dreams "offset waking experience," a hungry person would tend to dream of eating.

Check Your Understanding 2

Read the following passage. Then circle the letter of each answer that is most firmly based on the given information. Finally, read the explanations of the answers below.

> What makes a good opening line? Sociologists have actually observed and studied how people react to typical "pickup lines." For example, in a bar, the most preferred opening line is "Do you want to dance?" The least preferred is "Bet I can outdrink you." In a restaurant, you'll have the most success with a sincere question like "I haven't been here before. What's good on the menu?" But stay away from "cute" remarks like "I bet the strawberry shortcake isn't as sweet as you are." In the supermarket, you might try "Can I help you to the car with that?" Avoid asking "Do you really eat that junk?" And in the laundromat try "Want to go get a cup of coffee while we're waiting?" But never, never remark "Those are some nice undies you've got there."

1. You can conclude from the passage that first impressions are based
   a. on more than looks.
   b. only on looks.
   c. only on pickup lines.

2. The passage suggests that what you first say to a potential date
   a. is unimportant.
   b. is all that matters.
   c. will probably influence your success with that person.

3. Based on the passage, which of the following opening lines is likely to be most successful?
   a. Haven't I seen you in a beauty contest somewhere?
   b. Hi, my name is Jeff.
   c. You look like a girlfriend I dumped.

4. The implied main idea of the passage is that according to some sociologists,
   a. the cuter and more original a pickup line is, the better.
   b. simple, sincere-sounding pickup lines are most effective.
   c. pickup lines at the laundromat are more likely to be effective than pickup lines at a bar.

Explanations

1–2. The answer to the first question is *a*. Opening lines are not part of a person's looks, yet the passage implies that pickup lines are an important part of first impressions. However, experience tells us that looks also count, which is why answer *c* is not correct.

And since opening lines do affect first impressions, we must conclude that they are also likely to influence success with potential dates. So the answer to question 2 is *c*.

3. The answer to the third question is *b*. The passage suggests that the most successful opening lines are simple, sincere, and straightforward. Of the three choices in question 3, the only opening line that meets that standard is answer *b*.

4. The answer to question 4 is *b*. Since the passage says to "stay away from 'cute' remarks," we can conclude that answer *a* is not sound. Answer *b*, however, is supported by all the details of the passage. All of the recommended pickup lines are simple and sincere—they reflect the speakers' true wishes in down-to-earth questions: "Do you want to dance?"; "I haven't been here before. What's good on the menu?"; "Can I help you to the car with that?"; and "Want to get a cup of coffee while we're waiting?"

Nothing in the passage is about where pickup lines are more likely to be more effective, which is why answer *c* is wrong.

INFERRING PURPOSE AND TONE IN READING

An important part of critical reading is to realize that behind everything you read is an author. This author is a person with a reason for writing a given piece and with a personal point of view. To fully understand and evaluate what you read, you must recognize *purpose*—the reason the author writes. You must also be aware of *tone*—the expression of the author's attitude and feeling. Learning an author's purpose and tone requires inference skills.

Purpose in Reading

Authors write with a purpose in mind, and you can better evaluate what is being said by inferring what that purpose is. Three common purposes are:

- **To inform**—to give information about a subject. Authors with this purpose wish to give their readers facts. The following sentence, for instance, was written to inform.

> Chocolate is a product of the seed of the cacao tree of Central and South America.

The author is simply communicating factual information about chocolate.

- **To persuade**—to convince the reader to agree with the author's point of view on a subject. Authors with this purpose may give facts, but their main goal is to promote an opinion. Here's a sentence that is intended to persuade:

> It's about time that our company created a policy of not testing products on animals.

The author wishes to persuade people in the company to support a policy of not using animals in testing.

- **To entertain**—to amuse and delight; to appeal to the reader's senses and imagination. Authors with this purpose entertain in various ways, through fiction and nonfiction. Here's an example of something written to entertain:

> My boss is so dumb he once returned a necktie because it was too tight.

The exaggerated point of the anecdote is mainly meant to amuse.

Check Your Understanding

Read each of the three selections below and decide whether the author's main purpose is to inform, to persuade, or to entertain. Write what you think is the purpose of each selection in the space provided. Then read the explanations that follow.

1. You must take responsibility to ensure your children's success in school. You should read to your children and also let them see you reading and enjoying books. Then they will approach reading as something fun and desirable.

    Purpose: _____

2. During the Civil War, Clara Barton worked as a volunteer nursing the wounded and sick, often during a battle. Soldiers called her the "angel of the battlefield."

    Purpose: _____

3. I don't know which is harder, taking my body to the doctor or my car to the garage. Both worry me. I'm always afraid they'll find something I didn't know about. The only advantage to taking my body to the doctor over taking my car to the garage is that the doctor never asks me to leave it overnight.

Purpose: _____

Explanations

The purpose of the first paragraph is *to persuade* parents to give children a head start in learning. The author is trying to encourage parents to contribute to their children's mental development. In contrast, the main purpose of the second item is *to inform*—it provides information about Clara Barton. The author does not hope that the reader will do or favor anything. In the third passage, the playful comparison between a car and the author's body tell us that the author's main goal is *to entertain* with humor.

Tone in Reading

A writer's tone reveals the attitude he or she has toward a subject. Tone is expressed through the words and details the writer selects. Just as a speaker's voice can project a range of feelings, a writer's voice can project one or more tones, or feelings: anger, sympathy, hopefulness, sadness, respect, dislike, and so on. Understanding tone is, then, an important part of understanding what an author has written. To infer tone, you must take into account the author's message and choice of words.

To appreciate the differences in tones that writers can use, read the following statements of people who have won a sports event:

"I'm grateful to have won this medal for running. My opponents are wonderful athletes, and I was lucky to beat them today." (*Tones:* modest, humble; generous)

"Hand over that medal. I've passed the test, and I'm the best." (*Tones:* arrogant, haughty; humorous, amusing)

"Oh, my God. I won, I won. I can't believe it." (*Tones:* excited, thrilled; shocked, disbelieving)

On the next page is a list of words commonly used to describe tone. Note that two different words may refer to the same tone or similar tones—for example, *matter-of-fact* and *objective*, or *comic* and *humorous*. Brief meanings are given in parentheses for some of the words.

A List of Words That Describe Tone

objective	matter-of-fact
modest	humble
generous	appreciative
kind	humorous
amusing	confident
surprised	lighthearted
excited	thrilled
sentimental	shocked
disbelieving	uncertain
anxious	depressed
critical	bitter

arrogant *(conceited)*
optimistic *(looking on the bright side of things)*
ironic *(meaning the opposite of what is expressed)*
sarcastic *(making sharp or wounding remarks; ironic)*
scornful *(looking down on someone or something)*
revengeful *(wanting to hurt someone in return for an injury)*

Note: Most of the words in this box reflect a feeling or judgment. In contrast, *matter-of-fact* (sticking only to the facts) and *objective* (without prejudice, not affected by personal feelings) describe communication that does not express personal bias or feeling.

A Note on Irony

One commonly used tone is that of irony. When writing has an ironic tone, it says one thing but means the opposite. Irony is found in everyday conversation as well as in writing. Following are two examples; notice that the quotation in each says the opposite of what is meant.

> After eating a greasy hamburger with french fries and a few beers, someone might say, "Wow, I'm feeling healthier already."

> A fan might say of Whitney Houston, "Poor woman, born without looks or a singing voice."

Irony also refers to situations in which what happens is the opposite of what we might expect. We could call it ironic, for example, if a man bites a dog. So another way for writing to be ironic is to describe such situations. Here are a couple of examples of this type of irony:

A gangster who had many bodyguards to protect him from rivals died by slipping in the bathtub and drowning.

After shopping all day for a special party dress, Emily ended up buying the very first one she had tried on.

Check Your Understanding

Below are three statements expressing different attitudes about a difficult final test. Three different tones are used:

objective   confident   ironic

For each statement, write the tone that you think is present, and then read the explanations.

_____ 1. My history final is sure to be lots of fun, and it will last for only three hours.

_____ 2. The history final will include an essay section and a multiple-choice section.

_____ 3. I've kept up with assignments all semester, and I've reviewed all of the important material. So I should do pretty well on my history final.

Explanations

1. Item 1 has an *ironic* tone. The speaker is saying the opposite of what he means. He really means that the test will not be fun and that it will last entirely too long.

2. In item 2, the speaker communicates only facts about the test. She reveals no point of view—positive or negative—about those facts. Thus we can say that the speaker's tone is *objective*.

3. We can describe the tone of item 3 as *confident*—the speaker is confident about doing well on the final.

➤ *Practice*

A. After reading each passage, circle the letter of the answer that is most logically supported by the given information. Use the hints provided to help you answer each question.

> The story is told of an Amish man who was taking a long train trip. Following Amish tradition, he had left school at an early age to work in the fields. He began talking to his seatmate, who he learned was a university professor. The Amish fellow proposed a game. He said, "Since you are so well educated, how about I ask you a question, and if you can't answer it you give me a dollar? And since I have only a sixth-grade education, you ask me a question, and if I can't answer it, I give you fifty cents?" The professor agreed, and the Amish man asked his question. "If it takes an elephant three days to climb Mount Rushmore, how many potato peelings would it take to shingle a doghouse?" The professor pulled out a dollar and handed it to him. "You've got me. What's the answer?" The Amish man said, "I don't know either. Here's your fifty cents."

1. We can infer that the Amish man's question
   a. actually had no answer.
   b. was based on actual experience.
   c. could have easily been answered.

   Hints: The question is not scientific. (For example, what size is each potato peeling?) Also, it is not about a realistic problem.

2. The story implies that
   a. the Amish man was not as intelligent as the professor.
   b. the university professor was rude.
   c. being educated is not the same as being smart.

> The famous writer Dorothy Parker (1893–1967) once ran into a movie star after the star's most recent and highly publicized suicide attempt. Parker patted the woman's arm and murmured, "Better luck next time." When Parker heard that President Calvin Coolidge, known as "Silent Cal," was dead, she asked, "How can they tell?" In her review of one Broadway play, she wrote that *"The House Beautiful* is the play lousy." And she remarked of the actress Katherine Hepburn in another play that she showed a range of emotions "from A to B."

3. The implied main idea of the passage is that Parker was famous for her
   a. sweetness.
   b. good taste.
   c. sharp wit.

4. We can conclude that President Coolidge
   a. had a very lively personality.
   b. was a bitter enemy of Parker's.
   c. was a quiet, unexpressive person.

   Hint: All we learn about the president (besides that he died) is Parker's comment and that he was known as "Silent Cal."

5. We can infer that
   a. Hepburn once also starred in *The House Beautiful*.
   b. Parker thought that Hepburn's acting was dull.
   c. Parker and Hepburn had been close friends.

B. In the space provided, indicate whether the primary purpose of each sentence is to inform (**I**), to persuade (**P**), or to entertain (**E**).

   _____ 6. The *ZIP* in *ZIP code* stands for the national Zoning Improvement Plan.

   _____ 7. More money should be spent on buying our city police officers up-to-date weapons.

   _____ 8. If athletes get athlete's foot, what do astronauts get? The answer is: missile toe.

C. Each of the following passages illustrates one of the four different tones in the box below. In the space provided, put the letter of the tone that applies to each passage. Two tones will not be used.

a. sentimental	b. depressed	c. optimistic	d. sarcastic

   _____ 9. Let me list some of the reasons I'm happy that my sister Sophie is marrying Tom "Big Shot" Lewis. First, Tom is such a considerate human being. He realizes that doing conventional "nice" things, like remembering his girlfriend's birthday or giving her a Christmas present, would just distract her from the important things in life, like ironing his shirts. Secondly, he's got such potential. It's true that he's not working now; in fact, since we've known him he hasn't held a job for more than two months. But I'm sure any day now his plan to become a traveling disk jockey is going to materialize. Then he'll be able to pay Sophie back all the money she's lent him.

_____ 10. Since I flunked out of school, I haven't felt interested in much of anything. I guess I should be looking for a job or reapply for admission, but I don't have the energy. I don't know why I did so badly last term. It's not that the work was that hard. I just couldn't concentrate on any of my subjects. After a while it was so much easier to stay in bed than make the effort to get to class. Some of my teachers really tried to help me, but I didn't have much to say to them. They probably thought I hate them, but I don't. I just wasn't worth the time they were taking with me.

SCORE: Number right (_____) x 10 = _____%

Name _____

Section _____ Date_____

INFERENCES: Mastery Test 1

A. In the space provided, indicate whether the primary purpose of each sentence is to inform (**I**), to persuade (**P**), or to entertain (**E**).

_____ 1. In a country as wealthy as ours, 40 percent of the nation's children should not be living in poverty.

_____ 2. Almost all of Antarctica is covered with a sheet of ice about 6,500 feet thick.

_____ 3. Do you know where to find the most fish? Between the head and the tail.

B. Read each passage below. Then circle the letter of the answer to each item that is most logically supported by the words and information given.

> Trial lawyers point out that eyewitness accounts of crimes—often used to build a case against a suspect—are not always reliable. Experiments back up their claim. In one experiment, for example, a group of students was shown a film of a car accident. Then they were questioned about the film. Some were asked, "How fast was the white sports car going when it passed the barn?" A week later, all the students were asked whether there had been a barn in the film. Nearly 20 percent of the students who had been asked the initial question "remembered" the barn. In fact, there was no barn in the film.

4. The implied main idea of the passage is:
   a. Experiments support trial lawyers' claim that eyewitness testimony is not always reliable.
   b. Students are less reliable than many first-hand witnesses in trials.
   c. There are many ways in which our memories can be "tricked" into false remembering.

5. We can infer that eyewitnesses in court
   a. are highly accurate.
   b. are one of the least reliable sources of evidence.
   c. can be influenced into giving untrue testimony without realizing it.

A small private plane developed engine trouble while still many miles from a suitable landing strip. The pilot, realizing there was nothing he could do to keep the plane in the air, rushed back to where his three passengers sat and explained the predicament. He added, "I am a married man with two small children. I regret to tell you there are only three parachutes aboard." And with that, he grabbed one of the parachutes and bailed out.

One of the passengers reacted quickly to the pilot's exit. "I am a brilliant scientist!" he announced. "I am the world's smartest man! The world cannot do without me!" And with that, he too bailed out.

The other two passengers, an elderly priest and a Boy Scout, were quiet for a moment. "Son," the priest said finally, "I am old and have lived a full life. I am ready to meet my Maker."

"You'll have to cancel it, Father," the Boy Scout answered, smiling. "The world's smartest man just bailed out with my backpack!"

6. The main idea of the passage is:
   a. It is dangerous to fly in small private planes, especially when there are insufficient parachutes.
   b. A priest is more likely to be heroic and generous than a pilot and a scientist.
   c. No matter how smart someone is, he or she needs to examine the facts closely before acting.

In a certain country, when people became too old to work, someone would load them into a basket, carry them up to the mountain, and leave them there for the wolves to eat.

One day a son looked at his elderly father and thought, "Father is now too old to work. I will take him up to the wolves." So he got the basket and as he was putting his father in it, the old man spoke. "Son," he said, "when you return, remember to bring back the basket—because next time it will be your turn."

7. We can conclude from the story that
   a. the father was lying to his son.
   b. the father felt his son was doing the right thing.
   c. the father wanted his son to have second thoughts about his plan.

8. The main purpose of the story is
   a. to inform readers of a true custom among family members in another country.

b. to persuade readers to treat the elderly as they would want to be treated when they are older.

c. to amuse readers with an comical story about a father and son.

   At the very bottom of the American social ladder are the homeless. They are people whose worldly goods fill a few shopping bags. Social workers usually find that these people once were better off, but that some unexpected misfortune led to their losing their home. An apartment building, for example, is sold to a developer, and its poor tenants are evicted. A breadwinner loses his or her job because of a plant closing or a prolonged illness. A woman leaves an abusive husband but cannot afford an apartment on her own. Whatever the cause, the result is the same: a person, a couple, a mother and her children, or an entire family living on the street. Having fallen from a higher rung on the social ladder, many of the homeless are unable to regain their position.

9. The purpose of the passage is
   a. to inform.
   b. to persuade.
   c. to entertain.

10. We can conclude from the passage that inexpensive housing
    a. is often unavailable.
    b. would help people avoid homelessness.
    c. both of the above.

SCORE: Number right (_____) x 10 = _____%

INFERENCES: Mastery Test 2

Circle the letter of the answer to each item that is most logically supported by the passage.

A.   Did you ever have one of those days? You know, one of those days when your alarm clock mysteriously goes off at 4:08 a.m., and you never get back to sleep? Then you cancel plans in order to stay home and watch your favorite TV show, only to have it preempted by a news report.

It's one of those days when your scarf gets caught in the taxi cab just before it pulls away from the curb. It's a day where a lunch in the park turns into bird droppings on your sandwich, and your new car breaks down in traffic for no particular reason.

This is the day you realize you have no clean clothes for your date tonight. It's a day when you remember you left your keys on the kitchen table after you locked the front door. It's a day your teacher gives you a pop quiz the one time you didn't read the chapter. For those who don't know, it's called Monday.

1. The author's main purpose in writing this passage is
   a. to inform.
   b. to persuade.
   c. to entertain.

2. The author's tone can be described as
   a. critical.
   b. uncertain.
   c. amused.

B.   Sharon is a person whose life seems filled with conflict. I rarely have a conversation with her without being reminded of that fact. For example, she constantly complains to me that people "do her wrong." "And I thought she was my friend!" is her constant refrain. Before I knew Sharon well, I sympathized with her incredible bad luck. Now, however, I think I understand the situation better. Sharon expects her friends to show her unconditional love and acceptance, no matter how she behaves. Even when she stands her friends up, tells them lies, and takes advantage of them, she is astonished when they withdraw their friendship. Despite her constant experience of losing friends, she doesn't realize that she is responsible for the situation.

3. The speaker of the passage
   a. is Sharon's sister.
   b. is no longer on speaking terms with Sharon.
   c. has kept up her relationship with Sharon.

4. The tone of the passage can be described as
   a. critical.
   b. sentimental.
   c. uncertain.

C. (5-10) Read the following passage from *Homecoming*, an autobiography by Floyd Dell (1887-1969). Then check the **six** statements which are most logically supported by the information given.

That fall, before it was discovered that the soles of both my shoes were worn clear through, I still went to Sunday school. And one time the Sunday school superintendent made a speech to all the classes. He said that these were hard times, and that many poor children weren't getting enough to eat. It was the first that I had heard about it. He asked everybody to bring some food for the poor children next Sunday. I felt very sorry for the poor children.

Also, little envelopes were distributed to all the classes. Each little boy and girl was to bring money for the poor, next Sunday. The pretty Sunday school teacher explained that we were to write our names, or have our parents write them, up in the left-hand corner of the little envelopes. . . . I told my mother all about it when I came home. And my mother gave me, the next Sunday, a small bag of potatoes to carry to Sunday school. I supposed the poor children's mothers would make potato soup out of them. . . . Potato soup was good. My father, who was quite a joker, would always say, as if he were surprised, "Ah! I see we have some nourishing potato soup today!" It was so good that we had it every day. My father was at home all day long and every day, now; and I liked that, even if he was grumpy. . . .

Taking my small bag of potatoes to Sunday school, I looked around for the poor children; I was disappointed not to see them. I had heard about poor children in stories. But I was told just to put my contribution with the others on the big table in the side room.

I had brought with me the little yellow envelope with some money in it for the poor children. My mother had put the money in it and sealed it up. She wouldn't tell me how much money she had put in it, but it felt like several dimes. Only she wouldn't let me write my name on the envelope. I had learned to write my name, and I was proud of being able to do it. But my mother said firmly, no, I must not write my name on the envelope; she didn't tell me why. On the way to Sunday school I had pressed the envelope against the coins until I could tell what they were; they weren't dimes but pennies.

_____ 1. At the time, the author did not realize he was a poor child himself.

_____ 2. The author actually did not like potato soup.

_____ 3. The family had potato soup every day because it was so good.

_____ 4. The family had potato soup every day because it was so inexpensive.

_____ 5. The father's comment on potato soup showed his interest in nutrition.

_____ 6. The father's remark about potato soup was a sarcastic comment on their poverty.

_____ 7. The author's mother didn't want his name on the envelope because she was ashamed of their small donation.

_____ 8. The author's father probably lost his job.

_____ 9. The author must have gotten several pairs of new shoes that fall.

_____ 10. The author soon stopped going to Sunday school.

SCORE: Number right (_____) x 10 = _____ %

INFERENCES: Mastery Test 3

The following story is a heartwarming example of how good things can happen by accident. The story also provides the opportunity for you to apply your understanding of inferences to a full-length selection. To help you continue to strengthen your work on the skills taught in previous chapters, there are also questions on

- vocabulary in context
- central point and main ideas
- supporting details
- transitions.

Words to Watch

Following are some words in the reading that do not have strong context support. Each word is followed by the number of the paragraph in which it appears and its meaning there. These words are indicated in the selection by a small circle (°).

mystified (2) puzzled
tentative (22) unsure, hesitant

A FRIEND ON THE LINE

Jennings Michael Burch

Even before I finished dialing, I somehow knew I'd made a   1
mistake. The phone rang once, twice—then someone picked it up.

"You got the wrong number!" a husky male voice snapped   2
before the line went dead. Mystified°, I dialed again.

"I said you got the wrong number!" came the voice. Once   3
more the phone clicked in my ear.

How could he possibly know I had a wrong number? At that   4
time, I worked for the New York City Police Department. A cop is
trained to be curious—and concerned. So I dialed a third time.

"Hey, c'mon," the man said. "Is this you again?"   5

"Yeah, it's me," I answered. "I was wondering how you knew   6
I had the wrong number before I even said anything."

"You figure it out!" The phone slammed down.   7

I sat there awhile, the receiver hanging loosely in my fingers. I   8
called the man back.

"Did you figure it out yet?" he asked.   9

"The only thing I can think of is . . . nobody ever calls you."   10

"You got it!" The phone went dead for the fourth time.   11
Chuckling, I dialed the man back.

"What do you want now?" he asked.   12

"I thought I'd call . . . just to say hello."   13

"Hello? Why?"   14

"Well, if nobody ever calls you, I thought maybe I should."   15

"Okay. Hello. Who is this?"   16

At last I had gotten through. Now he was curious. I told him   17
who I was and asked who he was.

"My name's Adolf Meth. I'm eighty-eight years old, and I   18
haven't had this many wrong numbers in one day in twenty years!"
We both laughed.

We talked for ten minutes. Adolf had no family, no friends.   19
Everyone he had been close to had died. Then we discovered we
had something in common: he'd worked for the New York City
Police Department for nearly forty years. Telling me about his days
there as an elevator operator, he seemed interesting, even friendly. I
asked if I could call him again.

"Why would you wanta do that?" he asked, surprised.   20

"Well, maybe we could be phone friends. You know, like pen   21
pals."

He hesitated. "I wouldn't mind . . . having a friend again." His   22
voice sounded a little tentative°.

I called Adolf the following afternoon and several days after   23
that. Easy to talk with, he related his memories of World Wars I and
II, the Hindenburg disaster and other historic events. He was
fascinating. I gave him my home and office numbers so he could
call me. He did—almost every day.

I was not just being kind to a lonely old man. Talking with   24
Adolf became important to me, because I, too, had a big gap in my
life. Raised in orphanages and foster homes, I never had a father.
Gradually, Adolf took on a kind of fatherly importance to me. I
talked about my job and college courses, which I attended at night.

Adolf warmed to the role of counselor. While discussing a   25
disagreement I'd had with a supervisor, I told my new friend, "I
think I ought to have it out with him."

"What's the rush?" Adolf cautioned. "Let things cool down.   26
When you get as old as I am, you find out that time takes care of a
lot. If things get worse, *then* you can talk to him."

There was a long silence. "You know," he said softly, "I'm   27
talking to you just the way I'd talk to a boy of my own. I always
wanted a family—and children. You're too young to know how that
feels."

No I wasn't. I'd always wanted a family—and a father. But I   28
didn't say anything, afraid I wouldn't be able to hold back the hurt
I'd felt for so long.

One evening Adolf mentioned his eighty-ninth birthday was   29
coming up. Buying a piece of fiberboard, I designed a two-by-five-
foot greeting card with a cake and eighty-nine candles on it. I asked
all the cops in my office and even the police commissioner to sign
it. I gathered nearly a hundred signatures. Adolf would get a kick
out of this, I knew.

We'd been talking on the phone for four months now, and I   30
thought this would be a good time to meet face to face. So I decided
to deliver the card by hand.

I didn't tell Adolf I was coming; I just drove to his address one   31
morning and parked the car up the street from his apartment house.

A postman was sorting mail in the hallway when I entered the   32
building. He nodded as I checked the mailboxes for Adolf's name.
There it was. Apartment 1H, some twenty feet from where I stood.

My heart pounded with excitement. Would we have the same   33
chemistry in person that we had on the phone? I felt the first stab of
doubt. Maybe he would reject me the way my father had rejected
me when he went out of my life. I tapped on Adolf's door. When
there was no answer, I knocked harder.

The postman looked up from his sorting. "No one there," he   34
said.

"Yeah," I said, feeling a little foolish. "If he answers his door   35
the way he answers his phone, this may take all day."

"You a relative or something?"   36

"No. Just a friend."   37

"I'm really sorry," he said quietly, "but Mr. Meth died day   38
before yesterday."

Died? Adolf? For a moment, I couldn't answer. I stood there in 39
shock and disbelief. Then, pulling myself together, I thanked him
and stepped out into the late-morning sun. I walked toward the car,
misty-eyed.

Then, rounding a corner, I saw a church, and a line from the 40
Old Testament leaped to mind: "A friend loveth at all times." And
especially in death, I realized. This brought a moment of
recognition. Often it takes some sudden and sad turn of events to
awaken us to the beauty of a special presence in our lives. Now, for
the first time, I sensed how very close Adolf and I had become. It
had been easy, and I knew this would make it even easier the next
time, with my next close friend.

Slowly, I felt a warmth surging through me. I heard Adolf's 41
growly voice shouting, "Wrong number!" Then I heard him asking
why I wanted to call him again.

"Because you mattered, Adolf," I said aloud to no one. 42
"Because I was your friend."

I placed the unopened birthday card on the back seat of my car 43
and got behind the wheel. Before starting the engine, I looked over
my shoulder. "Adolf," I whispered, "I didn't get the wrong number
at all. I got you."

Reading Comprehension Questions

Vocabulary in Context

1. The word *chemistry* in "Would we have the same chemistry in
   person that we had on the phone? I felt the first stab of doubt"
   (paragraph 33) means
   a. science background.
   b. mutual attraction.
   c. voices.
   d. weak beginning.

Central Point and Main Ideas

2. Which statement best expresses the central point of the selection?
   a. People should be more polite while talking on the telephone.
   b. People who have worked for the same employer tend to have
      much in common.

    c. There ought to be a way for people without families to meet one another and develop family-like relationships.

    d. Through an accidental phone call, the author experienced the joy of a father-like friend.

3. The main idea of paragraphs 25 and 26 is expressed in
    a. the first sentence of paragraph 25.
    b. the first sentence of paragraph 26.
    c. the second sentence of paragraph 26.
    d. the last sentence of paragraph 26.

Supporting Details

4. The author
    a. had a strong relationship with his father, who died a few years earlier.
    b. grew up in orphanages and foster homes and never had a father in his life.
    c. really didn't mind growing up without a family of his own.
    d. became like a father to Adolf Meth.

5. When the author went to visit Adolf, he
    a. brought along his supervisor.
    b. began to worry that Adolf would reject him.
    c. immediately sensed that something was wrong with Adolf.
    d. had already called to make sure Adolf would be expecting him.

Transitions

6. The sentence below expresses a relationship of
    a. time.
    b. contrast.
    c. illustration.
    d. cause and effect.

    Talking with Adolf became important to me because I, too, had a big gap in my life. (Paragraph 24)

7. A blank has been inserted in the excerpt on the following page. Which transition would logically fit in the blank?
    a. *In contrast*
    b. *Because*
    c. *For instance*

Adolf warmed to the role of counselor. _____,
while discussing a disagreement I'd had with a supervisor, I told
my new friend, "I think I ought to have it out with him."

"What's the rush?" Adolf cautioned. "Let things cool
down. . . ." (Paragraphs 25–26)

Inferences

8. In paragraph 40, the author implies that
   a. he hadn't realized quite how important Adolf was to him until he
      was gone.
   b. Adolf Meth knew he was going to die soon.
   c. Adolf Meth lived very close to the author's home.
   d. his love for Adolf died when the old man died.

9. From the reading we can conclude that
   a. friends can be found through accidental meetings.
   b. nothing can at all resemble the relationships we have with our
      real family.
   c. there is little that the elderly can learn from the young.
   d. there is little that the young can learn from the elderly.

10. The reading suggests that
   a. the author feels terribly guilty because he did not visit Adolf
      before he died.
   b. the author never did make the phone call he set out to make at
      the start of the story.
   c. a person who outlives his or her friends and family can be very
      lonely.
   d. Adolf would have rejected the author had they met in person.

SCORE: Number right (_____) x 10 = _____ %

6

Summarizing and Outlining

Summarizing and outlining are two skills that will help you with a good deal of your college work: from notetaking in class to writing study notes for exams to preparing papers, speeches, and reports.

UNDERSTANDING SUMMARIES

All of us make summaries in everyday life. For example, in response to someone's question, we might summarize our day by saying:

"I had a good day" or "I had a bad day."

Or we might offer a slightly more specific summary:

"I had an exciting day" or "I had a depressing day" or "I had a busy day."

Or our summary might be even more detailed:

"I had a busy day. I had three classes at school this morning, spent the afternoon in the library doing homework, and then worked at my part-time job for five hours in the evening."

When we make such general statements, we are providing summaries. A *summary* can be defined as the reduction of information to its more important points. Just as we can summarize the numerous details of our day, so we can summarize the numerous details in college course materials. Read the following passage from a textbook, and then look at the summary of it that follows.

When reading, decide upon your purpose and then adjust your speed for the level of understanding required. Don't read everything at the same rate. There are times when it makes sense to read faster. When you read easy material or when your purpose in reading is entertainment, speed up. A common belief is that reading faster ruins enjoyment. That is not true. When you were in first grade, you probably read at a rate of ten to fifty words per minute. Now you may read one hundred to five hundred words per minute, a full ten times faster! Did you lose any of the enjoyment of books? Of course not, and in fact, you may enjoy books more now than when you read slowly. However, there are also times when it makes sense to read more slowly. For technical reading or any reading materials you wish to study, slow down. Take notes often, reread difficult passages, and read as slowly as necessary for full comprehension.

Summary of Passage:

Adjust your rate of reading for the level of understanding required. There are times when it makes sense to read faster and times when it makes sense to read more slowly.

Important Points About Summarizing

1   A summary includes the main idea and often the major supporting details of a selection. The length of a summary will depend upon your purpose and the material. Just as a general guideline, though, a paragraph might be summarized in a sentence or two, and an article might be summarized in a paragraph. An entire textbook chapter might be reduced to about three or so pages of notes.

Now look back at the summary of the passage about reading speed. Note that it includes the main idea (stated in the first sentence of the passage) and both major details.

2   Depending on your purpose, a summary can be in the words of the author or in your own words, or in a combination of the two. If you are summarizing textbook material or a class lecture, you may be better off using the words of the author or of your teacher, especially where definitions of important terms are involved.

Check Your Understanding

To get practice in summarizing, read the passage below. Then decide which of the four statements that follow accurately summarizes the information in the passage.

> More and more, top Hollywood movie people are now doing work for television. First of all, some big movie names have become television producers. Oliver Stone, well known for *Platoon*, *J.F.K.*, and other films, made his TV debut as producer of a mini-series for ABC. George Lucas of *Star Wars* fame produced an ABC series. In addition, successful Hollywood directors have started to do TV directing. For instance, Steven Spielberg, director of *E.T.*, directed TV's *Amazing Stories* series. Penny Marshall, who directed the film *A League of Their Own*, also directed the first episode of the TV series based on that film. Furthermore, more and more Hollywood actors are turning up on the small screen. Holly Hunter and Joanne Woodward, for instance, have appeared in cable television movies.

Circle the letter of the item that best summarizes the passage.
a. Hollywood once looked down on television. And television directors and actors considered movies a step up.
b. More and more, top movie people are working for television. Oliver Stone, Steven Spielberg, and Joanne Woodward are among those who have worked for TV.
c. More and more, top Hollywood people are doing work for television. Some big Hollywood names have been producers, directors, and actors for TV productions.
d. Oliver Stone, director of successful films, made his TV debut as the producer of an ABC miniseries. In addition, Holly Hunter and Joanne Woodward have appeared in cable television movies.

Here is how you could have found the best summary for the passage on Hollywood people working in television—and how you can go about summarizing any passage:

1   Find the basic parts of the passage: its main idea and major supporting details. Remember, a summary will always include the main idea and often the major details as well. A careful rereading of the passage above reveals that it lists three types of Hollywood people who work on TV. The main idea, then, is the general idea stated in the first sentence: "More and more, top movie people are doing work for television." The major details are facts about the three types of workers in TV: producers, directors, and actors.

2   You may find it very helpful while summarizing to do a mini-
outline of the passage, in which you number the supporting details.
On scratch paper or in the textbook margin or simply in your head,
you could create the following for the passage about television:

Main idea: More and more, top Hollywood people are doing work
for television.

Major details: 1. Producers
                     2. Directors
                     3. Actors

Such an outline shows you the main parts of the passage at a glance
and is therefore a useful guide to writing a summary.

3   By now you may know that the best summary of the above passage
is summary *c*. That summary includes the main idea and the three
major supporting details. Summary *a* includes only producing and
directing; it omits acting. Summary *b* begins with the main idea, but
it goes on to mention only minor details. Summary *d* is about only
minor details.

UNDERSTANDING OUTLINES

As you have seen, very often a good way to summarize something is to
outline it first. An outline is itself a summary in which spaces, numbers,
and letters are used to set off the main idea and the supporting details of a
selection. For example, the passage on page 107 about reading speed
could have been outlined as follows:

Adjust your rate of reading to the level of understanding required.
   1. Speed up for some materials
      a. Easy material
      b. Material meant for entertainment
   2. Slow down for some materials
      a. Technical materials
      b. Materials for study

Important Points About Outlining

1   Most outlines start with a main idea (or a title that summarizes the main idea) followed by major and perhaps minor details. The major and minor details are each marked with numbers or letters. The outline above on reading speed includes both major details, which are numbered, and minor details, which are lettered.

2   When doing an outline, put all major details at the same distance from the margin. In the outline on reading speed, for instance, both major details are placed at the same distance from the margin. As you can see, the minor details should be lined up together even further from the margin.

Note that an outline proceeds from the most general to the most specific, from the main ideas to major details to minor details.

Check Your Understanding

To get practice in outlining, read the following passage. Then decide which of the three choices that follow—A, B, or C—best condenses and organizes the information in the passage.

With discount pricing, companies offer various types of price reductions. One type of price reduction is a trade discount, which is offered by the producer to the wholesaler or retailer. An interior decorator, for example, may buy furniture from a manufacturer at a discount and then resell it to a client. There is also the quantity discount, which is offered to buyers who order large quantities of a product. These buyers receive a price break because they are cheaper to serve. They reduce the cost of selling, storing, and shipping products and of billing customers. Finally, a cash discount is a price reduction offered to people who pay in cash or who pay promptly.

A. Companies have various expenses.
   1. A trade discount is offered by the producer to the wholesaler or retailer.
   2. An interior decorator may buy furniture at a discount from a manufacturer and then resell it to a client.
   3. A quantity discount is offered to buyers who order large quantities.
   4. A cash discount is sometimes given to people who pay in cash or who pay promptly.

B. With discount pricing, companies offer various types of price reductions.
   1. Trade discounts
   2. Producer
   3. Wholesaler
   4. Retailer
   5. Buyers who order large quantities of a product
      a. Cheaper to serve
      b. Reduce the cost of selling, storing, and shipping products and of billing
   6. A cash discount
   7. To people who pay in cash
   8. To people who pay promptly

C. Types of price reductions in discount pricing
   1. Trade discount—by producer to wholesaler or retailer
   2. Quantity discount—to quantity buyers (because they reduce costs)
   3. Cash discount—to those who pay in cash or who pay promptly

To find the best of the three outlines, you must do the same thing you would do if you were outlining the passage yourself: Identify the main idea and major and minor details. A careful reading of the passage reveals that it is a list of types of price reductions used in discount pricing. The topic sentence is thus the first sentence: "With discount pricing, companies offer various types of price reductions." The major details are the three types of price reductions listed: trade discounts, quantity discounts, and cash discounts. The outline that best reflects the passage will have a heading that either states or summarizes the main idea. The body of the outline will name and briefly define each item listed.

Having analyzed the passage, let's look back at the above three outlines.

- Outline A names in its heading "various expenses," not the "types of price reductions" listed in the passage. In addition, that outline doesn't distinguish between major details and minor details (the example about an interior decorator is a minor detail that illustrates the first major detail). So outline A is incorrect.

- Outline B is also incorrect. The major and many minor details, and parts of each, are all numbered in the same series and at the same distance from the margin. The two items listed as minor details are really just one point—the buyers are cheaper to serve *because* they reduce the costs.

• Outline C is the correct outline. Its heading tells what the passage lists; the three major details, including brief definitions, are listed below the heading.

➤ *Practice*

Summarizing

1. Circle the letter of the best summary of the selection that follows.

Most popular accounts of lawlessness in the Old West appear to be greatly exaggerated. Bat Masterson, who, according to legend, killed thirty men in gunfights, actually killed three. Billy the Kid supposedly killed one man for each of his twenty-one years of life. He apparently killed only three. Kansas's cattle towns, legend holds, witnessed a killing every night. But in fact in Abilene, Caldwell, Dodge City, Ellsworth, and Wichita, a grand total of forty-five homicides took place during a fifteen-year span. In Deadwood, South Dakota, where Wild Bill Hickok was shot in the back while playing poker in 1876, only four homicides took place in the town's most violent year. And in Tombstone, Arizona, the site of the shootout at the OK Corral, only five men were killed in the city's deadliest year.

a. According to legend, Bat Masterson killed thirty men in gunfights. In reality, he killed only three. Similarly, Billy the Kid was said to have killed twenty-one men, but he apparently killed only three.

b. Most popular accounts of lawlessness in the Old West seem to be greatly overstated. Famous bandits killed many fewer men in reality than in legend, and the towns famous for lawlessness saw few killings.

c. Wild Bill Hickok was shot in the back while playing poker in 1876. That happened in Deadwood, South Dakota, where only four killings took place in the town's most violent year.

d. Five Kansas cattle towns reputed to have witnessed a killing every night in fact saw only forty-five homicides during a fifteen year span. In Deadwood, South Dakota, only four homicides took place in the town's most violent year.

2-3. Complete the summary of the following passage.

> Absolutely everything you do is caused by either internal or external motivation. If you are internally motivated, you are performing the activity because you enjoy it. The activity is rewarding in itself. For example, assume you like to watch football games on Sunday afternoons. Just watching the game brings good feelings. A friend who finds football games uninteresting would not have this internal motivation.
>
> Now, assume you want this friend to join you. You might have to provide an external motivator. An external motivator supplies an outside reward. Perhaps you could offer your friend some tasty snacks or concert tickets or cash for watching the game with you. These outside rewards would provide external motivation for sitting through a boring experience.

(Begin your summary here with a statement of the main idea.)

———————————————————————————————

———————————————————————————————

When you do something because you enjoy it, you are being internally motivated. *(Now add the second major detail.)*

———————————————————————————————

———————————————————————————————

Outlining

4. Circle the letter of the outline that best condenses and organizes the following passage. (*Hint:* Note that the major details are introduced with addition transitions.)

> The aging of the American population is the result of several trends. First, survival rates have improved steadily since the nineteenth century. Improvements in public health and nutrition have meant that more and more infants and children grow to adulthood. A second reason is increased lifespan, due in part to medical advances. In 1900, only two in five Americans lived to be at least 65 years old; today the figure is three out of four. Between 1960 and 1980, the number of Americans age 65 and older more than doubled. At the same time, the number of "old-old" grew four

times larger, reaching 1.6 million. All told, the elderly population of the United States grew faster than the population of India.

A third reason for the aging of the American population is the dropping birthrate. The "boom" in older people has been paired with a "bust" in births. With the exception of the baby boom period, birthrates have dropped steadily since 1800. Estimates are that by 2030 the proportion of Americans age 65 and older will have climbed from 12 to 21 percent.

A. Trends leading to the aging of the American population
 1. Steadily improving survival rates since the 19th century
   a. Improvements in public health
   b. Improvements in nutrition
 2. Increased lifespan, due in part to medical advances
 3. A declining birth rate

B. The aging of the American population
 1. The result of several trends
 2. Steadily improving survival rates since the 19th century
 3. Improvements in public health
 4. Improvements in nutrition
 5. Increased lifespan, due in part to medical advances
 6. A dropping birth rate

C. Trends leading to the aging of the American population
 1. Steadily improving survival rates since the 19th century
 2. Improvements in public health
 3. Improvements in nutrition
   a. Increased lifespan, due in part to medical advances
   b. A dropping birth rate

5-8. Complete the outline of the following passage. (***Hint:*** Note that the major details are introduced with addition transitions.)

The Head Start program has some serious problems. First is uneven quality of teaching. Some centers fail to meet even minimum standards of performance. Also, there is not enough emphasis on management skills. Management of many local programs is so poor, some say, that expanding Head Start will be difficult. Further, Head Start staff receive poor salaries. Higher salaries would attract higher quality workers. And finally, according to some studies, Head Start's effects fade if children don't get enrichment programs in elementary school.

Serious problems of _____

    1. _____

    2. _____

    3. _____

    4. Fading effects without elementary-school enrichment programs

SCORE: Number right (_____) x 12.5 = _____%

SUMMARIZING AND OUTLINING: Mastery Test 1

A. Summarizing

1. Circle the letter of the best summary of the following selection.

An important result of medical advances is an increase in the number of conditions thought to be of medical concern. In the not-too-distant past, birth and death usually occurred at home. Family members and friends were there or close by. Now most people are born and die in a hospital, surrounded by bright lights and expensive machines. People who were addicted to alcohol or drugs were once considered sinful or lacking in willpower. Now they are considered "sick." Problems that used to be accepted as part of life—baldness, wrinkles, small breasts, sleeplessness—are now deemed proper matters for medical attention. Some criminologists have even defined antisocial behavior as a medical problem. Lawbreakers of all kinds, from the shoplifter to the mass murderer, may potentially be labeled "sick."

a. Today people with addictions are considered sick, not sinful, and problems that used to be accepted as part of life are now considered medical matters.

b. According to some criminologists, even antisocial behavior is a medical problem. Lawbreakers of all types, from the shoplifter to the mass murderer, may someday be labeled as "sick."

c. Medical advances have made some conditions medical matters that once were not. Such conditions include birth and death, addictions, and various problems once accepted as part of life.

d. People used to be born and die at home, with family members and friends nearby. Now, thanks to medical advances, most people are born and die in a hospital, surrounded by bright lights and expensive machines.

2. Complete the summary of the following passage by adding the missing major details.

Self-disclosure is a way of revealing yourself to others. It has three key aspects. First, it must be intended. If you accidentally tell a friend that you're thinking about quitting a job, that act is not self-disclosure. Furthermore, the information must be meaningful.

Volunteering trivial facts, opinions, or feelings—that you like fudge, for example—hardly counts as disclosure. Third, the information being disclosed should not be widely known by others. There's nothing noteworthy about telling others that you are depressed or elated if they already know that.

Self-disclosure, a way of revealing yourself to others, must be intended, _____

_____

B. Outlining

3. Circle the letter of the outline that best condenses and organizes the following passage.

   Bird communication can be separated into two categories. First is song: a complicated, repeated pattern of sounds used to warn off a competing male or to attract a female. Many of those sounds, of course, are vocal, but not all of them. Birds also "sing" with their bodies. Thus the rhythmic tapping of a woodpecker's beak is a song, as are the sounds made by a woodcock's vibrating feathers. Birds make other sounds that cannot be called songs, but are known as calls. A call is defined as a short, sharp sound used to rally the flock or warn other birds of the presence of an enemy. There are various types of calls. For instance, migrating birds often utter a "contact" call, especially when flying at night when travelers may not be able to see one another. Flocking birds also have special calls for feeding, assembling, and taking flight. For instance, Canadian geese signal a take-off with loud honking cries.

   A. Bird communication
      1. Song
      2. Vocal sounds
      3. Bodily sounds
      4. Calls
      5. Types of calls

   B. The two categories of bird communication
      1. Song: a complicated repeated pattern of sounds used to warn off a competing male or to attract a female.
         a. Vocal
         b. Body sounds

  2. Calls: short sounds used to rally the flock or warn other birds of
     the presence of an enemy
     a. Migrating birds, for example, use contact call, especially
        when flying at night
     b. Flocking birds, for example, have feeding, assembling and
        take-off calls

C. Bird songs
  1. Complicated, repeated pattern of sounds
  2. Used to warn off a competing male or to attract a female
  3. Many of the sounds are vocal
  4. Birds also made sounds with their bodies
     a. Rhythmic tapping of a woodpecker's beak
     b. Woodcock's vibrating feathers

4-8. Complete the outline of the following passage.

   There are a number of ways you can limit your intake of
pesticides. First, try to buy fresh vegetables in season. When
prolonged storage and long-distance shipping are not required,
there's less need for chemicals that resist spoilage. Also, wash
vegetables carefully. Third, peel vegetables with wax coatings,
which washing does not remove. Trim away tops and the very outer
leaves from leafy vegetables. Those leaves may contain most of the
harmful chemicals in a vegetable. Finally, to avoid even small
amounts of harmful chemicals in vegetables, you can buy organic
produce. Organic produce is available not only in health-food
stores, but also in some farmer's markets and big-city supermarkets.
"Organic" usually means that the food has been grown without
chemical fertilizers or pesticides.

Ways to _____

  1. _____

  2. Wash vegetables carefully.

  3. _____

  4. _____

  5. _____

SCORE: Number right (_____) x 12.5 = _____%

Name _____

Section _____ Date_____

SUMMARIZING AND OUTLINING: Mastery Test 2

A. Summarizing

1. Circle the letter of the best summary of "One Less Sucker Lives" (pages 17–19). Review the reading as much as necessary as you work on this question.

   a. The author was tricked into giving money to a man who came to her office and claimed the bakery company truck he drove had broken down. As he asked someone to lend him money to get back to his company, he seemed embarrassed. And he had a lot of identification. So the author lent him the money. She never saw him again and soon discovered he didn't work for the bakery company. She was angered not so much by the loss of money, but by having been cheated and made more cynical.

   b. The author knows that we were brought up to believe it is right to help our neighbors. In addition, she says that one of the greatest commandments given by the Almighty had to do with how we treat each other. But she also feels it is probably true that there is a sucker born every minute. So she has become more cynical than ever and much less likely to help out someone in need by lending that person money.

   c. A man wearing regular work clothes came to the author's office looking very uncomfortable. He approached the door and entered very shyly. He claimed that he was a driver for the Arnold Baking Company and that his truck had broken down on the highway nearby. He said he would bring the office staff some bread from his truck if someone would lend him the money he needed to get back to the company. He seemed extremely embarrassed to be asking for money. To prove that he wasn't lying, he showed the author a lot of credit and identification cards, including an Arnold Baking Company ID card with his picture on it.

2. Circle the letter of the best summary of "Winning the Job Interview Game" (pages 54–56). Review the reading as much as necessary as you work on this question.

a. A job interview is among the most dreaded things in life. For instance, you must wait in an outer room with strangers all applying for the same job. Everyone knows that only one person will get the job. Then you must look calm while being interviewed even though you are quite anxious. To do well at the interview, be prepared for certain questions that often come up in interviews.

b. You can make yourself stand out at a job interview by dressing in business clothing, arriving early, and following the interviewer's lead in doing some small talk at the beginning of the interview. In addition, be prepared for some common interview questions, such as "What are your weaknesses?" and "Why did you apply for this job?"

c. When you go for a job interview, wear business clothing. Also, be prepared to tell the interviewer something about yourself. You might tell him or her about where you were born and raised, where your family lives now, and where you went to school. You also might talk about what jobs you've had and why you're looking for a new job.

B. Outlining

3-5. Complete the following outline based on "American Family Life: The Changing Picture" (pages 35–38). Review the reading as much as necessary as you work on this question.

Changes in Three Parts of American Life That Weaken Family Togetherness

1. Work
   a. Two changes
      1) A greater percentage of mothers working
         a) Need for two paychecks
         b) Increase in single mothers

      2) _____

      _____

    b. The consequences: after-school care out of the home or self-care for children

2. Meals
    a. The change: Fast food, take-out, and heat-n-serve meals instead of home-cooked meals

    b. The consequence: _____

    _____

3. _____
    a. Two changes
      1) Numerous shows on television
      2) Availability of computer games
    b. The consequence: Family members spending their time in front of their separate screens

SCORE: Number right (____) x 20 = _____ %

Name _____

Section _____ Date_____

SUMMARIZING AND OUTLINING: Mastery Test 3

If the word *mall* makes your heart beat faster, if shopping is your favorite sport, and if your lifestyle would change drastically if you had no credit cards, then this selection may give you some welcome insight. It also provides the opportunity for you to apply your understanding of summarizing and outlining to a full-length reading. To help you continue to practice the skills taught in previous chapters, there are also questions on

- vocabulary in context
- central point and main ideas
- supporting details
- transitions
- inferences.

Words to Watch

Following are some words in the reading that do not have strong context support. Each word is followed by the number of the paragraph in which it appears and its meaning there. These words are indicated in the selection by a small circle (°).

descend on (2): attack
cliché (4): overused saying

LET'S GO SHOPPING

Anita Rab

"Let's go shopping!"   1

The words echo across America like a battle cry. Every day,   2
we head for the department store, discount center, or mall, cash and credit cards in hand. We scan the store ads like hungry people reading a menu. We descend on° the counters and racks of goods as if on a treasure hunt. We pick the counters and racks clean and go home exhausted, but fulfilled. We have just had another fix of our favorite drug: shopping.

Why is America a nation of consumer junkies? There are 3
several reasons.

First of all, Americans believe in competition, even for 4
possessions. The old sports cliché°, "Winning isn't everything—it's
the only thing," also applies to our feelings about buying. We
simply have to own the cars, appliances, clothes, and furniture our
neighbors and friends own. If we don't, we feel like losers.

The Coopers' four-year-old car, for instance, seems fine until 5
the Ballards next door buy a brand-new model. Suddenly every
paint chip and dent on the older model seems enormous. The
Coopers begin to wonder what their "old clunker" says about them.
Are people pitying them for driving it? Are they whispering that the
Coopers must not be doing too well? Do they think the Coopers are
cheap? Then the Coopers will show them! Determined to stay ahead
in the game, the Coopers visit the new car lots. They "just have to"
replace their car. Forget the fact that a few weeks ago they thought
their car was okay. Their idea of an "okay car" changed when the
Ballards purchased a new one.

The Coopers are victims of the competitive urge. That urge 6
tells us that people's success in life is measured by what they own.
So we admire the ones who own three cars or enough shoes to fill a
walk-in closet. By buying a new car, the Coopers are satisfying that
urge. The problem is that this urge never stays satisfied for long.
Next week, the Ballards may install a swimming pool.

A second reason for America's need to shop is our belief that 7
"new is better." In other countries, poorer people make do with what
they have. A sewing machine or bicycle will be lovingly repaired.
Children play with toys made of "junk" that Americans would have
put in the wastebasket. Many of us don't realize that it is possible to
fix a broken toaster, mend torn clothing, or be awakened by a wind-
up clock.

Manufacturers encourage this "new is better" attitude—for a 8
good reason. They'll make more money if we buy a new model as
soon as the old one fails. They've even invented items that are
meant to be used once and discarded. These items aren't limited to
paper plates and napkins. Now there are also disposable razors,
cameras, and contact lenses. Also, fix-it shops are getting rare. Why
should we repair the old when we can buy the new? As a result,
junkyards and dumps are filled with still-usable items we no longer
want. We don't reuse or recycle, which would save us money.

Instead, we throw away.

Finally, our buying habit is encouraged by the media.   9
Television and print ads carry tempting messages. These ads tell us
that their stereo, vacuum cleaner or car is what we need to be happy.
Or they tell us that buying a certain product will make us more
attractive. All the shampoo, makeup, and cologne ads stress the
same message. A single item, they insist, can transform us into the
ideal self each of us dreams about.

In fact, the media never stop telling us that we've got to have   10
the best. Unless a television show or movie is about poor people, the
setting is almost always sparkling new. And it's crammed with
expensive furniture and appliances. The unspoken message is "This
is how people are supposed to live. Are your home, your car, your
belongings this nice? If not, there's something wrong with you."

In this country, shopping fills a psychological need. We are   11
truly hooked on passing cash or plastic over a counter and receiving
something new in return. Like any addiction, it's one that can never
be fully satisfied. It just keeps on eating away at us. It will continue
to do so until we see it once and for all as the addiction that it is.

Reading Comprehension Questions

Vocabulary in Context

1. The word *transform* in "All the shampoo, makeup, and cologne ads
   stress the same message. A single item, they insist, can transform us
   into the ideal self each of us dreams about" (paragraph 9) means
   a. sell.
   b. change.
   c. talk.
   d. confuse.

Central Point and Main Ideas

2. Which sentence best expresses the central point of the selection?
   a. The media encourage the public to want new things.
   b. Americans are addicted to shopping for several reasons.
   c. Shopping can be exhausting but rewarding.
   d. The common addiction to shopping helps American
      manufacturers.

3. Which sentence best expresses the main idea of paragraphs 4–6?
   a. The competitive urge is one reason for Americans' shopping addiction.
   b. To avoid feeling like losers, the Ballards like to stay ahead of their neighbors.
   c. The Coopers decided their four-year-old car was a clunker.
   d. If the Ballards get a swimming pool, the Coopers will want one too.

Supporting Details

4. The author states that to make more money, manufacturers
   a. keep raising prices.
   b. make toasters that cannot be fixed.
   c. recycle old clothing into new products.
   d. sell items meant to be used only once and then thrown away.

Transitions

5. The major details of the selection are introduced with the transitions
   a. *for instance* and *first of all.*
   b. *first of all, second,* and *finally.*
   c. *but, another, so, next* and *until.*
   d. *now, also, instead, so, next,* and *finally.*

6. In this reading, the author
   a. lists types of consumer junkies.
   b. narrates a series of events in the order in which they happened.
   c. discusses the causes of America's shopping addiction.
   d. contrasts various addictions.

Inferences

7. The author suggests that one reason Americans are addicted to shopping is to
   a. raise their self-esteem.
   b. get richer.
   c. support products that they can reuse or recycle.
   d. buy things they really need.

8. The author's tone can be described as
   a. forgiving.
   b. revengeful.
   c. uncertain.
   d. concerned.

Summarizing and Outlining

9. Which of the following best outlines paragraphs 9–10?
   A. Another reason for the American addiction to shopping is media encouragement.
      1. Ads tempt people to buy more.
      2. The settings in TV shows and movies also encourage people to buy more.

   B. The media never stop telling us that we've got to have the best.
      1. Few TV shows and movies are about poor people.
      2. TV often shows settings filled with expensive furniture and appliances.

10. Which statement best summarizes the entire selection?
    a. Every day, Americans need to satisfy their urge to shop by heading for department stores, discount centers, and malls. They then go home exhausted, but temporarily fulfilled.
    b. Americans are addicted to shopping because of their urge to compete, their belief that new things are best, and the media encouragement to shop.
    c. People like the Coopers are victims of the urge to compete through what they buy. Behind that urge is the belief that people's success in life is measured by what they own.
    d. There are complicated psychological and social reasons behind America's various addictions.

SCORE: Number right (_____) x 10 = _____%

Part II

INTERMEDIATE READINGS

1

The Monsters in My Head
Frank Langella

Preview

For a child alone in bed at night, a monster can seem as real as the room. You may remember your own nighttime terrors. Perhaps you recall lying in bed stiff with fear as you heard noises or saw shadows outside your bedroom window. In this essay, Frank Langella tells what he has learned about fighting night monsters. He also explains that they are just the first in a series of "monsters," most of which appear in broad daylight.

Words to Watch

tufts (1): bunches growing together at the base
clapboard (1): a type of house siding in which long narrow boards overlap each other
ritual (6): ceremony, custom
macho (6): overly aggressive
amorphous (7): without a definite form
agony (7): intense suffering
apprentice (7): trainee
summer stock (7): summer theater productions
overwhelmingly (8): powerfully
aloft (9): in the air, overhead

I was sure he was coming to get me. First a hard step on the gravel and then a foot dragging behind. Step-drag, step-drag. I lay frozen in my bed. The long alleyway between our family house and the neighbor's was

1

hardly three feet wide. It was dark and covered with black dirt, gravel and tufts° of weeds and grass just barely able to survive the sunless space. The two windows of my room faced the clapboard° wall of our neighbor's house, and Venetian blinds remained permanently closed against the nonview.

It was the mid-1940s. I had just seen a movie about a mummy. I don't remember the name of it. Just the image, so powerful even still, of a man wrapped in grayish cloth around his ankles, legs, body up to the top of his head. Eyes and mouth exposed, one arm drawn up against his chest, elbow close to his side, hand clawed. The other arm dangling alongside the leg that dragged. Several strips of cloth hung loosely from that arm, swaying with each step-drag, step-drag. I don't remember where he was coming from or going to in the movie. It doesn't really matter. I knew that he was coming for me.   2

For so many nights I heard him as I lay alone in my bed. My heart pounded as I waited for the good foot to land. A pause, then the slow drag. I would get up from the bed, pull the blind as little as I could away from the glass; and, with my chin just a little over the window ledge, I would stare hard into the dark alley. There were no outdoor lights, so I never could see him clearly. But he was there. He stopped when he saw me. I would get back into bed and wait. He usually left. Sometimes I fell asleep, and he returned, waking me. Other nights, he spared me and moved on.   3

I never told anyone about him. I don't know why. Shame, I suppose. It was that he seemed to be my private terror, and as much as I was frightened of him, I was also frightened of losing him. One night, he deserted me forever, and I was not to think of him again for forty years, until my own son, this year, at age four, began calling out in the night: "Daddy, Daddy! There's a monster in my room. Come kill him." His room, several floors above the street, looks out over a New York alleyway to a brick wall. The windows are covered with louvered shutters. I found him sitting up in bed, eyes wide, staring at the tilted louvers, pointing at his monster. "He's coming in the window, Daddy. He's going to get me."   4

I grabbed a pillow and did a dutiful daddy fight with the monster, backing him up against the closet door, beating him toward the shutters, leaping onto the window seat, and driving him back out into the night. He was a sizeless, faceless creature to me. My son told me he was blue, with big teeth.   5

This ritual° went on for weeks. Sometimes, several times a night. I continued my battle, and, as I tucked him back under the covers, I explained that Daddy would keep the monster from him always. I was bigger and stronger; as long as I was there, no monster was going to get   6 my boy. I was wrong. No matter how hard I battled, the monster returned when my son wanted him to. I was forced to accept the fact that my macho° approach to protecting him from his fears wasn't working. My dad never told me he would save me from my monsters. I don't think he knew they existed.

As I thought back to my mummy and his eventual disappearance, I realized that he had never really gone away. He was with me still. He changed shapes as rapidly as I grew up. He became a wild bear at the foot of my bed. Then, later, an amorphous° flying object swooping over my head. In later years, he was my first day at kindergarten, the agony° of my early attempts at the diving board. He was hurricanes and the ocean, a mysterious death next door to us, my brother's ability to outdo me in all sports. He was my hypodermic needles, even early haircuts. Still later, my first date, my first night away from home, at sixteen, alone in a small boardinghouse as an apprentice° in summer stock°. The first woman to say no, the first woman to say yes. And then, he became my ambition, my fear of failure, struggles with success, marriage, husbandhood, fatherhood. There's always a foot dragging somewhere in my mind, it seems.

My son called out again. This time I went into his room, turned on the light and sat down facing him. His eyes were wild with fear, wilder than the earlier nights we had gone through this ritual. I asked him to listen, but he couldn't hear me. He kept screaming and pointing at the windows. "Kill him, kill him for me, daddy!" he cried. He grabbed the pillow and tried to get me to do my routine. I felt I needed to speak to him without the ritual happening first. When, at last, I could quiet him, I said with trembling voice that I was never going to kill the monster again. I explained that this was his monster. He had made him up, and only he could kill him. I told him that the monster was in his head and leapt out whenever he wanted him to. I said that he could make him go away whenever he chose, or that he could turn him into a friendly monster if he liked. He sat expressionless. He had never stared at me so hard. I said again that I would no longer perform this particular battle for him, but that I loved him and would always love him. A slow and overwhelmingly° beautiful smile that I shall never forget came to his face and he said: "You mean, I can make him do anything I want?" "Yes," I said, "you're in charge of him."

I went back to bed and lay there waiting for the return of the monster. He didn't come back that night and has never again appeared in that form. Sometimes he's being driven from the living room by my son with his He-Man sword aloft°, its scabbard stuck down the back of his pajamas as he cries out, "I am The Power." And sometimes he is under the covers in the big bed when the whole family plays tent. We just ask him, politely, to leave. He stays for dinner now and then. He's everything from ten feet tall to a small tiny creature in the cup of my son's hand. He's blue, green, and sometimes he's a she.

As my son grows, I know we will be able to face his monsters   10 together. And now, when all I was once so sure of has become a mystery to me, I'm hoping he'll be able to help me face the unknown ones yet to visit themselves upon me.

READING COMPREHENSION QUESTIONS

Vocabulary in Context

1. The word *deserted* in "One night, he [the imaginary mummy] deserted me forever, and I was not to think of him again for forty years" (paragraph 4) means
   a. killed.
   b. left.
   c. scared.
   d. defeated.

Central Point and Main Ideas

2. Which sentence best expresses the central point of this selection?
   a. Like his son, Langella was afraid of imaginary monsters as a child.
   b. Because his father did not help him fight the monsters of his youth, Langella wanted to help his son conquer his monsters.
   c. We can conquer fears of various forms by facing them ourselves with support from loved ones.
   d. "Monsters" usually appear at night, when children are alone and frightened of the dark.

3. Which sentence best expresses the main idea of paragraphs 1–3?
   a. The author grew up in the mid-1940s.
   b. Young children should not be allowed to watch mummy movies.
   c. The author's imaginary mummy had a dragging leg and hand.
   d. Many nights as a child in bed, the author imagined a very frightening mummy was coming to get him.

4. Which sentence best expresses the main idea of paragraph 7?
   a. Most of us fear failure.
   b. The author realized his fears took on different forms throughout his life.
   c. Langella was afraid of school and performed poorly in sports.
   d. If the author had never seen the mummy movie, he never would have been afraid.

Supporting Details

5. When he was young, the author
   a. slept on the second floor above the street.
   b. never told anyone about the mummy he feared in bed.
   c. fought the mummy with a pillow.
   d. never attended even one horror movie.

6. Langella's son's first monster was
   a. a mummy.
   b. always hiding in the closet.
   c. a werewolf.
   d. blue with big teeth.

7. The major details of paragraph 7 are
   a. ways the author has overcome his fears.
   b. the high and low points of the author's life.
   c. regrets the author has about his life.
   d. fears the author has faced throughout his life.

Transitions

8. The relationship between the two parts of the sentence below is one
   of
   a. time.
   b. contrast.
   c. cause and effect.
   d. illustration.

   There were no outdoor lights, so I never could see him clearly.
   (Paragraph 3)

Inferences

9. We can infer that the author feels his macho approach to protecting
   his son didn't work because
   a. Langella didn't make the fight look believable.
   b. Langella was still afraid of his own monsters.
   c. only Langella's son could get rid of his monster.
   d. Langella had never tried to kill his monsters for him.

10. From the last paragraph of the essay, we can infer that the author
    believes
    a. he must face his fears without support from anyone else.
    b. he will continue to have fears to face.
    c. one can never really overcome a fear.
    d. his son will reach a point when he has no fears.

OUTLINING

Complete the following outline of the story by writing in the letters of the outline parts in their correct order.

The Monsters in My Head

1. _____

2. The author's son's terror over a monster

3. _____

4. _____

5. The author's realization that life presents a continuous string of fears

6. _____

7. The son's taking charge of his own fear

8. The author's expectation that he and his son will support each other as each faces his own fears

Items Missing from the Outline
   a. The author's "fights" with his son's monster
   b. The author's childhood experiences with a monster
   c. The author's explanation to his son that he must take charge of his own fears
   d. The author's realization that he cannot fight his son's fears for him

DISCUSSION QUESTIONS

1. Did you have any monsters that haunted your childhood? How did you deal with them?

2. As Langella says, fears don't just go away as we grow older. (To see some of Langella's later fears, reread paragraph 7.) What were some of your later fears—and how have you dealt with them?

3. A title can often give us a strong hint about the central point of a piece. At first, this essay may seem to be mainly about Langella's son's monster, yet the title—"The Monsters in My Head"—is about the author's "monsters." What does this tell us about what the author means to say in this reading?

4. Can you think of any situations in which fear can actually be helpful?

2

A Small Victory
Steve Lopez

Preview

Following are two articles by *Philadelphia Inquirer* columnist Steve Lopez. The first article is about a problem: An older woman was starving to death because her health needs slipped between the cracks of Medicare. The second article is about a solution to her problem. As you finish the first article, see if you can guess what that solution might be.

Words to Watch

dog days (1): the hot, humid summer days between early July and early September
gleaming (2): shining
metropolis (2): big city
glances (2): flashes
shimmer (2): shine
bureaucracy (6): a system in which complex rules interfere with effective action
inventory (15): the amount of goods on hand
recurrence (38): reappearance
exclusively (40): entirely
sprawling (44): spread out (and therefore hard to deal with)
cynical (53): distrustful of people's motives
compiled (57): put together

First column, written on July 22:

On the dog days° of summer, ten floors above Camden [New Jersey], Ruby Knight sets the fan at the foot of her bed and aims it at Philadelphia. Then she sits in the window, breeze at her back, and lets her thoughts carry her across the river to the city where she grew up.

She is 71 and has lived—since her husband passed on—in a high-rise near the Ben Franklin Bridge toll plaza. The neighborhood isn't the greatest, but from the tenth floor, Philadelphia is a gleaming° metropolis°. The city sprouts above the river, and the sun glances° off skyscrapers that shimmer° in the July heat.

Mrs. Knight watches the boats and ships on the river, the cars on the bridge. She looks to North Philly and thinks back on her eighteen proud years as a crossing guard at 17th and Ridge. And she worries about tomorrow.

Mrs. Knight, in the quiet of her home, is slowly starving.

She beat cancer: Her doctor calls it a near miracle. But now she's wrestling a worse kind of beast.

Bureaucracy°.

Joseph Spiegel, a Philadelphia surgeon, tells the story:

In 1986, a tumor filled Mrs. Knight's throat. Spiegel removed her voice box and swallowing mechanism. Mrs. Knight was fed through a tube to her stomach. It was uncomfortable and painful, but she was happy to be alive.

Although she couldn't speak, she learned to write real fast and took to carrying a note pad around. She gets help from an older sister, Elizabeth Woods, who herself beat a form of lung cancer that's often a quick killer.

The doctor was impressed by Mrs. Knight's fight. "She said she was placing her faith in my hands and the Lord's," he says.

Mrs. Knight had several more operations. But over the years, no sign of cancer. And five months ago—she smiles at the memory—Spiegel removed the tube. She was able to swallow again. After four years.

Little did she know the end of one problem was the start of another.

Instead of pouring her liquid nutrition down the tube, Mrs. Knight now drank it. The same exact liquid.

But Medicare, which paid when it went down the tube, refused to pay when it went down her throat.

Mrs. Knight, who lives on a fixed and meager income, kept the liquid cans in the corner of her living room, an open inventory°. She would look at those cans as if they represented the days left in her life. And she began rationing.

Mrs. Knight says her fighting weight is close to 100. When it   16
dropped noticeably, she went to the doctor, but had trouble making her
point.

"I think she was a little embarrassed that she couldn't afford to buy   17
the stuff," Spiegel says.

She had lost about ten pounds since her last visit, down to the high   18
eighties. She was on her way, Spiegel says, to starving herself to death.

Spiegel got an emergency supply of the liquid—she goes through   19
about six cans a day at one dollar a can—and began calling Medicare. If
she ends up in the hospital, Spiegel argued, it'll cost Medicare a lot more
than six dollars a day.

But Medicare, with built-in safeguards against intentional or   20
accidental use of common sense, wouldn't budge.

"This is a federally funded program and we have specific guidelines   21
for what we can pay for and can't pay for," Jan Shumate said in an
interview. She's director of "Medicare Part B Services" in the Columbia,
South Carolina claims office.

But it's the same liquid.   22

"Yes, I understand that."   23

It costs less than hospitalization.   24

"Yes, I understand that, but we're mandated to go by the rules."   25

Even if it costs more money?   26

"My only solution I can suggest is if she files again and it gets   27
denied, she can request an informal review."

The reasoning is Medicare can't pay for every substance somebody   28
claims to need for survival.

Spiegel says Mrs. Knight needs this drink. She can't eat or drink   29
much of anything else. He has told her he may have to put the tube back
in her stomach, so Medicare will pay again.

At the mere suggestion, Mrs. Knight loses it. No way. Her sister is   30
with her, the two of them confused by it all. They've beaten cancer,
cheated the days, and now this.

Mrs. Knight hustles to the bathroom and returns with the scale. She   31
puts it by her bed, gets on. The needle hits 83. She stands at the window,
frail against the Philadelphia skyline, grace and dignity showing through
her despair.

The two sisters look at the cans in the corner. There's enough for   32
one month, but Mrs. Knight will try to stretch it. On her pad, she writes:

"My trial. God's got to do something."   33

(Dr. Spiegel is at 215-545-3322.)   34

Follow-up column, written on July 29:

It's the kind of thing I don't get around to often enough. But today, I 35
think some thanks are in order.

The problem is, I won't be able to get to everyone. I don't even 36
know where to begin.

Maybe with last week's column. 37

Those who looked in this corner last Sunday saw a story about 38
Ruby Knight, a retired crossing guard in North Philadelphia. She had
throat cancer real bad at one time, but Dr. Joseph Spiegel removed a
tumor and Mrs. Knight has gone nearly five years without a recurrence°.

It took four years for Mrs. Knight, now 71, to learn how to swallow 39
again. And it was a big day for her about six months ago when Spiegel
removed the feeding tube from her stomach. Finally, she could swallow.

Problem was, she couldn't eat or drink regular food because of 40
discomfort. Her diet was still, exclusively°, a nutritional supplement
called Ensure Plus.

Now here's the deal. 41

When Mrs. Knight poured it down the tube, it was covered by 42
Medicare. When she drank the same stuff, Medicare refused to cover it.

Medicare reasons that if you don't need a tube, you don't need a 43
special diet. The rule exists to avoid abuse.

"The idea is a good one," Spiegel says. "But Medicare is the 44
biggest, most sprawling° bureaucracy of all." He says its inability to
make reasonable exceptions often hurts the elderly poor.

Spiegel tried to get Medicare to change its mind, arguing that it 45
would cost the government a lot more if he had to surgically implant the
tube back in Mrs. Knight's stomach. But he got nowhere.

"We're mandated to go by the rules," a Medicare spokeswoman told 46
me when I asked for an explanation.

Meanwhile, Mrs. Knight, without anyone's knowledge, was 47
working on her own solution. She had begun rationing her Ensure Plus.

She kept a careful count of the cans, figuring she needed at least four 48
a day to survive. Mrs. Knight stacked the fifty-one cans in her Camden
living room, measuring the supply each day against her fixed income.

As Spiegel put it, "she was slowly starving herself." She went from 49
nearly one hundred pounds to eighty-three.

When I went to visit, I found one of the sweetest, most unassuming 50
people I have met. Mrs. Knight's sister, Elizabeth Woods, is the same
way. She's 76 and also beat cancer. They live in the same high-rise
apartment house with a fabulous view of Philadelphia, and they help each
other through the days.

Mrs. Knight can't speak, but she gets her points across just fine. She writes almost as fast as you can talk and she has a world-class hug. 51

The day after the column, Spiegel and his staff got to their Pine Street office at 8 a.m. There were seventy-four messages on the machine. By noon, there were 150. By closing time Monday, more than four hundred people had called. 52

"You can get cynical° about things," Spiegel says, "but then there's this outpouring of help from people. It's just astounding." 53

People called for two reasons. Compassion and anger. Everyone knows somebody who's been seriously ill. Everyone has had trouble with bureaucracy. 54

Ruby Knight hit the daily double. 55

And I would like to begin now with the thank-yous. First to Dr. Spiegel for his sense of compassion and outrage. To his staff—Lori, Gina, Maria, Sally, Laura, Monica and Mike—for patiently handling calls, letters and donations. "It was kind of fun," Maria says. 56

And thanks to readers whose names fill thirteen typed pages compiled° by Spiegel's staff. One person gave a year's supply of Ensure Plus. One donated twenty cases. Some sent prayers, holy cards, religious medals. 57

Some thanked Mrs. Knight for her years as a crossing guard at 17th and Ridge. Some people sent as much as four hundred dollars. One sent three one-dollar bills and a note: "I wish I could send more." 58

One sent ten dollars and this note: "May God bless you. I lost my dear husband to leukemia two and a half years ago." 59

Some called Medicare to complain. Some called Ensure Plus, where spokeswoman Sharon Veach said she thought the company could arrange to provide a lifetime supply, if needed. 60

Friday at noon, Spiegel, Maria and Mike drove to Camden and dropped in on Mrs. Knight with thirty cases of Ensure Plus and a list of donors. 61

Mrs. Knight was beside herself, humble, gracious, overwhelmed. She and her sister kept looking at each other, shaking their heads. 62

"I'm speechless," Mrs. Knight wrote on her pad, and then laughed. 63

She said she would pray for everyone. She kept scribbling that she wishes there were some way she could express thanks and love for the kindness of strangers. 64

And I told her that she had. 65

READING COMPREHENSION QUESTIONS

Vocabulary in Context

1. The word *meager* in "Mrs. Knight . . . lives on a fixed and meager income" (paragraph 15) means
   a. stolen.
   b. avoidable.
   c. very small.
   d. enormous.

2. The word *mandated* in " 'This is a federally funded program and we have specific guidelines for what we can pay for and can't pay for. . . . we're mandated to go by the rules' " (paragraphs 21 and 25) means
   a. not allowed.
   b. scared.
   c. mistaken.
   d. required.

Central Point and Main Ideas

3. Which statement best expresses the central point of the selection?
   a. The elderly poor usually suffer unnecessarily.
   b. Individuals were able to solve a problem that bureaucracy failed to handle.
   c. Mrs. Knight's diet is made up almost completely of a liquid supplement.
   d. Ruby Knight lost her voice box to throat cancer.

4. The main idea of paragraph 52 is
   a. Many people read the author's column about Mrs. Knight.
   b. Dr. Spiegel and his staff begin their work day at 8 a.m.
   c. Dr. Spiegel's office is a busy one.
   d. Many people called Dr. Spiegel in response to the author's column.

Supporting Details

5. Even though she could now swallow, Mrs. Knight
   a. could comfortably take only Ensure Plus.
   b. had lost her taste for regular food.
   c. preferred to feed herself through a tube.
   d. wanted to go to the hospital.

6. Dr. Spiegel's argument to Medicare was that
   a. the government should pay for whatever a person needs to survive.
   b. Mrs. Knight had suffered greatly because of her cancer.
   c. it would cost the government less if Mrs. Knight didn't have a tube in her stomach.
   d. keeping Mrs. Knight out of the hospital would be helpful because the hospitals are already too full.

Transitions

7. The relationship between the two sentences below is one of
   a. addition.
   b. time.
   c. contrast.
   d. cause and effect.

   Spiegel tried to get Medicare to change its mind, arguing that it would cost the government a lot more if he had to surgically implant the tube back in Mrs. Knight's stomach. But he got nowhere. (Paragraph 45)

8. The second sentence below begins with a word that shows
   a. addition.
   b. time.
   c. contrast.
   d. cause and effect.

   And I would like to begin now with the thank-yous. First to Dr. Spiegel for his sense of compassion and outrage. (Paragraph 56)

Inferences

9. Which of the following statements would the author of this selection be most likely to agree with?
   a. Medicare's rules are totally senseless.
   b. People helped Mrs. Knight because they knew they would be praised in the newspaper.
   c. Ensure Plus is too expensive.
   d. The Medicare system should find a way to make reasonable exceptions.

10. When the author refers to Mrs. Knight, his tone is
    a. humorous and amused.
    b. totally objective.
    c. admiring and affectionate.
    d. critical and disbelieving.

SUMMARIZING

Circle the letter of the passage that best summarizes "A Small Victory."

a. A Philadelphia surgeon had an elderly throat cancer patient who was fed a liquid diet through a tube to her stomach. When the tube was removed, she still needed to drink the liquid diet, but didn't have the money to pay for it. Finally, in response to the article about her, she got help.

b. Because of the inflexibility of Medicare, Mrs. Knight, a poor, elderly woman, was slowly starving to death. Medicare would not pay for the liquid diet she needed after recovering from throat cancer. However, her problem was solved when, in response to an article about her, numerous people sent her help and good wishes.

c. Since Medicare is a huge, sprawling bureaucracy, it is unable to respond readily to exceptions. As a result, people with special needs are often unable to get the help from Medicare that they need. However, when people are told about such problems, they are willing to provide some help themselves.

DISCUSSION QUESTIONS

1. What do you think would have happened if Dr. Spiegel and Steve Lopez hadn't helped Mrs. Knight?

2. In paragraph 20, Lopez writes that Medicare has "built-in safeguards against intentional or accidental use of common sense." What does he mean by "intentional or accidental use of common sense"? What does this statement tell us about Lopez's view of Medicare?

3. According to the article, Medicare refused to pay for Mrs. Knight's liquid diet because of a rule that "exists to avoid abuse." What type of abuse do you think the rule is meant to avoid? Do you believe that such abuse is common?

4. Why did the author, Steve Lopez, include Dr. Spiegel's telephone number at the end of the first article? What does that tell us about Lopez's view of human nature?

3

A Father's Story
Clark DeLeon

Preview

There are events in our lives which we look forward to and which we will never forget. For many people, the birth of a child is one such event. The author of this selection shares with us his experience in becoming a father. Notice how the words he has chosen draw the reader into the emotion of the event as well as the physical details.

Words to Watch

spontaneous (3): unplanned
unruly (5): hard to control
prenatal (7): before birth
transition (21): a time during labor when the mother gets the urge to push but should not because there isn't yet room for the baby to come through
audible (21): able to be heard
incision (30): cut
gloating (39): self-satisfied
paternalistic (39): fatherly
incubator (43): a heated container for premature babies
sublime (47): heavenly
prologue (47): introduction

This column is written with a smile. Why shouldn't it be? It concerns one of the greatest experiences of my life. The birth of my son. By my wife. With my help.

Where to begin?

His name is Daniel Clark. He was unplanned. Spontaneous°. A love child.

When Sara and I found out, I don't think there was any question as to how he would be delivered. Naturally. With her eyes wide open and alert and with my support.

A neighbor turned us on to Booth Memorial Hospital, a maternity hospital on City Line Avenue. Booth has one doctor, John Franklin, a tall, thin man in green sneakers with an unruly° moustache who specialized in natural, husband-assisted childbirth.

He didn't press the issue. When we saw him the first time, he asked us how we would like to have the baby delivered and if money was any problem because, if it was, things would be worked out.

Sara did a lot of reading, about six books altogether. My prenatal° bible was a book called *Husband-Coached Childbirth* by Robert A. Bradley, M.D.

Sara and I attended a couple of concentrated classes in what to expect during labor, how to breathe, when to push, how to relax and what is going on inside the mother when the baby has decided to make the big move.

Although we were prepared on Sunday morning when the first series of contractions set in, we were a little surprised since the due date was a month away.

It is a day I'll never forget. It began with me limping into the house at 8 a.m. Sunday morning after a rugby tournament in Allentown and the accompanying party, which left me sleeping it off on the side of a road until 7 a.m. Sara was on the couch where she had fallen asleep waiting for me. When I woke her I explained. She said she was happy I was safe, and then she mentioned that she had felt a contraction just an hour before.

By 11 a.m. we were pretty sure. We began getting any business done that needed attention, making a few phone calls, eating some breakfast, smiling at each other.

"Hello, Dr. Franklin. This is Mr. DeLeon."

"Hi, how are you?"

"Okay. I think we're going to have a baby today."

"Fine, fine. What's been happening?"

"Well, she started having contractions early this morning, and she's had a show of some blood and mucus. Right now the contractions are four minutes apart, about forty-five seconds long."

"All right, then. Why don't you come in and we'll have a look."   17

We arrived about 4 p.m. Dr. Franklin examined Sara. If it wasn't   18
time to enter, we were going to pick up a friend's camera at Sara's
mother's house. But we were ready.

Sara was really excited. We walked up to the labor room. Made   19
some more phone calls since it was definite and arranged to have the
camera brought down to the hospital.

Sara was beautiful during labor. When the contractions began to   20
increase, she would clutch my hand and we would do the breathing
exercise together. In through the nose, out through the mouth. Very
slowly, about six times a minute. Deep breaths while trying to relax
completely. Let the uterus do the work, Sara; it will be your turn soon.

As Sara approached transition°, she would fall asleep between   21
contractions. This was a most uncomfortable time. I did what I could,
rubbing her forehead with a cold cloth, offering water or ice chips,
stroking her hair, but my most important function was to be the rational,
loving mind when she was deep in a contraction. At this point, the
breathing must change to short, shallow breaths. An audible° pant which
sounds like hout, hout, hout, hout, hout. She is in pain at this point, and I
had her look at me rather than think about the contraction.

If I was ever close to a breaking point, it was during this.   22

"Sara . . . Sara, look at me. Hout, hout, hout, hout, hout, hout . . ."   23

"Howwt, hout, hou . . . Oh, Clark, Clark, I wish it was over, hout,   24
hout. . . ."

But never once did she ask for any anesthesia. During transition,   25
which lasted for about half an hour, Sara began to get the urge to push.
When this happens, the breathing again changes. In order not to push,
Sara would take the short breaths, but on every third one she emptied her
lungs by blowing. Hout, hout, blow. Hout, hout, blow.

Soon Dr. Franklin, who was periodically checking up (there were   26
three other women in labor at the time. Sunday was an unusually busy
night), examined Sara and said it was time to push.

Now if you ever wondered about the word labor I can tell you it   27
means what it sounds like—hard work. Sara would grab her knees until
her breath gave out, take another breath and push again. Push until her
face was beet red. Push until the blood vessels in her squeezed eyelids
stood out purple and large. Push until the contraction was over and
exhaustion overcame her and I would let her slump back against her
pillow, to sleep, until the next contraction.

When about a dime's worth of the baby's head was visible, we   28
moved to the delivery room. Sara's legs were settled into stirrup-type
braces and strapped in. There were two handles on the side of the

delivery table for her to hold onto and pull herself up during contractions.

At this point, all we could do was cheer Sara on during a 29
contraction because there was nothing more the doctor could do until the
baby's head appeared some more. Sara pushed for about a half hour.
When Dr. Franklin saw it was not coming easily, he decided on an
episiotomy. An episiotomy is a surgical cut which facilitates the exit of
the baby when there is any trouble because of a first child or a large baby.

Both Sara and I were able to observe the entire operation. She from 30
a mirror, me from leaning over. I was told to tie up my surgical mask
before the incision° was made. Now I didn't look much different than the
doctor and a fourth year med student who assisted during the birth and
labor. We were all dressed in light hospital green uniforms, floppy
slippers, hair nets and surgical masks.

After the episiotomy, the baby moved down a little more but not 31
enough. Sara was almost completely exhausted. She had been pushing
hard for an hour.

"Just a little more, baby, just a little more." 32

I don't know how many times I said that. Each time hoping it was 33
true. It was a long delivery. Dr. Franklin said that after an hour he tries to
help the baby out because it is not good for either the mother or child to
be caught in a half-way position too long.

He decided to help the baby's head emerge a bit by using forceps. 34
They look like two large stainless steel shoe horns. He positioned them,
and on the next contraction half of the baby's head was visible.

Now Sara was able to see our baby. Her eyes swallowed the rest of 35
her face when she looked into the mirror. "Oh, Clark. Look at him. Look
at him!"

And I did. 36

On the next contraction his entire head was visible. 37

My jaw dropped to the floor. There he was. He even opened his 38
eyes. I was holding Sara's shoulders for the next and final contraction
and then . . . out he came. Arms legs feet umbilical cord. We laughed.
There he is. There he is. The doctor held him up. I still hadn't seen
whether he was a boy or girl. Then I followed a tiny stream of water
which was tinkling on the doctor's arm. I looked up and there he was. A
son. A SON. A son whose first act as a post-natal human being was to
pee on the doctor. A chip off the old block.

Sara and I went bananas. A son. I could see right away that he was 39
perfect. I don't mean in the gloating° paternalistic° manner of most new
fathers. I was a trained observer, an objective journalist. I know a perfect
baby when I see one, and this baby was perfect. The most beautiful baby
in the world.

While they were ministering to the little critter, clamping his cord   40
and washing his mouth out, I grabbed the camera and took a couple of
pictures before the cord was cut. Somehow, even in my haste, they turned
out.

They wrapped him in a blanket and then Sara asked to hold him.   41
But she told the nurse to give him to me first, and minutes after Daniel
Clark's birth his father held him. Look at him. Look at those hands. He
even has eyelashes. His eyes are open. He's looking at me. Look at those
eyes! Perfect, I tell you. Perfect.

While we were waiting for the afterbirth, Sara looked up and said,   42
"It was so easy!" And she meant it. Whatever pain she had felt didn't
matter now. The sight of her baby was the perfect anesthesia.

After Sara was sewn up and we had taken pictures, the baby was   43
put into an incubator° to warm up. It's a cold 70-degree world to come
into when you've spent the last nine months in a 98.6 degree pleasure
resort where everything was taken care of automatically.

Delivery completed, Sara stepped off the table with some help. She   44
tried to walk back to her room, but this was just a little too much for her
after all the work she had been through. She fainted in my arms, and we
settled her into a wheelchair.

When we got to the recovery room, a phone call was made to each   45
of our parents and some friends. The baby was brought into the room in
the incubator, and within an hour of delivery Daniel Clark was at his
mother's breast nursing.

There is so much more to tell about, but I realize that I've probably   46
taken up enough room for three regular columns, so I'll have to
abbreviate.

Being a witness and participant in the birth of a child can only be   47
described as fulfillment approaching the sublime°. To watch that mound
of flesh grow and swell on Sara's stomach was only the prologue° to a
reality which so few men or even women are able to share. If there is a
bond of love and trust between two people, the sharing of the fruit of that
love should be done together with mind, heart and eyes open.

I love you, Sara. I love you, Dan. We did it together.   48

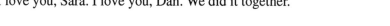

READING COMPREHENSION QUESTIONS

Vocabulary in Context

1. The word *facilitates* in "An episiotomy is a surgical cut which facilitates the exit of the baby" (paragraph 29) means
   a. prevents.
   b. delays.
   c. heals.
   d. makes easier.

2. The words *ministering to* in "While they were ministering to the little critter, clamping his cord and washing his mouth out, I grabbed the camera" (paragraph 40) mean
   a. praying for.
   b. caring for.
   c. talking to.
   d. pointing at.

Central Point and Main Ideas

3. Which sentence best expresses the central point of the selection?
   a. The author believes his son is the most beautiful baby ever born.
   b. For the author and his wife, the natural birth of their son was a joyous experience.
   c. The author's wife did not remember the pain of labor after the baby's birth.
   d. The author and his wife decided to have their baby delivered naturally.

4. Which sentence best expresses the main idea of paragraph 39?
   a. DeLeon was a trained journalist, so he could write about the experience.
   b. The parents were overjoyed by the sight of their newborn son.
   c. The author's baby was the most beautiful child ever born.
   d. The author was able to look at the baby as a professional, not a father.

Supporting Details

5. The author and his wife
   a. had planned for years to have this baby.
   b. took classes together to prepare for the birth.
   c. kept the baby's arrival a secret.
   d. decided to deliver the baby at home.

6. After the baby was born,
   a. the author was so excited that he forgot to take pictures.
   b. Sara did not want to go through another delivery like this one.
   c. Sara wanted her husband to hold the baby first.
   d. Sara walked back to her room.

Transitions

7. Authors generally present events in the order in which they happened. Time transitions help to make their order clear. For example, there are a few time transitions in paragraph 10. Write two of those transitions in these blank spaces:

   _____   _____

8. The sentence below expresses a relationship of
   a. time.
   b. addition.
   c. contrast.
   d. illustration.

   She tried to walk back to her room, but this was just a little too much for her. . . . (Paragraph 44)

Inferences

9. The author implies that
   a. he knew a lot about childbirth before his wife got pregnant.
   b. the article is about his first child.
   c. his wife should have had more medication.
   d. he felt useless throughout his wife's labor and delivery.

10. This article begins and ends in a tone of
    a. surprise.
    b. joy.
    c. confusion.
    d. amusement.

SUMMARIZING

Circle the letter—*a, b,* or *c*—of the passage that best completes the following summary of "A Father's Story."

The author's wife, Sara, became pregnant with an unplanned child. The parents planned for a natural childbirth. One Sunday morning, a month earlier than expected, Sara began having labor pains. That afternoon, they entered the hospital.

a. When Sara and the author got to the recovery room, he called their parents and some friends with the news: Sara had given birth to a beautiful baby boy. Soon after, the baby was at his mother's breast nursing.

b. DeLeon participated in the birth, an experience he found extremely fulfilling. Sara worked hard during the natural childbirth, assisted by DeLeon. The doctor did an episiotomy and used forceps to ease the birth. After a long delivery, the new parents were overjoyed at the sight of their baby boy. Within an hour, the baby was at his mother's breast nursing.

c. The birth of the child was very moving to the author. He expresses great love for his wife and son. He is delighted that he participated with his wife in his son's birth, making the experience very special.

DISCUSSION QUESTIONS

1. Why do you think the author and his wife decided to go through natural childbirth? Would you (or did you) make the same decision? Why or why not? What advantages of natural childbirth are mentioned in the article?

2. How would you describe the tone of paragraph 39? Objective or impassioned? Direct or ironic? Explain your choices.

3. If you have ever given birth to a child or watched the birth of a child, did you have feelings similar to those expressed by DeLeon? Have you had other experiences in your life that you might describe as "fulfillment approaching the sublime" (paragraph 47)?

4. Many people get involved emotionally while reading this selection. How does DeLeon get readers emotionally involved in his experience?

4

A Suicide at Twelve— Why, Steve? Richard E. Meyer

Preview

After a suicide, those who are left behind question what went wrong. They think back closely on the person's life to look for warning signs they may have missed. Such reflection is perhaps even more likely to occur when it is a child that has died. As you read this article about the death of a boy, look for clues about what was wrong, and ask yourself how this tragedy might have been stopped.

Words to Watch

thatch (1): thick covering, such as hair

subtle (3): not obvious

resigned himself (9): accepted the situation as unavoidable

vestry (10): room in a church where clergypeople's robes and other sacred objects are stored

allotted (21): assigned

discounts (28): minimizes, considers unimportant

fortified (29): strengthened

terrarium (33): container holding small plants

accumulated (70): grew in number

pediatric psychiatrist (80): a mental health doctor specializing in children

celebrated (81): performed

Requiem Mass (81): a mass for a dead person

He lived to be almost thirteen. Walnut eyes. Brown thatch°. Boy   1
Scout. Altar boy. He grew up in white, middle-class America. He played
football, and he played baseball. His mother, father, two brothers, and
sister loved him. On the fourth day of the eleventh month of his twelfth
year, a sunny afternoon in suburban Cincinnati, he walked down his
favorite trail in the woods behind his house, climbed a tree, knotted a
rope, and hanged himself.

Why, Steve?   2

In the past year, at least 210 others as young as Steve Dailey killed   3
themselves in the United States. Reported suicides among the very young
have more than doubled in twenty years. Even adjusted for population
growth, the rate has climbed. The story of Steve Dailey, all-American
boy, is an American tragedy: a story about the good life and the
possibilities it offers for hidden pressure, subtle° loneliness, quiet
frustration—and unanswered questions.

Why, Steve?   4

Steven Dailey was born July 30, 1961, in the Cincinnati suburb of   5
Clifton. One month after his first birthday, his parents, Sue and Charles
Dailey, presented him with a brother, Mike. The two boys would become
good friends. When Steve was two or a little older, Grandpa Rafton, in
charge of the tailors at MacGregor, the sporting goods company which
made uniforms for the Cincinnati Reds, presented Steve and Mike with
baseball uniforms of their own, cut in the Reds' own patterns from the
Reds' own cloth. Steven's had pitcher Jimmy O'Toole's old number, 31,
sewn on the back.

Almost from the day he was married, Charles Dailey worked with   6
Boy Scouts, first as an assistant scoutmaster for a year, then as a
scoutmaster for five. When Steve and Mike were still toddlers, he took
them along to Scout meetings. One night, he told a meeting of Scout
parents: "You know, these boys are growing up awfully fast. If you're
ever going to get to know your sons, you better get to know them now—
because soon they're going to be at an age when you can't really get to
know them."

In the second grade, Steve entered St. Catherine's School, in the   7
parish where the Daileys had moved in the suburb of Westwood. His
father became a volunteer football coach in St. Catherine's growing
athletic program. Steve Dailey was big enough to play second level, or
"pony," football. But he got paired in practice against a youngster
everybody called Mugsy. "After Mugsy kind of tore him up a few times,
he decided that maybe he ought to play 'bandits' a year and kind of find
out what it's all about first," his father remembers. "Bandits" are the
beginners. "That kinda bugged the devil out of me," Steve's father says.

Charles Dailey thinks he probably told his son he was disappointed. "But Steve says, 'Well, I just don't want to play "pony" ball. I'm just not good enough.' And it was probably a good choice on his part. But that was at the stage when I really wanted him to be the best football player in the world, you know. And I wanted him to be better."

Steve preferred quieter pursuits. He started a stamp collection. At   8
seven, he caught his first fish—a little bluegill he tugged from the lake at Houston Woods State Park on a camping trip with his family. In 1969, when he was eight years old, Steve joined the Cub Scouts. He advanced to Webelos, where he met Dan Carella, who would become his assistant scoutmaster. Just before becoming a full-fledged Boy Scout, Steve was given Cub Scouting's highest award, the Arrow of Light.

Steve was graduated from the "bandits" after a year of learning the   9
fundamentals of football. He played "pony" football for two years. But he was a large boy, and he found himself paired off against Mugsy again. Charles Dailey resigned himself°: "Steve didn't mind getting knocked down, getting blocked out and all that kind of stuff; but he just did not have the—what?—the killer instinct."

In school, Steve got B's and C's. He received his First Communion,   10
was confirmed, and learned how to serve Mass. He was a faithful altar boy who kept his serving appointments on holidays and vacations. But he wasn't above draining the last few drops of altar wine—or clowning with the incense in the vestry°. By 1972, when he was eleven, Steve was well on his way toward his most important goal: to become an Eagle Scout. He worked at it steadily. By now his father was a Scout commissioner. He went along with Steve and his troop on most of their hikes and campouts. And he counseled Steve on five of the dozen merit badges he earned.

"Steve went after the merit badges that took a little more brains and   11
thought," says Dan Carella. "He was sensitive—not a rough kid. He wasn't a real loner, but he wasn't outgoing as much as some of the other kids. He liked to be with the older boys and the grown-ups. But there were a lot of older boys and younger ones, and he was in-between. That's one of the reasons he had no real close buddies. I can't remember ever seeing him with any close buddy."

At home, Steve and Mike started a beer-can collection. Steve   12
learned to play chess. He read Hardy Boy mysteries. He got a new ten-speed bicycle for Christmas. And he went on a month-long camping trip to California with the whole family: Mike, sister Kay, and a new Dailey, his smallest brother, Jamie. Everybody visited Disneyland.

Back home, Sue and Charles Dailey noticed something—Mike was   13
always outside playing baseball with the kids in the neighborhood. Steve

preferred being alone. He worked on Scout projects or watched color television. His father thought it was because the other kids made up street rules for their game—and Steve insisted on playing by the correct rules.

By now Steve's father was athletic director at St. Catherine's. Steve worked long hours at fund-raising for the Dads' Club, which sponsored the parish teams. He took over the popcorn concession at basketball tournaments. "He'd get upset when I'd suggest he take a break and try to get some other kid to replace him so he could go watch the games," says Jay Deakin, past president of the Dads' Club.   14

During the 1972–1973 school year, Steve played "pee-wee" football, one level above "pony." So did Mugsy. "Steve always fought him off, but he'd get beat all the time," his father says. "There'd be nights when Steve'd say, 'Oh, he really wiped me out!'"   15

"It didn't frighten Steve to get hit," says coach Ray Bertran. "However, some boys, they go out and they look to hit the other kid. He wasn't that way. In 'pee-wee' I guess he was the biggest kid, but he just wasn't that aggressive."   16

Steve wasn't on the starting team. But one October evening, he came home from practice smiling.   17

"What happened?" asked his father.   18

"Boy, I really wiped him out tonight. I really got him."   19

Steve meant Mugsy. It was probably the only time that ever happened, Charles Dailey says.   20

Steve never missed a Scout meeting. He added up the requirements to become an Eagle, allotted° himself so much time to accomplish each, and put himself on a rigid schedule.   21

"Steve was really good at Scouting," says Charles Dailey, "and I really had a lot of pride in that."   22

Steve set his heart on a trip to the Philmont Scout Ranch in New Mexico, and started working at Scout projects to earn his way. He planned to work at a Scout car wash. And he never missed a Scout paper drive.   23

But he didn't go in for Scout roughhousing or free-for-alls. "Steve had sort of soft feelings," remembers Carella. "He was a very personal boy. He stuck up for the guys who were being picked on. During the district camporee in Mt. Airy Forest, there were a couple of kids who—well, they weren't mamma's boys, but they just didn't know how to handle themselves. A lot of the boys preferred to tent with other kids. But Steve said, 'Well, I'll go with them.'"   24

Last fall, Steve's father told him he had to play a fall sport. "I was thinking in terms of football," says Charles Dailey. But St. Catherine's had started soccer. Steve said he'd rather play that.   25

"He was aggressive on the soccer team," says football coach   26

George Kugler. Dan Carella describes him as "a good soccer player." But soccer was not the prestige sport at St. Catherine's.

"Football at St. Catherine's is king," says Bill Coffey, a history   27
teacher.

Carella discounts° any attempt by Charles Dailey to pressure his   28
son to play football. But he adds: "There probably was some pressure in
the situation. His father is athletic director. The situation says, 'Hey, how
come you're not playing, Steve?'"

To make enough money to go to the Philmont Scout Ranch, Steve   29
wanted a summer job. His father arranged for the job with a company
that shares space in the Cardinal Engineering Building, where he works
as a civil engineer. But he didn't tell Steve about the arrangement. Better,
he thought, to have Steve ask—and think he got the job himself. Lump in
his throat, Steve accompanied his father to the Cardinal Building one
morning in April. Fortified° by a cup of chocolate milk and a donut from
a bakery along the way, Steve marched in—and came out with a job
making catalogs and cleaning up for seventy-five cents an hour starting
when school let out this summer.

"Boy, he was a king then," Charles Dailey remembers.   30

Steve also got a newspaper route, with the weekly *Press*, which   31
circulates in Westwood. That money would go toward Philmont. And he
made arrangements with Aunt Beth McGinnis to mow her lawn for two
dollars whenever it needed it. That would go toward Philmont, too.

In his own way, Steve Dailey was shy. When his mother went from   32
room to room at night to check on her brood, she always got a kiss from
Mike, a kiss from Kay, and a kiss from Jamie. But never from Steve.
Kissing embarrassed him. His mother always thought: "Well, he'll come
to me when he's ready."

On Mother's Day, Sunday, May 12, her children brought Sue Dailey   33
breakfast in bed. Steve presented her with a terrarium° he'd made in
Scouts. And he put his arms around her and kissed her. By now, though,
school wasn't going entirely well. Steve wasn't doing his homework for
language arts. That was Margaret Linahan's class. And Steve was getting
a D.

"In content subjects, like science and social studies, I suppose he   34
could take his own path. But in English grammar there is only one way to
go," Mrs. Linahan smiles. "As long as I'm your teacher." She told Sue
and Charles Dailey their son's grades were falling.

"Hey, is something bothering you?" Steve's father asked him.   35

"No," Steve said.   36

"Hey, you know, if you fail anything you're going to be grounded in   37
the yard the whole summer."

In Bill Coffey's history class, Steve slipped from an A to a B or B-plus. Coffey was one of his favorites. He, in turn, appreciated Steve's sense of humor. "In the last few weeks, he didn't talk as much," Coffey remembers. "He didn't participate. And his dry wit was no longer as present." 38

Steve paid a sentimental visit to Sister Marie Russell's fourth-grade classroom. "I wondered why he was not with his class," she recalls, eyes puzzled behind her glasses. "Why was he wandering in the hall? And why was he by himself? You'd think a twelve-year-old would be with the boys." 39

Though Steve was never what Bill Coffey calls "Joe Popularity," he was well-liked—and he was good friends with Ted Hutchinson, for instance, and Rick Flannery. But Charles Dailey was unaware that Steve had any close friends. He never went to any of his friends' houses to play—and never invited any of them to his house to play. 40

With spring came baseball, and a peak of activity in the Dailey household. "We would have to fix a pot of stew, where you could keep heating it up when people would come in and out, or chili, or something like that," Sue remembers. Her husband says: "Sometimes we'd just eat, and then the person that wasn't here, he'd have to warm up the stuff that was left." 41

Steve played on an intermediate-ability team. He was a starter. But manager Ray Kendrick says, "I'm not sure he really liked sports, at least not baseball. He wasn't that enthusiastic abut it. . . ." 42

But now Charles Dailey headed in his spare time an athletic organization at St. Catherine's that totaled 110 coaches, almost all of them fathers who had volunteered. Four football teams . . . fourteen baseball teams . . . ten basketball teams . . . track . . . soccer . . . softball . . . volleyball . . . kickball. The parish sports budget totaled $11,491. 43

Steve's father says, "This year I think he wanted to play soccer again. But I told him that there wasn't any way, because in high school, well, he's just not going to be a soccer man . . . because he's plain too big, and never was real fast. I still had the hopes that this year he would finally find out, with the size and all on his side, that he would become more aggressive." 44

Steve Dailey, twelve years old, stood 5 feet 5 inches, and weighed 140 pounds. 45

"Steve, you ready for football?" coach George Kugler asked him. "You ought to play. Get some fundamentals. You're gonna be a big kid. You can make tackle." 46

Ted Hutchinson remembers Steve Dailey saying: "My dad wants me to play football, but I'd rather play soccer." 47

Two weeks before the end of school, Bill Coffey asked him: "Steve, 48
you gonna play football?"

"Yeah, I guess I have to," he shrugged. "My Dad wants me to lose 49
ten pounds because of the weight limit."

Steve put himself on another schedule, this time with weights. 50
Across the top of a piece of notebook paper he marked places for the
dates of each day until fall. Beneath that, he charted sit-ups, bench
presses, snatches, lifts, push-ups, windmills, jumping jacks; he measured
an oval in his backyard with a tape and started running laps.

Affectionately, Charles Dailey teased him about being a "big lop"— 51
the nickname he'd been given when he'd grown to be 6 feet 2 inches, as a
young man. But Mike told him Steve didn't like it. And he stopped.

On Sunday, May 26, Steve helped haul stones and build a form for 52
the concrete foundation to a utility shed-workshop his father was putting
up behind the house. He hurt his back and missed school on Monday. He
missed baseball practice, too. And that was the second time—the first
had been a short while before when he'd had to stay at home with Kay
and Jamie while his mother took Mike to the doctor.

"Then he didn't show up for one of our games," says Ray Kendrick, 53
the baseball manager. Charles Dailey thinks it was a make-up game. "I
started someone else in his place," Kendrick says.

That week, smiling, Steven told Sister Marie Russell about his 54
summer job. But he didn't dress up for Roaring Twenties Day in Bill
Coffey's history class. Ted Hutchinson remembers: "He just sat there."
And that week, Coffey remembers, he discussed Japanese hara-kiri in
class. He recalls no reaction from Steve.

On Saturday, June 1, Steve's father took him to a Scout show. He 55
bought Steve a souvenir patch. That evening Steve worked on his
personal management merit badge, for which he drew up a budget. It set
a fixed amount aside each month for the trip to Philmont. After dinner, he
tried to show his family photo slides of Philmont, but the projector bulb
blew out.

On Sunday, June 2, Steve helped clean the family camper for a 56
Scout canoe trip the coming weekend. He wire-brushed the rust from its
wheels and painted them white.

On Monday, June 3, he rode his bicycle in front of his house and hit 57
a hole in the pavement. It pitched him over the handlebars. A neighbor
was sure he'd been hurt, but he got up, looked around to be certain nobody
had seen him, and got back on his bike. One of its pedals was bent.

On Tuesday, June 4, two days before the end of school, Sue Dailey 58
volunteered to staple the PTA bulletin together at St. Catherine's. She
met Steve in the hall on his way to history. He called out, "Hi, Mom."

Margaret Linahan kept him after school to finish an assignment.   59
When he got done, he found that Aunt Beth had already left. She was to
have picked him up and taken him to her house so he could earn more
Philmont money mowing the lawn. But she had biscuits in the oven and
couldn't wait.

Steve walked home. He called his father at work: "I just want to tell   60
you that Monday I wrecked my bike."

"Oh? Did you get hurt?"   61

"Yeah, I hurt my hand, and you know, it's pretty sore. I think I   62
might have broken it."

Charles Dailey didn't think it was all that bad, or his son would   63
have mentioned it before. He and Steve talked about the bicycle. Steve's
father remembers saying, without raising his voice: "We'll take a look at
it, and if you broke it that means you're going to have to pay for it."

"You know, I can't play ball, so I don't want to go to practice,"   64
Steve said.

"Well, you know, I think you ought to go, because you've missed a   65
few times, and if you're going to be part of the team you've got to go to
practices, too."

"Well, I'm not gonna take my glove."   66

"I think that you ought to take the glove and all and just go on up."   67

Steve handed the telephone receiver to his mother, and she hung it   68
up. Steve walked out the back door. He had tears in his eyes. He went to
the garage, found the rope, carried it down the trail to a dead tree in the
woods.

His father found his body the next morning. The baseball glove was   69
nearby.

The terrible *ifs* accumulated°:   70

Dan Carella: "If he'd come to me . . ."   71

Sister Marie Russell: "Oh, if only I would have known, I would   72
have gone out of my way to get him and really talk to him . . ."

Margaret Linahan: "If I wouldn't have kept him after school . . ."   73

Beth McGinnis: "If I would have just waited for him . . ."   74

Sue Dailey: "If I'd only said he didn't have to go to baseball   75
practice . . ."

Charles Dailey: "If I had gone back there [to the woods that night], he   76
might have been able to keep his weight off the rope for a period of time,
or something like that, and, you know, you could have helped him . . ."

Steve's father says a police officer friend told him the rope wasn't   77
tied, but only looped, around the tree limb. He believes his son didn't
intend to die—but that the rope had held accidentally.

"Yet I don't question the fact that he got the rope and he went back   78 there and he had tied the rope around his neck. You know, I just can't believe that Steve would really do that. Except that he had to have done it, I guess."

Other police officers and county coroner Philip Holman determined   79
that the fastening around the tree limb was secure enough to rule out an accident. They declared Steve a suicide.

"Not infrequently, suicides are caused by intense anger or   80
frustration," says Dr. Fedor Hagenauer, a pediatric psychiatrist° at the University of Cincinnati. "Because this anger or frustration is addressed at people who are very important, children have a lot of guilty feelings about them. And then, because of the guilty feelings, and because the anger or frustration has to come out in some way, they might try to take it out on themselves . . . even with a token gesture, or going through the motions . . . maybe with a fantasy that they'll be rescued at the last minute . . . and they'll do it thinking, 'Everybody will see how unhappy I am and they'll learn and give in to what I'm unhappy about.'" It would have been impossible, he said, to predict Steve's fate.

The Rev. James Conway, who celebrated° Requiem Mass° at St.   81
Catherine's, doesn't think Steve was morally responsible for his death.

During the Mass, Boy Scouts presented gifts to God symbolizing   82
Steve's life. At Mike's suggestion, one was a soccer ball.

READING COMPREHENSION QUESTIONS

Vocabulary in Context

1. The word *rigid* in "He added up the requirements to become an Eagle, allotted himself so much time to accomplish each, and put himself on a rigid schedule" (paragraph 21) means
   a. inexpensive.
   b. strict.
   c. short.
   d. well-known.

2. The word *prestige* in "But soccer was not the prestige sport at St. Catherine's. 'Football at St. Catherine's is king,' says Bill Coffey" (paragraphs 26–27) means
   a. least exciting.
   b. easiest.
   c. important.
   d. most expensive.

Central Point and Main Ideas

3. Which of the following sentences from the reading best expresses the central point of the selection?
   a. "Reported suicides among the very young have more than doubled in twenty years." (Paragraph 3)
   b. "The story of Steve Dailey, all-American boy, is an American tragedy: a story about the good life and the possibilities it offers for hidden pressure, subtle loneliness, quiet frustration—and unanswered questions." (Paragraph 3)
   c. "Steven Dailey was born July 30, 1961, in the Cincinnati suburb of Clifton." (Paragraph 5)
   d. "The Rev. James Conway, who celebrated Requiem Mass at St. Catherine's, doesn't think Steve was morally responsible for his death." (Paragraph 81)

4. Which statement best expresses the main idea of paragraph 7?
   a. Despite his father's wish that he continue with pony football, Steve decided to play with a lower-level team.
   b. Steve Dailey's father became a volunteer football coach for St. Catherine's growing athletic program.
   c. Fathers and their sons often have disagreements about football.
   d. Steve Dailey got paired up in practices with Mugsy, an aggressive football player.

5. Which of the following would make the best topic sentence for paragraphs 8 and 9 of the reading?
   a. Steve did not want to play football because he was afraid of getting hit.
   b. Scouting was a major part of Steve's life.
   c. Steve was a well-rounded young man.
   d. Steve's personality was better suited to calm activities than to rough ones like football.

Supporting Details

6. Before Steve's death,
   a. his grades started dropping.
   b. he kept his problems to himself.
   c. he didn't dress up for Roaring Twenties Day.
   d. all of the above.

Transitions

7. The relationship between the two parts of the sentence below is one of
   a. addition.
   b. contrast.
   c. illustration.
   d. cause and effect.

   > "My dad wants me to play football, but I'd rather play soccer."
   > (Paragraph 47)

Inferences

8. We can infer that Steve played football and baseball
   a. in order to release his frustration.
   b. because he believed the sports would make him popular.
   c. because he was naturally talented at these sports.
   d. in order to please his father.

9. From the last conversation between Steve and Charles Dailey (paragraphs 60–68), we can infer that
   a. the damage to the bicycle was easier for Steve to talk about than his inner problems.
   b. Steve's father rarely took him to the doctor for sports injuries.
   c. Steve was disappointed because he couldn't play ball.
   d. Steve killed himself because he wrecked his bicycle.

10. Based on the information in the essay, the reader can infer that Steve's father
    a. had planned on meeting him in the woods the night of Steve's death.
    b. never really understood Steve's wishes and problems.
    c. physically abused Steve.
    d. believes that Steve was murdered.

SUMMARIZING

Circle the letter—*a, b,* or *c*—of the passage that best completes the following summary of "A Suicide at Twelve—Why, Steve?"

From an early age, Steve Dailey was involved in his father's interests of sports and scouting. Steve excelled at scouting, but not football, his father's choice of sports. Although he was large for his age, Steve lacked the aggressive personality needed for football. Instead, Steve preferred soccer, a less important sport at his school where his father was coach and then athletic director. When Steve was twelve, his life seemed to be going well, but there were some trouble spots. His grades and class participation had dropped; he had no close friends; and he avoided playing baseball, again, his father's choice of sports, not his own.

a. One day, Steve had an accident on his bicycle which left one of its pedals bent. The next day, Steve phoned his father at work to tell him about the accident. Although Steve reported that he thought he broke his hand, his father insisted he go to baseball practice. Further, he warned that Steve would have to pay to have the bike repaired. However, Steve never showed up for baseball practice and, that night, Steve's father found the baseball glove beside a dead tree in the woods.

b. One afternoon, Steve committed suicide. One psychiatrist who is familiar with his case believes that children feel a great deal of guilt when they are angry at people they should love, such as their parents, coaches, or teachers. Because the anger has to come out in some way, the children often take it out on themselves. However, their suicide attempts might only be token gestures meant to get attention, but not to take their lives. Some people believe this sort of "token gesture" was what Steve really intended to do that fateful night.

c. One day, after an argument with his father about baseball practice, Steve went to some nearby woods and hung himself. When he was found, his family and friends questioned what had troubled the young boy so much that he took his own life. One psychiatrist believes that Steve's suicide could not be predicted, and that he may have hoped to be rescued. Such suicides, he said, are caused by great anger, frustration, and guilt.

DISCUSSION QUESTIONS

1. Why do you think Steve committed suicide? Could the adults in Steve's life have avoided the suicide by treating him differently? Whatever your answers, give your reasons.

2. Charles Dailey said about Steve: "But that was at the stage when I really wanted him to be the best football player in the world, you know" (paragraph 7). Why do you think Steve's father wanted him to be the best football player in the world? Why do you suppose he wouldn't have been equally happy to have Steve become the best soccer player in the world?

3. Do you think all young men would have responded to Steve's situation as Steve did? If so, explain why you think so. If not, what might be the difference between Steve and others in a similar situation?

4. Throughout the selection, the question, "Are you going to play football, Steve?" appears a number of times. Do you think sports are given too much emphasis in today's schools? What are the advantages and disadvantages of sports programs? Specifically, is the emphasis on competition a good one or a bad one? Why?

5

Do It Better!
Ben Carson, M.D.,
with Cecil Murphey

Preview

If you suspect that you are now as "smart" as you'll ever be, then read the following selection. It is about Dr. Ben Carson, who was sure he was "the dumbest kid in the class" in school. Carson tells how he turned his life totally around from what was a sure path of failure. Today he is a famous neurosurgeon at Johns Hopkins University Hospital in Baltimore, Maryland.

Words to Watch

inasmuch as (13): since
potential (18): capacity for development and progress
solely (20): alone
rebellious (46): resisting authority
indifferent (58): uninterested
astonished (81): surprised

"Benjamin, is this your report card?" my mother asked as she 1
picked up the folded white card from the table.

"Uh, yeah," I said, trying to sound casual. Too ashamed to hand it to 2
her, I had dropped it on the table, hoping that she wouldn't notice until after I went to bed.

It was the first report card I had received from Higgins Elementary   3
School since we had moved back from Boston to Detroit, only a few
months earlier.

I had been in the fifth grade not even two weeks before everyone   4
considered me the dumbest kid in the class and frequently made jokes
about me. Before long I too began to feel as though I really was the most
stupid kid in fifth grade. Despite Mother's frequently saying, "You're
smart, Bennie. You can do anything you want to do," I did not believe her.

No one else in school thought I was smart, either.   5

Now, as Mother examined my report card, she asked, "What's this   6
grade in reading?" (Her tone of voice told me that I was in trouble.)
Although I was embarrassed, I did not think too much about it. Mother
knew that I wasn't doing well in math, but she did not know I was doing
so poorly in every subject.

While she slowly read my report card, reading everything one word   7
at a time, I hurried into my room and started to get ready for bed. A few
minutes later, Mother came into my bedroom.

"Benjamin," she said, "are these your grades?" She held the card in   8
front of me as if I hadn't seen it before.

"Oh, yeah, but you know, it doesn't mean much."   9

"No, that's not true, Bennie. It means a lot."   10

"Just a report card."   11

"But it's more than that."   12

Knowing I was in for it now, I prepared to listen, yet I was not all   13
that interested. I did not like school very much and there was no reason
why I should. Inasmuch as° I was the dumbest kid in the class, what did I
have to look forward to? The others laughed at me and made jokes about
me every day.

"Education is the only way you're ever going to escape poverty,"   14
she said. "It's the only way you're ever going to get ahead in life and be
successful. Do you understand that?"

"Yes, Mother," I mumbled.   15

"If you keep on getting these kinds of grades you're going to spend   16
the rest of your life on skid row, or at best sweeping floors in a factory.
That's not the kind of life that I want for you. That's not the kind of life
that God wants for you."

I hung my head, genuinely ashamed. My mother had been raising   17
me and my older brother, Curtis, by herself. Having only a third-grade
education herself, she knew the value of what she did not have. Daily she
drummed into Curtis and me that we had to do our best in school.

"You're just not living up to your potential°," she said. "I've got   18
two mighty smart boys and I know they can do better."

I had done my best—at least I had when I first started at Higgins 19
Elementary School. How could I do much when I did not understand
anything going on in our class?

In Boston we had attended a parochial school, but I hadn't learned 20
much because of a teacher who seemed more interested in talking to
another female teacher than in teaching us. Possibly, this teacher was not
solely° to blame—perhaps I wasn't emotionally able to learn much. My
parents had separated just before we went to Boston, when I was eight
years old. I loved both my mother and father and went through
considerable trauma over their separating. For months afterward, I kept
thinking that my parents would get back together, that my daddy would
come home again the way he used to, and that we could be the same old
family again—but he never came back. Consequently, we moved to
Boston and lived with Aunt Jean and Uncle William Avery in a tenement
building for two years until Mother had saved enough money to bring us
back to Detroit.

Mother kept shaking the report card at me as she sat on the side of 21
my bed. "You have to work harder. You have to use that good brain that
God gave you, Bennie. Do you understand that?"

"Yes, Mother." Each time she paused, I would dutifully say those 22
words.

"I work among rich people, people who are educated," she said. "I 23
watch how they act, and I know they can do anything they want to do.
And so can you." She put her arm on my shoulder. "Bennie, you can do
anything they can do—only you can do it better!"

Mother had said those words before. Often. At the time, they did 24
not mean much to me. Why should they? I really believed that I was the
dumbest kid in fifth grade, but of course, I never told her that.

"I just don't know what to do about you boys," she said. "I'm going 25
to talk to God about you and Curtis." She paused, stared into space, then
said (more to herself than to me), "I need the Lord's guidance on what to
do. You just can't bring in any more report cards like this."

As far as I was concerned, the report card matter was over. 26

The next day was like the previous ones—just another bad day in 27
school, another day of being laughed at because I did not get a single
problem right in arithmetic and couldn't get any words right on the
spelling test. As soon as I came home from school, I changed into play
clothes and ran outside. Most of the boys my age played softball, or the
game I liked best, "Tip the Top."

We played Tip the Top by placing a bottle cap on one of the 28
sidewalk cracks. Then taking a ball—any kind that bounced—we'd stand
on a line and take turns throwing the ball at the bottle top, trying to flip it

over. Whoever succeeded got two points. If anyone actually moved the cap more than a few inches, he won five points. Ten points came if he flipped it into the air and it landed on the other side.

When it grew dark or we got tired, Curtis and I would finally go   29
inside and watch TV. The set stayed on until we went to bed. Because Mother worked long hours, she was never home until just before we went to bed. Sometimes I would awaken when I heard her unlocking the door.

Two evenings after the incident with the report card, Mother came   30
home about an hour before our bedtime. Curtis and I were sprawled out, watching TV. She walked across the room, snapped off the set, and faced both of us. "Boys," she said, "you're wasting too much of your time in front of that television. You don't get an education from staring at television all the time."

Before either of us could make a protest, she told us that she had   31
been praying for wisdom. "The Lord's told me what to do," she said. "So from now on, you will not watch television, except for two preselected programs each week."

"Just *two* programs?" I could hardly believe she would say such a   32
terrible thing. "That's not—"

"And *only* after you've done your homework. Furthermore, you   33
don't play outside after school, either, until you've done all your homework."

"Everybody else plays outside right after school," I said, unable to   34
think of anything except how bad it would be if I couldn't play with my friends. "I won't have any friends if I stay in the house all the time—"

"That may be," Mother said, "but everybody else is not going to be   35
as successful as you are—"

"But, Mother—"   36

"This is what we're going to do. I asked God for wisdom, and this   37
is the answer I got."

I tried to offer several other arguments, but Mother was firm. I   38
glanced at Curtis, expecting him to speak up, but he did not say anything. He lay on the floor, staring at his feet.

"Don't worry about everybody else. The whole world is full of   39
'everybody else,' you know that? But only a few make a significant achievement."

The loss of TV and play time was bad enough. I got up off the floor,   40
feeling as if everything was against me. Mother wasn't going to let me play with my friends, and there would be no more television—almost none, anyway. She was stopping me from having any fun in life.

"And that isn't all," she said. "Come back, Bennie."   41

I turned around, wondering what else there could be.   42

"In addition," she said, "to doing your homework, you have to read 43
two books from the library each week. Every single week."

"Two books? Two?" Even though I was in fifth grade, I had never 44
read a whole book in my life.

"Yes, two. When you finish reading them, you must write me a 45
book report just like you do at school. You're not living up to your
potential, so I'm going to see that you do."

Usually Curtis, who was two years older, was the more rebellious°. 46
But this time he seemed to grasp the wisdom of what Mother said. He did
not say one word.

She stared at Curtis. "You understand?" 47

He nodded. 48

"Bennie, is it clear?" 49

"Yes, Mother." I agreed to do what Mother told me—it wouldn't 50
have occurred to me not to obey—but I did not like it. Mother was being
unfair and demanding more of us than other parents did.

The following day was Thursday. After school, Curtis and I walked 51
to the local branch of the library. I did not like it much, but then I had not
spent that much time in any library.

We both wandered around a little in the children's section, not 52
having any idea about how to select books or which books we wanted to
check out.

The librarian came over to us and asked if she could help. We 53
explained that both of us wanted to check out two books.

"What kind of books would you like to read?" the librarian asked. 54

"Animals," I said after thinking about it. "Something about animals." 55

"I'm sure we have several that you'd like." She led me over to a 56
section of books. She left me and guided Curtis to another section of the
room. I flipped through the row of books until I found two that looked
easy enough for me to read. One of them, *Chip, the Dam Builder*—about
a beaver—was the first one I had ever checked out. As soon as I got
home, I started to read it. It was the first book I ever read all the way
through even though it took me two nights. Reluctantly I admitted
afterward to Mother that I really had liked reading about Chip.

Within a month I could find my way around the children's section 57
like someone who had gone there all his life. By then the library staff
knew Curtis and me and the kind of books we chose. They often made
suggestions. "Here's a delightful book about a squirrel," I remember one
of them telling me.

As she told me part of the story, I tried to appear indifferent°, but as 58
soon as she handed it to me, I opened the book and started to read.

Best of all, we became favorites of the librarians. When new books came in that they thought either of us would enjoy, they held them for us. Soon I became fascinated as I realized that the library had so many books—and about so many different subjects. 59

After the book about the beaver, I chose others about animals—all types of animals. I read every animal story I could get my hands on. I read books about wolves, wild dogs, several about squirrels, and a variety of animals that lived in other countries. Once I had gone through the animal books, I started reading about plants, then minerals, and finally rocks. 60

My reading books about rocks was the first time the information ever became practical to me. We lived near the railroad tracks, and when Curtis and I took the route to school that crossed by the tracks, I began paying attention to the crushed rock that I noticed between the ties. 61

As I continued to read more about rocks, I would walk along the tracks, searching for different kinds of stones, and then see if I could identify them. 62

Often I would take a book with me to make sure that I had labeled each stone correctly. 63

"Agate," I said as I threw the stone. Curtis got tired of my picking up stones and identifying them, but I did not care because I kept finding new stones all the time. Soon it became my favorite game to walk along the tracks and identify the varieties of stones. Although I did not realize it, within a very short period of time, I was actually becoming an expert on rocks. 64

Two things happened in the second half of fifth grade that convinced me of the importance of reading books. 65

First, our teacher, Mrs. Williamson, had a spelling bee every Friday afternoon. We'd go through all the words we'd had so far that year. Sometimes she also called out words that we were supposed to have learned in fourth grade. Without fail, I always went down on the first word. 66

One Friday, though, Bobby Farmer, whom everyone acknowledged as the smartest kid in our class, had to spell "agriculture" as his final word. As soon as the teacher pronounced his word, I thought, *I can spell that word.* Just the day before, I had learned it from reading one of my library books. I spelled it under my breath, and it was just the way Bobby spelled it. 67

If I can spell "agriculture," I'll bet I can learn to spell any other word in the world. I'll bet I can learn to spell better than Bobby Farmer. 68

Just that single word, "agriculture," was enough to give me hope. 69

The following week, a second thing happened that forever changed 70 my life. When Mr. Jaeck, the science teacher, was teaching us about volcanoes, he held up an object that looked like a piece of black, glass-like rock. "Does anybody know what this is? What does it have to do with volcanoes?"

Immediately, because of my reading, I recognized the stone. I   71
waited, but none of my classmates raised their hands. I thought, *This is strange. Not even the smart kids are raising their hands.* I raised my hand.

"Yes, Benjamin," he said.   72

I heard snickers around me. The other kids probably thought it was   73
a joke, or that I was going to say something stupid.

"Obsidian," I said.   74

"That's right!" He tried not to look startled, but it was obvious he   75
hadn't expected me to give the correct answer.

"That's obsidian," I said, "and it's formed by the supercooling of   76
lava when it hits the water." Once I had their attention and realized I knew information no other student had learned, I began to tell them everything I knew about the subject of obsidian, lava, lava flow, super-cooling, and compacting of the elements.

When I finally paused, a voice behind me whispered, "Is that   77
Bennie Carson?"

"You're absolutely correct," Mr. Jaeck said and he smiled at me. If   78
he had announced that I'd won a million-dollar lottery, I couldn't have been more pleased and excited.

"Benjamin, that's absolutely, absolutely right," he repeated with   79
enthusiasm in his voice. He turned to the others and said, "That is wonderful! Class, this is a tremendous piece of information Benjamin has just given us. I'm very proud to hear him say this."

For a few moments, I tasted the thrill of achievement. I recall   80
thinking, *Wow, look at them. They're all looking at me with admiration. Me, the dummy! The one everybody thinks is stupid. They're looking at me to see if this is really me speaking.*

Maybe, though, it was I who was the most astonished° one in the   81
class. Although I had been reading two books a week because Mother told me to, I had not realized how much knowledge I was accumulating. True, I had learned to enjoy reading, but until then I hadn't realized how it connected with my schoolwork. That day—for the first time—I realized that Mother had been right. Reading is the way out of ignorance, and the road to achievement. I did not have to be the class dummy anymore.

For the next few days, I felt like a hero at school. The jokes about   82
me stopped. The kids started to listen to me. *I'm starting to have fun with this stuff.*

As my grades improved in every subject, I asked myself, "Ben, is   83
there any reason you can't be the smartest kid in the class? If you can
learn about obsidian, you can learn about social studies and geography
and math and science and everything."

That single moment of triumph pushed me to want to read more.   84
From then on, it was as though I could not read enough books. Whenever
anyone looked for me after school, they could usually find me in my
bedroom—curled up, reading a library book—for a long time, the only
thing I wanted to do. I had stopped caring about the TV programs I was
missing; I no longer cared about playing Tip the Top or baseball
anymore. I just wanted to read.

In a year and a half—by the middle of sixth grade—I had moved to   85
the top of the class.

Note: This selection is taken from the book *Think Big* by Ben Carson and Cecil
Murphey. For information on how to obtain the book, turn to page 564.

READING COMPREHENSION QUESTIONS

Vocabulary in Context

1. The word *trauma* in "I loved both my mother and father and went
   through considerable trauma over their separating. For months
   afterward, I kept thinking that my parents would get back together,
   . . . but he never came back" (paragraph 20) means
   a. love.
   b. knowledge.
   c. distance.
   d. suffering.

2. The word *acknowledged* in "One Friday, though, Bobby Farmer,
   whom everyone acknowledged as the smartest kid in our class, had
   to spell 'agriculture' as his final word" (paragraph 67) means
   a. denied.
   b. recognized.
   c. forgot.
   d. interrupted.

Central Point and Main Ideas

3. Which sentence best expresses the central point of the selection?
   a. Children who grow up in single-parent homes may spend large
      amounts of time home alone.
   b. Because of parental guidance that led to a love of reading, the
      author was able to go from academic failure to success.

    c. Parents should stay committed to their marriages when their children are young.

    d. Today's young people watch too much television day after day.

4. Which sentence best expresses the main idea of paragraphs 61–64?

    a. Books about rocks gave the author his first practical benefits from reading.

    b. Curtis took little interest in what his brother had learned about rocks.

    c. The author found a piece of agate by the railroad tracks.

    d. Studying rocks can be a fascinating experience.

Supporting Details

5. The author's mother

    a. was not a religious person.

    b. spoke to his teacher.

    c. had only a third-grade education.

    d. had little contact with educated people.

6. The major details in paragraphs 65–82 are

    a. books that Bennie Carson read.

    b. new skills Bennie Carson had gained.

    c. various people in Bennie Carson's elementary school class.

    d. two events that convinced Bennie Carson of the importance of reading books.

Transitions

7. The sentence below contains a transition that shows

    a. addition.

    b. contrast.

    c. illustration.

    d. cause and effect.

> . . . I hadn't learned much because of a teacher who seemed more interested in talking to another female teacher than in teaching us. (Paragraph 20)

8. The major details in paragraphs 65–82 are signaled by the addition words

    a. *two, other.*

    b. *two, one.*

    c. *one, other, finally, next.*

    d. *first, second.*

Inferences

9. We can conclude that the author's mother believed
   a. education leads to success.
   b. her sons needed to be forced to live up to their potential.
   c. socializing was less important for her sons than a good education.
   d. all of the above.

10. We can infer that Bennie Carson believed he was dumb because
    a. in Boston he had gotten behind in school.
    b. other students laughed at him.
    c. he had done his best when he first started at Higgins Elementary School, but still got poor grades.
    d. all of the above.

SUMMARIZING

Circle the letter—*a, b,* or *c*—of the passage that best completes the following summary of "Do It Better!"

At the beginning of fifth grade, Bennie Carson did poorly in school and believed he was stupid. After school, he and his brother would play outside and watch TV. Their hard-working mother believed her sons were not living up to their potential and that they needed a good education to escape poverty. So one day she set up some rules about finishing homework and not watching much TV. Also, each boy had to read two library books every week. Bennie learned to love his reading. His first practical experience with information from books came when he found rocks outside to identify.

a. The boys passed railroad tracks on the way to school, and Bennie began to pay attention to the crushed rocks between the railroad ties. Soon identifying the stones along the tracks became his favorite game. His knowledge of rocks also helped him in school when the teacher held up an object and asked, "Does anybody know what this is?" Nobody else in class knew what it was, but Bennie knew it was obsidian. He finally raised his hand, named the object, and also gave a lot of information about obsidian and volcanoes.

b. But it was two events in school that convinced him of the importance of reading. Because of his reading, he knew a difficult spelling-bee word, which made him think that perhaps he was not so dumb after all. Also, what he had read about rocks enabled him one day to give an impressive answer in class. The positive reactions he received from the teacher and students encouraged him to become a constant reader. By the middle of sixth grade, he was at the top of his class.

c. Bennie had always been a poor speller. His class had a spelling bee every Friday afternoon, and Bennie always missed his first word. One day, the smartest kid in the class got "agriculture" as his final word. Bennie was surprised to realize he could spell that difficult word, as he had learned it the day before from one of his library books. This greatly boosted his confidence.

DISCUSSION QUESTIONS

1. Why did Bennie consider himself the "dumbest kid in class"? How do you think this perception of himself affected his schoolwork?

2. The author recalls his failure in the classroom as an eight-year-old child by writing, "Perhaps I wasn't emotionally able to learn much." Why does he make this statement? What other things in a child's home or social life might interfere with his or her education?

3. Part of Carson's mother's plan for helping her sons to improve their schoolwork was limiting their television watching to two programs a week. How much of a role do you think this limit played in the success of her plan? Do you agree with her that unrestricted television watching can be harmful to children?

4. Carson's mother instructed him, "Education is the only way you're ever going to escape poverty." How true do you think this statement is today? What obstacles do poor students face in getting an education?

6

Tickets to Nowhere
Andy Rooney

Preview

We've all heard or read about lucky people who have won millions of lottery dollars. One California man, for example, won over ten million dollars on his very first lottery ticket. Stories like that are enough to keep many people hopefully "investing" in the lottery week after week. In this selection, Andy Rooney describes just such a person.

Words to Watch

gushed (6): flowed suddenly and plentifully
slithered (6): slid from side to side
fidgeted (12): moved nervously
clutched (13): held tightly

Things never went very well for Jim Oakland. He dropped out of   1
high school because he was impatient to get rich but after dropping out
he lived at home with his parents for two years and didn't earn a dime.

He finally got a summer job working for the highway department   2
holding up a sign telling oncoming drivers to be careful of the workers
ahead. Later that same year, he picked up some extra money putting
flyers under the windshield wipers of parked cars.

Things just never went very well for Jim and he was 23 before he   3
left home and went to Florida hoping his ship would come in down there.

177

He never lost his desire to get rich but first he needed money for the rent so he took a job near Ft. Lauderdale for $4.50 an hour servicing the goldfish aquariums kept by the cashier's counter in a lot of restaurants.

Jim was paid in cash once a week by the owner of the goldfish   4
business and the first thing he did was go to the little convenience store near where he lived and buy $20 worth of lottery tickets. He was really determined to get rich.

A week ago, the lottery jackpot in Florida reached $54 million. Jim   5
woke up nights thinking what he could do with $54 million. During the days, he daydreamed about it. One morning he was driving along the main street in the boss's old pickup truck with six tanks of goldfish in back. As he drove past a BMW dealer, he looked at the new models in the window.

He saw the car he wanted in the showroom window but   6
unfortunately he didn't see the light change. The car in front of him stopped short and Jim slammed on his brakes. The fish tanks slid forward. The tanks broke, the water gushed° out and the goldfish slithered° and flopped all over the back of the truck. Some fell off into the road.

It wasn't a good day for the goldfish or for Jim, of course. He knew   7
he'd have to pay for the tanks and 75 cents each for the fish and if it weren't for the $54 million lottery, he wouldn't have known which way to turn. He had that lucky feeling.

For the tanks and the dead goldfish, the boss deducted $114 of Jim's   8
$180 weekly pay. Even though he didn't have enough left for the rent and food, Jim doubled the amount he was going to spend on lottery tickets. He never needed $54 million more.

Jim had this system. He took his age and added the last four digits   9
of the telephone number of the last girl he dated. He called it his lucky number . . . even though the last four digits changed quite often and he'd never won with his system. Everyone laughed at Jim and said he'd never win the lottery.

Jim put down $40 on the counter that week and the man punched   10
out his tickets. Jim stowed them safely away in his wallet with last week's tickets. He never threw away his lottery tickets until at least a month after the drawing just in case there was some mistake. He'd heard of mistakes.

Jim listened to the radio all afternoon the day of the drawing. The   11
people at the radio station he was listening to waited for news of the winning numbers to come over the wires and, even then, the announcers didn't rush to get them on. The station manager thought the people running the lottery ought to pay to have the winning numbers broadcast, just like any other commercial announcement.

Jim fidgeted° while they gave the weather and the traffic and the   12
news. Then they played more music. All he wanted to hear were those
numbers.

"Well," the radio announced said finally, "we have the lottery   13
numbers some of you have been waiting for. You ready?" Jim was ready.
He clutched° his ticket with the number 274802.

"The winning number," the announcer said, "is 860539. I'll repeat   14
that. 860539." Jim was still a loser.

I thought that, with all the human interest stories about lottery   15
winners, we ought to have a story about one of the several million losers.

READING COMPREHENSION QUESTIONS

Vocabulary in Context

1. The expression *his ship would come in* in "he . . . went to Florida
   hoping his ship would come in down there. He never lost his desire
   to get rich" (paragraph 3) means
   a. he would decide what to do.
   b. he would get a job on a ship.
   c. he would travel worldwide.
   d. he would get lucky.

2. The word *deducted* in "For the tanks and the dead goldfish, the boss
   deducted $114 of Jim's $180 weekly pay" (paragraph 8) means
   a. taxed.
   b. gave as a bonus.
   c. subtracted.
   d. delayed.

Central Point and Main Ideas

3. Which statement best expresses the central point of the selection?
   a. Jim Oakland desperately needed money.
   b. Many people play the lottery each year.
   c. Jim Oakland, like millions of others, wasted his money and
      dreams on the lottery.
   d. Jim Oakland was unsuccessful at everything he tried.

4. Which statement best expresses the main idea of paragraphs 5–8?
   a. The fish tanks slid forward when Jim slammed on the truck's
      brakes.
   b. While daydreaming about winning the lottery, Jim saw a BMW
      car he wanted.

    c. Jim daydreamed so much about winning money that he lost money by being careless.

    d. Jim was a very poor driver.

Supporting Details

5. Jim dropped out of high school because
    a. he moved to Florida.
    b. he was eager to get rich.
    c. he got a good job.
    d. his grades were poor.

6. Jim wasn't upset when he broke some goldfish tanks because
    a. he thought his boss wouldn't charge him for the broken tanks.
    b. the broken tanks and dead fish would cost only a small part of his paycheck.
    c. he thought he would finally win the lottery.
    d. he had saved up a lot of money.

Transitions

7. The relationship of the second sentence below to the first is one of
    a. time.
    b. addition.
    c. contrast.
    d. illustration.

    Jim fidgeted while they gave the weather and the traffic and the news. Then they played more music. (Paragraph 12)

Inferences

8. We can conclude from paragraph 9 that Jim
    a. was good in math.
    b. did not date very often.
    c. kept his dreams about the lottery to himself.
    d. never dated the same girl for long.

9. Andy Rooney implies that Jim's idea of success for himself was
    a. reaching a goal he had worked hard for.
    b. getting a degree and a career.
    c. being lucky.
    d. all of the above.

10. We might conclude from this reading that Andy Rooney thinks
    a. lotteries tempt some people to throw away money they should use for other things.

b. Jim would have been more successful if he had at least finished high school and been willing to work hard.

c. it's very foolish to count on something you are unlikely to get.

d. all of the above.

SUMMARIZING

Circle the letter—*a, b,* or *c*—of the passage that best completes the following summary of "Tickets to Nowhere."

While some people win millions of dollars at lotteries, most aren't so lucky. An interesting example is Jim Oakland. Because Jim wanted to get rich quickly, he dropped out of high school. However, he then lived at home with his parents for two years without working. After finally getting a job one summer, he went to seek his luck in Florida, where he got a job servicing goldfish aquariums. Still determined to get rich, he bought twenty dollars worth of lottery tickets every week.

a. When the jackpot reached $54 million, Jim thought a lot about it. He woke up nights thinking about how he could use the winnings. During the days, he daydreamed about winning the lottery. One morning he was daydreaming while driving six of his boss's tanks of goldfish. Driving past a BMW dealer, he glanced at the new model in the window. He was thinking about which model he would buy once he won the lottery. As a result, he lost track of traffic and ended up slamming his breaks to avoid hitting the car in front of him. The tanks broke, the fish slid out, and he ended up owing his boss $114.

b. When the jackpot reached $54 million, he daydreamed so much about winning that he was careless while driving for work with some fish tanks. He ended up owing his boss $114 for broken tanks and dead fish. But Jim felt his financial problems would soon be solved by the lottery. He bought double the number of tickets as usual. On the day of the drawing, he listened to the radio all afternoon. The winning number was finally announced, and it wasn't Jim's.

c. When the jackpot reached $54 million, Jim woke up nights thinking about how he might spend the money. He bought double the amount of tickets as usual. On the day of the lottery, he listened to the radio all afternoon. The announcers, however, did not rush to tell listeners who won the lottery. Jim became nervous while the station broadcast weather and traffic information and the news. Finally, the winning number was announced, and it wasn't Jim's.

DISCUSSION QUESTIONS

1. If you were giving advice to Jim Oakland, what would you tell him?

2. As you read Rooney's piece, did you think Jim would win or lose the lottery? What about Rooney's choice of details made you think that?

3. Do you know anyone who has depended too much on luck and too little on his or her own abilities? What is that person like, and why do you think he or she behaves that way? Even if you don't know anybody like Jim Oakland, what reasons can you think of for a person to behave as he did?

4. Think about the positive and negative aspects of lotteries. On balance, do you think they do more harm than good, or vice versa? Explain.

7

Giving Emotional Support
Kim Wilkes

Preview

Can you remember receiving any praise lately? Or insults? If so, then you will know what author Kim Wilkes means when she says that "words are powerful tools." For various reasons, some people get in the habit of putting others down. According to Wilkes, however, positive support can be good for both the giver and the receiver.

Words to Watch

self-image (3): how a person sees and feels about himself
siblings (4): brothers and sisters
cycle (6): repeated series of events
highlight (12): outstanding feature
strings attached (13): something expected in return

Lois Talbot is treasurer of the Lawnside Parent-Teacher   1
Association. Recently she reported to the group on a fundraising drive. Watching her, the audience saw a reasonably calm, well-dressed woman. But Mrs. Talbot didn't feel calm. As always when she was about to speak before a group, she felt frightened and shaky. As she faced the crowd, she thought she heard her fifth-grade teacher's impatient voice. The voice was saying, "Lois, can't you do *anything* right? Stop mumbling! Speak up! Oh, just sit down and let someone else talk!" Feeling like a shy

eleven-year-old, Mrs. Talbot gulped nervously. Her hands left sweaty smears on her notecards. She wished she could sink through the floor.

Jed Stuart had supervised one of his company's warehouses for   2
nearly four years. He'd done an excellent job. One day, his boss offered him a new job. It involved supervising the company's whole warehouse operation. But Jed turned down the promotion. His self-image was strongly based on the frequent scoldings his father gave him when he was young: "I can't trust you with any responsibility! Just when I think I can depend on you, you mess things up!" Jed's good record at work proved he could handle the job. But that inner voice told him he would fail.

The old saying goes, "Sticks and stones may break my bones, but   3
words can never harm me." But the truth is that words are powerful tools. When people hear constant negative, hurtful remarks, they develop a low self-opinion. Such a poor self-image° is difficult to overcome. On the other hand, supportive comments help people develop confidence and a positive self-image.

From the earliest days of our childhoods, we build a mental picture   4
of ourselves. It is based largely on what we hear from the people most important to us. At first, that means our parents, siblings°, teachers and friends. Later, spouses, co-workers and other adults add to the picture. Our "memory bank" is filled with people's reactions to us.

Sadie is a single woman in her 70's. Her face is sweet and pleasant.   5
But her dress and hairstyle are as plain as she can make them. It is difficult for Sadie to look another person in the face. Rarely will she speak unless she's spoken to first. She is so withdrawn that people hardly notice she is around. One of Sadie's strongest childhood memories is what her mother often told visitors: "Sadie is such a plain, dull little thing that no one will ever pay much attention to her." Sadie's natural shyness increased every time she heard her mother's words.

Like Sadie, people who often hear negative remarks about   6
themselves usually develop a negative self-image. In addition, people who've *received* little emotional support find it difficult to *give* emotional support. So the cycle° continues: people who feel badly about themselves make those around them feel badly too. Mrs. Talbot's teacher, Jed's father, Sadie's mother may have all had poor self-images. Their low self-esteem affected how they treated the children in their care.

Why do so many people find it hard to give emotional support?   7
There are three major reasons.

- First, many of us simply don't realize how our words affect   8
  others. We may not intend to hurt others, but that's still the effect.
  "I was really excited when my parents came to visit my high

school," said Gina. "But on the way home, all they talked about was the artwork done by one of my classmates. I remember thinking, 'I bet they wish *she* was their daughter instead of me.'"

- Second, an insecure person may have a strong need to put others down. "I always worry that my performance at work doesn't measure up," confessed Jerry, a worker at a city hospital. "It makes me uncomfortable when other people do better than me. So I look for things to say that will bring them down. I guess I figure if I can make them feel bad, I'll feel better by comparison. The bad thing is, I can't appreciate anything about anyone else. And I *still* think I'm no good."   9

- And third, some people are afraid to make positive remarks about others. They find it risky to show affection or respect. "There are many times I'd like to give someone a compliment, but I just can't," said Helen. "In a way, giving a compliment means you're offering your friendship. It's opening yourself up to someone else. I'm afraid to do that. It would hurt so much if they rejected me. It's safer just not to try."   10

Fortunately, anyone can learn to be emotionally supportive. Just as physical exercise benefits the body, certain mental exercises improve our attitude towards others. Here are three good exercises to help you develop the habit of being supportive.   11

- Look for positive qualities in others. You have many chances to offer sincere compliments every day. Get in the habit of telling co-workers when they do a good job. Or tell a neighbor, "Your beautiful garden is a highlight° of my morning walk." And don't forget the people closest to you. A child would like to hear, "You've gotten to be a really big help to me in the kitchen." Or tell a spouse, "The meal you cooked was delicious."   12

- Don't give out emotional support that has "strings attached°." Compliments should stand on their own. They shouldn't be accompanied by warnings or advice. For example, just tell your son, "Your room looks terrific!" Don't add, "Why can't you keep it that way?"   13

- Finally, take time to notice when someone needs support. Don't wait to be asked for it. A child will often openly ask for approval—"Look at my painting! Isn't it pretty?" But adults are generally less frank about their need for support. A grown-up who faces an important meeting at work isn't likely to say, "Please tell me I'll do a good job!" But he needs to hear it all the same.   14

People react positively to those who are supportive of them. So as   15
you work on encouraging others, you will also help improve your own
self-image. You'll be starting a cycle of giving that will strengthen your
own self-esteem as well.

READING COMPREHENSION QUESTIONS

Vocabulary in Context

1. The word *withdrawn* in "Rarely will she speak unless she's spoken
   to first. She is so withdrawn that people hardly notice she is around"
   (paragraph 5) means
   a. outgoing.
   b. short.
   c. shy.
   d. intelligent.

2. The word *frank* in "A child will often openly ask for approval. . . .
   But adults are generally less frank about their need for support"
   (paragraph 14) means
   a. frightened.
   b. honest.
   c. quiet.
   d. angry.

Central Point and Main Ideas

3. Which statement best expresses the central point of the essay?
   a. An insecure person may feel the need to put others down.
   b. Lois Talbot, Jed Stuart, and Sadie are examples of people who
      were criticized as children.
   c. People can learn to be supportive, building up others as well as
      themselves.
   d. People find it hard to give emotional support for three main
      reasons.

4. Which sentence best expresses the main idea of paragraphs 7–10?
   a. People find it hard to give emotional support because they don't
      realize how words affect others.
   b. There are three main reasons people find it hard to give
      emotional support.
   c. Many people don't intend to hurt others, but they do.
   d. Some people find it risky to show affection or respect to others.

5. Which sentence best expresses the main idea of paragraphs 11–14?
   a. There are three exercises that help people develop the habit of being supportive.
   b. Exercise can improve both the body and the mind.
   c. We have many chances to offer sincere compliments every day.
   d. People should not expect to get something in return for emotional support.

Supporting Details

6. According to Wilkes, our mental picture of ourselves is based largely on
   a. our outward appearance, including the clothes we wear.
   b. the reactions to us of our family, friends, and co-workers.
   c. our grades and activities in school.
   d. what we read and our religious beliefs.

7. According to Wilkes, when you give emotional support to someone,
   a. that person is more likely to develop a low self-image.
   b. you will have difficulty finding a sincere compliment.
   c. you are only seeking approval for yourself.
   d. that person is more likely to react positively to you.

Transitions

8. The relationship between the two sentences below is one of
   a. addition.
   b. contrast.
   c. illustration.
   d. time.

   > When people hear constant negative, hurtful remarks, they develop a low self-opinion. . . . On the other hand, supportive comments help people develop confidence and a positive self-image. (Paragraph 3)

Inferences

9. The author implies that our attitudes about ourselves
   a. can change.
   b. are more negative than positive.
   c. are more positive than negative.
   d. are set for life when we are children.

10. The tone of this essay is
    a. cruel and sarcastic.
    b. entertaining and amusing.
    c. optimistic and encouraging.
    d. frustrating and embarrassing.

OUTLINING

Complete the following outline of "Giving Emotional Support" by filling in the missing major detail and the three missing minor details.

Central point: Despite our difficulties in giving emotional support, we can learn to be supportive, helping others and ourselves.

1. Introduction: Support or negative remarks affect people's self-image. *(Paragraphs 1–6)*
    a. People who hear negative comments develop a poor self-image, but those who hear positive comments develop confidence.
    b. People with a poor self-image find it hard to give emotional support, contributing to a cycle of low self-image in a family.

2. People find it hard to give emotional support for three main reasons. *(Paragraphs 7–10)*
    a. Many people don't realize how their words affect others.
    b. _____
    c. Some people are afraid to risk supporting others.

3. _____
    (Paragraphs 11–14)
    a. Get in the habit of looking for positive qualities in others and complimenting them.
    b. _____
    c. _____

4. Conclusion: By supporting others, you begin a cycle that includes support for yourself as well. *(Paragraph 15)*

DISCUSSION QUESTIONS

1. In paragraph 5, the author writes: "Sadie's natural shyness increased every time she heard her mother's words." Why do you think her mother's words affected Sadie in this way?

2. In paragraph 12, the author writes: "You have many chances to offer sincere compliments every day." From this we can conclude that the author feels that it's not a good idea to offer insincere compliments. Why might sincere compliments be better than insincere ones?

3. In the last paragraph of the essay, the author explains that when a person supports other people, his or her own self-esteem will also benefit. Can you think of any other ways people benefit from supporting others? For example, what other benefits might a parent, a boss, or a teacher gain?

4. Many adults still remember the encouragement of a supportive relative or even the compliment that a teacher wrote on a paper. Do you still remember the special support someone gave you when you were younger? Explain who this person was, how he or she supported you, and how that support may have influenced you.

8

Chicken Gizzards
James A. Perkins

Preview

Do the children in your family fight over who gets to sit in the front seat of the car? Do you compete with a housemate over sections of the Sunday newspaper? If so, you know how a running contest over something unimportant can take on a life of its own. In this selection, author and teacher James Perkins remembers such a competition in his own family.

Words to Watch

flanked by (1): having at its sides
gizzard (2): part of a bird's digestive system
crude (3): roughly done
strategy (5): a plan of action
dyed-in-the-wool (5): out-and-out, complete
greenhorns (5): inexperienced people
sullenly (7): silently and in ill humor
groused (7): complained, grumbled

Daddy and his daddy, Pap, and Daddy's brother-in-law, Uncle   1
Eddie, all loved to eat. Whenever our family got together it was around a table, a table loaded with food. I always hoped for ham, but their favorite was fried chicken, and there was usually a heaping platter of fried chicken flanked by° steaming bowls of green beans and mashed potatoes and gravy.

Besides liking chicken, they all three liked the gizzard° best of all, and down underneath of those wings and drumsticks and thighs and whatnot was the one gizzard. I think it all started one Sunday when Pap picked up the platter, smiled sheepishly, and said, "Would any of y'all like this here chicken craw?" "Don't mind if I do," said Daddy, and he forked the gizzard right off the platter. Pap's eyes went hard. He just sat there holding that empty platter with both hands. Finally he set it down and said, "I see." From then on we all saw that it was war, and it lasted for years.

At first it was rather crude°. Daddy took a wing and passed the chicken to Uncle Eddie. He slid the back off the platter and casually swept the gizzard with it. I could tell by the way they looked at him when he set the empty platter down that he had broken the rules and the last easy victory had been won.

Piece by piece another Sunday's chicken was eaten, and the three of them finally sat there staring at the gizzard. When Pap's wife, Lucy, asked, "One of you going to eat that thing?" she was ignored. Finally Pap made his move. There was an awful din of clashing metal and screaming. Pap forked the gizzard. Daddy, like an old time sheriff letting the hired gun slap leather first, nailed that gizzard to the platter with a fork, and Uncle Eddie, who, being right-handed, was at a disadvantage having to reach across, stuck his fork in the back of Pap's hand.

It was about then that strategy° was introduced. "My Gawd. It looks like Fronk's barn's on fire," yelled Pap. Daddy and Uncle Eddie didn't see any fire out the window. When they turned back they didn't see any gizzard either, and Pap was laughing so hard he nearly choked on it. After that there were so many visions that you would have thought we were a family of Roman Catholics instead of dyed-in-the-wool°, dull-as-paint Presbyterians. Pap saw things out the window. Daddy saw things out the back door. Uncle Eddie, who sat facing the china cupboard, was again at somewhat of a disadvantage. One time he told about the woman selling Bibles door to door, whose panties fell off right in the middle of the sales spiel, and gobbled the gizzard whole while Pap and Daddy were laughing. Another time he just sat there staring up at the ceiling. That didn't work. Pap said, "You can't treat us like a bunch of greenhorns° at the county fair. That ceiling's been up there since the house was built, and I ain't taking my eyes off that gizzard."

Toward the end nobody believed anybody or anything. One Sunday afternoon the fire bell rang and the three of them just sat there staring at the gizzard, each of them convinced that one of the other two had paid Curly Beckett to ring the bell.

It all came to an end on a Thanksgiving. They hunted all morning and came in to a big chicken dinner. When all the wings and legs and whatnot were gone, there on the platter were three gizzards. "Mr. Macklin gave them to me extra when I bought the chicken," said Lucy. They ignored her. They just sat there sullenly° looking at those three gizzards. Pap finally forked one of them and groused°, "Who the Hell ever heard of a chicken havin' three gizzards?"

READING COMPREHENSION QUESTIONS

Vocabulary in Context

1. The word *din* in "There was an awful din of clashing metal and screaming" (paragraph 4) means
   a. great silence.
   b. breaking.
   c. question.
   d. loud noise.

2. The word *spiel* in "he told about the woman selling Bibles door to door, whose panties fell off right in the middle of the sales spiel" (paragraph 5) means
   a. floor.
   b. talk.
   c. day.
   d. goal.

Central Point and Main Ideas

3. Which statement best expresses the central point of the selection?
   a. All the men in the author's family liked chicken gizzards.
   b. Competition can be more fun than winning the prize.
   c. The dinner hour can be a conversation time for families.
   d. Daddy, Pap, and Uncle Eddie played tricks on one another.

4. Which statement best expresses the main idea of paragraph 2?
   a. The three men began a fight over the gizzard which lasted many years.
   b. Since there is only one gizzard, it is the most important piece of the chicken.
   c. Daddy did not show Pap the respect that the older man expected.
   d. Families often argue over silly things.

5. Which statement best expresses the main idea of paragraph 5?
   a. Uncle Eddie once won the gizzard by telling a funny story about a woman who sold Bibles.
   b. Family dinners at the author's house were always interesting.

    c. The men eventually used tricks to try to win the gizzard.

    d. Pap saw Fronk's barn burning.

Supporting Details

6. Lucy was
    a. the hired servant.
    b. Pap's wife.
    c. Mr. Macklin's daughter.
    d. Uncle Eddie's wife.

7. The "gizzard war" finally ended when
    a. Lucy started serving ham instead of chicken.
    b. the men realized how silly their behavior was.
    c. there were three chicken gizzards on the platter.
    d. Uncle Eddie stuck Pap with a fork.

Transitions

8. Narratives usually benefit from time transitions. On the lines below, write three of the time transitions used throughout this reading.

    _____   _____   _____

Inferences

9. We can conclude from the last paragraph of the selection that the men
    a. were happy when Lucy got extra gizzards from Mr. Macklin.
    b. were tired of the "gizzard war."
    c. had come to dislike gizzards.
    d. were disappointed at the end of the "gizzard war."

10. The tone of this reading is
    a. disappointed yet realistic.
    b. comic and informal.
    c. mean-spirited and critical.
    d. sentimental and compassionate.

OUTLINING

Complete the following outline of the story by writing in the letters of the outline parts in their correct order.

Chicken Gizzards

1. _____

2. _____

3. _____

4. _____

    a. Eventually, however, Pap, Daddy and Uncle Eddie resorted to tricks in order to get the gizzard.

    b. The competition was ended one Thanksgiving when three gizzards were on the platter.

    c. The competition began one Sunday when Daddy took the gizzard Pap wanted.

    d. At first, efforts to "win" the gizzard were rather straightforward.

DISCUSSION QUESTIONS

1. How did the nature of the battles for chicken gizzards change over time?

2. The story ends when Lucy buys each of the men a chicken gizzard to eat. From this action, how do you think Lucy felt about the men's competition? How do you think the author felt about it?

3. Have you ever participated in or known of a similarly odd and fun competition? How did it end?

4. Although a fight over chicken gizzards might be rare, competition among family members for seemingly insignificant things is not. Why do you think there is so much competition among family members? Does this competition have any positive purposes?

9

From Nonreading to Reading
Stacy Kelly Abbott

Preview

As an adult, Abbott had to face a hard fact: he could not read well enough to function in society. Was it too late to learn? As Abbott describes his attempts to improve his situation, he also provides valuable insight into what factors create a non-reader.

Words to Watch

exposure to (2): experiencing the influence of (something)
reinforcement (4): support
peers (6): people of the same class, age, etc., such as classmates
taunting (7): insulting in a sarcastic way
overwhelming (8): overpowering
jargon (8): the specialized vocabulary of a given field
retain (11): keep in mind, remember
abstractly (11): about general ideas (not specific things), theoretically

Reading is the key to success in American society. Everything our   1
society is and does depends on that one word. In addition to the thousands of illiterates we hear about on television and in magazines, there is an unspoken and silent category of people never mentioned. This is the group of people who can read, but not quite well enough to feel

comfortable or successful with it. According to *Time* magazine, "There are over seventy-five million illiterate people in America. Another forty million are termed 'marginal readers.'" This is the group that I fit into. I am not totally comfortable with reading, but I am able to get by. Slowly and gradually the role of reading in my life is changing from nonexistent to partially existent to existent.

As early as I can remember there were never any recreational books in our home. It just was not something that was thought to be needed—or wanted, for that matter. My wife tells me that the most important thing for a preschooler to have is exposure to° reading. They need to have books to look at and "play" read. She has bought our daughter an entire library, and she is only one. Sometimes when I think about it, I think, "It's not fair! Why didn't my parents buy me books and read to me like my wife does to our daughter?" Of course, until my wife told me, I never knew books were supposed to be a part of your early childhood. This was my very first setback in reading. I had absolutely no exposure to any type of stories, poetry, or even picture books before I entered kindergarten. This was my first step on a road to nonreading.

I remember being excited when I entered kindergarten. In my memory, I was not slower or behind the other children. First grade was about the same. I kept up fairly well and though I do not remember learning the actual mechanics of reading, I still learned to read at the first grade level. The thing to remember is that this was twenty-three years ago, and school has gotten much harder now. I probably would not be able to keep up now because they give homework.

What I learned in school was the end of it. I had absolutely no reinforcement° at home of what I learned at school. It was at this point that drugs and alcohol were entering my life. My father was an alcoholic, and my three brothers and sisters were all teenagers at this time in my life. My two brothers had already dropped out of school, and my sister was well on her way too. Drugs and alcohol were not considered wrong at my house. They were an everyday part of my life. I did not know everyone else's home was not like that. It was inevitable that I try them when they were so readily available. This was my next step on the road to nonreading.

Second grade was where major problems began surfacing. I was held back in second grade, and my second year I was placed into Resource classes. I could no longer fit into regular classes. I could not read past a first grade level. Second grade is where most of my memories of early school are. It was here that my self-esteem plummeted downward. I realized I was slower than the other children. Sometimes children can be really cruel. They teased and told me I was stupid.

School and my self-esteem continued on this downward path for several years. Around junior high it seemed to get worse. This is when Resource became an embarrassment. It was shameful to be so "stupid." It was not so bad when I was in the Resource class because most of the others were about on my level. Reading aloud in front of this group was sort of calming. It was not bad at all. But I still had to take some regular classes. This was where the humiliation was horrible. I could read a little, but reading in front of this group of peers° was impossible. I just stuttered along. This is how the remainder of my school career went. Resource was satisfying, but regular classes were awful. Somehow I stuck with school and did not quit.

All my brothers and sisters dropped out, but they still lived at home. Drugs and alcohol were still readily available. I do not recall exactly when, but sometime while I was in high school my brother found out that I could not read. He began teasing and taunting° me. It was horrible. I was one of those millions of marginal readers who graduated from high school barely able to function in American society. I made sure I maintained a job where no reading was required. Life was fine for several years, but I was still continuing down the road to nonreading.

The beginning of the change in my life came when I became active in my church. It is common for young men in my church to serve a mission. This idea was not so bad, except for all the reading and learning required to be successful was overwhelming°. My desire to get my life in order finally convinced me to serve a mission. I learned to read much better, but only on church-related things. It was kind of like learning a jargon° for a job. I really still did not read very well at all.

About a year after I came home from my mission, I got married. It was then that I realized what bad shape I was really in. I had accumulated several delinquent bills simply because I could not read the contents of late notice letters. I even almost lost my home. By this time in my life, my fear of reading aloud haunted me. When I was in school I had more of a "don't care" attitude and really did not care what other people thought too much anymore. Now I really cared what people thought of me. I did not want my wife to think any less of me because of my problem. My wife convinced me that I was okay and she could help me learn to read better.

With her urging, I began college in the summer of 1990. I had been married for a year and had a daughter who was one week old. I read on an elementary school level, and my fear of reading aloud was a nightmare. My wife assured me that she had been through four years of college and had never had to read aloud. I took her word for it. I was taking a developmental reading class, and the very first day of class the teacher called on me to read a passage aloud. Somehow I struggled

6

7

8

9

10

through it, humiliated and all. When I told my wife what happened, she could not believe it! But she still reassured me that I could do it. I went and spoke with the teacher about my problem, and she was very understanding. All during the summer and fall my wife helped me by reading all my material onto tape and making notes for me. I was quickly seeing all the benefits reading had. Those few years had started me on the path to becoming a reader.

I struggled with school and worked really hard. We discovered that   11
the Texas Rehabilitation Commission could help with fees and tutors for reading. They sent me for testing, and it was discovered that I had a visual-spatial learning disability. This explained why it was so hard for me to retain° things and think abstractly°, both of which are required in college. Once the problem was discovered, it made it easier for me to deal with. Now I knew I was not stupid; I just had to learn to get around this. Though this explained the problem, it did not solve it! I still had to learn to read at a higher level. I have received all my textbooks on tape to help me read my books. I have purchased a phonics program to help me with my reading, and it is going slow but steady. I am making my way down the road of active reading.

As I look back over the past four years I see all the things that have   12
happened to make me see how important reading is. I am not where I want to be yet, but I will be in a year or two. I can say this with confidence now. I see reading now as a key to unlocking my whole future, especially my financial future. No more will there be the fear of having to fill out an application for employment in front of someone. I will be able to fill it out with ease, because I will know how to READ. No more will there be the fear of my daughter asking me to read her a book and me having to say "not right now." No more will there be the fear of delinquency letters because of my inability to read. Reading has truly come from a totally nonexistent part of my life to a very existent and essential part of my life. Reading has simply helped me "to be."

READING COMPREHENSION QUESTIONS

Vocabulary in Context

1. The word *inevitable* in "It was inevitable that I try [drugs and alcohol] when they were so readily available" (paragraph 4) means
   a. unavoidable.
   b. unlikely.
   c. good.
   d. deadly.

2. The word *plummeted* in "Second grade is where most of my memories of early school are. It was here that my self-esteem plummeted downward. I realized I was slower than the other children" (paragraph 5) means
   a. increased.
   b. fell quickly.
   c. renewed.
   d. was noticed.

Central Point and Main Ideas

3. Which statement best expresses the central point of the selection?
   a. There were no recreational books in the author's home while he was growing up.
   b. Abbott has improved his reading by getting his textbooks on audio tape and by buying a phonics program.
   c. There are forty million marginal readers in the United States.
   d. Despite a difficult youth and a learning disability, Abbott is learning to read, giving him hope for his future.

4. Which statement best expresses the main idea of paragraph 2?
   a. Abbott's wife has purchased an entire library for their daughter.
   b. The first obstacle to Abbott's reading was the lack of books in his home as a child.
   c. Abbott never knew how important books were to children until his wife told him.
   d. There are numerous story, poetry, and picture books available for preschool children.

5. Which statement best expresses the main idea of paragraph 4?
   a. Drugs and alcohol were not considered wrong in Abbott's home.
   b. The next obstacles to Abbott's reading were his family's lack of support for school and their use of drugs and alcohol.
   c. Abbott's brothers dropped out of school, and their sister was on her way to dropping out.
   d. Children often imitate what they see their parents or siblings doing.

Supporting Details

6. According to the selection, marginal readers
   a. are completely illiterate.
   b. are rare in the United States.
   c. can read only enough to get by.
   d. are very comfortable with reading and have often attended college.

7. Abbott improved his reading
   a. with hard work.
   b. with his wife's encouragement.
   c. by working around a learning disability.
   d. all of the above.

Transitions

8. The sentence below expresses a relationship of
   a. time.
   b. addition.
   c. contrast.
   d. cause and effect.

   About a year after I came home from my mission, I got married.
   (Paragraph 9)

Inferences

9. We can conclude from the essay that the type of reading disability Abbott has
   a. was not identified when he was a child.
   b. had little to do with his academic problems.
   c. is extremely common.
   d. all of the above.

10. We might infer from the selection that people with learning disabilities
    a. are unlikely to learn to read.
    b. may deal with the disability better if it has been fully identified.
    c. will never be able to think abstractly.
    d. will not become readers unless the disability is identified when they are very young.

OUTLINING

Complete the following outline by filling in the letters of the missing major and minor details, which are listed below the outline in random order.

Central point: Overcoming the problems of his youth and his reading disability, Abbott is improving his reading and is hopeful about his future.

1. For Abbott, there were two steps at home on the road of nonreading.

a. There was a lack of books when he was a child.

b. _____

2. In school from second grade on, Abbott experienced difficulty in reading, humiliation, and low self-esteem.

3. Abbott's life began to change when he served a church mission and improved his reading of church-related material.

4. _____

5. _____

6. Abbott now knows that reading will soon be a key to a better future.

Items Missing from the Outline

a. After marrying, Abbott realized how harmful poor reading was and that he could improve.

b. Abbott entered college and found out he had a certain learning disability, which he is learning to work around.

c. There were frequent use of drugs and alcohol and a lack of support for school.

DISCUSSION QUESTIONS

1. Abbott was surprised when his wife said that their baby daughter should be exposed to books. Obviously, a one-year-old is not going to learn to read. Do you think it makes sense to provide books for such a young child?

2. Abbott was excited about beginning school, but by the time he was in second grade, school had become a humiliating experience because of his difficulties with reading. Is there anything the school could have done differently to help Abbott succeed?

3. Abbott refers repeatedly to the humiliation of being a poor reader. Why do you think he was willing to "go public" with his problem by writing this essay?

4. What influences in Abbott's life saved him from accepting his status as a non-reader?

10

Television Changed My Family Forever
Linda Ellerbee

Preview

Everyone realizes that television has changed our lives greatly. But how? People who never lived in a world without TV may not fully understand its impact on our lives. Television producer and writer Linda Ellerbee has no such disadvantage. In this selection, she tells what her childhood was like before and after her family had a television set.

Words to Watch

cadence (2): rhythmic flow
commie pinko (18): communist
ambrosia (19): dish usually made with coconut, oranges, cherries, sour cream, and pineapple
circumstances (20): conditions, situations
inconsequential (20) unimportant

Santa Claus brought us a television for Christmas. See, said my parents, television doesn't eat people. Maybe not. But television changed people. Television changed my family forever. We stopped eating dinner at the dining-room table after my mother found out about TV trays. We kept the TV trays behind the kitchen door and served ourselves from pots on the stove. Setting and clearing the dining-room table used to be my job; now, setting and clearing meant unfolding and wiping out TV trays, then, when we'd finished, wiping and folding our TV trays. Dinner was served in time for one program and finished in time for another. During dinner we used to talk to one another. Now television talked to us. If you had something you absolutely had to say, you waited until the commercial, which is, I suspect, where I learned to speak in thirty-second bursts. As a future writer, it was good practice in editing my thoughts. As a little girl, it was lonely as hell. Once in a while, I'd pass our dining-room table and stop, thinking I heard our ghosts sitting around talking to one another, saying stuff.

Before television, I would lie in bed at night listening to my parents   2
come upstairs, enter their bedroom and say things to one another that I couldn't hear, but it didn't matter, their voices rocked me to sleep. My first memory, the first one ever, was of my parents and their friends talking me to sleep when we were living in Bryan and my bedroom was right next to the kitchen. I was still in my crib then. From the kitchen I could hear them, hear the rolling cadence° of their speech, the rising and falling of their voices and the sound of chips.

"Two pair showing."   3

"Call?"   4

"Check."   5

"Call?"   6

"Call." *Clink.*   7

"I raise." *Clink Clink.*   8

"See your raise and raise you back." *Clink clink clink.*   9

"Call." *Clink Clink.*   10

"I'm in." *Clink.*   11

"I'm out."   12

"Let's see 'em."   13

It was a song to me, a lullaby. Now Daddy went to bed right after   14
the weather and Mama stayed up to see Jack Paar (later she stayed up to see Steve Allen and Johnny Carson and even Joey Bishop, but not David Letterman). I went to sleep alone, listening to voices in my memory.

Daddy stopped buying Perry Mason books. Perry was on television   15
and that was so much easier for him, Daddy said, because he could never remember which Perry Mason books he'd read and was always buying the wrong ones by mistake, then reading them all the way to the end before he realized he'd already read them. Television fixed that, he said, because although the stories weren't as good as the stories in the books, at least he knew he hadn't already read them. But it had been Daddy and Perry who'd taught me how fine it could be to read something you liked twice, especially if you didn't know the second time wasn't the first time. My mother used to laugh at Daddy. She would never buy or read the

same book again and again. She had her own library card. She subscribed to magazines and belonged to the Book-of-the-Month Club. Also, she hated mystery stories. Her favorite books were about doctors who found God and women who found doctors. Her most favorite book ever was *Gone with the Wind,* which she'd read before I was born. Read it while she vacuumed the floor, she said. Read it while she'd ironed shirts. Read it while she'd fixed dinner and read it while she'd washed up. Mama sure loved that book. She dropped Book-of-the-Month after she discovered *As the World Turns.* Later, she stopped her magazine subscriptions. Except for *TV Guide.* I don't know what she did with her library card. I know what she didn't do with it.

Mom quit taking me to the movies about this time, not that she'd   16
ever take me to the movies very often after Mr. Disney let Bambi's mother get killed, which she said showed a lack of imagination. She and Daddy stopped going to movies, period. Daddy claimed it was because movies weren't as much fun after Martin broke up with Lewis, but that wasn't it. Most movies he cared about seeing would one day show up on television, he said. Maybe even Martin & Lewis movies. All you had to do was wait. And watch.

After a while, we didn't play baseball anymore, my daddy and me.   17
We didn't go to baseball games together, either, but we watched more baseball than ever. That's how Daddy perfected The Art of Dozing to Baseball. He would sit down in his big chair, turn on the game and fall asleep within five minutes. That is, he appeared to be asleep. His eyes were shut. He snored. But if you shook him and said, Daddy, you're asleep, he'd open his eyes and tell you what the score was, who was up and what the pitcher ought to throw next. The Art of Dozing to Baseball. I've worked at it myself, but have never been able to get beyond waking up in time to see the instant replay. Daddy never needed instant replay and, no, I don't know how he did it; he was a talented man and he had his secrets.

Our lives began to seem centered around, and somehow measured   18
by, television. My family believed in television. If it was on TV, it must be so. Calendars were tricky and church bells might fool you, but if you heard Ed Sullivan's voice you *knew* it was Sunday night. When four men in uniforms sang that they were the men from Texaco who worked from Maine to Mexico, you *knew* it was Tuesday night. Depending on which verse they were singing, you knew whether it was seven o'clock or eight o'clock on Tuesday night. It was the only night of the week I got to stay up until eight o'clock. My parents allowed this for purely patriotic reasons. If you didn't watch Uncle Milty on Tuesday nights, on Wednesday mornings you might have trouble persuading people you

were a real American and not some commie pinko° foreigner from
Dallas. I wasn't crazy about Milton Berle, but I pretended I was; an extra
hour is an extra hour, and if the best way to get your daddy's attention is
to watch TV with him, then it was worth every joke Berle could steal.

Television was taking my parents away from me, not all the time,   19
but enough, I believed. When it was on, they didn't see me, I thought.
Take holidays. Although I was an only child, there were always
grandparents, aunts, uncles and cousins enough to fill the biggest holiday.
They were the best times. White linen and old silver and pretty china.
Platters of turkey and ham, bowls of cornbread dressing and sweet
potatoes and ambrosia°. Homemade rolls. Glass cake stands holding
pineapple, coconut, angel food and devil's food cakes, all with good
boiled icing. There was apple pie with cheese. There were little silver
dishes with dividers for watermelon pickles, black olives and sliced
cranberry jelly. There was all the iced tea you'd ever want. Lord, it was
grand. We kids always finished first (we weren't one of those families
where they make the kids eat last and you never get a drumstick). After
we ate, we'd be excused to go outside, where we'd play. When we
decided the grown-ups had spent enough time sitting around the table
after they'd already finished eating, which was real boring, we'd go back
in and make as much noise as we could, until finally four or five grown-
ups would come outside and play with us because it was just easier, that's
all. We played hide-and-seek or baseball or football or dodge ball.
Sometimes we just played *ball*. Sometimes we just played. Once in a
while, there would be fireworks, which were always exciting ever since
the Christmas Uncle Buck shot off a Roman candle and set the
neighbor's yard on fire, but that was before we had a television.

Now, holiday dinners began to be timed to accommodate the   20
kickoff, or once in a while the halftime, depending on how many games
there were to watch; but on Thanksgiving or New Year's there were
always games so important they absolutely could not be missed under
any circumstances°, certainly not for something as inconsequential° as
being "it" and counting to ten while you pretended not to see six children
climb into the backseat of your car.

"Ssshhh, not now, Linda Jane. The Aggies have the ball."   21

"But you said . . . you promised. . . ."   22

"Linda Jane, didn't your daddy just tell you to hush up? We can't   23
hear the television for you talking."

Note: This selection is taken from the book *Move On* by Linda Ellerbee. For
information on how to obtain the book, turn to page 564.

READING COMPREHENSION QUESTIONS

Vocabulary in Context

1. The word *accommodate* in "Now, holiday dinners began to be timed to accommodate the kickoff, or once in a while the halftime, depending on how many games there were to watch" (paragraph 20) means
   a. suit.
   b. replace.
   c. ignore.
   d. postpone.

Central Point and Main Ideas

2. Which sentence best expresses the central point of the selection?
   a. Television changed Ellerbee's family for the worse.
   b. Television always damages family relations.
   c. Television replaced much of the reading in the Ellerbee household.
   d. Linda Ellerbee was pleased when television became a major part of her family's activities.

3. Which sentence best expresses the main idea of paragraph 15?
   a. Ellerbee's father read mysteries, but her mother liked other types of books.
   b. Television changes people's lives in various ways.
   c. Once Ellerbee's mother and father had television, they gave up reading.
   d. Ellerbee's mother would never read something twice, but Ellerbee learned it can be interesting to reread a book she likes.

4. The main idea of paragraph 18 is expressed in its
   a. first sentence.
   b. third sentence.
   c. fourth sentence.
   d. last sentence.

Supporting Details

5. The author may have learned to speak quickly and edit her thoughts because
   a. her parents thought that children should spend more time reading than talking.
   b. she was permitted to speak freely only during television commercials.
   c. she read mystery books that helped her to communicate in a brief and clear manner.

d. her family spent so much time playing cards they did not take time to converse with each other.

6. Television changed the Ellerbee family's life by
   a. eliminating eating dinner around the dining room table.
   b. cutting down on their pleasure reading and game playing.
   c. eliminating family interaction on holidays.
   d. all of the above.

Transitions

7. Ellerbee uses numerous time transitions to indicate her family's lifestyle before and after television. Find two of those transitions in paragraph 1, and write them in the blank spaces below.

   _____   _____

Inferences

8. The author implies that
   a. her family never did converse with each other much.
   b. for her as a young person, television's advantages outweighed its disadvantages.
   c. because of television, her parents paid too little attention to her.
   d. television's effects on her family were very limited.

9. In paragraphs 20–23, the author implies that
   a. football games should not be shown on TV.
   b. she felt it wasn't important for adults to play hide-and-seek with her and the other children.
   c. it is important for adults to find time to play with children.
   d. it would be better for children to play football than hide-and-seek.

10. The tone of this selection can be described as
    a. fearful.
    b. optimistic.
    c. resentful.
    d. forgiving.

OUTLINING

Complete the following outline of "Television Changed My Family Forever" by filling in the blank spaces. The missing items are listed in random order below the outline.

Central point: Television hurt the Ellerbee family's lives and interfered with family interaction.

1. The family started eating dinner in front of television instead of talking together around the dining-room table.

2. _____

_____

3. Television replaced reading for Ellerbee's parents.

4. _____

_____

5. Ellerbee and her father no longer played baseball or went to ball games.

6. The family's life was centered around, and measured by, television.

7. _____

_____

Items Missing from the Outline

- Family fun on holidays was replaced by adult interest in watching games on TV.
- Watching television eliminated much of the adult conversation and togetherness in the Ellerbee household.
- The family stopped going to movies.

DISCUSSION QUESTIONS

1. What were some of the ways in which the Ellerbee family's lives changed after they bought a television?

2. Ellerbee is unhappy about the negative effect television watching had on her family. However, many people argue that television can have a positive influence on its watchers. What might be some of the positive aspects of television?

3. Ellerbee writes that television changed the way her family ate, relaxed, and even communicated. What are some other inventions of the past fifty years that have changed lifestyles? For each invention you name, describe a specific way it has altered lifestyles.

4. Ellerbee discusses the specific, personal effects television watching had on herself and her family. Think about the effects television watching has had on society as a whole. What are some ways it has changed the way we behave, think, and learn?

11

Hard Times for the Town of the Dead
Gail Saffron

Preview

The American way of death is changing. The traditional American funeral involves burying relatives in the family burial plot. However, that practice is gradually giving way to a new type of funeral. In this reading, the author explains the change and the reasons behind it. She does so by focusing on a town where funerals have been the main industry.

Words to Watch

cremation (4): burning (a dead body) to ashes
hearse (7): a vehicle that carries a dead body to a house of worship
          or to a cemetery
hustle and bustle (11): busy activity

America's funeral business has undergone significant changes in recent years. Nowhere have those changes made a bigger impact than in Colma, California. For years, people have been dying to get into Colma. And for good reason. Most of the land in this small town is used for graveyards.

Ever since 1901, funerals have been Colma's biggest business. At that time, nearby San Francisco was running out of open space. To save land, a law was passed forbidding any more burials in the city. The town

1

2

of Colma had plenty of open space. It encouraged new cemeteries and funeral homes to locate there.

Over the years, three-fourths of Colma's two square miles of land 3 became cemeteries. Today, only 750 people live in Colma. The dead far outnumber them. Besides ordinary graves, Colma's burial grounds have huge tombs or monuments for the famous or wealthy people who rest there. One of these is newspaper publisher and multi-millionaire William Randolph Hearst. He is buried in a tomb that looks like an ancient Greek temple. Another permanent resident of Colma is Lefty O'Doul, a former major league baseball player. Carved on his headstone is an account of his baseball career. A visitor can learn that Lefty won two Most Valuable Player awards and hit .349 lifetime. In all, one and a half million people are buried in the town. For Colma, death has been good business.

Today, though, the funeral business in Colma—and across 4 America—has been hit by hard times. There are two reasons for this change. One is that people are taking longer to die. The other is that when they do die, their loved ones often choose cremation° instead of burial.

Americans live longer today than ever before. Our average life span 5 now is seventy-five years. In 1950, it was sixty-eight. Even though more people live in America now, they take longer to die. The result is that the annual death rate has not changed. Funeral homes have the same number of potential "customers" this year—about two million—as they did twenty years ago.

However, the number of people being laid to rest in cemeteries is 6 going down every year. Cypress Lawn, the second-largest cemetery in Colma, handled 2,129 burials in 1977. In 1992, it had only 1,487. The reason is that more and more people are choosing cremation instead. Less than ten years ago, only about 12 percent of Americans were cremated. Today, the figure is 17 percent. By the year 2000, this is expected to rise to 24 percent. In some areas of the country, cremation is more popular still. San Diego, California, handles more than half of its deaths this way.

Why has cremation become so popular? There are several reasons. 7 One is simply that it is cheaper. The cost of a funeral and burial is now $4,100, more than many families can afford. (This rise reflects the increased cost of managing a funeral home today. In 1970, for example, a new hearse° cost about $7,000. Today, it can cost over $35,000.) By contrast, a simple cremation may be had for $500. Afterwards, the ashes can be scattered at sea.

Cost is not the only reason for the growing popularity of cremation, 8 though. As our lifestyles change, so do our "death-styles." At one time, families lived for generations in the same town. When family members died, they were buried in the family plot. People made special trips—

especially on religious holidays—to visit the graves of their parents and grandparents. Often, these trips became afternoon outings for the whole family.

But today, Americans move more often, and families are scattered. People may live thousands of miles from the family plot. Often, they don't even know where their grandparents are buried. Visiting a gravesite is no longer a common thing to do on a holiday afternoon. And, since the cemetery is less central to the family, so is burial. Many people feel a simple cremation is more dignified.   9

For the town of Colma, changing attitudes toward death mean changes in the way people there live. A new highway has been built through what was once part of Eternal Home Cemetery. Another cemetery sold fifty acres of land to a developer. Now a shopping center stands there.   10

People in Colma used to laugh about their town's reputation. They even made jokes about the dead far outnumbering the living. They put up signs and bumper stickers saying "It's Great to Be Alive in Colma" and "Town of the Silent Majority." Today, many Colma residents—the living ones—miss what used to be a peaceful, quiet lifestyle. Once, death was their main industry. Today, Colma is being forced into the hustle and bustle° of modern life.   11

READING COMPREHENSION QUESTIONS

Vocabulary in Context

1. The word *span* in "Our average life span now is seventy-five years" (paragraph 5) means
   a. period of time.
   b. view of the world.
   c. type of activity.
   d. size or weight.

2. The word *potential* in "The result is that the annual death rate has not changed. Funeral homes have the same number of potential 'customers' this year . . . as they did twenty years ago" (paragraph 5) means
   a. poor.
   b. possible.
   c. steady.
   d. famous.

Central Point and Main Ideas

3. Which of the following best expresses the central point of the essay?
   a. America's funeral business has undergone significant changes in recent years.
   b. Many people feel that cremation is cheaper and more dignified than burial.
   c. Funerals have been Colma's biggest business since 1901.
   d. American families are more scattered today than they once were.

4. Which sentence best expresses the main idea of paragraphs 7–9?
   a. While a funeral and burial may cost $4,100, a simple cremation costs only $500.
   b. As people's style of living changes, so does the style of their funeral.
   c. Cremation has become more popular for several reasons.
   d. Many people feel that a simple cremation is more dignified than a burial.

Supporting Details

5. Nationally, the number of people who die each year
   a. is steadily increasing.
   b. is steadily decreasing.
   c. is staying about the same.
   d. cannot be calculated.

6. The number of people who are being cremated is increasing because
   a. costs of burials have greatly increased.
   b. visiting the family gravesite is no longer so important in America.
   c. some Americans believe cremation is more dignified than burial.
   d. all of the above.

Transitions

7. The sentence below expresses a relationship of
   a. time.
   b. addition.
   c. cause and effect.
   d. contrast.

   . . . since the cemetery is less central to the family, so is burial. (Paragraph 9)

Inferences

8. From the reading we can infer that
   a. San Francisco will soon allow burials in the city.
   b. cremation will probably continue to grow in popularity.
   c. the cost of a funeral and burial is likely to decrease greatly.
   d. in the near future, Americans will not be so scattered as they are now.

9. The main purpose of this article is
   a. to inform.
   b. to persuade.
   c. to entertain.

10. The tone of this reading is mainly
    a. angry.
    b. objective.
    c. mournful.
    d. critical.

OUTLINING

Following is an outline of the information in "Hard Times for the Town of the Dead." Complete the outline by filling in the missing central point, major detail, and minor detail. The missing points are listed in random order on the next page.

Central point: _____

_____

1. Americans are living longer, so funeral homes have the same number of possible funerals as they did twenty years ago.

2. _____

   _____

   a. _____

   _____

   b. Visiting gravesites is no longer common, so family burial plots are less important than they once were.

   c. Many Americans feel that a simple cremation is more dignified than burial in a coffin.

Items Missing from the Outline
- Cremation is much cheaper than coffin burial.
- Two reasons explain why the funeral business in Colma and across America has been hit by hard times.
- For several reasons, more and more people are being cremated instead of being buried.

DISCUSSION QUESTIONS

1. Saffron writes, "Many people feel a simple cremation is more dignified" than a burial. Do you agree? Why or why not? How would you like your loved ones to handle your funeral?

2. Would you have wanted to live in Colma when it was almost entirely a cemetery town? How did the people in Colma feel about it? Why do you think they felt that way?

3. Where in the reading does Saffron show that she is using Colma as an illustration of the funeral business throughout America? Why do you think she focused on Colma, rather than on the national funeral business in general? In other words, what did her article gain by the use of that example?

4. What reasons can you think of to explain the fact that "Americans live longer today than ever before"? What might be some effects of people having longer life spans?

12

The Role of Reading in My Life
Grant Berry

Preview

The author once was happy to think that after high school, he would never have to read another book. Surely he would never *want* to read another. Yet today he is in college, where he enrolls in English classes for the pleasure of it. In this essay, he describes what changed his attitude about reading—and about himself.

Words to Watch

tedious (3): boring
nil (3): zero
tread (3): the part of the bottom of a shoe that touches the ground
fumbling (5): searching awkwardly
emerging (5): coming out
potential (6): unused or undeveloped ability
deprivation (9): lack of economic and social necessities
Neanderthal (10): a person lacking refinement and skill

I can remember how the veins popped out on Mrs. Lingstrom's   1
forehead when she got angry. And I'll never forget the way she exposed
the ugly pinkish-blue underside of her tongue, rolling it back like a carpet
beneath her front teeth whenever she caught me talking to my best buddy
Jack. Mrs. Lingstrom was my first grade teacher; she introduced me to

the letter people. Unfortunately, I don't remember introducing the letter people to each other to form words. It may seem strange, but I can't remember learning how to read. My earliest school recollections involve swingsets, monkey-bars, and marbles. I wanted to whip every boy in first grade, not be the best reader. I had little use for the written word back then, and wouldn't until I was an adult.

My parents poured a good foundation for me; they read to me   2
whenever I waved a book at one of them. Sometimes my Dad will still recite "I'm a rootin', tootin' cowboy and my name is Cowboy Dan, I can ride 'em, rope 'em, wrangle as good as any man." He would stand with toes pointed outward, knees bent, and arms swinging at his sides. My mom and dad both say they could read that book to me without ever looking at the words. However, I outgrew my parents' laps and matured to read for myself only when I had to. Clicking on Fred Flintstone, George Jetson, and Gilligan was easier than turning pages, and I was also having a little trouble reading.

Reading for me was slow and tedious°. My eyes walked over words   3
like a snail trudging through mud. I couldn't focus on what I was reading, which allowed my young, active mind to wander far from my reading material. I would often finish a page and not remember a single word I had just read. Not only was reading a slow process, but my comprehension was nil°. I wasn't dumb; in fact, I was at a high English level. However, reading rated next to scraping dog poop from the tread° of my sneakers. I didn't yet know that reading could be like playing the guitar: the more you do it, the better you get. As far as reading was concerned, I thought I was stuck in the same slow waltz forever.

In junior high and high school, I read only when it was absolutely   4
essential. For example, I had to find out who Spiderman was going to web, or how many children Superman was going to save each month. I also had to find out which girls were popular on the bathroom walls. I'm ashamed to say that my mother even did a book report for me, first reading the book. In high school, when I would choose my own classes, I took art and electronics rather than English.

After graduation, I figured I'd never have to read another book. My   5
first job, and every job since, has involved working with my hands and not my head. I enjoyed my work, but after the money ran out, the month would keep going. One evening my wife's cousin called and said he had a way that we could increase our income. I asked, "How soon can you get here?" He walked us through a six-step plan of selling and recruiting, and when he was finished, my wife and I wanted in. Fumbling° around inside his large briefcase, he told us we needed the proper attitude first. Emerging° with a small stack of books, he said, "Read these!" Then he

flopped the books into my lap. I groaned at the thought of reading all those volumes. If this guy wanted me to develop a good attitude, giving me books was having the opposite effect. However, I wanted to make some extra cash, so I assured him I would try.

I started reading the books each night. They were self-help, positive-mental-attitude manuals. Reading those books opened up my world; they put me in touch with a *me* I didn't know existed. The books told me I had potential°, possibly even greatness. I took their message in like an old Chevrolet being pumped full of premium no-lead gasoline. It felt so good I started reading more. Not only did I read at night, I read in the morning before I went to work. I read during my breaks and lunch hour, waiting for signal lights to turn green, in between bites of food at supper, and while sitting on the toilet. One of the books I read said that there is no limit to the amount of information our brains will hold, so I began filling mine up.

The process of reading was slow at first, just as it had been when I was a kid, but it was just like playing the guitar. If I struck an unclear chord, I would try it again, and if I read something unclear, I would simply read it again. Something happened: the more I read, the better I got at it. It wasn't long before I could focus in and understand without reading things twice. I began feeling good about my reading skills, and because of the types of books I was reading, I started feeling good about *myself* at the same time.

The income from my day job blossomed while the selling and recruiting business grew demanding, disappointing, and fruitless. We stopped working that soil and our business died, but I was hooked on reading. I now laid aside the self-help books and began reading whatever I wanted. I got my first library card, subscribed to *Sports Illustrated*. I found a book of short stories, and I dove into poetry, as well as countless newspaper articles, cereal boxes and oatmeal packages. Reading, which had been a problem for me, became a pleasure and then a passion.

Reading moved me. As I continued to read in a crowded lunch room, sometimes I stumbled across an especially moving short story or magazine article. For example, a young Romanian girl was saved from starvation and deprivation° by an adoptive couple from the U.S. I quickly jerked the reading material to my face to conceal tears when she entered her new home filled with toys and stuffed animals. Not only did reading tug at my emotions, it inspired me to make a move.

All those positive-mental-attitude books kept jabbing me in the ribs, so last fall I decided to give college a try. I loved reading so much that I decided I'd like to touch others the way that I had been touched. The only snag in this idea was that I didn't know if I could write. I started out with a pair of English courses, and I was encouraged to enter the essay contest on the topic of "Taking Charge of My Life." I won a third place award. Words, whether someone else's or my own, consumed me. In my second college quarter, I discovered the works of Shakespeare, Hawthorne, and Hemingway. I was thrilled to get inside the minds of Flannery O'Connor, Edgar Allan Poe, and Robert Browning. The skill of these geniuses humbles me. I feel like a Neanderthal° scratching on cave walls compared to them. Nevertheless, all that thinking-big stuff I dumped into my brain keeps me believing.

I know reading is the reason I am in school today. The self-help   11
material I read made me feel as if I were capable of becoming somebody if I was willing to put forth the effort. My improved reading skills are proof that I can succeed at whatever I want—and writing is what I want. Reading gave me a hunger which is greater than my body's desire for food: to reach others with the written word. I may not be the second coming of Mark Twain, but my new-found love of reading has encouraged me to try to be.

READING COMPREHENSION QUESTIONS

Vocabulary in Context

1. The word *trudging* in "Reading for me was slow and tedious. My eyes walked over words like a snail trudging through mud" (paragraph 3) means
   a. racing easily.
   b. looking.
   c. sliding.
   d. moving slowly and with difficulty.

2. The word *snag* in "The only snag in this idea was that I didn't know if I could write" (paragraph 10) means
   a. advantage.
   b. difficulty.
   c. reason.
   d. opportunity.

Central Point and Main Ideas

3. Which statement best expresses the central point of the selection?
   a. As a child, the author found reading slow and tedious.
   b. The author read a number of self-help books that his cousin gave him.
   c. We must improve our education system from the early grades on up.

d. Serious reading improved Berry's ability to read, his self-esteem, and the quality of his life.

4. Which statement best expresses the main idea of paragraph 6?
   a. There is no limit to the amount of information our brains will hold.
   b. Self-improvement books should be required reading.
   c. Once the author began reading self-help books, he didn't want to stop.
   d. The author often read before going to work in the morning and during his lunch hour.

5. Which statement best expresses the main idea of paragraph 7?
   a. In addition to reading, the author has also learned how to play the guitar.
   b. At first, Berry found reading the self-help books a slow and difficult process.
   c. The more Berry read uplifting books, the more skilled he became at reading and the better he felt about himself.
   d. The author read a number of self-help books.

Supporting Details

6. The author didn't read much as a child because
   a. his parents had never read to him.
   b. he had trouble reading and found television watching easier.
   c. his first grade teacher was not a good teacher of reading.
   d. he already knew how to read.

7. The author began improving his reading
   a. as a senior in high school.
   b. during his first few jobs.
   c. after beginning college.
   d. when his wife's cousin gave him some manuals.

Transitions

8. The relationship of the second sentence below to the first is one of
   a. time.
   b. addition.
   c. contrast.
   d. illustration.

   In junior high and high school, I read only when it was absolutely essential. For example, I had to find out who Spiderman was going to web, or how many children Superman was going to save each month. (Paragraph 4)

Inferences

9. We can infer that almost all of the jobs the author has held
   a. have required him to do a lot of reading.
   b. have guaranteed him advancement and high salaries.
   c. have not required a lot of reading, but haven't paid very well.
   d. required a college education.

10. The author implies that reading can
    a. inform.
    b. inspire.
    c. affect emotions.
    d. all of the above.

OUTLINING

Complete the following outline by filling in the letters of the missing central point and major and minor details, which are listed on the next page in random order.

Central point: _____

1. Even though his parents read to him as a child, Berry found reading to be slow and dull.
2. In high school, he avoided all but the simplest and lightest reading.
3. He went on to do enjoyable manual work, but was dissatisfied with his income.
4. To begin a part-time business, Berry read self-help manuals, which benefited him in two ways.
   a. The self-help books improved Berry's ability and confidence in reading.
   b. _____
5. _____
6. _____
7. Berry entered college, hoping to become a writer, but unsure that he could.
8. In college, he discovered some of the great writers, and, by being a winner in a writing contest, he learned that he can write.

Items Missing from the Outline

    a. Berry put aside self-help books and went on to read a variety of materials.

    b. By finally reading, Berry improved his reading skills, his self-image, and his life.

    c. The information in the self-help books built up his self-esteem.

    d. The part-time business failed, but income from Berry's day job grew.

DISCUSSION QUESTIONS

1. Why does Grant Berry begin his essay with an unflattering description of his first-grade teacher? What does he seem to suggest by starting the essay in that way?

2. Berry says that "clicking on Fred Flintstone, George Jetson, and Gilligan was easier than turning pages." Do you agree that watching TV can interfere with a child's development as a reader? Why or why not?

3. Why do you think the self-help books he read had such a powerful effect upon Berry? Have you ever read a self-help book? What effect, if any, did it have on you?

4. The self-help books led Berry into a second job. That job became disappointing and he eventually dropped it. Why didn't Berry's new-found enthusiasm disappear along with the job? What in your life has helped you deal with disappointment?

13

Old Before Her Time
Katherine Barrett

Preview

If you are lucky, you will live to a ripe, old age. But is living a long life really lucky in American society? Patty Moore, at the age of twenty-six, turned herself into an eighty-five-year-old woman to see how we Americans treat our senior citizens. What she found out may not only surprise you, but also make you rethink your attitudes about older people.

Words to Watch

singular (1): unusual
perceived (2): seen
gerontology (4): the scientific study of aging
animated (4): lively
throng (4): crowd
nonentity (4): someone of no importance
lark (4): a carefree adventure
condescended (6): acted superior
laboriously (11): with great effort
manipulate (11): control
splotches (11): spots
navigate (11): walk through
jostled (11): bumped
vulnerable (12): defenseless
anathema (14): something to be avoided at all cost

disillusion (15): disappoint
nattily (21): neatly and stylishly
jauntily (21): cheerfully
seclusion (22): isolation
encounter (22): meeting
revel (23): take much pleasure
abysmally (24): terribly
flexible (24): able to adjust to change
trauma (24): painful emotional experience

This is the story of an extraordinary voyage in time, and of a 1
young woman who devoted three years to a singular° experiment. In
1979, Patty Moore—then aged twenty-six—transformed herself for the
first of many times into an eighty-five-year-old woman. Her object was
to discover firsthand the problems, joys and frustrations of the elderly.
She wanted to know for herself what it's like to live in a culture of youth
and beauty when your hair is gray, your skin is wrinkled and no men turn
their heads as you pass.

Her time machine was a makeup kit. Barbara Kelly, a friend and 2
professional makeup artist, helped Patty pick out a wardrobe and showed
her how to use latex to create wrinkles, and wrap Ace bandages to give
the impression of stiff joints. "It was peculiar," Patty recalls, as she
relaxes in her New York City apartment. "Even the first few times I went
out I realized that I wouldn't have to act that much. The more I was
perceived° as elderly by others, the more 'elderly' I actually became . . . I
imagine that's just what happens to people who really are old."

What motivated Patty to make her strange journey? Partly her 3
career—as an industrial designer, Patty often focuses on the needs of the
elderly. But the roots of her interest are also deeply personal. Extremely
close to her own grandparents—particularly her maternal grandfather,
now ninety—and raised in a part of Buffalo, New York, where there was
a large elderly population, Patty always drew comfort and support from
the older people around her. When her own marriage ended in 1979 and
her life seemed to be falling apart, she dove into her "project" with all her
soul. In all, she donned her costume more than two hundred times in
fourteen different states. Here is the remarkable story of what she found.

Columbus, Ohio, May 1979. Leaning heavily on her cane, Pat 4
Moore stood alone in the middle of a crowd of young professionals. They
were all attending a gerontology° conference, and the room was filled
with animated° chatter. But no one was talking to Pat. In a throng° of
men and women who devoted their working lives to the elderly, she

began to feel like a total nonentity°. "I'll get us all some coffee," a young
man told a group of women next to her. "What about me?" thought Pat.
"If I were young, they would be offering me coffee, too." It was a bitter
thought at the end of a disappointing day—a day that marked Patty's first
appearance as "the old woman." She had planned to attend the
gerontology conference anyway, and almost as a lark° decided to see how
professionals would react to an old person in their midst.

Now, she was angry. All day she had been ignored . . . counted out   5
in a way she had never experienced before. She didn't understand. Why
didn't people help her when they saw her struggling to open a heavy
door? Why didn't they include her in conversations? Why did the other
participants seem almost embarrassed by her presence at the
conference—as if it were somehow inappropriate that an old person
should be professionally active?

And so, eighty-five-year-old Pat Moore learned her first lesson: The   6
old are often ignored. "I discovered that people really do judge a book by
its cover," Patty says today. "Just because I looked different, people
either condescended° or they totally dismissed me. Later, in stores, I'd
get the same reaction. A clerk would turn to someone younger and wait
on her first. It was as if he assumed that I—the older woman—could wait
because I didn't have anything better to do."

New York City, October 1979.   Bent over her cane, Pat walked   7
slowly toward the edge of the park. She had spent the day sitting on a
bench with friends, but now dusk was falling and her friends had all gone
home. She looked around nervously at the deserted area and tried to
move faster, but her joints were stiff. It was then that she heard the barely
audible sound of sneakered feet approaching and the kids' voices. "Grab
her, man." "Get her purse." Suddenly an arm was around her throat and
she was dragged back, knocked off her feet.

She saw only a blur of sneakers and blue jeans, heard the sounds of   8
mocking laughter, felt fists pummeling her—on her back, her legs, her
breasts, her stomach. "Oh, God," she thought, using her arms to protect
her head and curling herself into a ball. "They're going to kill me. I'm
going to die. . . ."

Then, as suddenly as the boys attacked, they were gone. And Patty   9
was left alone, struggling to rise. The boys' punches had broken the latex
makeup on her face, the fall had disarranged her wig, and her whole body
ached. (Later she would learn that she had fractured her left wrist, an
injury that took two years to heal completely.) Sobbing, she left the park
and hailed a cab to return home. Again the thought struck her: What if I
really lived in the gray ghetto . . . what if I couldn't escape to my nice
safe home. . . ?

Lesson number two: The fear of crime is paralyzing. "I really 10
understand now why the elderly become homebound," the young woman
says as she recalls her ordeal today. "When something like this happens,
the fear just doesn't go away. I guess it wasn't so bad for me. I could
distance myself from what happened . . . and I was strong enough to get
up and walk away. But what about someone who is really too weak to run
or fight back or protect herself in any way? And the elderly often can't
afford to move if the area in which they live deteriorates, becomes
unsafe. I met people like this and they were imprisoned by their fear.
That's when the bolts go on the door. That's when people starve
themselves because they're afraid to go to the grocery store."

New York City, February 1980. It was a slushy, gray day and Pat 11
had laboriously° descended four flights of stairs from her apartment to go
shopping. Once outside, she struggled to hold her threadbare coat closed
with one hand and manipulate° her cane with the other. Splotches° of
snow made the street difficult for anyone to navigate°, but for someone
hunched over, as she was, it was almost impossible. The curb was
another obstacle. The slush looked ankle-deep—and what was she to do?
Jump over it? Slowly, she worked her way around to a drier spot, but the
crowds were impatient to move. A woman with packages jostled° her as
she rushed past, causing Pat to nearly lose her balance. If I really were
old, I would have fallen, she thought. Maybe broken something. On
another day, a woman had practically knocked her over by letting go of a
heavy door as Pat tried to enter a coffee shop. Then there were the
revolving doors. How could you push them without strength? And how
could you get up and down stairs, on and off a bus, without risking a
terrible fall?

Lesson number three: If small, thoughtless deficiencies in design 12
were corrected, life would be so much easier for older people. It was no
surprise to Patty that the "built" environment is often inflexible. But even
she didn't realize the extent of the problems, she admits. "It was a terrible
feeling. I never realized how difficult it is to get off a curb if your knees
don't bend easily. Or the helpless feeling you get if your upper arms aren't
strong enough to open a door. You know, I just felt so vulnerable°—as if I
was at the mercy of every barrier or rude person I encountered."

Ft. Lauderdale, Florida, May 1980. Pat met a new friend while 13
shopping and they decided to continue their conversation over a sundae
at a nearby coffee shop. The woman was in her late seventies, "younger"
than Pat, but she was obviously reaching out for help. Slowly, her story
unfolded. "My husband moved out of our bedroom," the woman said
softly, fiddling with her coffee cup and fighting back tears. "He won't
touch me anymore. And when he gets angry at me for being stupid, he'll

even sometimes . . . " The woman looked down, embarrassed to go on. Pat took her hand. "He hits me . . . he gets so mean." "Can't you tell anyone?" Pat asked. "Can't you tell your son?" "Oh, no!" the woman almost gasped. "I would never tell the children; they absolutely adore him."

Lesson number four: Even a fifty-year-old marriage isn't   14 necessarily a good one. While Pat met many loving and devoted elderly couples, she was stunned to find others who had stayed together unhappily—because divorce was still an anathema° in their middle years. "I met women who secretly wished their husbands dead, because after so many years they just ended up full of hatred. One woman in Chicago even admitted that she deliberately angered her husband because she knew it would make his blood pressure rise. Of course, that was pretty extreme. . . . "

Patty pauses thoughtfully and continues. "I guess what really made   15 an impression on me, the real eye-opener, was that so many of these older women had the same problems as women twenty, thirty or forty. Problems with men . . . problems with the different roles that are expected of them. As a 'young woman' I, too, had just been through a relationship where I spent a lot of time protecting someone by covering up his problems from family and friends. Then I heard this woman in Florida saying that she wouldn't tell her children their father beat her because she didn't want to disillusion° them. These issues aren't age-related. They affect everyone."

Clearwater, Florida, January 1981.   She heard the children   16 laughing, but she didn't realize at first that they were laughing at her. On this day, as on several others, Pat had shed the clothes of a middle-income woman for the rags of a bag lady. She wanted to see the extremes of the human condition, what it was like to be old and poor, and outside traditional society as well. Now, tottering down the sidewalk, she was most concerned with the cold, since her layers of ragged clothing did little to ease the chill. She had spent the afternoon rummaging through garbage cans, loading her shopping bags with bits of debris, and she was stiff and tired. Suddenly, she saw that four little boys, five or six years old, were moving up on her. And then she felt the sting of the pebbles they were throwing. She quickened her pace to escape, but another handful of gravel hit her and the laughter continued. They're using me as a target, she thought, horror-stricken. They don't even think of me as a person.

Lesson number five: Social class affects every aspect of an older   17 person's existence. "I found out that class is a very important factor when you're old," says Patty. "It was interesting. That same day, I went back to my hotel and got dressed as a wealthy woman, another role that I occasionally took. Outside the hotel, a little boy of about seven asked if I would go shelling with him. We walked along the beach, and he reached out to hold my hand. I knew he must have a grandmother who walked with a cane, because he was so concerned about me and my footing. 'Don't put your cane there, the sand's wet,' he'd say. He really took responsibility for my welfare. The contrast between him and those children was really incredible. The little ones who were throwing pebbles at me because they didn't see me as human. And then the seven-year-old taking care of me. I think he would have responded to me the same way even if I had been dressed as the middle-income woman. There's no question that money does make life easier for older people, not only because it gives them a more comfortable lifestyle, but because it makes others treat them with greater respect."

New York City, May 1981. Pat always enjoyed the time she spent   18
sitting on the benches in Central Park. She'd let the whole day pass by, watching young children play, feeding the pigeons and chatting. One spring day she found herself sitting with three women, all widows, and the conversation turned to the few available men around. "It's been a long time since anyone hugged me," one woman complained. Another agreed. "Isn't that the truth. I need a hug, too." It was a favorite topic, Pat found—the lack of touching left in these women's lives, the lack of hugging, the lack of men.

In the last two years, she had found out herself how it felt to walk   19
down Fifth Avenue and know that no men were turning to look after her. Or how it felt to look at models in magazines or store mannequins and know that those gorgeous clothes were just not made for her. She hadn't realized before just how much casual attention was paid to her because she was young and pretty. She hadn't realized it until it stopped.

Lesson number six: You never grow old emotionally. You always   20
need to feel loved. "It's not surprising that everyone needs love and touching and holding," says Patty. "But I think some people feel that you reach a point in your life when you accept that those intimate feelings are in the past. That's wrong. These women were still interested in sex. But more than that, they—like everyone—needed to be hugged and touched. I'd watch two women greeting each other on the street and just holding onto each other's hands, neither wanting to let go. Yet, I also saw that there are people who are afraid to touch an old person . . . they were afraid to touch me. It's as if they think old age is a disease and it's catching. They think that something might rub off on them."

New York City, September 1981. He was a thin man, rather nattily°   21
dressed, with a hat that he graciously tipped at Pat as he approached the bench where she sat. "Might I join you?" he asked jauntily°. Pat told him

he would be welcome and he offered her one of the dietetic hard candies that he carried in a crumpled paper bag. As the afternoon passed, they got to talking . . . about the beautiful buds on the trees and the world around them and the past. "Life's for the living, my wife used to tell me," he said. "When she took sick she made me promise her that I wouldn't waste a moment. But the first year after she died, I just sat in the apartment. I didn't want to see anyone, talk to anyone or go anywhere. I missed her so much." He took a handkerchief from his pocket and wiped his eyes, and they sat in silence. Then he slapped his leg to break the mood and change the subject. He asked Pat about herself, and described his life alone. He belonged to a "senior center" now, and went on trips and had lots of friends. Life did go on. They arranged to meet again the following week on the same park bench. He brought lunch—chicken salad sandwiches and decaffeinated peppermint tea in a thermos—and wore a carnation in his lapel. It was the first date Patty had had since her marriage ended.

Lesson number seven: Life does go on . . . as long as you're flexible   22
and open to change. "That man really meant a lot to me, even though I never saw him again," says Patty, her eyes wandering toward the gray wig that now sits on a wig-stand on the top shelf of her bookcase. "He was a real old-fashioned gentleman, yet not afraid to show his feelings— as so many men my age are. It's funny, but at that point I had been through months of self-imposed seclusion°. Even though I was in a different role, that encounter° kind of broke the ice for getting my life together as a single woman."

In fact, while Patty was living her life as the old woman, some of   23
her young friends had been worried about her. After several years, it seemed as if the lines of identity had begun to blur. Even when she wasn't in makeup, she was wearing unusually conservative clothing, she spent most of her time with older people and she seemed almost to revel° in her role—sometimes finding it easier to be in costume than to be a single New Yorker.

But as Patty continued her experiment, she was also learning a great   24
deal from the older people she observed. Yes, society often did treat the elderly abysmally° . . . they were sometimes ignored, sometimes victimized, sometimes poor and frightened, but so many of them were survivors. They had lived through two world wars, the Depression and into the computer age. "If there was one lesson to learn, one lesson that I'll take with me into my old age, it's that you've got to be flexible°," Patty says. "I saw my friend in the park, managing after the loss of his wife, and I met countless other people who picked themselves up after something bad—or even something catastrophic—happened. I'm not

worried about them. I'm worried about the others who shut themselves away. It's funny, but seeing these two extremes helped me recover from the trauma° in my own life, to pull my life together."

Today, Patty is back to living the life of a single thirty-year-old, and she rarely dons her costumes anymore. "I must admit, though, I do still think a lot about aging," she says. "I look in the mirror and I begin to see wrinkles, and then I realize that I won't be able to wash those wrinkles off." Is she afraid of growing older? "No. In a way, I'm kind of looking forward to it," she smiles. "I know it will be different from my experiment. I know I'll probably even look different. When they aged Orson Welles in *Citizen Kane* he didn't resemble at all the Orson Welles of today."

But Patty also knows that in one way she really did manage to capture the feeling of being old. With her bandages and her stooped posture, she turned her body into a kind of prison. Yet, inside she didn't change at all. "It's funny, but that's exactly how older people always say they feel," says Patty. "Their bodies age, but inside they are really no different than when they were young."

READING COMPREHENSION QUESTIONS

Vocabulary in Context

1. The word *transformed* in "In 1979, Patty Moore—then aged twenty-six—transformed herself . . . into an eighty-five-year-old woman" (paragraph 1) means
   a. awakened.
   b. changed.
   c. protected.
   d. confused.

Central Point and Main Ideas

2. Which statement best expresses the central point of the selection?
   a. Patty Moore learned the important lesson that life goes on as long as you're flexible and open to change.
   b. Patty Moore acted like an elderly woman over two hundred times.
   c. By making herself look old, Patty Moore learned what life is like for the elderly in America.
   d. Elderly people are often ignored and paralyzed by the fear of crime.

3. Which sentence best expresses the main idea of paragraphs 4–6?
   a. Patty Moore attended a gerontology conference dressed as an old person with a cane.
   b. Gerontology professionals devote their working lives to the elderly.
   c. In stores, clerks waited on "younger" people before helping Moore.
   d. At a conference and in stores, Moore learned that people often ignore the elderly.

4. Which statement best expresses the main idea of paragraphs 7–10?
   a. Pat Moore spent a day in October, 1979, in a New York City park.
   b. Pat Moore was badly beaten by some boys, but she was strong enough to get up and walk away.
   c. From being attacked and from talking with the elderly, Moore learned that fear of crime can paralyze older people.
   d. Crime in large cities such as New York can be particularly cruel and violent.

Supporting Details

5. At the time Moore began to disguise herself as an elderly woman, she was
   a. twenty-six.
   b. recently divorced.
   c. an industrial designer.
   d. all of the above.

6. What did Pat learn from the older, nattily dressed man who shared chicken salad sandwiches with her?
   a. The elderly are very sensitive to extremes of weather.
   b. Even a fifty-year-old marriage isn't necessarily a good one.
   c. As long as you are flexible and open to change, life goes on.
   d. All of the above.

Transitions

7. The relationship of the two parts of the sentence below is one of
   a. time.
   b. addition.
   c. comparison.
   d. cause and effect.

   She looked around nervously at the deserted area and tried to move faster. . . . It was then that she heard the barely audible sound of sneakered feet approaching. . . . (Paragraph 7)

Inferences

8. We can conclude that Moore may have disguised herself as an elderly woman over two hundred times in fourteen states because
   a. she and her friend Barbara Kelly continuously worked at perfecting Moore's costumes.
   b. people in the various locations discovered her true identity, so she had to move regularly.
   c. she wanted to see how the elderly were seen and treated all over the country, rather than just in one area.
   d. she was having trouble finding locations with large numbers of elderly people.

9. From paragraph 2, we could infer that
   a. many older people wear Ace bandages.
   b. people sometimes view themselves as others see them.
   c. Barbara Kelly also disguised herself as an elderly woman.
   d. the elderly don't look all that different from the very young.

10. The author implies that Moore's experiences as an old woman
   a. were not typical of real elderly people.
   b. did Moore more harm than good.
   c. were helpful to Moore personally and professionally.
   d. should never be repeated by anyone.

SUMMARIZING

Circle the letter—*a, b,* or *c*—of the passage that best begins the following summary of "Old Before Her Time."

a. Patty Moore, a young industrial designer and loving granddaughter, learned to disguise herself as an old woman. She wanted to see how the elderly are treated. Appearing as an elderly woman many times in fourteen states, she learned several lessons. The first was learned at a gerontology conference and in stores, where she found that older people are often ignored.

b. Patty Moore, an industrial designer, decided to attend a gerontology conference disguised as an elderly woman. In the crowd of people whose profession studies and serves the elderly, she was largely ignored. No one helped her when she struggled to open a heavy door. Nobody included her in conversations. In addition, in stores she was often made to wait until the clerk had helped someone younger. This was how Moore learned that the old are often ignored.

c. Patty Moore, a young industrial designer and loving granddaughter, learned to disguise herself as an elderly woman. A professional makeup artist showed Moore how to use latex to make it appear she had wrinkles. She also helped Moore pick out a wardrobe suited to an elderly woman. Finally, she showed Moore how to wrap Ace bandages on parts of her body to make it look like she had the stiff joints of an old woman.

Later, in a park in New York City, Moore was attacked by some boys who stole her purse and beat her badly. From that attack and the comments of some older people, she learned crime can paralyze the elderly. She also learned that correcting certain designs in the environment would greatly improve life for the elderly; that because many elderly considered divorce impossible, they remained in bad marriages; that the poor elderly are treated worse than the wealthy elderly; and that people never grow too old for romantic attention and affectionate contact. Finally, she learned that despite difficulties, life can be good if you're open to change.

DISCUSSION QUESTIONS

1. Think about the elderly people that you know. What experiences have they had, if any, that are similar to the ones Patty Moore had? In what ways can you tell that "inside they are really no different than when they were young" (paragraph 26)? In what ways might that not be true?

2. Why do you think that old people are honored in some countries, yet often ignored or mistreated in American society? Also, according to Patty Moore, having money "makes others treat [older people] with greater respect" (paragraph 17). Do you agree? Why might this be true?

3. What do you think was the author's purpose in writing the article—to inform, to persuade, to entertain, or a combination of any of those three? How do the seven lessons listed in the article fit in with the author's purpose?

4. How might Patty Moore's experiences influence how you treat the elderly?

14

Days of Discovery
Helen Keller

Preview

Most people learn language by hearing words and seeing them spoken. As an infant, however, Helen Keller had scarlet fever, which left her blind and deaf. In this excerpt from her autobiography, Keller (who was born in 1880 and died in 1968) tells how she learned language and what that meant to her. She later went on to graduate from Radcliffe College and become a famous writer, educator, and lecturer.

Words to Watch

vaguely (2): uncertainly
penetrated (2): entered
lingered (2): remained
preyed upon (2): greatly depressed
languor (2): exhaustion
had succeeded (2): had come after
tangible (3): touchable
groped (3): moved uncertainly
plummet and sounding-line (3): tools that measure the depth of water
flushed (5): full of spirit
uncomprehending (5): without understanding
tussle (6): struggle
dashed (6): threw so as to break
keenly (6): greatly
quiver (8): tremble

The most important day I remember in all my life is the one on   1
which my teacher, Anne Mansfield Sullivan, came to me. I am filled with

wonder when I consider the immeasurable contrast between the two lives which it connects. It was the third of March, 1887, three months before I was seven years old.

On the afternoon of that eventful day, I stood on the porch, dumb, expectant. I guessed vaguely° from my mother's signs and from the hurrying to and fro in the house that something unusual was about to happen, so I went to the door and waited on the steps. The afternoon sun penetrated° the mass of honeysuckle that covered the porch, and fell on my upturned face. My fingers lingered° almost unconsciously on the familiar leaves and blossoms which had just come forth to greet the sweet southern spring. I did not know what the future held of marvel or surprise for me. Anger and bitterness had preyed upon° me continually for weeks and a deep languor° had succeeded° this passionate struggle.

Have you ever been at sea in a dense fog, when it seemed as if a tangible° white darkness shut you in, and the great ship, tense and anxious, groped° her way toward the shore with plummet and sounding-line°, and you waited with beating heart for something to happen? I was like that ship before my education began, only I was without compass or sounding-line, and had no way of knowing how near the harbour was. "Light! give me light!" was the wordless cry of my soul, and the light of love shone on me in that very hour.

I felt approaching footsteps. I stretched out my hand as I supposed to my mother. Someone took it, and I was caught up and held close in the arms of her who had come to reveal all things to me, and, more than all things else, to love me.

The morning after my teacher came she led me into her room and gave me a doll. The little blind children at the Perkins Institution had sent it and Laura Bridgman had dressed it; but I did not know this until afterward. When I had played with it a little while, Miss Sullivan slowly spelled into my hand the word "d-o-l-l." I was at once interested in this finger play and tried to imitate it. When I finally succeeded in making the letters correctly I was flushed° with childish pleasure and pride. Running downstairs to my mother I held up my hand and made the letters for *doll*. I did not know that I was spelling a word or even that words existed; I was simply making my fingers go in monkey-like imitation. In the days that followed I learned to spell in this uncomprehending° way a great many words, among them *pin, hat, cup* and a few verbs like *sit, stand,* and *walk*. But my teacher had been with me several weeks before I understood that everything has a name.

One day, while I was playing with my new doll, Miss Sullivan put my big rag doll into my lap also, spelled "d-o-l-l" and tried to make me understand that "d-o-l-l" applied to both. Earlier in the day we had had a tussle° over the words "m-u-g" and "w-a-t-e-r." Miss Sullivan had tried to impress it upon me that "m-u-g" is *mug* and that "w-a-t-e-r" is *water,* but I persisted in confounding the two. In despair she had dropped the subject for the time, only to renew it at the first opportunity. I became impatient at her repeated attempts and, seizing the new doll, I dashed° it upon the floor. I was keenly° delighted when I felt the fragments of the broken doll at my feet. Neither sorrow not regret followed my passionate outburst. I had not loved the doll. In the still, dark world in which I lived there was no strong sentiment or tenderness. I felt my teacher sweep the fragments to one side of the hearth, and I had a sense of satisfaction that the cause of my discomfort was removed. She brought me my hat, and I knew I was going out into the warm sunshine. This thought, if a wordless sensation may be called a thought, made me hop and skip with pleasure.

7   We walked down the path to the well-house, attracted by the fragrance of the honeysuckle with which it was covered. Someone was drawing water and my teacher placed my hand under the spout. As the cool stream gushed over one hand she spelled into the other the word *water* first slowly, then rapidly. I stood still, my whole attention fixed upon the motions of her fingers. Suddenly I felt a misty consciousness as of something forgotten—a thrill of returning thought; and somehow the mystery of language was revealed to me. I knew then that "w-a-t-e-r" meant that wonderful cool something that was flowing over my hand. That living word awakened my soul, gave it light, hope, joy, set it free! There were barriers still, it is true, but barriers that could in time be swept away.

8   I left the well-house eager to learn. Everything had a name, and each name gave birth to a new thought. As we returned to the house every object which I touched seemed to quiver° with life. That was because I saw everything with the strange, new sight that had come to me. On entering the door I remembered the doll I had broken. I felt my way to the hearth and picked up the pieces. I tried vainly to put them together. Then my eyes filled with tears; for I realized what I had done, and for the first time I felt repentance and sorrow.

9   I learned a great many new words that day. . . . It would have been difficult to find a happier child than I was as I lay in my crib at the close of that eventful day and lived over the joys it had brought me, and for the first time longed for a new day to come.

Note: This selection is taken from the book *The Story of My Life* by Helen Keller. For information on how to obtain the book, turn to page 564.

READING COMPREHENSION QUESTIONS

Vocabulary in Context

1. The word *confounding* in "Miss Sullivan had tried to impress it upon me that 'm-u-g' is *mug* and that 'w-a-t-e-r' is *water,* but I persisted in confounding the two" (paragraph 6) means
   a. forgetting.
   b. confusing.
   c. creating.
   d. breaking.

2. The word *vainly* in "I remembered the doll I had broken. I felt my way to the hearth and picked up the pieces. I tried vainly to put them together. Then my eyes filled with tears" (paragraph 8) means
   a. unsuccessfully.
   b. modestly.
   c. skillfully.
   d. with great luck.

Central Point and Main Ideas

3. Which statement best expresses the central point of the selection?
   a. When Helen Keller was almost seven years old, Anne Sullivan came to be her teacher.
   b. Learning to communicate in sign language can be a challenging task for people of all ages.
   c. Helen Keller had suffered great anger and bitterness before Anne Sullivan arrived in her home.
   d. When Helen Keller was almost seven, Anne Sullivan opened the world of language and thought to her.

4. Which statement best expresses the main idea of paragraph 7?
   a. Miss Sullivan took Keller outside to the well-house.
   b. By the well-house, Keller, with Miss Sullivan's help, suddenly understood the mystery of language.
   c. Miss Sullivan placed Keller's hand under a stream of water.
   d. Keller faced many difficult barriers in her life, but they could eventually be overcome.

5. Which statement best expresses the main idea of paragraph 8?
   a. Understanding the mystery of language gave Keller new emotions and a great desire to learn.
   b. Keller tried without success to fix the doll she had broken.
   c. Keller felt repentance and sorrow for breaking the doll Miss Sullivan had given her.

d. After Keller understood what words were, the objects she touched seemed to tremble with life.

Transitions

6. The relationship between the two parts of the sentence below is one of
   a. addition.
   b. contrast.
   c. cause and effect.
   d. illustration.

   > I guessed vaguely from my mother's signs and from the hurrying to and fro in the house that something unusual was about to happen, so I went to the door and waited on the steps. (Paragraph 2)

Supporting Details

7. The first word that Helen Keller fully understood was
   a. *doll.*
   b. *teacher.*
   c. *mug.*
   d. *water.*

8. After understanding the nature of words, Keller
   a. quickly became tired of learning.
   b. regretted breaking the doll her teacher had brought her.
   c. could not cry.
   d. became angry and bitter over the years without language.

Inferences

9. We might infer from the reading that Keller had been angry and bitter because
   a. she could not travel on a ship.
   b. she was impatient for spring to come.
   c. she lacked understanding and knowledge.
   d. people were hurrying about in the Keller household.

10. In paragraph 8, Keller writes: "Everything had a name, and each name gave birth to a new thought." We can assume by that she means
    a. she discovered the names of people in her house.
    b. her experience gave her teacher much to think about.
    c. words made it possible for her to think specific thoughts.
    d. she finally learned her teacher's name and what her teacher was thinking.

SUMMARIZING

Circle the letter of the passage that best summarizes "Days of Discovery."

a. Helen Keller had spent the first six years of her life in confusion; she would often be angry or bitter without really understanding why. Then, in March, 1887, Anne Mansfield Sullivan arrived at her home. Although Keller didn't know it at the time, Sullivan was to become her teacher and life-long friend.

b. Helen Keller's teacher, Anne Sullivan, gave her a doll which had been sent by the blind children at the Perkins Institute. After allowing Keller to play with it for awhile, Sullivan next gave her a large rag doll. In this way, Sullivan tried to explain to Keller that a word can represent an idea. Specifically, she tried to show that the word *doll* could represent both Keller's new doll and her old rag one.

c. For the first six years of her life, Helen Keller lived in a world of confusion and anger. However, with the arrival of her teacher, Anne Sullivan, Keller's world changed. Sullivan taught Keller sign language and, most importantly, made her understand that words represent things and ideas. It was this lesson that opened the world of language and thought to Keller.

DISCUSSION QUESTIONS

1. In paragraph 1, Keller writes, "The most important day I remember in all my life is the one on which my teacher, Anne Mansfield Sullivan, came to me. I am filled with wonder when I consider the immeasurable contrast between the two lives which it connects." What does Keller mean by *the two lives*? In what ways were those two lives different?

2. In paragraph 3, Keller uses the image of being "at sea in a dense fog" with "no way of knowing how near the harbour was." What is she trying to communicate in that paragraph? In other words, what does the fog represent? The harbour and the light?

3. Keller writes in paragraph 5 that she "learned to spell in this uncomprehending way a great many words." What didn't she comprehend about words that she later came to understand? Also, why might she have at first confused the words *water* and *mug*?

4. Helen Keller was deprived of two of the five senses which most writers of description can call upon. Still, she manages to enrich her descriptions with sharp sensory details. Find some of them. Which senses do they appeal to?

15

Homeless Bound
Roy Rowan

Preview

Wearing old clothes, unshaven, and with a beat-up pack strapped to his back, a reporter from *People* magazine disguised himself as a homeless person. This story is his account of what it is like to live for two weeks among the homeless.

Words to Watch

apprehensive (1): uneasy, anxious
marauding (1): raiding
consternation (2): discouragement
shorn (2): stripped
desolation (2): loss
exhilarating (2): refreshing
hunkering (2): squatting
demeaning (2): lowering in status, degrading
profusion (4): large amount
queasy (6): uncomfortable
doled (6): given
oblivion (8): a state of being forgotten
devastated (13): ruined
gargantuan (15): huge
retreat (17): a peaceful, quiet place
cliques (20): groups
chronic (21): continuous

poignant (21): touching, moving
fetid (22): bad-smelling
dubbed (24): named
proliferation (24): build-up, accumulation
converted (24): changed
chime (25): join
caravan (26): group of vehicles
deprivation (27): loss
caustically (28): stingingly
deceptively (29): in a way that fools
deinstitutionalizing (30): releasing from institutions
flounder (30): struggle
pummeled (30): beaten
accosted (30): approached and spoken to in an unfriendly way
cubicle (34): small space
salvaged (35): saved
prodding (37): poking
chasm (40): marked difference
miasma (42): unhealthy atmosphere

I had decided to try to learn more about these victims of ¹
homelessness by stepping into their lives, and yet as that day approached,
I felt myself becoming more and more apprehensive°. I had heard horror
stories about the knifing and shooting of homeless men, mostly senseless
attacks by marauding° youth packs. One old man had been doused with
gasoline and set afire. I had also heard about wild free-for-alls started by
"crackheads" in the big armory shelters of Manhattan and Brooklyn.
"Better sleep with your shoes on or they'll be stolen," I was warned.
"Your glasses too."

The day was clear and crisp when I arrived at the Staten Island ferry ²
terminal. I had fifty dollars stashed in various pockets in small bills, but
no house keys, checks, credit cards, driver's license, or any identification
other than my Medicare card. To my wife's consternation° I had removed
my gold wedding band for the first time in thirty-seven years. Shorn° of
all these accoutrements, I felt peculiarly weightless. Worse, the
desolation° made me feel that perhaps I had made a horrible mistake.
Sharing a soldier's danger as a war correspondent, as I had done, was
strangely exhilarating°, yet the prospect of hunkering° down with these
derelicts seemed only demeaning°.

I parked my pack next to an old geezer and asked him if it was ³
possible to spend the night in the terminal. "Yes," he said. "The cops
usually don't bother you." He said his name was Philip Nachamie, and he

had lived there for three weeks. "Once I worked as a clerk for E. F. Hutton," he explained, pointing in the direction of Wall Street. "Just a few blocks from here."

I decided to board the next boat. Standing on the open bow with the cold wind whipping my face, I felt suddenly uplifted by the beauty of New York. The profusion° of steel and glass soaring skyward from Manhattan's southern tip, Miss Liberty standing proudly with sun glinting on her gilded torch, the spidery span of the Verrazano Bridge stretching across the harbor's mouth—all striking human accomplishments in a city where thousands lived on the street.

I hadn't been to Staten Island for years, but a social worker had mentioned a place called Project Hospitality, a few blocks from the ferry. A sign on the door warned DON'T EVEN THINK OF DOING DRUGS HERE. A friendly woman at the front desk told me to sign in. "We'll be serving dinner in an hour," she said. "But you can have coffee now."

I still felt queasy° in my new role, but I poured myself a cup and sat down. About forty men and women filled the chairs that lined the room. Dinner consisted of mushy Swedish meatballs on a heaping mound of brown rice. Two peanut butter sandwiches were also doled° out to each "client," as the homeless are referred to in drop-in centers like this. I pocketed mine for breakfast. "Sorry, but there are no beds available tonight on Staten Island," the woman at the front desk informed me.

I decided to spend the night crossing back and forth on the ferry. Its throbbing engines lulled me right to sleep, but as the ferry docked, a cop rapped his club against the back of my seat. The police, I came to learn, are viewed by the homeless as both enemy and protector. I slipped into the terminal through an exit, then reboarded the boat without paying. By 5 a.m. I had made half-a-dozen round trips, snatching twenty-minute naps en route. Finally I joined the snorers slumped on the benches in the Manhattan terminal.

When the new day dawned, I was camped between a pair of talkative New Englanders. Anthony Joseph Robert Quinn proclaimed himself a lace-curtain Irishman from Boston. His downfall apparently came from growing up with too much money and an unquenchable thirst for whiskey. Having quit Boston College to join the Army in World War II, he married a "very artistic lady" who eventually departed for Palm Beach with his and her money. But I couldn't pry loose the secret of what sent him into oblivion°. "You don't have an extra shirt in that pack, lad?" he inquired. "There's nothing under this coat." I had two extra and gave him one. "Bless you. Care for an eye-opener?" he asked, pulling out a pint.

Cecile Sanscartier, an aging but still twinkly-eyed blond woman, was originally from New Bedford, Massachusetts. She moved to New York City, where her husband drove a taxi. One night, she says, he was parked in front of Metropolitan Hospital, and he was shot and killed by holdup men. For several years after his death, Cecile worked in a stationery store but kept falling behind in her rent. Reluctantly last summer she entered a city shelter, where she says, "I was scared of being robbed or raped, and felt like a prisoner. Here I can walk out through the turnstile any time I want." She had been living at the ferry terminal for two months.

After only one night there, I was eager to find a bed. My back   10
ached, and I felt groggy from lack of sleep. I consulted the *Street Sheet* —a nonprofit annual publication, distributed free to New York's homeless, which lists the places they can go for food, shelter, clothing, medical assistance, and legal aid. It included the McAuley Water Street Mission. Within walking distance, it seemed like a good place to begin looking. At McAuley's, you must attend a midday, two-hour Bible class to get a ticket for dinner, a bed, and breakfast. "Food for the soul before food for the body," its homeless lodgers are told, although none seem eager for the religious nourishment. After the Bible class, I spent the rest of the afternoon at a nearby public library writing notes for this article. Warm, with clean bathrooms as well as books and newspapers, branch libraries are homeless havens.

Returning to McAuley's at 5:30 p.m., I joined about ninety men in   11
the chapel. Most were young blacks. First we stored our belongings for the night in a padlocked closet. Then we were interviewed. I was "Roy Brown from Chicago," the cover I had decided to use. "No, I don't have any identification. My wallet was snatched at the bus terminal when I arrived." Many of the homeless, I knew, carried no identification.

Finally we filed downstairs for a thick meat soup that looked more   12
like slabs of beef in gravy. Then everybody marched up to the dormitory, found their assigned bunks, and stripped for the communal showers. Hospital gowns were given out to sleep in because our clothes were hauled away on wheeled racks so they wouldn't be stolen. By seven-thirty everybody was in bed, the aged, handicapped, and grossly overweight having been awarded lower bunks.

Many men at McAuley's were regulars: some with jobs but no place   13
to live, others out looking for work. But none had surrendered to homelessness. There was a laid-off garbage collector from the Bronx, an unemployed bartender from Ireland, a sugar worker from St. Croix whose home had been devastated° by Hurricane Hugo, a political refugee from South Africa. "Why," he asked, "does a country like yours, that gives so much food to Africa, have so many hungry people?"

I returned to McAuley's three consecutive nights, making a couple   14
of friends there whom I would be happy to meet again. One was Jimmy Pate, a highly intelligent black man with a close-cropped salt-and-pepper

beard. He had managed a Salvation Army shop on Long Island and worked as a messenger in Manhattan. But as a periodic boozer, he would begin swigging gin and get fired. "I haven't had a drink for two weeks," he boasted. "Time to look for a job."

Another was Mark Fitzgerald, a gargantuan° Canadian with a black   15
beard so thick all you could see was a pair of blue eyes peeking out above it. He came from Churchill, on Hudson Bay below the Arctic Circle, where "polar bears," he said, "roam the streets like stray dogs." New York he called the "Trapezoid City. No matter what you do, you end up in a trap."

A linebacker in high school in Beaver, Pennsylvania, Fitzgerald   16
once dreamed of a pro-football career. Instead he found work in a Canadian oil field. A series of job changes back in the United States followed, and with each he seemed to pick up more weight, until he tipped the scales at more than four hundred pounds. Finally last December, at twenty-nine, he was hit with a massive heart attack in New York. "They jump-started me twice and kept me in intensive care for ten days," he reported. "That cleaned out my bank account."

Despite his own problems, Mark took pity on me. "I'll buy you a bus   17
ticket to St. Christopher's Inn when I get my next welfare check," he promised. St. Christopher's, he explained, is a retreat° in Garrison, New York, for homeless men. It bothered me not being able to level with Mark. But if word got out about what I was doing, it could have been dangerous. "How come you ask so many questions, man?" a McAuley regular had already wondered. My last night there, the director asked if I would like a permanent job manning the front desk. Clearly it was time to move on.

I had been spending my days trudging the streets, investigating   18
different drop-in centers and soup kitchens listed in the *Street Sheet*. Some, I discovered, like the Holy Apostles church in mid-Manhattan, serve hot, sit-down meals for one thousand men and women. *Voices to and from the Streets*, a free homeless newsletter published by the South Presbyterian Church in suburban Dobbs Ferry, even runs a column called "Dining Out with Rick C." that rates the soup kitchens for "atmosphere, service and cuisine." Sunday breakfast at St. Bartholomew's Church on Park Avenue received a four-star rating in all three categories. "'Bum's Rush' is really unnecessary here," it reported, since "everyone has a ticket." But I found Saturday breakfasts at St. Agnes even better. "The coffee cake here is top shelf," commented a toothless table mate, who also advised me, "Stay out of Grand Central. Too many guys over there eager to cut up a white face."

After dinner I checked into the Moravian Coffee Pot, considered a   19
safe haven for older homeless men and women. At first, the reverend in charge was pessimistic about my chances of being assigned to a shelter.

But after spying my week-old whiskers and hearing my sad story about being robbed, I was put on a school bus bound for St. Clement Pope Roman Catholic Church in Queens.

During the next few days, I found many surprises among the hundred Coffee Pot clients. There were teachers with master's degrees, shopkeepers, file clerks, secretaries, chambermaids, day laborers, a lawyer, even a TV actor who played in *The Defenders*, and a former opera singer who now sang on Sundays in the First Moravian Church next door. Most were nicely spruced up, since two showers and long racks of donated clothing were available upstairs. Yet they sat around in segregated black or white cliques°, complaining about everything from their free meals to the high rent and taxes that had driven them into the street. Consumed by their own misfortune, they showed little concern for each other. When it was announced that a woman there had died during the night, the news hardly caused a murmur. "I like rich people," a black woman confided. "Poor people are too cruel to each other."   20

Many Coffee Pot regulars, I was told, draw SSI (Supplemental Security Income) from the federal government for ailments that supposedly prevent them from working. But nobody appeared sick, except for the chronic°, croupy cough that plagues practically all the homeless, and which I, too, had picked up. Several times I was tempted to stand up and shout, "Why don't you all go out and get jobs?" Instead, I'd go out myself, prowling the city till dark, seeking homeless people with more poignant° stories. I must have looked pretty grubby. Women, I now noticed, leaned away from me on buses and subways.   21

It was beginning to sink in that sitting around crowded, fetid° drop-in centers, standing pressed together in long soup-kitchen lines, and sleeping side by side in shelters, the homeless had precious few moments alone. No wonder so many preferred the parks or streets, where even a cold packing crate to sleep in provided some privacy.   22

In four nights the Coffee Pot dispatched me to three shelters, each more comfortable than the last. Manhattan's famed Riverside Church, my final resting place so to speak, was called the "Helmsley Palace shelter." Pasta or some other tasty hot dish was served. The beds were well spaced in the men's choir room. There was a shower and a TV.   23

Already into my second week, the time had come to tough it out with the hard-core homeless in places like Tompkins Square Park on the Lower East Side, where police and squatters have been waging continuous warfare; Penn Station, dubbed° the "Panama combat zone" because of a proliferation° of drugs and guns; the Bowery; Brooklyn; and the big Bellevue shelter, converted° from a hospital.   24

In Tompkins Square Park, with the temperature hovering around 20   25 degrees F., I warmed myself over a trash-can fire with a group of shivering men, amusing themselves by reeling off their old penitentiary numbers. They eyed me suspiciously when I didn't chime° in with mine.

That night I decided to stay on the street as long as my feet could   26
take the cold. Dinner came from a Salvation Army mobile kitchen parked near City Hall. Too cold to sit around, I walked slowly up through Chinatown and SoHo back to the East Village. Along the way many men were leaning against buildings or slumped in doorways, waiting for the "Midnight Run," a church caravan° from suburbia that distributes sandwiches and blankets.

"Be careful crossing the street," I kept reminding myself. The sleep   27
deprivation° that dims the consciousness of every homeless person was beginning to slow my own reactions. Quite a few street dwellers, I'd heard, get hit by cars.

Then I walked three miles back to the Battery. About 2 a.m. I   28
decided to head for John Heuss House, a drop-in center for the chronically homeless and mentally ill, partly supported by Wall Street's Trinity Church. "You don't have a single scrap of paper with your name on it?" the night duty officer asked caustically°. Eventually he told me to shove some chairs together and stretch out, as others had done. Every time I reached for a chair, a mentally disturbed man grabbed it away. Only after the duty officer threatened to toss him into the street did I lie down.

Some of the mentally unstable homeless people, I found, sound   29
deceptively° sane. Bill Roth, thirty-three, a Long Island letter carrier for eight years, was holding forth brilliantly in Grand Central about the collapse of Communism in Eastern Europe, when he casually mentioned that boxing promoters were sure he could whip Mike Tyson, despite their eighty-pound difference. Later he admitted having been hospitalized for alcoholism and mental problems.

Deinstitutionalizing° these troubled people, I realized, not only   30
forces them to flounder° helplessly; it also allows them to inflict their insanity on everyone around them—sometimes violently. Right after my homeless stint ended, a deranged man in a midtown subway station was pummeled° to death by a passenger he had accosted° and spat on.

The next night I was determined to find a real bed. I went back to   31
Staten Island, but with no success. I tried the nearly all-black drop-in center on Bond Street in Brooklyn. James Conway, a homeless chef, who had just been released from the hospital, warned me that a bloody battle royal had erupted there the previous day. I wasn't feeling too comfortable anyway. A black woman had pointed at me and yelled, "Hey, look at the macadamia nut," when I walked in.

Then I remembered that Mark Fitzgerald, my McAuley friend, had 32
high praise for the Fulton Hotel in the Bowery. But a room there, he said,
costs $6.50. (Bus, subway, and ferry fares, cough medicine, and repairs to
my backpack had already used up thirty-five of my fifty dollars.) Finally
I decided to try some panhandling—not an appealing idea, although a
man at the Coffee Pot had boasted of picking up $240 in one day.

It was already dark when I arrived in Little Italy, a district of posh 33
restaurants bordering on the Bowery. The streets were filled with fur-
coated women from uptown. "Could you help a fella out?" I kept asking.
In forty minutes I collected four quarters, a dollar, and a fiver, although
my heart wasn't in it. I felt dishonest playing on the sympathy of
strangers, knowing that I didn't really need their help.

The Fulton Hotel turned out to be a Chinese flophouse named Fu 34
Shin, where a four-by-six-foot windowless, tableless, chairless cubicle°
now costs $8.50. There was barely room to squeeze in between the wall
and the bed, covered with a grimy green blanket showing worrisome
brown burn holes. A light bulb hung from a false ceiling constructed of
wrapping paper and chicken wire.

Here, at least, was a warm place of my own to shed my smelly 35
clothes and sleep. But the cubicle, I discovered about 1 a.m., wasn't
really all mine. That's when the cockroaches began running across my
face. I sat up in bed the rest of the night reading a *New York Times*
salvaged° from a sidewalk trash can. By then I was almost looking
forward to the Bellevue shelter with its thousand beds.

I wasn't sure they would let me into this city-run, older men's 36
refuge. I lacked the required Human Resources Administration case
number. But it was Martin Luther King, Jr.'s, birthday, and the place was
down to a skeleton staff. I gave my real name and handed the man at the
admitting office my Medicare card for identification. It was 5 p.m.
"You'll have to wait till midnight for an emergency bed," he advised. He
issued me a dinner slip and pointed down a long, dimly lit corridor to a
waiting room where some fifty other emergency-bed candidates were
congregated.

This was an angry bunch of men—mad at the armed guards there to 37
keep order, mad at each other, and mad at the world for the way it had
treated them. "Sit up!" snapped a guard, prodding° a skinny black fellow
sprawled on the floor. "Go 'way, asshole," responded the man. "Is my
lying down a security problem?" The guard prodded him again. "You
don't even know why I'm lying here, asshole. I got two bullet holes in
me." The guard finally gave up, and the bullet holes were never
explained.

A trembly, eighty-year-old, bewhiskered white man kept trying to 38
stand up and walk to the bathroom, only to fall back in his chair. The
guards ignored him. So did the others in the room. I desperately wanted
to offer a steadying hand. Yet, as a reporter, I also wanted to see what
would happen. Finally I watched a dark wet spot spread across the old
man's lap. Humiliated, he never looked down.

From time to time a woman came and called a few names—the 39
lucky recipients of emergency beds. But at 1 a.m. about twenty of us
were still waiting. "Okay, you guys are going to Post Five," barked one
of the guards. He led us down two flights to an abandoned lobby and
pointed at the marble floor. "Sleep here. You can go outside to pee." The
price of homelessness, I had come to understand, is not the hard surfaces
you sometimes have to sleep on or the soup kitchen meals that usually
leave a strong aftertaste in your mouth. It is the dehumanizing loss of
dignity.

After two weeks I felt saturated with these depressing sensations 40
and ready to write. My grubbiness was also becoming unbearable. Sitting
in the rear car of the train going home (where my neighbors never ride), I
wondered if I would ever run into any of my homeless friends again.
Would the deep chasm° separating us make such an encounter
embarrassing, even though I now know there are talented, intelligent
individuals out there among all the derelicts? Never again would I look
away when a homeless person approaches. It might be somebody I know.

There are a few I would very much like to see. I would like to find 41
out if Phillip Norde, a handsome thirty-eight-year-old Trinidadian who
says he was the first black man to model clothes on the fashion runways
of Europe for Gucci, Valentino, Giorgio Armani, and Missoni, managed
to stay off drugs. Having recently returned from a crack rehab center in
Vermont, he lives at the Wards Island shelter under the Triborough
Bridge. He fears that his problem is genetic. His father and grandfather
were both alcoholics. "But crack," he says, "takes over your body, your
mind, and your soul."

One man at the Coffee Pot, I believe, will surely break free. He's a 42
Fordham University graduate and a teacher whose periodic mental
breakdowns have left him homeless. Nevertheless, he calls his situation
"a temporary walk on the downside" and feels his positive attitude won't
permit him to stay stuck in that miasma°. "You can live without money,"
he says, "but you can't live without plans." That, I realized, is what had
made two weeks of homelessness endurable for me. I always knew I
would be going home.

READING COMPREHENSION QUESTIONS

Vocabulary in Context

1. The word *dispatched* in "In four nights the Coffee Pot dispatched me to three shelters, each more comfortable than the last. . . . my final resting place so to speak, was called the 'Helmsley Palace Shelter.' . . . There was a shower and a TV" (paragraph 23) means
   a. misled.
   b. sent.
   c. lent.
   d. described.

2. The words *spruced up* in "Most [of the clients] were nicely spruced up, since two showers and long racks of donated clothing were available upstairs" (paragraph 20) mean
   a. full.
   b. healthy.
   c. cleaned and neat.
   d. warmed up.

3. The word *posh* in "It was already dark when I arrived in Little Italy, a district of posh restaurants bordering on the Bowery. The streets were filled with fur-coated women from uptown" (paragraph 33) means
   a. little known.
   b. very cheap.
   c. fashionable.
   d. dirty.

Central Point and Main Ideas

4. Which of the following best expresses the central point of the selection?
   a. There is a big difference between the services of various shelters and soup kitchens for homeless people in New York City.
   b. Even though the basic needs of the homeless in New York may be met, they suffer from a loss of dignity.
   c. Homelessness is a problem in the United States.
   d. Homeless people are often sick and dirty because they have no money for medicine and soap.

5. The main idea of paragraph 20 is stated in its
   a. first sentence.
   b. second sentence.
   c. third sentence.
   d. last sentence.

Supporting Details

6. The author feels that mentally unstable homeless people
   a. are always easy to spot.
   b. are very strong.
   c. have to struggle helplessly after being released from institutions.
   d. should not be allowed in shelters.

7. The author discovered that almost all homeless people
   a. have a croupy cough.
   b. are mentally ill.
   c. have been hospitalized.
   d. all of the above.

Transitions

8. *Complete the passage:* The author introduces in paragraphs 14–16 two friends at McAuley's he "would be happy to meet again." The two friends are introduced with the addition transitions *one* and

   _____.

Inferences

9. We might conclude that Mark Fitzgerald called New York the "Trapezoid City" (in paragraph 15) because
   a. he was a geometry teacher and gave geometric names to every city.
   b. he was a Canadian who felt trapped in a foreign country.
   c. he felt his overweight condition confined him to New York City.
   d. he thought the city offered no good means of escape from homelessness.

10. From paragraph 20, we might conclude that
    a. most homeless people are well educated.
    b. the homeless at the Coffee Pot often fought with each other.
    c. the Coffee Pot is run by homeless people.
    d. having great problems can make one less sympathetic to others.

SUMMARIZING

Circle the letter of the best summary of "Homeless Bound."

a. Roy Rowan spent two weeks as a homeless person in New York City. During that time, he met a wide variety of homeless people, some of whom he would be very happy to see again. They included a very bright man whose alcoholism kept getting him fired. Another was a very heavy man who had experienced a massive heart attack.

He had to be kept in intensive care for ten days, which cleaned out his bank account. Rowan realized that he could endure homelessness because he always knew, unlike the other "homeless," that he'd soon be going home.

b. Roy Rowan spent two weeks as a homeless person in New York City. He went to public places, soup kitchens, and shelters. Some were surprisingly comfortable. Others were very uncomfortable. During this time, he met a wide variety of homeless people. A surprising number were talented, bright people who were down on their luck. There were also many hard-core homeless, including mentally ill people, former prisoners, and some elderly people. Center personnel and even homeless people sometimes treated the homeless poorly. Rowan learned that people become homeless for many reasons and that the worst part of being homeless is a degrading loss of dignity.

c. Author Roy Rowan spent two weeks as a homeless person in New York City. During that time, he stayed at a variety of public places, soup kitchens, and shelters, both pleasant and unpleasant. He began his stay on and near the Staten Island Ferry. Then he stayed for a few nights at the McAuley Water Street Mission, where a filling meal, showers, and beds were available. Then he went to the Moravian Coffee Pot, which sent him to increasingly comfortable shelters. Finally, the author went to places for the hard-core homeless. After two weeks, he was ready to get back to his real life and begin writing about the homeless.

DISCUSSION QUESTIONS

1. The author spent two weeks as a homeless person in order to learn more about victims of homelessness. What do you think he found that he didn't expect to find? What did he find that surprises you?

2. At the end of his article, Rowan says he feels that the Fordham University graduate and teacher "will surely break free" of homelessness. Why do you think Rowan feels that man will escape homelessness? Of all the homeless people mentioned in the article, which ones do you think are most likely to escape homelessness? Why?

3. Why do you think the drop-in centers refer to the homeless people who stay there as "clients"?

4. What are the various causes for homelessness mentioned in the article? What do you think individuals can do, if anything, to keep such things from making them homeless? What could society do?

16

A Love Affair with Books
Bernadete Piassa

Preview

When Bernadete Piassa was a child, she was discouraged from reading, yet she loved to read. In this essay, she tells how she managed to remain a devoted reader and how books have repaid her well for that devotion. For her, books are not just an occasional light pastime or a homework assignment. Throughout her life they have been her "friends," "guides," and "most faithful lovers."

Words to Watch

intrinsic (1): fundamental, essential
appalled (6): shocked
intriguing (6): interesting
sadistic (9): cruel
ardor (9): love and passion
exult (9): rejoice
seduces (13): attracts
infatuated (13): passionately fascinated
precision (13): exactness
subversive (15): turning people against something
lackluster (15): dull

When I was young, I thought that reading was like a drug which I 1
was allowed to take only a teaspoon at a time, but which, nevertheless,

had the effect of carrying me away to an enchanted world where I experienced strange and forbidden emotions. As time went by and I took that drug again and again, I became addicted to it. I could no longer live without reading. Books became an intrinsic° part of my life. They became my friends, my guides, my lovers. My most faithful lovers.

I didn't know I would fall in love with books when I was young and started to read. I don't even recall when I started to read and how. I just remember that my mother didn't like me to read. In spite of this, every time I had an opportunity I would sneak somewhere with a book and read one page, two pages, three, if I were lucky enough, always feeling my heart beating fast, always hoping that my mother wouldn't find me, wouldn't shout as always: "Bernadete, don't you have anything to do?" For her, books were nothing. For me, they were everything.

In my childhood I didn't have a big choice of books. I lived in a small town in Brazil, surrounded by swamp and farms. It was impossible to get out of town by car; there weren't roads. By train it took eight hours to reach the next village. There were airplanes, small airplanes, only twice a week. Books couldn't get to my town very easily. There wasn't a library there, either. However, I was lucky: My uncle was a pilot.

My uncle, who owned a big farm and also worked flying people from place to place in his small airplane, had learned to fly, in addition, with his imagination. At home, he loved to sit in his hammock on his patio and travel away in his fantasy with all kinds of books. If he happened to read a bestseller or a romance, when he was done he would give it to my mother, who also liked to read although she didn't like me to. But I would get to read the precious book anyway, even if I needed to do this in a hiding place, little by little.

I remember very well one series of small books. Each had a green cover with a drawing of a couple kissing on it. I think the series had been given to my mother when she was a teenager because all the pages were already yellow and almost worn-out. But although the books were old, for me they seemed alive, and for a long time I devoured them, one by one, pretending that I was the heroine and my lover would soon come to rescue me. He didn't come, of course. And I was the one who left my town to study and live in Rio de Janeiro, taking only my clothes with me. But inside myself I was taking my passion for books that would never abandon me.

I had been sent to study in a boarding school, and I was soon appalled° to discover that the expensive all-girls school had even fewer books than my house. In my class there was a bookshelf with maybe fifty books, and almost all of them were about the lives of saints and the miracles of Christ. I had almost given up the hope of finding something to read when I spotted, tucked away at the very end of the shelf, a small book already covered by dust. It didn't seem to be about religion because it had a more intriguing° title, *The Old Man and the Sea*. It was written by an author that I had never heard of before: Ernest Hemingway. Curious, I started to read the book and a few minutes later was already fascinated by Santiago, the fisherman.

I loved that book so much that when I went to my aunt's house to spend the weekend, I asked her if she had any books by the man who had written it. She lent me *For Whom the Bell Tolls*, and I read it every Sunday I could get out of school, only a little bit at a time, only one teaspoon at a time. I started to wait anxiously for those Sundays. At the age of thirteen I was deeply in love with Ernest Hemingway.

7

When I finished with all his books I could find, I discovered Herman Hesse, Graham Greene, Aldous Huxley, Edgar Allan Poe. I could read them only on Sundays, so, during the week, I would dream or think about the world I had discovered in their books.

8

At that time I thought that my relationship with books was kind of odd, something that set me apart from the world. Only when I read the short story "Illicit Happiness," by Clarice Lispector, a Brazilian author, did I discover that other people could enjoy books as much as I did. The story is about an ugly and fat girl who still manages to torture one of the beautiful girls in her town only because her father is the owner of a bookstore, and she can have all the books she wants. With sadistic° refinement, day after day she promises to give to the beautiful girl the book the girl dearly wants, but never fulfills her promise. When her mother finds out what is going on and gives the book to the beautiful girl, the girl runs through the streets hugging it and, at home, pretends to have lost it only to find it again, showing an ardor° for books that made me exult°. For the first time I wasn't alone. I knew that someone else also loved books as much as I did.

9

My passion for books continued through my life, and it had to surmount another big challenge when, at the age of thirty-one, I moved to New York. Because I had almost no money, I was forced to leave all my books in Brazil. Besides, I didn't know enough English to read in this language. For some years I was condemned again to the darkness; condemned to live without books, my friends, my guides, my lovers.

10

But my love for books was so strong that I overcame even this obstacle. I learned to read in English, and was finally able to enjoy my favorite authors again.

11

Although books have always been part of my life, they still hold a mystery for me, and every time I open a new one, I ask myself which pleasures I am about to discover, which routes I am about to travel, which

12

emotions I am about to sink in. Will this new book touch me as a woman, as a foreigner, as a romantic soul, as a curious person? Which horizon is it about to unfold to me, which string of my soul is it bound to touch, which secret is it about to unveil for me?

Sometimes, the book seduces° me not only for the story it tells, but   13
also because of the words the author uses in it. Reading Gabriel Garcia Marquez's short story "The Handsomest Drowned Man in the World," I feel dazzled when he writes that it took "the fraction of centuries for the body to fall into the abyss." The fraction of centuries! I read those words again and again, infatuated° by them, by their precision°, by their hidden meaning. I try to keep them in my mind, even knowing that they are already part of my soul.

After reading so many books that touch me deeply, each one in its   14
special way, I understand now that my mother had a point when she tried to keep me away from books in my childhood. She wanted me to stay in my little town, to marry a rich and tiresome man, to keep up with the traditions. But the books carried me away; they gave me wings to fly, to discover new places. They made me dare to live another kind of life. They made me wish for more, and when I couldn't have all I wished for, they were still there to comfort me, to show me new options.

Yes, my mother was right. Books are dangerous; books are   15
subversive°. Because of them I left a predictable future for an unforeseeable one. However, if I had to choose again, I would always choose the books instead of the lackluster° life I could have had. After all, what joy would I find in my heart without my books, my most faithful lovers?

READING COMPREHENSION QUESTIONS

Vocabulary in Context

1. The word *surmount* in "My passion for books . . . had to surmount another big challenge when, at the age of thirty-one, I moved to New York. . . . For some years I was condemned again . . . to live without books" (paragraph 10) means
   a. overcome.
   b. create.
   c. locate.
   d. show.

Central Point and Main Ideas

2. Which statement best expresses the central point of the selection?
   a. Books, which Piassa finds essential, have greatly influenced and enriched her life.
   b. After growing up in a small, secluded town in Brazil, the author decided to move to New York.
   c. People who grow up where books are not readily available are more likely to appreciate them.
   d. Piassa has enjoyed reading such authors as Ernest Hemingway and Gabriel Garcia Marquez.

3. Which statement best expresses the main idea of paragraph 9?
   a. Piassa was overjoyed to learn from the short story "Illicit Happiness" that she was not alone in her passion for books.
   b. "Illicit Happiness" is a story about a bookstore owner's daughter who tortures another girl by withholding a book.
   c. Clarice Lispector is a Brazilian author who wrote the touching short story "Illicit Happiness."
   d. Books can help us remember we are not alone in the world.

4. The main idea of paragraph 13 is best expressed in its
   a. first sentence.
   b. second sentence.
   c. third sentence.
   d. last sentence.

Supporting Details

5. Problems the author faced include
   a. being criticized by her mother for reading.
   b. not having a big choice of books available to her in Brazil.
   c. having to learn English as an adult.
   d. all of the above.

6. The boarding school Piassa attended in Rio de Janeiro
   a. had no books.
   b. mainly had religious books.
   c. discouraged reading of all kinds.
   d. was not near any of Piassa's family.

Transitions

7. The two parts of the sentence below have a relationship of
   a. time.
   b. addition.
   c. contrast.
   d. cause and effect.

   > Because I had almost no money, I was forced to leave all my books in Brazil. (Paragraph 10)

Inferences

8. We can conclude that Piassa compares reading to drug addiction because
   a. she was discouraged from reading just as people are discouraged from taking drugs.
   b. she needed to read books and addicts need drugs.
   c. books carried her "away to an enchanted world" and drugs also take people away from reality.
   d. all of the above.

9. We can infer that Piassa's aunt's copy of *For Whom the Bell Tolls* was probably
   a. extremely expensive.
   b. a shortened version.
   c. eventually given to Piassa.
   d. not in English.

10. Piassa implies her mother did not want her to read because her mother
    a. could not read herself.
    b. thought books were too expensive.
    c. thought books would encourage Piassa to leave home.
    d. did not have any books around the house.

SUMMARIZING

Circle the letter—*a, b,* or *c*—of the passage that best completes the following summary of "A Love Affair with Books."

Bernadete Piassa has had a passion for books since her childhood, even though her mother didn't like her to read. In her small Brazilian hometown, there were few books, but she often managed to find something to sneak away with and read. She was later sent to a boarding school in Rio de Janeiro. The only place she could find good books there was at her aunt's house, where she often stayed on Sundays. She eagerly looked forward to those Sundays. Piassa's passion for books continued.

a. However, when she moved to New York at the age of thirty-one, she had to give up books for a while. She had been unable to bring her own books along, and she didn't know English well enough to read it. Eventually, she learned English. Then she was again able to enjoy the pleasures of stories and the richness of words. She now feels that her mother discouraged reading so that Piassa would be satisfied to remain at home and live a traditional life. Piassa is grateful to books for inspiring her to choose a more exciting life and for providing comfort and options when things haven't turned out as planned.

b. She has enjoyed not only the wonderful stories she has read through the years, but also the rich language used by the authors. One author whose words delighted her is Gabriel Garcia Marquez, in his short story "The Handsomest Drowned Man in the World." In that story he wrote that it took "the fraction of centuries for the body to fall into the abyss." The rich phrase "the fraction of centuries" dazzled Piassa, and she read it over and over.

c. Piassa feared that her relationship with books meant that she was a strange person. But a short story titled "Illicit Happiness" provided her with the example of a beautiful girl who also loved books. She knew then that she was not alone, and the passion for books continued then in her life. She was even able to deal with the obstacle that confronted her when she came to America and did not know enough English to read in the language. Because her love of books motivated her to learn English, she was once again able to enjoy her favorite authors. Books continue to hold a mystery for her, and each new book is a journey into a new world of travels and new pleasures.

DISCUSSION QUESTIONS

1. In her essay, Piassa writes that she became addicted to reading. In what ways was her passion for reading like a drug addiction? Can you think of other positive things besides reading to which people can become "addicted"?

2. The author's mother discouraged her from reading. What was the attitude of the adults in your house to reading? Were you encouraged or discouraged to read?

3. What was the experience of reading like for you in school? Explain why it was a positive or a negative experience.

4. Generally, parents would like their children to read more. What ways would you suggest to encourage young children to read?

17

Coping with Nervousness
Rudolph F. Verderber

Preview

Imagine sitting among friends and telling them a long story about something that happened to you. You would probably express yourself in a relaxed manner. Now imagine yourself standing in front of a large class, telling the students and teacher exactly the same thing you told your circle of friends. This time, you probably would not be so relaxed. In fact, it is likely that your legs would be trembling, your heart pounding, and your mouth dry. Public speaking can be a very nerve-racking experience. However, there are ways to deal with the nervousness. In this selection from the widely-used college textbook *Communicate!* (7th edition, Wadsworth, 1993), Rudolph F. Verderber provides information that may make your future speaking assignments less painful.

Words to Watch

virtually (2): almost
channel (3): direct
adrenaline (4): a hormone that stimulates and strengthens parts of the body
compound (5): increase
flabbergasted (5): amazed
eliciting (5): drawing out
by the same token (8): using the same line of reasoning
psyching . . . up (9): preparing (oneself) psychologically
conveyed (9): communicated

initial (10): first

gestures (13): expressive movements of the hands, body, or head

Most people confess to extreme nervousness at even the thought   1
of giving a speech. Yet you must learn to cope with nervousness because
speaking is important. Through speaking, we gain the power to share
what we are thinking with others. Each of us has vital information to
share: we may have the data needed to solve a problem; we may have an
idea for a procedure that will save money for our company or group; we
may have insights that will influence the way people see an issue. We can
only imagine the tremendous loss to business, governmental, educational,
professional, and fraternal groups because anxiety prevents people from
speaking up.

Let's start with the assumption that you are indeed nervous—you   2
may in fact be scared to death. Now what? Experience has proved that
virtually° anyone can learn to cope with the fear of public speaking.
Consider the following points:

1. *You are in good company.* Not only do most beginning speakers   3
suffer anxiety at the thought of speaking in public, but many
experienced speakers confess to nervousness when they speak as
well. Now, you may think, "Don't give me that line—you can't
tell me that [fill in the name of a good speaker you know] is
nervous when speaking in public!" Ask the person. He or she
will tell you. Even powerful speakers like Abraham Lincoln and
Franklin D. Roosevelt were nervous before speaking. The
difference in nervousness among people is a matter of degree.
Some people tremble, perspire, and experience shortness of
breath and increased heartbeat. As they go through their speech,
they may be so preoccupied with themselves they lose contact
with the audience, jump back and forth from point to point, and
on occasion forget what they had planned to say. Others,
however, may get butterflies in their stomachs and feel weak in
the knees—and still go on to deliver a strong speech. The secret
is not to get rid of all of your feelings but to learn to channel°
and control your nervousness.

2. *Despite nervousness, you can make it through a speech.* Very   4
few people are so bothered by anxiety that they are unable to
proceed with the speech. You may not enjoy the experience—
especially the first time—but you can do it. In fact, it would be
detrimental if you were *not* nervous. Why? Because you must be
a little more aroused than usual to do your best. A bit of

nervousness gets the adrenaline° flowing—and that brings you to speaking readiness.

3. *Your listeners aren't nearly as likely to recognize your fear as you might think.* "The only thing we have to fear," Franklin Roosevelt said, "is fear itself." Many speakers compound° their fear out of anxiety that their audiences will perceive their nervousness—and that makes them even more self-conscious and nervous. The fact is that people, even speech instructors, will greatly underrate the amount of stage fright they believe a person has. Recently, a young woman reported that she broke out in hives before each speech. She was flabbergasted° when other students said to her, "You seem so calm when you speak." Try eliciting° feedback from your listeners after a speech. Once you realize that your audience does not perceive your nervousness to the degree that you imagine, you will remove one unnecessary source of anxiety.   5

4. *The more experience you get in speaking, the better you become at coping with nervousness.* As you gain experience, you learn to think more about the audience and the message and less about yourself. Moreover, you come to realize that audiences, your classmates especially, are very supportive, especially in informative speech situations. After all, most people are in the audience because they want to hear you. As time goes on, you will come to find that having a group of people listening to *you alone* is a very satisfying experience.   6

Now let's consider what you can do about your nervousness. Coping with nervousness begins during the preparation process and extends to the time you actually begin the speech.   7

The best way to control nervousness is to pick a topic you know something about and are interested in. Public speakers cannot allow themselves to be saddled with a topic they don't care about. An unsatisfactory topic lays the groundwork for a psychological mind-set that almost guarantees nervousness at the time of the speech. By the same token°, selecting a topic you are truly interested in will help you focus on what you want to communicate and so lay the groundwork for a satisfying speech experience.   8

A second key to controlling nervousness is to prepare adequately for your speech. If you feel in command of your material and delivery, you'll be far more confident. During the preparation period, you can also be "psyching yourself up°" for the speech. Even in your classroom speeches, if you have a suitable topic, and if you are well prepared, your   9 audience will feel they profited from listening to you. Before you say, "Come on, who are you trying to kid!" think of lectures, talks, and speeches you have heard. When the speaker seemed knowledgeable and conveyed° enthusiasm, weren't you impressed? The fact is that some of the speeches you hear in class are likely to be among the best and most informative or moving speeches you are ever going to hear. Public speaking students learn to put time and effort into their speeches, and many classroom speeches turn out to be surprisingly interesting and valuable. If you work at your speech, you will probably sense that your class looks forward to listening to you.

Perhaps the most important time for coping with nervousness is shortly before you give your speech. Research indicates that it is during the period right before you walk up to give your speech and the time when you have your initial° contact with the audience that your fear is most likely to be at its greatest.   10

When speeches are being scheduled, you may be able to control when you speak. Are you better off "getting it over with," that is, being the first person to speak that day? If so, you may be able to volunteer to go first. But regardless of when you are scheduled to speak, try not to spend your time thinking about yourself or your speech. At the moment the class begins, you have done all you can to be prepared. This is the time to focus your mind on something else. Try to listen to each of the speeches that comes before yours. Get involved with what each speaker is saying. When your turn comes, you will be far more relaxed than if you had spent the time worrying about your own speech.   11

As you walk to the speaker's stand, remind yourself that you have ideas you want to convey, that you are well prepared, and that your audience is going to want to hear what you have to say. Even if you make mistakes, the audience will be focusing on your ideas and will profit from your speech.   12

When you reach the stand, pause a few seconds before you start and establish eye contact with the audience. Take a deep breath to help get your breathing in order. Try to move about a little during the first few sentences—sometimes, a few gestures° or a step one way or another is enough to break some of the tension. Above all, concentrate on communicating with your audience—your goal is to share your ideas, not to give a performance.   13

READING COMPREHENSION QUESTIONS

Vocabulary in Context

1. The words *cope with* in "you must learn to cope with nervousness because *speaking is important*" (paragraph 1) mean
   a. concentrate on.
   b. regret.
   c. handle.
   d. imagine.

2. The word *detrimental* in "Despite nervousness, you can make it through a speech. . . . In fact, it would be detrimental if you were *not* nervous. Why? Because you must be a little more aroused than usual to do your best" (paragraph 4) means
   a. helpful.
   b. expensive.
   c. harmful.
   d. funny.

Central Point and Main Ideas

3. Which sentence best expresses the central point of the selection?
   a. Nearly everyone feels nervous when they speak in public.
   b. It is possible to control the fear of public speaking.
   c. You can control the nervousness of speaking by picking a topic that interests you.
   d. Even famous speakers report feeling nervous before giving speeches.

4. Which sentence best expresses the main idea of paragraph 3?
   a. Nearly everyone gets nervous before giving a speech, but good speakers are able to channel and control their nervousness.
   b. Franklin D. Roosevelt and Abraham Lincoln were nervous before speaking.
   c. Giving a speech can be a stressful experience.
   d. Speakers who tremble, perspire, and experience shortness of breath and increased heartbeat may lose contact with the audience.

5. Which sentence best expresses the main idea of paragraphs 7–13?
   a. When preparing a speech, choose a topic you know something about and are interested in.
   b. You will feel far more confident about a speech if you prepare adequately for it.
   c. There are various things you can do to cope with nervousness during the preparation and beginning of a speech.
   d. According to research, it is just before you walk up to give your speech and the time of your first contact with the audience that your fear is likely to be at its greatest.

Transitions

6. The relationship of the second sentence below to the first is one of
   a. addition.
   b. illustration.
   c. contrast.
   d. cause-effect.

   > As you gain experience, you learn to think more about the audience and the message and less about yourself. Moreover, you come to realize that audiences, your classmates especially, are very supportive, especially in informative speech situations. (Paragraph 6)

Supporting Details

7. Nervousness
   a. is rarely experienced by people who give speeches on a regular basis.
   b. can actually help a speaker to do his or her best.
   c. cannot be effectively controlled.
   d. always interferes with the effectiveness of a speech.

8. The audience
   a. is usually able to tell how nervous a speaker is.
   b. should never be allowed to make direct eye contact with the speaker.
   c. usually underestimates the nervousness of a speaker.
   d. rarely is interested in classroom speeches.

Inferences

9. The author suggests that
   a. it is best to concentrate on other things right before giving a speech.

b. you should revise your speech up until the last possible moment.

c. it is always best to try to be the first speaker of the day.

d. with proper preparation, you will not be nervous once your speech begins.

10. The tone of this reading is

a. optimistic and helpful.

b. outspoken and critical.

c. sympathetic and forgiving.

d. excited and joyous.

OUTLINING

Complete the outline by filling in the missing major and minor details. The missing items are listed in random order below the outline.

Central point: You can cope with the nervousness of public speaking.

A. Introduction: Since speaking is important, it's important to learn to cope with nervousness.

B. _____

_____

1. Even good speakers get nervous; they just learn to channel and control their nervousness.

2. Nervousness won't stop you from completing a speech, and it will even help you.

3. Your nervousness during a speech won't show nearly as much as you might think it will.

4. The more experience you get in speaking, the better you become at coping with nervousness.

C. _____

_____

1. Pick a topic you know something about and are interested in.

2. _____

_____

3. Try to control your nervousness just before you walk up to give your speech.

a) Try to schedule your speech at a comfortable time.

b) Focus your mind on something other than your speech.

4. _____

_____

a) As you walk to the speaker's stand, focus on your ideas and the fact that you're well-prepared.

b) When you reach the stand, do a few things to break some of the tension.

1. Pause a few seconds and establish eye contact with the audience.

2. Take a deep breath.

3. Move about a little during your first few sentences.

4. Concentrate on communicating with your audience.

Items Missing from the Outline

There are various ways to cope with the nervousness of speaking.
Prepare adequately for your speech.
Use coping methods for walking to the speaker's stand and just after.
Experience has shown that people can learn to cope with nervousness.

DISCUSSION QUESTIONS

1. What have your public speaking experiences been like? Have some speeches gone better than others? If so, what were the differences, and what do you think were the reasons for those differences? What did you find helpful in preparing and giving speeches?

2. Why do you think speaking on a topic you know a great deal about and are interested in could be helpful? Can you think of any examples from the speeches you've given or heard?

3. You may need to give speeches in your classes, but do you think you will have to speak in public after you graduate from school? In what situations might you have to give a speech or even a presentation to a small group?

4. Obviously, Verderber feels nervousness is no reason not to speak in public. What other activities have you willingly done despite the fact that they made you nervous in some way? Was being nervous in these situations advantageous? If so, how?

18

The Price of Hate: Thoughts on Covering a KKK Rally
Rachel L. Jones

Preview

Reporters observe events in order to report on them. They are therefore usually on the sidelines. But when Rachel L. Jones, as a reporter with *The Miami Herald*, covered a Ku Klux Klan rally, she became one of the rally's victims. In this essay, she explains how that event changed her— and how it didn't change her.

Words to Watch

>*mechanism* (2): system, ability
>*burly* (5): heavy and muscular
>*fray* (5): uproar
>*feigned* (9): pretended
>*clinical* (13): without feeling
>*proffered* (16): offered
>*jangled* (16): upset
>*siblings* (17): brothers and sisters
>*trauma* (17): shock
>*naive* (18): innocent, lacking in experience
>*vitriol* (31): bitterly abusive expression
>*visceral* (32): instinctive

striving (34): struggling
resolve (35): determination
epithets (36): insults, terms of abuse
rabble (38): mob
ingenious (38): clever
warily (39): guardedly
diffuse (41): soften
demented (43): insane

I was sitting at my computer terminal when I overheard someone in the office mention his concern because he thought a black couple was moving into a house on his street.   1

He was standing only four feet away from me, yet lacked a mechanism° that would prevent him from making racist statements in front of a black person. I stopped typing and stared at his back. He froze momentarily, and the woman he was talking to glanced at me.   2

I didn't confront him. I had to transmit copy to St. Petersburg and then leave to cover a graduation. Besides, my stomach was churning. Just seven days earlier, at a Ku Klux Klan rally in Clearwater, I had stood only four feet away from a Tarpon Springs man who told me he was tired of "the n—s getting everything."   3

I'd be lying if I said that the possibility of covering a Ku Klux Klan rally didn't cause me a few moments' concern about my physical well-being. But when another reporter came over to tell me about the May 28th Klan rally in front of Clearwater City Hall, I reasoned, "It's just another assignment. I am a reporter, and I know my life isn't all budget meetings."   4

I must admit to a curiosity about the Klan, and it seemed a good opportunity to take a look at that sideshow of human nature. Now, I *could* have asked to be excused from that particular assignment. As a police reporter, my Saturdays are sometimes very busy. Had I approached my editor to delicately decline, we could have both made ourselves believe it was only natural to send a burly° young man into the fray°. Anything could have happened that day—traffic accidents, drownings, first-degree murders at the jail.   5

I couldn't be two places at once, could I?   6

But two days before the event, I turned to my editor and asked, "I AM covering the rally on Saturday, aren't I?"   7

She didn't miss a beat. Yes, of course. Just a short story, unless the streets were running with blood or something.   8

I jokingly told her about the only slightly feigned° horror of my older sister, who shrieked into the phone, "They're letting a black   9 reporter cover the KLAN?"

At the Klan rally, the man from Tarpon Springs saw my press badge and figured I was a part of something he called the "Black Associated Press," which he swore was denying white journalism graduates jobs. Mr. Tarpon told me that n—s weren't qualified to get the jobs they were getting through affirmative action, and that America is for white people.

I paused momentarily and asked what he thought should be done about black people. He didn't know or care.

"Send 'em all to hell," he said, while I took notes.

It's funny—it was all so clinical°. My voice held an even tone, and while he talked I searched his contoured face for some glimmer of recognition on his part that *I* was a human being, and the words that he spat just might hurt me.

Just as I later waited for Mr. Welcome Wagon to turn around and apologize for his blunder, I waited for the Tarpon Springs man to show some spark of humanity, but he finished his conversation and walked away.

My stomach was still churning hours later as I relived that rally. The whole experience was like being scalded, like having something sharp raked over my flesh until it was raw.

After it was over I went home and drank a shot from the bottle of brandy I'd bought last Christmas. In Harlequin romances, handsome princes always proffered° hard liquor to soothe the jangled° nerves of a distraught heroine.

But I was alone, and I was no heroine. That night, every noise from the apartment upstairs made me jump, and the pattern of trees against the curtains frightened me as I tossed and turned. I called three of my siblings°, but other than offering sympathy, they felt helpless to ease my trauma°.

I had been so naive° about the whole assignment. The thing is, I never thought it would change me. I figured it would be difficult, but I didn't want it to *change* me.

What you must understand about the Klan is that its members and supporters have been stripped of their humanity. I gained that insight and feel stronger for it. It was easy enough on one level to say, "These people are stupid, so I shouldn't be bothered by what they say."

But that was cold comfort as I walked across the City Hall parking lot, feeling a numbness creep through my arms and legs. I thought I must have been walking like the Scarecrow in *The Wizard of Oz*, but figured if I could just make it to the church across the street, I'd be fine.

At the church, I asked to use the phone and was sent down a hall and to the left. My fingers felt like sausages as I tried to use the rotary dial, muttering curses as I fouled up several times. Finally managing to reach an editor, I was coherent enough to give her information for a brief summary of the rally.

But when the next editor picked up the phone, I dissolved in tears 22 after three words. He was puzzled, and I think unaware of what was wrong at first. I whimpered that I was sorry and didn't know what was wrong either. I gasped and caught a few breaths before describing in a wavering voice what had happened.

He tried calming me down to discuss the facts. How many people 23 attended? Had there been any clashes? What did police have to say? I planned to write a full story.

The editor said maybe we should just ignore the event. He asked if 24 any of the Klan members had been abusive to me. I mumbled, "Uh hum," and the tears flowed fresh. He told me to get as much police information as I could and to call him back later.

I placed the phone on the hook and buried my face in my hands, 25 letting the sobs come freely. The man who had let me use the church phone brought me a box of tissues and a Coke.

After I splashed my face with cold water and controlled the sobs, I 26 headed back to the rally, just as the Klansmen were loading up to leave. Shouts of "white supremacy" rang through the air as they rolled out, and my photographer walked over to give me the Klansmen's names. I turned away, telling her that I probably wouldn't use them anyway.

"I didn't think it would affect me," I whispered. 27

"Don't cry. They aren't worth it, Rachel," she said. 28

But even then, it had started to change me. . . . 29

When you have stared into the twisted face of hate, you must 30 change. I remember watching the documentary *Eyes on the Prize*, in particular the segment on the desegregation of Little Rock High School in 1957, and being disturbed by the outpouring of rage against those nine students.

The whites who snarled into the camera back then had no 31 explanation for their vitriol° and violence other than that the students were black, and they didn't care who knew it. They weren't going to let those n—s into the school, no matter what.

I've struggled all my life against a visceral° reaction to that kind of 32 racism. I have been mistreated because of my color, but nothing ever came near to what those students went through on a daily basis.

That and countless other examples let me know what I'd been 33 spared, and I decided to choose the path of understanding, realizing that some people are always going to fear or even hate me because of my color alone.

It's a burden blacks must carry no matter how high a level of achievement they reach, and I sought to incorporate that into my own striving°. Watching films of what hate turned those people into made me choose to reject it, to deal with people individually and not tarnish all whites with the same obscene images. *I would not hate.*

But as one Klan supporter muttered, "N— b—," at me as I weaved my way through the crowd, that resolve° crumbled. It stung as much as if he *had* slapped me or thrown something.

The leader shouted taunts and epithets° at a black woman who was infuriated by the proceedings, and who had even lunged at several people in the small group of supporters.

As the black woman walked away, the leader shouted, "Why don't you go back to Nee-gor Africa where you came from!" I laughed because he sounded foolish, but he saw me and sent a fresh stream of obscenity my way.

A Jewish woman who came to protest was heaped with stinging abuse, and the rabble° was ingenious° in its varied use of sexual and racial obscenities directed toward her.

Other reporters and photographers eyed me warily° throughout the rally, watching for my reactions to the abuse. When the leader started passing out leaflets and avoided my outstretched hand, a photographer asked for two and brought me one.

I said thank you. He said quietly, "You're very, very welcome," and was embarrassed when I caught his eye.

When it was all over, several police officials called me brave. But I felt cold, sick and empty. I felt like such a naive fool. I felt bitter. So this is what it feels like, I thought. Why *shouldn't* I just hate them right back, why couldn't I diffuse° this punch in the gut?

What is noble about not flinching in the face of hate? Slavery, lynchings, rape, inequality, was that not enough? If they want to send me to hell, shouldn't I want to take them along for the ride?

But I still couldn't hate. I was glad I had cried, though. It defied their demented° logic. It meant I was human.

READING COMPREHENSION QUESTIONS

Vocabulary in Context

1. The word *churning* in "I didn't confront him. I had to . . . leave to cover a graduation. Besides, my stomach was churning" (paragraph 3) means
   a. stirred up.
   b. full.
   c. digesting.
   d. quiet.

2. The word *coherent* in "I walked across the City Hall parking lot, feeling a numbness creep through my arms and legs. . . . Finally managing to reach an editor, I was coherent enough to give her information for a brief summary of the rally" (paragraphs 20 and 21) means
   a. awake.
   b. puzzled.
   c. logical.
   d. kind.

Central Point and Main Ideas

3. Which statement best expresses the central point of the selection?
   a. Despite the abuse she suffered at a KKK rally, the author refuses to hate.
   b. Racial slurs are all too common in the workplace.
   c. The KKK held a rally on May 28th in front of the Clearwater City Hall.
   d. During the rally, other reporters and photographers watched the author.

4. Which statement best expresses the main idea of paragraphs 4–7?
   a. The author learned that the KKK was going to hold a rally on May 28th.
   b. Reporters are often asked to cover events which might make them feel uncomfortable.
   c. Despite concern for her physical well-being, the author wanted to cover the KKK rally.
   d. As a reporter, the author was often busy on Saturdays.

5. Which statement best expresses the main idea of paragraphs 36–38?
   a. A black woman was very angry about what was happening.
   b. Klan members shouted insults at a black woman, the author, and a Jewish woman.

c. The Klan leader shouted insults at an angry black woman.

d. The author laughed at the leader of the Klan because he sounded foolish.

Supporting Details

6. The author states that members of the KKK
   a. recognize their victims' feelings.
   b. have lost their humanity.
   c. aren't really prejudiced.
   d. hate only African-Americans.

7. After attending the rally, Rachel Jones realized she had previously been
   a. jealous.
   b. prejudiced.
   c. inexperienced.
   d. bitter.

Transitions

8. The relationship between the two sentences below is one of
   a. addition.
   b. illustration.
   c. contrast.
   d. cause and effect.

   When it was all over, several police officials called me brave. But I felt cold, sick and empty. (Paragraph 41)

Inferences

9. We can infer that
   a. the author feels no one has suffered greater abuse than she has.
   b. it is easy to ignore prejudice when it is aimed directly at you.
   c. the KKK rally affected the author more than she had expected.
   d. after all, covering the KKK rally had little effect on the author.

10. We can infer from the article that the KKK members who demonstrated
    a. did not look at people as individuals.
    b. disliked only African-Americans.
    c. had lost jobs to members of the Black Associated Press.
    d. were friends with the office worker who made a racist statement in front of Jones.

SUMMARIZING

Circle the letter of the best summary of "The Price of Hate: Thoughts on Covering a Ku Klux Klan Rally."

a. The author, Rachel L. Jones, a police reporter, overheard a white man in her office say that he was concerned about a black couple moving into a house on his street. Jones, an African-American, was sitting just a few feet away from the man, yet that hadn't prevented him from making a racist statement.

   That incident was especially painful to Jones because it happened shortly after she had covered a Ku Klux Klan rally in Clearwater, Florida. At the rally, she interviewed a man from Tarpon Springs who was a member of the Klan. He told her that African-American reporters were denying white people jobs. When she asked him what he thought should be done about black people, he said, "Send 'em all to hell." The entire interview was done in unemotional tones. As she took notes, she could see no recognition within the man that she was a human being capable of being hurt. Although she waited for him to show some small evidence of humanity, he finished his conversation and walked away.

b. The author, Rachel L. Jones, a police reporter, was assigned to cover a Ku Klux Klan rally in Clearwater, Florida. Being African-American, Jones was concerned about her safety at the rally, but her professionalism and curiosity made her determined to go.

   Her experience at the rally, however, was more difficult than she had imagined. Klan members insulted African-Americans, including the author, and a Jewish woman. Being the target of hate was very painful. It took strength and courage for her just to walk to a nearby church and call in her report to her editors. Before she hung up, she had begun crying.

   She realizes that the experience has changed her in some way. Despite the racism she had faced in her life, she had chosen to reject hate. But being insulted with obscenities and watching others being insulted at the rally gave her bitter feelings and the temptation to hate. In the end, however, she could not. She had seen first-hand how hate could strip people of their humanity.

c. At times during her life, the author, Rachel L. Jones, had been mistreated because of her color, but she had never experienced firsthand the bitter hatred of the Ku Klux Klan. In fact, although she recognized that covering the Ku Klux Klan rally might put her in physical danger, she insisted on keeping the assignment. She admitted to being curious about "that sideshow of human nature."

After covering the rally, Jones thought back to the hatred African Americans have had to endure. Particularly, she remembered watching the documentary *Eyes on the Prize*. This documentary included a segment on the desegregation of Little Rock High School in 1957. The author was astonished at the senseless hatred the students had to endure.

About a week after covering the Ku Klux Klan rally, the author heard a white man in her office state that he was worried about a black couple moving into a house on his street. He said this despite the fact that she was sitting only four feet away from him. After witnessing during the same week a Ku Klux Klan rally and a racist remark by an officemate, Jones felt disgusted and noted that her "stomach was churning."

DISCUSSION QUESTIONS

1. Rachel Jones writes that she had been "naive about the whole assignment" to cover the KKK rally and that she hadn't wanted it to change her. How was she inexperienced and naive? How did the rally change her? Do you think Jones would have gone to the KKK rally had she known what the experience would be like? Give your reasons for your answer.

2. Why did Jones mention the documentary about the desegregation of Little Rock High School? In other words, what do her comments about that event add to her essay?

3. Jones had told herself, "These people are stupid, so I shouldn't be bothered by what they say." Why do you think that thought was "cold comfort" on the day of the rally?

4. What examples of kindnesses did Jones include in this essay? Why do you think she included them?

19

The Art of Flying Solo
Jean Seligmann

Preview

The American lifestyle has changed. In the fifties, the typical American family included one breadwinner, Dad, and a stay-at-home mom. A home-cooked meal was waiting on the dinner table each night. Divorce and remarriage were unusual. Today working mothers, fast foods, divorce, and stepparents are common facts of life. And now, as this *Time* magazine article explains, more and more Americans are finding themselves in yet another lifestyle pattern. They are living alone.

Words to Watch

bay (1): a distance away
harbor (1): hold inside us
ostracized (1): excluded
grueling (3): exhausting
demographer (4): someone who studies the characteristics of
                    human populations
stigma (5): stain on one's reputation
chic (5): fashionable
severe (7): extreme
acknowledging (8): admitting
status (8): condition
traumatic (8): a painful emotional experience
revels (12): takes great pleasure

surrogate (14): substitute
perks (14): benefits
atrophies (14): weakens
hurled (15): spoken forcefully
exhilarating (15): causing great cheerfulness

We grow up, most of us, with the expectation that when we're 1
really grown up, we'll be sharing a tube of toothpaste with someone else.
Someone to rub feet with when we wake up shivering at 3 a.m., to hold
the ladder when the overhead light bulb needs changing. Someone who'll
keep at bay° the terror many of us harbor° of ending up alone, isolated
and ostracized°. Yet the reality is that a huge and growing number of
Americans, by choice or by chance, have no one to squint at when they
wake up in the morning. At 35 or 75, whether they like it or not—and
many say they do—they're home alone.

What's it like to be not only the head of the household, but all its 2
arms and legs as well? Monica Walker, 34, an equity portfolio manager
for a Chicago investment firm, grew up in Texas with four brothers. "All
of my life I've had to do certain things alone," she says, "because I was a
female in a house of all men." Her family is Roman Catholic, and when
she was younger, she assumed she'd be married with children by the time
she was 34. "But that was only based on growing up in an environment
where my mother and her friends said these things," she now believes.

Before moving to Chicago in 1991, Walker turned down a marriage 3
proposal from her boyfriend in Dallas—and there have been others as
well. Her mother, she says, still thinks she should be married and worries
about her safety. Most of her high school and college friends are married,
and when they discover she lives by herself, says Walker, their first
comment is often something like: "Don't you want to be married?" But
after a grueling° workweek, she relishes coming home, alone, to her quiet
apartment in the city's Streeterville district. "Sometimes I just want to
read," she says. "I don't want to get my hair washed. I want to put on a T
shirt and wool socks and not have to talk to anybody."

According to the 1990 census, almost a quarter of the 94 million 4
U.S. households consisted of just one person, up from 17 percent in
1970. And the raw mass of people living in them has more than doubled,
soaring from 11 million then to 23 million now. We may think of them as
old and lonely, but many, like Walker, are neither. According to a new
census report, about a quarter are younger than 35, another quarter are 35
to 55, and 40 percent are 65 and older. In most cases, says Census Bureau
demographer° Jeanne Woodward, "it's a hard call to say whether [living
alone] is a choice or a consequence."

As a group, people living alone have taken another dramatic step on   5
the path away from the close-knit, extended families so common just a
few decades ago. Why are they doing it? For one thing, they're benefiting
from a decrease in the social stigma° of flying solo. In the past, the
tongue-clicking assumption was that if a man wasn't married, he must be
gay, and if a woman wasn't, she must be undesirable. Now, going it alone
has become socially acceptable, even chic°, in many circles. Americans
are surviving longer, too, and staying healthy enough to live
independently. We're marrying later and divorcing more often than we
used to. Financial comfort has also contributed to the rise in one-person
households. "Living alone is a luxury," declares Nina Hagiwara, 38, a
divorced librarian at San Francisco State University, "but I think once
you do it, you can't go back."

For David C'DeBaca, 46, living alone is more of a comfortable   6
habit than a luxury—one that's been with him since he left the military at
24. A builder of expensive custom-made Spanish colonial furniture, he
lives in the village of La Cienega, New Mexico, in a house that he built
himself. "I always seem to have known I was going to be single a long
time," he says. "I like being alone, always have." He dates about twice a
month and has come close to marriage in the past, he says, "but I don't
feel I have to try to make it happen." One reason it may not, he says, is
that "women over 30 are set in their ways—like me. I understand."

Visiting time: He does suffer occasional bouts of severe°   7
loneliness. "About twice a year I get really down," he says. "It lasts a few
days but I always seem to find my way clear." He relies on a network of
six especially close friends—both male and female—who, he says,
instinctively sense the problem when it comes up. "So I spend some
serious visiting time. We go to the movies, people-watch at the mall or go
to this theater or that art gallery."

Acknowledging° solo status° can be traumatic°. When Sandy   8
Goodenough, 43, a health-care administrator, bought her own condo in
Cambridge, Massachusetts, ten years ago, she says, "It was scary. I
thought at the time: Does this mean I'm making a statement that I'll
always be alone? When I look back on it, it seems really silly. You have
to live your life as it is."

Living alone can be frightening, says Philadelphia psychologist   9
Michael Broder, who has counseled singles for twenty years. "There's a
fear that something will happen to them and no one will know about it,
that they'll get sick and there will be no one to take care of them," he
says. "There's a fear that when major life events occur, there will be no
one to share that with." Solos tend to take exceptional security

precautions, although they are no more likely to become crime victims than members of larger households.

Robin Leeds, 38, is a political consultant and community organizer 10 who's concerned about protecting herself. Six years ago she bought her six-room condominium in a Boston brownstone. Back then, she carried a police whistle for personal safety, but now she relies on a network of women friends who check in with each other by phone on a daily basis. If she spends the evening out with a pal, they call each other later to make sure they both got home safely. "When you live alone, you really do have to build an outside support network," says Leeds. "If I had not grown up as a feminist, I'd probably not find all this as easy."

For the 51 percent of women living alone who are widows, being 11 suddenly solo is often not so easy. After her husband of 37 years died four years ago, Dione Donnelly, 60, says weekends were especially tough. She's come to dislike weddings, always leaving before the dancing begins and she finds herself without a partner. She misses sharing the change of seasons, especially the times when she and her husband would go to their second home on Wisconsin's Green Lake to enjoy the first snowfall or the autumn colors. Worse, she says, "People who had been our friends for thirty years, I never hear from. . . . But the thing that bothers me the most is not having someone to share all the small everyday details that couldn't possibly interest anybody else."

Big world: There are, however, some consolations. Married in 12 1952 at 20, Donnelly had a husband who expected a clean house, dinner on the table when he came home—and a wife who didn't work outside the home. "I never had anything to talk about with people," she says. "I was just a housewife." Then she got a real-estate license. "It gave me opportunities to see that there was a big world out there," she says. Today she looks forward to weekends—her busiest time as an agent. And she revels° in the small freedoms that now are hers. "If I don't feel like eating dinner," she declares, "I don't make dinner."

Living alone doesn't exclude having a serious relationship—and 13 having one doesn't necessarily lead to living together. Chris Mack, 43, a wastewater-treatment specialist, bought a house in Portland, Ore., for herself five years ago, shortly after breaking off a romantic liaison. Mack, who is a lesbian, doesn't plan to join households with her current girlfriend of more than three years. "I like to know the rake is where I left it," she says. Furthermore, Mack doubts anyone would put up with some of her habits. "I'll play the same music over and over a trillion times," she says. "I like to sing, and I have a lousy voice."

Lynn Michael Cohen, alone since his rocky three-year marriage 14 ended in divorce in 1986, is also not about to share his four-story, five-bedroom house in the east San Francisco Bay city of Richmond. He says it's just the right size for him and his eight-year-old tabby cat, Cindy, whom he calls his surrogate° child. Having lived by himself most of his adult life, Cohen, 53, found marriage a strain, a violation of his privacy. Now, while he enjoys the company of friends, he prefers hiking by himself in the rugged Point Reyes area north of San Francisco. "I'm not a loner," he insists. "Not in the sense that I'm cut off from the universe. But I like to live alone. I come and go pretty much as I please and I don't have to explain what's what and where I'm going." For Cohen, an engineer and software developer, "it's these little perks° that any relationship would have to compete with to make me give them up. And there's no doubt in my mind that your ability to compromise atrophies° after nonuse."

Perhaps what most separates people who live by themselves from   15
those who don't is the time they have to muse about the texture of their lives. Most would agree that going it alone is something of a tradeoff. To be sure, the pictures may get hung a little crooked, the aching back may go unrubbed. But it's also the fulfillment of that other childhood fantasy, hurled° defiantly at the all-powerful parents: "When I grow up, I'm going to do exactly what I please." Now, more of us than ever before are getting a chance to find out if that freedom is really as exhilarating° as it sounded back then.

READING COMPREHENSION QUESTIONS

Vocabulary in Context

1. The word *relishes* in "after a grueling workweek, she relishes coming home, alone, to her quiet apartment. . . . 'Sometimes . . . I want to put on a T shirt and wool socks and not have to talk to anybody'" (paragraph 3) means
   a. denies.
   b. enjoys.
   c. walks.
   d. resists.

2. The word *bouts* in "For David C'DeBaca, 46, living alone is more of a comfortable habit than a luxury. . . . He does suffer occasional bouts of severe loneliness. 'About twice a year I get really down,' he says" (paragraphs 6–7) means
   a. periods.
   b. jobs.

c. habits.

d. possibilities.

Central Point and Main Ideas

3. Which statement best expresses the central point of the selection?
   a. There are many alternatives to the traditional family.
   b. Living alone can be a frightening and lonely experience.
   c. The number of people who live alone is increasing for various reasons.
   d. People who are alone tend to take exceptional safety precautions.

4. Which statement best expresses the main idea of paragraph 5?
   a. There are several reasons for the increase in the number of people who are living alone.
   b. It's difficult to live with someone after living alone.
   c. Americans are marrying later and divorcing more often.
   d. Living alone has become fashionable in some circles.

5. Which statement best expresses the main idea of paragraphs 9–10?
   a. Robin Leeds, a woman who lives alone in Boston, once carried a police whistle for safety.
   b. People who live alone are often frightened and take special safety precautions.
   c. People living alone are not more likely to become crime victims than others.
   d. One disadvantage of living alone is that there is no one to help you when you are sick.

Supporting Details

6. Today, living alone has become
   a. more difficult to do.
   b. more socially acceptable.
   c. less expensive.
   d. all of the above.

7. According to the article, people often live alone
   a. to gain safety.
   b. to save money.
   c. to develop a career.
   d. to gain freedom.

Transitions

8. The relationship between the following two sentences is one of
   a. time.

    b. illustration.

    c. contrast.

    d. cause and effect.

> For the 51 percent of women living alone who are widows, being suddenly solo is often not so easy. . . . There are, however, some consolations. (Paragraphs 11–12)

Inferences

  9. From the comments of C'DeBaca (paragraph 7) and Leeds (paragraph 10), we can infer that people who live alone

    a. tend to have fewer friends than others.

    b. may have friends who take on roles often played by family members.

    c. are sure to end up moving in with friends.

    d. are unlikely to have close friends of the opposite sex.

  10. From the article, we might conclude that

    a. people who live alone tend to enjoy coming and going as they please.

    b. living alone means less compromise.

    c. today there are various lifestyle choices.

    d. all of the above.

SUMMARIZING

Circle the letter—*a, b,* or *c*—of the passage that best completes the following summary of "The Art of Flying Solo."

> According to Census Bureau reports, more and more adults of all ages are living alone. One reason is that it has become more socially acceptable. Also, Americans live longer and are staying healthy enough to live alone longer. In addition, they are marrying later and divorcing more often. Also, they are more able to afford living alone.

  a. For some, living alone means having networks of friends to help one get over loneliness and to feel more secure. Many women who live alone are widows, who often find living alone more lonely than those who have chosen to live alone. However, even widows can find benefits to living alone, such as a new career. In addition, living alone doesn't necessarily exclude a serious relationship. Finally, despite its disadvantages, living alone offers a great deal of personal freedom.

b. According to Nina Hagiwara, 38, a divorced librarian at San Francisco State University, living alone is a financial luxury, but well worth it. David C'DeBaca, 46, finds living alone more a comfortable habit than a luxury. He has lived alone since he was 24. While he has come close to marriage a few times, he feels he doesn't "have to try to make it happen." He realizes that people over 30 are set in their ways, making marriage less and less likely. Anyway, like other people who live alone, he has found a network of friends to enrich his life and help him get over times of loneliness.

c. Today, about 23 million people live alone, compared to 11 million in 1970. Of those people, about a quarter are younger than 35, another quarter are 35 to 55, and 40 percent are 65 and older. Examples of those who choose to live alone include Chris Mack, 43, a wastewater-treatment specialist. Mack bought her own home in Portland, Oregon, shortly after the end of a romance. Mack now has another serious relationship, but continues to live alone. She feels her odd habits make her someone that would be hard to live with.

DISCUSSION QUESTIONS

1. Have you ever lived alone for an extended period of time? What advantages did you find to living alone? What disadvantages?

2. The authors contrast living alone on purpose and living alone because one's mate has died. Why and how do you think living alone by choice differs from living alone by necessity?

3. In paragraph 4, the authors quote Census Bureau demographer Jeanne Woodward as saying, ". . . it's a hard call to say whether [living alone] is a choice or a consequence." What do you think she meant by that? If you were to live alone, would it be through choice or as a consequence?

4. What did Lynn Michael Cohen mean when he said that "there's no doubt in my mind that your ability to compromise atrophies after nonuse" (paragraph 14)? Do you agree?

20

A Drunken Ride, A Tragic Aftermath
Theresa Conroy and Christine M. Johnson

Preview

We have all heard many warnings against drinking and driving. However, witnessing a drunk driving accident can be far more convincing. If you have not seen such an accident, this article will be a useful substitute. You will not easily forget the accident and its terrible aftermath, as described by the authors.

Words to Watch

vehicular homicide (6): killing with a vehicle
spawning (8): producing in large number
carnage (19): corpses
appalled (59): filled with horror
catharsis (62): refreshing release of emotional tension
fathom (64): understand
tamperproof (65): unable to be falsely changed
curtail (68): cut back on
impair (76): weaken
faculties (76): abilities
incarcerate (79): put in prison

vicariously (94): by imagining someone else's experience
adherence (95): sticking
subsidized (97): financed
peer-group (97): made up of people of a similar age, grade, etc.
welling (104): rising

When Tyson Baxter awoke after that drunken, tragic night—with a   1
bloodied head, broken arm, and battered face—he knew that he had
killed his friends.

"I knew everyone had died," Baxter, 18, recalled. "I knew it before   2
anybody told me. Somehow, I knew."

Baxter was talking about the night of Friday, September 13, the   3
night he and seven friends piled into his Chevrolet blazer after a beer-
drinking party. On Street Road in Upper Southampton, he lost control,
rear-ended a car, and smashed into two telephone poles. The Blazer's cab
top shattered, and the truck spun several times, ejecting all but one
passenger.

Four young men were killed.   4

Tests would show that Baxter and the four youths who died were   5
legally intoxicated.

Baxter says he thinks about his dead friends on many sleepless   6
nights at the Abraxas Drug and Alcohol Rehabilitation Center near
Pittsburgh, where, on December 20, he was sentenced to be held after
being found delinquent on charges of vehicular homicide°.

"I drove them where they wanted to go, and I was responsible for   7
their lives," Baxter said recently from the center, where he is undergoing
psychological treatment. "I had the keys in my hand, and I blew it."

The story of September 13 is a story about the kind of horrors that   8
drinking and driving is spawning° among high school students almost
everywhere, . . . about parents who lost their children in a flash and have
filled the emptiness with hatred, . . . about a youth whose life is burdened
with grief and guilt because he happened to be behind the wheel.

It is a story that the Baxter family and the dead boys' parents agreed   9
to tell in the hope that it would inspire high school students to remain
sober during this week of graduation festivities—a week that customarily
includes a ritual night of drunkenness.

It is a story of the times.   10

The evening of September 13 began in high spirits as Baxter,   11
behind the wheel of his gold Blazer, picked up seven high school chums
for a drinking party for William Tennent High School students and

graduates at the home of a classmate. Using false identification, according to police, the boys purchased one six-pack of beer each from a Warminster Township bar.

The unchaperoned party, attended by about fifty teenagers, ended about 10:30 p.m. when someone knocked over and broke a glass china cabinet. Baxter and his friends decided to head for a fast-food restaurant. As Baxter turned onto Street Road, he was trailed by a line of cars carrying other party goers.   12

Baxter recalled that several passengers were swaying and rocking the high-suspension vehicle. Police were unable to determine the vehicle's exact speed, but, on the basis of the accounts of witnesses, they estimated it at fifty-five miles per hour—ten miles per hour over the limit.   13

"I thought I was in control," Baxter said. "I wasn't driving like a nut; I was just . . . driving. There was a bunch of noise, just a bunch of noise. The truck was really bouncing.   14

"I remember passing two [cars]. That's the last I remember. I remember a big flash, and that's it."   15

Killed in that flash were: Morris "Marty" Freedenberg, 16, who landed near a telephone pole about thirty feet from the truck, his face ripped from his skull; Robert Schweiss, 18, a Bucks County Community College student, whose internal organs were crushed when he hit the pavement about thirty feet from the truck; Brian Ball, 17, who landed near Schweiss, his six-foot-seven-inch frame stretched three inches when his spine was severed; and Christopher Avram, 17, a premedical student at Temple University, who landed near the curb about ten feet from the truck.   16

Michael Serratore, 18, was thrown fifteen feet from the truck and landed on the lawn of the CHI Institute with his right leg shattered. Baxter, who sailed about ten feet after crashing through the windshield of the Blazer, lost consciousness after hitting the street near the center lane. About five yards away, Paul Gee, Jr., 18, lapsed into a coma from severe head injuries.   17

John Gahan, 17, the only passenger left in the Blazer, suffered a broken ankle.   18

Brett Walker, 17, one of several Tennent students who saw the carnage° after the accident, would recall later in a speech to fellow students: "I ran over [to the scene]. These were the kids I would go out with every weekend.   19

"My one friend [Freedenberg], I couldn't even tell it was him except for his eyes. He had real big, blue eyes. He was torn apart so bad. . . ."   20

Francis Schweiss was waiting up for his son, Robert, when he received a telephone call from his daughter, Lisa. She was already at Warminster General Hospital.

"She and Robbie and his friends were in a bad accident and Robbie was not here" at the hospital, Schweiss said. "I got in my car with my wife; we went to the scene of the accident."

There, police officers told Francis and Frances Schweiss that several boys had been killed and that the bodies, as well as survivors, had been taken to Warminster General Hospital.

"My head was frying by then," Francis Schweiss said. "I can't even describe it. I almost knew the worst was to be. I felt as though I were living a nightmare. I thought, 'I'll wake up. This just can't be.'"

In the emergency room, Francis Schweiss recalled, nurses and doctors were scrambling to aid the injured and identify the dead—a difficult task because some bodies were disfigured and because all the boys had been carrying fake driver's licenses.

A police officer from Upper Southampton was trying to question friends of the dead and injured—many of whom were sobbing and screaming—in an attempt to match clothing with identities.

When the phone rang in the Freedenberg home, Robert S. and his wife, Bobbi, had just gone upstairs to bed; their son Robert Jr. was downstairs watching a movie on television.

Bobbi Freedenberg and her son picked up the receiver at the same time. It was from Warminster General. . . . There had been a bad accident. . . . The family should get to the hospital quickly.

Outside the morgue about twenty minutes later, a deputy county coroner told Rob Jr., 22, that his brother was dead and severely disfigured; Rob decided to spare his parents additional grief by identifying the body himself.

Freedenberg was led into a cinderblock room containing large drawers resembling filing cabinets. In one of the drawers was his brother, Marty, identifiable only by his new high-top sneakers.

"It was kind of like being taken through a nightmare," Rob Jr. said. "That's something I think about every night before I go to sleep. That's hell. . . . That whole night is what hell is all about for me."

As was his custom, Morris Ball started calling the parents of his son's friends after Brian missed his 11:00 p.m. curfew.

The first call was to the Baxters' house, where the Baxters' sixteen-year-old daughter, Amber, told him about the accident.

At the hospital, Morris Ball demanded that doctors and nurses take him to his son. The hospital staff had been unable to identify Brian—until Ball told them that his son wore size 14 shoes.

Brian Ball was in the morgue. Lower left drawer.   35

"He was six foot seven, but after the accident he measured six foot   36
ten, because of what happened to him," Ball said. "He had a severed
spinal cord at the neck. His buttocks were practically ripped off, but he
was lying down and we couldn't see that. He was peaceful and asleep.

"He was my son and my baby. I just can't believe it sometimes. I   37
still can't believe it. I still wait for him to come home."

Lynne Pancoast had just finished watching the 11:00 p.m. news and   38
was curled up in her bed dozing with a book in her lap when the doorbell
rang. She assumed that one of her sons had forgotten his key, and she
went downstairs to let him in.

A police light was flashing through the window and reflecting   39
against her living room wall; Pancoast thought that there must be a fire in
the neighborhood and that the police were evacuating homes.

Instead, police officers told her there had been a serious accident   40
involving her son, Christopher Avram, and that she should go to the
emergency room at Warminster General.

At the hospital she was taken to an empty room and told that her   41
son was dead.

Patricia Baxter was asleep when a Warminster police officer came   42
to the house and informed her that her son had been in an accident.

At the hospital, she could not immediately recognize her own son   43
lying on a bed in the emergency room. His brown eyes were swollen
shut, and his straight brown hair was matted with blood that had poured
from a deep gash in his forehead.

While she was staring at his battered face, a police officer rushed   44
into the room and pushed her onto the floor—protection against the
hysterical father of a dead youth who was racing through the halls,
proclaiming that he had a gun and shouting, "Where is she? I'm going to
kill her. I'm going to kill him. I'm going to kill his mother."

The man, who did not have a gun, was subdued by a Warminster   45
police officer and was not charged.

Amid the commotion, Robert Baxter, a Lower Southampton   46
highway patrol officer, arrived at the hospital and found his wife and son.

"When he came into the room, he kept going like this," Patricia   47
Baxter said, holding up four fingers. At first, she said, she did not
understand that her husband was signaling that four boys had been killed
in the accident.

After Tyson regained consciousness, his father told him about the   48
deaths.

"All I can remember is just tensing up and just saying something,"   49
Tyson Baxter said. "I can remember saying, 'I know.'

"I can remember going nuts."   50

In the days after the accident, as the dead were buried in services   51
that Tyson Baxter was barred by the parents of the victims from
attending, Baxter's parents waited for him to react to the tragedy and
release his grief.

"In the hospital he was nonresponsive," Patricia Baxter said. "He   52
was home for a month, and he was nonresponsive.

"We never used to do this, but we would be upstairs and listen to   53
see if Ty responded when his friends came to visit," she said. "But the
boy would be silent. That's the grief that I felt. The other kids showed a
reaction. My son didn't."

Baxter said, however, that he felt grief from the first, that he would   54
cry in the quiet darkness of his hospital room and, later, alone in the
darkness of his bedroom. During the day, he said, he blocked his emotions.

"It was just at night. I thought about it all the time. It's still like   55
that."

At his parents' urging, Baxter returned to school on September 30.   56

"I don't remember a thing," he said of his return. "I just remember   57
walking around. I didn't say anything to anybody. It didn't really sink
in."

Lynne Pancoast, the mother of Chris Avram, thought it was wrong   58
for Baxter to be in school, and wrong that her other son, Joel, a junior at
William Tennent, had to walk through the school halls and pass the boy
who "killed his brother."

Morris Ball said he was appalled° that Baxter "went to a football   59
game while my son lay buried in a grave."

Some William Tennent students said they were uncertain about how   60
they should treat Baxter. Several said they went out of their way to treat
him normally, others said they tried to avoid him, and others declined to
be interviewed on the subject.

The tragedy unified the senior class, according to the school   61
principal, Kenneth Kastle. He said that after the accident, many students
who were friends of the victims joined the school's Students Against
Driving Drunk chapter.

Matthew Weintraub, 17, a basketball player who witnessed the   62
bloody accident scene, wrote to President Reagan and detailed the grief
among the student body. He said, however, that he experienced a

catharsis° after reading the letter at a student assembly and, as a result, did not mail it.

"And after we got over the initial shock of the news, we felt as though we owed somebody something," Weintraub wrote. "It could have been us and maybe we could have stopped it, and now it's too late. . . ." 63

"We took these impressions with us as we then visited our friends who had been lucky enough to live. One of them was responsible for the accident; he was the driver. He would forever hold the deaths of four young men on his conscience. Compared with our own feelings of guilt, [we] could not begin to fathom° this boy's emotions. He looked as if he had a heavy weight upon his head and it would remain there forever." 64

About three weeks after the accident, Senator H. Craig Lewis (D., Bucks) launched a series of public forums to formulate bills targeting underage drinking. Proposals developed through the meetings include outlawing alcohol ads on radio and television, requiring police to notify parents of underage drinkers, and creating a tamperproof° driver's license. 65

The parents of players on William Tennent's 1985–1986 boys' basketball team, which lost Ball and Baxter because of the accident, formed the Caring Parents of William Tennent High School Students to help dissuade students from drinking. 66

Several William Tennent students, interviewed on the condition that their names not be published, said that, because of the accident, they would not drive after drinking during senior week, which will be held in Wildwood, N.J., after graduation June 13. 67

But they scoffed at the suggestion that they curtail° their drinking during the celebrations. 68

"We just walk [after driving to Wildwood]," said one youth. "Stagger is more like it." 69

"What else are we going to do, go out roller skating?" an eighteen-year-old student asked. 70

"You telling us we're not going to drink?" one boy asked. "We're going to drink very heavily. I want to come home retarded. That's senior week. I'm going to drink every day. Everybody's going to drink every day." 71

Tyson Baxter sat at the front table of the Bucks County courtroom on December 20, his arm in a sling, his head lowered and his eyes dry. He faced twenty counts of vehicular homicide, four counts of involuntary manslaughter, and two counts of driving under the influence of alcohol. 72

Patricia Ball said she told the closed hearing that "it was Tyson Baxter who killed our son. He used the car as a weapon. We know he killed our children as if it were a gun. He killed our son." 73

"I really could have felt justice [was served] if Tyson Baxter was the only one who died in that car," she said in an interview, "because he didn't take care of our boys."

Police officers testified before Bucks County President Judge Isaac S. Garb that tests revealed that the blood-alcohol levels of Baxter and the four dead boys were above the 0.10 percent limit used in Pennsylvania to establish intoxication.

Baxter's blood-alcohol level was 0.14 percent, Ball's 0.19 percent, Schweiss's 0.11 percent, Avram's 0.12 percent, and Freedenberg's 0.38 percent. Baxter's level indicated that he had had eight or nine drinks—enough to cause abnormal bodily functions such as exaggerated gestures and to impair° his mental faculties°, according to the police report.

After the case was presented, Garb invited family members of the dead teens to speak.

In a nine-page statement, Bobbi Freedenberg urged Garb to render a decision that would "punish, rehabilitate, and deter others from this act."

The parents asked Garb to give Baxter the maximum sentence, to prohibit him from graduating, and to incarcerate° him before Christmas day. (Although he will not attend formal ceremonies, Baxter will receive a diploma from William Tennent this week.)

After hearing from the parents, Garb called Baxter to the stand.

"I just said that all I could say was, 'I'm sorry; I know I'm totally responsible for what happened,'" Baxter recalled. "It wasn't long, but it was to the point."

Garb found Baxter delinquent and sentenced him to a stay at Abraxas Rehabilitation Center—for an unspecified period beginning December 23—and community service upon his return. Baxter's driver's license was suspended by the judge for an unspecified period, and he was placed under Garb's jurisdiction until age 21.

Baxter is one of fifty-two Pennsylvania youths found responsible for fatal drunken-driving accidents in the state in 1985.

Reflecting on the hearing, Morris Ball said there was no legal punishment that would have satisfied his longings.

"They can't bring my son back," he said, "and they can't kill Tyson Baxter."

Grief has forged friendships among the dead boys' parents, each of whom blames Tyson Baxter for their son's death. Every month they meet at each other's homes, but they seldom talk about the accident.

Several have joined support groups to help them deal with their losses. Some said they feel comfortable only with other parents whose children are dead.

Bobbi Freedenberg said her attitude had worsened with the passage   88
of time. "It seems as if it just gets harder," she said. "It seems to get
worse."

Freedenberg, Schweiss, and Pancoast said they talk publicly about   89
their sons' deaths in hopes that the experience will help deter other
teenagers from drunken driving.

Schweiss speaks each month to the Warminster Youth Aid Panel—a   90
group of teenagers who, through drug use, alcohol abuse, or minor
offenses, have run afoul of the law.

"When I talk to the teens, I bring a picture of Robbie and pass it   91
along to everyone," Schweiss said, wiping the tears from his cheeks. "I
say, 'He was with us last year.' I get emotional and I cry. . . .

"But I know that my son helps me. I firmly believe that every time I   92
speak, he's right on my shoulder."

When Pancoast speaks to a group of area high school students, she   93
drapes her son's football jersey over the podium and displays his
graduation picture.

"Every time I speak to a group, I make them go through the whole   94
thing vicariously°," Pancoast said. "It's helpful to get out and talk to kids.
It sort of helps keep Chris alive. . . . When you talk, you don't think."

At Abraxas, Baxter attended high school classes until Friday. He is   95
one of three youths there who supervise fellow residents, who keep track
of residents' whereabouts, attendance at programs, and adherence° to the
center's rules and regulations.

Established in Pittsburgh in 1973, the Abraxas Foundation provides   96
an alternative to imprisonment for offenders between sixteen and twenty-
five years old whose drug and alcohol use has led them to commit crimes.

Licensed and partially subsidized° by the Pennsylvania Department   97
of Health, the program includes work experience, high school education,
and prevocational training. Counselors conduct individual therapy sessions,
and the residents engage in peer-group° confrontational therapy sessions.

Baxter said his personality had changed from an "egotistical,   98
arrogant" teenager to someone who is "mellow" and mature.

"I don't have quite the chip on my shoulder. I don't really have a   99
right to be cocky anymore," he said.

Baxter said not a day went by that he didn't remember his dead   100
friends.

"I don't get sad. I just get thinking about them," he said. "Pictures   101
pop into my mind. A tree or something reminds me of the time. . . .
Sometimes I laugh. . . . Then I go to my room and reevaluate it like a
nut," he said.

Baxter said his deepest longing was to stand beside the graves of his   102
four friends.

More than anything, Baxter said, he wants to say good-bye.   103

"I just feel it's something I have to do, . . . just to talk," Baxter said,   104
averting his eyes to hide welling° tears. "Deep down I think I'll be hit
with it when I see the graves. I know they're gone, but they're not gone."

READING COMPREHENSION QUESTIONS

Vocabulary in Context

1. The word *deter* in "Freedenberg, Schweiss, and Pancoast said they
   talk publicly about their sons' deaths in hopes that the experience
   will help deter other teenagers from drunken driving" (paragraph
   89) means
   a. punish.
   b. pay.
   c. prevent.
   d. hide.

2. The word *averting* in "I just feel it's something I have to do, . . . just
   to talk," Baxter said, averting his eyes to hide welling tears"
   (paragraph 104) means
   a. opening.
   b. turning aside.
   c. drying.
   d. thinking of.

Central Point and Main Ideas

3. The authors express the central point of their article in
   a. the first sentence of the article.
   b. the sentence that makes up paragraph 4.
   c. the sentence that makes up paragraph 8.
   d. the first sentence of paragraph 11.

4. Which sentence best expresses the main idea of paragraphs 21–47?
   a. The families of the victims learned what had happened.
   b. A great deal of disturbance can follow an accident.
   c. The family of Robert Schweiss learned that he was killed in the
      accident.
   d. The hospital emergency room is a difficult place after a terrible
      accident.

Supporting Details

5. The parents of the boys who died are **not**
   a. joining support groups.
   b. speaking to teenagers about the accident.
   c. making peace with Tyson Baxter.
   d. meeting with each other.

6. _____ TRUE OR FALSE? Of all the teens in the car, Baxter had the highest blood-alcohol level.

7. In paragraphs 8–10, the authors state that the accident
   a. was one of the worst of its time.
   b. happened all too quickly.
   c. is an example of many other such accidents.
   d. is a fictional story.

Transitions

8. The sentence below expresses a relationship of
   a. time.
   b. addition.
   c. illustration.
   d. contrast.

   After Tyson regained consciousness, his father told him about the deaths. (Paragraph 48)

Inferences

9. From the comments made at court by the parents of the victims, we can infer that the parents
   a. did not blame their own sons for their underage drinking.
   b. believed Baxter had gotten false identification for their sons.
   c. felt all of the victims that survived should be punished.
   d. wanted Baxter to have to return to school right away.

10. We can infer from the statements made by seniors in paragraphs 67–71 that
    a. many students at Baxter's high school had not heard of his accident.
    b. graduation parties will be strictly chaperoned.
    c. many students do not understand all the dangers of alcohol abuse.
    d. the drinking age is lower in Wildwood than in other places.

SUMMARIZING

Circle the letter of the passage that best summarizes paragraphs 61–71 of "A Drunken Ride, A Tragic Aftermath."

    a. Students reacted in various ways to the accident. According to the high school principal, some students joined the school's Students Against Driving Drunk chapter. One student, Matthew Weintraub, wrote a letter explaining the grief of the student body. His comments showed that some students felt guilt over the accident: "It could have been us and maybe we could have stopped it, and now it's too late. . . ." Some students said they would not drive after drinking during senior week.

    b. According to the school principal, the tragedy unified the senior class. Some of the students' reactions were described in a letter by one seventeen-year-old student, Matthew Weintraub. Weintraub expressed the grief and guilt felt by some fellow students, as well as their recognition of the heavy burden carried by the driver. He originally intended to mail the letter to President Reagan. However, after reading it at a student assembly, he decided that the letter had already served the purpose of releasing tension for him, and he didn't mail it.

    c. There were various student and community responses to the accident. It seemed to unify the high school seniors, and many friends of the victims joined the school's Students Against Driving Drunk chapter. Students were reported to feel guilt and sadness. Also, a state senator held forums to develop laws against underage drinking. The parents of the school's basketball team, which lost two players to the accident, formed a group to discourage student drinking. Finally, some seniors decided that, while they would still drink during senior week, they would not drive after drinking.

DISCUSSION QUESTIONS

1. The authors write in paragraph 14: "'I thought I was in control,' Baxter said. 'I wasn't driving like a nut; I was just . . . driving.'" What does this tell us about the effects of alcohol on drivers?

2. To what extent do you think Tyson Baxter was responsible for the accident? Do you feel his passengers were at fault too in any way? If so, to what extent were they also responsible? Is there anyone else that you think is partly to blame for the accident?

3. Is Tyson Baxter's life ruined forever? Or can he, in time, return to a "normal" life?

4. Why do you think drinking and driving is so common among high school students? How common do you think it is among college students? What do you think schools, parents, students, and society in general can do to discourage students from drinking and driving?

21

The Strange, True Story of Dracula
Richard M. Robinson

Preview

You are probably familiar with the famous villain Dracula. As the following reading reveals, this bad guy of novels and movies is based on a historical person. How much of the Dracula that thrills modern audiences is fact? How much is fiction? Was the real Dracula also a villain? The author answers these questions as he explains how such legendary figures can develop.

Words to Watch

vampires (2): dead bodies that come back to life and suck the blood of sleeping victims
patriot (3): a person who loves his country
resemblance (3): similarity
origin (3): beginning
accounts (6): reports
source material (11): original material that is used to study a historical subject
werewolves (11): people who have been changed into wolf-like creatures
sexual symbolism (13): images that represent sexuality

W*olves howl in the night. A young girl cries out, then is silenced.*   1
A rustling is heard, as of great bat-wings rising through the darkness. At

dawn the girl's body is found, dead but strangely peaceful, with a faint smile on her face. She is pale, drained of blood, with two tiny puncture-marks on her neck. Count Dracula has struck again!

That scene, or one like it, has been repeated in dozens of Hollywood movies through the years. Count Dracula, lord of the vampires°, is one of the most popular villains of horror stories. His evil deeds never fail to thrill us. Yet hardly anyone knows the true story of Count Dracula. Most of us imagine that he was simply made up, like Frankenstein's monster.   2

The popular Dracula of the movies—who rises from his coffin at night to drink blood—was indeed made up. This version of the Dracula story was first told by an author named Bram Stoker, who wrote the novel *Dracula* in 1897. But Bram Stoker's Dracula was based partly on old legends and partly on fact. There really was a Count Dracula, who lived hundreds of years ago in Transylvania. In his own lifetime he was famed for his cruelty. Yet to many people he was also a patriot° and a hero. The true adventures of the Count, and how he turned from a fifteenth-century warrior into a villain of Hollywood horror movies, are the strangest of all the tales of Dracula. The story of Dracula shows how a single seed of fact can grow into a tree of legend and fantasy with hardly any resemblance° to its historical origin°.   3

The story begins in Transylvania, which is today part of the country of Romania. In the fifteenth century, Transylvania lay between Hungary and the Ottoman Turkish Empire. The Hungarians and Turks fought over Transylvania for centuries. The wars were also wars of religion. The Hungarians and the Transylvanians were Christians, while the Ottoman Turks were Muslims. As is the case with many religious wars, the fighting went on with great cruelty on both sides.   4

One of the Christian leaders in the wars was Vlad III, Prince of Walachia. He was called Dracul, or "Dragon," for his fierceness in battle against the Turks. After he died, his place was taken by his son, also named Vlad. This Vlad called himself "Son of the Dragon"—or, in Romanian, Dracula.   5

Other people soon gave him a different name: Vlad Tepes, or Vlad the Impaler. Impaling was a cruel punishment of the time, in which the victim was dropped onto a sharp wooden stake and left there until he died. According to old accounts°, Vlad the Impaler, or Dracula, impaled his enemies by the hundreds. He committed other cruelties as well. Once, when an ambassador from a rich Italian city refused to take off his hat, Vlad had the hat nailed to the unfortunate man's head.   6

But Vlad was not known only for his cruelty. To the poor people of Walachia he was a hero. Most of Vlad's victims, after all, were rich   7 merchants and nobles who oppressed the poor. Vlad was also, like his father, a fierce fighter against the hated Turks. One Greek historian called him a "hero of Christianity" after he defeated the Turkish Sultan in 1461.

Vlad made the mistake, though, of impaling too many powerful   8
nobles. He had become Prince of Walachia in 1456. By 1462 he made so many enemies that the king of Hungary had him arrested and thrown into prison. Vlad remained in prison until 1476. Then the king—needing a good fighter against the Turks—released him and restored him to the princely throne of Walachia. After only a few months, though, Prince Vlad was assassinated. The historical Dracula was dead. (There is, however, no evidence that the killer drove a stake through Vlad's heart.)

The story of Vlad Dracula's cruelty continued to spread through   9
Europe, even after he died. The printing press was a new invention at this time, and it was used to print up "news sheets" about interesting and lurid events. These news sheets were the *National Enquirer* of that time. To the true stories of Dracula, many imaginary ones were added. But as the years went by, other stories became more popular, and the tales of Vlad Dracula gradually faded from public view.

Dracula remained forgotten for more than four hundred years. But   10
in the late 1700's and early 1800's, "gothic" stories—what we now call horror stories—became popular in England. Writers began to search for old legends and tales of superstition that could be used in horror novels. One writer, John-William Polidori, wrote a book called *The Vampire* in 1819, for a horror-story competition. (The novel *Frankenstein,* by Mary Shelley, was written for this same competition.)

Writers found that southeastern Europe—including Transylvania—   11
was a good area to find source material° for horror stories. The people of Transylvania had many superstitions, including ones about werewolves° and vampires. The fashion for gothic horror was still strong in the late 1800's, when Bram Stoker stumbled upon the legends of Vlad Dracula.

The original Dracula legends never made him out to be a vampire,   12
but that did not bother Stoker. When he found the tales of Dracula, he realized they were what writers call a "hook"—a bit of history or legend that could be the basis for a good story. In Stoker's Dracula story the true Prince Vlad, impaler and Turk-fighter, was hardly involved at all.

Instead, Stoker turned Dracula into a perfect gothic villain. In the   13
novel, Count Dracula was handsome in a frightening sort of way. At a time when polite people never talked about sex, Stoker filled his novel with sexual symbolism°—the fatal kiss, the bite, Dracula's power to enslave his victims through desire. When the novel was published, in 1897, it was an immediate hit. People loved it.

Today, more than ninety years later, people still love it. Yet the   14
Dracula we all know has hardly a thing to do with the real Prince Vlad
Dracula. Where the truth about Dracula didn't fit into a good story, it has
been ignored and forgotten. Where something that never happened would
make the story better (such as having Dracula drink blood), storytellers
haven't hesitated to add it to the story.

This is the way that most famous legends have grown. History's   15
"witches" and King Arthur were as different from their legends as Prince
Vlad was from the Dracula of the movies. Meanwhile, Vlad the Impaler,
the warrior who died over five hundred years ago, lives on—greatly
changed—in our imaginations. It will take more than a wooden stake
through the heart to kill the legend of Dracula.

READING COMPREHENSION QUESTIONS

Vocabulary in Context

1. The word *rustling* in "A rustling is heard, as of great bat wings
   rising through the darkness" (paragraph 1) means
   a. conversation.
   b. roaring sound.
   c. series of soft sounds.
   d. long silence.

2. The word *lurid* in "The story of Vlad Dracula's cruelty continued to
   spread. . . . The printing press was a new invention at this time, and
   it was used to print up 'news sheets' about interesting and lurid
   events. These news sheets were the *National Enquirer* of that time"
   (paragraph 9) means
   a. shocking.
   b. dull.
   c. peaceful.
   d. science.

Central Point and Main Ideas

3. Which sentence best expresses the central point of the selection?
   a. Southeastern Europe has inspired writers looking for ideas for
      horror stories such as *Dracula*.
   b. Like many famous legends, the legend of Dracula is mainly
      fiction, but with a historical basis.
   c. The original Dracula was known for impaling his enemies,
      mostly the rich and powerful.

    d. The story of Count Dracula was first told by Bram Stoker, who in 1897 wrote his novel about a human vampire.

4. Which sentence best expresses the main idea of paragraph 6?
    a. Impaling was a cruel punishment of the fifteenth century.
    b. Dracula was also called Vlad Tepes, or Vlad the Impaler.
    c. Among Dracula's many enemies was an ambassador from a rich Italian city.
    d. Dracula was known for his cruelty.

Supporting Details

5. The real Dracula was
    a. a hero to some.
    b. known for his cruelty.
    c. the son of a fierce soldier.
    d. all of the above.

6. _____ TRUE OR FALSE? The publishers of the news sheets of the 1400s were very careful to print only facts.

Transitions

7. The first word of paragraph 7 signals that its relationship to paragraph 6 is one of
    a. addition.
    b. contrast.
    c. time.
    d. cause and effect.

8. Paragraph 8 is organized according to a time order—a series of events presented in the order in which they happened. The author uses time transitions to help readers follow the sequence of events. In the blanks below, write two time transitions that are used in paragraph 8.

_____   _____

Inferences

9. We can infer that "The Strange, True Story of Dracula" was written mainly
    a. to inform readers about the creation of legends.
    b. to persuade readers not to believe everything they read.
    c. to entertain readers with comical stories about legends.
    d. none of the above.

10. The last sentence of this reading implies that the legend of Dracula
    a. is lifeless.
    b. will soon die.
    c. is dangerous.
    d. is likely to live on.

OUTLINING

Complete the following "outline" of the reading by filling in the two missing paragraph numbers.

1. Introduction *(Paragraphs 1 to 3)*

2. The Story of the Real Dracula *(Paragraphs 4 to ____)*

3. The Making of the Legendary Dracula *(Paragraphs ____ to 13)*

4. Conclusion *(Paragraphs 14–15)*

DISCUSSION QUESTIONS

1. Why do you think the legend of Dracula has remained so popular over the years? What fascination does the story hold for people?

2. The author writes that despite the fact that the historical Dracula was known for his cruel punishments, he was a hero to his own people. Why do you believe people are often willing to overlook cruelty in their heroes?

3. The author explains how a real person can develop into a legendary character. What famous people of our century could become legendary characters in the future, and why might they become legendary?

4. Robinson writes that exaggerated stories about Vlad Dracula appeared in news sheets printed after his death. He calls these sheets "the *National Enquirer* of that time." Why do you think people are so eager to read stories they know are not entirely true? Do you purchase *The National Enquirer* or other tabloid newspapers? If so, what about them do you find appealing?

22

Dealing with Colds
Cathie Cush

Preview

According to scientists, the common cold is not (despite its name) caused by cold weather. However, it is all too common. Some of us deal with a cold by ignoring it as much as possible. Many of us use one or more of the many remedies available on drugstore and supermarket shelves. Some of us turn to Mother's chicken soup and/or doses of vitamin C. And to prevent a cold, many of us follow Mother's advice to dress warmly and avoid the dampness. Which of these approaches are supported by science? This selection provides some interesting answers.

Words to Watch

informed (5): educated
muzzle (6): the part of an animal's head that sticks out, including the nose, mouth, and jaws
decongestant (11): a medicine or treatment that lessens congestion
secretions (12): materials that are produced by the body
supplements (16): things added (as to the diet) to strengthen

You're rundown and tired. Your throat feels as if you just   1
swallowed sandpaper. When the doctor speaks, her voice comes from very, very far away.

"I'm sorry," she says. "You have an infectious rhinovirus. I'm afraid   2
there is no cure."

You nod silently, accepting the news.   3

"The good news is," she continues, "the infection should run its   4
course in about ten days. In the meantime, get plenty of rest and take an
over-the-counter remedy to relieve that sore throat and congestion."

Sound simple? Of course. But in order to relieve your cold   5
symptoms, you'll need to make some informed° choices.

Since the earliest days of civilization, humans have tried to beat the   6
common cold. In the first century A.D., a Roman author suggested that
cold sufferers "kiss the hairy muzzle° of a mouse" to relieve their
symptoms. Colonial Americans had an even more unusual remedy. They
would place salted pork and onions inside a dirty sock and wear it around
their necks.

Today we are hardly closer to combating any of the two hundred   7
viruses that cause the common cold. Colds still strike old and young, men
and women, rich and poor. The cold victim may suffer from sore throat,
muscle aches, chills, fever, headache, stuffy nose, coughing, sneezing,
and congestion—or just one or two of these annoying symptoms. The
cold will probably last from seven to ten days, then go away, regardless
of whether the sufferer has taken modern medicines or spent a week
kissing mouse muzzles. But while your cold runs its course, you probably
can minimize your misery. Just do what the doctor ordered—take one of
the many cold remedies available on the drugstore shelf.

A century ago, traveling salesmen roamed the West selling magic   8
lotions supposed to cure everything from bellyache to baldness. While
today's cold remedies are far more effective than yesterday's phony cure-
alls, many are designed to relieve a very broad range of symptoms. Some
contain as many as five active ingredients. The challenge is finding the
remedy or remedies to control your symptoms without paying for
ingredients you don't need. These extra features raise the cost of the
medicine and can also produce unwanted side effects. In fact, in order to
get enough of one ingredient that is really useful to you, you may have to
overdose on another.

Antihistamines are a very good example of ingredients that are   9
generally unnecessary. These substances, which are active elements in
many cold remedies, are very effective against the runny nose, itching
and sneezing caused by an allergy. Several tests, however, have shown
that antihistamines do little to relieve cold symptoms. In addition,
antihistamines frequently cause drowsiness. At best, this drowsiness can
be a nuisance; at worst, it can be dangerous for those who have to drive
or operate heavy machinery.

Most of the other ingredients usually found in cold remedies are   10
effective against cold symptoms. But you may not need all of those

ingredients at the same time.

For example, if a stuffy nose is your only complaint, all you may need is a decongestant° to shrink swollen tissues and help you breathe freely. Then the only decision you have to make is whether to use a spray or drops or swallow a tablet or capsule. Unfortunately, none of these options is without a drawback. Sprays or drops may be the best choice. They act quickly, taking effect in as little as five minutes. However, their continued use can lead to "rebound congestion." The drops and sprays can irritate sensitive nasal passages, eventually causing more swelling instead of relieving it. Decongestant tablets or capsules won't produce rebound congestion, but they may take as long as an hour to work. They're also likely to cause sleeplessness and dry mouth. Most importantly, because these oral products can increase blood pressure even in people with low blood pressure, they are potentially dangerous for everyone.

To be properly treated, a cough needs to be identified as being either productive or nonproductive. A productive cough—one that brings up material from your airways and lungs—is useful in helping you recover, so you should encourage the clearance of material from your lungs by "loosening up" the mucus. To do this, use an expectorant, which thins secretions° so that they can be removed more easily by coughing. Although there are many over-the-counter cough remedies containing expectorants, the best expectorant is water, especially in warm liquids such as soup. Moistening the air with a humidifier will also help.

A nonproductive cough—a dry cough bringing up no mucus—can be treated with a suppressant, one of several medications that quiet the urge to cough. One of these is the narcotic codeine, which is available in many states only by prescription. It can also cause a variety of side effects, including lightheadedness, nausea, and vomiting. Another suppressant is an antihistamine that causes drowsiness. The safest and most effective suppressant is an ingredient called dextromethorphan, which is found by itself and in combination with other ingredients in syrups and lozenges. Codeine, antihistamines and dextromethorphan work directly on the brain. Medicated cough drops can help calm the need to cough by soothing or numbing the throat with menthol or camphor. Some cough syrups contain both an expectorant and a suppressant. But it's silly to pay for both because if you need one, you don't need the other.

Like a cough, a sore throat can be treated from the brain's pain center, using aspirin. Or it can be treated directly, with throat lozenges or sprays that numb the irritated area. Taking aspirin in a spray or chewing gum, however, doesn't seem to do the trick. Plain old aspirin tablets do help ease sore throats as well as the other aches and pains that often come with colds. If aspirin's all you need, there's no reason to pay for any other ingredients.

Whatever you take, it pays to read labels and warnings on cold   15
remedies and to stay within recommended doses. If you're not sure what to take, ask your druggist or doctor.

Finally, the best way to "treat" a cold is to avoid getting one.   16
Surprisingly, research shows that dampness and cold weather have nothing to do with colds. Instead, we get them through direct contact with cold viruses—usually by touching people who are carrying these germs. Colds are more common in winter because people are indoors and closer together. One way to avoid colds, then, is to wash your hands often when you are near someone with a cold. Several studies indicate that large doses of vitamin C might also prevent a cold (and limit the length and severity of a cold once it's caught). So another means of avoiding colds is to take daily supplements° of 500 to 1000 milligrams of vitamin C. Clearly, prevention is easier and less expensive than catching a cold, and it sure beats trying to kiss a mouse's whiskers.

READING COMPREHENSION QUESTIONS

Vocabulary in Context

1. The word *minimize* in "while your cold runs its course, you probably can minimize your misery . . . take one of the many cold remedies available" (paragraph 7) means
   a. lessen.
   b. learn from.
   c. experience.
   d. increase.

2. The word *options* in "Then the only decision you have to make is whether to use a spray or drops or swallow a tablet or capsule. Unfortunately, none of these options is without a drawback" (paragraph 11) means
   a. sprays.
   b. illnesses.
   c. choices.
   d. complaints.

Central Point and Main Ideas

3. Which sentence best expresses the central point of the selection?
   a. Some cold medicines have five active ingredients.
   b. There are ways to relieve and avoid colds.

c. There have been some unusual attempts to cure the common cold.

d. There is no cure for the common cold.

4. Which sentence best expresses the main idea of paragraph 9?

 a. Antihistamines are an example of unnecessary and harmful ingredients in cold medicines.

 b. Medicines can sometimes cause drowsiness.

 c. Antihistamines are very effective against the runny rose, itching and sneezing caused by an allergy.

 d. Researchers have done a number of tests to determine the effectiveness of antihistamines.

5. Which sentence best expresses the main idea of paragraphs 12–13?

 a. A productive cough is one that brings up material from the airways and lungs.

 b. A nonproductive cough can be treated with a suppressant.

 c. There are two types of coughs—productive and nonproductive.

 d. Productive and nonproductive coughs are treated differently.

Supporting Details

6. Colds are caused by

 a. viruses.

 b. cold weather.

 c. dampness.

 d. wind.

7. Warm soup acts as an

 a. antihistamine.

 b. expectorant.

 c. suppressant.

 d. decongestant.

Transitions

8. The sentence below expresses a relationship of

 a. addition.

 b. contrast.

 c. illustration.

 d. cause and effect.

 Colds are more common in winter because people are indoors and closer together. (Paragraph 16)

Inferences

    9. From paragraph 7 we can infer that
      a. what we call a cold is really one of many related infections.
      b. all colds are the same.
      c. we are likely to discover a cure for the common cold soon.
      d. women and men have very different experiences with colds.

  10. The author recommends washing "your hands often when you are near someone with a cold" because
      a. you might infect that person with some other sickness.
      b. cleanliness is a good habit to get into.
      c. soap fights certain cold symptoms.
      d. washing will get rid of any cold viruses on your hands.

OUTLINING

Complete the following outline by filling in the missing major and minor details.

Central point: You can relieve and avoid colds.

  A. You can't cure a cold, but you can relieve it.
    1. There have been ineffective remedies used throughout history.
    2. Today's remedies are more effective, but may contain ingredients you don't need.
      a. Many cold remedies include antihistamines, which are useful for fighting allergy symptoms, not colds.
      b. Many cold remedies include more ingredients than you need, so choose remedies to suit your symptoms.
        1) Different types of decongestants have advantages and disadvantages.
          a) Sprays or drops act quickly but can lead to rebound congestion.
          b) _____
          c) All decongestants can increase blood pressure.
        2) Choose a cough medicine that suits your cough.
          a) Use an expectorant for productive coughs.
          b) _____

3) Treat a sore throat with aspirin, throat lozenges or sprays.

4) Also use aspirin to ease the other aches and pains of a cold.

B. There are two ways to avoid catching a cold.

1. _____

2. _____

DISCUSSION QUESTIONS

1. How do you usually care for a cold? Will you try anything new in the future as a result of reading this article?

2. Since antihistamines have been shown to do little to relieve colds, why do you think drugmakers add them to cold remedies?

3. The author mentions a couple of very unusual ways people have tried to fight colds. Have you heard of any other unusual methods subscribed to by family members or friends? Do you have any pet theories of your own? What are they?

4. This article explains how to avoid catching a cold, but what can someone who already has a cold do to help keep others from catching it?

23

Good People Don't Make Headlines
Claude Lewis

Preview

"One bad apple," the old saying goes, "can spoil the whole bunch." Unfortunately, we often let a handful of criminals spoil the way we see an entire race. African-Americans, in particular, often are victims of this way of thinking. In this selection, newspaper columnist Claude Lewis, an African-American, introduces us to a few people who might open our eyes.

Words to Watch

> *malingerers* (2): people who avoid work by pretending to be unable to work
> *jaundiced* (5): prejudiced
> *assailed* (5): attacked with criticism
> *exclusive* (5): leaving out all others (except the select group)
> *domain* (5): field of activity
> *capacity* (11): ability
> *devotion* (12): love and loyalty

It's nobody's fault, I suppose, but it bothers me that the reputations of most groups are made by those who do ill rather than by those who do good.

Nearly every time you hear about welfare, for example, images of   2
blacks come to mind because the rumor is that most people on welfare
are black malingerers°, people who contribute little and who are "drains
on society," as the saying goes.

Many of the people responsible for big-city crime are blacks; no   3
question about that. But thousands of crimes are committed every day by
others. We don't hear very much about them, or not in the same way.

Few weeks pass without some reader sending me—as some   4
unsigned writer did on Tuesday—newspaper clippings of blacks
responsible for bank holdups, violent attacks, theft, drug abuse, child
abuse and a lot more.

I am convinced these jaundiced° historians, who usually don't have   5
the courage to sign their names, also know that while too many blacks
live outside the law, so, too, do millions of other Americans. Too many
other Americans have babies outside of marriage, or use abortions as a
birth control technique, or engage in illegal activities. Yet I am regularly
assailed° by people who would have me believe differently. None of
these negative experiences are the exclusive° domain° of blacks.

I got to thinking about this recently when a friend, Frank Donahue,   6
who is a talented *Inquirer* librarian, asked me whether I had seen the
obituary of decorated Philadelphia police officer Douglas Mallory, who
at 39 died of a heart attack.

Inquirer staff writer Donna St. George did a fine job on Thursday in   7
telling us about Mallory. She did it by quoting the officer's friends and
family. Vickilynn, his wife, summed up her husband's life in a stunningly
simple way.

As committed as he was to the job, Mallory found his greatest   8
pleasures in family life, his wife told St. George.

"He loved his girls," his wife said. "He would get up in the morning   9
and help me get their lunches together. He would drive them to school
every day. He was a good father to them, someone they could count on.
He would laugh with them, play with them. He had it all for them and
was there when they needed him.

"He was an outstanding father to them, and I'm just glad I had the   10
chance to be married to him," she said in a way that would have made her
late husband very proud.

I suspect that what made Mallory so outstanding is that he was so   11
terribly ordinary in the very best sense of the word. What made him so
valuable was his capacity° for caring, an attribute that most people
possess, though it often remains hidden.

There are thousands of Americans, both black and white, who are   12
heroes and heroines in their homes. But so often, we overlook their hard

work and strong devotion°. Too often we don't realize that without the contributions of such people, all of society would be the poorer.

Another individual whom St. George wrote about in Thursday's obituary section was Roberta Pride, who died in her home this week after teaching school for twenty-nine years. Pride, who taught many years in West and North Philadelphia, refused to give up on her students. Instead, she inspired many of them to do their best, despite the fact that many had problems no youngster should ever know. 13

Her husband, Theodore, is wise enough to realize that though she loved him dearly, "she worshiped the ground" their sons walked on. That's precisely how passionate parents should love their children. 14

The point I'm struggling to make is a simple one: Most people are decent, hardworking, loving, even though the headlines of our society are too often made by those who live outside the law, who never learned that the real joy in life is in helping, loving, giving and assisting others who might otherwise wind up on the junk heap of humanity. 15

Arlene M. B. Rexon also was among the many Americans who died last week. She served her community of Haddonfield with a nearly fierce devotion. She worked with so many civic and religious organizations there's not space here to list them. And what makes her so very special is that there are so many others who go through life, almost unnoticed, who are also taken for granted. 16

Every once in a while, all of us ought to look past the noisy headline makers to those who quietly perform good works that often go unnoticed. 17

There are millions of people who deserved to be called "special." Officer Mallory and Roberta Pride, who were black, were among them. They were both a credit to their race. So was Arlene M. B. Rexon, a 62-year-old white woman, a credit to her race. But the race I'm talking about in all three instances is the *human* race. 18

READING COMPREHENSION QUESTIONS

Vocabulary in Context

1. The words *engage in* in "Too many other Americans have babies outside of marriage or . . . engage in illegal activities" (paragraph 5) mean
    a. warn about.
    b. take part in.
    c. disapprove of.
    d. are afraid of.

2. The word *attribute* in "What made him so valuable was his capacity for caring, an attribute that most people possess, though it often remains hidden" (paragraph 11) means
   a. answer.
   b. award.
   c. quality.
   d. opinion.

Central Point and Main Ideas

3. Which sentence best expresses the central point of the selection?
   a. Our society needs more people like the police officer, teacher, and community volunteer described in the article.
   b. Although the news media connect blacks with social problems, most blacks are like people everywhere: decent, hardworking, and loving.
   c. Obituaries reveal what a person was really like.
   d. The police, teachers, and volunteers include millions of hardworking, loving people.

4. Which sentence best expresses the main idea of paragraph 16?
   a. Arlene Rexon was one of the many good people who do not get much recognition.
   b. Arlene M. B. Rexon also died last week.
   c. There are many people who go through life almost unnoticed.
   d. Like many others, Arlene Rexon was taken for granted.

Supporting Details

5. The author feels that
   a. headlines are often untrue.
   b. blacks rarely commit crimes.
   c. whites rarely commit crimes.
   d. many ordinary people of all races are special.

6. Officer Mallory, according to the article and his wife,
   a. was decorated.
   b. died of a heart attack.
   c. was a loving family man.
   d. all of the above.

Transitions

7. The relationship between the two sentences below is one of
   a. contrast.
   b. time.

    c. illustration.

    d. cause and effect.

> Many of the people responsible for big-city crime are black; no question about that. But thousands of crimes are committed every day by others. (Paragraph 3)

8. This article is largely organized as a list of items—a list of examples of ordinary people who are special. The last two people listed are introduced with the addition transitions

    a. *another, also.*

    b. *second, next.*

    c. *in addition, moreover.*

    d. *furthermore, last of all.*

Inferences

9. The author suggests that the real joy in life comes from

    a. teaching troubled young people.

    b. helping and loving others.

    c. working for civic and religious organizations.

    d. being recognized in the headlines for our achievements.

10. In the last paragraph of his essay, the author implies that

    a. people must compete against each other to be called special.

    b. there are more good black people than good white people.

    c. we should not always be labeling people by race.

    d. Arlene M. B. Rexon was more special than Roberta Pride.

SUMMARIZING

Circle the letter of the best summary of "Good People Don't Make Headlines."

    a. Three ordinary people described in obituaries are examples of the many ordinary people who live decent, hardworking, and loving lives. Douglas Mallory, who died at 39 of a heart attack, was a decorated police officer who was a devoted father. Roberta Pride was a long-term teacher who inspired troubled young people to do their best. She was a passionate parent to her own children. Arlene M. B. Rexon served her community by working with many civic and religious organizations.

b. The author regrets that the reputations of most groups are made by those who do ill rather than by those who do good. He is tired of having welfare and big-city crime, for example, always associated with African-Americans. He points out that many other people also engage in such negative behavior. Having babies outside of marriage and using abortions for birth control are not only done by black people. Unfortunately, the author is constantly attacked by those who criticize only African-American offenders.

c. Lewis feels that people too often associate particular problems only with certain groups, such as African-Americans, because they appear in the news. Criminal and other negative behaviors are engaged in by many others as well. Furthermore, he notes, most people of all races are decent, hardworking and loving, but they don't get the media attention that the lawbreakers get. Examples are three ordinary people described in recent obituaries: a decorated police officer who was a loving family man, a dedicated mother and teacher, and a woman devoted to civic and religious organizations.

DISCUSSION QUESTIONS

1. Why does Lewis include Roberta Pride and Arlene M. B. Rexon in his list of heroes and heroines? In what way were these women like Officer Mallory?

2. Lewis suspects that Officer Mallory was "so outstanding" because "he was so terribly ordinary in the very best sense of the word." What do you think Lewis means by this statement?

3. Lewis used people in recent obituaries to illustrate his point that there are many special people who "quietly perform good works that often go unnoticed." If you had written the essay, what people from your own life could you have used as examples? What about those people makes them special?

4. Lewis begins his essay by writing: "It's nobody's fault, I suppose, but it bothers me that the reputations of most groups are made by those who do ill rather than by those who do good." Do you agree that people associate groups with criminals and others "who do ill" that show up in the news? If so, what can be done to counteract this tendency? And do you agree that it's nobody's fault?

24

Keys to
College Success
Sheila Akers

Preview

Some students feel that the ability to do well in school is a natural gift. They don't realize that ability is in large part learned. If you haven't yet picked up ways to succeed in college, or if you've forgotten what you once knew, this article can help. The four steps described here can mean the difference between wasting time and making the most of it.

Words to Watch

vague (2): unclear
incredibly (8): unbelievably
initiative (8): sense of responsibility for taking action
overwhelming (8): too much to handle
floundering (9): struggling
bristle (12): are thickly filled
intimidating (17): threatening

Every year, college catches numerous freshmen by surprise. They simply didn't realize how much more difficult college can be than high school. They also may not have understood that college teachers would treat them as responsible adults. First-year students often learn too late that instructors will not remind them when assignments are due or tests are given. Some freshmen are so bowled over by the challenges of

1

college that they give up before learning all is not hopeless. However, any student who really wants to can learn the keys to college success: control your time, get off to a strong start, apply study skills, and learn to concentrate.

CONTROL YOUR TIME

Jerry had a typically busy college schedule. He was taking five classes, as well as working in the school library. He liked to play basketball at least one night a week, and a date or party usually occupied another evening. Five weeks into the semester, Jerry realized he was in serious trouble. He was behind in his reading in every class. A major mid-term paper was due soon, and he had only a vague° idea what his topic would be. Nevertheless, he felt that he was constantly studying. Other people he knew had schedules as busy as his, and yet they were keeping up. What was wrong?

Jerry's sense that he was "always studying" came from the fact that he generally carried his books around with him. And, in fact, he did glance at them often. But those frequent few minutes of reading were sandwiched between a hundred other tasks: eating lunch, talking with friends, making phone calls. Rarely did Jerry sit down with the specific intention of studying a particular topic for a planned period of time. The hours, days, and weeks were slipping away, leaving Jerry with very little to show for them.

Jerry needed some education in the first key to succeeding in college: taking control of your time. This means *knowing* what you have to do and *planning* ahead for classes, projects, and tests. One important means of time control is using a large monthly calendar to give you an "at-a-glance" view of due dates and other special events. Check with your calendar often. It can keep you from losing track of time and being surprised by how soon you must hand in your term paper or take a biology midterm. Another means of time control is making up a weekly study schedule. In other words, plan specific blocks of time during your week when you will study. In making a weekly schedule, first fill in the hours when you have unbreakable commitments to class time, work time, and so on. Then look for chunks of free time—at least one hour long— that you can use for studying. A study schedule can help you make efficient use of your time by capturing those free hours that would otherwise drift away, leaving you wondering why you accomplished so little. A final method of time control is a "to-do" list. On a "to-do" list, you jot down the goals you want to accomplish during the day, or over the next several days. Such a list might contain reminders of everything

2

3

4

from buying a CD to reading Chapter 3 of your psychology text. A "to-do" list brings together all the stray "I have to. . ." ideas that cross your mind each day. Crossing items off a "to-do" list can give you a real feeling of satisfaction. You also have the pleasant sensation that you are controlling your tasks and responsibilities, not the other way around.

GET OFF TO A STRONG START

Marissa walked empty-handed into her first American history class.   5
She remembered that in high school nothing ever happened on the first day of class. To her surprise, the professor began a lecture immediately. She borrowed a pen and paper from a classmate to take notes, but sat helplessly as the prof directed students to look at a map in the textbook.

At the end of the hour, the professor handed out a schedule of due   6
dates for assignments. Marissa saw with relief that the major term paper was not due until the day before Christmas vacation. On a beautiful late-summer day, that seemed unimaginably far away.

The week after Thanksgiving, Marissa became uneasily aware that   7
some of her classmates were handing in their history term papers. She realized that she had a major research project ahead of her, not to mention other exams to study for. Suddenly worried, she spent most of the next week in the library, trying to pull together the resources she needed to begin the paper. She found that the topic she had chosen was a popular one. Most materials relating to it had already been checked out. With a week and a half to go, Marissa not only hadn't finished her term paper—she didn't even know what it would be about.

Marissa was ending the term as she began it: unprepared. She had   8
never learned a second key to college success: making a strong start at the beginning of each new semester. Wasting time at the start of the term and then having to play "catch-up" is a sure route to failure in college. Making a strong start means being disciplined enough to study, read, and initiate time-control measures even though "It's only the first week" or "I don't have a test for three weeks." You have to go even to those first classes ready to take notes. You should buy your books right away, despite the long line at the bookstore. In addition, you should find out the names and phone numbers of one or two people in each class so you can borrow their notes if you miss class. Another part of making a strong start is giving some thought to those end-of-the-semester papers and projects, even if December or May seems incredibly° far away. It takes additional energy to do some early research in the library, and it takes some initiative° to discuss a term paper idea early on with a professor, but getting off to a quick start has important benefits. You space out your

work, for one thing, so that you don't face a marathon week of putting together a project or paper. And you eliminate the psychological pressure you feel when you put off tasks until the job seems overwhelming°.

APPLY STUDY SKILLS

Enrique had always done pretty well in high school. Most of his classes there had emphasized class discussions, and he learned easily by that method. Most of his high school exams had been true-or-false or multiple-choice types, and he had performed well on them. He was unhappily surprised, then, to find himself floundering° in college. 9

His professors lectured at what seemed to Enrique a terrific pace. He tried to copy down everything they said, but he found it impossible to both listen and write at the same time. His college courses required a lot of reading—difficult reading. Faced with page after page of solid type, with rarely a picture or photograph for variety, Enrique felt overwhelmed. He found himself staring for minutes at the same paragraph, stymied by words he didn't understand. He realized he was turning pages automatically, but not really absorbing what he was reading. As he looked ahead to the endless pages that made up a textbook chapter, he wondered how he would ever plow through them. 10

College examinations were more difficult than Enrique had expected, too. He couldn't do well merely by remembering facts accurately. Instead, he was asked to write long essays to show that he really understood the material the class had covered. By mid-term, Enrique was terribly discouraged. He had almost concluded that he just didn't have what it took to do well in college. 11

Enrique's problem was not a lack of intelligence. It was that he didn't know about the third key to success in college. That key is learning and using study skills. Study skills include knowing how to take class notes; how to read texts skillfully by previewing, marking, and taking notes on them; and how to study for objective or essay exams. Without these essential skills, the time you spend attending class and studying may be of little help in earning a good grade. Just as you have to learn new skills on a job, you have to learn the skills needed to do well in college. Some students know these skills by the time they arrive on a college campus—they may have been taught them in high school or "picked them up" on their own. Other students slide by in high school without knowing these skills and, because they have a high-school diploma, feel they are ready for college. They aren't. College lectures cover more information, and with more sophistication, than high school lectures. College textbooks are harder to read; they bristle° with dozens 12 of new terms and present difficult theories and concepts. College tests are tougher, and they are graded according to higher standards. Only a firm grasp of study skills will enable you to survive, and succeed, in this setting. If you feel that your study skills are weak, get help immediately. Most colleges have study skills workshops or courses, so take advantage of them. Campus learning or tutoring centers often have guides to college study skills free for the asking. And campus bookstores carry many books that can help you learn and practice essential study and reading skills.

LEARN TO CONCENTRATE

Laura was delighted with her off-campus apartment. She and her roommates had furnished it, she thought, with everything they could ever need. They had a stereo, several radios, and a color TV. In the evenings the girls loved to bring their books into the comfortable living room and study together as they listened to music and chatted. Friends would often drop in, and the roommates would make popcorn or nachos for their guests before getting back to the books. Often the group would end up going out together before the evening ended. 13

Laura felt her life was almost ideal—except for her grades. She was shocked by her first set of marks after moving into the apartment. Her performance had slipped in every single class. "What's happened to you?" one favorite professor asked Laura in surprise. 14

What had happened was that Laura, in her enthusiasm over living independently with friends, had forgotten the final key to college success: the art of concentration. 15

This skill seems to get more difficult every year. Television rarely challenges its viewers to watch anything that requires concentration or to give a subject more than ten minutes' worth of attention at a time. And much of the reading we do in daily life requires less concentration than ever. Newspapers specialize in brief stories with limited vocabularies and many color pictures. Books on the best-seller list are filled with cartoons, jokes, and diagrams of exercise techniques. Switching from this kind of mental fluff to the intense concentration needed to study college material is indeed a challenge. 16

If your ability to concentrate is "flabby," there are several steps that will get you into shape. First, have a positive attitude toward studying. No matter how unattractive your task seems, think of it as a means to a goal that is important to you—getting a college degree. Next, keep yourself in good physical shape. Exhaustion or illness effectively shuts down your ability to concentrate. Also, create a good study environment. Have a place in your dorm room, apartment, or house where you keep all 17 your class-related materials and where you have the basics for a productive study session: a good light, paper, pens, a typewriter, a calculator, and so on. You will save yourself time if your setting is well-equipped, and your concentration will not be interrupted because you have to find a note pad. Before you begin to study, jot down a brief list of goals for the study session. For example, you might write: "(1) Read Chapter 10 in soc., (2) Memorize definitions for chemistry, (3) Rough draft of English essay." Having specific, doable goals can make the session less intimidating°. Finally, control your concentration by noticing when your mind wanders and making the conscious effort needed to pull it back. This can be done as simply as making a check mark with a pencil whenever you find your mind losing concentration. The deliberate effort to begin concentrating again should strengthen your ability and make concentration for longer periods possible.

Time control, a strong start at the beginning of the semester, study   18
skills, and concentration are the four keys to success in school. If you make the effort to learn and use these keys, you will open the door to the kind of life you want.

READING COMPREHENSION QUESTIONS

Vocabulary in Context

1. The word *initiate* in "Making a strong start means being disciplined enough to study, read, and initiate time-control measures even though 'It's only the first week'" (paragraph 8) means
   a. forget.
   b. scatter.
   c. notice.
   d. begin.

2. The word *stymied* in "He found himself staring for minutes at the same paragraph, stymied by words he didn't understand" (paragraph 10) means
   a. encouraged.
   b. blocked.
   c. considered.
   d. interested.

Central Point and Main Ideas

3. The author expresses her central point in
   a. the first sentence of the reading.
   b. the last sentence of paragraph 1.

    c. the first sentence of paragraph 18.

    d. both *b* and *c*.

4. Which statement best expresses the main idea of paragraph 12?

    a. To do well in college, students need to brush up on, or learn, study skills.

    b. Some students who were successful in high school struggle in college.

    c. College textbooks are more difficult to read than high school textbooks.

    d. Most colleges have tutoring centers.

5. Which statement best expresses the main idea of paragraph 16?

    a. Newspapers often print only brief stories with limited vocabularies.

    b. Television and popular reading have hurt many students' ability to concentrate.

    c. College textbooks often have lengthy, complicated passages that require deep concentration.

    d. Watching television does not require deep concentration.

Supporting Details

6. According to the author,

    a. students should include only school work on "to-do" lists.

    b. "to-do" lists will help students remember when long-term projects are due.

    c. items on a "to-do" list should never be crossed out.

    d. "to-do" lists help students to achieve daily goals.

7. The author states that it can be easier to concentrate

    a. when given a large volume of work.

    b. close to the end of the semester.

    c. when work is broken up into specific, doable goals.

    d. when slightly tired.

Transitions

8. Paragraph 4 lists three ways to take control of your time. The three methods are introduced with the addition transitions

    a. *one, another, final.*

    b. *first, second, third.*

    c. *first of all, also, finally.*

    d. *one, in addition, last of all.*

9. Paragraph 17 lists several steps to take to improve concentration. Most of those steps are introduced with an addition transition. Write two of those transitions in the blanks below.

_____ _____

Inferences

10. Akers implies that students who get off to a strong start at the beginning of the semester
    a. experience intense pressure as the semester continues.
    b. have difficulty working at a high level for the rest of the semester.
    c. don't get overwhelmed by the workload.
    d. often forget about end-of-the-semester papers and projects.

OUTLINING

Fill in the points that are missing in the following outline based on "Keys to College Success." (The numbers of the paragraphs covered by the outline are included.)

Central point: Students can do well in college by learning the four keys to college success.

1. Control your time. *(Paragraph 4)*

   a. Mark a large monthly calendar with due dates.

   b. _____

   c. Use "to-do" lists.

2. _____

   _____ *(Paragraph 8)*

   a. Study, read and begin time-control measures from the beginning of the semester.

   b. Be ready to take notes even at the first class.

   c. Buy your books right away.

   d. Find out the names of one or two students in each class so you can borrow their notes if you miss class.

   e. Begin working on end-of-semester projects early.

3. Use good study skills, and get help in strengthening your skills if necessary. *(Paragraph 12)*

   a. Certain skills are vital to college success.

     1) College students must know how to take class notes.

     2) College students must know how to read texts skillfully.

     3) College students must know how to study for exams.

   b. There are ways for students to learn the vital study skills.

     1) Colleges offer study skills workshops or courses.

     2) Free guides to college study skills are often available on campus.

     3) Campus bookstores carry helpful books on study and reading skills.

4. Concentrate effectively. *(Paragraph 17)*

   a. _____

   b. Stay in good physical shape.

   c. Create a good study environment.

   d. Before each study session, write down a short list of goals for that session.

   e. _____

DISCUSSION QUESTIONS

1. Could your studying benefit from time-control measures? What steps do you already take to manage your time? When do you do most of your studying? Are there any hours that you waste because they fall between work or class time?

2. How have you worked on your study skills? For example, what note-taking methods have you developed, and how do you work on your vocabulary? What services does your school offer to help students improve their study skills?

3. Where do you usually study, and what would Akers feel are the advantages and disadvantages of that place? If your study environment leaves something to be desired, how might you improve or replace it?

4. The author claims that television has hurt many people's ability to concentrate. How does television try to keep the viewer's attention? Do you think watching television has affected your ability to concentrate? If you think it has, what could you do about it?

25

The Battle for My Body
Richard Rhodes

Preview

What can be done to protect children from abusive parents? You may ask this question as you read the following selection. It is taken from a book that Richard Rhodes has written about his boyhood. Rhodes describes with chilling detail the way that his father and stepmother performed as parents. Despite the challenging vocabulary, you'll probably feel compelled to keep reading.

Words to Watch

conflated (1): mentally combined two events
bewildering (1): greatly confusing
debut (1): appearance
sadistically (4): done to get pleasure from causing pain
detonate (4): cause to explode
grossly (4): very badly
disproportionate (4): out of proportion
provocation (4): annoyance
coercive (5): forcing
intermittent (5): off-and-on
intact (5): undamaged
abrasions (5): scrapes
indignation (5): resentment
demarcated (5): marked the limits of

undermining (6): weakening
physiology (6): bodily processes
radically (6): extremely
manipulating (6): controlling
assault (6): attack
induce (8): cause
simultaneously (10): at the same time
hydraulic (10): of fluids
improvised (13): made up at that moment
omniscient (15): all-knowing
receptacle (17): container
asserting (17): making it known
fiat (17): command
devising (17): inventing
restraint (18): holding back
stealthily (18): secretly
patent (18): out in the open

My father knew the woman who became my stepmother before we 1
began boarding at her house. One evening in the winter of 1947 Dad took
us to a Kansas City road-show production of the Grand Ole Opry, the first
live entertainment I remember from childhood, and it seems to me she
joined us for the show, sitting on the other side of Dad, turning his head.
It may be that I've conflated° her bewildering° debut° with the honky-
tonk dazzle of the Opry, with lights and flash and crowd. Since I didn't
know Dad had a private life, I didn't know where this small, heavily
perfumed, tough-looking woman had come from; like the road show, she
might have been unloaded from a truck. It was obvious that he wanted my
older brother, Stanley, and me to like her. I don't think we did. After nine
years of boardinghouses we had sensitive bullshit detectors, and her voice
was southern and honeyed, cunning, edged with menace.

According to my school records, we moved into her house in 2
February 1947. But memory keeps time differently from school records. I
have trouble believing that all that Stanley and I lived through during our
stepmother years occupied only twenty-eight months of our lives, until
we were removed by the Jackson County juvenile court to the relative
safety of the Andrew Drumm Institute for Boys in July 1949.

My stepmother was born in Texas, in 1899, which means she was 3
forty-eight years old in 1947. She was a short woman with white skin, a
full head of dark hair, large breasts. She used makeup heavily, powder
over a pancake base, a pucker of red lipstick, thick mascara if not false
eyelashes, and her small, usually open-toed shoes had stilt heels and

platform soles to boost her height. None of this matters particularly, except that she was evidently a mantrap, someone who bushwhacked husbands and cleaned them out. She'd been married four or five times before. Dad became her plow horse; she worked him for more than fifteen years, until he died of cancer of the stomach in 1965. Stan thinks she married once more after that.

We never did call her Mother, nor did she ever even remotely   4
deserve the name. To tame Stanley and me, to make us new men, she tinkered sadistically° with control worked out on the surface and the interior of our bodies. She lived by rigid systems of rules; to transgress even the least of those rules might detonate° an outburst of rage that even to a ten-year-old seemed grossly° disproportionate° to the provocation°. Since we were children, and had few rights in the first place, since our father was too cowardly to defend us from brutalization, everything became possible for her.

Slapping us, kicking us, bashing our heads with a broom handle or a   5
mop or the stiletto heel of a shoe, slashing our backs and the backs of our legs with the buckle of a belt, our stepmother exerted one kind of control over us, battery that was immediately coercive° but intermittent° and limited in effect. We cowered, cringed, screamed, wrapped our heads protectively in our arms, danced the belt-buckle tango, but out of sight and reach we recovered our boundaries more or less intact°. The bodily memory of the blows, the heat of the abrasions°, the caution of pain, the indignation°, and the smoldering rage only demarcated° those boundaries more sharply.

More effective control required undermining° our boundaries from   6
within. As diseases do, our stepmother sought to harness our physiology° to her own ends. Compelling us to eat food we didn't like—cayenne gravy, mint jelly, moldy bread—is hardly more coercion than most parents impose, not that custom justifies it. Our stepmother tinkered more radically° with manipulating° what we took into our bodies and what we expelled. The techniques she developed led eventually to a full-scale assault°.

At ten years of age I no longer wet the bed, but I needed the toilet at   7
night. The only bathroom in the house opened directly inside her bedroom door. I used it whenever I had to, sometimes more than once a night, until she announced one day in a fury that I was getting up at night unnecessarily and disturbing her sleep. I should make sure I relieved myself before I went to bed, she told me, because from then on I was forbidden to use the bathroom at night. "I married your *father*, not you," she added mysteriously.

Telling someone not to do something to induce° them to do it is a   8
powerful form of suggestion. Dutifully, I went to the bathroom just
before climbing to my upper bunk on the north wall of the sleeping
porch, but as soon as Stanley turned out the lights and we settled down to
sleep I felt my bladder fill. I lay awake then for hours. I tried to redirect
my thoughts, tell myself stories, recite numbers, count sheep. I clamped
my sphincters until they cramped and burned. Lying on my back, hurting
and urgent, I cried silently to the ceiling low overhead, tears running
down my face without consolation, only reminding me of the other flow
of body fluid that my stepmother had blocked. When clamping my
sphincters no longer worked I pinched my penis to red pain.

Sometimes I fell asleep that way and slept through. Once or twice I   9
wet the bed. That villainy erupted in such monstrous humiliation that I
learned not to repeat it. Thereafter I added struggling to stay awake to
struggling to retain my urine.

One desperate night I decided to urinate out the window. There were   10
two windows in the porch back wall. They opened ten feet above the
yard. I waited until I was sure Stanley was solidly asleep, climbed down
my ladder, and slipped to the nearer window. Two springloaded pins had
to be pulled and held out simultaneously° to open it. That wasn't easy to
coordinate, especially since I was bent over with cramping. The window
fit its frame badly. It jammed and squeaked going up. I forced it up six
inches and then a foot, high enough, stood on tiptoe, my little penis barely
reaching over the sill, and let go. I'd hoped the hydraulic° pressure would
be sufficient to drive the stream of urine through the screen, missing the
ledge and the frame, but the angle was bad. I dribbled. My urine ran down
the ledge and out under the screen frame. That meant it would leave a
telltale stain down the outside wall. I tried forcing the stream into a higher
arc and managed to pulse it in splashes through the screen. It sprayed out
into the night air below a blank silver moon.

I'd barely begun when I heard noise—the bedroom door, footsteps   11
in the dining room, the kitchen door swinging. I clamped off the flow in a
panic—it was hard to stop—popped my dripping penis back into my
pajamas, warm urine running down my leg, and stood at the window
waiting. I prayed to God it wasn't my stepmother.

Dad stepped through the doorway, half-awake. "What's going on?"   12
he said softly.

"It was stuffy in here," I improvised°. "I opened the window to get   13
some air."

"You don't want to disturb your Aunt Anne," he told me, giving my   14
stepmother the name we were supposed to call her. "Better close that
thing and get on back to bed."

I wasn't sure if he knew what I was doing or not. Probably not. I 15
closed the window. He padded off. I'd managed to alleviate my urgency
enough to get to sleep. To my amazement—I suppose I believed her
omniscient°—my stepmother only grumbled the next morning about
people up at night prowling around. Even so, I knew I couldn't use the
window anymore. I'd have to find some other way.

    I had plenty of time at night to think. I needed a way to store my 16
urine, a chamber pot. The top of the closet that Stanley and I shared
formed a deep storage shelf, level with the head of my bed. Stanley and I
stashed our junk there—books, comic books, cigar boxes of crayons and
pencils, homemade wooden swords. There were dozens of empty mason
jars in the basement. I could bring up some jars, I worked out, urinate
into them at night, hide them on the junk shelf, and empty them the next
day when no one was looking.

    Accumulating jars was easy. I brought them up from the basement 17
one at a time. Stanley and I used them anyway to collect fireflies and
bugs and they all looked alike. Arranging them in the dark to relieve my
urgent bladder was harder. Dad's and our stepmother's bed was on the
other side of the wall behind the closet. We couldn't hear through the
wall unless she and Dad were fighting, but I didn't dare take chances.
She hadn't only forbidden me to use the bathroom at night. Because
she'd offered me no alternative receptacle°, she'd effectively forbidden
me to urinate at night, asserting° by that fiat° that she, not I, controlled
my bladder. Devising° an alternative, as I'd done, was challenging her
authority over my body. I also had every reason to believe that if she
caught me with a mason jar of urine she'd forbid me that release as well
and I'd be worse off than I was before.

    So I didn't open a jar to relieve myself as soon as the house quieted 18
down. I continued my ritual of restraint°, of clamping my sphincters and
pinching my penis, until I could no longer bear the pain. Only then, an
hour or more after bedtime, did I dare to ease a jar stealthily° from its
hiding place, slip it under the covers to muffle any sound, and slowly
unscrew its heavy zinc lid. After I'd waited awhile longer to be sure no
one had heard, I turned on my side, released my penis, bent it over the
rough lip of the jar tilted down into the sag of my mattress, and
tentatively, squirting and clamping, emptied my bladder. I thought I could
fill a jar and sometimes I nearly did. To avoid overflow I pressed a finger
along the inside of the jar; when the warm urine wet it I knew I needed to
stop. Hot with shame, I would screw the lid back on, struggling
sometimes to start the threads straight. Then I had the concealment
problem in reverse. I had to move the jar filled with urine back onto the

junk shelf, and with the evidence now patent°, I was even more terrified of being heard. It didn't take me as long to return the jars to the shelf as it did to fetch them, but I worked tense with caution and froze every time my bunk springs squeaked.

Disposing of the jars turned out to be the hardest part. I was afraid   19
to move them when our stepmother was home and she seldom left the house after school or during the evening. Jars of urine began accumulating on the shelf behind the junk. They didn't smell—I screwed the lids tight enough to prevent that—but the liquid turned a darker yellow and grew gray cobwebs of mold. Once in a while I had a chance to dispose of them, one or two at a time. I let Stanley in on the secret. He didn't disapprove beyond warning me of the danger. "You better hadn't let her catch you," he told me. A dozen jars collected on the shelf.

I was away all one Saturday morning doing a job, running errands or   20
cleaning out someone's garage. When I got home Stanley met me coming through the backyard and hissed me aside to a conference. "She almost found the jars," he whispered. I turned white. "It's okay," he said. "I got rid of them. She got mad about all the junk on the shelf and told me to clean it off. She was standing there watching me. I started cleaning stuff off but I kept moving it around to hide your jars. I got to where I didn't see how I could hide them any longer and just then the phone rang and she went off and started jawing. I hurried up and ran the jars down the back steps and hid them out here under the old tarp. She went off after that and I came out and emptied them. Whew! They smelled bad. They smelled like dead fish." It was a close call and he wasn't happy with me for exposing him to it. After that he helped me keep them emptied.

To this day, forty years later, once a month or so, pain wakes me.   21
Falling asleep with urine in my bladder or unmoved rectal stool, I still reflexively tighten my pelvic muscles until my sphincters cramp. My stepmother still intermittently controls my body even at this distant and safe remove. I sit on the toilet those nights in the silence of my house forcing my sphincters to relax, waiting out the pain in the darkness, remembering her.

Note: This selection is taken from the book *A Hole in the World* by Richard Rhodes. For information on how to obtain the book, turn to page 564.

READING COMPREHENSION QUESTIONS

Vocabulary in Context

1. The word *transgress* in "She lived by rigid systems of rules; to transgress even the least of those rules might detonate an outburst of rage" (paragraph 4) means
   a. write.
   b. remember.
   c. follow.
   d. disobey.

2. The word *alleviate* in "I'd managed to alleviate my urgency enough to get to sleep" (paragraph 15) means
   a. increase.
   b. lessen.
   c. awaken.
   d. hide.

Central Point and Main Ideas

3. Which statement best expresses the central point of the selection?
   a. The author's stepmother controlled him and his brother by violence and by controlling their bodies.
   b. The author's stepmother was a short woman who was married at least five times.
   c. The author and his brother were moved to the Andrew Drumm Institute for Boys in July 1949.
   d. Child abuse is probably more common than many people believe it is.

4. Which statement best expresses the main idea of paragraph 16?
   a. The author had plenty of time at night to think.
   b. The author and his brother shared a closet with a deep storage shelf.
   c. The author planned a way he could urinate at night.
   d. The author planned on finding empty mason jars in the basement.

Supporting Details

5. The author decided he shouldn't urinate out the window because
   a. his stepmother caught him.
   b. opening the window made too much noise.
   c. he woke his brother up.
   d. his father noticed a stain on the outside wall.

6. Being unable to use the bathroom at night brought Rhodes
    a. physical pain.
    b. feelings of shame.
    c. long-term physical problems.
    d. all of the above.

Transitions

7. The sentence below expresses a relationship of
    a. time.
    b. addition.
    c. contrast.
    d. cause and effect.

    Because she'd offered me no alternative receptacle, she'd effectively forbidden me to urinate at night. . . . (Paragraph 17)

8. The pattern of organization of paragraph 20 is time order—one event is followed by another. Authors use time transitions to make the order of events clear. Fill in the blanks below with two of the four time transitions in paragraph 20.

    _____   _____

Inferences

9. The author implies that the worst kind of control of him and his brother was
    a. the whippings.
    b. the verbal abuse.
    c. the control of their bodies.
    d. none of the above.

10. We can infer from this selection that the author's father
    a. had not been married before.
    b. knew about the jars of urine the author stored.
    c. was also controlled by Anne.
    d. all of the above.

SUMMARIZING

Circle the letter—*a, b,* or *c*—of the passage that best completes the following summary of "The Battle for My Body."

As boys, Richard Rhodes and his brother lived with a cruel, controlling stepmother from whom their father did not protect them. For over two years, she abused Rhodes and his brother physically and mentally, until they were sent to an institution for boys. Her physical beatings were cruel. Worse and more effective, however, were her efforts to control their bodies. She even forbade Rhodes to use a bathroom at night. That rule caused him great psychological and physical pain as he lay awake trying to keep from needing a bathroom. He tried urinating out a window, but opening the window made too much noise. He finally thought of a plan.

a. He would bring up some empty mason jars from the basement. There were dozens of them there. He would urinate in the jars at night and hide them on a shelf in the closet he shared with his brother. That closet was filled with things that would hide the jars— books, art supplies, homemade wooden swords. He brought the jars up to the bedroom one at a time. Since he and his brother used the jars to collect insects, he didn't look suspicious carrying such a jar.

b. He would urinate into jars he brought up from the basement and hide them on a closet shelf. Later, he would secretly empty them. Despite his fear of his stepmother, Rhodes went ahead with the plan. He still painfully controlled his urges until long after bedtime to avoid being caught. The hardest part of the plan, however, was emptying the jars unseen. Forty years later, the author is still sometimes bothered at night by the pain of the same cramps he had as a boy trying to keep from needing to go to the bathroom.

c. He would urinate into jars at night and hide them on a closet shelf. As a result, jars of urine began to accumulate on the closet shelf. Once there were as many as a dozen jars there. Luckily, they had no odor—since Rhodes screwed each jar tightly shut. Eventually, the author told his brother about what he was doing with the jars.

DISCUSSION QUESTIONS

1. In what ways did the stepmother try to control the author and his brother? Why do you think she tried so hard to control them?

2. Rhodes uses two comparisons (in paragraphs 1 and 6) to help him communicate his view of his stepmother. He compares her to a road show and to a disease. How would *you* describe Rhodes's stepmother?

3. There's not much in this reading about the author's father. Based on what is written about him in this excerpt, what kind of man do you think he was?

4. Child abuse is a real problem in many families. Have you or has anyone you know been a victim of child abuse? What steps do you think a person must take to heal himself or herself after such abuse?

Part III

LONGER
READINGS

1

Why Me?
Sammy Davis, Jr.

Preview

Sammy Davis, Jr., the popular entertainer, died in 1990 of cancer. He wrote two autobiographies, *Yes, I Can* and *Why Me?* The following selection from *Why Me?* details a major experience in his life. The year is 1942, and Davis has just been drafted into the recently integrated Army. Sheltered from prejudice by his family, he is unprepared for the racial discrimination he meets. In this excerpt, Davis explains how his experiences make him determined to become a star.

Note: For ease of reference, the Words to Watch are explained at the bottoms of the pages on which they appear.

A PFC° was sitting on the steps of a barracks°, sewing an emblem onto a shirt. I walked over to him. "Excuse me, buddy. I'm a little lost. Can you tell me where 202 is?"   1

He jerked his head, indicating around the corner. "And I'm not your buddy, you black bastard!" He turned back to his sewing.   2

The corporal standing outside 202 checked my name against a list on a clipboard. "Yeah—well, you better wait over there till we figure out what to do with you."   3

It was 1942. I was at the Infantry's Basic Training Center at Fort Francis E. Warren in Cheyenne, Wyoming. I sat on the steps where he'd pointed. Other guys were showing up and he checked them off against his   4

PFC (1): private first class
barracks (1): a building for housing soldiers

list and told them, "Go inside and take the first bunk you see." I looked
away for a moment and heard him saying, "Sit over there with Davis."

A tall, powerfully built guy dropped his gear alongside mine. "My   5
name's Edward Robbins." We shook hands and he sat down next to me.
One by one, men were arriving and being sent inside but no one else was
told to wait with us. Finally, it was clear that we were the only ones being
held outside while all the white guys were going right in.

The corporal went inside. We were sitting in front of a screen door,   6
so I could hear every word he was saying. "Look, we got a problem.
Those niggers out there are assigned to this company. I'm gonna stick
'em down at that end. You two guys move your gear so I can give 'em
those last two bunks."

Another voice said, "Hey, that's right next to me. I ain't sleepin'   7
near no dinge."

"Look, soldier, let's get something straight right off. I'm in charge   8
of this barracks and . . ."

"I ain't arguin' you're in charge. I'm only sayin' I didn't join no   9
nigger army."

Edward and I looked straight ahead.   10

"What about the can? Y'mean we gotta use the same toilets as them?"   11

"That's right, soldier. They use the same latrine we all use. Now   12
look, we ain't got no goddamned choice. They used to keep 'em all
together, but now for some goddamned reason somebody decided to
make us the first integrated outfit in the Army and they sent 'em here. We
just gotta put up with 'em . . ."

It was impossible to believe they were talking about me.   13

"Yeah, but I still ain't sleepin' next to no nigger."   14

"What the hell's the Army need 'em for? They'll steal ya blind   15
while ya sleep and they're all yeller bellies . . ."

"Awright, knock it off. I don't want 'em any more than you do, but   16
we're stuck with 'em. That's orders."

There was the sound of iron beds sliding across the wooden floor.   17
The corporal beckoned° from the doorway. "Okay, c'mon in," he
snapped, "on the double." We picked up our gear and followed him
through the door. I felt like a disease he was bringing in.

There were rows of cots on both sides with an aisle down the center.   18
The guys were standing in groups. They'd stopped talking. I looked
straight ahead. I could feel them staring as we followed the corporal
down the aisle. He pointed to the last two cots on one side. "These are

---

beckoned (17): called over with a signal, such as a wave

yours. Now, we don't want no trouble with you. Keep your noses clean, do as you're told, and we'll get along." He walked away.

I looked around the barracks. The bed nearest ours was empty. All 19 the cots were about two feet apart from each other except ours, which were separated from the rest by about six feet—like we were on an island.

A few of the men sort of smiled and half waved hello. Some 20 wouldn't look over at us. The nearest, a tall, husky guy who must have been a laborer or an athlete, kept his back turned.

A sergeant came in and from the center of the barracks announced, 21 "I'm Sergeant Williams. I'm in charge of this company and I . . ." His glance fell on the space between the beds. He turned to the corporal. "What the hell is that?"

The corporal explained how he'd handled things. Sergeant Williams 22 listened, then spoke sharply. "There is only one way we do things here and that's the Army way! There will be exactly three feet of space, to the inch, between every bed in this barracks. You have sixty seconds to replace the beds as you found them. *Move!*"

He came over to me. "What's your name, soldier?" 23

"Sammy Davis, Jr." 24

"Did you arrive at this barracks first or tenth or last or what?" 25

"About in the middle." 26

"Did you choose this bunk?" 27

"Well, no. I was told . . ." 28

He looked around. By this time the barracks had been rearranged. 29 "All right, Davis. Move your gear one bunk over." He turned to Edward. "You do the same."

He addressed us all. "No man here is better than the next man 30 unless he's got the rank to prove it."

I sat on the end of my bunk, the shock gone, anger growing inside 31 of me until my legs were shaking. I couldn't give them the satisfaction of seeing how they'd gotten to me. I saw one of the other guys polishing his boots. That was a good idea. The boots were a brand-new, almost yellow leather, and we'd been told to darken them with polish. I took off my watch and laid it safely on the bed. It had been a present from my father and Will*, a gold chronograph, the kind the Air Force pilots were using. I'd been dying to own one. It cost them $150, so the rent didn't get paid, but Will said, "We always had the reputation as the best-dressed act in show business. Can't let 'em think different about us in the Army."

---

*Before Sammy entered the service, he and his father were both part of a song-and-dance act with Will called the Will Mastin Trio.

I opened my shoeshine kit, took out the polish and brush, and began   32
rubbing the polish into the leather, doing the same spot over and over,
working so hard that I could blank out everything else from my mind.
Suddenly another pair of boots landed at my feet. "Here, boy, you can do
mine too."

I looked up. It was the guy who had the bed next to me, and he'd   33
already turned away. I grabbed for the boots, to throw them at his head—
but I didn't want to make trouble. I put them down beside his bed.

"Hey, boy, don't get me wrong. I expected t'give you a tip. Maybe   34
two bits for a good job."

"I'm no bootblack. And I'm no boy either."   35

"Whoa now, don't get uppity, boy." He shrugged and walked over   36
to Edward. "Here y'are, boy. You can do 'em."

"Yes, suh! Glad t'do 'em, suh."   37

"Well, that's more like it. And you don't have to call me sir. Just   38
call me Mr. Jennings. Y'see, in the Army you only call the officers sir."

"Yes, suh, Mr. Jennings. And my name is Edward. Anything you   39
needs . . ."

I wanted to vomit. I was alone in that barracks.   40

Jennings was talking to a couple of the other guys. "This may work   41
out okay. One of 'em's not a half-bad nigger." He came by Edward's
bunk with three more pairs of boots. Edward's face fell for a second but
he brightened up right away. "Yes, suh, you just leave 'em here and I'll
take care of 'em."

"You oughta thank me for settin' up this nice little business for you."   42

"I do thank you." He smiled broadly. "Oh, yes, suh. I thanks you   43
kindly."

Edward was avoiding my eyes. Eventually he looked up and moved   44
his head just the slightest bit. For a split second he opened up to me and I
saw the humiliation he was enduring. I hoped he'd look up again so I
could let him know I was sorry I'd judged him. Perhaps this was how he
had to live, but I wasn't going to take it from anybody. I wasn't going to
let anybody goad me into fights and get myself into trouble either. I was
going to mind my own business and have a clean record.

Jennings flopped onto his bunk. He sat up, reached over, and took   45
my watch off my bed. "Say, this ain't a half-bad watch." He looked at me
suspiciously.

"Put it back."   46

"Hold on, now. My, but you're an uppity one." He stood up. "Hey,   47
Phillips . . . catch!" He tossed the watch across the barracks. I ran to get it
back, but just as I reached Phillips he lobbed it over my head to another
guy, who threw it back to Jennings. I ran after it, knowing how ridiculous

I looked getting there just as Jennings threw it over my head again, that I shouldn't chase after it, that I was only encouraging them, but I was afraid they'd drop it and I couldn't stop myself.

"Atten-*shun!!!*" Every head in the barracks snapped toward the 48 doorway. Sergeant Williams walked straight to Jennings. "What've you got there?"

Jennings showed him my watch. 49

"Whose is it?" 50

Jennings shrugged. 51

"It's mine." 52

Sergeant Williams brought it to me. Jennings grinned. "Hell, Sarge, 53 we were just kiddin' around."

"You're a wise guy, Jennings. In the Army we respect another 54 man's property. You just drew KP for a week." He left the barracks.

Jennings looked at me with more hatred than I had ever seen on a 55 man's face. "I'll fix you for this, black boy."

Hours after lights-out I lay awake. How many white people had felt 56 like this about me? I couldn't remember any. Had I been too stupid to see it? I thought of the people we'd known—agents, managers, the acts we'd worked with—those people had all been friends. I know they were. There were so many things I had to remember: the dressing rooms—had we been stuck at the ends of corridors off by ourselves? Or with the other colored acts? No. Dressing rooms were assigned according to our spot on the bill. And the places we stayed? They *were* almost always colored hotels and rooming houses, but I'd never thought of them like that. They were just *our* rooming houses. But did we *have* to go to them? Didn't we just go to them because they knew us and because they were the cheapest? Or wasn't that the reason? Sure, there were people who hadn't liked us, but it had always been: "Don't pay attention, Poppa, he's just jealous 'cause we got a better act." Or: "They don't like us 'cause we're in show business." And I'd never questioned it. I remembered several times Will telling me, "Someday you'll understand." But I didn't understand and I couldn't believe I ever would.

Most of the men in our barracks gave me no problems, either 57 because they didn't care or because after a day of Basic they were too tired to worry what the hell I was. But there were about a dozen I had to look out for. They clustered around Jennings and their unity alone was enough to intimidate° anybody who might have wanted to show

---

intimidate (57): make fearful

friendliness toward me. When that group wasn't around, the others would be pleasant, but as soon as one of them showed up, it was as if nobody knew me. The sneers°, the loud whispers, the hate-filled looks were bad enough, but I didn't want it to get worse. I tried to keep peace with Jennings without Tomming° him as Edward was doing. I hoped that if I was good at my job he'd respect me, but when I was good on the rifle range he hated me all the more. If I was bad he laughed at me. I found myself walking on eggs to stay out of his way, casually but deliberately standing on a different chow line, always finding a place at one of the tables far away from him in the mess hall.

I was fastening the strap on my watch before evening mess and it   58
slipped off my wrist and fell to the floor next to Jennings's bed. Before I could reach it he stood up and ground it into the floor with the heel of his boot. I heard the crack. He lifted his foot, smiling coyly°. "Oh! What *have* I gone and done? Sure was foolish of you to leave your watch on the floor. Too bad, boy. Tough luck."

The glass was crushed and the gold was twisted. The winding stem   59
and the hands were broken off and mangled°. I put the pieces on the bed and looked at them, foolishly trying to put them together again.

"Awwww, don't carry on, boy. You can always steal another one."   60

I looked at him. "What've you got against me?"   61

"Hell, I ain't got nothin' against you, boy. I like you fine."   62

I knew I should swing at him or something, but I was so weakened   63
from the hurt of it that I couldn't get up the anger. I wrapped the pieces in some paper and put it in my pocket. Maybe it could still be fixed.

Overnight the world looked different; it wasn't one color anymore.   64
I could see the protection I'd gotten all my life from my father and Will. I appreciated their loving hope that I'd never need to know about prejudice and hate, but they were wrong. It was as if I'd walked through a swinging door for eighteen years, a door which they had always secretly held open. But they weren't there to hold it now, and when it finally hit me it was worse than if I'd learned about it gradually and knew how to move with it.

---

sneers (57): mocking smiles
Tomming (57): slavishly serving (This word comes from Uncle Tom, a slave character in the novel *Uncle Tom's Cabin* by Harriet Beecher Stowe.)
coyly (58): in a manner pretending innocence
mangled (59): damaged

Sergeant Williams walked out of the mess hall with me. "I was looking over the service records and I see that you were in show business. We have shows at the service club every Friday. If you'd care to help out I'm sure it would be appreciated, and perhaps you might enjoy doing it." 65

After the show, I was standing backstage with one of the musicians, a guy from another company, and I suggested we go out front and have a Coke. He said, "Maybe we'd better go over to the colored service club. We don't want trouble." 66

"Trouble? I just entertained them for an hour. They cheered me. Hey, look, God knows I don't want trouble, but there's gotta be a point where you draw the line. Now, I don't know about you, but I'm thirsty and I'm going in for a Coke." 67

A few of the guys who'd seen the show saw us walking in and made room for us at their table. Jennings was seated with four of his buddies. They looked over at me and smiled or smirked°, I couldn't be sure which. I sat with a group from our barracks and it was the best hour I'd spent in the Army. I luxuriated° in it. I had earned their respect; they were offering their friendship and I was grabbing for it. 68

After an hour or so I said good night and headed for the door. As I passed Jennings's table he stood up. "Hey, Davis, c'mon over here and let's get acquainted." He was smiling, holding out his hand. It would have been satisfying to brush him off, but if he was trying to be friendly it seemed better to accept it and keep the peace. "I was going to the barracks . . ." 69

"Hell, you got time for one little drink with us." He pulled out a chair for me. "Man, where'd you learn to dance like that? I swear I never saw a man's feet move so fast. By the way, notice I ain't callin' you boy." 70

"Have a beer, Davis." One of the guys pushed a bottle toward me. "Here y'are," Jennings said. 71

"If you don't mind, I'd rather have a Coke." 72

"Hey, old buddy, you're in the Army. It's time you got over that kid stuff. Try it. You're gonna like it." 73

The others were watching me. One of them grinned. "Yeah, you gotta learn to drink if you're gonna be a soldier." 74

Jennings said, "Listen, you're gonna insult me in a minute. Any man who won't drink with me . . ." 75

"Okay, I'll try it." 76

---

smirked (68): smiled in a false, offensive manner
luxuriated (68): took great pleasure

"That's better. Now I'll tell you how to drink beer. It can't be sipped   77
like whiskey or Coke. To really get the taste of beer you've gotta take a
good long slug."

The others nodded and raised their bottles. Jennings said, "Here's to   78
you." I picked up my bottle to return their toast. I had it halfway to my
mouth when I realized it wasn't cold. It was warm. As it came close to
my nose I got a good whiff of it. It wasn't beer.

"Hell, don't smell it, man. Drink it!"   79

I took another smell and all at once I understood the smiles, the   80
handshakes, the friendliness from Jennings. Somebody had taken the
bottle empty into the men's room and came back with it filled.

Jennings was saying, "Come on, drink up, boy . . ."   81

I put the bottle on the table. The faces in front of me zoomed in like   82
a movie close-up and I could see every bead of perspiration, every blink
of their eyes. The noise in the room was growing loud then low, loud then
low. Suddenly I snapped out of it. "Drink it yourself, you dirty louse."

Jennings laughed. "He even curses like a Coke drinker." I tried to   83
stand up but my chair wouldn't move. He had his foot behind a leg of it,
trapping me. The hate was back in his face. "You wanta live with us and
you wanta eat with us and now you came in here to drink with us. I
thought you loved us so much you'd wanta . . ."

I felt a warm wetness creeping over the side of my shirt and pants.   84
While he'd been talking he had turned the bottle upside down and let it
run out on me. I stared at the dark stain spreading over the khaki cloth,
cringing° from it, trying to lean away from my wet shirt and wet pants.
My pocket was too soaked to put my hand in for my handkerchief.

Jennings jumped up, pointing to me, jeering° loudly, "Silly niggers   85
can't even control themselves. This little fella got so excited sittin' with
white men—look what he did to himself."

I was out of the chair and on top of him. I had my hands on his   86
throat with every intention of killing him. I loved seeing the sneer
replaced by shock as I squeezed tighter and tighter, my thumbs against
his windpipe. He was gasping for breath. In a desperate effort he swung
around fast, lifting me off the floor. My own weight dragged me off him
and I flew through the air and crashed into one of the tables. Within
seconds the area was cleared as though we were in a ring together.

Until this moment it hadn't been a fight, it had been an attack by   87
115 pounds of rage propelled by blind impulse. I hadn't known it was

---

cringing (84): drawing back
jeering (85): mocking rudely

going to happen any more than Jennings had. The weeks of taking it, of looking for peace, of avoiding trouble, had passed, and it just happened, like a pitcher overflows when you put too much into it.

But we both knew it was going to be different now: he was a foot taller than me and half again my weight, or more, and without the advantage of surprise I was like a toy to him. He was taking his time, grinning to his friends, caressing the knuckles of one hand with the palm of the other. He raised his fists and began circling, licking his lips, anticipating the pleasure he was going to take out of me. 88

I flew into him with every bit of strength I had. His fist smashed into my face. Then I just stood there watching his other fist come at me, helpless to make myself move out of the way. I felt my nose crumble as if he'd hit an apple with a sledgehammer. The blood spurted out and I smelled a dry horrible dusty smell. 89

"Get up, you yellow-livered black bastard, you stinking coon nigger. . . ." I hadn't realized I was on the floor. I got to my feet and stumbled toward him. He hit me in the stomach and I collapsed. I was gasping for breath but no air was coming in and I was suffocating. Then suddenly I could taste air, and the figures in front of my eyes straightened out and became people again. I got up and went for him. He was methodically hitting me over and over again, landing four to every one of my punches, but they weren't hurting me anymore, they were just dull thuds against my body. Then his fist was beating down on the top of my head like a club. Someone shouted, "Don't hit 'im on the head, Jen. Y'can't hurt a nigger 'cept below the forehead." He kept pounding me and I grabbed his shirt with one hand to keep myself from falling so I could hit him in the face with my other hand. I had to stay on my feet and keep hitting him, nothing else mattered, and I was glad to trade being hit ten times for the joy of feeling my fist smash into his face just once. I hung on and kept hitting him and hitting and hitting. . . . 90

A guy named O'Brien, from my barracks, was holding a wet cloth against my face. "You'll be okay," he said. "The bleeding's stopped." 91

We were outside. I was propped up against the side of the PX. Another guy was there. Miller. He smiled. "You might feel better to know that you got in your licks. You closed one of his eyes and you broke his nose. He's wearing it around his left ear." I started to laugh but a shock of pain seared my lips. My head was pounding like it was still being hit. 92

They walked me to the barracks. Sergeant Williams was waiting in the doorway. He shook his head in disgust. "Very smart! Well, get over to the infirmary with Jennings." He walked into his bedroom. 93

I had sent Jennings to the infirmary. What beautiful news. Gorgeous! Miller and O'Brien were waiting to take me there. I shook my 94 head and thanked them. I wasn't going to give Jennings the satisfaction of seeing me in the infirmary, not if my nose fell off entirely.

I got into bed. The bruises were murder. Still, the worst pain wasn't   95
so bad that I wouldn't do it again. Jennings had beaten me unconscious and hurt me more than I'd hurt him, but I had won. He was saying, "God made me better than you," but he lost the argument the minute he had to use his fists to prove it. All he'd proven is that he was physically stronger than me, but that's not what we were fighting over.

I'd never been so tired in my life, but I couldn't sleep. I hated   96
myself for those weeks of tiptoeing around trying to avoid trouble. I'd been insane to imagine there was anything I could do to make a Jennings like me. I hadn't begun to understand the scope° of their hatred. I was haunted by that voice yelling, "Y'can't hurt a nigger 'cept below the forehead." My God, if they can believe that, then they don't even know what I am. I'm a whole other brand of being to them.

There was so much to think about. How long would I have gone on   97
not knowing the world was made up of haters, guys in the middle, Uncle Toms . . . I couldn't believe I was going to spend the rest of my life fighting with people who hate me when they don't even know me.

We were loaded with Southerners and Southwesterners who got   98
their kicks out of needling° me, and Jennings and his guys never let up. I must have had a knock-down-drag-out fight every two days. I had scabs on my knuckles for the first three months in the Army. My nose was broken again and getting flatter all the time. I fought clean, dirty, any way I could win. They were the ones who started the fights, and I didn't owe them any Marquis of Queensberry rules. It always started the same way: a wise guy look, a sneer—once they knew how I'd react, they were constantly maneuvering° me into fights. To them it was sport, entertainment, but for me the satisfaction which I had first derived° diminished° each time, until it was just a chore I had to perform. Somebody would say something and my reaction would be: oh, hell, here we go again. But I had to answer them. Invariably°, I'd walk away angrier than when the fight had started. Why should I have to keep getting my

---

scope (96): extent
needling (98): teasing and irritating
maneuvering (98): influencing
derived (98): gotten
diminished (98): decreased
invariably (98): constantly

face smashed? Why did I have to prove what no white man had to prove?

I kept in touch with my father and Will by phone. "We're makin' 99 ends meet, Poppa. They ain't what you'd call huggin' and kissin' but we're gettin' by till the day you come home. So do your job in the Army and then get back as fast as you can." I never bothered to tell them what my job in the Army was exactly.

The guy in front of me finished with the washbasin, and as I moved 100 forward, a big Southerner, Harcourt, grabbed me by the T-shirt and yanked me back so hard that I stumbled clear across the room, hit the wall, and fell down.

"What's *that* for?" 101

He drawled, "Where I come from niggers stand in the back of the 102 line."

I got up, gripped my bag of toilet articles, and with all the strength I 103 had, hit him in the mouth with it. The force and shock knocked him down. I stood over him, fists ready. But he made no attempt to get up. Blood was trickling out of his mouth. He wiped it away with his towel, then looked at me. "But you're still a nigger."

Sergeant Williams was standing in the doorway. He motioned for 104 me to follow him to his room and closed the door. "Sit down, Davis." He offered me a cigarette and I took it. "That's not the way to do it, son. You can't beat people into liking you."

The moment I heard, "You're still a nigger," I'd known that. 105

"You've punched your way across the camp. Have you stopped the 106 insults? After you beat them up, did they respect you?"

"When a guy insults me, what should I do, Sergeant? Curtsy and tell 107 him thanks?"

"You've got to fight a different way, a way where you can win 108 something lasting. You can't hope to change a man's ideas except with a better idea. You've got to fight with your brain, Sammy, not with your fists."

It seemed as though I passed Harcourt a hundred times a day, and I 109 was haunted by that voice: "You're still a nigger." He never said another word to me, but his eyes were saying it in the way they passed over me— as though I wasn't there.

We finished Basic and took our physicals for overseas duty. I was 110 rejected because of an athletic heart. I didn't qualify for any of the Army's specialist schools where I might have bettered myself. My lack of education closed everything to me. They didn't know what to do with me, so somebody sent down an order, "Put him through Basic again," probably hoping that by the time I came out I'd be somebody else's problem. When

I came out I was sent back in again, like a shirt that hadn't been done right. Four times. I was disgusted with myself. Outside a club or a theater I was totally unequipped for the world, just another uneducated laborer.

I was on latrine duty and I passed Sergeant Williams's room. The 111 door was open and he was on his bed, reading. He must have had a hundred books in there. "These all your books, Sergeant?"

"Yes. Would you like to read one?" 112

I wanted to, but I'd never read a book and I was afraid of picking 113 something ridiculous and making a fool of myself.

He sat up. "You'll get a lot more out of them than you do from 114 those comic books you read." He chose a book and gave it to me. "Start with this one. You may not enjoy it right away but stick with it."

It was *The Picture of Dorian Gray* by Oscar Wilde. After taps, I 115 went into the latrine, where the lights stayed on, and sat on the floor reading until after midnight. The next day I bought a pocket dictionary at the PX° and started the book from the beginning again, doing my reading in isolated places so people wouldn't see me looking up words.

When I'd finished it I gave it back to Sergeant Williams and we 116 talked about it. He handed me more and we had discussions as I finished them. He took a book from his shelves. *The Complete Works of Shakespeare.* "Now you're going too far. I mean, I never spent a day in school in my life."

His voice had a slight edge to it. "I never said you should be 117 ashamed of no schooling. But it's not something to be proud of either."

He gave me Carl Sandburg's books about Lincoln, books by 118 Dickens, Poe, Mark Twain, and a history of the United States. I read *Cyrano de Bergerac*, entranced° by the flair° of the man; by the majesty of speeches I read aloud in a whisper, playing the role, dueling in dance steps around the latrine; imagining myself that homely°, sensitive man, richly costumed in knee breeches, plumed hat, a handkerchief tucked into my sleeve, a sword in my hand. I feasted on the glory of the moment when, making good his threat, he drove the actor from the stage, and as the audience shouted for their money back, tossed them his last bag of gold and admitted to Le Bret, "Foolish? Of course. But such a magnificent gesture." And it was. Glorious! I put my hand in my pocket, and clutching a fistful of silver, I slipped out into the night, sword in

---

PX (115): Post Exchange, a store at a military base
entranced (118): spellbound
flair (118): smart style
homely (118): unattractive

hand, to drive the actor from the stage. Then, as fops° and peasants alike shouted for their money back, I bowed and hurled my handful of coins into the air. They landed clanging against the side of the barracks. A light went on. A voice yelled, "Corporal of the guard!" I ran like hell.

The more education Sergeant Williams gave me, through his books 119 and our discussions, the greater a hunger I developed for it. When I ran through his books I found others at the post library and then reread the ones he had.

As I got offstage at the service club, a fellow standing in the wings 120 came over to me. "That was one hell of a show you just did. Will you have a drink with me? My name is George M. Cohan, Jr.*"

We sat together and he said, "You've heard about the show every 121 camp's going to be doing for the intercamp competition? Well, with all the stuff you know and with my dad's special material, which I know backwards, I'll bet we could get that assignment. All the guys trying for it will just be using stuff out of the Special Services books. But with us writing our own, something fresh, we couldn't miss."

We auditioned for the general and then we were invited to describe 122 the show we'd do. While we talked, a WAC° captain, his adjutant°, found enough stumbling blocks to build a wall around the entire camp and she said she'd let us know in about a week.

Outside, George said, "Well, she's the power as far as our show's 123 concerned. We've got to butter her up."

We thought up excuses to go to her office and always brought 124 bunches of flowers that we'd picked. The captain seemed to be swinging over to our side, so we redoubled our efforts.

I stopped off to leave some new material we'd worked out. She 125 asked, "You were a professional entertainer, Davis?"

"Yes, Captain. Since I was three." 126

"Tell me something about it." She leaned back, listening, waving 127 away clerks who tried to speak to her. Her interest triggered a stream of show talk and "the old days" poured out of me. She smiled. "When I first heard your ideas they seemed so professional that frankly I doubted you'd be able to execute them. But now that I understand your background, and

---

fops (118): men overly concerned with their appearance

*The son of George M. Cohan, a famous entertainer, playwright, and writer of popular songs, including "Yankee Doodle Dandy."

WAC (122):   Women's Army Corps, a branch of the Army before integration of men and women in the armed services

adjutant (122): an officer who assists the commanding officer

from what I know of George, I'm convinced you and he are more than up to the job. I'd like you two to work out a budget for props and costumes as soon as you can." She walked me to the door, shook hands with me, and smiled. "I probably shouldn't say this but you boys have quite an edge over the others. We'll have the official word by Friday."

Leaving, I felt like doing a Fred Astaire number, tap-dancing across   128
the tops of the row of desks leading to the front door. I was a specialist. Show business had given me something to offer the Army.

As I started toward my barracks, a couple of headquarters clerks   129
called out to me. One of them, a PFC with a heavy Southern drawl, smiled. "The captain told us to take you to meet her at Building 2134."

I grinned. "Her wish is my command." Maybe she wanted me to   130
look at props and scenery they'd used in other shows. We walked about half a mile, to a semi-deserted part of the camp, to barracks that weren't in use. I followed the PFC into 2134. One of the men closed the door behind us. They shoved me into the latrine. Four others were in there, obviously waiting for us.

"Sorry, nigger, but your lady love won't be here."   131

"What is this?"   132

"Nothin' but a little meeting some of us in the office thought we   133
oughta have with you." They took hold of my arms. The PFC spit in my face. I tried to reach up to wipe it away but I couldn't move my arms. "Oh, I'm sorry. Here, I'll wipe it for you." He slapped me across the face, then backhanded me.

The seven of them crowded around me. The PFC was breathing   134
heavily and a vein in his forehead was pulsing quickly. "We've been watching you makin' eyes at the captain for a week now, and we decided we oughta have a little talk with you."

"Making eyes? Wait a minute . . ."   135

He hit me again. "Niggers don't talk 'less they're spoken to." He   136
punched me in the stomach and I collapsed, hanging by the arms from the two guys who were holding me. "Now, like I was sayin', we just get so sick seein' you playin' up to her, and bringin' her flowers, and tryin' to make time—not to say the captain would give an ape-face like you the time of day, but we figured we should smarten you up some so you won't be makin' such a fool of yourself.

"Now, what you gotta learn is that black is black and it don't matter   137
how white it looks or feels, it's still black, and we're gonna show you a little experiment to prove it so's you won't think we're tryin' to fool you none."

One of the others was stirring a can of white paint. Two of them   138
ripped my shirt open and tore it off me. The PFC had a small artist's

paintbrush, which he dipped into the paint. They held me in front of a mirror. Across my chest he wrote, "I'm a nigger!" Then he wrote something on my back. When he was finished with that he took a larger brush and began to cover my arms and hands with white paint, going back and forth over the hair on my arms until every strand was plastered down.

"Now," he said, "we're gonna let this paint dry so we can finish our 139 lesson. So while we're waiting, you c'n give us a little dance."

They let go of my arms. My legs felt like cardboard buckling under 140 me. Two of them were blocking the door and the other five were surrounding me.

"Come on, Sambo, give us a little dance!" 141

I stood motionless, dazed. The PFC said, "Guess he don't 142 understand English." They held me again while he picked up the brush and wrote on my forehead, grinning, taking great pleasure in his work, doing it slowly, carefully. When he finished they dragged me back to the mirror. He'd written "Coon" in white paint that was starting to drip into my eyebrows.

"Now listen," he said, "you gotta understand me. When I tell you 143 we wanta see you dance for us, then you gotta believe we wanta see you dance. Now, we're trying to be gentlemen about this. We figure you don't teach a hound nothin' by whipping him, so we're trying to be humane and psychological with you, but if we're takin' all this trouble on your education, then you gotta show a little appreciation and keep us entertained durin' all the time we're givin' up for you. So, come on, Sambo, you be a good little coon and give us a dance."

They let go of my arms again. The PFC punched me in the stomach. 144 "Dance, Sambo." When I got my wind back I started tapping my feet, incredulous°, numbed.

"That's better, Sambo. A little faster . . ." 145

I danced faster, stumbling over my own legs. 146

"Faster, Sambo, faster. . ." 147

As I got near the PFC, he hit me in the stomach again. "Didn't you 148 hear me say faster, Sambo?" They made me keep dancing until I couldn't raise my feet off the ground.

"Okay, that's enough of that. You're not that good." He turned to 149 the others. "I really thought we were gonna have us a treat, didn't you?" They all nodded and acted disappointed. "Well, I guess we can't be mad 'cause you don't dance good. Anyway, we gotta get back to your education."

---

incredulous (144): unbelieving

I could feel the paint tightening on my skin.   150

"Now, we figure you've got the idea you're the same as white   151
'cause you're in a uniform like us and 'cause you dance at the shows and
you go in and sit down with white men and because you think you got
manners like a white man with the flowers you give our women. So we
gotta explain to you how you're not white and you ain't never gonna be
white no matter how hard you try. No matter what you do or think, you
can't change what you are, and what you are is black and you better get it
outta your head to mess around with white women.

"Now, look at your arm. Looks white, don't it? Well, it ain't. Watch   152
and see." He poured turpentine on a rag and began wiping my arm in one
spot. When my skin showed through the paint, he grinned. "There.
Y'see? Just as black 'n' ugly as ever!"

He rubbed some turpentine on his own arm. "See the difference? No   153
matter how hard I keep rubbin', it's still white. So, like I said, white is
white and black is black." He poured the rest of the turpentine down the
drain.

"Okay, you ugly little nigger bastard. We're lettin' you off easy this   154
time. I mean, we coulda been nasty and painted all the rest of you, but we
figured you're a smart nigger and you'll get the idea fast, so because
we're peace-lovin' fellas we don't wanta hurt you none, so we didn't do
that. Now we're gonna be leaving you here, but remember that we did
you this favor, see? And if you should decide to tell anybody anything
about our little lesson, well, we'd just have to admit we caught you
makin' passes at the captain and that sure wouldn't do neither of you no
good, and then besides that we'd have to find you again and give you
another lesson, 'cept we'd have to try harder to make you understand,
like maybe open up your skin a trifle° and show you it's black under
there too. So just take our little lesson in the spirit we meant and we're
willin' to let bygones be bygones and you'll stay away from the captain,
right? Okay, Sambo, we'll be goin' now . . ."

Then I was alone. I looked at myself in one of the mirrors. I wanted   155
to crawl into the walls and die. I sat down on the floor and cried.

I looked at the part of my arm they had cleaned with turpentine. I   156
rubbed the skin and watched it change color under the pressure, then
darken as the blood flowed through again. How could the color of skin
matter so much? It was just skin. What is skin? Why is one kind better
than another? Why did they think mine made me inferior?

I stayed there for an hour, maybe two hours. I lost track of time,   157

---

trifle (154): little bit

trying to understand it. Why should they want to do this to me? I'd have given my life to hear my father say, "Hell, Poppa, they're just jealous of our act." I wanted to believe anything but that people could hate me this much.

As the paint hardened it drew on my skin. It was starting to pull the hairs on my arms and it itched terribly. I tried to wipe some of it off with toilet paper, but it tore and stuck to the paint and only made it worse. I had to get back to the barracks. I dreaded being seen. Some of the guys would laugh and some would feel sorry for me and one would be as bad as the other. But I wanted Sergeant Williams to see me. I wanted to hear him tell me again, "You've got to fight with your brain." 158

It was already dark. Most of the camp was in the mess halls, so it was easy to hide behind buildings back to the barracks. It was empty. I got my towel and after-shave lotion and went into the latrine. I poured half a bottle on the towel and rubbed until it hurt, but it didn't help at all. There were voices outside, Sergeant Williams and some of the guys. I hid in the shower, praying they wouldn't come in. When I heard the other guys' steps going toward their bunks I ducked into Sergeant Williams's room. 159

He closed the door. "Who did it?" I shook my head. "Don't be a fool. You don't have to fear them. They'll be court-martialed and sent to the stockade for years. . . ." 160

I wasn't afraid. I just wanted it to be over. If they were arrested there'd be a trial and everybody in camp would know about it. I just wanted to forget that it ever happened. 161

There was no pity in his face—just sadness. Not only for me but for the depth of what he could read into what had happened. He left the room, cautiously, so nobody would see me, and sent to the motor pool for turpentine. Then he locked the door, soaked his towel, and began wiping the paint off my skin. For the next hour and a half he didn't say one word. I sat there naked to the waist until he was finished. Then he gave me soap and a brush and sent me to the shower room. 162

Bits of paint clung to my pores. I stood under the hot water rubbing until rashes° of blood trickled to the surface, brushing until I'd scraped the last speck of white out of my skin. 163

I got into bed. *Nobody, nobody in this world is ever going to do this to me again. I'll die first.* 164

The band was playing the overture. George made room for me to peek through the curtain. Among all the faces, I saw Harcourt from my barracks. How can you run out and smile at people who despise you? 165

---

rashes (163): outbreaks

How can you entertain people who don't like you?

I did my opening number, forcing myself to concentrate on the one   166
thing I was out there to do: entertain the audience.

As I was taking my bow, enjoying the applause, I glanced at   167
Harcourt. He wasn't applauding. Our eyes met and I caught something in
his face that I'd never seen there before. It wasn't warmth or respect—he
was trying to show no recognition at all. At that moment I knew that
because of what I could do on a stage he could never again think, "But
you're still a nigger." Somehow I'd gotten to him. He'd found something
of me in six minutes of my performance which he hadn't seen in the
barracks in all those months.

My talent was the weapon, the power, the way for me to fight. It   168
was the only way I might hope to affect a man's thinking. The same man
who had caused the question had provided the answer. The man who had
shown me that my fists could never be enough was showing me how to
fight with whatever intelligence and talent God had given me.

We played the show for a week and when I was on that stage it was   169
as though the spotlight erased all color and I was just another guy. I could
feel it in the way they looked at me, not in anything new that appeared in
their faces, but in something old that was missing. While I was
performing they forgot what I was and there were times when even I
could forget it. Sometimes offstage I passed a guy I didn't know and he
said, "Good show last night." It was as though my talent was giving me a
pass from their prejudice. I didn't hope for camaraderie°. All I wanted
was to walk into a room without hearing the conversation slow down,
and it was happening. I was developing an identity around camp and it
was buying me a little chunk of peace.

I was transferred into Special Services and for eight months I did   170
shows in camps across the country, gorging° myself on the joy of being
liked. I dug down deeper every day, looking for new material, inventing
it, stealing it, switching it—any way that I could find new things to make
my shows better—and I lived twenty-four hours a day for that hour or
two at night when I could stand on that stage, facing the audience,
knowing I was dancing down the barriers between us.

I walked around the camp remembering my first months in   171
Cheyenne. Now that I was leaving the Army I had a detached° feeling

---

camaraderie (169): friendship
gorging (170): filling greedily
detached (171): uninvolved emotionally

about it, as though it had happened to someone else. But it was me all right, and I wasn't about to let myself forget it. I'd gone into the Army like a kid going to a birthday party, and I'd seen it. They'd taught me well all that my father and Will had so lovingly kept from me.

I'd learned a lot in the Army and I knew that above all things in the world I had to become so big, so strong, so important that those people and their hatred could never touch me. My talent was the only thing that made me a little different from everybody else, and it was all that I could hope would shield me *because* I was different. 172

I'd weighed it all, over and over again: What have I got? No looks, no money, no education. Just talent. Where do I want to go? I want to be treated well. I want people to like me and be decent to me. How do I get there? There's only one way I can do it with what I have to work with. I've got to be a star! I have to be a star like another man has to breathe. 173

Note: This selection is taken from the book *Why Me?* by Sammy Davis, Jr. For information on how to obtain the book, turn to page 564.

READING COMPREHENSION QUESTIONS

Vocabulary in Context

1. The word *execute* in " 'When I first heard your ideas they seemed so professional that frankly I doubted you'd be able to execute them. But now that I understand your background, and from what I know of George, I'm convinced you and he are more than up to the job. . . . ' " (paragraph 127) means
   a. write.
   b. remember.
   c. recognize.
   d. carry out.

Central Point and Main Ideas

2. Which sentence best expresses the central point of the selection?
   a. Davis went through basic training in Cheyenne, Wyoming.
   b. Davis's Army experiences taught him about racial prejudice and that his talent could protect him from it.
   c. While in the Army, Davis learned the value of reading and of literature, with the help of Sergeant Williams.
   d. The Army brought Davis into contact with many different types of people.

3. Which sentence best expresses the main idea of paragraph 64?
   a. Davis appreciated his father's and Will's wish to protect him from prejudice and hate.
   b. The war was changing the world.
   c. Overly protected by his father and Will, Davis was unprepared for the racial discrimination he met.
   d. Davis missed his father and Will.

4. Which sentence best expresses the main idea of paragraph 169?
   a. The camp show played for a week.
   b. Soldiers began to tell Davis that the show was good.
   c. Davis didn't hope for real friendship from the soldiers in his audiences.
   d. Through the camp show, Davis's talent led others to treat him without prejudice.

Supporting Details

5. Jennings
   a. had no friends in the barracks.
   b. wasn't much bigger than Davis.
   c. became friendly with Sergeant Williams.
   d. went out of his way to make Davis's life miserable.

6. Davis learned that his fights would
   a. put him in the infirmary.
   b. not hurt him much physically.
   c. never earn him the respect he wanted.
   d. get him in trouble with the WAC captain.

7. After being painted white, Davis
   a. had his attackers court-martialed.
   b. went to the infirmary for help.
   c. called his father and Will for support.
   d. received assistance from Sergeant Williams.

Transitions

8. In general, Davis presents the events of his Army years in an organizational pattern of
   a. time order.
   b. contrast.
   c. cause and effect.
   d. definition and example.

Inferences

9. We can conclude that Sergeant Williams
   a. was not prejudiced against African-Americans.
   b. was a well-read man.
   c. encouraged Davis's desire to learn.
   d. all of the above.

10. Davis implied that he came to see stardom as a way to
    a. get out of the Army.
    b. become rich.
    c. be accepted.
    d. help his family.

SUMMARIZING

Circle the letter—*a, b,* or *c*—of the passage that best completes the following summary of the reading from *Why Me?*

Sammy Davis, Jr., first became aware of prejudice when he entered the Army in Cheynne, Wyoming. The Army was being integrated, and some of the men in his barracks were very prejudiced. They harassed him from the first day, and Davis often got into fights. But the fights never won him the respect of those who hated him.

In the meanwhile, Davis began to educate himself with the help of a sergeant's library and encouragement. Also, he and George M. Cohan, Jr., decided to audition for the camp show for an intercamp competition. To increase their chances, they became especially friendly with the WAC captain who assisted the man in charge of the show.

a. A group of prejudiced soldiers interpreted Davis's actions as romantic interest in the captain. They attacked and tormented him, leaving him covered in white paint. He refused to accuse his attackers against the advice of his sergeant, who personally cleaned the paint off Davis. Davis wanted to avoid a trial and publicity. Soon after, he performed in the camp show and discovered that because of his talent, the prejudiced soldiers treated him with acceptance. He had similar positive experiences after being transferred into Special Services and doing shows in camps across the country for eight months. By the time his Army service was done, Davis saw his talent as a way to avoid prejudice. As a result, he became determined to become a star.

    b. A group of prejudiced soldiers interpreted Davis's actions as romantic interest in the captain. They took him to a semi-deserted part of camp on a false pretense. They then said they were going to teach him a lesson for "makin' eyes at the captain." They proceeded to hit Davis, paint "I'm a nigger!" in white across his chest, and cover him with white paint. Then they forced him to dance. When they left, Davis sat down on the floor and cried. Later, he went into his sergeant's room. The sergeant wanted Davis to name the people who had attacked him, but Davis wanted to avoid a trial and publicity. The sergeant then sent for some turpentine and cleaned the paint off Davis. Davis later performed at the camp show and in Special Services until his service in the Army was up.

    c. At first the captain discouraged Davis and Cohan. Then one day she and Davis had a conversation about his background. She was very interested and told him, ". . . now that I understand your background, and from what I know of George, I'm convinced you and he are more than up to the job." She asked them to work out a budget for props and costumes as soon as possible. Eventually, they were chosen for the intercamp competition. Davis wondered how he could perform for people he knew hated him for his color. But once he got out on the stage, he forced himself to concentrate on entertaining the audience. His talent impressed his fellow soldiers, who started treating him more as if he were "just another guy."

DISCUSSION QUESTIONS

1. Davis at first fought prejudice with his fists. Give examples from the passage that show why he came to feel that physical fighting was not the best way to combat prejudice. Why do you think Davis's talent was a more powerful weapon against prejudice than his fists?

2. Davis was protected from prejudice as he was growing up by his father and Will. Do you think this protection was harmful or beneficial to Davis? Explain your answer.

3. Do you think Davis should have told Sergeant Williams who attacked him? Why?

4. What is your reaction to this piece? Were you surprised by the amount of racism Davis had to combat? Do you believe such violent racism is a thing of the past, or do you think it still exists today? Explain your answer.

2

Mister Rogers
Jeanne Marie Laskas

Preview

"Would you be mine? Could you be mine? Won't you be my neighbor?"
Do you, like many Americans, fondly recognize these words from the
theme song of the children's TV show *Mister Rogers' Neighborhood*? If
so, you may wonder what kind of man Fred Rogers is in private life and
why his show—and he—are still so popular. You'll find some answers to
those questions in this article, published in *Life* magazine in 1992,
twenty-five years after the show began.

When Fred Rogers arrived at Boston University for commencement exercises last spring, he was carrying his father's plain black
graduation robe, which he wanted to wear. But all the other graduates
would be in red robes, the BU people explained. Wouldn't he rather wear
one of those instead? "Well, OK," Rogers said, and he put on the shiny
new garment. "This sure is fancy, my goodness!" he said, looking more
like a kid playing dress-up than a man about to receive his twenty-fifth
honorary doctorate.

A Presbyterian minister, Rogers was scheduled to give the
invocation°. People are often surprised to learn that Rogers, 64, is a
clergyman, and yet that fact is at the root of almost everything about him.
When he was ordained° in 1963, he chose television as the medium for

1

2

---

invocation (2): prayer said at the beginning of a public ceremony
ordained (2): formally appointed a clergyman

his ministry and children as his congregation. The result is *Mister Rogers' Neighborhood*, the longest-running program on public television. February will mark its twenty-fifth anniversary on national television.

Surely none of the somber° deans or other regally° dressed   3
academics sitting on stage at BU were prepared for what happened when the name Fred Rogers was announced to the class of 1992.

"Wooooo!" shouted 5,400 graduates, jumping to their feet. "Mister   4
Rogers! Aaaaoooo!" they yelled, and some threw their caps like Frisbees into the sky. "Mister Rogers! Woooooo! Tweeeet! Aaaaoooo!"

This was, after all, Rogers' audience. The kids who grew up   5
watching *Mister Rogers' Neighborhood* are today's college students. They believe in him. They don't hesitate to stand up and cheer for him.

A decade ago Mister Rogers was treated far less respectfully.   6
Remember Eddie Murphy, Cheech and Chong, Johnny Carson and other comedians who made people laugh by poking fun at Mister Rogers? Perhaps the intensity of the program set those people off. Rogers' persona° is unlike anything you're liable to see on television: slow, deliberate, gentle. Children accept it because it is so like them: genuine. Adults can feel threatened by it, perhaps because it recalls for them a lost child within. For some, it's easier to make fun of Mister Rogers than it is to figure him out.

You don't see as many satires anymore. For one thing, young adults   7
today have Mister Rogers in their souls; they grew up with him. For another, he has aged gracefully. Making fun of Mister Rogers would be like making fun of your own grandfather.

Nowadays, it's hip to love Mister Rogers. The cheering in the   8
stadium went on for minutes, growing louder and louder. "Wooo! Tweeet! Mister Rogers!" Finally, the graduates broke into the "wave," jumping in sequence like fans do at football games. It was quite a sight, all those red robes going up and down. Rogers stood before them, smiling shyly, wondering how he would ever put these wild kids in the mood for praying. Then he leaned into the microphone, and in his tiniest voice he asked, "Will you sing with me?"

Timidly, he began singing, "It's a beautiful day in the   9
neighborhood," the opening song of his program. It seemed like such a weird thing to do. It seemed like such a courageous thing to do. And therein lies the key to Mister Rogers' appeal: It's his capacity to be weak that makes him so strong.

---

somber (3): serious, solemn
regally (3): royally
persona (6): public image

It worked. ". . . Would you be mine? Could you be mine? Won't   10
you be my neighbor. . . ." The graduates knew all the words, and they
joined in, arm in arm, swaying back and forth in their red robes, and the
stadium was tamed with song.

Fred Rogers lives in Pittsburgh, where *Mister Rogers' Neighborhood*   11
is produced. The life he leads is disciplined, peaceful and quiet. He swims
every morning at 6:30 at a local pool, where he weighs in at precisely 143
pounds. He is a strict vegetarian. He doesn't drink or smoke, rarely goes to
parties and gets to bed by 9:30. His favorite place on earth is The Crooked
House, a rickety° old home in Nantucket, Massachusetts, to which he
retreats every summer. He is a voracious° reader, and when he finds he
needs to unwind, he likes to improvise° on one of his two grand pianos.
Music is his second love. His first is Joanne, his wife of forty years, who
is a concert pianist. They met in college. A jolly woman with a Southern
drawl, she rolls through life with infectious laughter. "Oh, that is
wonderful, just wonderful!" she is liable to say about the simplest
discovery—a spider web, a shadow, a pretty piece of chocolate.

Mr. and Mrs. Rogers live in an elegant apartment in a neighborhood   12
called Oakland, the university section of town. They have two sons, John,
30, who works in real estate in Topeka, Kansas, and James, 33, a hospital
technician who lives with his wife and son just a few blocks from his
parents. Rogers has always been careful to keep his family out of the
media spotlight. But he will tell you that his grandson, four-year-old
Alexander, is the current light of his life. "Alexander teaches me to be
present in the moment," he says. They play together—and most of the
ideas for *Mister Rogers' Neighborhood* now come from Alexander.

Rogers still writes all the scripts for his program, in addition to all   13
the songs, in addition to working and doing the voices for most of the
puppets. He is careful never to use the word "show" when referring to the
program. He is not an actor. There is no showmanship here.

Studio A in the WQED building in Pittsburgh turns into a colorful,   14
somewhat mystical place each time the *Neighborhood* set—a modest
contraption° that hasn't changed much over the years—is brought in. The
furniture and curtains are outdated. The puppets are crude; the mouths of
most don't even move. *Mister Rogers' Neighborhood* has the appearance

---

rickety (11): likely to fall apart
voracious (11): very eager
improvise (11): make up music while playing
contraption (14): invention designed for a particular purpose

of something a kid could put on in his own living room. The significance? This is a place just like home. This is a visit from a favorite uncle, or grandfather, or some other grownup who has time just for you.

Every day he greets you singing the same song. Every day he takes   15
off his sport coat and puts on a sweater. (He has a large, colorful collection of these sweaters, most made by his mother. One hangs on permanent exhibition at the Smithsonian Institution, not far from Archie Bunker's chair.) Every day he takes off his shoes, puts on his sneakers. The ritual—as in a church service—has a way of lulling you. Every day you know what to expect. This place is dependable. This place is safe.

The viewer travels from Mister Rogers' living room to the   16
Neighborhood of Make-Believe, from reality to fantasy, the journey teaching you something about the world. Not your ABCs. Not how to count from one to ten in Spanish. His lessons are about war, love, divorce, competition, death. Each week the program tackles a new theme—through stories. The emotions surrounding the death of a loved one, for instance, were explored when Mister Rogers discovered that one of his goldfish had died. He faced the fact of its death. He grieved. He buried it. Running parallel to this were the troubles in the Neighborhood of Make-Believe, where the trolley had jumped its tracks. The neighbors thought the trolley was dead. They explored their own feelings of loss. And then Mister Rogers brought his audience back to the real world and told the true story of what happened when he was a boy, and his best friend, his dog, Mitzi, died. He talked about how sad you feel when you are left alone by the one you love.

The program's target audience is children aged two to five, who   17
might also tune in to the more dazzling world of *Sesame Street*, with its quick cuts and graphics slick enough to keep adults amused. Two Yale psychologists once did a study comparing the programs and found that kids follow the *Neighborhood* stories better than the zippy world of *Sesame Street*—and that *Mister Rogers' Neighborhood* improved the children's imaginative play. Scholars hail the program as perhaps the healthiest fare on TV for children. "Children's television is a disgrace," says George Gerbner of the University of Pennsylvania, who has been conducting a study of television programming for twenty-five years. "It treats children as consumers to be manipulated°. There is no one else doing what Rogers does. He treats children as human beings. It's a shame that he's the only one."

The central message on *Mister Rogers' Neighborhood* is always the   18

---

manipulated (17): influenced

same, and it's stated over and over again: You are special. You are worthwhile, no matter what you are on the outside. Your insides are what matter.

It is a deceptively simple lesson in self-esteem that children seem to   19
gulp down whole, as if satisfying a tremendous hunger.

Just as Fred Rogers did when he was a boy.   20

Rogers was born in Latrobe, a small industrial town in western   21
Pennsylvania that also produced golfer Arnold Palmer and Rolling Rock
beer. He lived in the great big red brick house on Weldon Street. The
Rogerses were a wealthy family; his father was president of the McFeely
Brick Company, one of the largest employers in the area. Rogers'
childhood was solitary. He was sickly, an only child until he turned 11,
when his parents adopted a baby girl. His mother, who was known for her
enormous generosity, doted on° him and feared always for his safety. He
was not allowed to play outside by himself. She tried to cure him of his
hay fever by providing him with an air-conditioned room, where he spent
an entire summer, day and night. An overweight, lonely boy, he coped
with life's traumas through his puppets and through music.

The brightest spot in the young boy's life was his maternal   22
grandfather, Fred McFeely, the man after whom Rogers was named. (Mr.
McFeely would eventually end up as a character in the Neighborhood.)
His grandfather let him climb on the giant stone wall—by himself! His
grandfather let him run free. His grandfather always had some fascinating
thing to show him, and together they liked to order stuff from Sears.

One day, when one of their visits was coming to an end, his   23
grandfather turned to him and said, "You know, you made this day a
really special day. Just by being yourself. There's only one person in the
world like you. And I happen to like you just the way you are."

That was it. That was the message that went soaring like an arrow   24
into his heart, never to budge.

In a way, Fred Rogers has spent the rest of his life trying to become   25
the same kind of force to millions that his grandfather was to him.

Rogers never planned to go into television. He planned to be a   26
musician or a minister, or both. He went to Rollins College in Florida to
study music composition, and by his senior year he had been accepted at
Pittsburgh Theological Seminary.

That was 1951. When he came home for Easter vacation, he   27
confronted television for the first time. "I just hated it," he recalls.
"Grown men were throwing pies at each other." He thought that the

---

doted on (21): adored

medium had potential for better things, and so he decided on a new career. "Everyone was so flabbergasted," he says, "because literally, I was supposed to start in the seminary in September."

He got a job in New York City on the *NBC Opera Theatre*, then *Your Lucky Strike Hit Parade* and *The Kate Smith Hour.* He was moving up the ladder, having been promoted to network floor director, when, in 1953, he startled everybody once again by deciding to leave NBC for a job with the nation's first community-supported public television station, Pittsburgh's WQED-TV. "The people at NBC said, 'You're out of your mind! That place isn't even on the air yet!' And I said, 'Well, something tells me that's what I'm supposed to do.'" 28

He wrote and produced *The Children's Corner*, in partnership with a friend named Josie Carey. Though he wasn't seen on camera, Rogers worked the puppets. He also enrolled at Pittsburgh Theological Seminary, where his education included training in child psychology at Pittsburgh's Arsenal Family and Children Center, founded by Dr. Benjamin Spock and Margaret McFarland, with consulting help from Erik Erikson. He was ignited by his studies and particularly by noted child psychologist McFarland, who helped him to explore the way children experience the world. He consulted with her almost daily until she died in 1988. 29

And yet McFarland claimed that Rogers was the one who taught her about children. "He is able to empathize° in a unique° way," she once said. "He is one of the rare individuals who hasn't shed his own childhood experiences." 30

In the end, it was the marriage of television, psychology and theology that provided the atmosphere in which Rogers thrived. The prototype° of *Mister Rogers' Neighborhood* was a fifteen-minute program called *Misterogers*, provided in 1963 by the Canadian Broadcasting Corporation, which resembled the Neighborhood of Make-Believe segments of today. Revamped and extended to a half-hour format that incorporated visits with Mister Rogers in his living room, it was next seen on a local Pittsburgh station. In 1967 the Sears-Roebuck Foundation agreed to fund the program and make it available to all public television stations nationally. Today, *Mister Rogers' Neighborhood* is broadcast on more than three hundred stations and watched by more than eight million households a week. 31

---

empathize (30): identify with another's feelings
unique (30): very unusual
prototype (31): original that serves as a model

At each morning's taping there are kids running through Studio A. 32
Many are fans who have written letters; Rogers receives about a hundred
a week and responds to each one personally. Children with special needs
are often invited to visit the set.

"Hey, you're the real Mister Rogers!" Brian Campbell cries out 33
when he sees his hero walk into Studio A. A plump little boy, somewhat
awkward, Brian, 10, has Williams syndrome, a condition that causes mild
mental retardation and congenital° heart defects. He's come all the way
from Arlington, Texas, to meet Mister Rogers.

"And you're the real you," Rogers says, bending down to shake 34
Brian's hand. "You're so brave to shake my hand."

"I am special, aren't I, Mister Rogers?" Brian says. 35

"Yes, you are." 36

"You know what, Mister Rogers?" Brian says. "You are my friend." 37
With that, the boy starts singing a song from the *Neighborhood.* "You are
my friend, you are special. . . ." Rogers puts his arm around him and
sings along quietly. The crew in the studio grows silent. "Good for you,
Brian," Rogers says when the song is over. "Good for you!"

"Can I give you a big hug, Mister Rogers?" Brian asks. 38

Fred Rogers opens his arms, and Brian Campbell falls inside. 39

"I love you, Mister Rogers," Brian says. 40

Brian's mother is completely undone by this exchange. "This is the 41
highlight of my life," she says.

"I'm telling you, you get blown away when you start paying 42
attention to what Fred is doing," says Teresa Edmondson, a 35-year-old
production intern. "They need a *Mister Rogers* show for adults. It is
profound! At my age, going back to school, a single mother, divorced,
you know, I have a lot of doubts about myself. And when I listen to Fred,
he is speaking to me too. Every human being's life is worth something. I
come into this studio, and it's like every day I get a little jolt of self-
esteem. I should have been watching this show my whole life."

That attitude might account for why most people who start working 43
for *Mister Rogers' Neighborhood* never leave. One by one crew members
will tell you, with enormous pride, "Oh, yeah, Fred and I are good
friends."

Johnny Costa is one of Rogers' closest friends, which many people, 44
even Costa, find surprising. "We're opposites, me and Fred," Costa says,
sitting at his piano in the corner of Studio A. A noted jazz pianist, Costa

---

congenital (33): present since birth

is a somewhat bawdy°, crusty° musician who puts the rich jazz combinations underneath Rogers' simple melodies, providing depth and texture. He has been here since the program started.

"Me, I'll enjoy a good steak," Costa says. "Now Fred, he would   45
never think of eating a steak. And I'll enjoy a glass of wine. Fred doesn't drink. Fred, he would never swear. Me, I would swear. You follow me?

"But gee, if you strip away the facades and you think about the   46
important things, we are almost exactly like brothers. We want the same things. We want beauty in music. We want a certain love that comes out. We often talk about heaven and about meeting Beethoven up there. Sometimes I'll say, 'But Fred, I may end up in hell.' And he'll tell me he thinks because of the music I give people, I'll end up in heaven. Boy, that makes me feel good. Wouldn't that make you feel good?"

Over on the set, Fred Rogers and young Brian Campbell are still   47
playing. Brian makes the trolley go, then feeds the fish, while Rogers follows along, crouching down to Brian's level. The producer wants to turn this studio back into a place of work. "Come on, Fred," she says. But Rogers has one more thing to say to Brian. He gets on his knees and looks the child square in the eye. "You blessed my space today, Brian," he says.

Brian considers this. "Well, I'm glad you're here, Mister Rogers,"   48
he says. "But we'll probably never see each other again after today, will we?"

"We can still be television neighbors," Rogers says. "Can't we?"   49

"O.K.," Brian says, adding, "I am special, Mister Rogers, aren't I?"   50

"Yes, you are."   51

As a minister, Rogers has never thought of his television program,   52
or Studio A, or any part of the world as a place to preach. "I never wanted to superimpose° anything on anybody," he says. "I would like to think that I can create some sort of atmosphere that allows people to be comfortable enough to be who they are. And consequently, if they are, they can grow from there.

"A lot of this—all of this—is just tending soil."   53

What, in the end, was Fred Rogers' message to the Boston   54
University Class of 1992?

---

bawdy (44): unrefined, vulgar
crusty (44): rude, bad-tempered
superimpose (52): add on

At the baccalaureate service, he quoted from Saint-Exupéry's *The*   55
Little Prince: *"essentiel est invisible pour les yeux. . . .* What is essential
is invisible to the eye."

And then he said, "It's not the honors and the prizes and the fancy   56
outsides of life which ultimately nourish our souls. It's the knowing that
we can be trusted, that we never have to fear the truth, that the bedrock°
of our very being is good stuff." He went on to ask, "What is essential
about you that is invisible to the eye?" And he paused for a long time.
Then he recited a song from his program called "It's You I Like": "It's
you I like. It's not the things you wear. It's not the way you do your hair,
but it's you I like. The way you are right now. The way deep down inside
you. Not the things that hide you—not your diplomas, they're just beside
you. But it's you I like, every part of you."

A stillness fell over the crowd. The people seemed to travel inward,   57
looking for some part of themselves that they had long since forgotten—
or some part they had not yet found.

Or something else entirely. Whatever it was, a lot of them cried.   58

READING COMPREHENSION QUESTIONS

Vocabulary in Context

1. The word *lulling* in "Every day he greets you singing the same
   song. . . . Every day he takes off his shoes, puts on his sneakers. The
   ritual . . . has a way of lulling you. . . . This place is dependable.
   This place is safe" (paragraph 15) means
   a. surprising.
   b. calming.
   c. disappointing.
   d. entertaining.

2. The word *shed* in "McFarland claimed that Rogers was the one who
   taught her about children. . . . 'He is one of the rare individuals who
   hasn't shed his own childhood experiences' " (paragraph 30) means
   a. believed.
   b. remembered.
   c. described.
   d. lost.

---

bedrock (56): foundation

3. The word *facades* in "'We're opposites, me and Fred,' Costa says, sitting at his piano. . . . 'But gee, if you strip away the facades and you think about the important things, we are almost exactly like brothers'" (paragraphs 44 and 46) means
   a. surface appearances.
   b. meals.
   c. names.
   d. musical combinations.

Central Point and Main Ideas

4. Which sentence best expresses the central point of the selection?
   a. The college students of today have grown up with the *Mister Rogers' Neighborhood* program.
   b. Fred Rogers was inspired by some loving comments from his grandfather.
   c. When Fred Rogers spoke at a Boston University commencement, the students cheered loudly for him, sang with him, and were greatly moved by his comments.
   d. Fred Rogers, a gentle and loving man on TV and in real life, remains popular because of his emphasis on the inborn goodness of everyone.

5. Which sentence best expresses the main idea of paragraphs 28–31?
   a. Rogers worked on a number of television shows as a young man, including *The Kate Smith Hour* and *The Children's Corner*.
   b. In 1953, Rogers left commercial TV for public TV.
   c. Combining TV, psychology, and theology, Rogers built a successful career in television.
   d. *Mister Rogers' Neighborhood* was patterned after a fifteen-minute Canadian show called *Misterogers*.

Supporting Details

6. The set for the *Mister Rogers' Neighborhood* program is
   a. clean and modern.
   b. outdated but comforting.
   c. always changing.
   d. filled with state-of-the-art puppets.

7. Mr. Rogers
   a. began his TV career in children's programs.
   b. answers his fan mail himself.
   c. now has a show that is filmed in Canada.
   d. always planned to go into television.

Transitions

8. The second sentence below expresses a relationship of
   a. time.
   b. addition.
   c. contrast.
   d. cause and effect.

> Rogers' persona is unlike anything you're liable to see on television: slow, deliberate, gentle. Children accept it because it is so like them: genuine. (Paragraph 6)

Inferences

9. When Rogers said, "I would like to think I can create some sort of atmosphere that allows people to be comfortable enough to be who they are. And consequently, if they are, they can grow from there. A lot of this—all of this—is just tending soil" (paragraphs 52–53), he implied that
   a. he wishes to create a positive environment in which people can blossom.
   b. he is an experienced and loving gardener.
   c. he wishes for young people eventually to gain the religious beliefs he holds.
   d. he hopes the young people at the graduation are well-prepared for life.

10. The author's general tone reveals that her attitude toward Fred Rogers is
    a. pessimistic.
    b. excited and playful.
    c. respectful and admiring.
    d. both positive and negative.

OUTLINING

The following outline shows the general structure of the selection. Complete the outline by filling in the three missing parts in the correct order. The missing parts are listed in random order after the outline.

1. Introduction: Boston U. commencement—how Fred Rogers was received and how he began his presentation

2. _____

3. _____

4. _____

5. Relationships: Brian Campbell, Teresa Edmondson, Johnny Costa

6. Conclusion: Fred Rogers' message at the Boston U. commencement and how it was received

Items Missing from the Outline

His current show and its success
His background: childhood, professional education, and previous work
His current life

DISCUSSION QUESTIONS

1. Did you ever watch *Mister Rogers' Neighborhood* as a child? As a grownup? What were your reactions to the show?

2. Why do you think Laskas included the anecdote about Brian Campbell in her article? In other words, what does that anecdote tell readers about the public Mister Rogers and the real Fred Rogers?

3. Fred Rogers included in his speech this quotation from *The Little Prince:* "What is essential is invisible to the eye." What does that mean, and why do you think he chose this quotation for his audience?

    How does this quotation relate to Johnny Costa's comment that "if you strip away the facades and you think about the important things, we are almost exactly like brothers"?

4. Some people consider Fred Rogers to be a hero. Would you agree? Does he embody any of the qualities that you would associate with a hero?

3

I Know Why the Caged Bird Sings
Maya Angelou

Preview

Maya Angelou came into the public eye when she delivered a poem at the inauguration of President Bill Clinton. She had written the poem especially for the occasion. But she was already known to the millions of people who had read one or more installments of her moving autobiography. The following excerpt is taken from the first and most popular of her autobiographical books, *I Know Why the Caged Bird Sings*. It describes her sexual abuse at the hands of her mother's friend, a Mr. Freeman. At the time, she was eight years old. Her nickname was Ritie, and she was living in St. Louis with her mother, her older brother, Bailey, and Mr. Freeman.

Mother was competent° in providing for us. Even if that meant getting someone else to furnish the provisions°. Although she was a nurse, she never worked at her profession while we were with her. Mr. Freeman brought in the necessities and she earned extra money cutting poker games in gambling parlors. The straight eight-to-five world simply didn't have enough glamour for her, and it was twenty years later that I first saw her in a nurse's uniform.

1

---

competent (1): capable
provisions (1): necessary supplies

Mr. Freeman was a foreman in the Southern Pacific yards and came   2
home late sometimes, after Mother had gone out. He took his dinner off
the stove where she had carefully covered it and which she had
admonished° us not to bother. He ate quietly in the kitchen while Bailey
and I read separately and greedily our own Street and Smith pulp
magazine. Now that we had spending money, we bought the illustrated
paperbacks with their gaudy° pictures. When Mother was away, we were
put on an honor system. We had to finish our homework, eat dinner and
wash the dishes before we could read or listen to *The Lone Ranger,*
Crime Busters or *The Shadow.*

Mr. Freeman moved gracefully, like a big brown bear, and seldom   3
spoke to us. He simply waited for Mother and put his whole self into the
waiting. He never read the paper or patted his foot to the radio. He
waited. That was all.

If she came home before we went to bed, we saw the man come   4
alive. He would start out of the big chair, like a man coming out of sleep,
smiling. I would remember then that a few seconds before, I had heard a
car door slam; then Mother's footsteps would signal from the concrete
walk. When her key rattled the door, Mr. Freeman would have already
asked his habitual question, "Hey, Bibbi, have a good time?"

His query° would hang in the air while she sprang over to peck him   5
on the lips. Then she turned to Bailey and me with the lipstick kisses.
"Haven't you finished your homework?" If we had and were just
reading—"O.K., say your prayers and go to bed." If we hadn't—"Then
go to your room and finish . . . then say your prayers and go to bed."

Mr. Freeman's smile never grew, it stayed at the same intensity°.   6
Sometimes Mother would go over and sit on his lap and the grin on his
face looked as if it would stay there forever.

From our rooms we could hear the glasses clink and the radio   7
turned up. I think she must have danced for him on the good nights,
because he couldn't dance, but before I fell asleep I often heard feet
shuffling to dance rhythms.

I felt very sorry for Mr. Freeman. I felt as sorry for him as I had felt   8
for a litter of helpless pigs born in our backyard sty in Arkansas. We
fattened the pigs all year long for the slaughter on the first good frost, and
even as I suffered for the cute little wiggly things, I knew how much I

---

admonished (2): warned
gaudy (2): showy
query (5): question
intensity (6): strength

was going to enjoy the fresh sausage and hog's headcheese they could give me only with their deaths.

Because of the lurid° tales we read and our vivid° imaginations and, probably, memories of our brief but hectic lives, Bailey and I were afflicted—he physically and I mentally. He stuttered, and I sweated through horrifying nightmares. He was constantly told to slow down and start again, and on my particularly bad nights my mother would take me in to sleep with her, in the large bed with Mr. Freeman.   9

Because of a need for stability°, children easily become creatures of habit. After the third time in Mother's bed, I thought there was nothing strange about sleeping there.   10

One morning she got out of bed for an early errand, and I fell asleep again. But I awoke to a pressure, a strange feeling on my left leg. It was too soft to be a hand, and it wasn't the touch of clothes. Whatever it was, I hadn't encountered the sensation in all the years of sleeping with Momma. It didn't move, and I was too startled to. I turned my head a little to the left to see if Mr. Freeman was awake and gone, but his eyes were open and both hands were above the cover. I knew, as if I had always known, it was his "thing" on my leg.   11

He said, "Just stay right here, Ritie, I ain't gonna hurt you." I wasn't afraid, a little apprehensive°, maybe, but not afraid. Of course I knew that lots of people did "it" and they used their "things" to accomplish the deed, but no one I knew had ever done it to anybody. Mr. Freeman pulled me to him, and put his hand between my legs. He didn't hurt, but Momma had drilled into my head: "Keep your legs closed, and don't let nobody see your pocketbook."   12

"Now, I didn't hurt you. Don't get scared." He threw back the blankets and his "thing" stood up like a brown ear of corn. He took my hand and said, "Feel it." It was mushy and squirmy like the inside of a freshly killed chicken. Then he dragged me on top of his chest with his left arm, and his right hand was moving so fast and his heart was beating so hard that I was afraid that he would die. Ghost stories revealed how people who died wouldn't let go of whatever they were holding. I wondered if Mr. Freeman died holding me how I would ever get free. Would they have to break his arms to get me loose?   13

Finally, he was quiet, and then came the nice part. He held me so   14

---

lurid (9): sensational
vivid (9): lively
stability (10): lack of change
apprehensive (12): uneasy

softly that I wished he wouldn't ever let me go. I felt at home. From the way he was holding me I knew he'd never let me go or let anything bad ever happen to me. This was probably my real father and we had found each other at last. But then he rolled over, leaving me in a wet place and stood up.

"I gotta talk to you, Ritie." He pulled off his shorts that had fallen to   15
his ankles, and went into the bathroom.

It was true the bed was wet, but I knew I hadn't had an accident.   16
Maybe Mr. Freeman had one while he was holding me. He came back with a glass of water and told me in a sour voice, "Get up. You peed in the bed." He poured water on the wet spot, and it did look like my mattress on many mornings.

Having lived in Southern strictness, I knew when to keep quiet   17
around adults, but I did want to ask him why he said I peed when I was sure he didn't believe that. If he thought I was naughty, would that mean that he would never hold me again? Or admit that he was my father? I had made him ashamed of me.

"Ritie, you love Bailey?" He sat down on the bed and I came close,   18
hoping. "Yes." He was bending down, pulling on his socks, and his back was so large and friendly I wanted to rest my head on it.

"If you ever tell anybody what we did, I'll have to kill Bailey."   19

What had we done? We? Obviously he didn't mean my peeing in the   20
bed. I didn't understand and didn't dare ask him. It had something to do with his holding me. But there was no chance to ask Bailey either, because that would be telling what we had done. The thought that he might kill Bailey stunned me. After he left the room I thought about telling Mother that I hadn't peed in the bed, but then if she asked me what happened I'd have to tell her about Mr. Freeman holding me, and that wouldn't do.

It was the same old quandary°. I had always lived it. There was an   21
army of adults, whose motives and movements I just couldn't understand and who made no effort to understand mine. There was never any question of my disliking Mr. Freeman, I simply didn't understand him either.

For weeks after, he said nothing to me, except the gruff hellos   22
which were given without ever looking in my direction.

This was the first secret I had ever kept from Bailey and sometimes   23
I thought he should be able to read it on my face, but he noticed nothing.

I began to feel lonely for Mr. Freeman and the encasement° of his big   24

---

quandary (21): state of confusion
encasement (24): enclosure

arms. Before, my world had been Bailey, food, Momma, the Store, reading books and Uncle Willie. Now, for the first time, it included physical contact.

I began to wait for Mr. Freeman to come in from the yards, but   25
when he did, he never noticed me, although I put a lot of feeling into "Good evening, Mr. Freeman."

One evening, when I couldn't concentrate on anything, I went over   26
to him and sat quickly on his lap. He had been waiting for Mother again. Bailey was listening to *The Shadow* and didn't miss me. At first Mr. Freeman sat still, not holding me or anything, then I felt a soft lump under my thigh begin to move. It twitched against me and started to harden. Then he pulled me to his chest. He smelled of coal dust and grease and he was so close I buried my face in his shirt and listened to his heart, it was beating just for me. Only I could hear the thud, only I could feel the jumping on my face. He said, "Sit still, stop squirming." But all the time, he pushed me around on his lap, then suddenly he stood up and I slipped down to the floor. He ran to the bathroom.

For months he stopped speaking to me again. I was hurt and for a   27
time felt lonelier than ever. But then I forgot about him, and even the memory of his holding me precious melted into the general darkness just beyond the great blinkers of childhood.

I read more than ever, and wished my soul that I had been born a boy.   28
Horatio Alger was the greatest writer in the world. His heroes were always good, always won, and were always boys. I could have developed the first two virtues, but becoming a boy was sure to be difficult, if not impossible.

The Sunday funnies influenced me, and although I admired the   29
strong heroes who always conquered in the end, I identified with Tiny Tim. In the toilet, where I used to take the papers, it was tortuous to look for and exclude the unnecessary pages so that I could learn how he would finally outwit his latest adversary°. I wept with relief every Sunday as he eluded° the evil men and bounded back from each seeming defeat as sweet and gentle as ever. The Katzenjammer kids were fun because they made the adults look stupid. But they were a little too smart-alecky for my taste.

When spring came to St. Louis, I took out my first library card, and   30
since Bailey and I seemed to be growing apart, I spent most of my Saturdays at the library (no interruptions) breathing in the world of penniless shoeshine boys who, with goodness and perseverance°, became

---

adversary (29): opponent
eluded (29): cleverly escaped
perseverance (30): steadily sticking to a purpose despite difficulties

rich, rich men, and gave baskets of goodies to the poor on holidays. The little princesses who were mistaken for maids, and the long-lost children mistaken for waifs°, became more real to me than our house, our mother, our school or Mr. Freeman.

During those months we saw our grandparents and the uncles (our only aunt had gone to California to build her fortune), but they usually asked the same question, "Have you been good children?" for which there was only one answer. Even Bailey wouldn't have dared to answer No.   31

On a late spring Saturday, after our chores (nothing like those in Stamps*) were done, Bailey and I were going out, he to play baseball and I to the library. Mr. Freeman said to me, after Bailey had gone downstairs, "Ritie, go get some milk for the house."   32

Mother usually brought milk when she came in, but that morning as Bailey and I straightened the living room her bedroom door had been open, and we knew that she hadn't come home the night before.   33

He gave me the money and I rushed to the store and back to the house. After putting the milk in the icebox, I turned and had just reached the front door when I heard, "Ritie." He was sitting in the big chair by the radio. "Ritie, come here." I didn't think about the holding time until I got close to him. His pants were open and his "thing" was standing out of his britches by itself.   34

"No, sir, Mr. Freeman." I started to back away. I didn't want to touch that mushy-hard thing again, and I didn't need him to hold me any more. He grabbed my arm and pulled me between his legs. His face was still and looked kind, but he didn't smile or blink his eyes. Nothing. He did nothing, except reach his left hand around to turn on the radio without even looking at it. Over the noise of music and static, he said, "Now, this ain't gonna hurt you much. You liked it before, didn't you?"   35

I didn't want to admit that I had in fact liked his holding me or that I had liked his smell or the hard heart-beating, so I said nothing. And his face became like the face of one of those mean natives the Phantom was always having to beat up.   36

His legs were squeezing my waist. "Pull down your drawers." I hesitated for two reasons: he was holding me too tight to move, and I was sure that any minute my mother or Bailey or the Green Hornet would   37

---

waifs (30): homeless children

*Stamps was a town in Arkansas where Ritie and Bailey had lived with their grandmother, who assigned them many more chores than their mother had.

bust in the door and save me.

"We was just playing before." He released me enough to snatch down my bloomers, and then he dragged me closer to him. Turning the radio up loud, too loud, he said, "If you scream, I'm gonna kill you. And if you tell, I'm gonna kill Bailey." I could tell he meant what he said. I couldn't understand why he wanted to kill my brother. Neither of us had done anything to him. And then.

Then there was the pain. A breaking and entering when even the senses are torn apart. The act of rape on an eight-year-old body is a matter of the needle giving because the camel can't. The child gives, because the body can, and the mind of the violator cannot.

I thought I had died—I woke up in a white-walled world, and it had to be heaven. But Mr. Freeman was there and he was washing me. His hands shook, but he held me upright in the tub and washed my legs. "I didn't meant to hurt you, Ritie. I didn't mean it. But don't you tell . . . Remember, don't you tell a soul."

I felt cool and very clean and just a little tired. "No, sir, Mr. Freeman, I won't tell." I was somewhere above everything. "It's just that I'm so tired I'll just go and lay down a while, please," I whispered to him. I thought if I spoke out loud, he might become frightened and hurt me again. He dried me and handed me my bloomers. "Put these on and go to the library. Your momma ought to be coming home soon. You just act natural."

Walking down the street, I felt the wet on my pants, and my hips seemed to be coming out of their sockets. I couldn't sit long on the hard seats in the library (they had been constructed for children), so I walked by the empty lot where Bailey was playing ball, but he wasn't there. I stood for a while and watched the big boys tear around the dusty diamond and then headed home.

After two blocks, I knew I'd never make it. Not unless I counted every step and stepped on every crack. I had started to burn between my legs more than the time I'd wasted Sloan's Liniment on myself. My legs throbbed, or rather the insides of my thighs throbbed, with the same force that Mr. Freeman's heart had beaten. Thrum . . . step . . . thrum . . . step . . . STEP ON THE CRACK . . . thrum . . . step. I went up the stairs one at a, one at a, one at a time. No one was in the living room, so I went straight to bed, after hiding my red-and-yellow-stained drawers under the mattress.

When Mother came in she said, "Well, young lady, I believe this is the first time I've seen you go to bed without being told. You must be sick."

I wasn't sick, but the pit of my stomach was on fire—how could I tell her that? Bailey came in later and asked me what the matter was. There was nothing to tell him. When Mother called us to eat and I said I wasn't hungry, she laid her cool hand on my forehead and cheeks. "Maybe it's the measles. They say they're going around the neighborhood." After she took my temperature she said, "You have a little fever. You've probably just caught them."

Mr. Freeman took up the whole doorway. "Then Bailey ought not to   46
be in there with her. Unless you want a house full of sick children." She answered over her shoulder, "He may as well have them now as later. Get them over with." She brushed by Mr. Freeman as if he were made of cotton. "Come on, Junior. Get some cool towels and wipe your sister's face."

As Bailey left the room, Mr. Freeman advanced to the bed. He   47
leaned over, his whole face a threat that could have smothered me. "If you tell . . ." And again, so softly, I almost didn't hear it—"If you tell." I couldn't summon up the energy to answer him. He had to know that I wasn't going to tell anything. Bailey came in with the towels and Mr. Freeman walked out.

Later Mother made a broth and sat on the edge of the bed to feed   48
me. The liquid went down my throat like bones. My belly and behind were as heavy as cold iron, but it seemed my head had gone away and pure air had replaced it on my shoulders. Bailey read to me from *The Rover Boys* until he got sleepy and went to bed.

That night I kept waking to hear Mother and Mr. Freeman arguing. I   49
couldn't hear what they were saying, but I did hope that she wouldn't make him so mad that he'd hurt her too. I knew he could do it, with his cold face and empty eyes. Their voices came in faster and faster, the high sounds on the heels of the lows. I would have liked to have gone in. Just passed through as if I were going to the toilet. Just show my face and they might stop, but my legs refused to move. I could move the toes and ankles, but the knees had turned to wood.

Maybe I slept, but soon morning was there and Mother was pretty   50
over my bed. "How're you feeling, baby?"

"Fine, Mother." An instinctive answer. "Where's Bailey?"   51

She said he was still asleep but that she hadn't slept all night. She   52
had been in my room off and on to see about me. I asked her where Mr. Freeman was, and her face chilled with remembered anger. "He's gone. Moved this morning. I'm going to take your temperature after I put on your Cream of Wheat."

Could I tell her now? The terrible pain assured me that I couldn't.   53
What he did to me, and what I allowed, must have been very bad if already God let me hurt so much. If Mr. Freeman was gone, did that mean Bailey was out of danger? And if so, if I told him, would he still love me?

After Mother took my temperature, she said she was going to bed   54 for a while but to wake her if I felt sicker. She told Bailey to watch my face and arms for spots and when they came up he could paint them with calamine lotion.

That Sunday goes and comes in my memory like a bad connection 55 on an overseas telephone call. Once, Bailey was reading *The Katzenjammer Kids* to me, and then without a pause for sleeping, Mother was looking closely at my face, and soup trickled down my chin and some got into my mouth and I choked. Then there was a doctor who took my temperature and held my wrist.

"Bailey!" I supposed I had screamed, for he materialized suddenly, 56 and I asked him to help me and we'd run away to California or France or Chicago. I knew that I was dying and, in fact, I longed for death, but I didn't want to die anywhere near Mr. Freeman. I knew that even now he wouldn't have allowed death to have me unless he wished it to.

Mother said I should be bathed and the linens had to be changed 57 since I had sweat so much. But when they tried to move me I fought, and even Bailey couldn't hold me. Then she picked me up in her arms and the terror abated for a while. Bailey began to change the bed. As he pulled off the soiled sheets he dislodged the panties I had put under the mattress. They fell at Mother's feet.

In the hospital, Bailey told me that I had to tell who did that to me, 58 or the man would hurt another little girl. When I explained that I couldn't tell because the man would kill him, Bailey said knowingly, "He can't kill me. I won't let him." And of course I believed him. Bailey didn't lie to me. So I told him.

Bailey cried at the side of my bed until I started to cry too. Almost 59 fifteen years passed before I saw my brother cry again.

Using the old brain he was born with (those were his words later on 60 that day) he gave his information to Grandmother Baxter, and Mr. Freeman was arrested and was spared the awful wrath° of my pistol-whipping uncles.

I would have liked to stay in the hospital the rest of my life. Mother 61 brought flowers and candy. Grandmother came with fruit and my uncles clumped around and around my bed, snorting like wild horses. When they were able to sneak Bailey in, he read to me for hours.

The saying that people who have nothing to do become busybodies is 62 not the only truth. Excitement is a drug, and people whose lives are filled

---

wrath (60): anger

with violence are always wondering where the next "fix" is coming from.

The court was filled. Some people even stood behind the churchlike   63
benches in the rear. Overhead fans moved with the detachment° of old
men. Grandmother Baxter's clients were there in gay and flippant°
array°. The gamblers in pin-striped suits and their makeup-deep women
whispered to me out of blood-red mouths that now I knew as much as
they did. I was eight, and grown. Even the nurses in the hospital had told
me that now I had nothing to fear. "The worst is over for you," they had
said. So I put the words in all the smirking° mouths.

I sat with family (Bailey couldn't come) and they rested still on the   64
seats like solid, cold gray tombstones. Thick and forevermore unmoving.

Poor Mr. Freeman twisted in his chair to look empty threats over to   65
me. He didn't know that he couldn't kill Bailey . . . and Bailey didn't lie
. . . to me.

"What was the defendant wearing?" That was Mr. Freeman's   66
lawyer.

"I don't know."   67

"You mean to say this man raped you and you don't know what he   68
was wearing?" He snickered° as if I had raped Mr. Freeman. "Do you
know if you were raped?"

A sound pushed in the air of the court (I was sure it was laughter). I   69
was glad that Mother had let me wear the navy-blue winter coat with
brass buttons. Although it was too short and the weather was typical St.
Louis hot, the coat was a friend that I hugged to me in the strange and
unfriendly place.

"Was that the first time the accused touched you?" The question   70
stopped me. Mr. Freeman had surely done something very wrong, but I
was convinced that I had helped him to do it. I didn't want to lie, but the
lawyer wouldn't let me think, so I used silence as a retreat.

"Did the accused try to touch you before the time he or rather you   71
say he raped you?"

I couldn't say yes and tell them how he had loved me once for a few   72
minutes and how he had held me close before he thought I had peed in
my bed. My uncles would kill me and Grandmother Baxter would stop
speaking, as she often did when she was angry. And all those people in

---

detachment (63): lack of interest
flippant (63): improper
array (63): clothing
smirking (63): smiling in an offensive way
snickered (68): laughed in a sly, partly held-back way

the court would stone me as they had stoned the harlot in the Bible. And Mother, who thought I was such a good girl, would be so disappointed. But most important, there was Bailey. I had kept a big secret from him.

"Marguerite, answer the question. Did the accused touch you before the occasion on which you claim he raped you?" 73

Everyone in the court knew that the answer had to be No. Everyone except Mr. Freeman and me. I looked at his heavy face trying to look as if he would have liked me to say No. I said No. 74

The lie lumped in my throat and I couldn't get air. How I despised° the man for making me lie. Old, mean, nasty thing. Old, black, nasty thing. The tears didn't soothe my heart as they usually did. I screamed, "Ole, mean, dirty thing, you. Dirty old thing." Our lawyer brought me off the stand and to my mother's arms. The fact that I had arrived at my desired destination by lies made it less appealing to me. 75

Mr. Freeman was given one year and one day, but he never got a chance to do his time. His lawyer (or someone) got him released that very afternoon. 76

In the living room, where the shades were drawn for coolness, Bailey and I played Monopoly on the floor. I played a bad game because I was thinking how I would be able to tell Bailey how I had lied and, even worse for our relationship, kept a secret from him. Bailey answered the doorbell, because Grandmother was in the kitchen. A tall white policeman asked for Mrs. Baxter. Had they found out about the lie? Maybe the policeman was coming to put me in jail because I had sworn on the Bible that everything I said would be the truth, the whole truth, so help me, God. The man in our living room was taller than the sky and whiter than my image of God. He just didn't have the beard. 77

"Mrs. Baxter, I thought you ought to know. Freeman's been found dead on the lot behind the slaughterhouse." 78

Softly, as if she were discussing a church program, she said, "Poor man." She wiped her hands on the dishtowel and just as softly asked, "Do they know who did it?" 79

The policeman said, "Seems like he was dropped there. Some say he was kicked to death." 80

Grandmother's color only rose a little. "Tom, thanks for telling me. Poor man. Well, maybe it's better this way. He was a mad dog. Would you like a glass of lemonade? Or some beer?" 81

Although he looked harmless, I knew he was a dreadful angel counting out my many sins. 82

---

despised (75): hated

"No, thanks, Mrs. Baxter. I'm on duty. Gotta be getting back."   83

"Well, tell your ma that I'll be over when I take up my beer and   84
remind her to save some kraut for me."

And the recording angel was gone. He was gone, and a man was dead   85
because I lied. Where was the balance in that? One lie surely wouldn't be
worth a man's life. Bailey could have explained it all to me, but I didn't dare
ask him. Obviously I had forfeited° my place in heaven forever, and I was
as gutless as the doll I had ripped to pieces ages ago. Even Christ Himself
turned His back on Satan. Wouldn't He turn His back on me? I could feel
the evilness flowing through my body and waiting, pent up°, to rush off my
tongue if I tried to open my mouth. I clamped my teeth shut, I'd hold it in. If
it escaped, wouldn't it flood the world and all the innocent people?

Grandmother Baxter said, "Ritie and Junior, you didn't hear a thing.   86
I never want to hear this situation nor that evil man's name mentioned in
my house again. I mean that." She went back into the kitchen to make
apple strudel for my celebration.

Even Bailey was frightened. He sat all to himself, looking at a   87
man's death—a kitten looking at a wolf. Not quite understanding it but
frightened all the same.

In those moments, I decided that although Bailey loved me he   88
couldn't help. I had sold myself to the Devil and there could be no
escape. The only thing I could do was to stop talking to people other than
Bailey. Instinctively, or somehow, I knew that because I loved him so
much I'd never hurt him, but if I talked to anyone else that person might
die too. Just my breath, carrying my words out, might poison people and
they'd curl up and die like the black fat slugs that only pretended.

I had to stop talking.   89

I discovered that to achieve perfect personal silence all I had to do   90
was to attach myself leechlike to sound. I began to listen to everything. I
probably hoped that after I had heard all the sounds, really heard them
and packed them down, deep in my ears, the world would be quiet
around me. I walked into rooms where people were laughing, their voices
hitting the walls like stones, and I simply stood still—in the midst of the
riot of sound. After a minute or two, silence would rush into the room
from its hiding place because I had eaten up all the sounds.

In the first weeks my family accepted my behavior as a post-rape,   91
post-hospital affliction. (Neither the term nor the experience was

---

forfeited (85): lost because of an offense
pent up (85): held in

mentioned in Grandmother's house, where Bailey and I were again staying.) They understood that I could talk to Bailey, but to no one else.

Then came the last visit from the visiting nurse, and the doctor said   92
I was healed. That meant that I should be back on the sidewalks playing handball or enjoying the games I had been given when I was sick. When I refused to be the child they knew and accepted me to be, I was called impudent° and my muteness° sullenness°.

For a while I was punished for being so uppity° that I wouldn't   93
speak; and then came the thrashings, given by any relative who felt himself offended.

[Because of Maya's continuing refusal to talk, she and Bailey were sent to stay with her grandmother in Arkansas. It was there that she met a remarkable woman who encouraged her to begin speaking again.]

Note: This selection is taken from the book *I Know Why the Caged Bird Sings* by Maya Angelou. For information on how to obtain the book, turn to page 564.

READING COMPREHENSION QUESTIONS

Vocabulary in Context

1. The word *afflicted* in "Bailey and I were afflicted—he physically and I mentally. He stuttered, and I sweated through horrifying nightmares" (paragraph 9) means
   a. adored.
   b. troubled.
   c. pleased.
   d. trusted.

2. The word *abated* in "Mother said I should be bathed and the linens had to be changed. . . . Then she picked me up in her arms and the terror abated for a while" (paragraph 57) means
   a. repeated.
   b. decreased.
   c. comforted.
   d. misled.

---

impudent (92): disrespectful
muteness (92): silence
sullenness (92): moodiness
uppity (93): full of pride, snobbish

Central Point and Main Ideas

3. Which sentence best expresses the central point of the selection?
   a. Children are often abused by those they know and trust.
   b. Childhood sexual abuse caused the author great physical and psychological pain.
   c. As a child, the author and her brother lived in St. Louis with her mother and her mother's boyfriend.
   d. If justice is not officially served, then people may take it into their own hands.

4. Which sentence best expresses the main idea of paragraph 72?
   a. Ritie was afraid her uncles and grandmother would become angry with her.
   b. Ritie's childish fears kept her from telling the truth about Mr. Freeman.
   c. Ritie was especially fearful of disappointing her brother.
   d. In Ritie's mind, she was somehow like the harlot in the Bible.

Supporting Details

5. At first, Ritie didn't tell anyone about being raped because
   a. she was afraid Mr. Freeman would hurt Bailey.
   b. no one ever believed her.
   c. she couldn't speak well.
   d. she wanted her mother to marry Mr. Freeman.

6. Ritie believed that Mr. Freeman died because
   a. he left her mother.
   b. she lied in court.
   c. he had raped her.
   d. he wasn't punished by the court.

Transitions

7. As in all narratives, the details of this reading are organized into a
   a. list of items.
   b. time order.
   c. contrast pattern.
   d. cause-and-effect pattern.

Inferences

8. From paragraph 14 we can conclude that
   a. Ritie longed for physical affection.
   b. Mr. Freeman was Ritie's real father.
   c. Mr. Freeman had sexually abused other children.
   d. Ritie still feared Mr. Freeman might die.

9. In paragraph 88, the author's tone can be described as
   a. joyful.
   b. hopeless.
   c. confident.
   d. comforting.

10. From paragraphs 91–93, we can infer that the adults in Ritie's life
    a. understood how guilty Ritie felt.
    b. were angry at Bailey.
    c. wanted Ritie to act like a grownup.
    d. were frustrated by Ritie's silence.

SUMMARIZING

Circle the letter—*a, b,* or *c*—of the passage that best completes the following summary of the reading from *I Know Why the Caged Bird Sings.*

Eight-year-old Ritie and her older brother, Bailey, lived with their mother and her boyfriend, Mr. Freeman. Mr. Freeman sexually abused Ritie twice without penetration. He threatened to kill Bailey if she told anyone. Though confused by the sexuality, Ritie welcomed Mr. Freeman's affection on those occasions. In between them, he ignored her. She soon forgot about the incidents and buried herself in reading. A few months later, Mr. Freeman forced Ritie into intercourse, causing her to pass out from the pain. He cleaned her up and again warned her not to tell anyone, and she didn't. However, her weak condition and the discovery of her stained panties made it clear that someone had raped her. By then, Mr. Freeman had moved out.

a. Ritie was brought to the hospital, where Bailey convinced her to tell who had raped her. Mr. Freeman was arrested, and Ritie very much enjoyed the rest of her stay in the hospital. Her mother and grandmother brought her gifts, and her uncles also visited. When Bailey was sneaked in, he read to her for hours. Later, Ritie had to attend and testify at Mr. Freeman's trial. Confused by her experiences with Mr. Freeman, Ritie felt that she was wrong for having been with him in such circumstances. She thought her uncles, grandmother, and mother would all be disappointed in her and that Bailey would be disappointed that she had kept it all secret from him. So when the defense lawyer asked if Mr. Freeman had ever touched her before the rape, she lied and said no.

b. After Ritie was hospitalized, Bailey told her to tell who had raped her so that another little girl wouldn't be hurt. Ritie explained that if she told, the man might kill Bailey. Bailey assured her that the man could not kill him, and she believed Bailey. She knew he would never lie to her. So she told Bailey, who told Grandma Baxter. Mr. Freeman was soon arrested and then put on trial. When Ritie was asked at the trial if he had ever touched her before the rape, she lied. Mr. Freeman was found guilty and sentenced to a year and a day in prison, but his sentence was quickly suspended. He was released the afternoon of the day he was sentenced. Soon after, he was found dead.

c. Ritie was brought to the hospital, where Bailey convinced her to tell who had raped her. Mr. Freeman was soon brought to trial, where Ritie, fearful of others' judgment, lied when asked if he had ever touched her before the rape. Mr. Freeman was sentenced to a year and a day in jail, but his sentence was suspended. He was found dead soon after his release. Ritie thought he died because she had lied in court. As a result, she decided she had to quit speaking to anyone but Bailey, whom she figured she loved so much that her words would not kill him. Her silence eventually angered the adults.

DISCUSSION QUESTIONS

1. How important a figure was Bailey in Ritie's life?

2. Ritie misunderstood what had happened to her—and what happened to Mr. Freeman. Explain how her misunderstanding made the experience even worse.

3. What do you think Angelou meant in comparing Mr. Freeman to the litter of helpless pigs (in paragraph 8)? How did the effects of Mr. Freeman's death contrast with the effects of the death of the pigs?

4. Statistics tell us that many children are sexually abused by adults, often relatives or friends of a family. What do you think can be done to help stop the sexual abuse of children?

4

Taking Charge
of My Life

Preview

The stories that follow are taken from the book *Taking Charge of My Life,* a collection of personal essays. They were among the hundreds submitted by college students in a scholarship program conducted by Townsend Press. Each of the students had taken at least one college developmental reading or writing course. To apply, students wrote a paper on the challenges, internal and external, that they faced in getting to college. The essays were judged for both content and form—for the power of the details as well as the overall effectiveness of the writing. Like the editors and teachers who judged the submissions, you may find reading the essays to be an inspiring experience.

1   RICKI GUTIERREZ
Oklahoma City Community College, Oklahoma City, Oklahoma

I had been drunk and high for the better part of nine months. I was living in an ex-lover's apartment while he was paying the bills and waiting for me to get it together and get a job. He was on the verge of throwing me out. I had been doing things for a long time that were against my moral values, hanging out with people with whom I said I would never hang out. I was doing things for money I said I would never do. I was forty pounds overweight, thirty-two years old, and a high

1

school dropout. I felt hopeless—completely and thoroughly hopeless. I had been out the night before with an ex-con drinking and carrying on.

I felt so much shame because of my behavior that I could not hold my head up. I thought of my son who had lived with his father since age three; he was now fourteen. I felt more guilt than I could stand about all the times I had stood him up, for all the times I lied to him, been late to pick him up, and neglected him when he was with me. I thought of the few friends I had left that were fed up with me because they never knew what I was going to do anymore. I felt alone and worthless.

I was drinking rum that night, straight shots of rum. I sat alone in the apartment and drew the conclusion that the world would be a much better place if I were not here. I believed this with all my heart, so I went across the breezeway where Jerry (my ex) was staying, at his mother's apartment. I took a full bottle of an anti-depressant that had been prescribed for his mother, without anyone noticing. I went back to the unkempt° apartment I was existing in. Then, I went to the phone to call a friend that was supposed to have come over for spaghetti, but had stood me up. I took another shot of rum while I talked to my friend. I counted out fifty pills in one pile and fifty in another. Then, I scooped up the first pile of pills, crammed them in my mouth, took the glass of water off the table, and began to swallow. I then said good-bye to my friend. I said I would talk to her later, not letting on for a minute what I was doing. I hung up the phone and swallowed the second fifty pills. After that, I walked over to the sofa to lie down and die.

Some hours later, when I came to in intensive care, I felt so disgusted, disappointed, ashamed, and angry. I wanted to run or disappear. "Why the hell am I still here?!" my mind screamed. I spent five days in intensive care before being escorted by the police to the Crisis Center, a detoxification center in the city where I lived. I felt as if I were walking around dead, not only because it's so hard to come off drugs and alcohol, but because I was carrying around the weight of my entire life. I left after seven days, again ushered by the police, but this time to the state hospital. I was so afraid, for the state mental hospital is where I always feared I belonged. And I was nothing less than terrified of being locked up in a "nut ward."

Instead of the mental hospital, I was sent to the neighboring drug and alcohol treatment center. This is where I was to begin the long and slow road to recovery, back to myself. I was told while I was there that I had a disease called alcoholism and that I was not a bad person, in spite

2

3

4

5

---

unkempt (3): messy, not tidy

of what I had always believed. I heard the stories of the courageous people that come to the treatment center from Alcoholics Anonymous. They said they had made some of the same or similar choices in life that I had made. They had been involved in destructive relationships such as I had been. Nevertheless, they were making changes in their lives. They said I could too.

I had reached a point in my life where I felt I could sink no lower. It seemed I couldn't die, yet I found the thought of living life as I had been unbearable. After hearing the stories of the people in Alcoholics Anonymous, I had something that I hadn't had for a very long time. I had a glimmer of hope. A counselor told me that my life was worth living, that I had a lot to offer, and that I was capable. The first time I heard the words, "You are capable," I felt stunned; I asked her to repeat the words. I found myself standing in the hall, as this woman was telling me that I was capable, with a big question mark on my face. It was as if I had never before heard these positive kinds of things. While growing up, I heard negative messages much more than I had heard anything that soothed my soul like the words the counselor was now saying to me.

In the thirty-one days that I was in the treatment center, I began a journey inward. I've been told by counselors and by my new friends that, while the journey is very painful at times, the only way out of the pain is to go back through it and face it head-on. I had denied the facts of my childhood long enough; in fact, I had almost denied the facts to my grave. When I was asked about my childhood, my response was always something of this nature: "My mother did the best she could do." I would focus on the few pleasant things and tell these things only, unless I was very drunk. And, on occasion, I would tell some of the darker things. The truth of the matter is, while my mother may have been doing the best she could do, it was by no stretch of the imagination good enough.

Before I was born, my mother had already been married three times and had three small girls besides myself. While married to her third husband, she began drinking and dancing with her husband's best friend. She became pregnant with me by this friend of her husband's. I was told this story by one of my sisters at about the age of twelve. My first memory is around the age of three. My mother led me by the hand into a baby-sitter's apartment. I felt afraid to stay with this man, and my sisters seemed afraid also. After my mother left, the man made pallets on the floor and asked us who wanted to sleep with him. For some reason I was chosen, and as we were lying there, in the still dark night, the man whispered something to me. He placed my small three-year-old hand on something soft and clammy. I felt squeamish. My hand jerked away from what it felt. The man whispered something else to me, and once again, he placed my hand there, this time squeezing my hand after he placed it where he wanted it. I knew this time not to move my hand. The man finally went to sleep; so did I.

The first of a long line of men in my mother's life that I remember   9 was a tall, olive-complected, dark-haired man. My sisters and I were in bed; my mother was sleeping with this man in another part of the small house. I awakened the next morning to this man scolding and shaming me for wetting in the bed. I was not much older than three.

Soon after, another olive-complected, dark-haired man entered our   10 lives. I remember his broad shoulders and dark eyes. The first time I saw him, he bent down to lift my small body from the floor. I felt his very large hands slip under my armpits as he lifted me up to his chest, holding my face at his. I felt timid° and shy as I looked at him. I got the feeling that this man was going to be my daddy, and I wanted a daddy. He placed me back on the ground with as much ease as when he picked me up. He then offered me a piece of candy, and I turned to go and play alone. My sisters were no longer living with us; they were now living with their fathers. Mother married this man, whose name was Freddie, and the hope I had for a father soon turned into one of the most startling° and gruesome° nightmares of my life.

Freddie and my mother spent many hours in their bedroom. One   11 time I crept to the door and peeked in at them; later my mother went to the bathroom, and Freddie came to the room where I was now playing, grabbed me by the collar, and said in a low whisper while looking straight into my eyes, "If you ever do that again, I will kill you."

I was still wetting the bed at age 4. Freddie told my mother he   12 would "break me" of wetting the bed. One morning I awakened to Freddie yanking the cover off me. He saw that I had, indeed, wet the bed. He then pulled me violently from the bed and stuck my face in the wet circle, rubbed my nose in it as if I were a dog. He tried to "break" me in this manner often.

Next, he informed me that if I were going to act like a baby and wet   13 the bed, I would be treated like a baby: I would have to wear a diaper the next time I wet the bed. He seemed very pleased with this new idea. I felt afraid and absolutely helpless. I was at the mercy of this man, and he had none. Although my mother was in the house while much of this was going on, she was simply not available. Why, I don't know.

---

timid (10): fearful
startling (10): surprising
gruesome (10): causing horror and disgust

The next day I was not only wearing a diaper, but I was made to parade up and down the sidewalk in front of our house so that the kids that were playing outside would see. I tried to walk softly so the children wouldn't see me. I remember well how I longed to become invisible. We moved often; therefore, I never had a chance to put down roots or get to know the neighboring children; but, at times like these, I can't say that I really wanted to get acquainted with my neighbors. I felt so ashamed, and less than human.

Freddie didn't like me around; so, often, when we had our meals, he and my mother would sit in the living room and eat together while I sat at the table alone. One night, I spilled my milk. Freddie came over to the chair where I sat, placed his hand on the back of my head, lifted me up, lowered me to my knees on the floor, pushed my head down, and said, "Lick it up."

Later when I reached school age, nothing changed except the houses we lived in and my mother's husbands. When I would have homework, my mother would send me to my room to do it. When I came out of the room to be tested by her and I didn't get it right, she would scream that she had things to do, and "What in the hell have you been doing in there anyway?" She would slap me across the face, take me by the arm and shove me back into my room. After that I would cry so hard I couldn't think. I soon quit bringing my homework home. I lied and said I didn't have any homework.

This is not an attempt to bash Freddie, my mother, or anyone else that has crossed my path over the years, but child abuse is real, and it does interfere with a person's ability to succeed in our world. These are grotesque° stories, and hard to read, I'm sure. They are equally as hard for me to relive as I write; nevertheless, these are things that have shaped my opinion of and feelings for myself and the world in which I live. These are the obstacles I've had to overcome to get into college, and these are the obstacles I will have to continue crossing in order to get my degree.

I want to overcome the abuse of my childhood. I want to live, and I want the education I feel I was robbed of as a child due to physical, mental, emotional, and sexual abuse and the instability of moving from place to place.

I'm taking charge of my life in these ways: I have not seen my mother in two years. I have been in therapy for three and a half years. My relationship with my son is improving, and I haven't had a drink or a drug in over two and a half years. I finished my first semester of college

grotesque (17): very odd

with the highest grades possible in effective reading, study skills, spelling, and College Writing II.

If I win this scholarship, I will use the money to continue my 20 education. I want to be a part of the mainstream of life, to be able to take care of myself, pay my bills, take vacations, enjoy life, and contribute to society in a positive way.

2 RUBY ROLON
Roane State Community College, Harriman, Tennessee

In 1953 on the 31st of May, I was born. I had beautiful parents who 21 loved me and helped me to grow into a person I liked very much. But on June 8, 1964, my father died. That began a whole new life for me. It was a life that I hope no child would ever have to live through, though I believe millions of children do.

Things seem to change when there is a death in the family. You 22 experience feelings you never knew existed in you, such as anger, jealousy, hurt, fear, and loneliness. You don't just feel these things; you start acting them out. So it was in my case.

My mother began drinking heavily after my father's death. She 23 would stay out all night, leaving the six of us alone to take care of ourselves. I thought we did pretty well. We could go anywhere, do anything. We didn't have any supervision at all.

I missed my mother. She wasn't the mother that got up every 24 morning and made us breakfast. She wasn't the mother that helped decorate Valentine boxes or bake cookies for us anymore. I remember my brother and me sharing a can of peas. I hated peas! But I learned to eat them because no one cooked.

I longed for my mother's attention. I wanted her to see that I was 25 growing into a young woman, but that didn't seem very important to her. She wanted the alcohol. We were second to her.

One of my sisters had married before Mom's drinking became 26 heavy. I was glad, because she wouldn't have to live like we did. She would be taken care of. I wanted to be loved too, most of all by my mother, but she could not separate herself from the bottle.

My older brother was thirteen at the time my mother began 27 drinking. By sixteen, he had been in trouble with the police, had stolen things, and God only knows what else went on in his life. Before his seventeenth birthday, he took a gun from someone and killed himself.

How alone he must have been. How hurt and afraid he must have 28 been of life. I never had a chance to tell him I loved him. I never had a chance to really know him. I wanted to know him more because he had grown into a person that you couldn't really understand. He was hardly ever home, and when he was, it was just briefly. I loved him, no matter what he thought of me.

Life went on for the rest of us. I existed, though not really wanting 29 to. I hated life. What was the reason for it? I saw no reason, no hope, no happiness. I HATED LIFE!

At sixteen, I decided I would quit school. Quitting was something I 30 had to do but didn't really want to do. The peer pressure was too much for me. I had been ridiculed and humiliated too many times about my clothes, my size, and my hanging out alone. I had no friends because no one wanted to get close to me.

Mom hadn't paid the bills, so the utilities had been cut off. We 31 washed our clothes by the side of the road at night. I don't remember how we cleaned our bodies. I think we had cold water, but I'm not sure. I just know that I didn't look nice or smell nice when I went to school. Mom never noticed. I wished she would have.

She did notice when I wanted to get married at eighteen. I had never 32 had a boyfriend, so I married the first man that asked me. I thought that I loved him, but I realized I just used him to escape that life of alcohol and misery. I never meant to hurt him. I never wanted to hurt anyone, ever.

I met another man that I thought could really make a difference in 33 my life. He did make a big difference. I wanted to commit suicide. He didn't love me. No one would ever love me! Why should I live?

I drank two bottles of pills. I was very tired of trying to get love. I 34 didn't know any other way. Not being loved hurt very much. I couldn't take any more hurting from anyone. I just wanted to die.

It didn't happen. I don't know why; it just didn't work. Someone 35 took care of me while I was "out." It wasn't the man I lived with. I awoke to find that I was pregnant.

I had tried so hard before to get pregnant. If I only had a child! 36 Someone I could love, someone to love me! Now I had a chance at life. I had a reason to live again! I knew that baby would be special. I just knew it!

I stayed another year with this baby's father. I had grown somehow. 37 I knew I had to be a responsible person. This was a life that I held in my hands. He was not going to be abandoned; he would not go hungry or go around dirty. He was special. Above all, he was loved.

I have married since then, and I have three children more. I'm very 38 blessed with my children. I don't have everything I need for my children, but they're very much loved. I'm trying to go to college now at thirty-nine years old. I've made this decision even though there are still many obstacles in my way. For example, I don't have the full support of my husband, although I wish I did. My children and I are going through trying times, but no one said it would be easy.

I'm determined to make it through because when I think of my past, 39 I think of their future. I also think of all the children in this world that are going through what I went through! I want to be there, if only for just one of them. As a social worker, maybe I can help save some child from a life full of hurt. I will make it through college and be a social worker because I am taking charge of my life! Then I can help others to make a difference.

3 STACY EBELING
Sheridan College, Sheridan, Wyoming

I learned to fail as a small child. The lessons taught in my family 40 had little to do with succeeding in school or life. I was a frail° and petite° girl who learned early that my ideas and perceptions° were worthless. I remember a time coming home after school when I was in the fourth grade. I was wearing my brown and white checkered dress. I was the first one to arrive of the four children. My mother was sitting in the kitchen talking to a friend and sipping coffee. I set my school books on the kitchen table and greeted them. Mom turned and asked me, "Is the wall black or white?" She was pointing at our white kitchen wall. I replied, "The wall is white." She slapped my face. My cheek stung and tears filled my eyes. I looked to her friend, who stoically° sat there and did nothing. At that moment, I tried to figure out what was happening. My mother then asked me again, "What color is the wall, Stacy?" Hurt and angry, I looked at her and said, "The wall is black." Mom looked at her friend and smiled. I picked up my school books and went to my room and cried. I learned in grade school that you do not challenge authority and that I was of little value.

My lessons in the classroom were sometimes as painful as they were 41 at home. I have a twin sister who is developmentally disabled. She had

---

frail (40: weak
petite (40): small
perceptions (40): views
stoically (40: calmly in the face of pain

always been in special education classes until our seventh grade year. She sat in the row to my right and one desk closer to the front of the classroom. Two boys sat in the same row with my sister, one of them in front of her and one behind her. We brought our lunches to school in a brown paper bag which we kept under our desks. On one occasion, the two boys began kicking Tracy's lunch back and forth between them. Tracy was too shy to stand up for herself. I was enraged that those boys were being mean to my sister. I whispered, "Stop it." The boy sitting beside me smashed her lunch with his foot and laughed at me. He then kicked her lunch back to his friend. I yelled, "Stop it!" The teacher had been writing on the blackboard with her back to the class. I heard her call my name: "Stacy, go to the back of the room." She grabbed a big ruler and followed me to the rear of the classroom and told me to bend over and put my hands on a table. She hit me three times while the class watched. She never asked me what happened. That day I was humiliated in school.

I went to five different high schools because my family moved so frequently. I don't recall anyone at school ever telling me what needed to be done to prepare to go on to college. No one ever helped me pick out classes. When I was sixteen and a sophomore in high school, my mother told me that I was smart enough to go to college. That same year, she and my stepfather bought me a new Ford Pinto. I sometimes drove friends to lunch off campus. On a fall afternoon, I came home right after school and was met by my mother. The first thing she said to me was, "There was a black boy in the back seat of your car today." I had taken three friends to lunch, and one of them was black. She took the car keys, and I no longer had a car. I was never allowed to drive a family vehicle again. Shortly after this, she kicked me out of the house. Survival was in and college was out. 42

After living with a teacher and his family for one year, I was allowed to move back home. My current stepfather was my first real father figure. He was the third stepfather, but he was also my first hope for a father. One Saturday night, we were downstairs sitting together watching television. He made a pass at me. I was frightened. I told my brother, hoping he would protect me. He confronted° my stepfather, who in turn told my mother. I had just graduated from high school, and Mother kicked me out again. She didn't believe my story. Not long after that I was married. 43

My husband had achieved all of his goals. He was satisfied with where he was in life. I worked off and on to supplement° our income. We 44

---

confronted (43): faced
supplement (44): add to

both came from dysfunctional° backgrounds where higher education was not a value. We repeated our programmed histories with each other and found our way to divorce court nine years later. I found myself alone with my four-year-old son. I met a male friend who tried to talk me into going to college. He wanted me to go to school. I wasn't ready. Financially and personally, the idea seemed impossible.

I had never been taught to plan ahead. Long-term goals were not   45
part of my existence. I had been a victim my entire life and had no insight into my condition. Depression and the resulting lack of self-esteem and self-confidence had become a way of life. There was no place in my life for school. Anyway, I was scared that I could fail again. I could feel as worthless as I did in our kitchen when I was in the fourth grade, or as humiliated as I was at the back of the room in the seventh grade, or as alone as I did when I was kicked out of my home.

I had a job selling janitorial supplies for a company that offered no   46
security or potential° for advancement. The owner never kept his promises regarding commissions and salary. I hated my job. I began to feel desperate. I was forced to stop and look in the mirror. Who was I? I was thirty-two years old and I had no identity, no real direction, and no purpose in my life. I wanted to lock myself up in my house and stay there. Something had to change. I had to take a risk. My male friend stood by me and encouraged me. I went to therapy. My therapist also encouraged me. I called the local college. I still didn't have the courage to go to the school yet. Two months later I called the college again. This time I made an appointment at the Learning Skills Center. It was tough for me to take that first step.

The staff wanted me to take some tests. The thought scared me. I   47
never excelled in school. I had not learned to value education. For the first time I wanted to do well, yet I feared failure. I took tests to explore my interests and to uncover what I was capable of doing at the collegiate level. The staff told me I was not ready to take on the courses offered without more preparation. These educators gave me an identity. I became an "adult returning student." I was one of the new generation seeking an education.

Sitting in class the first day was like being a kid again, but there I   48
was in an adult body. My pencil was rolling back and forth between my fingers nonstop! My foot tapped throughout that first class as if it had an independent source of energy. I lived through the first day of school.

It was quickly apparent that I did not know how to study. The   49

---

dysfunctional (44): damaging
potential (46): possibility

faculty had the foresight to see that I was enrolled in a class entitled "College Success." This teacher was dedicated to instilling° new skills in me that would ready me to face the world of academia. I needed to learn how to take notes, read a professor in order to succeed in any particular class, manage my time efficiently, prepare for tests, and successfully cope with stress in school.

The word "stress" does not adequately describe what came next. My ten-year-old son began to share me with textbooks. Suddenly, he was in competition with college prep math and a writing skills course. Cooking dinner, doing laundry, vacuuming the house, and paying bills also had to compete with these new demands on my limited resources. My social life died. Refusing to bury it entirely, I joined a support club at school. The group had dubbed itself ANTS for Adult Non-Traditional Students. I made new friends whose confidence in me exceeded my own. Just before the end of that first semester, they elected me president for the following school year. I had developed a desire to learn and to succeed. I was sure that I would barely pass two of my first three classes. When straight "A's" came in, I was ready to celebrate.

That semester was just the beginning. Next, it was on to courses like Introductory Algebra and English 101. A new wave of anxiety and fear swept over me. Furthermore, how was I going to stand up in front of the ANTS group and actually lead a meeting? Without realizing it, I took on the philosophy of a recovering alcoholic. I was now taking one day at a time. As the semester progressed, I maintained the attitude of giving my best effort. Some tests didn't go as well as others. I'd just do better on the next one. I was now a student. I was putting direction in my life. I had a future, in spite of my past!

I have not reached the summit of this peak yet. The economic recession discussed on the nightly network news is nothing compared to the financial dilemmas I face daily as a single parent in college. My child's new Cub Scout shirt meant careful sale shopping for that month's necessities. We will continue to carefully manage other resources as well in the years ahead before the sheepskin is in hand. Quality time with my child is a major objective enroute to the top of this mountain. I want an education to be as important to him as it now is to me. My desire is to succeed for both of us. He now brings his homework to the kitchen table and we work together.

The top of this mountain will be finishing my training as a physical therapist. However, this climb will not be my last; it is the preparation for

instilling (49): firmly planting

many more to come. My intellectual, emotional, and spiritual growth is a lifelong endeavor. I plan to share my success by sharing my story and my skills with others. I learned to fail as a child, and I am learning to succeed as an adult.

4   JUAN ANGEL
Blue Mountain Community College, Pendleton, Oregon

My name is Juan Angel. I am thirty years old, and I was born in Mexico.   54

As a child, I was alone for most of the time. My father was an alcoholic, and he abandoned my family and me when I was three years old. My mother had to struggle to survive by working from place to place in Mexico. Her good intentions to support me economically were not enough because of low salaries, so she eventually ended up working here in the United States.   55

I lived with some of my relatives in a little village in Mexico and worked from dawn to sunset and ate sometimes once a day. I felt totally condemned to die of starvation and hard work. My relatives spent the money that my mother sent me, claiming that I was just a child and didn't need it. As a defenseless child, I was innocent, ignorant, and lacked the courage to stand up against the abuse and the injustice. My Gramma, who lived in another little village, couldn't do anything about the oppression I suffered, and she probably didn't even know what was really happening in my life. My relatives covered everything up, and the complaints I made were ignored while my suffering continued to get worse. After five years of being mistreated, humiliated, and abused by my relatives, I decided to put an end to it, and I went to live with my Gramma.   56

When I moved into my Gramma's house, I started living a new lifestyle. By then, I was eight years old, and I felt for the first time proud of myself because I had made my first big decision in life.   57

My Gramma had some pigs, so I had to feed them. One day I was feeding them close to a water stream when I saw two boys passing by. They carried some books in their handbags. I saw them every day walking down a grassy road while I fed those pigs. My curiosity grew intensely, and one day I stopped them on their way back home. I asked them what they were doing, and they told me that they were attending school. I wanted to know if they knew how to read, and immediately they started reading and writing to show me. I simply couldn't believe it. When they left, I scratched my head and nodded for a moment, looking   58 toward the sky. I said, "Going to school! That's exactly the next step I have to work on." After I finished feeding those pigs, I went home. While I was walking home, I thought about how I would convince my Gramma to allow me to to go school. I knew it was going to be hard to convince her because there were around twenty boys in the village, and they were not attending school either, except those two whom I admired.

When I talked to her about my decision on going to school, she got 59 very upset, and she immediately thought about who would care for her pigs. I calmed her down by telling her that I would continue feeding them. She didn't accept my proposal at first, so I looked for the two boys and talked to them about my interest in going to school. They encouraged me to leave the house and forget about the pigs; they would help me to go. I thought it was not a bad idea, but I opposed it because my Gramma and I were living alone. In addition, the closest school was two miles away from the village. For those reasons I hesitated to make such a decision. I had spent two years growing pigs and hesitated about my next step.

Finally, I gave up and left my Gramma alone in the house. My 60 friends helped me find a place to sleep in town where the school was, and they gave me some food every day. They took me to the school, and I explained my situation to the principal; to my surprise, his name was Juan, also. He told me that my age (ten years old) wouldn't match the rules of the school. "You're too old," he said. He questioned me for about five minutes, and then he told me to come back the next day. He met with all the teachers, and after some deliberation°, they approved my enrollment as a new student. I was excited and happy about my achievement as a ten-year-old boy. On the other hand, I couldn't sleep very well at night because I remembered my Gramma very much. She was desperately looking for me, and she found me after a week. I cried while I explained to her why I had left home. She hugged me very hard, and then she went to talk to the principal about my desire to attend school. I never expected her to talk to the principal, but she did. I have never experienced so much happiness in my life as when I was ten years old.

I walked the two miles back and forth to school every day. In 61 addition, I had to feed the pigs early in the morning before I went to school and after I came home from school. I also chopped wood for cooking. I did chores at home as a responsible man in charge of a household. My Gramma and I lived happily for six years while I was in primary school.

---

deliberation (60): careful thought

After I finished my first six years in school, I had to make another   62
tough decision. I had to leave my Gramma completely alone because the
secondary school I wished to attend was in another town about three
hours away by bus. A few months before I took off, she began to suffer
from an acute° pain in her chest. I didn't want to leave her, but I did. I
wanted to stay in school as much as I could. I used to visit her every
weekend, but sometimes the lack of money made it impossible. When I
started my second year in the school, I began to worry about my
Gramma's health. Her chest pains were getting worse, and I received a
letter in which she said that she missed me very much.

A week later a friend of mine was looking for me at the school. He   63
told me that my Gramma was very sick. I immediately went to see her.
She was lying down with a blanket on the floor. When she saw me, she
hugged me very hard, and then she began to ask how my school was. I
could hardly answer her because my tears ran down my cheeks as never
before. She asked me not to cry, but I couldn't stop. She told me to
continue in school, and I promised her I would. A few minutes later, she
died in my arms, and I felt that everything was torn apart inside me. I
thought that I could never overcome the painful experience of losing my
Gramma forever.

My mother, who was here in the United States, got there in time for   64
the funeral. She asked me to come with her, but I refused her offer. She
came back to the United States, and I stayed in Mexico for another four
years of school. She continued asking me to join her. Finally, I gave in
and immigrated to the United States in 1988. I immediately attended an
English class at night and worked days. At the end of the year I got here,
my English teacher recommended me to a Hispanic program where I
could get my GED diploma. When I enrolled in the program, everything
was free, including a room in a dormitory. When I finished the program, I
had my GED. I then returned to my mother's house. I was unemployed,
and three months later, I started working on an irrigated farm, growing
alfalfa. I worked three years, and I quit because I wanted to find a more
flexible job which allowed me to go to college.

Now I'm working in a feed department on swing shift, and I'm   65
attending college in the morning. This department where I'm working
operates just in the wintertime, so I'm on the verge of being laid off. I'm
a part-time student at Blue Mountain Community College, and I would
like to continue attending college. I will keep trying to find ways to stay
in college.

---

acute (62): sharp

I have been confronting many obstacles in my life since my   66
childhood. I have challenged those obstacles, and I know by experience
how to overcome them. It has not been easy, but I always believe in
success through education. Even though I know the struggle is not over
yet, I will keep an optimistic smile toward the future.

5   REGINA RUIZ
Burlington County College, Pemberton, New Jersey

I feel funny. So very funny, telling you about my life, my feelings,   67
my secrets. I do not know how to welcome you into my heart and soul.
You see, nobody ever asked me what I thought or how I felt about life's
challenges. Or, maybe, they never really cared about what I thought.

My journey to Burlington County College began many years ago in   68
Caracas, Venezuela, where I was born and grew to a young lady full of
energy and life. My parents called me Regina because there was
something regal° about the sound. They had high hopes of my marrying a
local boy from a good, wealthy family. You know the kind—slick, black
hair, long sideburns, driving a sport car. The kind who brings you flowers
on every date and swears his undying love for you three days a week, and
the other days he is sleeping with Maria, the local social worker.

To get even, or because I was in a romantic haze°, I met and   69
married a U.S. Marine from Des Moines, Iowa, who was stationed at our
local Embassy, where I also worked.

Marriage, a home in America, and three beautiful children occupied   70
twenty-five years of my life.

Where did my life go? It went somewhere. But there is no lost-and-   71
found department for a life lost in the years.

The marriage was bad. It was so bad that I cried every night for all   72
those years. I would tell myself, "You are in a strange country—maybe
the customs are different. The children need me and I cannot admit
failure to my parents back in Venezuela."

As luck would have it, fate intervened°. My ex-Marine husband   73
found someone new and left me and the children with no money, very
hurt and depressed.

---

regal (68): royal
haze (69): fog
intervened (73): came in to alter a situation

I quickly took an inventory°—foreign-born, with not a great   74
command of the English language, no money, no job training and two
kids in college. The future looked bleak.

But it did not stop. My father died. I loved him so much, and he was   75
always my source of strength in need. Mother became ill.

I felt very hurt, lonely, angry, and very sorry for myself.   76

I remembered a saying my Dad would quote to me when things   77
were going wrong and the future looked black. He may have gotten this
quote from the Spanish edition of *Reader's Digest*. He would say, "My
dear, it is always the darkest when you are fresh out of matches."

"Dad, I am out of matches." Or so I thought.   78

I decided to make my life something worthwhile by helping people.   79
I wanted to help and heal. Maybe, at the same time, heal myself.

I appeared before the college doors with my knees shaking and full   80
of doubt. I wanted to be a nurse.

I enrolled in college. I was proud of myself for not falling into the   81
garbage pit waiting so close by.

Then the fun began—subjects which were very hard for me.   82

In order to survive, I managed to get two jobs to keep up with house   83
payments and food. The kids found college money by working and
appealing to their father.

I met my challenge on a daily basis. Now, my days begin long before   84
the sun makes its appearance. I stumble bleary-eyed° to the shower and
afterwards select the day's outfit. After a quick check in the mirror, I make
my way downstairs to prepare a quick breakfast along with my lunch, feed
the cat (who happens to be my alarm clock), and do what seems like a
million other small chores. Then I drive for forty-five minutes to the
Pemberton Campus, while studying my chemistry key notes on index
cards before a test. I would do this with tears in my eyes. You see, at the
same time I am worrying about the situation with my water heater that
slowly but surely is leaking and may not last until the new one can be
installed. In addition, I am anxious to schedule my exterminator's visit to
treat the termites discovered in my basement. My preoccupation with such
household woes is due to a cancelled appointment to have my furnace
cleaned, which resulted in a periodic spray of soot.

After a hectic morning of classes, I rush to my car for a hurried   85
thirty-minute ride to the office, where a desk piled high with import
documents is waiting for me, along with innumerable phone calls from

---

took an inventory (74): made a detailed list
bleary-eyed (84): having blurred eyes

the brokers, custom officials and suppliers. Meanwhile, an impatient boss wants to know the precise location of one of the fifty containers traveling between eastern Europe and Burlington, New Jersey.

As the clock winds toward 5:00 p.m., I get ready to travel back to   86
the Cinnaminson Campus for another round of classes. As I arrive on campus, I waste another thirty minutes searching for that nonexistent parking spot. My class continues until 10:00 in the evening, and I praise the Lord it doesn't last longer. By that time, I am beginning to see double. I slowly make my way to the car and begin the long commute home, counting in my mind how many customers I will see as a result of my second job—hairdressing. On evenings when I have no classes scheduled, I take appointments to cut hair or give permanents. As I arrive home, I find a hungry son and starving cat, both waiting to be fed. I usually cook something simple for us, then proceed to do the few dishes because I hate the thought of adding one more chore to my early morning schedule. By the time I finish getting ready for bed, it is midnight; I look up and see the stairway leading to the bedroom, which by then seems longer than the one outside the Philadelphia Museum of Art, and proceed to crawl in bed and into the arms of Morpheus°.

People question the wisdom of my studying to be a nurse. It may   87
take four or five years.

"You will never last," they tell me.   88

"You will be too old to lift a bed pan," they mock.   89

But I am not discouraged. There are twenty more courses ahead of   90
me before I get into the nursing area. While all these things challenge me, the greatest of all is to be able to hold my head high.

Somehow, just somehow, I think it might be all worth it—if I can   91
hold the hand of someone dying all alone in a cold hospital ward and whisper in their ear, "You are not alone, I am here, I am here, I will never leave you."

Maybe, just maybe, I will find that life that was lost. It is out there   92
somewhere.

But I know one thing—"I am in charge," and I will never let go   93
again. Never.

Morpheus (86): the god of dreams in Greek mythology

6   **LACEY WRAY**
D'Youville College, Buffalo, New York

Is bulimia a disease or just a habit? This question is frequently   94
asked by people of all ages. Many people say that it's a disease, and
others say that bulimia is just a bad habit that can be easily broken. I do
not claim to know the appropriate answer, but I have some ideas from my
own personal experience. My experience with bulimia began on January
6, 1988. I was fourteen years old and a freshman in high school, but I had
the self-confidence of a five-year-old who was starting kindergarten.

During the previous September my father and now ex-step-mom   95
invited me on a trip to North Carolina. I was extremely excited because
my mom had only let me go on one other vacation with my father. When
I went on the first vacation with my father, I was treated as a mere child,
and I was not permitted to venture° off and do things on my own. This
time it was going to be different. A week at the beach, gorgeous guys—
this was definitely a young teen's dream vacation. At least this was my
dream vacation until my father totally destroyed it. My father and I were
discussing our plans for the trip, and he made a comment that would
impact° my life forever. He very casually stated, as if he were only
asking me what I would like for dinner, "I hope you lose some weight
because I don't want to take a fat little girl with me to the beach!"

At that point I figured I'd lose the weight or I'd lose my chance for   96
a dream vacation. I began a slow diet with an average weight loss of two
pounds per week. I was happy, but my father just kept asking, "Aren't
you going on a diet?" I began binging° constantly because he upset me,
and then so that I wouldn't gain the weight, I began the cycle of binging
and purging°, bulimia at its best. Many people feel that purging is
difficult, but I found the task rather easy. In the beginning all that I
needed to do was touch the back of my throat with two of my fingers,
and I would begin vomiting. Eventually, I would eat and my body would
automatically begin purging.

Before I knew it, I had lost forty pounds in three months. I had   97
successfully pleased my father and in the process pleased myself. Even
though I stopped losing weight after the three months, I was still trapped

---

venture (95): dare to go
impact (95): have an effect upon
binging (96): satisfying oneself with large amounts (of food, drink,
            etc.) at a time
purging (96): emptying (in bulimia, vomiting)

in the cycle, and I couldn't escape. By the time we reached North Carolina, I had gone from a size 13-14 to a size 7-8. My skin had become extremely pale, and I was constantly tired. My hair had begun falling out, and my menstrual periods ceased.

It was at this point that I realized I had become extremely malnourished, and because of this I decided to start eating again. Within two months I had put on sixty pounds and felt as if I had betrayed my father. I decided to begin dieting again: this time the right way. I soon discovered it just isn't that easy to stop being bulimic. I felt as if the bulimia had taken over. Even though I tried to eat and not purge myself, it seemed as if my body was on automatic pilot. It was at this point that I admitted to myself, for the first time, that I had a disease. 98

For the past four years I have been on a diet roller-coaster. I would do fine for three or four days, and then I would willingly let the bulimia take over. Once I realized the bulimia had taken over, I would stop, but the cycle would soon start again. Gain weight, diet, bulimia, stop dieting, gain weight, etc. . . . 99

Well, finally for the first time since I began being bulimic, I have successfully escaped this self-destructive disease. I have been dieting, without letting the bulimia take over, since September 9, 1992. This may not seem to be an extremely long time to anyone else, but for me it seems like a lifetime. However, I constantly have the thought, "Go ahead; do it; it won't hurt you," in the back of my head. It may seem strange, but my disease has given me a greater understanding of alcohol and drug addiction. I truly can understand the need to "just do it." With the help of my understanding friend Brenda, I truly have the support I need. I am finally winning a battle I never thought would end. 100

Although I have friends whom I can talk to, I wish that I could be open with my mom and step-dad, but I am afraid they would feel as if it was their fault I have this problem or that they had raised me wrong. My father and I are no longer on speaking terms; I finally realized this wasn't the first incident in which he had made me feel insecure. However, I am still on speaking terms with my ex-step-mom. I recently told her what my father had said to me, and she became very angered by it. She was upset that I had not told her of this incident when it occurred, but she is still very supportive of me. Telling her of my problem was one of the first steps in my recovery. 101

I have one important message for others with this problem. Learn how to lean on your friends and family because sometimes a problem is too big to handle alone, and no one can expect you to have the strength of Superman. I always tried to succeed alone, but I now realize that sometimes a person has to ask for help in order to succeed. 102

If I had not asked for this help, I may not be alive today. I had   103
always wanted to go to college, but in my time of sickness this did not
matter to me. I am very glad for the chance I have been given to improve
upon my education and my ways of life. It frightens me to think that an
inner struggle, such as my inner struggle with bulimia, can destroy a
person's chance for a future. I hope that with the education I am
obtaining I can assist others to make a choice for life and a future, instead
of the choice of self-destruction.

7   GREG FRANCIS
Indiana University at Kokomo, Kokomo, Indiana

Alcoholism has ruined countless lives since the beginning of time.   104
It is a cunning°, baffling° disease that lures millions to destruction.
Sometimes the grip of alcohol is broken, and someone is set free. After
years of alcohol abuse, I was granted a miracle. After I was taught to live
without alcohol, I learned to take charge of my life.

My drinking career started at age thirteen. Alcohol gave me   105
confidence and a feeling of euphoria°. When I was drinking, I became
witty and spontaneous°. I remember thinking that it would be great if I
could feel that good every minute of every day. Alcohol had me under its
evil spell.

My parents monitored my activities closely, so I had to become   106
efficient at creating situations that would allow me to drink. During my
freshman year in high school, I would attend varsity sporting events just
long enough to borrow dollar bills from five or six of my friends. I would
then meet an older friend at a predetermined time and place to go out
drinking in his car.

Without realizing it, I gradually began limiting my activities to   107
those that involved drinking. I surrounded myself with people who drank
as much as or more than I did. If someone questioned my drinking, I tried
to avoid that person whenever possible. Alcohol was my best friend, and
my life became a quest° for a buzz.

---

cunning (104): tricky
baffling (104): puzzling
euphoria (105): high spirits
spontaneous (105): acting freely
quest (107): search

When I was fourteen, I was arrested for underage drinking at a 108
football game. I was not sorry for what I had done, and I didn't think
about the loved ones whom I had hurt. I only cared about drinking
without getting caught again. Alcoholics are crafty°, and I usually
managed to hide my drinking from my coaches and my parents, but not
from everyone.

After my arrest, the father of one of my friends, a recovering 109
alcoholic, tried to talk to me about getting help, but I didn't listen. I
believed my only problem was people like him trying to run my life. I
refused to believe I was an alcoholic, and no one could tell me otherwise.

High school sped by in a blur of parties and many drunk nights. 110
Although I was arrested a couple more times, my punishments were light.
In 1983, I graduated at the bottom of my class, even though my
comprehension test scores were well above average. College was not for
me, so I went to work.

Once I began working, I spent most of my money on alcohol. I 111
started binges that lasted days and sometimes weeks. I often woke up in
strange places and couldn't remember how I had gotten there. Each
morning I examined my car for evidence of a collision the night before. I
no longer drank to feel the euphoria that I had once experienced. I now
needed alcohol to function properly and to relieve the terror I felt when I
was sober. A shot and a beer in the morning would calm my hangovers
enough for me to show up for work.

During the summer of 1986, my mother was diagnosed with cancer 112
and given less than a year to live. I didn't use the time to comfort my
mother and help my family. Because I was working two jobs, I used this
as an excuse for not being around. Actually, when I was not at work, I
was drinking. I was enslaved by alcohol, and the master demanded my
full attention.

Mother died after six months. It is difficult to describe the guilt that 113
haunted me. Her death caused me to realize the stranglehold that alcohol
had on me. Although I was not strong enough to change, I hated what I
had become. I lived less than a block away from my parents, and instead
of visiting my mother, I chose to get drunk.

A year after my mother died, I was diagnosed with diabetes and was 114
ordered to follow a strict diet that did not include alcohol. I wanted to
stop drinking and was determined to do so. Actually I tried, but I couldn't
defeat the urge to drink. Consequently, I felt weak and pathetic, which
just led to another drink.

---

crafty (108): clever and sly

The combination of drinking and diabetes led to many brushes with   115
death. Friends began to avoid me because they never knew when they
would have to call an ambulance for me. Once a doctor told me that I had
a death wish after he had pulled me from a coma. He was much closer to
the truth than he realized.

In December of 1990, I was arrested for my third Operating While   116
Intoxicated offense. Because I was convicted of a class D felony, I was
sentenced to thirty days in jail. I also had to complete a sixty-day in-
patient alcohol abuse treatment program as well as sixty days of in-home
detention°.

I had finally hit rock bottom. After twelve years of heavy drinking,   117
I was ready to give up. I lost my job as well as my self-respect and the
respect of those I cared about. I felt as important as a lump of tobacco
that someone had spit on a sidewalk. Although I never tried suicide, I
didn't dismiss the idea either.

Then came my miracle! While I was incarcerated°, I began   118
attending Alcoholics Anonymous meetings that were conducted at the
jail. Listening to the discussions, I noticed that the lives of the
participants had been no different from mine. Their stories were not
exactly the same, but the feelings of hopelessness and despair were
identical. But now these men were happy. I wanted what they had.

After twenty-nine days, I was released from jail and ordered to go   119
directly to New Directions in Lafayette, Indiana, for the treatment
program. My head had finally cleared from a month away from alcohol,
and I had a desire to keep it that way. Nervous but excited and hopeful, I
entered the program.

Alcohol treatment was nothing like I had envisioned°. First, the   120
only females there were the cooks and a couple of counselors. Second,
although therapy sessions were conducted in groups, I was shown no pity
from my counselor or my peers°. I was actually expected to take
responsibility for my actions and for my recovery. The first two weeks
were hell. I wasn't allowed to use the phone or to have visitors. I felt as if
I were being attacked during group sessions. My counselor and peers,
always brutally honest, confronted me about my behavior. For a while, I
actually thought that jail was preferable.

---

detention (116): confinement
incarcerated (118): imprisoned
envisioned (120): imagined
peers (120): people of equal standing, being in the same situation,
            or of the same age, etc.

As time went on, I began to realize that in order to have a successful   121
recovery, both my attitude and behavior would have to change. Once I
started listening to criticism with an open mind, I began to grow. As part
of my treatment, I was given many writing assignments, and my
counselor encouraged me. She said that I had talent and that I should
develop it. As a result, I decided to pursue a college degree.

When I graduated from New Directions, I moved into a halfway   122
house in Indianapolis. Because the halfway house required its residents to
be employed, I had to live for a while at the Salvation Army until I found
a job. It was very difficult to obtain° employment because of my police
record and the fact that my driver's license had been suspended. Finally I
found work doing odd jobs for an oil company. Often I worked outside in
freezing temperatures at physically difficult jobs, but I could pay the bills.

The next step was to find a way to go to college. I had heard that   123
Vocational Rehabilitation Service would help with financial aid because
alcoholism is considered to be a handicap. So I talked with a counselor
who said that I was qualified to receive four years of schooling. I had to
complete some psychological testing in order to determine the amount of
brain damage I had received due to alcohol abuse. Fortunately, the tests
found no brain damage and an above average intelligence. My miracle
continued.

About two months later, when I had almost completed the admission   124
process at Indiana University-Purdue University at Indianapolis, I was
laid off from the oil company. I tried desperately to find new
employment, but my efforts were in vain. Had I still been drinking, I
would have crumbled under the pressure. But I was now sober, and I had
faith that no matter what happened, God would help me through.

At this same time, my older brother drowned in a pond close to his   125
home in Tennessee. The temptation to drink at the time of the funeral was
intense. But thanks to God and what I had learned while in treatment, I
stayed clean. I was able to grieve in a healthy manner, unlike when my
mother passed away.

When I returned to Indianapolis, everyone was very supportive. For   126
example, my landlord was patient about my rent. But I still couldn't find
a job, and after six weeks my residency was terminated°. At that point
my father suggested I move back home with him. I quickly made the
necessary phone calls and had everything transferred to Kokomo, where I
now reside. This delayed the financial aid from vocational rehabilitation,

---

obtain (122): get
terminated (126): ended

but everything was in order for late registration at Indiana University at Kokomo by the fall of 1992.

I have just completed my first semester with a grade point average   127
of 3.35, the best grades of my life. I hope to be a physical therapist and work with handicapped children. Since I also enjoy writing, I would like to incorporate it into my career.

There are still some hurdles to leap and bridges to cross. My   128
driver's license will be suspended for another eight years, making it difficult to use the school facilities and cutting down on job prospects. Some of my required classes are offered only during the day, and my father, who is my chauffeur, works from 6 a.m. to 3 p.m. But these are problems with which I can cope.

I would not be where I am today if I had not been forced to view   129
my life in an honest manner. Alcohol almost killed me many times, and I am still only one drink away from a life of hell. I have been sober for almost two years, and I have never felt happier or more serene. With God's grace, I will stay sober today. Tomorrow will take care of itself.

8   XINRONG LIU
Iowa Western Community College, Council Bluffs, Iowa

At my high school graduation, I received a card from my   130
counselor. On it, there was a poem:

> Only as high as I reach can I grow;
> Only as deep as I look can I see;
> Only as much as I dream can I be.

I have always kept this poem on the first page of my notebook, and   131
it has become an inspiration for me ever since. I was not raised in the United States. I came to this country when I was eighteen years old. My native language is Chinese, and I have been brought up with Chinese traditions. When I first landed at the Kansas City airport two years ago, I could only speak a few broken English words and did not have any clue of general conversation—I was absolutely lost.

For my first year in America, I was enrolled as a high school senior   132
in Shenandoah, Iowa. After growing up in a city of nine million people, it was a big change for me to live in a rural town in southwest Iowa. Along with being unable to communicate, I had to face a completely different kind of culture. From food to teenagers' lifestyle, everything was new to me, and I needed to adjust to it all. My life was turned upside down, and I was totally confused.

Among all the problems, language was the biggest. Although I had 133
been studying English at school, the American daily conversation was
totally different from what I learned in the textbook. I could not
understand the lecture in the classroom at all. In addition to speaking,
reading was also difficult for me. I had to stop every few lines to look up
words in the dictionary. Compared with other people, I spent twice as
much time on school work. I gave up social activities to work on my
language skills during weekends and vacations.

The extra amount of work was nothing compared with what I had to 134
face emotionally. In China, I was a good student, and things had always
come fairly easy for me. Now, I needed help everywhere. At school, I
tried everything to overcome my language disadvantage—talking to
people, recording lectures, and borrowing notes. However, the progress
seemed so slow that I felt I would never be able to get it. My grades
dropped and so did my confidence. Many times I cried in bed at night
and wondered why life was so rough on me. I wanted to give up and
forget the whole deal. When these moments came, I would close my
eyes, put the poem on my heart, and recite:

> Only as high as I reach can I grow;
> Only as deep as I look can I see;
> Only as much as I dream can I be.

Its magic inspiration and my determination of getting a higher education
have amazingly kept me going.

On top of these problems, I have had to worry about my financial 135
situation. Since it is impossible for me to get financial help from my
family, I have decided to put myself through college. I knew it would be
difficult, but I was willing to take the challenge because I treasure the
value of education. With the help of several people and a couple of
scholarships, I started at a community college. During the school year, I
worked as an assistant for two professors and at a restaurant on weekends.
My vacation time was spent in a factory as an assembly worker.

The road to college has not been easy for me. However, meeting all 136
the challenges along the way has made me tougher and more experienced
to face life's difficulties. Now that I have been in the United States for
more than two years, the language and the culture are not problems for
me any more. As a sophomore at Iowa Western Community College, I
have been keeping a 4.0 GPA on a 4.0 scale. While being a member of
the International Honor Society, my autobiography was published in the
fifteenth edition of *The National Dean's List*. At school, I have been
nominated as the most outstanding speech student and a two-term winner
of an academic scholarship.

While being able to overcome my difficulties, I remember those 137
people who are still having problems. I try to help them as I once was
helped. Understanding their anxiety and emotional frustrations has led
me to be a tutor in several courses. It is a real joy in my heart to see these
students make progress.

My second year in college has been much better than the first. 138
However, there is never an end to the challenges. Bettering my language
skill is a continuing task, and school expenses are still my main concern.
I have, however, learned to enjoy challenges. Trying my best and
overcoming the difficulties have been true thrills in my life.

During this time, I have been trying to contribute my ability to the 139
community. I give time to community services, help others whenever I
can, and most importantly, promote understanding between China and
America. I have been giving programs on China to various civic clubs and
church organizations around the area. It is very important to me to see a
good relationship between our two countries, for I love them both deeply.

I plan to get a B.S. degree in computer science and a secondary 140
degree in international studies. Studying in graduate school is also part of
the plan. A good education is one of many goals in my life. After
finishing school, I would like to contribute my talent and ability to the
society. With my bilingual and bicultural skills, I hope to work with
international affairs. Some day, if my dream comes true, I would like to
be an ambassador who devotes herself to promoting a better
understanding and relationship between China and the United States.

This is only my second year in college, and I have a long way to go 141
before achieving my goals. The battle with problems and difficulties will
never stop as long as I keep setting higher goals. In order to reach the
peak, I must have the confidence to overcome whatever is along the road.
Through all the challenges, I have learned a lesson: determination and
hard work make anything possible.

Deep in my heart, I will always believe in the poem: 142

> Only as high as I reach can I grow;
> Only as deep as I look can I see;
> Only as much as I dream can I be.

9   BETTIE JO MELLOTT
Ohio University Eastern, St. Clairsville, Ohio

Meg sat in a wheelchair in the cafeteria at the Columbus 143
Rehabilitation Center. With her useless limbs and facial scars, she looked
like a cerebral palsy patient, not like the victim of an industrial injury.

Actually, she had been raped, beaten, and left for dead by a prisoner at the correctional facility where she had been a medication nurse. Her body was permanently damaged, but her soul and spirit were on fire for life. Determination and gusto°, it just radiated° from everywhere, her eyes, her smile, and even the proud, upright way she sat in her wheelchair. I was immediately drawn to her. What an inspiration she became to me! We shared many similarities, but the greatest difference was that I improved and went home. She's still there. I felt so ashamed of my own fears and shortcomings regarding my injuries. My name is Bettie Jo (B.J.) Mellott. I am forty-three years old, a mother, and a full-time sophomore at Ohio University Eastern in St. Clairsville, Ohio.

At the time I met Meg in the rehabilitation center, I had encountered   144 severe trauma° in my own life, not only physically, as my body was now damaged, but my emotional psyche° was in a fragile state. It happened in January of 1989. I was severely injured as an L.P.N.° in the CCU° due to a lifting accident. The memories are vague and sketchy, but I do remember many days of lying in the hospital, pain coursing through my body. The worst feeling, however, was the sense of helplessness. When I got to go home, I was on weeks of bed rest followed by months of physical therapy, more treatments, tests, and several more hospitalizations. I had to use a walker to even be up for only minutes a day, then half-hours, then one, two, three hours, etc. I had problems with my balance, trying to use my legs. I was so weak physically and emotionally. Some days I didn't even want to try. I was so discouraged, having to face the reality that maybe I'd never be well, trying to make adjustments to the way my life was now.

My family was also struggling with me. My husband Herman, who   145 drives a school bus full time, now found himself in the role of both mother and father, trying to keep up with everything. That meant milking thirty-eight cows twice a day, seven days a week, keeping up with a large garden, cooking, cleaning, taking care of our two sons Mikel and Mark, who were 8 and 16 at the time. I could only come home on weekends and still wasn't much help to him. He was brave, but becoming exhausted with all the stress and hard work. My heart broke for him every time I saw his haggard° face and tired body. The thought crossed my mind

---

gusto (143): enthusiasm
radiated (143): spread out like rays
trauma (144): injury
psyche (144): inner being
L.P.N. (144): Licensed Practical Nurse
CCU (144): Coronary Care Unit
haggard (145): appearing exhausted

many times that he would want to chuck it all and just walk out or ask me to leave, but it never came to that. He stuck by me through it all, and I thank God for his dedication and unending love. The hardest part was knowing that I couldn't change things no matter how much I wanted to make them better. I kept hoping I'd get off the crutches I was using and would be whole again.

There was much that I couldn't change, but I was still determined to   146 take charge of my life. In September of 1991, after much soul searching for the courage to try, I signed up for a course at Ohio University Eastern, our local college, a Credit for Life Experiences class. I was very much afraid. My self-esteem was low. Up until this time, I had not been allowed to drive over ten miles at any one time, but just getting to college one way was nearly thirty-two miles and practically an hour's drive. Fortunately, this university has handicapped-parking facilities and an elevator in the building, so I could get to the classes I needed. I made four trips to the class, then had to finish the rest by mail, as I had to go back to the rehab center in Columbus for another three weeks.

During this stay, I agreed to an epidural nerve block. To my dismay,   147 I had an extreme reaction to the cortisone injected into my spinal column, which put me in the Ohio State University Hospital with a partial loss of vision in one eye for about three weeks and a temporary loss of the use of my right leg and hand. Needless to say, that set me back both physically and emotionally.

Upon release from the hospital, I decided that I wanted to attend   148 college full time this time for real (the initial class consisted of a teacher and four students). Now it would mean dealing with the "handicap" stigma. I walked using Canadian Crutches with an odd gait which drew attention to myself. I had also gained over sixty pounds since my injury, and I felt extremely fat and ugly. I was 42 years old, and almost all the other students seemed to be 18 and beautiful. I worried myself sick over everything imaginable. After much pleading with my neurosurgeon, he tentatively released me to attend full time. I also had to prove to Worker's Compensation that I could withstand the academic and physical demands, and show my family that I wasn't hurting myself with undue stress and all the physical demands necessary to attend two or three days a week, carrying a full-time load.

I withdrew all the money I had in my savings account, paid for my   149 tuition and books, and began winter quarter, scared to death I'd fail or flunk out, so much was riding on this trial period. In hindsight, I think all the negatives stacked against me were actually the incentives that made me that much more determined to try and prove to everyone and myself that I could succeed.

Somehow I made it through the winter quarter. It ended with my   150
making an A, a B+, and two C+'s for thirteen credit hours. I then signed
up for the spring quarter and held my breath. After the Bureau of
Worker's Compensation and the Doctor of Record evaluated me both
physically and academically, I was allowed to continue. I even received
assistance for tuition and supplies from the Bureau of Vocational
Rehabilitation. I began spring quarter full of enthusiasm, determined to
make better grades, take more classes, and complete as many courses as
possible to be able to graduate in three years rather than four. I was so
encouraged by my success and so motivated to learn more that I decided
to take summer classes. I attended full time, took twenty-one credit hours
and made the Dean's List with a 3.750 G.P.A.

All was not easy, however. I had run into my first academic   151
obstacle: English Composition. I never had a problem verbalizing my
thoughts, but apparently I had major shortcomings when it came to
writing down those same thoughts. I made mistakes including comma
splices, fragments, idea disorganization, and, in general, had forgotten
many ground rules of semantics. Fortunately, my professor, Mr. Patrick
Wood, was more than willing to help me overcome these drawbacks and
academic difficulties. One of his recommendations was that I take a
developmental course in writing, English 150, where the basics are re-
emphasized and can be internalized more readily through repetitious
lesson plans.

My many problems and the course Freshman Comp 151 ended with   152
my getting an incomplete. Thus, in fall quarter, I did indeed take the
developmental English course. Through sheer° perseverance° and skillful
guidance of the professor, I learned how to write full sentences, spell
words more accurately, punctuate a little more properly, and organize my
thoughts in a more functional way. At the end of the course, I made an A-
grade. I still made mistakes, as you have probably observed, but this was
a major victory for me. I now had confidence. Beginning in January
(winter quarter), I will use this confidence to retake English 151,
knowing that I am much better prepared to internalize writing concepts
and become a better writer.

In many ways, having an academic problem has made me   153
appreciate the educational process even more. I learned a long time ago
that life often involves struggle, but I am not a quitter. I have known
much pain in life. For instance, I was engaged twice to military men who

---

sheer (152): total
perseverance (152): continued and patient effort

were killed while in Vietnam. I lost my home to a fire and had to start completely over. My father was killed in an auto accident, and now this injury. I feel my faith has been tested repeatedly, yet I have risen to the occasion spiritually stronger. Therefore, attending college and overcoming academic obstacles is just one more stepping stone on the pathway to my future.

Fall quarter has just ended. I carried twenty-three credit hours, including one nursing class at a nearby technical school. (If a student at Ohio University Eastern attends full time, he can take one free course each semester at the technical school, which I did.) The course, Community Nursing Practices, is a requirement for an Associate Degree R.N.° Program. I am trying also to meet the academic requirements to sit for state boards for my R.N. license. My ultimate goal is to teach preventative health care in the Public Health Care System, or in some capacity in the high school or college level. I am also taking the appropriate classes to sit for the exam of Licensed Social Worker.   154

My goals are high, and the road ahead is not an easy one, but I am a survivor. In a paradoxical° kind of way, I know that I am gifted. I value living. I value giving. Each day is a struggle, but I want to make a difference in the lives of other Megs and Bettie Jo's who might give up because of their pain. I am thankful for the opportunity to learn, and I plan to make the most of it. My primary goals are threefold: to be a good mother and wife, to complete the college process, and to eventually become a licensed social worker.   155

My family and close friends have been very supportive of me, and we have been able to apply some of these same principles in other ways in our family life. My son Mikel, now twelve years old, has recently take on the responsibility of providing a foster home and care for a Pilot Dog puppy. His name is Harris, an eight-week-old golden retriever puppy. We shall keep him until he is thirteen months old. Then, he will return to the Pilot Dog, Inc. School, where he will undergo training to be a guide dog for a blind person. My son will be learning many valuable lessons through this experience that may ultimately make him a better human being.   156

As for myself, I still have over half of my education to complete. At present, I am registered for winter quarter. I will be taking twenty-seven credit hours to continue with my goal of graduating in three years. Yes, I will continue to pursue my dreams. I have taken charge of my life!   157

R.N. (154): Registered Nurse
paradoxical (155): seeming to contradict circumstances

There are many things beyond my control, but I have learned that taking charge means a daily deciding to enter life more fully. Life is full of obstacles, but it also is full of opportunities. It means trying, sometimes a lot of trying (e.g. this paper has involved some five rewrites). It also means the pursuit of dreams. 158

Ohio University Eastern will be beginning a Master's Degree for Rehabilitation Counselors program in June of 1994. Priority° is being given to females, those with disabilities, and also those who reside in an Appalachian region. I meet all of those. I have spoken via telephone to the contact person in charge of this pilot program, Dr. Lisa Lopez-Lever. I feel confident that I at least have a chance at this opportunity. It is opportunities like your Scholarship Program for Developmental Reading and Writing Students that may also play an important part in my future or the future of others who are just like me, trying very hard to get an education and help themselves and others along life's journey. 159

Note: You have read nine of the fifty essays in the book *Taking Charge of My Life*. For information on how to obtain the entire book, turn to page 564.

READING COMPREHENSION QUESTIONS

Vocabulary in Context

1. The word *incorporate* in "Since I also enjoy writing, I would like to incorporate it into my career" (paragraph 127) means
   a. avoid.
   b. include.
   c. sign.
   d. separate.

Central Point and Main Ideas

2. Which sentence expresses a central point that applies to all the essays in this reading?
   a. Alcoholism, drug abuse, and other addictions interfered with the authors' ability to take charge of their own lives.
   b. People should be required to get parenthood training before having children of their own.
   c. Despite great challenges, the authors have taken strong, positive steps to make their lives what they want them to be.

---

priority (159): first consideration

    d. The authors have learned that the only way for people to greatly improve their lives is to go to college and obtain a degree.

3. The main idea of paragraph 41 is best expressed in its
    a. first sentence.
    b. second sentence.
    c. third sentence.
    d. fourth sentence.

4. Which sentence best expresses the main idea of paragraph 46?
    a. The author was selling janitorial supplies for a company she did not like.
    b. The author was encouraged by her therapist and a friend.
    c. Lacking a sense of direction, the author, with encouragement, took the first step toward going to college.
    d. The author was thirty-two years old and working in a dead-end job for a janitorial supplies company.

Supporting Details

5. Some of the authors in this collection have had to overcome
    a. addictions.
    b. childhood problems.
    c. financial problems.
    d. all of the above.

6. All of the authors in this collection have
    a. poor health.
    b. at least one positive goal.
    c. helpful parents.
    d. a college degree.

Transitions

7. The supporting details of paragraph 19 are organized in a
    a. contrast pattern.
    b. cause-and-effect pattern.
    c. definition-and-example pattern.
    d. list-of-items pattern.

Inferences

8. From Ricki Gutierrez's and Stacy Ebeling's essays, we might conclude that
    a. children will develop the same way no matter what their parents do.

     b. teachers are more important than parents in a child's development.

     c. parental treatment greatly influences a child's self-esteem.

     d. parents should not remarry until their children are grown.

9. For many, or all, of the authors of these essays, the first step in improving their lives was to
   a. save some money.
   b. decide to change their lives.
   c. get married.
   d. change jobs.

10. These essays illustrate that for a person's life to improve, he or she must
    a. have extremely good luck.
    b. get therapy.
    c. marry and have children.
    d. realize he or she has the ability to change and grow.

SUMMARIZING

Circle the letter of the best summary of the reading from *Taking Charge of My Life*.

     a. All of the authors in the reading from *Taking Charge of My Life* have enrolled in college as a way to improve their lives. Most are studying to enter careers in which they will directly help others improve their lives. Among their goals are becoming a social worker, a nurse, a physical therapist, an ambassador, and a rehabilitation counselor. For these students, education is a path to a satisfying career.

     b. The readings from *Taking Charge of My Life* include essays by students enrolled in colleges around the country. Alcoholism and/or drug addiction have caused some of them pain and loss of hope. However, they have learned that they can escape their addiction and build a rich life. They have been helped in their personal growth by others, including members of Alcoholics Anonymous, personal therapists, friends, and family. Gaining insight into their past has been an important part of their recovery. Also important is learning that they have the ability to make something of themselves.

     c. All of the authors in the reading from *Taking Charge of My Life* have overcome great obstacles and are creating rich lives for themselves. Some suffered child abuse and a lack of self-confidence. Some had to overcome alcohol or drug addiction. Others had to adjust to an unfamiliar culture. They all came to realize that they could improve their own lives, often with the help and support of others. Now all of the authors are enrolled in college and are on their way to satisfying, useful careers.

DISCUSSION QUESTIONS

1. Some of the essay authors write about an event that was an important positive turning point in their lives. What was the turning point for Ricki Gutierrez (paragraphs 1–20)? For Regina Ruiz (paragraphs 67–93)? For Greg Francis (paragraphs 104–129)? What do those turning points have in common?

2. For all of the essay writers, going to college involved overcoming some obstacles. What obstacles have you overcome to get to college? What do you hope to accomplish in college?

3. For many of the essay writers, the support of a special teacher or friend was important as they decided to take charge of their lives. Who has given you special support in your life, and how do you think that person has helped you?

4. Some of the essay writers suffered from low self-esteem. What are some ways people can strengthen their self-esteem? How could you encourage high self-esteem in children? (Turn to the reading "Giving Emotional Support" on pages 183–186 to see one author's ideas on this subject.)

5

Alicia: My Story
Alicia Appleman-Jurman

Preview

During World War II the Nazis under Adolf Hitler attempted to destroy the Jewish people. The number of Jews who died then is estimated to be over six million. This selection is from Alicia Appleman-Jurman's story of her life as a Polish girl who survived the terrors of the Nazis. Today she lives in the United States, where she is a writer and lecturer.

The reading begins in 1941, when the German army under Hitler was invading countries across Europe. Alicia Jurman was a young Jewish girl living with her parents and brothers in a town in Poland. Russian soldiers who had occupied the town were now leaving, as they retreated from the advancing Germans. One day the Germans arrived, and Alicia's girlhood was about to turn into the worst of nightmares.

THE GERMAN OCCUPATION

As quickly as they had entered, the Russians disappeared from   1
Buczacz. It was the beginning of the fall of 1941. School had closed for the summer and classes had not yet resumed when the sound of guns was heard outside the city. Word had it that the Germans were close by. Then one morning all the Russians were gone, and with them some of our own townspeople, who, because they had supported the Russians, now feared reprisals° from the Germans.

---

reprisals (1): pay backs, retaliations

After the Russians left, there was wild looting in town. Windows   2
were smashed, stores ransacked°—even my father's china shop fell
victim to the mobs. Then it became quiet, and the townspeople waited for
their new captors. Our Jewish community was particularly concerned.
Would the Germans treat us as they did their own Jews? Many families
had fled to Poland from Germany when the war began in 1939. My father
had in fact worked to bring over a German Jewish doctor and his two
children—their mother had already died.

Then the Germans came. Mostly I remember the motorcycles. To   3
this day I shudder when I hear the roaring sound of a motorcycle outside
my house. No one really knew what would happen, and everyone was in
shock. I was mostly wondering if school would start on time and whether
Jewish children would be allowed to attend.

One day when I came down to breakfast my father was not there.   4

"Where is Papa?" I asked.   5

"Oh, he left early," said my mother as she served me my porridge.   6
"He has gone to register."

"Register? Register for what?"   7

My brother Bunio reached across me for a piece of bread.   8

"Haven't you heard that all men between the ages of eighteen and   9
fifty are to register at the police station?"

"No."   10

"Well, there you are," he said between bites.   11

"When will he be home?" I asked as my mother placed a glass of   12
milk before me.

"By midday, most likely," she said. "Now, Alicia, eat your   13
breakfast."

Midday came, and my father did not return. The sky had clouded   14
over, and at two o'clock we heard a sound like thunder outside the town,
coming from the direction of the Fador°.

By nightfall Papa still had not returned, and Bunio was sent to the   15
police station to find out what was happening. "Go back home," he was
told. "Your father will get home in due time."

It was obvious that Papa would not be coming home that night. My   16
mother did not sleep, and we children took turns sitting up with her. She
was very troubled. Although she tried not to show it, the tightly gripped
handkerchief in her hand revealed her anguish°.

---

ransacked (2): searched through for goods to steal
Fador (14): the meadowland that bordered the city of Buczacz
anguish (16): intense pain

In the early morning my mother left the house to meet with the men   17
who had formed a committee to represent the Jewish people to the
German authorities. They were later to be known as the Judenrat, but
then they were an unofficial committee consisting of a number of well-
known Jewish men. Mother was gone only a short while and, upon her
return, went straight into her bedroom. She was there a short time, then
hastily left the house again. I wanted to ask her where she was going, but
she was in such a hurry I decided not to; instead, I followed her. She went
into a building near our big synagogue°. As I waited for her to come out,
I saw more women enter the building, and a terrible fear gripped my
heart. Was this some kind of registration of mothers now? Would my
mama be gone the way Papa was? Then the door opened and Mother
appeared. Walking very stiffly, looking neither to the left nor to the right,
she went straight home. I waited a little while longer and followed her.

Now, with Mother safely home, I thought once more of my father.   18
Maybe he had returned home during my absence and I would find him
there.

I saw my brother Bunio leave the house, and, fearing that he might   19
reprimand° me for being out so early, I set upon him first.

"Bunio, where are you going so early and why are you leaving us   20
alone? Does Mama know you are going out?"

"She sent me to the police station to ask for news about Papa," he   21
said.

"May I come with you? Please, Bunio."   22

"Not now. You help Mama; she is very nervous right now."   23

Bunio was right. Mother was nervous but did not seem particularly   24
sad. She was lost in thought and did not even ask me where I had been
when I entered the kitchen. Bunio came home shortly with the same
answer. "Papa will return in time."

But Papa did not return. Three days passed, and we had not heard   25
from him. By this time the families who had had their men taken were
frantic. The realization that they had completely disappeared began to
sink in, followed by anger and desperation.

Both Bunio and Zachary made discreet° inquiries of their Christian   26
friends. No one had seen anything. If they knew something, they were
not going to tell. One of them mentioned the Fador; that was all. The

---

synagogue (17): house of worship and communal center for a
    Jewish congregation

reprimand (19): scold

discreet (26): careful, cautious

search for the missing men started. Bunio went to the Fador fearing the worst, but could find nothing, not so much as a trace. About six hundred leading citizens of our Jewish community had just vanished.

His news angered me. "You couldn't have looked very hard," I 27 accused him.

"Alicia, I looked everywhere." 28

"You couldn't have. You couldn't have." 29

"Alicia"—his voice was gentle—"I looked everywhere I could 30 think of."

My mother, listening to our argument, sat quietly, holding my 31 brother Herzl on her lap, looking drained of all strength. The ordeal was clearly showing on her now.

Zachary spoke. "Do you remember the thunder we heard the other 32 day? Don't you remember how odd we thought it?"

Suddenly I realized what he was hinting at. "It was thunder!" I 33 cried. "Don't tell me it wasn't."

"It could have been thunder, sweetheart, but I didn't think so then. I 34 think"—he looked at my mother, and with a choked voice added—"we should start preparing ourselves for the worst."

"No," I cried. "No! He is still somewhere, our father is still . . . I tell 35 you!"

My mother did not speak up. Did she believe this nonsense too? 36

"Well," I said, "if you can't find him, I will." 37

"Alicia, you won't find him," said Bunio, shaking his head. 38

"Yes, I will," I cried hotly. "And don't you try to stop me!" 39

I ran over the Fador into the woods. I went back and forth, calling 40 and calling. "Papa! It's Alicia! Papa, where are you?"

I must have walked for miles and miles, from the woods to the 41 Fador, crossing the river and back into the woods, calling, calling. I looked for anything—a scrap of clothing, anything that might suggest that a large group of people had been in the area. Several times I found something—a matchstick here, a broken cup there—but there was no sign of the people anywhere. Hours went by, and my throat was beginning to feel sore from all the calling, but I continued walking and calling, walking and calling. Suddenly I felt very tired and sat down on a log.

I don't know how long I sat there, when suddenly I heard a voice 42 calling my name. I sprang to my feet. "Papa!" I cried. "Papa, I am here!"

"Stay where you are," the voice called back. "I am coming." Then 43 the figure of my brother Zachary came into sight. Tears of disappointment welled in my eyes as I sat heavily back on the log. I didn't look up as he approached.

He reached out and stroked my hair.   44

"You are a mess," he said. I didn't raise my head. He sat down   45
beside me.

"It's time to go home now," he said softly. "Mama is worrying."   46

I looked over at him. There was so much of our father in Zachary—   47
the blond hair, the gray-blue eyes, the way he laughed, the sense of
strength. I saw all those things now, and the resemblance was comforting.

"Zachary," I asked, "do you think Papa is dead?"   48

He looked at me with eyes brimming with tears, then reached over   49
and pulled me close to him, saying, "I just don't know, sweetheart. I just
don't know." I rested my head against his chest and felt his strong arms
holding me close. "I looked everywhere," I told him. "I could not find
him. I could not find anything."

"I know."   50

"Zachary, what will we do without Papa?"   51

He kissed the top of my head. "We must hope for the best. You   52
know how our people think; we must hope. We will miss him very much,
but we must continue living."

"Are they to kill us all?"   53

He smiled. "No, sweetheart, not even if they tried." He stood up and   54
pulled me to my feet. "Come on now. Let's go home and tell Mama that
we are hungry and we want our dinner right away."

And so we walked home together, Zachary's strong arm around my   55
shoulder. We never saw our father again. None of the families of the six
hundred men ever did. Only one man escaped, and he immediately went
into hiding. It would be almost three years before I would find him and
learn what had really happened to my father. Not until 1967, when the
German SS officer in charge of the mass murder was found and brought
to trial, did I learn how the Germans had asked the Jewish community to
pay ransom for the release of the captives—after they had already been
murdered. My mother had given away all her remaining jewelry and
money to ransom my father, leaving us with no means of support.

MY FIRST ESCAPE

It was soon frighteningly clear to the Jewish people in Buczacz that   56
the elimination of the six hundred men was only the first step in a
methodical German plan. First the Germans removed all young and
influential men—civic, business and religious leaders—anyone who
could sway public opinion or who could inspire the people to resist. The
next step was to move the people out of their homes into one special area,
a ghetto. To do this, the Germans enlisted the help of the Ukrainian

police. Rumors were circulating that this was about to happen, and some families were already looking for a place to live in the selected area before the actual expulsion° from their homes.

We had friends who owned a small home in the new ghetto near the   57
Bashte meadow, not far from the river Stripa in the northern part of Buczacz. They agreed to let us have one room that we could use should the rumor prove true, in exchange for a monthly rent payment. Quietly we started moving some of our linens and dishes at night to what might become our new home. We were careful not to be obvious, since we did not want to be stopped by the Ukrainian police who were constantly patrolling our neighborhood.

What we feared happened one early morning in September. The   58
Ukrainian police came into our house and ordered us out. They stood there in their blue uniforms, guns pointing at us, watching every move we made. My mother had told us what might happen and had begged my brothers not to say anything and not to give the police a reason to arrest or shoot us. Even though we were somewhat prepared for the move, when it actually came it was a very painful experience. We took what we could carry. Anger and frustration brought tears to my eyes, but I did not let the policemen see them. Zachary noticed them and whispered to me in Hebrew, "*Chavivati*, my dear, we'll return to our home someday when the war is over; things don't last forever." Squeezing my hand, he smiled at me.

The anger that gripped my whole being lessened, and a wave of   59
tremendous love for my brother overcame me. Helping me carry my bundle with one hand while carrying his with the other, Zachary pulled me out of the house. I did turn my head for a last look at my home, but I knew that in the future I would try to avoid passing it.

On the way to our new neighborhood we met people who were also   60
being driven from their homes. They carried bundles, and some were crying openly.

We settled quickly into our new place. The first thing we did was   61
buy a small round iron stove with a plate on top to heat one pot: We were lucky to get it. We all doubled up in our beds. My youngest brother, Herzl, liked to sleep with his favorite brother, Bunio. At least Herzl was one member of our family who was young enough not to fully understand our situation.

New regulations followed our resettlement. All of the Jews had to   62
wear a white armband with a yellow Star of David on it. We were to stay

---

expulsion (56): being thrown out by force

home after sunset and were absolutely forbidden in most public places, such as parks, marketplaces, movies, schools, and main streets. Our center of civic life became the building that housed the Jewish council known in German as the Judenrat. It was located near the big synagogue, which had been closed. The punishment promised to anyone who dared enter the synagogue was death.

We avoided all public places except the marketplace. We went there 63 not to buy, but to sell. My mother took her linens to trade with the farmers—linens that had been handed down from her mother and grandmother. My little brother Herzl, now nine, bought and sold lighter flints. Mama did not allow my older brothers to go to the market for fear they might be arrested by the Ukrainian police and shot.

I was now eleven years old and my specialty was soap, an item that 64 was beginning to become very scarce. I would buy a bar of soap for ten zlotys° from a Jewish family who made it in their home and would try to sell it for twelve zlotys, or ten zlotys and a piece of bread. My customers were farmers who came to the city to trade their produce for clothing, soap, matches, flints, and other items. I would crouch among the wagons that gathered in the bustling° marketplace on Thursday. I had to keep low to avoid the Ukrainian policemen, who now regularly patrolled our city, especially on market day. If caught, you would lose your merchandise, be taken to the police station, and eventually shot. It was a very dangerous way to earn money, but I had to do it. I had a responsibility, my first of many yet to come.

One day in November, Bunio disappeared while on the way to get 65 some wood for our stove. We could not sleep during the night for worrying about him. Early in the morning Mama went to the Judenrat. She was told that the German and Ukrainian police had taken about one hundred boys to a work camp in Borki Wielki, about one hundred miles from Buczacz. But the Judenrat would be allowed to contact the boys, and they would be allowed to receive food packages, one every two weeks. About their eventual return, the Judenrat did not know but would work hard for their release. Mama came home very unhappy. Losing Bunio, that handsome, athletic boy, filled us with terrible anguish. Herzl grieved deeply for Bunio. Since Papa's disappearance, Bunio had been both brother and father to Herzl. I caught him crying silently several times, crying and rocking his small body back and forth. A poor, miserable nine-year-old boy.

---

zlotys (64): the basic unit of money in Poland
bustling (64): busy

We put all our energies into sending Bunio food packages. Every   66
two weeks a wagon with packages left from the Judenrat grounds for
Borki Wielki. The driver who owned the wagon was a Gentile. He
traveled with two Jewish men who held special travel permits. I was
always there to see the wagon off, to make sure that the package to Bunio
was safely in place. I always carried it there myself, hugging it close to
my heart. There were pieces of bread tenderly packed by my mother: Not
a crumb was missing from the pieces I carried back from the market in
my apron. I was tempted at times to break off a little corner to satisfy my
continuous hunger, but my love for my brother was greater than the
temptation, and I was proud of myself.

Two days after the wagon left we had news from my brother. He   67
was not allowed to write, but he sent oral messages. He was well, was
working hard in a stone quarry, and sent his love to us. I would wait to
see one of the men who traveled with the packages and beg him to tell
me more about Bunio. How does he look, how does he feel? Once the
man replied, "Oh, he is well. He, too, is asking many questions about his
family. I can see you are very close." Then he added gently, "You miss
your brother very much, don't you?" I just nodded and hurried away, not
wanting the man to see the tears that were suddenly blinding me.

Detaining° Jewish people for forced labor was a common practice   68
with the Germans, and the Ukrainians had adopted the custom with relish°.
I myself had been caught twice; the first time to polish furniture and floors
at the German police station. Most of the furniture was looted from Jewish
homes after the owners were thrown out. As I worked my way through the
massive wooden pieces, one item caught my eye. It was my father's
nightstand. Tears of anger sprang to my eyes as I began to recognize the
pieces of furniture—chairs, tables—all from our lovely home. I wiped
away the tears and began to polish my furniture. I remembered that there
was a hidden compartment inside the nightstand. My father showed it to
me once when I was in his bedroom. Quietly, so that I would not be
noticed, I tried to find it, but I couldn't. It gave me some measure of
satisfaction to believe that the Germans had not found it either.

The second time, I was caught in the afternoon and ordered to clean   69
the floors in my old school—and in my very own classroom. The room
had changed. Gone were the pictures of Stalin and Lenin. The Madonna
and Child were back in their former place. My armband with the Star of
David was slipping as I worked, so I took it off and placed it near the

---

detaining (68): holding under supervision
relish (68): great pleasure

Madonna. Shouldn't she, too, be wearing an armband like mine? Wasn't she missing the Jewish children?

I remember watching as the Christian children walked to school, 70 dressed in their pretty dresses and bright ribbons. They were lovely, and I envied not only their clothes but their freedom to be educated. It was a bitter experience.

I also remember that at one point the desire to learn overcame the 71 warnings I had received about staying away. One day I climbed a tree outside the window of my classroom and watched. Through the window I could see my former classmates sitting at their desks. One of these was my friend Slavka, whom I had known since we first came to Buczacz. She was a Gentile, but then, so were many of my friends.

It didn't take long for my presence to become known to those inside 72 the classroom. One by one heads turned, and I could see the children whispering together. When Slavka turned to look, our eyes met; she couldn't wave, of course, for fear of reprimand from the teacher. I was holding fast to the tree. Our exchange was bittersweet°—my misery at not being allowed in the school, her sympathy mingled with helplessness to correct the situation. In a moment she looked away and didn't turn around again.

I think the teacher also knew I was there, but she said nothing— 73 perhaps the sight of a lonely child desperate for knowledge touched her heart. I stayed up in that tree for quite a while, listening to the lesson, trying to memorize what was being said. It was so frustrating, so utterly maddening. I couldn't stand it. I absolutely could not stand it. So when the teacher asked the next question, a dozen hands shot up, including mine. Zip! I was out of that tree and flat on my back among the leaves on the ground, the breath completely knocked out of me. Looking straight up as I struggled to breathe, I could see a sea of faces at the window, all small, round little faces with noses pressed against the glass and mouths agape°. Slavka's face was among them. She peered down unhappily as the teacher rushed down the stairs and out the door to me.

"Are you all right?" she asked, helping me into a sitting position. 74

I nodded shakily. My breath was coming back in gasps. The teacher rubbed my back until I could breath normally, then she said, "Alicia, you know you can't come back here anymore." 75

I looked up at her forlornly°. "But I don't mind the tree," I said. 76

---

bittersweet (72): a mixture of bitterness and sweetness
agape (73): wide open
forlornly (76): desperately

She smiled, a smile I remembered so well from the times when she   77
taught our class geography. "It is dangerous, Alicia, and I don't mean the
tree. Do you understand?" She wiped the dirt from my sweater, and, in
doing so, her fingers brushed over the yellow Star of David on my
armband.

"Alicia," she said, "you understand, don't you?"   78
I did.   79

Our lives had suddenly taken on a routine that was as monotonous°   80
as it was frightening. I peddled soap at the marketplace together with my
brother Herzl, making sure not to be seen by the Germans or the
Ukrainian police. My mother and her friend Ruth found a place near the
river over the Bashte meadow where we lived. Some of the village farm
women passed there on the way to the city market to sell their produce. It
was a relatively safe place, but it was difficult to sell anything to those
women; they were convinced that they could get a better deal in the city.
Yet my mother and her friend managed to get some potatoes, some grain,
and sometimes a small bottle of sunflower oil.

Several weeks later Bunio was still in the work camp. We missed   81
him desperately and continued to send him packages. During this time
Zachary had not been content to sit. He and some friends began
patrolling our neighborhood, trying to organize some kind of resistance
group. But people were afraid to raise a hand against the Germans for
fear of retaliation°. For my proud brother, whose father had taught him to
fight so well, this was an extremely maddening situation.

In his quiet way he kept a watchful eye on us and his friends and their   82
families. He came to be loved by the people he visited, both old Buczacz
families and new arrivals from neighboring towns and villages. Our town
had become the center for all the Jewish people within hundreds of miles.

And they adored him, this handsome young man who made his   83
rounds almost daily through the streets of the crowded ghetto. The young
people even began singing songs Zachary had written. One I remember was
a plaintive° song about a grandfather holding his grandson on his lap and
telling the young child to always honor and remember his father, who had
been killed by the Nazi Germans, by saying the memorial Kaddish for him.

Some of Zachary's songs, and many others, were sung by the young   84
people when they gathered one evening at a friend's home. I had gone

---

monotonous (80): unchanging
retaliation (81): repayment, revenge
plaintive (83): sorrowful

there with Zachary and sat quietly listening to songs of love, brotherhood, and yearning for° life. Some songs were in Hebrew about Eretz Israel, the land of Israel. Sometimes a girl's sweet voice would start with a joyous tune, only to be interrupted in the middle by a heartbreaking sob. Life seemed so vigorous in these young people. I was moved by the beauty of the music, yet I was pained by the knowledge that death was so near.

Those thoughts were to haunt me again the following day. I had 85
been visiting two of my friends in their home. One of the boys was my own age and he was teaching me how to play chess. Their father was a physician whom my father had helped to escape from Germany. On the other side of the door we could hear the sound of boots tramping on the pavement, but there was always marching going on those days in Buczacz, and we had grown accustomed to it. Suddenly the front door was kicked open and several German policemen entered the house. Everyone inside—the doctor, his two children, and I—was ordered out.

The doctor pleaded with the policemen to let me go, pointing out 86
that I was not his child but was just visiting his children. "Please let her go home," he added with tears in his voice.

"Silence, damned Jew!" was the reply he received as the policemen 87
pushed us roughly toward the door. We had no choice but to go.

With guns pointing at us, we walked up Kolejova Street to the train 88
station. For a moment I thought we might be taken to the police station or the Fador, but we were not. In an hour we were at the farthest end of the train station. There were other Jewish people sitting on the grounds; SS troops were standing over them with pointed guns. We were in a state of shock. All of this had happened very quickly. Homes attacked, people marched out, and here we were at the station facing a freight train. We were to go somewhere in this train, but where? Where could they be taking women and children? Certainly not to a work camp. This is crazy, I thought; this is a crazy nightmare.

The herd of human captives grew larger and larger as more people 89
were added. We were kept there for a long time; at least two hours, it seemed. Fortunately we were allowed to sit. All the time, sitting and waiting, I wondered what was to become of us. After being chased out of our homes we were now being taken away from our city.

Oddly enough, my mind was not so much on my predicament° as it 90
was on my mother. How could I get a message to her? All this had

---

yearning for (84): desiring
predicament (90): difficult situation

happened swiftly and, it seemed, only in one section of the ghetto. The rest of the people in the ghetto were probably just beginning to realize what had happened. I worried about my mother—one son dead, her husband probably dead, one son imprisoned in a work camp, and her only daughter taken without a chance to say good-bye. I would be gone, there was no telling how long, maybe forever. And she would not know how I had disappeared.

Suddenly the locomotive of the waiting freight train started up and a   91
shrill whistle like a shriek of agony, pierced the air. A loud German voice commanded us to get into the boxcars. I held the hand of one of the boys, who in turn held his father's hand. We pulled each other up into the boxcars. There was crying and moaning because one of the SS° brutes was using a whip to speed up the loading of the cars.

The cars were very tightly packed, so most of the people were   92
forced to stand. Some of the smaller children were able to sit at their parents' feet, but I was older and quite tall for my eleven years. I stood.

After the last person had been packed aboard the train, the doors   93
were shut, and the car was plunged into near darkness, prompting cries from the people within.

We soon realized that the car was not entirely dark. Light could be   94
seen through cracks between the boards, and better still, there were small barred windows, open and without glass, which let enough light in so that once our eyes had adjusted, we could see fairly clearly.

The train started with a lurch° that threw several people off their   95
feet. It pulled slowly out of the station. Several men concentrated to see if they could tell what direction it would take; one man said north, another east, another southeast—they could not be sure.

As the train picked up speed, cold wind began to whistle through   96
the barred openings. It was November, and many people had been forced from their homes without a coat. I was wearing a sweater. I had left my coat at the doctor's home.

There was a young woman standing very near me, holding a baby.   97
She had wrapped it in her shawl to keep it warm, and I noticed that she kept shifting the child from arm to arm, trying to ease the strain of its weight on her shoulders. I reached over and touched her arm. She started, looking at me in surprise.

"Shall I hold the baby a little while?" I asked. "It would give you a   98
chance to rest."

SS (91): the SS troops, a special Nazi military unit
lurch (95): sudden swaying movement

She smiled, "Thank you, but no. I want to hold him as long as I can." 99

The trip wore on and on. One hour, two hours; it became quite late 100 in the afternoon. Some people had even fallen asleep standing up, leaning on the shoulders of their loved ones. Some tried to lie down on the floor between the legs of those standing. But this worked best for the small children.

I saw a man reach up and shake the bars on one of the windows. 101 "Hey!" he cried. "This bar is loose. Look!"

Another man reached over and tried the bar. It was true. Several men 102 worked their way through the mass of people to the window, taking turns wrenching at the steel bar. They pounded at it with the palms of their hands, wrapped shawls around it and pulled—anything to work it free.

Finally, after much effort, the bar pulled away from its bottom bolt 103 and could be twisted up and away from the window. But this still left too small an opening for anyone to squeeze through, so they continued working.

More time passed, and we could feel the train slowing down. 104 Someone was lifted to the window to see what was happening. "We are entering a mountain range," he said. "The incline is forcing the train to slow down."

With renewed vigor they pounded at the remaining bars until a 105 second one was pried free and could be twisted back. This left an opening large enough for children to escape. The man closest to the window kissed his eight-year-old son, told him to go to his grandmother's home, where his mother was, lifted him up, and pushed him through the opening into the bushes alongside the railway tracks. With tears in his eyes he turned and said, "Who is next?" There was silence. Most parents kept their children close and would not allow them to be pushed through the window. Only two more kissed their children and moved them toward the men at the window.

My father's friend, the doctor, was one of those helping pass the 106 children out of the train window. He reached down for me. "Come, Alicia," he said. "The train is traveling as slowly as it ever will. There is a slope covered with bushes with a stream at the bottom. Remember to roll when you hit the ground. Run and hide until the train leaves; then just follow the railroad tracks back home."

"But wait," I said, stepping back. "Help your own children first." 107

"No," he said. "They are staying with me." 108

"But why?" 109

"Alicia"—he squeezed my shoulder and looked at me sadly— 110 "Alicia, the world has gone insane when people do this kind of thing to other people."

His voice became husky, and he cleared his throat before 111 continuing. I could see that his eyes had become very wet. "I don't want to be part of the human race anymore," he said. "And anyway, what would my children do without a father? Their mother is dead. Where would they go? How could they live?

"No, they will go with me. We will suffer our fate together. But 112 you, Alicia, you have a mother; you have brothers. You have to try to return to them. Do you hear me?" He gripped my arms tightly. "You must live, Alicia. You must live." And with that he lifted me up and handed me over to another of the men. "She goes next," he said.

It was the most terrifying thing that had ever happened to me— 113 more terrifying than the time I met a wild boar in the forest in Rosulna. As I was pushed through the window I could see the slope far below me. To be pushed from a moving train . . . but I no longer had a say in the matter. I was going out that window and in a hurry.

In a moment I was flying through the air, and then crash! I hit a 114 bush. A big branch gave way under me, forming a kind of cradle for my body. "Roll, Alicia, roll." I kept hearing the doctor's instructions, and I rolled off the branch and down the hill, gaining speed as I went. I could hear what sounded like guns near me. Apparently the Germans had discovered our escape and were shooting at us.

But the train kept moving and I heard no more gunfire. After a 115 while I eased into a sitting position. I checked myself for damage. I was certainly banged up—my legs and face were scratched, my sweater torn, and my elbows and knees were bleeding. I was sore all over. Later I would find that my shoulders, back, and hips were covered with bruises. But nothing seemed to be broken. The bushes had cushioned my fall. The men in the train had known what they were doing.

I thought of my mother and brothers, and new strength flowed into 116 my battered body. I had to get home quickly. All I had to do, the doctor told me, was to follow the railway tracks.

But where was home? How far away? How long to get there? 117

I was running over the railroad tracks, frantic to escape from the 118 *train. I had just jumped out of a boxcar window and I thought I had escaped to safety but, to my great horror, the train was chasing after me and was trying to catch me. It was getting closer and closer. I could hear its loud whistle and the voice of the doctor who helped me escape urging me to run, run faster. Suddenly out of nowhere there was a river in front of me and I felt myself falling into the cold water. Somewhere in midair my fall had become a graceful dive and, when I finally hit the water, it was a feeling of great relief.*

The water was blue, and there were many fish swimming around. It 119
was so peaceful, and I let the current carry me. Slowly, very slowly, I
surfaced and I could hear voices from far away, as though from a long
tunnel. Then one voice became clearer.

"Her fever has broken. She will be all right now. Just keep her 120
covered."

I felt myself being lifted gently and put down again. I felt a spoon in 121
my mouth. I tried to swallow the warm liquid, but it hurt my throat. The
pain made me fully awake.

I was in bed, my head cradled in my mother's arm while she was 122
trying to spoon-feed me tea. I looked up at Mama, and I could see the
tears in her eyes. I turned my head to the right, and there stood my
brothers. Zachary had a big smile on his face—a smile that did not reach
his eyes, which were looking at me with great concern. Herzl stood there
with his mouth open, as though he were trying to say something but the
words would not come out.

I took another painful swallow, and then another, and just closed my 123
eyes. I was very tired. Suddenly it dawned on me that I was home. I
wanted to shout out loud. I am home! I am home again! But I didn't have
the strength.

A week passed before I was strong enough to be out of bed. I 124
returned to selling soap and getting bread to send to Bunio in the labor
camp. But when I slept, the nightmares took over again, and I relived my
escape from the train, the return home, the fever, and the pain. I woke up
in the mornings drenched in perspiration and shaking with fear. My
nightmares did not go unnoticed by my family. One morning I found
Zachary standing near my bed.

"Alicia, I would like to take a little walk. We will go over the 125
Bashte down the river, and just walk and talk."

"Zachary, do you think it is safe?" I asked. 126

"Oh, come on, you sleepyhead, get dressed." 127

He started pulling at my blanket. I threw my pillow at him and got 128
dressed quickly.

It was wonderful to walk with Zachary. When we reached the top of 129
the hill he spread a blanket on the ground and we sat down. I leaned my
head on his shoulder, and we just sat there looking at the river. After a
while I started talking. I told Zachary about my experience on the train. I
repeated the words the doctor had told me when I asked him to save his
children and explained how I followed the railroad tracks, how ill I had
felt. Finally, choking on tears, I told him that if I hadn't loved and
worried about my family so much, I would never have made it home.
Then my tears came and I cried and cried.

I don't know how long we sat there when Zachary said, "Here, 130
Alicia, take this. It's time to get back."

He handed me a handkerchief with a red apple in it. I used the 131
handkerchief but kept the apple. I couldn't eat it just then. How
wonderful of Zachary, I thought. He knew how much I loved apples.

When we were close to home Zachary stopped me and, taking my 132
hand, looked at me.

"Alicia, sweetheart, I know how painful this might be for you, but 133
could you repeat what you just told me to some people at the Judenrat?
They should know exactly what happened. It is very important."

"Zachary, I would do anything for you, you know that. You are the 134
best brother in the world, and I love you," I added in a whisper.

In a small room at the Judenrat we met two men. Zachary had 135
apparently arranged it, and they were waiting for us. They knew what had
happened, they said. There were two survivors: me and another girl who
was hurt and still in bed.

I did not look at the men as I told them my story, but when I 136
finished I glanced at them and saw that they were shaken and had tears in
their eyes.

"Please, Zachary, take your sister home and then come back," the 137
older of the men said.

"I will go home by myself," I said, and headed for the door. I had 138
just closed the door when I heard an angry voice coming from the room. I
recognized my brother's voice. He was very angry. For some reason he
was speaking in Hebrew. "*Lo!* [No!]" he kept saying, "we can't just sit
and wait. We will all be killed." And then, like thunder, a voice answered
him—also in Hebrew. "You want to fight? Then fight. But when the
Germans retaliate by killing hundreds of women and children, how will
you feel then? Can you bear the thought of such a mass murder? Do you
want this on your conscience? Do you? Speak up, Zachary!"

As the argument continued, I was afraid that this shouting was 139
going to get out of control, so I quickly opened the door and entered the
room. My heart turned over with pain when I saw my brother. He just
stood there with his head lowered and his fists clenched. He looked
completely defeated. I took his hand in mine and pulled him out of the
room. We walked home in silence.

I looked at Zachary just before we entered our home. He was his 140
old self again, but there was a certain look of determination about him
that I couldn't understand. . . .

Anne,

I will not be able to
meet with you tonight.
I forgot to call.
I will be working on
my research paper.
See you next wednesday

Cynthia

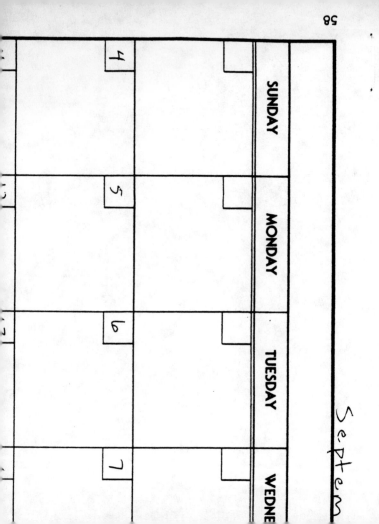

SUNDAY	MONDAY	TUESDAY	WEDNE
4	5	6	7

Septem

IN PRISON

[Two of Alicia's brothers are killed by the Germans. Alicia struggles to survive with her mother, younger brother, and remaining friends. Then one day there is a knock at the door.]

All of my nightmares became reality one late afternoon in 141 December 1942, about four o'clock. I had just returned from pumping water for our tiny household. I had set the water buckets down in their usual place in the hall and pushed the front door shut, when suddenly there was a heavy knock. I still had my gloves on, and my heavy shawl was wrapped high around my head, covering my nose and mouth against the bitter outside cold.

I opened the door and saw a Ukrainian policeman. He held a pencil 142 and a small notebook, and seemed to be checking things off some sort of list. "Frieda Jurman?" he asked.

I swallowed hard, and a wave of sickness swept over me. "Yes," I 143 said.

He made a check in his little book. "Come with me." 144

And so I went. I said nothing, fearing he would realize that my 145 voice was too high and childlike to belong to a woman. It may seem strange that he thought me an adult, but I was tall for a twelve-year-old, about five feet six inches, and the coat and shawl disguised my body well. The thing I most feared had happened. They had come for my mother. I wanted to get away from our house as soon as possible, so I walked quickly in the direction the policeman indicated.

He brought me directly to the police station, where I was put into a 146 cell with many others. It was a bare cell. The people were sitting on the stone floor all huddled together. I found a corner and sat down, pulling my legs up and encircling them with my arms. I put my head down and closed my eyes. I made up my mind that I wasn't going to cry or think about what was going to happen to all of us. Instead, I was trying to listen to what the women near me were saying. They were talking about a street action they were caught in. This was odd, because the policeman had come into our house to ask for my mother by name. Street actions were something new. We were now being picked up at random in the streets. What new horrors would that bring to the ghetto, I wondered.

Dawn was just breaking, when a prison guard came and unlocked 147 the door to our cell. "Everybody line up and go upstairs into the waiting room," he called out. The people who had remained awake were heavy with fatigue. I, like some others, had taken the opportunity to get some sleep; I knew I would need to be alert later.

As the line moved, I could see that the people were stooping and writing their names on a yellow ledger in front of a policeman seated behind a table. I blinked hard when I realized that I knew the policeman. I felt ill inside.   148

This man, who was helping murder my people, was the father of my childhood friend, Olga. As I came nearer, I watched him silently. He did not look much at the people who approached him, but kept his eyes on the ledger.   149

When it was my turn I stepped up, took the pencil, and wrote "Alicia Jurman" on the yellow paper. I did not sign my mother's name, as I feared Olga's father would recognize me, realize what had happened, and send for my mother. His eyes widened as he recognized the name. "Alicia"—he looked at me—"what are you doing here?"   150

I straightened my shoulders. "I was taken here like the others," I said. He seemed baffled; clearly there had been a mistake. All of the others were adults; they had not meant to include children in this action.   151

Olga's father looked around to see if any of the other policemen had noticed his outburst, then motioned for me to come closer.   152

"Look," he said, "the Germans will be here soon to take you away. When they get here, I want you to get down on your knees and beg for your life."   153

He searched my face for a nod or some other sign of acknowledgment, but I only stared back. His words "beg for your life" were still ringing in my ears. He looked uncomfortable under my gaze. "All right," he said. "Move on."   154

I took my place with the others. I still couldn't believe that Olga's father could be part of this. I still remembered when he had told his daughter how fortunate she was to have me help her with her homework and how glad he was that we were friends. Friends, I thought bitterly, and hatred began to settle into my heart. Will he accompany the Germans and help them shoot us? Will his bullet find its target in my heart or head?   155

It wasn't long before the Germans came. I could see by their uniforms that they were not the usual SS men, known to us as Hitler's most brutal killers, or even the Wehrmacht (army). They were the local German police.   156

As one of them explained that we were to be loaded into sleighs for a journey to another city, I watched Olga's father. Our eyes met. I could almost hear his thoughts. *Say it! Do it now!* I looked back at the German. He was winding down his talk; time was running out. Olga's father looked at the German, then at me again. Beg for your life, his eyes commanded me.   157

But I would not. Never! Never! I was frightened but angry at him, at the Germans, at the whole world. I wanted desperately to live, but I didn't think for a moment that going down on my knees before a heartless German murderer would save my life. If they released me, would they look for my mother again? Call it what you will, anger, dignity, courage, or just hatred. I couldn't beg, and the moment passed. `158`

Finally the German finished. The doors opened, and the people were being pushed outside. Suddenly Olga's father stood up and came over to me. Swiftly he swung his open hand at me. The blow caught me on the cheek. Throwing my head to one side. Then his hand swung back, connecting against my other cheek. The force of his slap threw me off my feet, onto the crowd of the people. Hands reached out to catch me, and I was quickly steadied. `159`

Olga's father stood in the middle of the room, his body stiff, his eyes glaring at me. Then something seemed to break inside him. He turned and went back to the table, where he sat down. He folded his hands in front of him and studied them. He did not look up again as we left the room. `160`

A blast of bitter cold air hit us as we stepped into the street. It must have been four or five in the morning, and the sky had taken on the eerie hue° it often had when it had shaken off the night but not yet accepted the day. `161`

At least now I knew we weren't going to be shot immediately, a fate we in Buczacz had come to expect for anyone caught in an action. Had that been the case, they would have taken us to the Fador, or the Bashte. But we had turned in the opposite direction and were now a long way from those places. `162`

Soon we drove past the ghetto. I craned my neck, straining to see our little house just beyond the hill. But I couldn't see it. I thought of my mother. Would she be asleep, or would she be pacing the floor, sick with panic and grief at having lost her fourth child in so short a time? If only she had known how much I loved her. Would it have comforted her or pained her even more, since she was helpless to save me? Tears that I had held back for a long time were finally streaming down my face. `163`

Then we were crossing the Black Bridge at the edge of the city. And suddenly we were in the country, traveling into the misty morning. `164`

Two Ukrainian policemen were assigned to each sleigh. One faced the horses and one faced us, holding a machine gun in his lap. Maybe if I waited until this man's back was turned, I could leap into the snow and `165`

---

hue (161): shade of color

run for cover. It wouldn't be so hard. I could roll into the ditch on the side of the road.

But what might happen then? Bunio had been killed because one of the other slave laborers had escaped. They might line up nine people from the sleigh and shoot them on the spot. They might even kill all sixty. Or they might simply find some unfortunate person to take my place. No, I just couldn't take that chance. 166

Our journey wore on and on. Six o'clock came, then seven, then eight. I could almost tell the time by the rising sun. 167

In the next village we passed children bearing knapsacks on their way to school. Their faces were partially hidden under shawls and hats, but I could catch glimpses of noses and cheeks red with the cold. As they stopped to let us pass, they looked from the policemen to us with puzzled eyes, not understanding but sensing—the way children often do—that something was wrong with the huddled people on the sleighs. 168

The sun rose higher; it was midday. I could see the outline of a city in the distance. It was a big city, much bigger than Buczacz. I had a terrible feeling as we headed toward it. 169

There was something familiar about that place. I had the feeling that I had been there before; a memory was fighting to break through to my consciousness. Did I really recognize that sign? Or did I just think so? I had seen the building before, hadn't I? But had I really? The streets were crowded, and sleighs had to pull to one side to let us pass. People in the streets were shouting things at us, cupping their hands around their mouths, or shaking their fists. "Cursed Jews! Christ killers!" Some spat in our direction. 170

It was around noon. We had been traveling about eight hours, when the sleighs arrived at a huge compound. They stopped while massive gates were pulled open and then continued through. As we pulled up before a large stone building, I saw that we were in a prison yard. 171

"It is Chortkov prison," I heard one man tell another. "They have brought us to Chortkov." 172

We were quiet. Everyone knew that this was the city where the Gestapo was headquartered, and the central base for murdering actions in ghettos, including Buczacz. Chortkov had distinct memories for me. It was in this city that I was blessed by the Chortkov rabbi, and it also was in this very prison that my brother Moshe died during the Russian occupation. 173

"Get out of the sleighs!" The order broke through my reminiscences and jerked me back to the present. Suddenly there were SS men everywhere, barking orders and insults. People were getting off the sleighs. Those who weren't fast enough were pulled or pushed to the 174 ground. Rifle stocks and long sticks seemed to fly through the air as the Nazis beat and jabbed us. Arms were lifted to shield faces and bodies from blows. All around me were cries of pain. More SS men appeared. They were wearing ski boots and carrying ski poles; I had the impression that they had stumbled onto our reception and decided to join their friends.

The woman in front of me caught a blow on the back of her neck   175
and dropped to her knees. An SS man was moving closer for a second strike.

"Get up," I urged her. I thought that if I could just get her to her   176
feet, maybe he wouldn't be so angry with her. I bent over and wrapped my arms around her waist, struggling to pull her up.

Crack! A sharp blow caught me right across the back, nearly   177
knocking the breath from my lungs as it drove me to my hands and knees. I gasped from surprise and pain. Looking up, I saw the SS man swinging his bamboo ski pole directly above me. The pole made a whistling sound as he whipped it through the air to beat me again and again.

I felt a click in my back, then knifelike pains that made it difficult   178
for me to inhale. I knew he had cracked some of my ribs. I squirmed to get away but could barely crawl, the pain was too great. Again and again he stuck me. Then I heard another click, different from the first, and the sound of wood splitting. The prong of the ski pole fell into the snow beside me. He had beaten me so hard, he had broken the pole. This enraged the SS man even more. "Damned Jew!" he screamed, kicking me with his heavy boots. I tried to shield my body, but he kicked at my arms and hands too. Then, as quickly as it had started, the abuse seemed to end. Orders were shouted for us to enter the building.

A woman helped me to my feet. "Come, Alicia, we have to go   179
inside now." I stared dumbly at her. She knew me. She knew my name. Mrs. Eckerberg had been caught in this madness with me. I didn't remember seeing her at the police station in Buczacz. Her presence was calming but disorienting° too. It was almost as though she had appeared out of thin air.

Mrs. Eckerberg tried to smile reassuringly, but I could see that she,   180
too, was in a great deal of pain. Blood ran down her cheek from a cut in her forehead. I felt my tired body relax against hers as we plodded slowly and painfully through the snow and into the building.

The prison was made entirely of stone. The solid walls had kept out   181
the warmth of the morning, and the chill went through my coat and shawl. Now we were ordered to remove our overcoats and put them on a

---

disorienting (179): confusing

huge pile, and then to stand in a circle. It was terribly difficult to get out of my coat; my bruised and stinging fingers fumbled painfully at the buttons. It was lucky that I had been wearing this coat at the time I was beaten; otherwise my back might have been broken.

Without my coat the cold felt even more bitter. In moments I was   182
shivering, which shook my cracked ribs, sending bursts of sharp pain through my back and chest.

Next we were ordered to remove all of our jewelry. No one resisted;   183
but those who were slow in unfastening snaps or pulling off rings were beaten. I saw some necklaces ripped from around necks, and knuckles made bloody by pulling off tight rings.

Quickly I began to remove my own jewelry, a pair of pierced   184
earrings I had worn since I was six years old. I was able to take one earring off easily, but the other one had always been a problem. The closer the Germans came, the more frantically I worked with the difficult earring, pulling and twisting.

Finally two Nazis stood before me, one holding a sack containing   185
all the jewelry, the other ready to help remove the pieces. Quickly I handed over the first earring. "I will have the other for you right away," I said in broken German, twisting at the gold ring.

The man did not hesitate for a moment but reached over, slapped   186
my hand away, and grasped the tight gold ring. He jerked his hand sharply downward, and pulled the earring out, tearing the earlobe. I felt dizzy as the blood flowed freely down my neck from the burning wound.

Suddenly my legs gave away, and I collapsed to the floor.   187
Unfortunately I did not faint, but remained conscious as two guards hurried over to kick me back to my feet. It was as though I were in the middle of a bad dream. I saw Mrs. Eckerberg reaching over to help me, but she was pushed back. I could hear the Germans shouting at me and could see the toes of their boots coming toward me, but their blows felt muffled.

I saw their mouths twisting grotesquely° and their teeth bared, but I   188
could not understand them. I could hear only a loud rushing in my ears, like a waterfall. Everything looked white and misty and seemed to be in slow motion. Finally I could not look anymore, but slumped my head forward against my chest, my eyes gazing unfocused at the stone floor.

I don't know how long I remained there unconscious. Sometime   189
later I felt myself put onto a sack and pulled along the floor. I was pulled

---

grotesquely (188): crookedly

roughly down the stone steps, each one jarring° my ribs with increasing pain. The pain actually seemed to reawaken my senses, because by the time I reached the cell door I felt more coherent°, more conscious of my surroundings. I was pushed to a corner while the other people were herded past, and then I was dragged in through the barred door. I heard the door clang shut behind me.

I awakened early the next morning to the sound of clanking metal and bootsteps. Several Germans had entered the cell and were ordering people to their feet, jabbing at them with the muzzles of their guns. I huddled in the corner, hoping I wouldn't be noticed. My body was stiff with cold and it hurt a lot to breathe. 190

About eight women were pushed outside the cell, and the rest of us were left alone. I tried to pull myself into a sitting position which took me quite a while to do. I had to move very slowly so as not to jar my ribs. The cell was freezing. I could feel the blood from my torn ear caked on my neck and face. When I scratched lightly I was able to flake much of it away. The ear itself was very tender and felt swollen. 191

I looked for Mrs. Eckerberg. And when I found her, I saw that she was very ill. Her head was all matted with blood from the wound on her head. When I called her name she opened her eyes, and to my great relief, she recognized me. 192

"Alicia, will you take care of my sons? You will do it for me? Please," she whispered. I couldn't sit for too long, so I lay down and pulled her head onto my hip. 193

I could hear sounds coming from the courtyard. There was a small window in our cell but it was too high, so we couldn't look outside. The sounds I heard were terrifying. There were the cries of people and shouts in German; but even more chilling, I could also hear snarling dogs. Soon the air was filled with the blended sound of barking dogs and the shrieks of human beings. 194

I pulled my sack over Mrs. Eckerberg and lay listening to the horrible sounds. How I would have loved to put my hands over my ears and muffle out the screams and growls, but I couldn't touch my torn ear. Many in the cell did cover their ears; others huddled together, weeping. Still others like myself lay still. No one could sleep. 195

Some time passed and it became quiet outside. Three women were returned to the cell. Each was dragged in and thrown on the floor; not one had had the strength to walk by herself. Cellmates moved forward to 196

---

jarring (189): bumping
coherent (189): able to think logically

help, but the poor unfortunates cried out at the touch of a hand on their ravaged bodies. Their arms and legs were torn by dog bites. We didn't have to ask about the others; we knew they had died. Two of these survivors also died during the day.

Throughout the day, every few hours more people were taken out to the courtyard. Many were torn by the dogs; others were beaten severely. Some were brought back to the cell; many were not. There was very little talking; people were immobilized by fear and suffering. Many stared straight ahead; some, like myself, tried to sleep off and on. The reasons I sought sleep were many; sleep erased the pain, the fear, the cold, and the hunger. I had not eaten nor had I had a drop of water in two days, but I sought sleep, especially because I didn't want to see the faces of the Nazis when they eventually pulled me out of the cell. 197

On the third day of my imprisonment a German guard brought in a bucket of water and a ladle. "Drink all you want," he told us. "When you want more, call out." The water was cold, with pieces of ice floating in it; we drank it all, and the bucket was refilled several times. But no food came that day or any other. We were slowly being starved to death. 198

Night came again, but the raids on the cells did not stop. Again and again we heard the screams in the courtyard; and never did as many return as had left. People began to die in the cell, either from the beatings or the dogs or exposure to the cold. 199

Poor Mrs. Eckerberg died one night just as I was trying to pour some water between her lips. She opened her eyes for a moment, looked at me, and died. I thought she went to sleep, but the woman next to me recognized death. Now she will not have to suffer anymore, I thought as I covered her face with my sack. 200

The Germans came in the next morning and went about the cell, kicking at us to see if we were still alive. Those who did not move were kicked again, more severely. And if they still didn't move, they were carried away for dead. I felt as though I ought to mourn poor Mrs. Eckerberg, who had brought me a bit of comfort days before, but actually I felt very little. I was beginning to die myself. I realized that a person could actually become one of the living dead; could go on living but feel nothing, not pain, not fear, not sorrow. I was very near to this state. 201

I was still able to think, and my thoughts went back to the time I was thrown out of the train. I was with the doctor, and heard him say again that he didn't want to be part of the human race anymore. Now I clearly understood what the doctor had meant. But then I heard him say to me, "You must live, Alicia. You must live." 202

My mind raced. I thought about my mother and brother. I thought of 203 their anguish over losing their family one by one. I also remembered how I had promised myself to protect my mother with my life. I felt the familiar sensation of hate burning within me.

Damned Nazis, I thought to myself. *I'll show you. I won't die. You* 204 *will not be able to kill me. I will live to see you pay for your crimes and to have your name erased from this world.*

When I awakened, I was no longer in the prison. I was in bed in a 205 darkened room, and I could see light coming in through the doorway. I didn't recognize the room at all. Was I dreaming? Or could I actually be dead, and at some stopping station on my way to heaven?

I felt terrible: hot, clammy, then cold and very ill. My joints ached 206 and my head hurt. I felt tightness around my back and chest. I tried to get out of the bed, but I was so weak that I could barely even roll over.

Soon after, a woman entered my room. 207

"Oh, you are awake!" she said. "That is wonderful. Oh, Jules"—she 208 called to someone in the outer room—"the girl is awake."

A man entered. He smiled at me. "So, dear one," he said, "how are 209 you feeling today?" He felt my forehead. "Hmm, still warm, but I believe you will recover now."

"Where am I?" I asked. 210

"In our home, in the Chortkov ghetto," the man answered. He was a 211 gentle man, and I felt very safe with him and the woman.

"I am Jules Gold, and this is my wife, Sala. You have been with us 212 for two weeks."

Two weeks! It didn't seem possible. I had been unconscious for 213 fourteen days.

"Do you feel like having a little tea, or soup?" the woman asked. 214

Until she mentioned food I had not thought of it, but suddenly I 215 realized I was ravenously° hungry.

"Yes, please," I replied. 216

While Mrs. Gold prepared my soup, Mr. Gold propped some 217 pillows behind my back and began to tell me the story of the last two weeks. I was in their home, Mr. Gold told me, because he had discovered me in a pile of dead bodies awaiting burial at the prison cemetery.

The earth had frozen badly, so the Germans called in additional help 218 to dig graves. Ghetto Jews were forced to bury the corpses of their own people who had died in prison. Mr. Gold, as a member of the Judenrat, accompanied the men from the ghetto to the cemetery so that in case the

---

ravenously (215): extremely

Germans decided to shoot them, he could at least try to plead for their lives.

Apparently, after I had become unconscious in the prison cell, I had been assumed dead, either by my cellmates or by the German guards. At any rate, my body had been thrown onto a pile of bodies, in the middle of the room, which was then carried outside and left in the snow for burial. Mr. Gold told me that when he picked me up, he thought he heard a moan, and then he realized that my body was warm. The Jewish burial party pretended to bury me and actually put me in the grave. But when the German guards left, they pulled me out, wrapped me in a coat, hid me under the straw of their sleigh, and brought me into the ghetto to Mr. Gold's home. Since then, he and Mrs. Gold had cared for me as though I were their own child, not knowing if I would live or die. For two weeks I had tossed and turned in the bed, moaning, talking in my sleep, sometimes calling for my mother, sometimes for my father. They had been very concerned that an action might take place while I was sick. It was a true miracle that I was still alive, and they were determined that I stay that way. Two angels from heaven, I thought. 219

Mrs. Gold brought in a cup of tea and a bowl of broth. 220

"Now, don't eat this too quickly," she cautioned. "You may get pains in your stomach." 221

I tried to do as she asked me, but in the end I gulped the soup down. It was thin and watery, but to me it tasted wonderful. When I finished, Mrs. Gold tucked the blanket tightly around me. 222

"Too much excitement at one time is not good for you," she said. "We will talk more later; but for now, try to get some more sleep." 223

I was still so weak that it wasn't at all difficult to drift back to sleep. But this time I was aware of the Golds coming into my room to check on me. I could tell the difference between day and night. I could hear voices as the couple talked in the next room. After two weeks of nonexistence I was overjoyed to be able to make use of my senses once more. 224

Every day I ate soup and bread for breakfast, lunch, and dinner. I was so hungry, I could have eaten around the clock. But I knew the Golds must have the same difficulties in getting food as every other Jewish family in Poland, and I knew they were giving me food they could have eaten themselves. I was deeply grateful for their sacrifice and felt very guilty about it. 225

As I grew stronger, we talked more and more. They wanted to know where I had come from, and how my family had been able to survive. I told them about the deaths of my three brothers; how my father had just disappeared and we believed he, too, was dead; how Mama, Herzl, and I peddled goods in the marketplace for bread and potatoes. . . . 226

"Alicia," asked Mr. Gold, "can you remember when you first became ill in the prison?" 227

"I don't really know exactly when, but it must have been on the third or fourth day." 228

"Did others become ill at that time?" 229

I told him I didn't know, but that many people had died during the time I was in the cell. I told him about Mrs. Eckerberg. 230

"Alicia," Mr. Gold continued to question me, "did you have typhoid before you came to Chortkov prison?" 231

"I was ill with typhus last winter, or rather early spring. Had I been ill with the same disease again?" I asked him. 232

"Not exactly; you had typhoid, which is a little different. But you are well now," he added quickly. 233

I was curious about his interest in the illness, so I asked some questions myself. Mr. Gold told me that we were apparently given water to drink that had been contaminated with disease. So that was it. The Germans had given us all the water we wanted to drink, which was not in character for them. 234

"Did all the people who came from Buczacz die in prison?" I asked Mr. Gold. 235

"No, some were released and sent back to Buczacz." 236

I understood it all now; the Nazis were trying to kill us by disease too. 237

I stayed about a month in Chortkov at the Golds' home. My health improved, but slowly. After three weeks I was finally able to get out of bed, but I was so weak I could barely stand. My ear had begun to heal, and my back didn't hurt so much, although it was still very tender. I continued to wear bandages to keep my ribs in place and knew that I would have to wear them for some time. 238

The first day I was able to stay out of bed for a while, Mrs. Gold gave me a pair of boy's pants and a shirt to wear. It surprised me that they had children's clothing. As I took them from her she must have seen the question in my eyes. 239

"They were our son's. He was killed before you came to stay with us." 240

I went over and hugged her. "I am very sorry," I said. 241

"Thank you, my dear," she said, patting my hand. "I am sure he would have liked you very much. Sometimes I feel as . . . as though our son returned. . . ." She could not complete her sentence because she started to cry. She didn't have to finish. I knew what she meant. How she must have loved me to give me her son's clothing. I remembered how Mama gave her sons' clothing to the Eckerberg boys. I thought, how heavy with sorrow are the hearts of Jewish mothers. 242

One evening about six weeks after they found me, Mr. Gold   243
returned home and announced that he had found a way to get me back to
Buczacz. "In two days you will be with your mother and brother," Mr.
Gold said as he put his arm around me.

"We will put you under the straw in a sleigh, where you will be nice   244
and warm and no one will even know you are there. Is that all right with
you?"

I nodded. Then something clicked in my mind. A sleigh driven by   245
whom? I hesitated whether to ask. I was afraid to hurt Mr. Gold's
feelings. But I had to ask.

"Mr. Gold, please forgive me for asking; I am really very grateful   246
for what you have done for me, but who is going to drive this sleigh into
Buczacz? I hope it is not some farmer. I have such bad memories . . ."

"You can trust me. You will be in very safe hands." He smiled.   247
"Good, then. Mama," he addressed his wife, "Alicia will be leaving in
two days. Let's see if we can find something warm for her to wear."

I burst into tears. Mr. Gold put his arms around me and held me   248
tightly. "Shush, darling, no more tears," he said. "Now is the time for us
all to be brave."

Two days later Mrs. Gold awoke very early, about half past four in   249
the morning. Mr. Gold was already awake. Because of the need for
secrecy, they lit only one candle. Mrs. Gold gave me a piece of bread and
some tea. She also gave me a small package, which I put in my coat
pocket. "Chew slowly, my dear," she said. "This will be your last food
until you get home."

Suddenly there was a knock on the door. "Ah," said Mr. Gold, "that   250
should be our friend." He told me to wait in the other room and then
opened the door. I heard some voices in a different language. For a moment
I thought it might be Hebrew, but I couldn't be sure. I felt excitement
mounting in me together with a certain amount of apprehension. Mrs. Gold
called for me to come out. There was a man in the kitchen who seemed to
fill up all the space there. He was big and burly°.

"So," he said, looking at me, "this is to be my traveling companion,   251
eh? We will do our talking now, little friend. Once we are on the road, we
take no chances."

The man's name was Ivan. He and Mr. Gold explained that they   252
were going to smuggle me out of the ghetto. I would have to be in a
potato sack under the straw; and whatever I heard, I was not to make a
sound. Once we were out of the city it would be a little easier. But now

---

burly (250): heavy and muscular

they had to put a kerchief over my mouth and nose, which I could remove when we left the city. Ivan would stop before the Black Bridge in Buczacz and let me off there. "Now," he said, "it is time to say good-bye. We must leave without delay."

I turned to the Golds. Mrs. Gold's eyes were brimming with tears as she hugged me tightly. "We will miss you, Alicia," she said. "Try not to forget us." 253

"I won't, Mrs. Gold," I said. "I won't ever forget you." 254

When I went to hug Mr. Gold, I could feel that he was warm. I touched his forehead and it was hot. 255

"I hope you are not getting sick, Mr. Gold," I asked with concern in my voice. 256

"It's all right, Alicia, don't worry. I have had typhus already, so if I get ill, I will get well again." 257

"I am sorry if you got sick because of me." 258

"No, no, child. Not because of you. There is a terrible epidemic in the ghetto. Don't worry, I will be all right. Good luck, Alicia. Take care, dear child." 259

"God bless you, Mr. Gold," I said, giving him a last kiss on his cheek, and then I quickly followed Ivan to the sleigh. 260

I stepped into a sack, which Ivan tied. He lifted me in his arms and pushed me under a kind of wooden platform on the bottom of the sleigh; then he put straw on top of me. The sleigh moved for a while and then it stopped. I heard voices, and things were put on top of my platform. Then we moved again. And then someone was asking something. I heard loud laughter and the words "the usual," and the sleigh moved on. Perhaps a half hour passed before we stopped again. People were talking and unloading the things that had been put on the sleigh earlier. Now I heard distinct voices saying, "We will not be able to bury them today. The earth is too frozen." 261

The sleigh jerked and moved on. I began to perspire when I realized that I had been under dead people and had been brought back to a cemetery again. Now I understood why they put a kerchief around my mouth and nose; to prevent me from making a noise. I was supposed to be dead too. 262

"You can remove your kerchief now," came Ivan's loud voice. "We are out of the city. Best go to sleep; it is a long way home for you!" 263

I stayed awake for the first hour or so of the trip, thinking about the Golds and about the prison and wondering what would await me back in Buczacz. I was filled with both joy and worry. Then I drifted off to sleep and slept through much of the remaining journey. When the sleigh stopped I found myself lifted out from under the wooden platform. Ivan 264 removed the sack and I stepped out. "Thank you very much for bringing me home," I said as I looked at Ivan. There was something abut his eyes that caught my heart. They were so sad. I was stunned. They simply did not suit this big man. Who was he anyway, I wondered.

"All right, I am off," said Ivan, and he jumped up on the seat. I watched him turn around to go back to Chortkov.   265

It had started snowing, the new flakes falling gently down on the older, hardened snow. I put out my hand and caught some. They looked so beautiful that I licked them with my tongue. My joints ached; I shivered as I made my way over the bridge, down the street, and into the ghetto. But it wasn't only the January weather that made me shiver—on many of the doorways I saw signs in Polish and German saying "typhoid." So, I thought bitterly, I was not the first to make it home. The typhoid was already here.   266

My anticipation mounted as I came closer and closer to our house. My heart sank when I saw the sign on our door. I paused for a minute to catch my breath and compose myself, then pushed the door open. It was deathly still inside our room. I looked around and saw Mama and Herzl lying in their beds. I approached slowly, fearfully, not knowing if I would find them dead or alive. Reaching the bed, I gently touched Mama's shoulder. Her head turned toward me and her eyes opened. She was very ill.   267

Then she smiled weakly. "Alicia," she whispered, "you have come home to us."   268

"Yes, Mama," I replied in a choking voice. "I have come home."   269

Note: This selection is taken from the book *Alicia: My Story* by Alicia Appleman-Jurman. For information on how to obtain the book, turn to page 563.

READING COMPREHENSION QUESTIONS

Vocabulary in Context

1. The word *baffled* in " 'I was taken here like all the others,' I said. He seemed baffled; clearly there had been a mistake. All of the others were adults" (paragraph 151) means
   a. calm.
   b. satisfied.
   c. puzzled.
   d. friendly.

Central Point and Main Ideas

2. Which sentence best expresses the central point of the selection?
   a. The Nazis were even worse to the Jews than the Russians had been.
   b. Alicia suffered horrors under the Nazis, which strengthened her determination to live.
   c. The Nazis killed Alicia's father and three of her brothers.
   d. World War II should have been avoided.

3. Which sentence best expresses the main idea of paragraph 66?
   a. Alicia was careful not to eat any of the bread she brought from the market for her brother.
   b. Two Jewish men were issued special travel permits to go to Borki Wielki.
   c. Bunio was imprisoned at Borki Wielki and had little food to eat.
   d. Alicia's family regularly sacrificed some of their own food in order to send some to Bunio.

4. Which sentence best expresses the main idea of paragraphs 267–269?
   a. Alicia was filled with anticipation to see her family again.
   b. Alicia's mother and brother Herzl were still alive.
   c. Alicia returned home to find her mother and brother Herzl sick with typhoid.
   d. Alicia returned home in January after being imprisoned, rescued, and nursed back to health.

Supporting Details

5. Alicia escaped death at Chortkov prison because
   a. Olga's father convinced Alicia to beg for her freedom.
   b. Mrs. Eckerberg hid her.
   c. Jules Gold found her in a pile of dead bodies and rescued her.
   d. she got typhoid and fled from the hospital.

6. Alicia realized that the German guards at Chortkov gave the Jews plenty of ice water to drink because
   a. the water contained deadly germs meant to kill Jews.
   b. the guards wanted to keep the Jews alive for more torture.
   c. some of the guards felt sorry for the prisoners.
   d. the guards wanted the Jews to get strong enough to work.

Transitions

7. As in all narratives, the details of this selection are organized mainly in a
   a. list-of-items pattern.
   b. time order.
   c. contrast pattern.
   d. cause-and-effect pattern.

Inferences

8. The author implies that when she attempted to participate in school lessons from a tree, the teacher felt
   a. sympathetic but fearful.
   b. angry and disgusted.
   c. courageous and revengeful.
   d. confused and hurt.

9. After Alicia came home from pumping water one late afternoon in December of 1942, she left with a Ukrainian policeman because
   a. he had come to arrest her.
   b. she wanted to save her mother's life.
   c. she recognized him.
   d. she was confused.

10. We can conclude that Olga's father slapped Alicia on both sides of her face because
    a. he hated all Jews.
    b. he was frustrated and angry because she refused to beg for her life.

   c. he thought she would try to escape.

   d. he was trying to hurt her enough so that she would have to be hospitalized and not sent on the train.

OUTLINING

Complete the following outline of the reading from *Alicia: My Story* by filling in the letters of the missing major and minor details, which appear in random order below the outline.

1. The Germans arrive, and Papa disappears.

2. _____

3. Bunio is taken away to forced labor (and eventually killed).

4. Alicia is forced into and escapes from a railroad boxcar and then makes her way home. (Zachary is later killed.)

5. Alicia is sent to Chortkov prison, where she is treated inhumanely.

   • Her coat and jewelry are taken, and she is badly beaten.

   • She is starved.

   • She is eventually given typhoid-infected water to drink.

   • _____

6. _____

   • She is found alive by Jules Gold, one of the men in a Jewish burial group.

   • Jules Gold takes her to his ghetto home, where he and his wife nurse her back to health.

   • _____

7. At home, Alicia finds her mother and brother sick with typhoid.

Items Missing from the Outline

   a. The Golds arrange for her to be smuggled back home.

   b. Alicia is rescued from the graveyard.

   c. Alicia's family is forced into a ghetto and a very restricted life.

   d. Unconscious, Alicia is brought with a pile of dead bodies out in the snow for burial.

DISCUSSION QUESTIONS

1. Judging from the reading, what qualities did Alicia have that might have helped her survive the Nazis?

2. The mass extermination of the Jews and others by the Nazis is often referred to as the Holocaust. Some people argue that the Holocaust never really occurred. What in Alicia's story supports the idea that there indeed *was* a Holocaust?

3. There were some non-Jews in Alicia's story that were sympathetic and kind to the Jews. Who were they? How can you explain the fact that so many other Germans did nothing to help the Jews?

4. Because of the violence, brutality, and emotional intensity of this passage, one might argue that college students should not be expected to read and respond to such readings. Do you agree or disagree with this argument? Why?

6

Watchers
Dean Koontz

Preview

This selection is the beginning of the popular novel *Watchers*, by Dean R. Koontz. The author of many entertaining thrillers, Koontz skillfully draws his readers into this strange, suspenseful story. He begins with a few fascinating characters in three unusual story lines. In the first, a lonely man goes hiking and meets a stray dog that is quite odd (to say the least). Together they flee from an unknown but terrifying danger. Next, a large man goes about the routine of his occupation—killing to order. Third, a timid thirty-year-old woman is threatened by an aggressive TV repairman. To see how their stories weave together, you'll have to get your hands on a copy of the book. Don't be surprised if the minute you finish this excerpt you'll rush out to do just that.

ONE

On his thirty-sixth birthday, May 18, Travis Cornell rose at five o'clock in the morning. He dressed in sturdy hiking boots, jeans, and a long-sleeved, blue-plaid cotton shirt. He drove his pickup south from his home in Santa Barbara all the way to rural Santiago Canyon on the eastern edge of Orange County, south of Los Angeles. He took only a package of Oreo cookies, a large canteen full of orange-flavored Kool-Aid, and a fully loaded Smith & Wesson .38 Chief's Special.

During the two-and-a-half-hour trip, he never switched on the radio. He never hummed, whistled, or sang to himself as men alone frequently do. For part of the drive, the Pacific lay on his right. The morning sea was broodingly° dark toward the horizon, as hard and cold as slate, but nearer shore it was brightly spangled° with early light the colors of pennies and rose petals. Travis did not once glance appreciatively at the sun-sequined water.

He was a lean, sinewy° man with deep-set eyes the same dark brown as his hair. His face was narrow, with a patrician° nose, high cheekbones, and a slightly pointed chin. It was an ascetic° face that would have suited a monk in some holy order that still believed in self-flagellation°, in the purification of the soul through suffering. God knows, he'd had his share of suffering. But it could be a pleasant face, too, warm and open. His smile had once charmed women, though not recently. He had not smiled in a long time.   3

The Oreos, the canteen, and the revolver were in a small green nylon backpack with black nylon straps, which lay on the seat beside him. Occasionally, he glanced at the pack, and it seemed as if he could see straight through the fabric to the loaded Chief's Special.   4

From Santiago Canyon Road in Orange County, he turned onto a much narrower route, then onto a tire-eating dirt lane. At a few minutes past eight-thirty, he parked the red pickup in a lay-by, under the immense bristly boughs of a big-cone spruce.   5

He slipped the harness of the small backpack over his shoulders and set out into the foothills of the Santa Ana Mountains. From his boyhood, he knew every slope, vale°, narrow defile°, and ridge. His father had owned a stone cabin in upper Holy Jim Canyon, perhaps the most remote of all the inhabited canyons, and Travis had spent weeks exploring the wild land for miles around.   6

He loved these untamed canyons. When he was a boy, black bears had roamed the woods; they were gone now. Mule deer could still be found, though not in the great numbers he had seen two decades ago. At least the beautiful folds and thrusts of land, the profuse° and varied brush, and the trees were still as they had been: for long stretches he   7

---

broodingly (2): moodily
spangled (2): glittering
sinewy (3): muscular and lean
patrician (3): noble
ascetic (3): serious
flagellation (3): whipping
vale (6): valley
defile (6): path
profuse (7): plentiful

walked beneath a canopy of California live oaks and sycamores.

Now and then he passed a lone cabin or a cluster of them. A few   8
canyon dwellers were half-hearted survivalists who believed the end of
civilization was approaching, but who did not have the heart to move to a
place even more forbidding. Most were ordinary people who were fed up
with the hurly-burly of modern life and thrived in spite of having no
plumbing or electricity.

Though the canyons seemed remote, they could soon be   9
overwhelmed by encroaching° suburbs. Within a hundred-mile radius,
nearly ten million people lived in the interconnecting communities of
Orange and Los Angeles Counties, and growth was not abating°.

But now crystalline°, revelatory° light fell on the untamed land with   10
almost as much substance as rain, and all was clean and wild.

On the treeless spine of a ridge, where the low grass that had grown   11
during the short rainy season had already turned dry and brown, Travis
sat upon a broad table of rock and took off his backpack.

A five-foot rattlesnake was sunning on another flat rock fifty feet   12
away. It raised its mean wedge-shaped head and studied him.

As a boy, he had killed scores of rattlers in these hills. He withdrew   13
the gun from the backpack and rose from the rock. He took a couple of
steps toward the snake.

The rattler rose farther off the ground and stared intensely.   14

Travis took another step, another, and assumed° a shooter's stance°,   15
with both hands on the gun.

The rattler began to coil. Soon it would realize that it could not   16
strike at such a distance, and would attempt to retreat.

Although Travis was certain his shot was clear and easy, he was   17
surprised to discover that he could not squeeze the trigger. He had come
to these foothills not merely to attempt to recall a time when he had been
glad to be alive, but also to kill snakes if he saw any. Lately, alternately
depressed and angered by the loneliness and sheer pointlessness of his
life, he had been wound as tight as a crossbow spring. He needed to
release that tension through violent action, and the killing of a few
snakes—no loss to anyone—seemed the perfect prescription for his

---

encroaching: (9) advancing
abating: (9) decreasing
crystalline: (10) clear
revelatory: (10) revealing
assumed: (15) took on
stance: (15) posture

distress. However, as he stared at this rattler, he realized that its existence was less pointless than his own: it filled an ecological niche°, and it probably took more pleasure in life than he had in a long time. He began to shake, and the gun kept straying from the target, and he could not find the will to fire. He was not a worthy executioner, so he lowered the gun and returned to the rock where he had left his backpack.

The snake was evidently in a peaceable mood, for its head lowered   18
sinuously° to the stone once more, and it lay still.

After a while, Travis tore open the package of Oreos, which had   19
been his favorite treat when he was young. He had not eaten one in fifteen years. They were almost as good as he remembered them. He drank Kool-Aid from the canteen, but it wasn't as satisfying as the cookies. To his adult palate, the stuff was far too sweet.

The innocence, enthusiasms, joys, and voracities° of youth can be   20
recalled but perhaps never fully regained, he thought.

Leaving the rattlesnake in communion with the sun, shouldering his   21
backpack once more, he went down the southern slope of the ridge into the shadows of the trees at the head of the canyon, where the air was freshened by the fragrant spring growth of the evergreens. On the west-sloping floor of the canyon, in deep gloom, he turned west and followed a deer trail.

A few minutes later, passing between a pair of large California   22
sycamores that bent together to form an archway, he came to a place where sunlight poured into a break in the forest. At the far side of the clearing, the deer trail led into another section of woods in which spruces, laurels and sycamores grew closer together than elsewhere. Ahead, the land dropped steeply as the canyon sought bottom. When he stood at the edge of the sunfall with the toes of his boots in shadow, looking down that sloped path, he could see only fifteen yards before a surprisingly seamless darkness fell across the trail.

As Travis was about to step out of the sun and continue, a dog burst   23
from the dry brush on his right and ran straight to him, panting and chuffing°. It was a golden retriever, pure of breed by the look of it. A male. He figured it was little more than a year old, for though it had attained the better part of its full growth, it retained° some of the

---

ecological niche (17): role within nature
sinuously (18): in a curving manner
voracities (20): eager appetites
chuffing (23): puffing
retained (23): kept

sprightliness° of a puppy. Its thick coat was damp, dirty, tangled, snarled, full of burrs and broken bits of weeds and leaves. It stopped in front of him, sat, cocked its head, and looked up at him with an undeniably friendly expression.

Filthy as it was, the animal was nonetheless appealing. Travis stopped, patted its head, and scratched behind its ears. 24

He half-expected an owner, gasping and perhaps angry at this runaway, to follow the retriever out of the brush. Nobody came. When he thought to check for a collar and license, he found none. 25

"Surely you're not a wild dog—are you, boy?" 26

The retriever chuffed. 27

"No, too friendly for a wild one. Not lost, are you?" 28

It nuzzled his hand. 29

He noticed that, in addition to its dirty and tangled coat, it had dried blood on its right ear. Fresher blood was visible on its front paws, as if it had been running so long and so hard over rugged terrain that the pads of its feet had begun to crack. 30

"Looks like you've had a difficult journey, boy." 31

The dog whined softly, as if agreeing with what Travis had said. 32

He continued to stroke its back and scratched its ears, but after a minute or two he realized he was seeking something from the dog that it could not provide: meaning, purpose, relief from despair. 33

"On your way now." He gave the retriever a light slap on its side, rose, and stretched. 34

The dog remained in front of him. 35

He stepped past it, heading for the narrow path that descended into darkness. 36

The dog bolted around him and blocked the deer trail. 37

"Move along, boy." 38

The retriever bared its teeth and growled low in its throat. 39

Travis frowned. "Move along. That's a good dog." 40

When he tried to step past it, the retriever snarled. It snapped at his legs. 41

Travis danced back two steps. "Hey, what's gotten into you?" 42

The dog stopped growling and just panted. 43

He advanced again, but the dog lunged at him more ferociously than before, still not barking but growling even deeper and snapping repeatedly at his legs, driving him backward across the clearing. He took eight or ten clumsy steps on a slippery carpet of dead spruce and pine 44

---

sprightliness (23): liveliness

needles, stumbled over his own feet, and fell on his butt.

The moment Travis was down, the dog turned away from him. It 45
padded across the clearing to the brink° of the sloping path and peered
into the gloom below. Its floppy ears had pricked up as much as a
retriever's ears can.

"Damn dog," Travis said. 46

It ignored him. 47

"What the hell's the matter with you, mutt?" 48

Standing in the forest's shadow, it continued to stare down the deer 49
trail, into the blackness at the bottom of the wooded canyon slope. Its tail
was down, almost tucked between its legs.

Travis gathered half a dozen small stones from the ground around 50
him, got up, and threw one of the missiles at the retriever. Struck on the
backside hard enough to be stung, the dog did not yelp but whipped
around in surprise.

Now I've done it, Travis thought. He'll go for my throat. 51

But the dog only looked at him accusingly—and continued to block 52
the entrance to the deer trail.

Something in the tattered beast's demeanor°—in the wide set dark 53
eyes or in the tilt of its big squarish head—made Travis feel guilty for
having stoned it. The sorry damn dog looked disappointed in him, and he
was ashamed.

"Hey, listen," he said, "*you* started it, you know." 54

The dog just stared at him. 55

Travis dropped the other stones. 56

The dog glanced at the relinquished° missiles°, then raised its eyes 57
once more, and Travis swore he saw approval in that canine face.

Travis could have turned back. Or he could have found another way 58
down the canyon. But he was seized by an irrational determination to
forge ahead, to go where he *wanted* to go, by God. This day of all days,
he was not going to be deterred or even delayed by something as trivial°
as an obstructive° dog.

He got up, shrugged his shoulders to resettle the backpack, took a 59
deep breath of the piny air, and walked boldly across the clearing.

---

brink (45): edge
demeanor (53) manner
relinquished (57): given up
missiles (57): weapons meant to be thrown
trival (58): unimportant
obstructive (58): presenting obstacles

The retriever began to growl again, softly but menacingly. Its lips 60
skinned back from its teeth.

Step by step, Travis's courage faded, and when he was within a few 61
feet of the dog, he opted for a different approach. He stopped and shook
his head and gently berated the animal: "Bad dog. You're being a very
bad dog. You know that? What's gotten into you? Hmmmm? You don't
look as if you were born bad. You look like a good dog."

As he continued to sweet-talk the retriever, it ceased growling. Its 62
bushy tail wagged once, twice, tentatively.

"That's a good boy," he said slyly, coaxingly. "That's better. You 63
and I can be friends, huh?"

The dog issued a conciliatory° whine, that familiar and appealing 64
sound all dogs make to express their natural desire to be loved.

"Now, we're getting somewhere," Travis said, taking another step 65
toward the retriever with the intention of stooping and petting it.

Immediately, the dog leaped at him, snarling, and drove him back 66
across the clearing. It got its teeth in one leg of his jeans, shook its head
furiously. He kicked at it, missed. As Travis staggered out of balance
from the misplaced kick, the dog snatched the other leg of his pants and
ran a circle around him, pulling him with it. He hopped desperately to
keep up with his adversary° but toppled and slammed to the ground
again.

"Shit!" he said, feeling immeasurably foolish. 67

Whining again, having reverted° to a friendly mood, the dog licked 68
one of his hands.

"You're schizophrenic°," Travis said. 69

The dog returned to the other end of the clearing. It stood with its 70
back to him, staring down the deer trail that descended through the cool
shadows of the trees. Abruptly, it lowered its head, hunched its shoulders.
The muscles in its back and haunches visibly tensed as if it were
preparing to move fast.

"What're you looking at?" Travis was suddenly aware that the dog 71
was not fascinated by the trail itself but, perhaps, by something *on* the
trail. "Mountain lion?" he wondered aloud as he got to his feet. In his
youth, mountain lions—specifically, cougars—had prowled these woods,
and he supposed some still hung on.

---

conciliatory (64): intended to overcome distrust
adversary (66): opponent
reverted (68): returned
schizophrenic (69): having contradictory moods

The retriever grumbled, not at Travis this time but at whatever had 72 drawn its attention. The sound was low, barely audible°, and to Travis it seemed as if the dog was both angry and afraid.

Coyotes? Plenty of them roamed the foothills. A pack of hungry 73 coyotes might alarm even a sturdy animal like this golden retriever.

With a startled yelp, the dog executed° a leaping-scrambling turn 74 away from the shadowed deer trail. It dashed toward him, past him, to the other arm of the woods, and he thought it was going to disappear into the forest. But at the archway formed by two sycamores, through which Travis had come only minutes ago, the dog stopped and looked back expectantly. With an air of frustration and anxiety, it hurried in his direction again, swiftly circled him, grabbed at his pants leg, and wriggled backward, trying to drag him with it.

"Wait, wait, okay," he said. "Okay." 75

The retriever let go. It issued one woof, more a forceful exhalation 76 than a bark.

Obviously—and astonishingly—the dog had purposefully 77 prevented him from proceeding along the gloomy stretch of the deer trail because something was down there. Something dangerous. Now the dog wanted him to flee because that dangerous creature was drawing nearer.

Something was coming. But what? 78

Travis was not worried, just curious. Whatever was approaching 79 might frighten a dog, but nothing in these woods, not even a coyote or a cougar, would attack a grown man.

Whining impatiently, the retriever tried to grab one leg of Travis's 80 jeans again.

Its behavior was extraordinary. If it was frightened, why didn't it 81 run off, forget him? He was not its master; it owed him nothing, neither affection nor protection. Stray dogs do not possess a sense of duty to strangers, do not have a moral perspective, a conscience. What did this animal think it was, anyway—a freelance Lassie?

"All right, all right," Travis said, shaking the retriever loose and 82 accompanying it to the sycamore arch.

The dog dashed ahead, along the ascending trail, which led up 83 toward the canyon rim, through thinning trees and brighter light.

Travis paused at the sycamores. Frowning, he looked across the 84 sun-drenched clearing at the night-dark hole in the forest where the

---

audible (72) able to be heard
executed (74): performed

descending portion of the trail began. What was coming?

The shrill cries of the cicadas° cut off simultaneously°, as if a   85
phonograph needle was lifted from a recording. The woods were
preternaturally° silent.

Then Travis heard something rushing up the lightless trail. A   86
scrabbling noise. A clatter as of dislodged stones. A faint rustle of dry
brush. The thing sounded closer than it probably was, for sound was
amplified as it echoed up through the narrow tunnel of trees.
Nevertheless, the creature was coming fast. Very fast.

For the first time, Travis sensed that he was in grave° peril°. He   87
knew that nothing in the woods was big or bold enough to attack him, but
his intellect was overruled by instinct. His heart hammered.

Above him, on the higher path, the retriever had become aware of   88
his hesitation. It barked agitatedly°.

Decades ago, he might have thought an enraged black bear was   89
racing up the deer trail, driven mad by disease or pain. But the cabin
dwellers and weekend hikers—outriders of civilization—had pushed the
few remaining bears much farther back into the Santa Anas.

From the sound of it, the unknown beast was within seconds of   90
reaching the clearing between the lower and higher trails.

The length of Travis's spine, shivers tracked like melting bits of   91
sleet trickling down a windowpane.

He wanted to see what the thing was, but at the same time he had   92
gone cold with dread, a purely instinctive fear.

Farther up the canyon, the golden retriever barked urgently.   93

Travis turned and ran.   94

He was in excellent shape, not a pound overweight. With the   95
panting retriever leading, Travis tucked his arms close to his sides and
sprinted up the deer trail, ducking under the few low-hanging branches.
The studded soles of his hiking boots gave good traction; he slipped on
loose stones and on slithery layers of dry pine needles, but he did not fall.
As he ran through a false fire of flickering sunlight and shadow, another
fire began to burn in his lungs.

Travis Cornell's life had been full of danger and tragedy, but he'd   96

---

cicadas (85): large flylike insects (the males make a loud, high sound)
simultaneously (85): at the same time
preternaturally (85): abnormally
grave (87): serious
peril (87): danger
agitatedly (88): in a disturbed manner

never flinched from anything. In the worst of times, he calmly confronted° loss, pain, and fear. But now something peculiar happened. He lost control. For the first time in his life, he panicked. Fear pried° into him, touching a deep and primitive level where nothing had ever reached him before. As he ran, he broke out in gooseflesh and cold sweat, and he did not know why the unknown pursuer should fill him with such absolute terror.

He did not look back. Initially, he did not want to turn his eyes   97
away from the twisting trail because he was afraid he would crash into a low branch. But as he ran, his panic swelled, and by the time he had gone a couple of hundred yards, the reason he did not look back was because he was afraid of what he might see.

He knew that his response was irrational. The prickly sensation   98
along the back of his neck and the iciness in his gut were symptoms of a purely superstitious terror. But the civilized and educated Travis Cornell had turned over the reins to the frightened child-savage that lives in every human being—the generic ghost of what we once were—and he could not easily regain control even though he was aware of the absurdity° of his behavior. Brute instinct ruled, and instinct told him that he must run, run, stop thinking and just run.

Near the head of the canyon, the trail turned left and carved a   99
winding course up the steep north wall toward the ridge. Travis rounded a bend, saw a log lying across the path, jumped but caught one foot on the rotting wood. He fell forward, flat on his chest. Stunned, he could not get his breath, could not move.

He expected something to pounce on him and tear out his throat.   100

The retriever dashed back down the trail and leaped over Travis,   101
landing surefootedly on the path behind him. It barked fiercely at whatever was chasing them, much more threateningly than when it had challenged Travis in the clearing.

Travis rolled over and sat up, gasping. He saw nothing on the trail   102
below. Then he realized the retriever was not concerned about anything in that direction but was standing sideways on the trail, facing the underbrush in the forest to the east of them. Spraying saliva, it barked stridently°, so hard and loud that each explosive sound hurt Travis's ears.

---

confronted (96): faced
pried (96): forcefully entered
absurdity (98): ridiculousness
stridently (102): harshly

The tone of savage fury in its voice was daunting°. The dog was warning the unseen enemy to stay back.

"Easy, boy," Travis said softly. "Easy." 103

The retriever stopped barking but did not glance at Travis. It stared 104 intently into the brush, peeling its pebbly black lips off its teeth and growling deep in its throat.

Still breathing hard, Travis got to his feet and looked east into the 105 woods. Evergreens, sycamores, a few larches. Shadows like swatches of dark cloth were fastened here and there by golden pins and needles of light. Brush. Briars. Climbing vines. A few well-worn toothlike formations of rock. He saw nothing out of the ordinary.

When he reached down and put a hand upon the retriever's head, 106 the dog stopped growling, as if it understood his intention. Travis drew a breath, held it, and listened for movement in the brush.

The cicadas remained silent. No birds sang in the trees. The woods 107 were as still as if the vast elaborate clockwork mechanism of the universe had ceased ticking.

He was sure that he was not the cause of the abrupt silence. His 108 passage through the canyon had not previously disturbed either birds or cicadas.

Something *was* out there. An intruder of which the ordinary forest 109 creatures clearly did not approve.

He took a deep breath and held it again, straining to hear the 110 slightest movement in the woods. This time he detected the rustle of brush, a snapping twig, the soft crunch of dry leaves—and the unnervingly° peculiar, heavy, ragged breathing of something big. It sounded about forty feet away, but he could not pinpoint its location.

At his side, the retriever had gone rigid°. Its floppy ears were 111 slightly pricked, straining forward.

The unknown adversary's raspy breathing was so creepy—whether 112 because of the echo effect of the forest and canyon, or because it was just creepy to begin with—that Travis quickly took off his backpack, unsnapped the flap, and withdrew the loaded .38.

The dog stared at the gun. Travis had the weird feeling that the 113 animal knew what the revolver was—and approved of the weapon.

Wondering if the thing in the woods was a man, Travis called out: 114

---

daunting (102): discouraging
unnervingly (110): frighteningly
rigid (111): stiff

"Who's there? Come on out where I can see you."

The hoarse breathing in the brush was now underlaid with a thick 115 menacing gnarl°. The eerie guttural° resonance° electrified Travis. His heart beat even harder, and he went as rigid as the retriever beside him. For interminable° ticking seconds, he could not understand why the noise itself had sent such a powerful current of fear through him. Then he realized that what frightened him was the noise's ambiguity: the beast's growl was definitely that of an animal . . . yet there was also an indescribable quality that bespoke° intelligence, a tone and modulation almost like the sound that an enraged man might make. The more he listened, the more Travis decided it was neither strictly an animal nor human sound. But if neither . . . then what the hell was it?

He saw the high brush stirring. Straight ahead. Something was 116 coming toward him.

"Stop," he said sharply. "No closer." 117

It kept coming. 118

Now just thirty feet away. 119

Moving slower than it had been. A bit wary° perhaps. But closing in 120 nevertheless.

The golden retriever began to growl threateningly, again warning 121 off the creature that stalked° them. But tremors were visible in its flanks, and its head shook. Though it was challenging the thing in the brush, it was profoundly frightened of a confrontation.

The dog's fear unnerved Travis. Retrievers were renowned for 122 boldness and courage. They were bred to be the companions of hunters, and were frequently used in dangerous rescue operations. What peril or foe could provoke° such dread in a strong, proud dog like this?

The thing in the brush continued toward them, hardly more than 123 twenty feet away now.

Though he had as yet seen nothing extraordinary, he was filled with 124 superstitious terror, a perception of indefinable but uncanny° presences.

---

gnarl (115): snarl, growl
guttural (115): harsh
resonance (115): strong, deep tone
interminable (115): unending
ambiguity (115): vagueness; ability to be interpreted in more than one way
bespoke (115): showed
wary (120): cautious
stalked (121): followed
provoke (122): bring about
uncanny (124): strangely disturbing

He kept telling himself he had chanced upon a cougar, just a cougar, that was probably more frightened than he was. But the icy prickling that began at the base of his spine and extended up across his scalp now intensified. His hand was so slick with sweat that he was afraid the gun would slip out of his grasp.

Fifteen feet. 125

Travis pointed the .38 in the air and squeezed off a single warning 126 shot. The blast crashed through the forest and echoed down the long canyon.

The retriever did not even flinch, but the thing in the brush 127 immediately turned away from them and ran north, upslope, toward the canyon rim. Travis could not see it, but he could clearly mark its swift progress by the waist-high weeds and bushes that shook and parted under its assault.

For a second or two, he was relieved because he thought he had 128 frightened it off. Then he saw it was not actually running away. It was heading north-northwest on a curve that would bring it to the deer trail above them. Travis sensed that the creature was trying to cut them off and force them to go out of the canyon by the lower route, where it would have more and better opportunities to attack. He did not understand how he knew such a thing, just that he *did* know it.

His primordial° survival instinct drove him into action without the 129 need to *think* about each move he made; he automatically did what was required. He had not felt that animal surety° since he had seen military action almost a decade ago.

Trying to keep his eye on the telltale tremble of the brush to his 130 right, abandoning his backpack and keeping only the gun, Travis raced up the steep trail, and the retriever ran behind him. Fast as he was, however, he was not fast enough to overtake the unknown enemy. When he realized that it was going to reach the path well above him, he fired another warning shot, which did not startle or deflect° the adversary this time. He fired twice into the brush itself, toward the indications of movement, not caring if it *was* a man out there, and that worked. He did not believe he hit the stalker, but he scared it at last, and it turned away.

He kept running. He was eager to reach the canyon rim, where the 131 trees were thin along the ridge top, where the brush was sparse°, and where a brighter fall of sunlight did not permit concealing shadows.

---

primordial (129): fundamental
surety (129): certainty
deflect (130): turn aside
sparse (131): thin

When he arrived at the crest a couple of minutes later, he was badly winded. The muscles of his calves and thighs were hot with pain. His heart thumped so hard in his chest that he would not have been surprised to hear the echo of it bouncing off another ridge and coming back to him across the canyon. `132`

This was where he had paused to eat some Oreos. The rattlesnake, which earlier had been sunning on a large flat rock, was gone. `133`

The golden retriever had followed Travis. It stood beside him, panting, peering down the slope they had just ascended. `134`

Slightly dizzy, wanting to sit and rest but aware that he was still in danger of an unknown variety, Travis looked down the deer trail, too, and scanned what underbrush he could see. If the stalker remained in pursuit of them, it was being more circumspect°, climbing the slopes without disturbing the weeds and bushes. `135`

The retriever whined and tugged once at Travis's pants leg. It scurried across the top of the narrow ridge to a declivity° by which they could make their way down into the next canyon. Clearly, the dog believed they were not out of danger and ought to keep moving. `136`

Travis shared that conviction. His atavistic° fear—and the reliance on instinct that it involved—sent him hurrying after the dog, over the far side of the ridge, into another tree-filled canyon. `137`

Vincent Nasco had been waiting in the dark garage for hours. He did not look as if he would be good at waiting. He was big—over two hundred pounds, six-three, muscular—and he always seemed to be so full of energy that he might burst at any moment. His broad face was placid°, usually as expressionless as the face of a cow. But his green eyes flashed with vitality, with an edgy nervous watchfulness—and with a strange hunger that was like something you expected to see in the eyes of a wild animal, some jungle cat, but never in the eyes of a man. Like a cat, in spite of his tremendous energy, he was patient. He could crouch for hours, motionless and silent, waiting for prey. `138`

At nine-forty Tuesday morning, much later than Nasco expected, the dead-bolt lock on the door between the garage and the house was disengaged with a single hard *clack*. The door opened, and Dr. Davis Weatherby flicked on the garage lights, then reached for the button that would raise the big sectional door. `139`

---

circumspect (135): cautious
declivity (136): a downward slope
atavistic (137): primitive, stemming from remote ancestors
placid (138): calm

"Stop right there," Nasco said, rising and stepping from in front of 140
the doctor's pearly-gray Cadillac.

Weatherby blinked at him, surprised. "Who the hell—" 141

Nasco raised a silencer-equipped Walther P-38 and shot the doctor 142
once in the face.

Sssnap. 143

Cut off in midsentence, Weatherby fell backward into the cheery 144
yellow and white laundry room. Going down, he struck his head on the
clothes dryer and knocked a wheeled metal laundry cart into the wall.

Vince Nasco was not worried abut the noise because Weatherby was 145
unmarried and lived alone. He stooped over the corpse, which had
wedged the door open, and tenderly put one hand on the doctor's face.

The bullet had hit Weatherby in the forehead, less than an inch 146
above the bridge of his nose. There was little blood because death had
been instantaneous, and the slug had not been quite powerful enough to
smash through the back of the man's skull. Weatherby's brown eyes were
open wide. He looked startled.

With his fingers, Vince stroked Weatherby's warm cheek, the side 147
of his neck. He closed the sightless left eye, then the right, although he
knew that postmortem muscle reactions would pop them open again in a
couple of minutes. With a profound gratefulness evident in his tremulous°
voice, Vince said, "Thank you. Thank you, Doctor." He kissed both of the
dead man's closed eyes. "Thank you."

Shivering pleasantly, Vince plucked the car keys off the floor where the 148
dead man had dropped them, went into the garage, and opened the Cadillac's
trunk, being careful not to touch any surface on which he might leave a clear
fingerprint. The trunk was empty. Good. He carried Weatherby's corpse out
of the laundry room, put it in the trunk, closed and locked the lid.

Vince had been told that the doctor's body must not be discovered 149
until tomorrow. He did not know why the timing was important, but he
prided himself on doing flawless work. Therefore, he returned to the
laundry room, put the metal cart where it belonged, and looked around
for signs of violence. Satisfied, he closed the door on the yellow and
white room, and locked it with Weatherby's keys.

He turned out the garage lights, crossed the darkened space, and let 150
himself out the side door, where he had entered during the night by
quietly voiding° the flimsy lock with a credit card. Using the doctor's
keys, he relocked the door and walked away from the house.

---

tremulous (147): unsteady
voiding (150): making useless

Davis Weatherby lived in Corona Del Mar, within sight of the   151
Pacific Ocean. Vince had left his two-year-old Ford van three blocks
from the doctor's house. The walk back to the van was very pleasant,
invigorating. This was a fine neighborhood boasting a variety of
architectural styles; expensive Spanish casas° sat beside beautifully
detailed Cape Cod homes with a harmony that had to be seen to be
believed. The landscaping was lush and well tended. Palms and ficus and
olive trees shaded the sidewalks. Red, coral, yellow, and orange
bougainvillaeas blazed with thousands of flowers. The bottlebrush trees
were in bloom. The branches of jacarandas dripped lacy purple blossoms.
The air was scented with star jasmine.

Vincent Nasco felt wonderful. So strong, so powerful, so alive.   152

Sometimes the dog led, and sometimes Travis took the lead. They   153
went a long way before Travis realized that he had been completely
jolted out of the despair and desperate loneliness that had brought him to
the foothills of the Santa Ana Mountains in the first place.

The big tattered dog stayed with him all the way to his pickup,   154
which was parked along the dirt lane under the overhanging boughs of an
enormous spruce. Stopping at the truck, the retriever looked back the way
they had come.

Behind them, black birds swooped through the cloudless sky, as if   155
engaged in reconnaissance° for some mountain sorcerer. A dark wall of
trees loomed° like the ramparts° of a sinister castle.

Though the woods were gloomy, the dirt road onto which Travis   156
had stepped was fully exposed to the sun, baked to a pale brown, mantled
in fine, soft dust that plumed around his boots with each step he took. He
was surprised that such a bright day could have been abruptly filled with
an overpowering, palpable° sense of evil.

Studying the forest out of which they had fled, the dog barked for   157
the first time in half an hour.

"Still coming, isn't it?" Travis said.   158

The dog glanced at him and mewled° unhappily.   159

"Yeah," he said, "I feel it too. Crazy . . . yet I feel it too. But what   160

---

casas (151): houses
reconnaissance (155): a survey
loomed (155): came indistinctly into view
ramparts 155): fortification
palpable (156): definite
mewled (159): cried weakly

the hell's out there, boy? Huh? What the hell is it?"

The dog shuddered violently. 161

Travis's own fear was amplified every time he saw the dog's terror 162
manifested°.

He put down the tailgate of the truck and said, "Come on. I'll give 163
you a lift out of this place."

The dog sprang into the cargo hold. 164

Travis slammed the gate shut and went around the side of the truck. 165
As he pulled open the driver's door, he thought he glimpsed movement in
nearby brush. Not back toward the forest but at the far side of the dirt
road. Over there, a narrow field was choked with waist-high brown grass
as crisp as hay, a few bristly clumps of mesquite, and some sprawling
oleander bushes with roots deep enough to keep them green. When he
stared directly at the field, he saw none of the movement he thought he
had caught from the corner of his eye, but he suspected that he had not
imagined it.

With a renewed sense of urgency, he climbed into the truck and put 166
the revolver on the seat beside him. He drove away from there as fast as
the washboard lane permitted, and with constant consideration for the
four-legged passenger in the cargo bed.

Twenty minutes later, when he stopped along Santiago Canyon 167
Road, back in the world of blacktop and civilization, he still felt weak
and shaky. But the fear that lingered was different from that he'd felt in
the forest. His heart was no longer drumming. The cold sweat had dried
on his hands and brow. The odd prickling of nape° and scalp was gone—
and the memory of it seemed unreal. Now he was afraid not of some
unknown creature but of his own strange behavior. Safely out of the
woods, he could not quite recall the degree of terror that had gripped him;
therefore, his actions seemed irrational.

He pulled on the handbrake and switched off the engine. It was 168
eleven o'clock, and the flurry of morning traffic had gone; only an
occasional car passed on the rural two-lane blacktop. He sat for a minute,
trying to convince himself that he had acted on instincts that were good,
right, and reliable.

He had always taken pride in his unshakable equanimity° and 169
hardheaded pragmatism°—in that if in nothing else. He could stay cool in

---

manifested (162): displayed
nape (167): the back of the neck
equanimity (169): calmness and self-control
pragmatism (169): practicality

the middle of a bonfire. He could make hard decisions under pressure and accept the consequences.

Except—he found it increasingly difficult to believe something   170
strange had actually been stalking him out there. He wondered if he had misinterpreted the dog's behavior and had imagined the movement in the brush merely to give himself an excuse to turn his mind away from self-pity.

He got out of the truck and stepped back to the side of it, where he   171
came face-to-face with the retriever, which stood in the cargo bed. It shoved its burly head toward him and licked his neck, his chin. Though it had snapped and barked earlier, it was an affectionate dog, and for the first time its bedraggled condition struck him as having a comical aspect. He tried to hold the dog back. But it strained forward, nearly clambering over the side of the cargo hold in its eagerness to lick his face. He laughed and ruffled its tangled coat.

The retriever's friskiness and the frenzied° wagging of its tail had   172
an unexpected effect on Travis. For a long time his mind had been a dark place, filled with thoughts of death, culminating in today's journey. But this animal's unadulterated° joy in being alive was like a spotlight that pierced Travis's inner gloom and reminded him that life had a brighter side from which he had long ago turned away.

"What was that all about back there?" he wondered aloud.   173

The dog stopped licking him, stopped wagging its matted tail. It   174
regarded him solemnly, and he was suddenly transfixed° by the animal's gentle, warm brown eyes. Something in them was unusual, compelling. Travis was half-mesmerized°, and the dog seemed equally captivated. As a mild spring breeze rose from the south, Travis searched the dog's eyes for a clue to their special power and appeal, but he saw nothing extraordinary about them. Except . . . well, they seemed somehow more expressive than a dog's eyes usually were, more intelligent and aware. Given the short attention span of any dog, the retriever's unwavering stare *was* damned unusual. As the seconds ticked past and as neither Travis nor the dog broke the encounter, he felt increasingly peculiar. A shiver rippled through him, occasioned not by fear but by a sense that something uncanny° was happening, that he was teetering on the threshold of an awesome° revelation°.

---

frenzied (172): wild
unadulterated (172): pure
transfixed (174): motionless in wonder
mesmerized (174): hypnotized
uncanny (174): mysterious
awesome (174): fearful, wondrous
revelation (174): something revealed

Then the dog shook its head and licked Travis's hand, and the spell 175
was broken.

"Where'd you come from, boy?" 176

The dog cocked its head to the left. 177

"Who's your owner?" 178

The dog cocked its head to the right. 179

"What should I do with you?" 180

As if in answer, the dog jumped over the truck's tailgate, ran past 181
Travis to the driver's door, and climbed into the pickup's cab.

When Travis peered inside, the retriever was in the passenger's seat, 182
looking straight ahead through the windshield. It turned to him and
issued a soft woof, as if impatient with his dawdling.

He got in behind the wheel, tucked the revolver under his seat. 183
"Don't believe I can take care of you. Too much responsibility, fella.
Doesn't fit in with my plans. Sorry about that."

The dog regarded him beseechingly°. 184

"You look hungry, boy." 185

It woofed once, softly. 186

"Okay, maybe I can help you that much. I think there's a Hershey's 187
bar in the glove compartment . . . and there's a McDonald's not far from
here, where they've probably got a couple hamburgers with your name
on them. But after that . . . well, I'll either have to let you loose again or
take you to the pound."

Even as Travis was speaking, the dog raised one foreleg and hit the 188
glove-compartment release button with a paw. The lid fell open.

"What the hell—" 189

The dog leaned forward, put its snout into the open box, and 190
withdrew the candy in its teeth, holding the bar so lightly that the
wrapping was not punctured.

Travis blinked in surprise. 191

The retriever held forth the Hershey's bar, as if requesting that 192
Travis unwrap the treat.

Startled, he took the candy and peeled off the paper. 193

The retriever watched, licking its lips. 194

Breaking the bar into pieces, Travis paid out the chocolate in 195
morsels°. The dog took them gratefully and ate almost daintily.

Travis watched in confusion, not certain if what had happened was 196
truly extraordinary or had a reasonable explanation. Had the dog actually

---

beseechingly (184): in a begging manner

morsels (195): small portions

understood him when he had said there was candy in the glove box? Or had it detected the scent of chocolate? Surely the latter.

To the dog, he said, "But how did you know to press the button to pop the lid open?" 197

It stared, licked its chops, and accepted another bit of candy. 198

He said, "Okay, okay, so maybe that's a trick you've been taught. Though it's not the sort of thing anyone would ordinarily train a dog to do, is it? Roll over, play dead, sing for your supper, even walk on your hind feet a little ways . . . yeah, those're things that dogs are trained to do . . . but they're not trained to open locks and latches." 199

The retriever gazed longingly at the last morsel of chocolate, but Travis withheld the goody for a moment. 200

The *timing*, for God's sake, had been uncanny. Two seconds after Travis had referred to the chocolate, the dog had gone for it. 201

"Did you understand what I said?" Travis asked, feeling foolish for suspecting a dog of possessing language skills. Nevertheless, he repeated the question: "Did you? Did you understand?" 202

Reluctantly, the retriever raised its gaze from the last of the candy. Their eyes met. Again Travis sensed that something uncanny was happening; he shivered not unpleasantly, as before. 203

He hesitated, cleared his throat. "Uh . . . would it be all right with you if I had the last piece of chocolate?" 204

The dog turned its eyes to the two small squares of the Hershey's bar still in Travis's hand. It chuffed once, as if with regret, then looked through the windshield. 205

"I'll be damned," Travis said. 206

The dog yawned. 207

Being careful not to move his hand, not holding the chocolate out, not calling attention to the chocolate in any manner except with words, he addressed the big tattered dog again: "Well, maybe you need it more than I do, boy. If you want it, the last bit's yours." 208

The retriever looked at him. 209

Still not moving his hand, keeping it close to his own body in a way that implied he was withholding the chocolate, he said, "If you want it, take it. Otherwise, I'll just throw it away." 210

The retriever shifted on the seat, leaned close to him, and gently snatched the chocolate off his palm. 211

"I'll be double-damned," he said. 212

The dog rose onto all fours, standing on the seat, which brought its head almost to the ceiling. It looked through the back window of the cab and growled softly. 213

Travis glanced at the rearview mirror, then at the side-mounted 214 mirror, but he saw nothing unusual behind them. Just the two-lane blacktop, the narrow berm°, the weed-covered hillside sloping down on their right side. "You think we should get moving? Is that it?"

The dog looked at him, peered out the rear window, then turned and 215 sat with its hind legs tucked to one side, facing forward again.

Travis started the engine, put the truck in gear, pulled onto Santiago 216 Canyon Road, and headed north. Glancing at his companion, he said, "Are you really more than you appear to be . . . or am I just cracking up? And if you are more than you appear to be . . . what the devil *are* you?"

At the rural eastern end of Chapman Avenue, he turned west toward 217 the McDonald's of which he'd spoken.

He said, "Can't turn you loose now or take you to a pound." 218

And a minute later, he said, "If I didn't keep you, I'd die of 219 curiosity, wondering about you."

They drove about two miles and swung into the McDonald's 220 parking lot.

Travis said, "So I guess you're my dog now." 221

The retriever said nothing. 222

TWO

Nora Devon was afraid of the television repairman. Although he 223 appeared to be about thirty (her age), he had the offensive cockiness of a know-it-all teenager. When she answered the doorbell, he boldly looked her up and down as he identified himself—"Art Streck, Wadlow's TV"— and when he met her eyes again, he winked. He was tall and lean and well-scrubbed, dressed in white uniform slacks and shirt. He was clean-shaven. His darkish-blond hair was cut short and neatly combed. He looked like any mother's son, not a rapist or psycho, yet Nora was instantly afraid of him, maybe because his boldness and cockiness seemed at odds with his appearance.

"You need service?" he asked when she hesitated in the doorway. 224

Although his question appeared innocent, the inflection° he put on 225 the word "service" seemed creepy and sexually suggestive to Nora. She did not think she was overreacting. But she had called Wadlow TV, after all, and she could not turn Streck away without explanation. An explanation would probably lead to an argument, and she was not a confrontational person, so she let him inside.

---

berm (214): unpaved edge of paved road
inflection (225): tone

As she escorted him along the wide, cool hallway to the living-   226
room arch, she had the uneasy feeling that his good grooming and big
smile were elements of a carefully calculated disguise. He had a keen
animal watchfulness, a coiled tension, that further disquieted her with
every step they took away from the front door.

Following her much too closely, virtually° looming° over her from   227
behind, Art Streck said, "You've got a nice house here, Mrs. Devon. Very
nice. I really like it."

"Thank you," she said stiffly, not bothering to correct his   228
misapprehension° of her marital status.

"A man could be happy here. Yeah, a man could be very happy."   229

The house was of that style of architecture sometimes called Old   230
Santa Barbara Spanish: two stories, cream-colored stucco with a red-tile
roof, verandas, balconies, all softly rounded lines instead of squared-off
corners. Lush red bougainvillaea climbed the north face of the structure,
dripping bright blossoms. The place was beautiful.

Nora hated it.   231

She had lived there since she was only two years old, which now   232
added up to twenty-eight years, and during all but one of them, she had
been under the iron thumb of her Aunt Violet. Hers had not been a happy
childhood or, to date, a happy life. Violet Devon had died a year ago. But,
in truth, Nora was still oppressed by her aunt, for the memory of that
hateful old woman was formidable°, stifling°.

In the living room, putting his repair kit beside the Magnavox,   233
Streck paused to look around. He was clearly surprised by the decor.

The flowered wallpaper was dark, funereal°. The Persian carpet was   234
singularly unattractive. The color scheme—gray, maroon, royal blue—
was unenlivened by a few touches of faded yellow. Heavy English
furniture from the mid-nineteenth century, trimmed with deeply carved
molding, stood on clawed feet: massive armchairs, footstools, cabinets
suitable for Dr. Caligari, credenzas that looked as if they each weighed
half a ton. Small tables were draped with weighty brocade°. Some lamps
were pewter with pale-gray shades, and others had maroon ceramic

---

virtually (227): in effect
looming (227) appearing
misapprehension (228): misunderstanding
formidable (232): causing great fear
stifling (232): smothering
funereal (234): gloomy
brocade (234): a heavy fabric

bases, but none threw much light. The drapes looked as heavy as lead; age-yellowed sheers hung between the side panels, permitting only a mustard-colored drizzle of sunlight to enter the room. None of it complemented° the Spanish architecture; Violet had willfully imposed her ponderous bad taste upon the graceful house.

"You decorate?" Art Streck asked.   235

"No. My aunt," Nora said. She stood by the marble fireplace, 236
almost as far from him as she could get without leaving the room. "This was her place. I . . . inherited it."

"If I was you," he said, "I'd heave all this stuff out of here. Could 237
be a bright, cheery room. Pardon my saying so, but this isn't you. This might be all right for someone's maiden aunt . . . She was a *maiden* aunt, huh? Yeah, thought so. Might be all right for a dried-up maiden aunt, but definitely not for a pretty lady like yourself."

Nora wanted to criticize his impertinence°, wanted to tell him to 238
shut up and fix the television, but she had no experience at standing up for herself. Aunt Violet had preferred her meek, obedient.

Streck was smiling at her. The right corner of his mouth curled in a 239
most unpleasant way. It was almost a sneer°.

She forced herself to say, "I like it well enough."   240

"Not really?"   241

"Yes."   242

He shrugged. "What's the matter with the set?"   243

"The picture won't stop rolling. And there's static, snow."   244

He pulled the television away from the wall, switched it on, and 245
studied the tumbling, static-slashed images. He plugged in a small portable lamp and hooked it to the back of the set.

The grandfather clock in the hall marked the quarter-hour with a 246
single chime that reverberated° hollowly through the house.

"You watch a lot of TV?" he asked as he unscrewed the dust shield 247
from the set.

"Not much," Nora said.   248

"I like those nighttime soaps. *Dallas, Dynasty,* that stuff."   249

"I never watch them."   250

"Yeah? Oh, now, come on, I bet you do." He laughed slyly. 251
"Everybody watches 'em even if they don't want to admit it. Just isn't

---

complemented (234): looked good with
impertinence (238): rudeness
sneer (239): mocking smile
reverberated (246): echoed over and over

anything more interesting than stories full of backstabbing, scheming, thieving, lying . . . and adultery. You know what I'm saying? People sit and watch it and cluck their tongues and say, 'Oh, how awful,' but they really get off on it. That's human nature."

"I . . . I've got things to do in the kitchen," she said nervously. "Call   252
me when you've fixed the set." She left the room and went down the hall through the swinging door into the kitchen.

She was trembling. She despised herself for her weakness, for the   253
ease with which she surrendered to fear, but she could not help being what she was.

A mouse.   254

Aunt Violet had often said, "Girl, there are two kinds of people in   255
the world—cats and mice. Cats go where they want, do what they want, take what they want. Cats are aggressive and self-sufficient by nature. Mice, on the other hand, don't have an ounce of aggression in them. They're naturally vulnerable°, gentle, and timid, and they're happiest when they keep their heads down and accept what life gives them. You're a mouse, dear. It's not bad to be a mouse. You can be perfectly happy. A mouse might not have as colorful a life as a cat, but if it stays safely in its burrow and keeps to itself, it'll live longer than the cat, and it'll have a lot less turmoil° in its life."

Right now, a cat lurked in the living room, fixing the TV set, and   256
Nora was in the kitchen, gripped by mouselike fear. She was not actually in the middle of cooking anything, as she had told Streck. For a moment she stood by the sink, one cold hand clasped in the other—her hands *always* seemed to be cold—wondering what to do until he finished his work and left. She decided to bake a cake. A yellow cake with chocolate icing. That task would keep her occupied and help turn her mind away from the memory of Streck's suggestive winking.

She got bowls, utensils, an electric mixer, plus the cake mix and   257
other ingredients out of the cupboards, and she set to work. Soon her frayed nerves were soothed by the mundane° domestic activity.

Just as she finished pouring the batter into the two baking pans,   258
Streck stepped into the kitchen and said, "You like to cook?"

Surprised, she nearly dropped the empty metal mixing bowl and the   259
batter-smeared spatula. Somehow, she managed to hold on to them and— with only a little clatter to betray her tension—put them into the sink to

---

vulnerable (255): capable of being hurt
turmoil (255): disturbance
mundane (257): ordinary

be washed. "Yes. I like to cook."

"Isn't that nice? I admire a woman who enjoys doing woman's 260 work. Do you sew, crochet, do embroidery, anything like that?"

"Needlepoint," she said. 261

"That's even nicer." 262

"Is the TV fixed?" 263

"Almost." 264

Nora was ready to put the cake in the oven, but she did not want to 265 carry the pans while Streck was watching her because she was afraid she would shake too much. Then he'd realize that she was intimidated by him, and he would probably get bolder. So she left the full pans on the counter and tore open the box of icing mix instead.

Streck came farther into the big kitchen, moving casually, very 266 relaxed, looking around with an amiable smile, but coming straight toward her. "Think I could have a glass of water?"

Nora almost sighed with relief, eager to believe that a drink of cold 267 water was all that had brought him here. "Oh, yes, of course," she said. She took a glass from the cupboard, ran the cold water.

When she turned to hand it to him, he was standing close behind 268 her, having crept up with catlike quiet. She gave an involuntary start°. Water slopped out of the glass and splattered on the floor.

She said, "You—" 269

"Here," he said, taking the glass from her hand. 270

"—startled me." 271

"Me?" he said, smiling, fixing her with icy blue eyes. "Oh, I certainly 272 didn't mean to. I'm sorry. I'm harmless, Mrs. Devon. Really, I am. All I want is a drink of water. You didn't think I wanted anything else—did you?"

He was so damned bold. She couldn't *believe* how bold he was, 273 how smart-mouthed and cool and aggressive. She wanted to slap his face, but she was afraid of what would happen after that. Slapping him—in any way acknowledging his insulting double entendres° or other offenses—seemed sure to encourage rather than deter him.

He stared at her with unsettling° intensity, voraciously°. His smile 274 was that of a predator°.

---

start (268): sudden jerking movement
double entendres (273): words with double meanings, with the
                              second meaning off-color
unsettling (274): upsetting
voraciously (274): greedily
predator (274): someone that victimizes others

She sensed the best way to handle Streck was to pretend innocence 275
and monumental thickheadedness, to ignore his nasty sexual innuendos
as if she had not understood them. She must, in short, deal with him as a
mouse might deal with any threat from which it was unable to flee.
Pretend you do not see the cat, pretend that it is not there, and perhaps the
cat will be confused and disappointed by the lack of reaction and will
seek more responsive prey elsewhere.

To break away from his demanding gaze, Nora tore a couple of 276
paper towels from the dispenser beside the sink and began to mop up the
water she had spilled on the floor. But the moment she stooped before
Streck, she realized she'd made a mistake, because he did not move out
of her way but stood over her, loomed over her, while she squatted in
front of him. The situation was full of erotic symbolism. When she
realized the submissiveness implied by her position at his feet, she
popped up again and saw that his smile had broadened.

Flushed and flustered, Nora threw the damp towels into the 277
wastecan under the sink.

Art Streck said, "Cooking, needlepoint . . . yeah, I think that's real 278
nice, real nice. What other things do you like to do?"

"That's it, I'm afraid," she said. "I don't have any unusual hobbies. 279
I'm not a very interesting person. Low-key. Dull, even."

Damning herself for being unable to order the bastard out of her 280
house, she slipped past him and went to the oven, ostensibly° to check
that it was finished preheating, but she was really just trying to get out of
Streck's reach.

He followed her, staying close. "When I pulled up out front, I saw 281
lots of flowers. You tend the flowers?"

Staring at the oven dials, she said, "Yes . . . I like gardening." 282

"I approve of that," he said, as if she ought to care whether he 283
approved or not. "Flowers . . . that's a good thing for a woman to have an
interest in. Cooking, needlepoint, gardening—why you're just full of
womanly interests and talents. I'll bet you do everything well, Mrs.
Devon. I mean everything a woman should do. I'll bet you're a first-rate
woman in every department."

If he touches me, I'll scream, she thought. 284

However, the walls of the old house were thick, and the neighbors 285
were some distance away. No one would hear her or come to her rescue.

I'll kick him, she thought. I'll fight back. 286

But, in fact, she was not sure that she would fight, was not sure that 287

---

ostensibly (280): seemingly on the surface

she had the gumption° to fight. Even if she did attempt to defend herself, he was bigger and stronger than she was.

"Yeah, I'll bet you're a first-rate woman in every department," he 288 repeated, delivering the line more provocatively° than before.

Turning from the oven, she forced a laugh. "My husband would be 289 astonished to hear that. I'm not too bad at cakes, but I've still not learned to make a decent piecrust, and my pot roast always turns out bone-dry. My needlepoint's not half bad, but it takes me forever to get anything done." She slipped past him and returned to the counter. She was amazed to hear herself chattering on as she opened the box of icing mix. Desperation made her garrulous°. "I've got a green thumb with flowers, but I'm not much of a housekeeper, and if my husband didn't help out— why, this place would be a disaster."

She thought she sounded phony. She detected a note of hysteria in 290 her voice that had to be evident to him. But the mention of a husband had obviously given Art Streck second thoughts about pushing her further. As Nora poured the mix into a bowl and measured out the required butter, Streck drank the water she had given him. He went to the sink and put the empty glass in the dishpan with the dirty bowls and utensils. This time he did not press unnecessarily close to her.

"Well, I better get back to work," he said. 291

She gave him a calculatedly distracted smile, and nodded. She 292 began to hum softly as she returned to her own task, as if untroubled.

He crossed the kitchen and pushed open the swinging door, then 293 stopped and said, "Your aunt really liked dark places, didn't she? This kitchen would be swell, too, if you brightened it up."

Before she could respond, he went out, letting the door swing shut 294 behind him.

In spite of his unasked-for opinion of the kitchen decor, Streck 295 seemed to have pulled in his horns, and Nora was pleased with herself. Using a few white lies about her nonexistent husband, delivered with admirable equanimity, she had handled him after all. That was not exactly the way a cat would have dealt with an aggressor, but it was not the timid, frightened behavior of a mouse, either.

She looked around at the high-ceilinged kitchen and decided it was 296 too dark. The walls were a muddy blue. The frosted globes of the overhead lights were opaque, shedding a drab, wintry glow. She

gumption (287): courage
provocatively (288): suggestively
garrulous (289): overly talkative

considered having the kitchen repainted, the lights replaced.

Merely to contemplate making major changes in Violet Devon's   297
house was dizzying, exhilarating°. Nora had redone her own bedroom
since Violet's death, but nothing else. Now, wondering if she could
follow through with extensive redecoration, she felt wildly daring and
rebellious. Maybe. Maybe she could. If she could fend off° Streck,
maybe she could dredge° up the courage to defy her dead aunt.

Her upbeat self-congratulatory mood lasted just twenty minutes,   298
which was long enough to put the cake pans in the oven and whip up the
icing and wash some of the bowls and utensils. Then Streck returned to
tell her the TV set was repaired and to give her the bill. Though he had
seemed subdued when he left the kitchen, he was as cocky as ever when
he entered the second time. He looked her up and down as if undressing
her in his imagination, and when he met her eyes he gave her a
challenging look.

She thought the bill was too high, but she did not question it   299
because she wanted him out of the house quickly. As she sat at the
kitchen table to write the check, he pulled the now-familiar trick of
standing too close to her, trying to cow° her with his masculinity and
superior size. When she stood and handed him the check, he contrived°
to take it in such a way that his hand touched hers suggestively.

All the way along the hall, Nora was more than half-convinced that   300
he would suddenly put down his tool kit and attack her from behind. But
she got to the door, and he stepped past her onto the veranda, and her
racing heart began to slow to a more normal pace.

He hesitated just outside the door. "What's your husband do?"   301

The question disconcerted° her. It was something he might have   302
asked earlier, in the kitchen, when she had spoken of her husband, but
now his curiosity seemed inappropriate.

She should have told him it was none of his business but she was   303
still afraid of him. She sensed that he could be easily angered, that the
pent-up violence in him could be triggered with minor effort. So she
answered him with another lie, one she hoped would make him reluctant
to harass her any further: "He's a . . . policeman."

---

exhilarating (297): cheering
fend off (297): turn away
dredge (297): gather
cow (299): frighten
contrived (299): managed
disconcerted (302): made uneasy

Streck raised his eyebrows. "Really? Here in Santa Barbara?" 304

"That's right." 305

"Quite a house for a policeman." 306

"Excuse me?" she said. 307

"Didn't know policemen were paid so well." 308

"Oh, but I told you—I inherited the house from my aunt." 309

"Of course, I remember now. You told me. That's right." 310

Trying to reinforce the lie, she said, "We were living in an 311
apartment when my aunt died, and then we moved here. You're right—
we wouldn't have been able to afford it otherwise."

"Well," he said, "I'm happy for you. I sure am. A lady as pretty as 312
you deserves a pretty house."

He tipped an imaginary hat to her, winked, and went along the walk 313
toward the street, where his white van was parked at the curb.

She closed the door and watched him through a clear segment of the 314
leaded, stained-glass oval window in the center of the door. He glanced
back, saw her, and waved. She stepped away from the window, into the
gloomy hallway, and watched him from a point at which she could not be
seen.

Clearly, he hadn't believed her. He knew the husband was a lie. She 315
shouldn't have said she was married to a cop, for God's sake; that was
too obvious an attempt to dissuade° him. She should have said she was
married to a plumber or doctor, anything but a cop. Anyway, Art Streck
was leaving. Though he knew she was lying, he was leaving.

She did not feel safe until his van was out of sight. 316

Actually, even then, she did not feel safe. 317

After murdering Dr. Davis Weatherby, Vince Nasco had driven his 318
gray Ford van to a service station on Pacific Coast Highway. In the public
phone booth, he deposited coins and called a Los Angeles number that he
had long ago committed to memory.

A man answered by repeating the number Vince had dialed. It was 319
one of the usual three voices that responded to calls, the soft one with a
deep timbre°. Often, there was another man with a hard sharp voice that
grated on Vince.

Infrequently, a woman answered; she had a sexy voice, throaty and 320
yet girlish. Vince had never seen her, but he had often tried to imagine
what she looked like.

---

dissuade (315): discourage
timbre (319): tone

Now, when the soft-spoken man finished reciting the number, Vince   321
said, "It's done. I really appreciate your calling me, and I'm always
available if you have another job." He was confident that the guy on the
other end of the line would recognize his voice, too.

"I'm delighted to hear all went well. We've the highest regard for   322
your workmanship. Now remember this," the contact said. He recited a
seven-digit telephone number.

Surprised, Vince repeated it.   323

The contact said, "It's one of the public phones at Fashion Island. In   324
the open-air promenade near Robinson's Department Store. Can you be
there in fifteen minutes?"

"Sure," Vince said. "Ten."   325

"I'll call in fifteen with the details."   326

Vince hung up and walked back to the van, whistling. Being sent to   327
another public telephone to receive "the details" could mean only one
thing: they had a job for him already, two in one day!

Later, after the cake was baked and iced, Nora retreated to her   328
bedroom at the southwest corner of the second floor.

When Violet Devon had been alive, this had been Nora's sanctuary°   329
in spite of the lack of a lock on the door. Like all the rooms in the large
house, it had been crammed with heavy furniture, as if the place served
as a warehouse instead of a home. It had been dreary in all other details
as well. Nevertheless, when finished with her chores, or when dismissed
after one of her aunt's interminable lectures, Nora had fled to her
bedroom, where she escaped into books or vivid daydreams.

Violet inevitably checked on her niece without warning, creeping   330
soundlessly along the hall, suddenly throwing open the unlockable
door, entering with the hope of catching Nora in a forbidden pastime or
practice. These unannounced inspections had been frequent during
Nora's childhood and adolescence, dwindling in number thereafter,
though they had continued through the final weeks of Violet Devon's
life, when Nora had been a grown woman of twenty-nine. Because
Violet had favored dark dresses, had worn her hair in a tight bun, and
had gone without a trace of makeup on her pale, sharp-featured face,
she had often looked less like a woman than like a man, a stern° monk
in coarse° penitential robes, prowling the corridors of a bleak°

---

sanctuary (329): a place of shelter
stern (330): serious
coarse (330): rough
bleak (330): gloomy

medieval° retreat to police the behavior of fellow monastics.

If caught daydreaming or napping, Nora was severely reprimanded° 331
and punished with onerous° chores. Her aunt did not condone laziness.

Books were permitted—if Violet had first approved of them— 332
because, for one thing, books were educational. Besides, as Violet often
said, "Plain, homely women like you and me will never lead a glamorous
life, never go to exotic places. So books have a special value to us. We
can experience most everything vicariously, through books. This isn't
bad. Living through books is even *better* than having friends and
knowing . . . men."

With the assistance of a pliable° family doctor, Violet had kept Nora 333
out of public school on the pretense of poor health. She had been
educated at home, so books had been her only school as well.

In addition to having read thousands of books by the age of thirty, 334
Nora had become a self-taught artist in oils, acrylics, watercolors, pencil.
Drawing and painting were activities of which Aunt Violet approved. Art
was a solitary pursuit that took Nora's mind off the world beyond the
house and helped her avoid contact with people who would inevitably
reject, hurt, and disappoint her.

One corner of Nora's room had been furnished with a drawing 335
board, an easel, and a cabinet for supplies. Space for her miniature studio
was created by pushing other pieces of furniture together, not by
removing anything, and the effect was claustrophobic°.

Many times over the years, especially at night but even in the 336
middle of the day, Nora had been overcome by a feeling that the floor of
the bedroom was going to collapse under all the furniture, that she was
going to crash down into the chamber below, where she would be
crushed to death beneath her own massive four-poster bed. When that
fear overwhelmed her, she had fled onto the rear lawn, where she sat in
the open air, hugging herself and shuddering. She'd been twenty-five
before she realized that her anxiety attacks arose not only from the
overfurnished rooms and dark decor of the house but from the
domineering° presence of her aunt.

On a Saturday morning four months ago, eight months after Violet 337

---

medieval (330): characteristic of the Middle Ages
reprimanded (331): scolded
onerous (331): burdensome
pliable (333): easily influenced
claustrophobic (335): uncomfortably closed in
domineering (336): overwhelming in power

Devon's death, Nora had abruptly been seized by an acute° need for change and had frantically reordered her bedroom-studio. She carried and dragged out all the smaller pieces of furniture, distributing them evenly through the other five crowded chambers on the second floor. Some of the heavier things had to be dismantled and taken away in sections, but finally she succeeded in eliminating everything but the four-poster bed, one nightstand, a single armchair, her drawing board and stool, the supply cabinet, and the easel, which was all she needed. Then she stripped off the wallpaper.

Throughout that dizzying weekend, she'd felt as if the revolution   338
had come, as if her life would never be the same. But by the time she had redone her bedroom, the spirit of rebellion had evaporated, and she had left the rest of the house untouched.

Now this one place, at least, was bright, even cheerful. The walls   339
were painted the palest yellow. The drapes were gone, and in their place were Levolor blinds that matched the paint. She had rolled up the dreary carpet and had polished the beautiful oak floor.

More than ever, this was her sanctuary. Without fail, upon passing   340
through the door and seeing what she had wrought°, her spirits lifted and she found some surcease° from her troubles.

After her frightening encounter with Streck, Nora was soothed, as   341
always, by the bright room. She sat at the drawing board and began a pencil sketch, a preliminary study for an oil painting that she had been contemplating for some time. Initially, her hands shook, and she had to pause repeatedly to regain sufficient control to continue drawing, but in time her fear abated.

She was even able to think about Streck as she worked and to try to   342
imagine just how far he might have gone if she had not managed to maneuver him out of the house. Recently, Nora had wondered if Violet Devon's pessimistic view of the outside world and of all other people was accurate; though it was the primary view that Nora, herself, had been taught, she had the nagging suspicion that it might be twisted, even sick. But now she had encountered Art Streck, and he seemed to be ample° proof of Violet's contentions°, proof that interacting too much with the outside world was dangerous.

---

acute (337): sharp
wrought (340): done
surcease (340): time away
ample (342): enough
contentions (342): claims

But after a while, when her sketch was half finished, Nora began to 343
think that she had misinterpreted everything Streck had said and done.
Surely he could not have been making sexual advances toward her. Not
toward *her*.

She was, after all, quite undesirable. Plain. Homely. Perhaps even 344
ugly. Nora knew this was true because, regardless of Violet's faults, the
old woman had some virtues, one of which was a refusal to mince
words°. Nora was unattractive, drab, not a woman who could expect to
be held, kissed, cherished. This was a fact of life that Aunt Violet made
her understand at an early age.

Although his personality was repellent, Streck was a physically 345
attractive man, one who could have his choice of pretty women. It was
ridiculous to assume he would be interested in a drudge° like her.

Nora still wore the clothes that her aunt had bought for her—dark, 346
shapeless dresses and skirts and blouses similar to those that Violet had
worn. Brighter and more feminine dresses would only call attention to
her bony, graceless body and to the characterless and uncomely lines of
her face.

But why had Streck said that she was pretty? 347

Oh, well, that was easily explained. He was making fun of her, 348
perhaps. Or, more likely, he was being polite, kind.

The more she thought about it, the more Nora believed that she had 349
misjudged the poor man. At thirty, she was already a nervous old maid,
as fear-ridden as she was lonely.

That thought depressed her for a while. But she redoubled her 350
efforts on the sketch, finished it, and began another from a different
perspective. As the afternoon waned she escaped into her art.

From downstairs the chimes of the ancient grandfather clock rose 351
punctually on the hour, half-hour, and quarter-hour.

The west-falling sun turned more golden as time passed, and as the 352
day wore on the room grew brighter. The air seemed to shimmer. Beyond
the south window a king palm stirred gently in the May breeze.

By four o'clock, she was at peace, humming as she worked. 353

When the telephone rang, it startled her. 354

She put down her pencil and reached for the receiver. "Hello?" 355

"Funny," a man said. 356

"Excuse me?" 357

---

mince words (344): control words for the sake of politeness
drudge (345): someone who through lack of imagination centers
   her life on dull physical tasks

"They never heard of him." 358

"I'm sorry," she said, "but I think you've got the wrong number." 359

"This is you, Mrs. Devon?" 360

She recognized the voice now. It was him. Streck. 361

For a moment, she could not speak. 362

He said, "They never heard of him. I called the Santa Barbara 363
police and asked to speak with Officer Devon, but they said they don't
have an Officer Devon on the force. Isn't that odd, Mrs. Devon?"

"What do you want?" she asked shakily. 364

"I figure it's a computer error," Streck said, laughing quietly. "Yeah, 365
sure, some sort of computer error dropped your husband from their
records. I think you'd better tell him as soon as he gets home, Mrs.
Devon. If he doesn't get this straightened out . . . why, hell, he might not
get his paycheck at the end of the week."

He hung up, and the sound of the dial tone made her realize that she 366
should have hung up first, should have slammed down the handset as
soon as he said that he'd called the police station. She dared not
encourage him even to the extent of listening to him on the phone.

She went through the house, checking all the windows and doors. 367
They were securely locked.

At McDonald's on East Chapman Avenue in Orange, Travis Cornell 368
had ordered five hamburgers for the golden retriever. Sitting on the front
seat of the pickup, the dog had eaten all of the meat and two buns, and it
had wanted to express its gratitude by licking his face.

"You've got the breath of a dyspeptic° alligator," he protested, 369
holding the animal back.

The return trip to Santa Barbara took three and a half hours because 370
the highways were much busier than they had been that morning.
Throughout the journey, Travis glanced at his companion and spoke to it,
anticipating a display of the unnerving intelligence it had shown earlier.
His expectations were unfulfilled. The retriever behaved like any dog on
a long trip. Once in a while, it *did* sit very erect, looking through the
windshield or side window at the scenery with what seemed an unusual
degree of interest and attention. But most of the time it curled up and
slept on the seat, snuffling in its dreams—or it panted and yawned and
looked bored.

When the odor of the dog's filthy coat became intolerable, Travis 371
rolled down the windows for ventilation, and the retriever stuck its head

---

dyspeptic (369): having indigestion

out in the wind. With its ears blowing back, hair streaming, it grinned the foolish and charmingly witless grin of all dogs who had ever ridden shotgun in such a fashion.

In Santa Barbara, Travis stopped at a shopping center where he 372 bought several cans of Alpo, a box of Milk-Bone dog biscuits, heavy plastic dishes for pet food and water, a galvanized tin washtub, a bottle of pet shampoo with a flea- and tick-killing compound, a brush to comb out the animal's tangled coat, a collar, and a leash.

As Travis loaded those items into the back of the pickup, the dog 373 watched him through the rear window of the cab, its damp nose pressed to the glass.

Getting behind the wheel, he said, "You're filthy, and you stink. 374 You're not going to be a lot of trouble about taking a bath, are you?"

The dog yawned. 375

By the time Travis pulled into the driveway of his four-room rented 376 bungalow on the northern edge of Santa Barbara and switched off the pickup's engine, he was beginning to wonder if the pooch's actions that morning had really been as amazing as he remembered.

"If you don't show me the right stuff again soon," he told the dog as 377 he slipped his key into the front door of the house, "I'm going to have to assume that I stripped a gear out there in the woods, that I'm just nuts and that I imagined everything."

Standing beside him on the stoop, the dog looked up quizzically°. 378

"Do you want to be responsible for giving me doubts about my own 379 sanity? Hmmmmmm?"

An orange and black butterfly swooped past the retriever's face, 380 startling it. The dog barked once and raced after the fluttering prey, off the stoop, down the walkway. Dashing back and forth across the lawn, leaping high, snapping at the air, repeatedly missing its bright quarry°, it nearly collided with the diamond-patterned trunk of a big Canary Island date palm, then narrowly avoided knocking itself unconscious in a head-on encounter with a concrete birdbath, and at last crashed clumsily into a bed of New Guinea impatiens over which the butterfly soared to safety. The retriever rolled once, scrambled to its feet, and lunged out of the flowers.

When it realized that it had been foiled, the dog returned to Travis. 381 It gave him a sheepish look.

"Some wonder dog," he said. "Good grief." 382

He opened the door, and the retriever slipped in ahead of him. It 383

---

quizzically (378): in a puzzled manner
quarry (380): a creature being hunted

padded off immediately to explore these new rooms.

"You better be housebroken," Travis shouted after it.   384

He carried the galvanized washtub and the plastic bag full of other   385
purchases into the kitchen. He left the food and pet dishes there, and took
everything else outside through the back door. He put the bag on the
concrete patio and set the tub beside it, near a coiled hose that was
attached to an outdoor faucet.

Inside again, he removed a bucket from beneath the kitchen sink,   386
filled it with the hottest water he could draw, carried it outside, and
emptied it into the tub. When Travis had made four trips with the hot
water, the retriever appeared and began to explore the backyard. By the
time Travis filled the tub more than half full, the dog had begun to urinate
every few feet along the whitewashed concrete-block wall that defined
the property line, marking its territory.

"When you finish killing the grass," Travis said, "you'd better be in   387
the mood for a bath. You reek°."

The retriever turned toward him and cocked its head and appeared   388
to listen when he spoke. But it did not look like one of those smart dogs
in the movies. It did not look as if it understood him. It just looked dumb.
As soon as he stopped talking, it hurried a few steps farther along the
wall and peed again.

Watching the dog relieve itself, Travis felt an urge of his own. He   389
went inside to the bathroom, then changed into an older pair of jeans and
a T-shirt for the sloppy job ahead.

When Travis came outside again, the retriever was standing beside   390
the steaming washtub, the hose in its teeth. Somehow, it had managed to
turn the faucet. Water gushed out of the hose, into the tub.

For a dog, successfully manipulating a water faucet would be very   391
difficult if not impossible. Travis figured that an equivalent test of his
own ingenuity° and dexterity° would be trying to open a child-proof
safety cap on an aspirin bottle with one hand behind his back.

Astonished, he said, "Water's too hot for you?"   392

The retriever dropped the hose, letting water pour across the patio,   393
and stepped almost daintily into the tub. It sat and looked at him, as if to
say, *Let's get on with it, you dink.*

He went to the tub and squatted beside it. "Show me how you can   394
turn off the water."

----

reek (387): smell bad
ingenuity (391): cleverness
dexterity (391): physical skill

The dog looked at him stupidly. 395

"Show me," Travis said. 396

The dog snorted and shifted its position in the warm water. 397

"If you could turn it on, you can turn it off. How did you do it? 398
With your teeth? Had to be with your teeth. Couldn't do it with a paw, for
God's sake. But that twisting motion would be tricky. You could've
broken a tooth on the cast-iron handle."

The dog leaned slightly out of the tub, just far enough to bite at the 399
neck of the bag that held the shampoo.

"You won't turn off the faucet?" Travis asked. 400

The dog just blinked at him, inscrutable°. 401

He sighed and turned off the water. "All right. Okay. Be a wiseass." 402
He took the brush and shampoo out of the bag and held them toward the
retriever. "Here. You probably don't even need me. You can scrub
yourself, I'm sure."

The dog issued a long, drawn-out *woooooof* that started deep in its 403
throat, and Travis had the feeling it was calling *him* a wiseass.

Careful now, he told himself. You're in danger of leaping off the 404
deep end, Travis. This is a damn smart dog you've got here, but he can't
really understand what you're saying, and he can't talk back.

The retriever submitted to its bath without protest, enjoying itself. 405
After ordering the dog out of the tub and rinsing off the shampoo, Travis
spent an hour brushing its damp coat. He pulled out burrs, bits of weeds
that hadn't flushed away, unsnarled the tangles. The dog never grew
impatient, and by six o'clock it was transformed°.

Groomed, it was a handsome animal. Its coat was predominantly 406
medium gold with feathering of a lighter shade on the back of its legs, on
its belly and buttocks, and on the underside of the tail. The undercoat was
thick and soft to provide warmth and repel water. The outer coat was also
soft but not as thick, and in some places these longer hairs were wavy.
The tail had a slight upward curve, giving the retriever a happy, jaunty°
look, which was emphasized by its tendency to wag continuously.

The dried blood on the ear was from a small tear already healing. 407
The blood on the paws resulted not from serious injury but from a lot of
running over difficult ground. Travis did nothing except pour boric-acid
solution, a mild antiseptic, on these minor wounds. He was confident that
the dog would experience only slight discomfort—or maybe none at all,

---

inscrutable (401): mysterious
transformed (405): changed greatly
jaunty (406): lighthearted

for it was not limping—and that it would be completely well in a few days.

The retriever looked splendid now, but Travis was damp, sweaty, and stank of dog shampoo. He was eager to shower and change. He had also worked up an appetite. 408

The only task remaining was to collar the dog. But when he attempted to buckle the new collar in place, the retriever growled softly and backstepped out of his reach. 409

"Whoa now. It's only a collar, boy." 410

The dog stared at the loop of red leather in Travis's hand and continued to growl. 411

"You had a bad experience with a collar, huh?" 412

The dog stopped growling, but it did not take a step toward him. 413

"Mistreated?" Travis asked. "That must be it. Maybe they choked you with a collar, twisted it and choked you, or maybe they put you on a short chain. Something like that?" 414

The retriever barked once, padded across the patio, and stood in the farthest corner, looking at the collar from a distance. 415

"Do you trust me?" Travis asked, remaining on his knees in an unthreatening posture. 416

The dog shifted its attention from the loop of leather to Travis, meeting his eyes. 417

"I will never mistreat you," he said solemnly°, feeling not at all foolish for speaking so directly and sincerely to a mere dog. "You must know that I won't. I mean, you have good instincts about things like that, don't you? Rely on your instincts, boy, and trust me." 418

The dog returned from the far end of the patio and stopped just beyond Travis's reach. It glanced once at the collar, then fixed him with that uncannily intense gaze. As before, he felt a degree of communion with the animal that was as profound as it was eerie—and as eerie as it was indescribable. 419

He said, "Listen, there'll be times I'll want to take you places where you'll need a leash. Which has to be attached to a collar, doesn't it? That's the only reason I want you to wear a collar—so I can take you everywhere with me. That and to ward off fleas. But if you really don't want to submit to it, I won't force you." 420

For a long time they faced each other as the retriever mulled over° the situation. Travis continued to hold the collar out as if it represented a gift rather than a demand, and the dog continued to stare into his new 421

---

solemnly (418): very seriously
mulled over (421): considered carefully

master's eyes. At last, the retriever shook itself, sneezed once, and slowly came forward.

"That's a good boy," Travis said encouragingly.   422

When it reached him, the dog settled on its belly, then rolled onto its   423
back with all four legs in the air, making itself vulnerable. It gave him a
look that was full of love, trust, and a little fear.

Crazily, Travis felt a lump form in his throat and was aware of hot   424
tears scalding the corners of his eyes. He swallowed hard and blinked
back the tears and told himself he was being a sentimental dope. But he
knew why the dog's considered submission affected him so strongly. For
the first time in three years, Travis Cornell felt needed, felt a deep
connection with another living creature. For the first time in three years,
he had a reason to live.

He slipped the collar in place, buckled it, gently scratched and   425
rubbed the retriever's exposed belly.

"Got to have a name for you," he said.   426

The dog scrambled to its feet, faced him, and pricked its ears as if   427
waiting to hear what it would be called.

God in heaven, Travis thought, I'm attributing human intentions to   428
him. He's a mutt, special maybe but still only a mutt. He may look as if
he's waiting to hear what he'll be called, but he sure as hell doesn't
understand English.

"Can't think of a single name that's fitting," Travis said at last. "We   429
don't want to rush this. It's got to be just the right name. You're no
ordinary dog, fur face. I've got to think on it a while until I hit the right
moniker°."

Travis emptied the washtub, rinsed it out, and left it to dry.   430
Together, he and the retriever went into the home they now shared.

Note: This selection is taken from the book *Watchers* by Dean Koontz. For
information on how to obtain the book, turn to page 564.

---

moniker (429): personal name, nickname

READING COMPREHENSION QUESTIONS

Vocabulary in Context

1. The word *flinched* in "Travis Cornell's life had been full of danger and tragedy, but he'd never flinched from anything. In the worst of times, he calmly confronted loss, pain, and fear" (paragraph 96) means
   a. drawn back.
   b. been taken.
   c. bought.
   d. stolen.

Main Ideas

2. Which statement best expresses the main idea of paragraphs 202–212?
   a. Although he felt foolish, Travis began to talk to the retriever.
   b. Talking to the retriever and watching its responses, Travis sensed that the dog understood language.
   c. Travis spoke to the retriever as if it were human.
   d. When Travis asked if he could have the last piece of chocolate, the dog looked away from the candy and out the window.

3. Which statement best expresses the main idea of paragraphs 336–338?
   a. Rebelling one weekend against the darkness of the house and the oppression of her aunt, Nora gave her bedroom a bright, cheerful look.
   b. Nora's bedroom had been cluttered with dark, heavy furniture which had been chosen by her aunt.
   c. Nora had often been overcome with anxiety over the overfurnished rooms and dark decor of her aunt's home.
   d. Nora redecorated her bedroom, giving it a bright, cheerful look.

4. Which sentence best expresses the main idea of paragraph 370?
   a. Since the highways were busier than they had been in the morning, Travis's drive to Santa Barbara took three and a half hours.
   b. Travis and the dog drove back to Santa Barbara.
   c. On the long ride back to Santa Barbara, Travis saw none of the unusual intelligence that the dog had shown earlier.
   d. During most of the ride back to Santa Barbara, the retriever slept or looked bored.

Supporting Details

5. Although the television repairman made offensive remarks, Nora Devon did not confront him because
   a. she feared he might hurt her Aunt Violet.
   b. she lacked the courage to stand up for herself.
   c. it seemed like the man's feelings would get hurt easily.
   d. she was too busy baking a cake.

6. Travis began to cry when the dog rolled on its back and let him put on its collar because he
   a. now knew for sure that the retriever could think like a human.
   b. had never before had a pet.
   c. felt needed for the first time in a long while.
   d. would not have been able to keep the dog if it didn't wear its collar.

Transitions

7. The relationship between the two parts of the sentence below is one of
   a. time.
   b. addition.
   c. contrast.
   d. cause and effect.

   > After murdering Dr. Davis Weatherby, Vince Nasco had driven his gray Ford van to a service station on Pacific Coast Highway. (Paragraph 318)

Inferences

8. We can conclude that Travis's time in the mountains
   a. will have little effect on his life.
   b. made him feel even lonelier.
   c. was very similar to the times he spent there when he was a boy staying at his father's cabin.
   d. got him out of his depressed mood in a way he had not foreseen.

9. From paragraph 151 we can infer that killing someone
   a. always depressed Vince.
   b. had worn Vince out.
   c. was easy for Vince.
   d. was the only thing on Vince's mind.

10. We can infer that Art Streck, the TV repairman, phoned Nora to say there was no Officer Devon in the police files because Streck
   a. feared Nora's husband would not get paid if his name wasn't in the computer.
   b. hoped Nora would call him back to repair her television set again some time.
   c. wanted Nora to know that he knew she was lying.
   d. wanted to show Nora that he had no interest in her after all.

SUMMARIZING

Watchers begins with three separate story lines. Circle the letter—*a, b,* or *c*—of the best summary of the parts about Travis Cornell.

   a. Travis Cornell goes to the foothills of the Santa Ana Mountains on his thirty-sixth birthday. He soon meets a very intelligent dog that warns him of an approaching danger. The dog, a handsome retriever, stands between Travis and a narrow path leading into a dark part of the canyon. Each time Travis tries to go further into the canyon, the dog blocks the way, growling, lunging, and snapping enough to persuade Travis. Eventually Travis instinctively realizes that something terrible is pursuing both him and the dog. Moving quickly and carefully, Travis and the dog flee through the mountain foothills and safely reach Travis's pickup. Eventually, Travis adopts the dog as his own. He wants to name the dog, but can't seem to think of just the right name.

   b. Travis Cornell goes to the foothills of the Santa Ana Mountains on his thirty-sixth birthday. He hopes to combat feelings of loneliness and despair by passing time in a place where he had once been happy. He soon meets a very intelligent retriever that warns him of an approaching dangerous creature of some sort. Frightened, Travis and the dog manage to avoid the creature and safely reach Travis's pickup. On the way home, Travis finds the dog appealing. In addition, he observes that the retriever, amazingly enough, seems to understand language. Travis decides not to bring the animal to a shelter, but to adopt it instead. At home, the dog responds with love and trust, giving Travis the feeling of being needed that he had been missing in his life.

   c. Travis Cornell goes to some mountain foothills on his thirty-sixth birthday. He plans to relax by hiking and killing rattlesnakes, childhood pastimes of his. However, when faced with a rattler, he no longer feels a strong desire to kill it. Eventually, Travis meets a very clever dog who warns him of an approaching danger. Together, they escape the canyons and drive away in Travis's pickup. In the pickup, Travis thinks out loud about giving the dog the chocolate bar in the glove compartment. Amazingly, the dog opens the glove compartment and removes the chocolate bar. Travis decides to test the dog's ability to understand language. He asks the retriever if it's okay if he has the last of the candy. The dog glances regretfully at the candy and then looks out the window. Travis realizes this is a very special dog.

DISCUSSION QUESTIONS

1. At the beginning of this reading, Travis Cornell goes hiking to fight his depression. How does Travis feel by the end of the selection? What has changed him?

2. One way that authors tell us about their characters is through the details of the story's setting. What does the description of Nora Devon's house tell readers about her?

3. How did this selection make you feel? Would you like to read the rest of the book? Why or why not? Why do you think thrillers are so popular?

4. As Travis Cornell becomes increasingly afraid, he allows his instincts to govern his actions. Rather than thinking logically, he simply flees the danger he senses is approaching. Have you ever been in a situation where your instincts took over? If so, describe the danger you felt and how your instincts may have helped you.

7

Candle in the Wind: The Ryan White Story
Beth Johnson Ruth

Preview

Ryan White wanted to be treated as a regular kid. But when he was thirteen years old, it was discovered he had AIDS. He then became both a social outcast and a beloved friend of celebrities. Both his attackers and supporters were often emotional in their point of view. Through it all, Ryan politely but persistently defended the rights of AIDS victims. In the process, he became an inspiring example of inner strength and courage for us all.

"Mom waited until after Christmas. Then she told me I had AIDS. I asked her, 'Am I going to die?' She said, 'We're all going to die someday.'" 1

With that exchange, Ryan White ceased to be a sick thirteen-year-old junior high student from Kokomo, Indiana. He became Ryan White, a social outcast who would not accept the label; Ryan White, national cause; Ryan White, the kid who put a face on the growing, ghostly AIDS epidemic. 2

Ryan was a reluctant celebrity. In the five years between the time he learned of his illness and his death in 1990, he made dozens of personal appearances, telling children and adults the facts about AIDS. Famous entertainers like Elton John and Michael Jackson became his friends. His picture was on the cover of *People* magazine; a movie was made about 3 his life; he met with the President. But through it all, Ryan's refrain never changed: again and again he insisted: "I'm just a regular kid." He'd tell it to Phil Donahue, Brooke Shields, or a classroom of fifth graders in New York. "All I've ever wanted is to be treated like everyone else."

It seemed true that Ryan was uncomfortable with his fame. He certainly would have traded the benefits of being famous for the anonymity° that would have been his had he been healthy—"Like that," Ryan once said with a snap of his fingers. But, while Ryan White may have wished to be a "regular kid," that was a destiny he was denied. Ryan's courageous good humor, the compassion he aroused for AIDS victims everywhere, his polite but persistent battle against ignorance and prejudice, lifted him far above the world of the everyday. 4

Even before he contracted AIDS, Ryan struggled against painful odds. Three days after he was born on December 6, 1971, he nearly bled to death after being circumcised. Doctors realized that Ryan had hemophilia, a condition that prevents the blood from clotting normally. A minor cut can be fatal; a bump or bruise can lead to joints painfully swollen with internal bleeding. Protecting their child from the ordinary run of cuts and scrapes can dominate° the lives of a hemophiliac's parents. Ryan's mother, Jeanne, decided early on not to overprotect her son. (Jeanne was divorced from Ryan's father, Wayne, when Ryan was five.) Bike riding, skateboarding, and playing on the playground were all parts of Ryan's young life. There were frightening "bleeds" and some emergency trips to the hospital, but in between accidents Ryan and his mother insisted that he be treated like any other child. 5

The near-normality of Ryan's life was made possible by Factor VIII, a concentrated clotting agent made from human blood. Once a month throughout her son's life, Jeanne White picked up a supply of Factor VIII from the hospital. She became expert in giving Ryan the injections he needed to keep his blood clotting normally. 6

In his autobiography, *Ryan White: My Own Story*, Ryan credits his experience with hemophilia with shaping his attitude towards his own life and health. He rejected physical therapy at the hospital in favor of exercising on his own: "Maybe I have an incurable disease, but I don't have to be a permanent invalid," he wrote. He also taught himself ways of dealing with pain through keeping his mind positive and active. Finally, he constantly compared his situation with that of other children he met at the hospital. His situation, he decided, could be a lot worse. 7

---

anonymity (4): being unknown
dominate (5): take over

"You can feel well no matter what's wrong with you," he declared. "I think that's the only way to think. Besides," he continued, "with Factor VIII, hemophilia didn't seem that bad."

Factor VIII gave Ryan White his life. Two or three times a week, his mother took a batch of Factor VIII from the refrigerator, tied a tourniquet around Ryan's thin arm, and injected the clotting agent. Ryan and Jeanne joked about "Old Faithful," a prominent vein in his right arm that was the spot of most of the injections. 8

Neither Ryan nor Jeanne ever knew which batch of Factor VIII was infected with the AIDS virus. It was most likely one used during Ryan's twelfth year of life. A batch of Factor VIII yields a dozen injections; Jeanne probably injected her son with AIDS-contaminated blood at least that many times. 9

The summer before his thirteenth birthday, Ryan didn't feel well. He began seventh grade with his class at Western Middle School in Kokomo, but just after his birthday in December, he became seriously ill. He was hospitalized with pneumocystis, a rare form of pneumonia. As he lay near death in Riley Children's Hospital in Indianapolis, doctors discovered the truth. Ryan had AIDS. 10

Ryan recovered from the pneumocystis crisis. After he spent Christmas in the hospital, his mother and minister arrived to tell him what the doctors had learned. After the initial shock had passed and Ryan started to regain his strength, he began looking forward to going back to school. However long he had left, the "regular kid" wanted to get on with his life. 11

It was not to be. Because of Ryan's huge medical bills and the expense of the drugs used to treat AIDS, Jeanne, a factory worker, filed suit against the company that produced the contaminated Factor VIII, trying to force them to pay for Ryan's treatment. The suit failed, but the Kokomo newspaper picked up on the story. Within hours, the word spread throughout Indiana—Ryan White had the deadly, mysterious disease called AIDS. 12

Throughout that winter and spring, Ryan was too weak to go back to school. But even as he stayed at home, he began to sense what kind of reception was waiting for him in the outside world. Few people in Kokomo understood the facts about AIDS. To them, AIDS was not simply a disease. It was something dirty and frightening, something associated with promiscuous° homosexuals and drug users. Ryan's younger sister, Andrea, was accused of having AIDS, too. At church, Ryan and his mother were asked to sit in a specific pew, so that everyone would know 13

---

promiscuous (13): not being selective about one's sexual partners

where they were. Fellow churchgoers pulled their children away from Ryan's side. People avoided public bathrooms after Ryan had been seen in them. At school, a boy asked a friend of Ryan's, "What kind of bread do fags eat? Ryan White bread."

But Ryan still believed that he would be avoided only by a few people who didn't know any better. By July, his health had improved to the point that he was itching to get back to school. Then Jeanne got the official word from Western Middle School officials. "They don't want you back, Ryan," she told him. "Even for a visit. They're afraid you'll infect the other kids."

Ryan was outraged. Everything he had learned in the months since he had been diagnosed told him that he posed no threat to his schoolmates. He missed his friends. He wanted to learn. Seeing his mother beginning to crumble before the insistence of Western Middle School that he remain at home made him all the angrier. "We *have* to fight, Mom," he told her. "If we don't, we won't be allowed to go anywhere or do anything. What they want to do isn't right. We can't let it happen to anybody else."

The battle was underway. The Indiana health commissioner announced that Ryan belonged in school. The Western school board voted to keep him out anyway. Teachers returned from vacation early to declare their refusal to have Ryan in their classrooms. A parent collected signatures on a petition in support of the school's stand.

At Ryan's insistence, Jeanne filed suit against Western, claiming that the school was discriminating against a handicapped child. A group of more than one hundred Western parents threatened to sue the school if Ryan was allowed in. Western offered to pay for a tutor for Ryan, but no one would take the job.

The rejection of Ryan by the students, teachers, and parents of Western Middle School was based on fear and ignorance of the truth about AIDS. Ryan could sympathize with their initial reaction. "I understood some of their fear of AIDS," he said later, "because we had fear, too, before I was diagnosed." What he couldn't understand was the community's refusal to accept the medical facts.

As Ryan and his doctors stated again and again, AIDS is not passed through casual contact. AIDS is contracted when an infected person's blood, semen, or vaginal secretions° enters another person's bloodstream. Most people get AIDS through having unprotected sex with an infected person. Other ways of catching AIDS include sharing an unsterilized hypodermic needle with an infected person (as in the use of illegal

---

secretions (19): substances produced by some part of the body

intravenous° drugs). Getting tattooed or having one's ears pierced with an unsterilized needle could also spread the virus. AIDS-infected mothers can transmit the virus to their babies through childbirth or breast feeding. Like Ryan, some people have contracted AIDS after receiving an injection or transfusion of infected blood or blood product. However, the nation's blood supply is now tested for the AIDS virus, so the chances of the disease being spread that way are very low. Normal classroom contact with Ryan White posed no danger of passing on AIDS. As evidence, Ryan noted that his mother and sister lived side by side with him, sharing food, the bathroom, and hugs and kisses, yet remained AIDS-free.

Despite these assurances, the parents of Kokomo were unconvinced. Rumors ran wild through the community. Couldn't their children catch AIDS from Ryan if they shared a drinking fountain, or sat on a toilet seat he had used? What if Ryan touched another child? What if he had a nosebleed in the hall? What if a child ate off a plate in the cafeteria that Ryan had used previously? 20

"Look," Ryan told anyone who would listen, "each of you is more dangerous to me than I am to you." He was right. AIDS is a virus that destroys the victim's immune system—the body's ability to fight off disease. An ordinary cold or flu that is easily shaken off by a healthy person can be extremely dangerous to someone with AIDS. People don't die of AIDS itself. They die of diseases that their bodies' weakened immune systems can no longer resist. 21

Finally the school offered a compromise: Ryan could listen in on his classes via a telephone hookup in his home. On the first day of school, local reporters crowded into Ryan's bedroom as he listened to his teachers over the phone. Ryan was frustrated not to be able to see the blackboard, not to hear his classmates' questions, not to hear his teachers well as they moved around the room. At lunchtime, a reporter asked Ryan how he liked the arrangement. "It stinks," he answered angrily. 22

The court battles continued as Ryan heard his lessons over the hated telephone. The attacks on the White family accelerated. Callers to a Kokomo talk radio show called Jeanne White a poor housekeeper and an unfit mother. They accused her of milking Ryan's condition for publicity. Jerry Falwell, president of Liberty University and the Moral Majority citizens' groups, stated that AIDS was God's punishment for the sins of homosexuals. He, too, criticized Jeanne White for "using" Ryan to give AIDS a "good name." 23

At the same time, outside of Kokomo, public sympathy for Ryan 24

---

intravenous (19): administered into veins

was growing. An Italian television talk show flew the Whites to Rome so Ryan could appear on their program. Italians who recognized Ryan on the street shook his hand and hugged him. He was a guest on the *CBS Morning News* and NBC's *The Today Show*. Actor Tom Cruise kidded around with Ryan at the NBC studio. AIDS patients and their families from all over the country contacted Ryan, thanking him for his courage in going public with his fight.

25   Finally, fifteen months after Ryan had left school, the state of Indiana ruled that Western had to let him in. On February 21, 1986, after the county health officer provided a medical certificate stating that he was healthy enough to attend school, Ryan arrived at Western. But 43 percent of his classmates stayed home. Others marched in front of the school carrying picket signs reading "Students Against AIDS." Rather than being reassured by the extra precautions Ryan and his mother had reluctantly agreed to—a separate bathroom and water fountain, disposable plates and eating utensils—Kokomo parents were more convinced than ever that his disease was contagious.

26   Before Ryan had been back at school a full day, he was called to the principal's office. There he learned that the Kokomo parents' group, now calling itself Concerned Citizens and Parents, had succeeded in getting a restraining order° from the county circuit court. Ryan could not attend school, said the order, until another hearing could be held to determine whether AIDS was a "communicable disease." Ryan was out again.

27   After the excitement of returning to school, this blow was almost more than even Ryan could bear. He and his mother went home, where he closed himself in his room to cry. "Am I ever going to win at anything?" he asked himself. "Tom Cruise and regular people in New York and Rome can look me in the eye and not be afraid, but my whole town seems to think AIDS is God's pest control."

28   When word got out that Ryan and Jeanne were continuing their struggle to have Ryan admitted to Western Middle School, the lid blew off the town's simmering hostility°. A letter to the editor of the *Kokomo Tribune* claimed that Ryan "constantly threatens to bite, scratch, or spit on children if things aren't done 'his way'. . . he spit[s] on the fresh produce [in a grocery store] . . . urinat[es] on restroom walls." At Easter services at the Whites' family church, parishioners pointedly turned away from Jeanne and Ryan when it was time to exchange a handshake of

---

restraining order (26): a legal order preventing something from taking place

hostility (28): opposition

peace. Jeanne's car was vandalized in the parking lot of the factory where she worked. Eggs, bottles, and garbage were tossed at Ryan's house. When Ryan or Jeanne appeared in public, they heard shouts of "Bitch!" and "Ryan White is a faggot!" Most frighteningly, a bullet was shot through the Whites' living room window.

Ryan was shocked by the vehemence of people's feelings towards   29
him. But he never lost his hope that, given enough time and education, people would cease being afraid of him and would accept him as a part of the community. "My mom always taught me to turn the other cheek, and that's what I did," he told an audience of schoolchildren on the *Donahue* show. He also became convinced that, because he remained unusually healthy for someone with full-blown AIDS, his life had a special purpose. He believed that God wanted him to keep up his fight on behalf of everyone who had ever suffered from unfair prejudice.

After three more weeks on the telephone hook-up, the date for   30
Ryan's hearing arrived. The Whites' lawyer had requested that it be held outside of Kokomo, in the town of Frankfort, Indiana. On April 10, the Whites arrived at the Frankfort courthouse. They were immediately encouraged by their reception there. Drivers went by honking, shouting, "Good luck, Ryan!" Some of Jeanne's co-workers wore buttons saying "Friends of Ryan White." Once in the courtroom, the judge wasted no time. "The restraining order is dissolved," he announced. Ryan was free to return to Western Middle School. Within an hour, he was back in class.

If Ryan thought that life would be pleasant once he returned to   31
school, he soon learned otherwise. Most of the outright hostility ceased, but Ryan was treated as anything but "a normal kid." Twenty-two children were taken out of school and enrolled in a newly-formed home study program. In the halls of Western, Ryan was treated with a mixture of fear and mocking. Other students flattened themselves against their lockers as he passed. Children refused to sit beside him in class. Life was only slightly less lonely than it had been at home. On Valentine's Day, when students were matched by a computer dating system, someone fixed the program so that Ryan was matched with other boys, and his sister, Andrea, with girls. Soon after that, Ryan's locker at school was trashed and spray-painted with anti-homosexual slogans.

Nothing—not even the invitation to a celebrity-studded AIDS   32
benefit party in New York, not appearing in a magazine ad with Elizabeth Taylor, not even receiving a phone call from his hero, rock star Elton John—could ease the hurt that Ryan felt. For almost a year and a half he had struggled for the right to go to school. Now he had won his battle, but he was alone. When school ended for the summer, Ryan was barred from the town swimming pools. He received news that several of the

teenage AIDS patients with whom he had become long-distance friends had died. In the fall, he became ill again and ended up back in Riley Hospital. Elton John called him in the hospital, promising to host him at an upcoming concert, but Ryan's thoughts had turned gloomy. "I don't want to die in Kokomo, Mom," he told Jeanne. In fact, he had picked out a place he would rather die. He'd noticed a peaceful-looking cemetery in the small town of Cicero, about an hour south of Kokomo. In July, 1987, the Whites moved to Cicero.

Getting out of Kokomo was a relief. Ryan's growing friendship with a crew of celebrities was fun—Olympic diving champion Greg Louganis kept in touch with Ryan and presented him with one of his gold medals. When a TV movie was made about Ryan's life and experience in Kokomo, the producers invited his family to a party in Malibu, California. At the party Ryan and his family rubbed shoulders with actors including Lukas Haas, who portrayed Ryan in the film; Bruce Willis; Demi Moore; and—wonder of wonders—Ryan's all-time favorite TV girl, Alyssa Milano, from the show *Who's The Boss*. Alyssa kissed Ryan and gave him a friendship bracelet from her arm. 33

Best of all was the White family's growing relationship with Elton John. The rock star had always dared to be unconventional—wearing rhinestone-spangled jackets, wild sunglasses, dangling earrings, and crazy hats. Ryan admired Elton's willingness to be different, and Elton in turn was impressed by Ryan's courage and persistence. When the Whites were in California to meet with the movie producers, Elton flew them in his private jet to two of his concerts. Ryan and Andrea wandered around backstage, wearing sweatshirts, scarves and sunglasses given to them by the rocker. Later Elton took them on a tour of Universal Studios and to Disneyland. Elton made it clear that he wasn't afraid of catching AIDS from Ryan: he shared cans of Coke with him, horsed around with him, hugged and kissed him. When fatigue caught up with Ryan at Disneyland, Elton pushed him in a wheelchair. 34

But Ryan's health was getting worse. An August, 1987, article about him in *People* magazine described in pathetic detail what AIDS was doing to him. "The disease is shutting down his body, system by system, raising colors on him in its advance like horrible campaign decorations— yellow when his liver falters, blue for his lungs. The worst of it, his mother says, is that he can never get warm anymore." In the humid August heat, Ryan sat around the house wearing a sweater, jacket, slippers, and a wool blanket. When he couldn't bear the cold anymore, he would hold his blue fingers over the burners of the kitchen stove. Scars on his hands showed where he came too close to the heat. He suffered from constant diarrhea, thrush (a mouth fungus), and herpes. He vomited 35 several times an hour, and his weight dropped to fifty-four pounds. Although he was always hungry, the mere act of eating exhausted him too much to finish more than a few bites.

Ryan was at rock-bottom, emotionally and physically. His hometown had rejected him. Apart from celebrities, he had no friends. He was nearly too ill to care. The *People* article declared that he was dying. 36

What happened next seemed almost miraculous to Ryan and his family. As the Whites settled into their new house in Cicero, the world opened its arms to them. The principal of Hamilton Heights High School assured Jeanne that Ryan would be welcome there. Better yet, Ryan began getting visitors. A neighbor came by with chocolate-chip cookies. Jill Stewart, president of the high school student body, dropped by to welcome Ryan to Cicero and make it clear that she intended to be his friend. Her friend Wendy Baker came by a few days later. Wendy and Jill brought Ryan photographs of all the teachers at Hamilton Heights, so that he would recognize them when they met. They introduced other friends to Ryan. At about the same time, Ryan's doctors began treating him with an experimental drug called AZT. Although AZT is not a cure for AIDS, it does slow the effects of the virus for some people. 37

The administrators of Hamilton Heights were determined that their experience with Ryan would be nothing like Western's. They asked Ryan to delay his enrollment that fall for two weeks. Instead of normal classes, the entire school spent that two-week period having a crash course on AIDS. Students and teachers spent their time attending lectures, films, and question-and-answer sessions with health experts. Students too shy to ask questions were encouraged to write unsigned notes and put them into a special locker. By the second week, Jill reported to her new friend, most of the unsigned notes were asking, "How can we help Ryan?" 38

By the time Ryan walked into Hamilton Heights High School for his first day of class, students and teachers alike were anxious to make him welcome. Wendy, Jill, and other student officers met Ryan at the door and helped him find his classrooms. In science class, a dark-haired girl named Heather McNew invited him to be her lab partner. Heather and Ryan were to become inseparable friends. The school janitor even handed Ryan a poem he had written. It read: "We are sorry for your fight / But for every day that you are here / We can see a little light." 39

When the Children's Television Workshop show *3-2-1-Contact* came to Hamilton Heights to make a program about Ryan and AIDS education, two of Ryan's classmates explained what had happened. "At Ryan's other school, peer pressure caused people to be against him," they said. "Here, peer pressure helped. People shared information in a positive way. Students passed it on to their parents and the townspeople. Here, it 40 became the thing to be for Ryan, not against him."

In Cicero, a new Ryan emerged. The days of stoically° turning the   41
other cheek were at an end. He had friends—lots of them. He was one of
the gang, riding to school with a group of kids, going out for pizza,
pulling pranks. He gained weight. He made the honor roll. He found a
summer job in a skateboard shop. His health improved so dramatically
that his doctor, Martin B. Kleiman of Indiana University Medical Center,
couldn't explain it.

"I can assure everyone Ryan has AIDS and it's still fatal," said Dr.   42
Kleiman. "But all the scientific data we had would not have pointed to
him being with us today and doing so well. Ryan has just blossomed, and
I don't know why. I'd like to think it's because I'm a good doctor, but I
can't take full credit. He's on no unusual drugs, no unusual therapy. He's
got a great attitude, and that plays a big part. He's optimistic, not a
quitter."

"Ryan is the happiest person I know," said his friend Jill Stewart,   43
who chauffeured him to school in her orange Toyota. "I've never seen
him in a bad mood, never heard him complain. You just feel good being
around Ryan. He's brought our whole school together."

The 1988-89 school year passed in a happy blur. Pretty Dee Laux   44
was Ryan's date for the school prom. With life becoming more normal,
Andrea was able to resume her hobby of competitive roller-skating. The
ordinary joys of life in Cicero were punctuated with extraordinary events.
The Whites and Heather McNew were invited to Los Angeles for an
AIDS benefit, where Ryan introduced Lakers star Kareem Abdul-Jabbar.
Rocker Michael Jackson invited the family and Heather to spend a day at
his ranch, playing with the superstar's collection of exotic° animals,
riding in his four-wheeler, and bouncing on his trampoline. Ryan reported
Michael to be "shy" and "just like a regular person," with whom he could
relax and talk easily. The two became good friends and were in touch
frequently after that visit. Michael even surprised Ryan with a new red
Mustang after his return to Indiana.

When Ryan was asked to address the President's Commission on   45
AIDS, he put his feelings into words:

"My life is better now," he told the Commission at their hearings in   46
Washington, D.C. After describing the horrors he had faced in Kokomo,
he told of the family's move to Cicero. "We did a lot of hoping and

---

stoically (41): showing great self-control in an emotional or
        painful situation

exotic (44): from other places

praying that the community would welcome us, and they did. For the first time in three years, we feel we have a home, a supportive school, and lots of friends. . . .

"I'm feeling great. I'm a normal happy teenager again. . . . I attend   47
sports functions and dances. My studies are important to me. I made the honor roll just recently, with two A's and two B's. I'm just one of the kids, and all because the students at Hamilton Heights High School listened to the facts, educated their parents and themselves, and believed in me.

"I believe in myself as I look forward to graduating from Hamilton   48
Heights High School in 1991.

"Hamilton Heights High School is proof that AIDS education in   49
schools works."

Ryan was at peace. "It's funny," reflected his mother. "Most kids   50
[Ryan's age] feel their lives are just beginning. But if Ryan died in two months, I would feel he's lived a very full life. All his wishes have come true. He's back in school. He's got friends."

"Sometimes I forget I have AIDS," Ryan remarked on one occasion.   51
"Or I could, if people didn't remind me."

Unfortunately, AIDS didn't forget about Ryan. In the fall of 1989,   52
illness began creeping over him once again. A painful hernia made his stomach push out, but his blood platelet count was too low to allow corrective surgery. Chills, laryngitis, and exhaustion tormented him. By October, he was too worn out to go to school. When Michael Jackson invited Ryan back to his ranch after Christmas, Ryan worried he wouldn't be well enough to go, but he couldn't bring himself to say no. At the secluded° ranch, Ryan sat in the sun without worrying about people staring at the sores and shingles on his skin. He had a wonderful time. When he left, Michael hugged him, saying, "Never give up. Do it for me."

Ryan didn't give up—ever. When he sensed that his failing health   53
this time signaled the final struggle, he faced the thought with his characteristic grace. He realized there was something he needed to say to his mother, and he said it. "I'm scared," he told her. Then he told her he wanted to talk about his funeral. He and Jeanne disagreed over what he should wear to be buried in. Jeanne suggested the tuxedo he had worn to the prom with Dee Laux. But Ryan was firm—he wanted to be comfortable, even in a coffin. He would wear jeans, a surf shirt, basketball shoes and the watch Michael Jackson had given him.

---

secluded (52): very private

He was relieved by his conversation about death. "I guess just 54
saying I was that scared helped. Plus, I always feel better if I make plans.
I started looking ahead again."

Another trip beckoned Ryan, this one to give an award to former 55
President Ronald Reagan at an AIDS benefit party in Los Angeles. In L.A.,
Ryan appeared on a television show with Los Angeles Raider Howie Long,
who had helped to put together the party. That night, Ryan met the
Reagans, stood on stage with Kareem Abdul-Jabbar and Long, and thanked
the volunteers for their help. Then, feverish and ill, he left the stage and
returned to his hotel, where he slept for an entire day. When he woke up, he
told his mother he wanted to see Dr. Kleiman, his doctor back in Indiana.

The family caught a night flight back to Indianapolis. Ryan was 56
admitted to Riley for the last time. His liver, spleen, and kidneys were all
failing. The effort to breathe was exhausting him. Dr. Kleiman told Ryan
and Jeanne that his best hope lay in putting Ryan into a drug-induced
coma and inserting a ventilator into his chest. With the machine breathing
for him, there was a possibility Ryan's worn-out body could summon
enough energy to allow his medications to do their work. Ryan, unable to
speak, scrawled a note. "Go for it." His mother held his hand and prayed.
Before he became unconscious, Ryan wrote one final word. It read
simply, "MOM?" At that moment, for all the maturity and courage that
made him seem so much older than his years, he became what he was: a
suffering young boy, needing his mother's reassurance. She smiled at him
and promised, "Everything's going to be all right, Ryan."

Ryan remained in a coma for a week. During that time, Riley 57
Hospital was swamped with calls, telegrams, visitors and flowers for
their eighteen-year-old patient. Elton John arrived and stayed with Jeanne
through the long bedside vigil°. The rock star filed phone messages,
tidied up, listened to Ryan's grandparents voice their grief, made phone
calls on the family's behalf, and installed bodyguards outside the
intensive care unit, to keep curiosity-seekers away.

Rocker John Cougar Mellencamp and the Rev. Jesse Jackson came 58
to visit. Michael Jackson telephoned, Elton holding the phone to Ryan's
ear in the hopes that Michael's voice might reach him. Jill, Heather, Dee,
Wendy, their parents, and other friends spent long days talking to the
unresponsive Ryan, playing him tapes of his favorite music, and speaking
of their love for him. Jeanne, remembering how concerned Ryan was
about "looking good" around his friends, moussed his hair into the buzz-
cut look he liked.

---

vigil (57): a period of wakeful watching

On Saturday evening, Elton left the hospital to make a brief   59
appearance at the Hoosierdome for the fourth annual Farm Aid benefit
concert. A thunderous ovation greeted him as he shakily announced,
"This one's for Ryan." He sat down at his piano to sing the bittersweet
"Candle in the Wind," a song he had written about the brief life of
Marilyn Monroe. The song finished, he rushed offstage and back to
Ryan's bedside. There he found Ryan's own fragile flame flickering for
the last time. His pupils were no longer responding to light, although his
heart, stubborn as ever, kept up its unsteady beat.

As the sun rose on April 8, 1990, Palm Sunday morning, Jeanne   60
asked her son to let go. "It's time, sweetheart," she murmured, stroking
his hand and face. "Goodbye, buddy; goodbye, my pumpkin." Finally the
green dial on Ryan's heart monitor clicked off.

Ryan's funeral was the largest ever held in Indiana. The famous   61
were there, of course. Elton led the congregation in a hymn and played a
song he had written for Ryan: "Skyline Pigeon," about a bird released
from captivity. First Lady Barbara Bush, Michael Jackson, Phil Donahue
and Marlo Thomas, Howie Long, Lukas Haas, were all there.

Ryan loved them all, and surely would have been pleased to see   62
them. But that wouldn't have been the greatest thrill to the boy who had
wanted above all else to be one of the crowd, to be accepted by his
community. Of the fifteen hundred people who packed the sanctuary and
hundreds more who stood outside in a drizzling rain, most were the
people whom Ryan had allied° himself with: ordinary folks, coping with
the hand life had dealt them as best they could. He had never believed
that he had dealt with his life in any extraordinary way. As his mother
said, remembering the funeral, "I bet he was looking down and laughing,
saying, 'I can't believe all you silly people are getting wet to see me.'"

Ryan White is gone, but the world is truly changed for his having   63
lived and died. AIDS-infected children are routinely enrolled in public
schools. Education programs about AIDS are a common feature in
schools around the country. The extent of the public's interest and
concern about AIDS was demonstrated after a heartrending cover story on
Ryan's death was published in *People* magazine. The story drew more
reader response than any other in the magazine's history. Many spoke of
the blessing Ryan's life had been to other AIDS sufferers. A woman who
had lost her husband to AIDS wrote that she would save the issue for her
two-and-one-half-year-old daughter, "so that when she is older and I tell
her about her father, I can also tell her about Ryan and his courageous

---

allied (62): associated

battle to have people with AIDS treated with kindness and respect."
Another letter-writer, himself diagnosed with AIDS, wrote, "[Ryan] has
given me something special. I can now face my eventual death from
AIDS and go out of this world with a proud heart and a courage that
wasn't there before."

"It seems to me you lived your life like a candle in the wind," Elton   64
sang of Ryan White during his last hours. The metaphor was a fitting one.
Physically, Ryan was never more than a spark of a boy, nothing much
besides skin and bones and close-cropped hair. To look at him, you'd
never think he had what it took to withstand the storms that buffeted° his
young life for so many years. And yet his flame glowed steadily, lighting
not only his own existence but that of hundreds of people who called
Ryan their friend, and thousands more whose lives were brightened by
the grace and courage of his example.

READING COMPREHENSION QUESTIONS

Vocabulary in Context

1. The word *contracted* in "Even before he contracted AIDS, Ryan
   struggled against painful odds" (paragraph 5) means
   a. described.
   b. got.
   c. avoided.
   d. recalled.

2. The word *vehemence* in "Ryan was shocked by the vehemence of
   people's feelings towards him. But he never lost his hope that, given
   enough time and education, people would cease being afraid of
   him" (paragraph 29) means
   a. warmth.
   b. strength.
   c. absence.
   d. hopefulness.

3. The word *unconventional* in "The rock star had always dared to be
   unconventional—wearing rhinestone-spangled jackets, wild
   sunglasses, dangling earrings, and crazy hats" (paragraph 34) means
   a. shy.
   b. greedy.

---

buffeted (64): struck repeatedly

c. rude.

d. unusual.

Central Point and Main Ideas

4. Which statement best expresses the central point of the selection?

a. Many people act out of fear when faced with AIDS victims.

b. Ryan White probably got the AIDS virus from an infected blood donor.

c. AIDS victims must continue to fight the fear and ignorance of the general public.

d. Ryan White dealt courageously with AIDS and people's ignorance of it, making life better for other victims.

5. Which statement best expresses the main idea of paragraph 13?

a. At first, Ryan was too weak to go back to school.

b. Children can be cruel to one another.

c. Because they feared AIDS, many residents of Kokomo treated Ryan and his family unkindly.

d. Many residents of Kokomo insulted Ryan White and his sister, Andrea.

6. The main idea of paragraph 24 is stated in its

a. first sentence.

b. second sentence.

c. third sentence.

d. last sentence.

Supporting Details

7. A person *cannot* get AIDS by

a. engaging in unprotected sex.

b. sharing an unsterilized needle with an infected person.

c. using the same bathroom as an infected person.

d. getting a transfusion of infected blood.

Transitions

8. The sentence below expresses a relationship of

a. time.

b. addition.

c. contrast.

d. cause and effect.

. . . a bump or bruise can lead to joints painfully swollen with internal bleeding. (Paragraph 5)

Inferences

9. From the way Ryan White was treated at the high school in Cicero, we can infer that
   a. many students there still did not understand how people get AIDS.
   b. Ryan had many relatives at that school.
   c. education can calm people's fears about AIDS.
   d. other AIDS victims had been students there before Ryan.

10. Elton John compared Ryan White to "a candle in the wind." We might conclude that the wind in this comparison symbolizes
    a. Ryan's doctors and nurses.
    b. Ryan's mother and sister.
    c. the illness that finally took Ryan's life.
    d. the love and acceptance Ryan experienced at Hamilton Heights High School.

OUTLINING

The following outline shows the general organization of the article "Candle in the Wind: The Ryan White Story." Complete the outline by filling in the letters of the descriptions of major details, which are listed in random order on the next page.

Central point: Ryan White's strength in fighting AIDS and public fears of AIDS inspired and helped many.

1. Introduction: A general overview of Ryan White

2. _____

3. _____

4. Ryan's desire go back to school in Kokomo and the local and nonlocal treatment of him

5. Ryan's decision to move to Cicero, his physical improvement and the local and nonlocal treatment of him

6. _____

7. Ryan's funeral

8. What Ryan gave to the world

9. Conclusion

Items Missing from the Outline

   a. Ryan's contraction of a rare form of pneumonia and the discovery that he had AIDS
   b. Ryan's final struggles and the support he received
   c. Ryan's hemophilia and how it led to his getting AIDS

DISCUSSION QUESTIONS

1. Although Ryan White was feared and opposed in Kokomo, he was welcomed at his school in Cicero. Why do you think the people in Kokomo were so fearful and unkind—even after they were told the facts about AIDS? Why did the people in Cicero act so differently to Ryan?

2. AIDS victims are often, but by no means always, homosexuals or drug abusers who have used infected needles. How might this fact have slowed understanding about the disease?

3. Do you know anyone with AIDS? If so, how is that person treated by others? How do that person's circumstances compare with those Ryan White faced?

4. The author quotes some of Ryan's classmates at Hamilton Heights High School in Cicero: "'At Ryan's other school, peer pressure caused people to be against him,' they said. 'Here, peer pressure helped.'" Think back to your high school days. How do you think peer pressure influenced you and others in your class? In what ways might it have made life difficult for some students?

8

"Murder" He Says
M. E. Kerr

Preview

The time is 1943, and the United States is at war against Germany and Japan. Young American men are being drafted, air-raids are taking place, and Americans are rationing supplies. But teenager Marijane Meaker (the girlhood name of author M. E. Kerr) and her friends are more interested in sex, romance, and love than in the war effort. Marijane, a tomboy and rebel, is growing up with her colorful parents in a small town in New York. In this excerpt, she and her boyfriend help her best friend, a girl named Ella Gwen, with a forbidden love.

A hot Friday night in August, and I am up in my room, waiting for   1
my date to arrive. I am listening to "Temptation" on a record that would
break into small pieces if I were to drop it.

My date is due at seven.   2

I'm fifteen. I'm going steady.   3

I'm wearing a black peasant skirt, a white peasant blouse, and   4
huaraches°. My stockings are painted on, from a bottle of suntan lotion,
and a fake white gardenia is pinned in my long blond hair, worn
pageboy style.

---

huaraches (4): flat sandals in which the uppers are made of
interwoven strips of leather

I'm always dressed a half hour early, but the rule in our house is that   5
you stay upstairs until your date arrives, and wait at least five minutes
after he's inside, before you show yourself. This is to give my father time
to scare him to death. This is also a way of not appearing eager.

"Always play hard to get," my father advises, "and if a boy starts to   6
tell you a joke you've heard before, pretend you haven't heard it. Laugh
hard after he tells it . . . unless it's dirty."

While I wait, I read from *The Fountainhead* by Ayn Rand. I'm not   7
reading the whole book, just "the good parts."

> *He had thrown her down on the bed and she felt the blood beating
> in her throat, in her eyes, the hatred, the helpless terror in her body.
> She felt the hatred and his hands; his hands moving over her body,
> the hands that broke granite.*

My best friend, Ella Gwen Logan, lent me the book, with "the good   8
parts" marked.

I had to smuggle it into the house and up to the bedroom.   9

I've already been warned by my mother that Ella Gwen is not a   10
good influence.

I hear the doorbell ring.   11

I hear my mother call out, "Come in, Donald!"   12

I put *The Fountainhead* back under my mattress and stand in front   13
of my bureau mirror, combing my hair and putting on Tabu°.

Donald is now entering our living room, where my father is looking   14
over his newspaper at him, grunting a hello.

My father is president of a mayonnaise factory, now dehydrating   15
onions for the government. The whole town stinks of onions, and this is a
great embarrassment to me.

My father served in the French army, way back in World War I, and   16
he affects° a French beret, which is more embarrassment. No one else's
father wears a beret.

No one else's father rides a bicycle back and forth to work in his   17
beret.

My father does many things I think are humiliating.   18

He is slightly deaf and wears a tiny black plug in his left ear. When   19
we are in church Sunday mornings, he makes a great production out of
removing the plug just as the minister is about to deliver his sermon. My
father pulls the plug out, reaches inside his suit jacket for the black box

---

Tabu (13): a perfume with a romantic image
affects (16): likes to wear

that goes with it, and wraps the cord around the box. At the end of the sermon, when the choir starts to sing, he takes the box out once more, unwinds the cord, and sticks the plug back into his ear.

This is the same man who sent me off to Sunday school, when I was little, with a question for my Sunday school teacher: What was the slipperiest day in Bethlehem? ("The day Joseph came through on his ass.")   20

Donald is now saying, "How are you tonight, sir?"   21

My father won't bother to answer that one.   22

He won't bother to put down his newspaper, either.   23

My father is showing Donald just what he thinks of Donald's notion that he is good enough to date my father's daughter.   24

My mother invites Donald to sit down, and Donald sits on the very edge of the davenport°.   25

My mother talks to him softly.   26

My parents are like the classic team of police detectives handling a guileful° suspect. One is rough and one is gentle. Donald is caught between them, alternately nodding in agreement with everything my mother says and stealing nervous glances across the room at my scowling° father.   27

Donald Dare is a local undertaker's son. He's sixteen. We've been going steady for a year, and we sign all our notes "Puddles of Purple Passion."   28

We have a song, too. "'Murder' He Says." ("He says 'Murder' he says, every time we kiss. . . .")   29

I wear a silver identification bracelet he gave me with "Murder" on the one side and "He Says" on the other.   30

The only time we kiss is when we say good night at my front door. It is a very fast kiss, mouths closed along with eyes, and he has never said "Murder" after. He has never tried to French kiss—some girls call it a soul kiss. When we talk about boys, we talk about this kind of kissing. We talk about boys trying to pet "below the neck," "below the waist." Our conversations take place in the girls' toilet at school, and in our bedrooms at pajama parties.   31

I always greatly exaggerate the difficulty I have controlling Donald.   32

But Donald and I go everywhere together, keeping our hands to ourselves when we're alone, holding hands in public. We need other eyes   33

---

davenport (25): sofa
guileful (27): deceitful, tricky
scowling (27): frowning

on us to be demonstrative°. We seek out the crowd and wrap our arms around each other.

I can't remember how our "romance" started.   34

Our friendship started with my curiosity about Dare's Funeral   35
Home.

That was when I was fourteen. I'd go down to the funeral parlor   36
with Donald after school, on warm spring days when he knew he didn't
have to ask me inside.

He'd never let any kids from school inside his house.   37

There were ramps all through the downstairs, to make it easier to   38
roll caskets from room to room. There were always overnight "guests,"
all dead. There was the sickly sweet smell of too many roses, gladioli,
daffodils, and lilies. There was the likelihood of running into strangers
who were crying.

We would sit outside in the yard, on the iron glider, and he would   39
complain to me.

"I'm not going to be an undertaker!"   40

"What's that building in the back?" I'd ask. I wanted to be a writer,   41
and I was curious about anything that was different.

Donald's house was definitely different.   42

"That's the shop," he'd answer me, and he'd get red.   43

"Is that where they work on the bodies?"   44

"That's where they take them."   45

"Did you ever go back there?"   46

"I've been back there, but I hate it back there, and he knows it."   47

His father, in conversation, was always "he" or "him." Donald   48
never said "my father."

We had a state prison in the center of our town, and Donald once   49
said, "I'd rather be a convict's son than an undertaker's son."

"Your father should have decided to have more children," I said. "If   50
you had brothers, one of them might have wanted to carry on the family
business."

"No brother of mine would want to be an undertaker, either."   51

"But at least you'd have a better chance if you had a brother. You   52
could flip a coin to see who'd be the undertaker."

"Well, I don't have a brother."   53

"If you had a sister, she'd probably have to do the cosmetic work on   54
all the corpses, just like your mother does."

"You know what he says? He says my wife will do that. He says   55

---

demonstrative (33): showing feelings openly

that's the way a family business works."

"Don't ask me to be your wife," I told him.   56

"I'd never ask anybody to be my wife if I planned to stay in this   57
town," Donald said, "but I don't plan to. I'm going to get out. I'll never
be an undertaker."

"I'm going to get out too," I said. "This town's too small for me."   58

"I really am going to get out," Donald said.   59

"I really am, too."   60

Finally either Donald got past his embarrassment over his house   61
around me, or I wore him down with my questions.

I got to go inside.   62

There were all sorts of rules in that house. All the window shades   63
had to be at the same level so it'd look good from the outside. Radios had
to be played very low. Donald's mother couldn't cook anything like
corned beef and cabbage that would make the house smell. All old "floral
tributes" had to be removed before they began wilting.

I saw my first dead people up close, their heads resting on oversized 64
satin pillows, hands folded one over the other as they lay stretched out in
their coffins. I saw Gorilla, the Dares' fat white angora cat, who sneaked
into the "slumber rooms" every chance he got, to sleep with the "guests."
I sat listening to Donald's plump, rouge-cheeked mother practice "Jesus
Is Tenderly Calling" on their pump organ in the parlor, next to the casket
selection room. I watched his tall, burly° father trudge° up from "the
shop" afternoons, for a cup of Lipton tea in their kitchen. He'd say he
was taking a break, and I'd imagine some corpse left with the blood
draining out of it, on a slab in the back building.

Donald and I got to like each other. We shared a rebel's hatred of a   65
small town where everyone knew everything you did; we shared a palms-
hitting-forehead astonishment over things parents expected you to do.

Sometimes he'd drive the hearse up to my house, and we'd sit in it   66
and listen to the radio.

My father'd say, "I don't want you sitting in the hearse with him!   67
Sit out in the open."

I wasn't allowed to go anywhere in a car with a boy, much less in a   68
hearse with one.

"Oh, Ellis," my mother'd say when she thought I was out of earshot   69
(I seldom was), "they don't *do* anything."

"It doesn't look good," he'd insist.   70

---

burly (64): big and muscular
trudge (64): walk tiredly

How Donald and I got from the glider in his yard, and the hearse in   71
our driveway, to dances in the school gym and "Puddles of Purple
Passion," I was never sure, but there he was on that August night in our
downstairs, being bullied by my father.

My father finally puts down his newspaper.   72
"Business is good tonight, Donald! Lots of obituaries in the paper.   73
Ha! Ha! Ha!"
My father always treated Donald the way he treated Skippy, our   74
family dog. He always spoke gruffly. ("Did you get your geometry
homework done, Skippy? You can't go out if you didn't!") He always
thought what he said to either of them was hilarious, but Donald and the
dog didn't think so. They just sat shivering in his presence.
Donald stands up as I enter the room. His mother has drilled   75
manners into him. ("If you're rude, people will remember it when their
loved ones pass and they'll call Dowd's instead of Dare's.")
Donald's very tall, like his father—my own father has to look up to   76
him—and he's skinny, since he claims everything that goes on in his
house makes him lose his appetite. Behind his back my father says he's
probably consumptive°, and calls him Famine.
Donald's wearing the pants to his glen plaid double-breasted suit, a   77
white shirt, and a gray V-neck sweater, with newly polished loafers.
He'd like to be wearing pegged° pants, as the other boys are, but the   78
only concession° to modern style that his father allows is a long gold
watch chain looped down the right side of his pants.
The boys stand around on downtown street corners twirling their   79
long watch chains. They're our town's version of zoot-suiters.
All the burden of what the only son of a funeral director feels is in   80
Donald's very light, sad blue eyes. He often looks close to tears. He never
smiles so you can see his perfect white teeth. Just a slight tip of his lips.
"Hi," he manages, and I manage "Hi" back, even though the notes   81
we pass in school always have umpteen *x*'s at the end. We are bolder on
paper than we are face to face. We both come from families who only
kiss on holidays when relatives arrive, or at airports and train stations.
Secretly, I once read a journal my father keeps, and hides behind   82
The Harvard Classics.
One entry read: *Our daughter is dating the local undertaker's son,*   83

---

consumptive (76): ill with a disease that wastes away the body
pegged (78): wide on top and narrow at the bottom
concession (78): giving in

Donald Dare: tall, dark, and harmless. Dares very little is my guess.

My father's eyes narrow. "Donald? I want her back at twelve 84
o'clock sharp!"

"Yes, sir. Twelve o'clock." 85

"Not five minutes after twelve, and not two minutes after twelve. 86
Twelve o'clock sharp."

My mother starts purring. "Are you going to Murray's after the 87
movie?"

"Yes." 88

Murray's is the hangout, where we go to drink Cokes, listen to the 89
jukebox, put salt in the sugar bowls, and tell the one about the traveling
salesman and the farmer's daughter.

I say nothing about our plan to connect with Ella Gwen Logan and 90
Hyman Ginzburg.

It is 1943. There is a world war raging. 91

My father puts ads in the local paper, apologizing for the onion 92
smell:

Ivanhoe Foods Has Gone to War!
Our onions are for field rations for our fighting men.
When you smell onions, pray for peace.

My mother saves fats and tin. 93

My older brother has just been commissioned° an ensign°, and 94
assigned to a carrier-based torpedo bomber squadron.

My father is an air-raid warden and patrols our neighborhood with a 95
flashlight, wearing a special white helmet, armband, and gas mask.

I am not allowed to speak to sailors, who pour into our small town 96
from Sampson Naval Base.

There is gas, shoe, meat, cheese, coffee, and butter rationing. 97

Boys who were ahead of me in high school are listed as dead or 98
missing in the local paper.

I will remember very little of this as I grow older. But I will never 99
forget Ella Gwen Logan and Hyman Ginzburg.

Ella Gwen's father was a dentist, in the days when going to the 100
dentist really hurt.

Dr. Logan never made it any easier. 101

---

commissioned (94): appointed
ensign (94): an officer in the United States Navy or Coast Guard

He was one of the meanest little men in town, the kind who 102
chuckled when you yelled, "Now *that* hurts!" and told you it didn't hurt
much.

He had a red face and darting brown eyes, no taller than five five, 103
with only one thing going for you if he was your dentist, and that was his
obsession with cleanliness.

He changed his little white coats after every patient, and kept a can 104
of 20 Mule Team Borax to scrub his hands with every five minutes at the
sink.

His radio was tuned to the local station, but you heard very little of 105
tunes like "Don't Get Around Much Anymore," "You'd Be So Nice to
Come Home to," and "As Time Goes By."

His sister, Ella Gwen's Aunt Mildred, was his nurse, and what you 106
heard mostly were their running conversations that went something like
this:

"I hear old man Finkelstein is selling his scrap metal to the Japs." 107
"I wouldn't put it past that kike!" 108
Or: 109
"What do you mean wops don't wash their salad bowls?" 110
"Wops don't. They just wipe them out with a dirty cloth after they 111
use them, which is why I don't order salad when I eat dago."

You'd go into his office and you'd hear about thirty minutes of their 112
harangues° on niggers, wops, kikes, polacks, hunkies, and spics. All the
while he hit every exposed nerve he could reach in your mouth with his
little silver pick.

Ella Gwen's mother was always "sick," usually upstairs in bed, in 113
their house on Apple Avenue. It wasn't until I was grown up that I
discovered she drank up there. Her sickness was the bottle, but none of us
kids knew that. She never lurched° around or acted loud or slurred her
words. When she did get herself downstairs in a robe, and Dr. Logan was
around delivering one of his tirades°, all she ever said was "Oh, Charlie."
She wouldn't say it in a condemning way. There'd be the little smile on
her mouth, as though he was some kind of cutup, doing and saying things
anyone would who had the nerve.

From these two Ella Gwen came, which ought to knock the socks 114
off the old saying "An apple never falls far from the tree."

---

harangues (112): long, emotional speeches
lurched (113): staggered
tirades (113): long emotional speeches

Ella Gwen was as unlike her family as a peacock is unlike sheep.   115
When we'd leave her house and all his frothing° bigotry, she'd walk
beside me, flame-faced, looking down, saying only, "I can't help it," in a
whisper.

She was a tiny, pretty, blue-eyed blonde. The boys were always   116
whistling at her and following her from school. But she wasn't allowed to
date until she was eighteen.

She had two years to go. Her nineteen-year-old brother was a   117
lieutenant in the Army, somewhere in England.

Ella Gwen's sex lecture from her mother had consisted of one   118
sentence: "Your brother can come home after doing it, take a shower, and
be a new man, but you would be ruined for life."

Ella Gwen put herself between all the school bullies and the ones   119
being bullied.

When we were in sixth grade, she stuck up for a minister's son   120
named Nelson Tutton. He was the only boy in our grade who didn't have
long pants. He was fat and frightened, and he wet his pants when he was
cornered by classmates. Reverend Tutton declared he'd stay in knickers°
until he stopped wetting. As long as he stayed in knickers, he got picked
on, he got scared, he peed.

His mother brought him to school every morning and waited for   121
him every afternoon, in the Tuttons' black Packard.

Coming and going, just inside the front door of school, he was   122
ambushed.

Ella Gwen charged to the rescue, pulling boys' hair, kicking their   123
shins, causing enough commotion to summon the teachers from their
classrooms and give Nelson time to escape.

Then there was Carrie Speck, freshman year, with bulbous acne, the   124
victim of the girls.

"If you squeeze Carrie," one of them became famous for saying,   125
"pus will come out."

Carrie was invited by Ella Gwen to come along to Murray's with us.   126
Ella Gwen passed her the only notes she got in classes, and sat with her
in school assemblies, and got her to join us in the bleachers at games.

Ella Gwen was a rescuer of losers and a bringer home of stray cats   127
and dogs, so sentimental she cried when Eddie Cantor sang his closing
song nights on the radio: "I love to spend each Wednesday with you. . . ."

She also spent as much time as I did in the town library, after   128

---

frothing (115): mean, petty
knickers (120): knee-length pants

school. The librarians, already in their coats, would have to dig us out of the stacks at closing time.

Ella Gwen could always find "the good parts" in novels, and she   129
loved what she called "real love poetry." Not Elizabeth Barrett Browning, with her timid

> *How do I love thee? Let me count the ways,*

but Oscar Wilde with

> *For all night long he murmured honeyed words,*
> *And saw her sweet unravished limbs, and kissed*
> *Her pale and argent body undisturbed,*
> *And paddled with the polished throat and pressed*
> *His hot and beating heart upon her chill and icy breasts.*

Hyman Ginzburg was the third after-school library addict in our   130
town.

He was almost eighteen. A tall, thin-haired Jewish refugee from   131
Nazi Germany, he wore little gold-trimmed eyeglasses, talked with an accent, collected stamps, and played both violin and piano. He spoke three languages and used "big words" in English.

He was as strange in our small upstate New York town as anyone   132
would be who'd landed from Mars on a spaceship. We didn't have that many Jews in town. People like my father weren't even sure "Jew" was what you could politely call one, and insisted on describing one as "a person of the Jewish persuasion."

No one in our town had ever had the name Hyman. The word itself   133
was never spoken, unless you were talking privately about the wedding night.*

Hyman Ginzburg made everything all the worse for himself by   134
refusing all invitations to go out for basketball. He was six foot four.

He said he didn't care for sports.   135

When they weren't calling him "a queer," they were calling him   136
"Hyman the Hopeless"; "Hopeless" for short.

They felt he really was.   137

It happened on an ordinary winter afternoon in the library.   138

---

*This comment refers to the hymen, a membrane at the opening of the vagina that is generally stretched or torn upon a female's first intercourse.

I had just "discovered" Thomas Wolfe. I had found a book by him   139
in the stacks, and opened it to

For you are what you are, you know what you know, and there are
no words for loneliness, black, bitter, aching loneliness, that gnaws
the roots of silence in the night.

Around the same time I would sit by our phonograph at home,   140
singing along with Frank Sinatra's record of "All or Nothing at All,"
playing it over and over.

My father would ask me, "What do you mean, half a love doesn't   141
appeal to you?"

You don't have to answer that kind of a question from a father . . .   142
but I don't know how I would have answered it even to myself. I, who
was going steady with Donald Dare—one fast kiss at the door and *pffft*,
with " 'Murder' He Says" for a love song?

I don't know what I thought I knew about black, bitter, aching   143
loneliness gnawing, either . . . but I was hugging Wolfe to me, rushing
through the stacks of the library, to find Ella Gwen and show the passage
to her.

In between the volumes of Louisa May Alcott and James Joyce,   144
they were standing. It was late afternoon, and the sun was coming
through an upper window, fixing them in a dagger of light.

The first thing I thought was that Hyman looked like a ninny°. He   145
had bad posture anyway, and he was stooped over, with his long neck
hanging out like a chicken's, the gold-rimmed glasses slipping down his
long, crooked nose. He had this deeply dizzy smile on his face. He
looked like he'd gone quietly mad.

Ella Gwen wasn't faring° well, either. She was gazing up at him   146
with a stunned expression, as though someone had just thrown a rock at
the back of her head. Her mouth hung open. She had wide, frightened,
Bambi eyes.

The two of them looked like a cartoon, until Hyman suddenly   147
leaned forward and put his mouth gently against hers.

I had never seen that anywhere but in the movies, while I was   148
eating Butterfingers and Tootsie Rolls, giggling and elbowing the girls on
both sides of me.

It was a long, long kiss, but in a few short seconds they had   149
outdistanced me.

---

ninny (145): fool
faring (146): getting along

I was left far behind, to date a boy with dead people in his   150
downstairs, who didn't even French kiss.

It was not just what I saw, either, there in the row of books from A   151
to J. It was what I felt, an electricity they had and I had never had. They
were wired for sound, and I was not even plugged in.

I plodded through the stacks toward the front of the library, trying to   152
remember all the other times the three of us were there. How had they
gotten from then to where they were without my knowing it?

"Oh, you're checking out my old pal Thomas Wolfe!" the librarian   153
exclaimed. "I remember how I felt when I first read him. I still love *You
Can't Go Home Again!*"

That was the last thing I wanted to hear.   154

She was an old maid who lived by herself in one room, at a place   155
called The Women's Union. She went to all the band concerts in Hoopes
Park on Saturday nights in summer, with another old maid who taught
second grade. Some evenings she ate alone in the window of Weddigen's
Restaurant on Genesee Street.

"Enjoy it, Marijane!"   156

I wished she wouldn't sing my name out like we knew each other   157
that well, or had anything in common.

In high school we watched the ones in love more than we watched   158
the ones who scored touchdowns, made baskets, had the leads in school
plays, sang at assemblies, or called out all the funny lines that disrupted
classes and got sent to the principal's office.

The ones in love were always on. You didn't have to wait until a   159
special day to see them, or go anyplace to find them, or do anything or
pay anything for the privilege of watching them.

They were always there.   160

They were different from us.   161

We were Jane and Robert and Tom and Marilyn and Eddie, but they   162
were JohnandJan, LarryandGloria, BillandDeenie.

They were even different from those of us who went steady like   163
they did. We had the name without the game. We were sheep going
through the motions of the herd. They were in the grip of something that
sent them on long walks by themselves down behind the stadium during
lunch hours, and kept them lingering by lockers long after the bell for
class rang.

We were ascending, even our voices were still childishly high as we   164
called out to each other. They were falling in love, descending, and their
tones were low and sensual. No dances in the gym were really underway
until they got there. No dancers danced quite the same way they did

together.

News of anything Hitler, Roosevelt, or Churchill did took second   165
place to news of any of their breakups. They were The Ones.

Of all the lovers in our small town, in 1943, HymanandEllaGwen   166
were The Golden Ones.

A Jewish leper would have been more welcome in Hyman's house   167
than Ella Gwen was. She was a *shiksa*—from the Hebrew *sheques*,
meaning "blemish." The Ginzburgs were Orthodox Jews. Ella Gwen was
pork, bacon, ham, oysters, and shrimp. She was a *goy*, as in the sentence
Dos ken nor a goy: "*That*, only a *goy* is capable of doing!"

Dr. Logan had only to hear that Ella Gwen "admired" someone in   168
her class with the name Hyman Ginzburg. The mere mention of that
name was enough to transform him into a raving madman, threatening to
pack her off to boarding school or send her to St. Louis to live with her
grandparents.

Hopeless Hyman, "the queer," became a new, dark, romantic hero,   169
and basketball was, after all, a "boy's" game.

JohnandJan, LarryandGloria, and BillandDeenie paled before   170
HymanandEllaGwen.

When we watched HymanandEllaGwen, we watched a love affair   171
that Shakespeare, MGM, or Cole Porter couldn't have made more
passionate and doomed.

They were our own Tristan and Iseult, Romeo and Juliet, Heloise   172
and Abelard.

We watched them as you'd watch someone young and dying, or   173
something splendid on its way to ruin.

Dear M. J.,   174

Can Hy call you when he wants to get in touch with me? You   175
must, never, never, never let anyone in your family know you're our
go-between if you agree. I know it's a lot to ask, but you're the only
one I can trust. We are so in love it hurts! Have you read This Is My
Beloved? *Hy gave me a copy. Our song is "You'll Never Know." He*
is such a doll! It is worth all the sneaking around we have to do. It
is worth everything in this world! Please let me know if we can
count on you! We were at Hunter's Point yesterday afternoon. It is
our place. Oh Gawd, it was beautiful! Love ya, EGL.

Dear Ella Gwen,   176

Hy can always call me. You can count on me. Natch! Where do   177
I get This Is My Beloved? *It's not in the library. Have you gone all*
the way? Don't answer that if you don't want to. Love ya. MJ

Dear M. J.,   178

Here is my copy of This Is My Beloved. *You'll see why it's not*   179
in the library. Read the underlined parts first.

I told Hy if it would help I would even become Jewish. I   180
honestly mean that! He told his father I said it, and his father said
saying a broche *over a chicken won't make it a fish. He said a*
female gentile can't become a Jew since she has the children and
she must be born a Jew. (A broche *is Jewish for blessing) So we are*
really up a creek without a paddle, since the Ginzburgs are as bad
as my own family when it comes to Hy and me. We are getting
desperate since he is eighteen now and will be drafted soon. He'll
call you tonight to say when and where I should meet him. I'm
saying I'm going to the Red Cross to roll bandages with you. We
will never never forget what you are doing for us. Love ya. EGL

P.S. I almost faint after we kiss for a long time and Hy says he   181
feels like a firecracker that has to go off. Never, never repeat any of
this!

Dear Ella Gwen,   182

Thanks for the book. I'll read it late tonight. Don't say you're   183
rolling bandages with me. Say you're going to see For Whom the
Bell Tolls, *which is where Donald and I are going. You know the*
plot already from the book by Ernest Hemingway, so you're safe if
your folks grill you. Love ya. MJ

P.S. Have you gone all the way?   184

Dear M. J.,   185

I got my first 70 ever (in English) in all my life! My father is   186
furious! He says he wonders what my mind's on when I'm doing my
homework. (If he knew he'd croak!) I can't go out week nights
anymore. Hy and I are skipping school Tuesday and going
someplace in his father's car. Neither of us cares what happens
anymore, except he'll have to go to war and then what'll we do? I
have never, never, never felt this way about anyone or thought
anyone could about anyone. Love ya. EGL

P.S. Almost.   187

One afternoon when I arrived home from school, I knew I was in   188
big trouble.

My mother was waiting for me in the hall.   189

She was carrying something in her hand, behind her back. One of   190
the afternoon soap operas was playing in the living room, through the
Stromberg-Carlson. She had walked away from it for this encounter.

There was a brand-new V-letter° from my brother in the silver tray on the hall table, but she wasn't pointing it out to me.

"What is this?" She whipped out the copy of *This Is My Beloved* 191 and held it up to my face, the same way she'd thrust a turd in a paper towel at Skippy's nose when we were housebreaking him.

"It's a book," I said.   192

"I know it's a book!"   193

"It's poetry."   194

"It's filth!"   195

"I wouldn't call it filth."   196

"What would you call it?" She was opening it with shaking hands, 197 until she came to

We need so little room, we two . . .
thus on a single pillow, as we move
nearer, nearer Heaven . . .

"Nearer, nearer Heaven" was gasped out, but her voice gained a 198 certain outraged momentum° as she spat out the last nine words:

until I burst inside you like a screaming rocket!

I couldn't think of anything to say. She was fighting to get her 199 breath back.

"Just *one* of the underlined parts," said my mother. "One of the *few* 200 underlined parts I can even read aloud!"

"I didn't underline them."   201

"Ella Gwen Logan underlined them!"   202

"Okay," I said.   203

"Oh, no, it is *not* okay," she said. "I don't want this kind of trash in 204 this house! I don't want you reading this kind of trash!"

"All it's about is people in love," I said.   205

"Is that what Ella Gwen Logan says it's about?"   206

"She doesn't have to. I can read."   207

"I don't want you to see Ella Gwen Logan anymore."   208

"Then I'll have to wear a blindfold to school."   209

"This is *not* a joke!"   210

From the living room, a woman's voice was delivering the Bell 211 Telephone commercial:

V-letter (190): a letter delivered by V(ictory)-mail, a special armed
              forces mailing system used during World War II
momentum (198): force

Give him a break. Evening is about his only chance to telephone home. He can get through easier if the wires aren't crowded—and his call means so much to him and the home folks . . . So please, don't call long distance between—

My mother was concluding a minilecture on Ella Gwen's history of   212
calling my attention to obscene literature with " . . . and you are not to take any more calls from Hyman Ginzburg! Tell him not to call here again! I know what's going on!"

"You've been going through my desk again!"   213

"Everyone in this town knows what's going on. The Logans are the   214
last to know what's going on right under their noses!"

"A person's desk is supposed to be private property."   215

"A person's desk is not supposed to be filled with secret plans that   216
help Ella Gwen Logan go off to Hunter's Point, to neck and pet, et cetera, with an older boy her parents don't approve of!"

"They don't et cetera, and you know *why* the Logans hate Hy! The   217
Logans are prejudiced!"

"That's the Logans' business. I don't have anything against Hyman   218
Ginzburg per se°, but I do have plenty against what the two of them are up to!"

"Why isn't that the two of them's business?"   219

"Because they're making it your business, that's why. Because   220
they're making you a party to what they're doing in the woods and in cars, and you tell her you're forbidden to have anything more to do with her!"

"She's my best friend."   221

"She *was* your best friend."   222

"She still is, whether I have anything to do with her or not."   223

"Then enjoy your memories of Ella Gwen Logan, because she is not   224
to come here, or to call here, and you are not to go there, or call there, and Hyman Ginzburg is not to call here. She's a bad influence on you!"

"All she did wrong was fall in love," I complained.   225

"All she did wrong," said my mother, slapping the thin book down   226
hard on the hall table, "is let her feelings for that boy get way out of hand!" She marched herself back into the living room. "*Way* out of hand!" she called over her shoulder.

Back to that hot August night of my date with Donald Dare.   227

---

per se (218): for himself

As we go down my front walk, I whisper to him, "Did you get it?"   228

"It's parked down on Marvin Avenue."   229

"The hearse or the flower car?"   230

"The flower car."   231

"You didn't park it in front of the McIntees', did you? If Mrs.   232
McIntee sees me getting into the flower car with you, she'll call my
mother just as sure as the sun'll come up tomorrow!"

"I parked it way down past old man Palmer's house."   233

We're holding hands as we walk along. Across the street, Mr. and   234
Mrs. Hunter are sitting side by side in wicker rockers on their front
porch, smiling at us, waving. Behind them, in their window, there's a
gold star hanging. Their son, Hooton, went down with the USS
Oklahoma when the Japs torpedoed it at Pearl Harbor. . . . Next to their
house, in the De Marcos' window, are three blue stars for Nick, Sam, and
Tony De Marco, all Marines now.

We are considered the street lovers. Neighbors out hosing their   235
Victory gardens or reading the evening paper on their porches brighten at
the sight of us, enjoying the idea Donald and I are off to a movie and
Murray's—young lovers still young enough not to be touched by the war.

The Dares' flower car looks like a long limousine with the back cut   236
out, leaving an open space. It is the show-flower car, the one that follows
the hearse to the cemetery, with eighty percent of all the floral tributes.
There is a smaller flower car, a station wagon, rushed to the cemetery
ahead of the hearse, with the other twenty percent, so the grave has some
decorations around it when the mourners arrive.

The show-flower car has a C sticker on its windshield, meaning it   237
qualifies for extra gas since it's needed for an essential business activity.

The only thing in the open space tonight is Hyman Ginzburg's   238
duffel bag.

Hyman is waiting in the front seat of the flower car. Perspiration   239
runs down his face, making it hard for him to keep his glasses on his
nose, and he's giving his wristwatch nervous glances.

The three of us are squeezed into the front seat.   240

"Walking out the front door was hard," Hyman says. "My father   241
said, 'Well, it's Shabbos°, but it's your last night, too, and it's still
Shabbos tomorrow when we put you on your train. So say goodbye to
your friends.'"

Hyman has orders to report to Fort Knox, Kentucky.   242

As we ride downtown, Spike Jones's band comes over the radio: 243

Shabbos (241): the Yiddish word for Sabbath

> *Ven der Fuehrer° says*
> *"Ve iss der Master race°,"*
> *Ve heil° (phhht!)*
> *Heil (phffft!)*
> *Right in der Fuehrer's face!*

"Over here they think Adolf Hitler's funny," Hy says.   244

"It's that mustache," Donald says.   245

Ella Gwen is waiting for us behind the Women's Union, where she   246
has told her family she was going to roll bandages for the Red Cross.
She's wearing a yellow jumper the color of her hair, a white blouse, and
brown-and-white spectator pumps.

She has managed to carry a shoulder bag and a knitting bag out of   247
her house, crammed with extra underwear, a dress, a nightie, a cardigan,
and blue jeans.

She tells us about it after she climbs in front, where she has to sit on   248
Hyman's lap.

We are in for an hour-and-a-half ride to Syracuse, New York.   249

As we drive out of town, we're all perspiring in the hot night and   250
singing along with the radio:

> *Don't sit under the apple tree*
> *With anyone else but me. . . .*

It is still light out, and we go over the big hills, past the lush   251
farmlands, and into the little town of Skaneateles, known for having the
coldest of all the Finger Lakes. It is the first thing we see, a slim streak of
bright-blue water, with a long green lawn in front of it. A band concert is
in full swing there, while out on the lake boats are letting down their sails
at buoys°. There are soldiers and sailors strolling near the bandstand with
girls, and old people wiping their necks with handkerchiefs, sitting on
benches, listening to "The Battle Hymn of the Republic."

Summers past, our families would bring us to this town to eat at   252
The Krebs, a famous restaurant, and to attend The Skaneateles Summer

---

Fuehrer (243): a word from German that means "leader" and refers
here to Hitler

Master race (243): people that considered themselves superior and
thus suited to rule over others (a concept behind
some of Hitler's activities)

heil (243): to salute someone with the enthusiastic German greeting
heil, which is how Hitler was often saluted

buoys: (251): floaters that mark danger points or channels

Theater, where "real" actors and actresses performed in plays like *Our Town.*

  We go on our way, along familiar roads, through hill-circled hamlets°, past Holsteins° heading in toward red barns, pointing out the sunset sinking in the treetops behind us. We see the first star of the evening in the slate-blue sky, and we make lots of nervous little jokes about what's going to happen when "they" finally find the notes left for them.   253

  "My father is going to have a conniption fit°!" Ella Gwen says.   254

  "Mine's going to say Kaddish°!"—Hy.   255

  When we get to the Syracuse station, we lose some of the high sense of adventure. We push our way through the thronged° terminal beneath big signs begging everyone to travel light. We trip over suitcases, bags, boxes, packages, and rope-tied bundles, while Hy rushes ahead for the tickets. We stand under a huge sign warning: **A SLIP OF THE LIP WILL SINK A SHIP!***   256

  Ella Gwen keeps thanking Donald and me and watching for Hy. Young men in white and khaki uniforms not much older than we are, are locked in embraces with their girls, their mothers, sisters, and grandmothers. A loudspeaker blares, announcing train arrivals and departures.   257

  Suddenly Hy is running toward us crying, "Track nine. That's us! Hurry, honey!"   258

  Ella Gwen reaches up to hug me, tears starting in her blue eyes. I hate myself for hearing the echo of my mother's voice, just for a second, "*Way* out of hand!"   259

  Kisses and promises to write, then Ella Gwen runs with Hy, almost losing one of her spectator pumps, which falls off her bare foot. She gets it back on; Hy's arm slips around her waist, they look back at us, laughing.   260

  One more time before they disappear up the tunnel leading to the trains, they stop a second to wave good-bye. We can't see Ella Gwen   261

---

  hamlets (253): small villages
  Holsteins: (253): dairy cows of a certain breed
  conniption fit (254): a fit of great anger
  Kaddish: (255): Jewish prayer said after the death of a relative
  thronged (256): crowded

  *This warning was meant to remind Americans not to reveal any troop movements or other information they may have learned from relatives in the Army.

through the onrushing crowd, only Hy, because he's so tall. He's wrinkled up his nose, mouthing the word "good-bye," looking like someone grimacing from a stab wound.

Then they are gone.   262

On the way back, Donald and I don't talk a lot. I ride way over on 263
the seat next to him. I can smell the Vitalis he puts on his hair.

We pass Burma Shave signs along the roadside, glimpsing their 264
messages in the headlights.

There are usually six in a row, saying things like: 265

> **Hardly a driver**
> **Is now alive**
> **Who passes**
> **On hills**
> **At 75**
> **Burma Shave**

For the first time, I realize the war has changed them, too. Donald 266
reads them aloud as we go by.

> **Let's make Hitler**
> **And Hirohito**
> **Look as sick**
> **As Benito**
> **Buy Defense Bonds**
> **Burma Shave**

We sit very close, for us, listening to music, songs about missing the 267
one you love, waiting for the one you love, coming home to the one you love. In my mind's eye I see Hy towering over my little best friend, his long arm reaching down around her waist, and the glint of his eyeglasses as they looked back laughing, her small hand blowing a kiss, the heavy knitting bag with her things in it on her arm.

At one point I say, "Their song was 'You'll Never Know.'" They 268
are already in the past tense.

Donald says, "Well, they made it. They got out."   269

When we finally get to Marvin Avenue, where we'll leave the 270
flower car, Donald says, "Okay, we saw *The More the Merrier* tonight. With Jean Arthur and Joel McCrea. My mother saw it last night, and I know all you need to know if you're cross-examined. . . . It's about a Washington government girl who—"

While he runs through the plot for me, I watch his face in profile. I 271 toy with the idea of terrifying him into speechlessness by saying right out, "I love you, Donald Dare, and this has been the best evening of my entire life!"

"Did you get all that?" he asks me.   272

"I got it. I'll walk in the house and say, 'Am I glad I'm not one of those poor girls who has to work for the government in Washington!'"   273

Donald imitates my mother's voice. "Why do you say that, dear?"   274

"She never calls me dear."   275

"Why do you say that, Marijane?"   276

"Well, poor Jean Arthur rented her half to this daffy old man—"   277

"Her half of what?"   278

"Her half of her four-room apartment in Washington, D.C. You know, Mother, apartments are impossible to get in big cities like Washington."   279

"Which is why you should thank your lucky stars you're living here with Daddy and me, darling."   280

I give his arm a punch. "She'd *never* call me darling!"   281

We're starting to laugh hysterically when Donald says, "It's seven to twelve. We're just going to make it!" He opens the door to the flower car.   282

We race through the vacant lot up from Marvin Avenue toward my house.   283

At the door we're out of breath.   284

We always had this corny little routine before the good-night kiss. It went: 285

I'll give you a ring—Donald.   286

What kind?—me.   287

Diamond.   288

Tonight he just says, "I'll call you tomorrow."   289

He kisses me. There is just the slightest flicker of his tongue against my lips, too slight to be *le baiser Francais*°, but we are certainly moving nearer, nearer Heaven, though at a snail's pace.   290

As Donald runs down our front walk, he stops halfway and jumps in the air, clicking his heels together.   291

"What's he running for?" my father says as I come through the front door.   292

The mantel clock is bonging twelve times.   293

"What were you spying at us through the venetian blinds for?"   294

"What's Famine's big hurry? Did someone die?" my father says.   295

---

le baiser Francais (290): French for "the French kiss"

"Was the movie good?" my mothers asks. 296

"Am I glad I'm not one of those poor girls who has to work for the 297 government in Washington, D.C.," I begin, walking into our living room.

Behind me, my father says, "The government's glad you're not, 298 too."

Note: This selection is taken from the book *ME ME ME ME ME—Not a Novel* by M. E. Kerr. For information on how to obtain the book, turn to page 564.

READING COMPREHENSION QUESTIONS

Vocabulary in Context

1. The words *obsession with* in "He had . . . only one thing going for you if he was your dentist, and that was his obsession with cleanliness. He changed his little white coats after every patient, and kept a can of 20 Mule Team Borax to scrub his hands with every five minutes" (paragraphs 103–104) mean
   a. avoidance of.
   b. abnormal interest in.
   c. great ignorance of.
   d. playing with.

Central Point and Main Ideas

2. Which sentence best expresses a central point of the selection?
   a. Wartime marriages are a big mistake.
   b. Fascinated with romance, Marijane and Donald help two lovers escape parental intolerance.
   c. Marijane and Donald were more passionate with each other when people were looking than when they were alone.
   d. Bigotry was a big problem facing Americans during the 1940s.

3. The main idea of paragraph 63 is expressed in its
   a. first sentence.
   b. second sentence.
   c. third sentence.
   d. last sentence.

4. Which sentence best expresses the main idea of paragraph 113?
   a. Marijane knew Ella Gwen's parents quite well.
   b. Ella Gwen's friends did not know that Mrs. Logan was an alcoholic.

    c. Ella Gwen's mother was a secret alcoholic who encouraged Mr. Logan's bigotry.

    d. Dr. Logan frequently gave long, bigoted speeches.

5. Which sentence best expresses the main idea of paragraphs 147–151?

    a. Marijane saw Ella Gwen and Hyman kissing passionately in the library.

    b. Marijane's boyfriend, Donald, did not French kiss.

    c. Ella Gwen and Hyman's passionate kiss made the author realize that her relationship with Donald was low on passion.

    d. The only other place Marijane had seen a sudden kiss like Hyman's was in the movies.

Supporting Details

6. Marijane's father thought that Donald was

    a. big trouble for his daughter.

    b. overweight.

    c. a real lover.

    d. harmless.

7. Mrs. Meaker forbade Marijane to see Ella Gwen because

    a. Ella Gwen was dating a Jew.

    b. Ella Gwen caused Marijane to miss curfew when they went on double dates.

    c. Mrs. Meaker thought Ella Gwen was a bad influence on what Marijane read.

    d. Mrs. Meaker knew that Ella Gwen's father was a bigot.

Transitions

8. Which of the following transitions would best fit the blank inserted between the sentences below?

    a. *In addition*

    b. *In contrast*

    c. *For example*

    d. *Therefore*

    Ella Gwen put herself between all the school bullies and the ones being bullied. _____, when we were in the sixth grade, she stuck up for a minister's son named Nelson Tutton. (Paragraphs 119–120)

Inferences

9. We can infer that Marijane considered Ella Gwen and Hyman's running away as
   a. a foolish mistake.
   b. something done only out of spite for their parents' attitudes.
   c. a romantic adventure.
   d. a good way to travel and see part of the country.

10. We can conclude that the main reason the author includes offensive words in paragraphs 107–112 is that
    a. she wants to show how bigoted Dr. Logan was.
    b. she herself is bigoted.
    c. she wants to show that in 1943 everyone was bigoted.
    d. she didn't realize that many people find these words offensive.

SUMMARIZING

Circle the letter—*a, b,* or *c*—of the passage that best completes the following summary of " 'Murder' He Says."

A teenager at the time of World War II, Marijane Meaker is going steady with the son of a local undertaker. Their romance has not been very passionate, but an evening they spend with Marijane's best friend and her boyfriend adds some fire to their relationship.

Marijane's best friend is Ella Gwen, a loving person who stands up for people who are bullied or teased. She and Marijane are often at the library. Also often there is an unpopular Jewish refugee from Germany named Hyman. One day at the library, Marijane sees Hyman and Ella Gwen French kissing. Marijane realizes then just how lacking in passion her relationship with Donald is. That kiss is the beginning of a passionate romance that is opposed by both of their parents. Hyman's parents, Orthodox Jews, are against a non-Jewish wife for their son. Ella Gwen's parents are prejudiced against Jews, among others. Marijane assists the lovers by passing messages between them.

a. One day, Mrs. Meaker forbids Marijane to associate with Ella Gwen. She is angry about the "filth" and "trash" in books that Marijane gets from Ella Gwen. Mrs. Meaker has found such a book under Marijane's mattress. She also forbids Marijane to take any more phone calls from Hyman. She tells Marijane that she knows that Ella Gwen and Hyman are conducting a romance against Ella Gwen's parents' wishes. Mrs. Meaker explains that she is not against dating a Jew. However, she is against Marijane getting involved in a deceitful and overly sexual relationship. She tells Marijane that Ella Gwen has allowed her feelings for Hyman to "get way out of hand." Despite Mrs. Meaker's feelings, Marijane considers Ella Gwen to be her best friend. So she agrees to help Ella Gwen run away with Hyman. One night, she and Donald do just that.

b. Marijane doesn't even remember how her own romance began. But she does remember that she and Donald became friends because of her curiosity about his father's funeral home. In fact, she finally got Donald to take her inside. There she saw dead people for the first time. She also saw that the family's white cat slept with the corpses every chance he got. Eventually somehow, her and Donald's relationship grew into a romance. Although they are going steady, Marijane realizes that their relationship differs from those of more passionate couples in school. Those couples are distinguished from other students because they seem to be truly in love. They are the couples that go on long walks alone and linger by their lockers long after the bell for class rings. That group includes Ella Gwen and Hyman, who decide to run away together the day before Hyman has to report to the Army.

c. Marijane and Donald agree to help Ella Gwen and Hyman run off together one night just before Hyman has to enter the Army. Mrs. Meaker has forbidden Marijane to associate with Ella Gwen. She is angry about the "filth" in books that Marijane gets from Ella Gwen. She is also angry about Ella Gwen's forbidden romance and Marijane's part in it. So Marijane tells her parents that she and Donald are going to the movies that night. Instead, Donald and Marijane drive Ella Gwen and Hyman the long distance to the Syracuse station. Ella Gwen and Hyman leave together by train. The romance and drama of the evening excites Marijane and Donald. On the ride home, Marijane toys with declaring her love for both Donald and their wonderful evening together. And at her door that night, Donald gives her a goodnight kiss that is ever so slightly closer to a French kiss than any he has given her before.

DISCUSSION QUESTIONS

1. The author prepares readers for Ella Gwen and Hyman's romance by telling us some key details about Ella Gwen. What details in the story help us understand why she was the type of person who might fall for and run away with someone like Hyman?

2. In what ways was Marijane embarrassed by her parents? Why do you think young people are so often embarrassed by their parents? Can you remember anything about your parents that embarrassed you? Would it still embarrass you today?

3. Did Marijane and Donald do the right thing in helping Ella Gwen and Hyman go against their parents' wishes? Would you do the same for your friends? Explain your answers.

4. Marijane and Ella Gwen spent a good deal of their time as teenagers underlining "the good parts" from romance novels and love poetry. Do you think their curiosity about sex would have been different had they grown up today, when television shows and movies are filled with sexual language and vivid sex scenes? Do you think they were better off not having had this exposure?

9

Dangerous Parties
Paul Keegan

Preview

On some college campuses, alcohol and sex are almost as common as textbooks. The result can be what is now known as "date rape" or "acquaintance rape." Not long ago, for instance, a group of drunk male students took advantage of a drunk female student at the University of New Hampshire. Paul Keegan, who went to that school, returned to explore the event and what followed. In this article, he tells what he learned.

I love the University of New Hampshire, its green lawns, its   1
beautiful turn-of-the-century structures, the little paths that snake through the woods to classroom buildings hidden in the trees. I went to college here from 1976 to 1980. It's Everyman's school, ten thousand kids on two hundred acres, cheap and easy to get into for New Hampshire students, expensive and more prestigious for the 39 percent from out of state. Almost everyone can find their niche° here, as I eventually did.

But it's the darker side of college life that took me back recently,   2
the side that can emerge at a place like UNH after a night of partying at a

---

niche (1): place that a person fits into

bar like the Wildcat. The Wildcat is a pizza-and-beer joint in Durham, a small town that for nine months of the year is overrun by students. Steve Karavasilis, the owner, will pour you a draft beer for a dollar or a pitcher for $3.75. The Wildcat's signature is a wall of windowpanes that creates a huge, moving mosaic° of Main Street. That's where guys sit down with a pitcher to watch girls.

Steve has hung a sign clearly stating that you can't be served unless   3
you are at least twenty-one. But somehow, last February 19, on a cold and clear Thursday night, two twenty-year-old sophomores named Chris and Jon, and a nineteen-year-old sophomore named Gordon, sat here and shared several pitchers of beer with a group of friends. The three were buddies who lived on the fourth floor of UNH's Stoke Hall. They were happy-go-lucky guys with a boyish charm and a bag of fraternity pranks. Jon and Gordon had recently become brothers at Sigma Alpha Epsilon. Jon, from Manchester, New Hampshire, was the character of the bunch, a slick° talker who always wore his SAE hat, even when he walked to the shower carrying his soap and shaving cream in a six-pack carton. Gordon was tall and good-looking, a little moody, some thought. He was from Rochester, New York. And Chris, of Lexington, Massachusetts, was not a fraternity brother, but he had lots of friends at SAE.

The boys arrived at the Wildcat that Thursday night sometime   4
between nine-thirty and ten o'clock and drank about six beers apiece. At about twelve-fifteen, they went out into the freezing night and headed back to their dorm, where they encountered an eighteen-year-old freshman named Sara who had been drinking heavily at a fraternity party. One by one, each of the three boys had sex with her. As the incident proceeded, witnesses said, Jon bragged in a hallway that he had a "train" going in his room and then gave his friends high fives, as a football player might do after scoring a touchdown.

Sexual assault, if that is what happened here, goes on at every   5
college in America. About one woman student in eight is raped, according to a government survey. 90 percent of these are victims of "acquaintance rape," defined as "forced, manipulated°, or coerced° sexual intercourse by a 'friend' or an acquaintance." Its most repugnant°

---

mosaic (2): picture made up of many parts
slick (3): smooth
manipulated (5): unfairly influenced
coerced (5): forced through use of power, threats, or pressure
repugnant (5): disgusting, offensive

extreme is gang rape. Bernice Sandler of the Association of American Colleges says she has documented evidence of more than seventy incidents of this nationwide in the past four or five years. They usually involve fraternities and drugs or alcohol, she says, and the men nearly always contend that it wasn't rape, that they were merely engaged in group sex with a willing partner.

That was precisely the defense used by the UNH boys when they were arrested five days later. Jon and Chris were charged with aggravated felonious sexual assault°, punishable by a maximum of seven and a half to fifteen years in prison, and Gordon with misdemeanor sexual assault°. All three pleaded innocent, claiming Sara was a willing and active participant in everything that went on. Sara says she had a lot to drink and does not remember what happened.

Like friends of mine who went to other schools, I remember hearing vague tales about such incidents. What makes this case unique is that everyone on campus soon learned the details of what happened that night, and the turmoil° that exploded was unlike anything UNH has experienced since the late sixties.

Four days after *Foster's Daily Democrat*, in nearby Dover, mistakenly reported that the boys had confessed to the crime, three life-sized male effigies° were hung from a ledge at UNH's Hamilton Smith Hall along with a huge banner that read BEWARE BOYS, RAPE WILL NOT BE TOLERATED. When the accused were allowed to stay on in Stoke Hall, someone sprayed a graffiti message to UNH President Gordon Haaland on the walkway leading to his office: GORDON, WHY DO YOU ALLOW RAPISTS TO STAY ON CAMPUS? And senior Terry Ollila was barred from taking part in the university's judicial proceedings° against the three because she was overheard saying, "I want to see these guys strung up by their balls."

Room 127 of Hamilton Smith Hall, where I struggled through Psychology 401, can feel claustrophobic° when all of its 170 seats are full. It was here, in late spring, that the controversy°, after simmering for

6

7

8

9

---

aggravated felonious sexual assault (6): a serious, major charge of sexual assault

misdemeanor sexual assault (6): a minor charge of sexual assault

turmoil (7): uproar, confusion

effigies (8): likenesses

judicial proceedings (8): legal events for judging

claustrophobic (9): uncomfortably closed in

controversy (9): debate

months, began to heat up again. Thanks to a shrewd° defense lawyer trying to reverse the tide of opinion running against his clients, the normally private student disciplinary hearings were held in public.

Jon, Chris, Gordon, and eleven other witnesses had their backs to the audience as they testified to the five Judicial Board members facing them across a large table. But they could feel the crowd close behind, hear the shuffling of feet, the coughing, the whispering. For four extraordinary evenings, witnesses nervously described what they had seen and heard, and the hearings soon became the hottest show in town. When sophomore John Prescott described how he had interrupted the alleged° assault, he could hear women behind him whispering encouragement: "Yeah, good answer." When the testimony became graphic°, the crowd gasped. At one point, when the defense began asking about the alleged victim's previous sex life, Sara's father leapt to his feet shouting.   10

Finally, in the early morning hours of May 7, the board found all three boys not guilty of sexual assault. Gordon, cleared of all charges, wept with relief. Jon and Chris were suspended for the summer and fall terms for violating a university rule entitled "Respect for Others."   11

It was at this point that the campus, poised° at the precipice° for months, went over the edge. Four days later, a hundred people, including Sara, turned out for an "educational forum" that turned into a shouting match and led Dan Garvey, the normally easygoing associate dean of students, to storm out of the room. The next day more than two hundred people showed up at a protest demonstration that was crashed by a group of about twenty fraternity members and boys from the fourth floor of Stokes. "Dykes!" they yelled. "Lesbians! Man-haters!" Then it got much uglier. "Look out, we're gonna rape *you* next!" shouted one. "I had Sara last night!" cried another.   12

Unrattled, the protesters acted out a satire of a rape trial and read a list of demands: the university should nullify° the hearings, make a public apology to Sara, and expel all three boys. As the group began marching to the office of Dean of Student Affairs J. Gregg Sanborn, they encountered Sanborn on the sidewalk. More than a dozen of them   13

---

shrewd (9): clever
alleged (10): said to be so, but without proof
graphic (10): described in clear detail
poised (12): balanced
precipice (12): steep cliff
nullify (13): cancel the decision of

surrounded him, linked arms, and said they wouldn't let him go until he promised to respond to their demands.

Sanborn agreed, but in his response he defended the university's handling of the affair. Demonstrators marched to his office, announced they were relieving him of his duties, and hung a HELP WANTED sign from the flagpole. After a weekend of altercations° between demonstrators, fraternity members, and other students, campus police arrested eleven protesters for criminal trespass. As the semester ended, a shaken President Haaland wrote an open letter advising everyone to return to UNH next fall "ready to examine our moral behavior."   14

Until then, I had followed the public agonies° of my school from a distance. Incidents like the one in Stoke Hall were rare, I knew, and most nights at UNH were probably filled with the warm times among good friends that I remembered so vividly. Still, each new development also triggered less pleasant memories about college life, until finally I decided that I had to go back and find out exactly what was going on at my old school—or, for that matter, at virtually° every school. In truth, though, I suspected I already knew.   15

When I moved into Stoke Hall as a freshman, in the fall of 1976, the place terrified me. It is a hulking, Y-shaped, eight-story monster, made of brick and concrete, crammed with 680 students. We called it the Zoo. It was named after Harold W. Stoke, president of UNH during the baby-boom years that made high-rise dorms necessary on campuses across America. After a tearful good-bye to my parents, I introduced myself to my roommate, who was stoned, and then I ventured° into the hallway to meet my new neighbors. They seemed much older than I, standing in front of their open doors bragging to each other about how much beer they'd drunk last night and how many times they'd gotten laid.   16

I lasted about two weeks in Stoke, then found an opening in another dorm. My new roommate was Ed, a born-again Christian with a terrible sinus condition who would sit on the edge of his bed and play his guitar, accompanying himself by wheezing through his nose. He was engaged in this favorite hobby the cold January afternoon I returned from the holidays with four friends. My buddies pushed me into the room, laughing and screaming and dancing and tackling each other. Devout Ed   17

---

altercations (14): heated arguments
agonies (15): sufferings
virtually (15): almost
ventured (16): dared to go

looked up from his guitar in disgust and amazement, wheezed, and said, "What happened to *you*?"

What was happening to me, dear Ed, wherever you are, is that I was   18
learning to drink, one of the two major components of a college education. The other, of course, is sex, and soon enough I learned about that, too.

When I returned to Durham last fall, I wasn't surprised to discover   19
that some things don't change. Drinking is still the number one social activity and beer the beverage of choice. As for sex, you want to try it but you're scared of it, so you usually get drunk before deciding anything. Thus, it's common to get drunk without having sex, but rare to have sex without being drunk.

Drinking remains a surefire way of getting to know someone in a   20
hurry. This is necessary partly because of the tendency of college kids to travel in packs. Everybody goes to parties, not on dates, to get to know people, and at that age, the last thing you want to be is different. There are also practical considerations: hardly anyone has a car. The students' universe is Durham and the campus, for at least the first two years. And on weekends, there isn't anything to do on campus but party.

What has changed dramatically, however, is where the kids party.   21
Today's students were incredulous° at my stories about the huge keg blowouts in our dorms. UNH banned kegs from dorms in 1979, my senior year, when New Hampshire raised the drinking age. Then, in 1986, the university stopped serving alcohol at the student union pub when it found itself in the embarrassing position of selling liquor to minors that it couldn't seem to keep out. This leaves just two options for freshmen and sophomores who aren't lucky enough to know an upperclassman with an apartment: they can drink in their rooms with the door shut, or they can go to fraternity parties.

Frats were decidedly uncool in the sixties but began to come back   22
in the mid-seventies. During my visit I couldn't help but notice all the new frat houses that had popped up. Today, UNH has fourteen frats with twelve hundred members. Their growing influence seems to have worsened the drinking problem. "All the drinking has gone underground," Paul Gowen, chief of the Durham police, told me. "At least bars are controlled environments where they're obligated to cut you off if you have too much to drink. But wearing a headband and marking it every time you chugalug a sixteen-ounce beer is not exactly what I would call a controlled environment."

---

incredulous (21): disbelieving

Madbury Road, also known as Fraternity Row, looks exactly as you   23
might expect: aristocratic old houses line one side of the street, set back
from the road on small hills, with wide lawns stretching in front. Several
frat members told me that a spate° of bad publicity in the last few years
over the usual offenses—alcohol poisonings, vandalism—had made this
a period of retrenchment° for the Greeks. Parties are now smaller and
more exclusive. Posted outside the door are signs that say BROTHERS
AND INVITED GUESTS ONLY. "Invited guests" means girls, preferably
freshmen. The logic is circular: girls go to frat parties because they're the
only place to drink and meet boys, who, in turn, joined the frat because
that's where the parties are where you drink and meet girls.

Fraternity Row is only half a block up the hill from Stoke Hall.   24
Forty percent of Stoke's residents last spring were freshman girls—250
of them —which makes the dorm an integral°, if unofficial, part of the
Greek system. Just out of high school, freshman girls are not yet wise to
the ways of fraternity boys. On any Thursday, Friday, or Saturday night
on Madbury Road, after about ten o'clock, you'll see clusters of girls
marching up from Stoke and the other dorms beyond, toward whichever
houses are having parties that night.

There they find the beer, and the boys. Because the fraternity   25
houses stand on private property, police can't go into a frat without
probable cause. To protect themselves from the occasional sting
operation, most frats now post at the door an enormous boy-man with a
thick neck who, with deadly seriousness, asks every girl who enters the
same question: "Are you affiliated with or related to anyone affiliated
with the liquor commission or any other law enforcement agency?" The
girls will either say "No" or "Jeez, you've asked me that *three* times"
before he lets them through.

One Friday night last fall I asked a fraternity member to take me to a   26
party, and he agreed on the condition that I not identify him or the
fraternity. We met at about eleven o'clock and walked to the frat house for
what is known, without a trace of irony, as a Ladies' Tea. We squeezed
past about eight guys standing near the door and descended a flight of
stairs into the darkness. My first sensation was the overpowering stench of
stale beer, and when we reached the bottom, I could see its source.
Enormous puddles covered most of the basement floor. Standing in it were
a couple of hundred kids jammed into a room the size of a two-car garage,

---

spate (23): a large outpouring
retrenchment (23): reduction
integral (24): necessary

picking up their feet and dropping them into the puddles—dancing—as rock blasted from two enormous speakers. The only illumination came from two flashing lights, one blue, the other yellow.

We pushed our way toward a long wooden bar with a line of frat   27
boys behind it. They stood watching a wave of girls surging° toward the corner where the beer was being poured, each girl holding an empty plastic cup in her outstretched hand. Two boys were pouring beers as fast as they could. My guide fetched two beers and told me one hundred tickets to the party were sold to girls, at three dollars apiece. Adding in girlfriends and sorority girls, he said, there were probably between one hundred fifty and two hundred girls in the house. "How many guys?" I shouted. "Oh, probably about seventy."

I asked how many kegs they'd bought tonight, and he led me behind   28
the bar, past the sign that said BROTHERS ONLY BEHIND BAR—NO EXCEPTIONS. In the corner stood a walk-in wooden refrigerator with a "Bud Man" cartoon character painted on the door. Twelve empty kegs were stacked outside it. We opened the refrigerator and found fourteen more fresh kegs of Busch, their blue seals unbroken. Two others were hooked up to hoses that ran out to the bar. My host told me that Anheuser-Busch has student representatives on campus who take the orders, and the local distributor's truck pulls right up to the back door to drop the kegs off. A guy pouring beer said they'd probably go through twenty kegs tonight.

I asked a stocky senior whose shirt was unbuttoned to the middle of   29
a hairless chest whether his frat gets into much trouble. "Oh, once in a while there will be some problems," he said. "You know, if somebody rapes somebody or if there's an alcohol thing." When I asked about the rape controversy he started to get angry.

"Everybody's singling fraternity guys out," he said. "I took a   30
women's studies class last spring because I heard it would be easy. Ha. There were about twenty-five girls and three guys. They started giving me all this shit just because I was in a fraternity. What was I going to say? 'Yes, I think rape is a good thing'? I don't need that shit. So I dropped it and took Introduction to Film," he concluded. "All I had to do for it was sit there and watch movies."

I asked if he thought the rape issue was mostly about girls having   31
sex and then changing their minds the next day. "Absolutely," he said. "I'll bet you guys twenty dollars each I could get laid tonight, no problem. But you know what? If I'm in bed with a girl and she says, 'I'm

---

surging (27): streaming

tired,' and then goes to sleep, you know what I'm thinking? I'm thinking handcuffs."

We walked back into the crowd and I asked where the bathroom was. My guide pointed to a door in a dark corner. When I pushed it open, I was assaulted by the stench of urine, and realized I was standing in a shower. Bits of soap were scattered around. A boy stood peeing on the tile floor. "So this is the urinal," I said, trying not to breathe. "Yep," he said, zipping up his pants, "just aim into the drain." 32

Later, at around one-thirty, I counted five couples on the dance floor making out. "You've Got to Give It to Me" by J. Geils was playing. Just before I left, I noticed a boy dancing with a very attractive girl. They were bathed in yellow light, circling a beer puddle. Her back was to me, but he saw that I was looking at her. The boy smiled broadly at me, knowingly, then looked at the girl, then back at me. It was all he could do to keep from giving me the thumbs-up sign. 33

That was a typical weekend night; what happened on the traumatic° night of February 19, 1987, I pieced together from police records, the testimony of witnesses, and conversations with most of the participants. 34

On that night, a freshman named Karen decided she was not in the mood to party with the other girls on the fourth floor of Stoke Hall. She was still upset about her grandfather, who had died in the fall. Also, a boy she liked was not treating her well. Karen told the others she'd rather just stay in her room and study. Her friend Sara, however, would have none of it. "Come on," she told Karen. "You never have any fun. What you need is to go out with your friends and have a good time." 35

This was typical Sara. She was popular, cute, fun-loving, and smart—she'd had a 3.9 grade point average the previous semester. She planned to be a biology major, and her friends marveled at how easily subjects like botany and chemistry came to her. But Sara was also a real partyer. It was not unusual for her to get everybody else on the floor psyched up to go out. And that night, excitement on the fourth floor was running high. There was a Ladies' Tea at Pi Kappa Alpha, a fraternity behind Stoke. The mood was infectious. Finally, Karen smiled and gave in. 36

Sara was in her room with her best friend, Michele, drinking rum and Cokes and listening to Steve Winwood. By the time they left for the party forty minutes later, Sara had consumed two rum and Cokes, and had finished up with a straight shot. Finally, a little after ten, Karen and two other girls, Noelle and Tracy, were ready, and all five headed out into 37

---

traumatic (34): shocking

the cold night. The temperature was hovering around zero as they walked to the three-story frat house they called Pike.

The basement wasn't yet crowded. Sara and Karen squeezed up to   38
the small curved bar. Each grabbed a plastic cup of beer and challenged the other to a chugging contest. Karen won. They laughed and went back for another. As the night wore on, Sara became preoccupied with a Pike brother named Hal who was pouring beer. Michele noticed that Sara was drinking fast so she'd have an excuse to return and talk with him. But Hal acted cold, which hurt Sara's feelings.

Within an hour, Michele saw Sara dancing wildly. Later, she saw   39
her leaning against a post, looking very spaced out. When Michele asked her something, Sara didn't seem to hear her. Linda, a freshman who also lived at Stoke, was looking for a friend when she noticed Sara leaning against the wall. "Where's Rachel?" Linda shouted. When Sara didn't respond, Linda repeated the question, this time louder. Sara merely stared straight ahead. Finally, Linda shook her and screamed, *"Where is she?"* This elicited° only a mumble, so Linda gave up.

At about twelve-thirty, Michele, Noelle, and Tracy decided to leave,   40
but Sara said she wanted to stay longer. Karen and Sara agreed there was no reason to leave, since they were both having a good time. They assumed they'd go back together later. At length, Karen staggered upstairs, threw up, and passed out. When she awakened she was lying on the floor near the bathroom. By then, the party was over and Sara was gone.

At about twelve-thirty that night, Jon, Chris, and Gordon were   41
returning to Stoke after their night at the Wildcat. The three sophomores were probably legally intoxicated but not out of control. Chris decided to go up to the fifth floor, while Jon and Gordon went to the fourth, where all three lived. They headed to one of the girls' wings, and on the way, dropped their pants around their ankles and raced down the hall, a favorite prank. They stopped to visit Laura, a dark-haired freshman who used to date Jon, and her roommate, Linda, who had tried to talk to Sara at the party. No one was in, so they left a note: "We came to see you in our boxer shorts—Jon and Chris."

On the way back to their wing, the two boys saw a girl in the   42
hallway. She was looking for Scott, she said. Noticing her shirt tail sticking out of the zipper of her pants, Gordon tugged on it playfully and said, "What's this?" Both boys laughed.

Before going into his room, Jon asked the girl if he could have a   43

---

elicited (39): brought out

goodnight hug, which, he says, she gave him. He then asked for a good-night kiss, and she complied°. When the couple backed toward the door, Gordon decided to leave the two of them alone. Without exchanging a word with her, Jon had sex with the girl in his room. After about twenty minutes, he walked down the hall to Gordon's room, where Gordon was already in bed. "I just did it with a girl; she's really horny," Jon told him. Still in his underwear, Gordon decided to check out what was happening. He says he entered Jon's room out of curiosity, without any sexual intentions. But once inside, he changed his mind.

Meanwhile, Jon raced up to the fifth floor to tell his roommate, 44 Chris, what was going on. The two went downstairs to their room. When they reached the door, the boys were surprised to see Linda and Laura, the girls they had left the note for about an hour earlier.

Wordlessly, Chris slipped into the room while Jon, in jeans and T-45 shirt, stayed outside with the girls, casually discussing the night's partying. The girls saw nothing unusual about Chris going into his own room at one-thirty in the morning, and Jon was being his normal smooth-talking self. But when they drifted near the door, according to the girls' account, Jon said, "Don't go in. Gordy's in there doing really bad things with a drunk girl." (Jon denies using the words *bad things* and *drunk*.)

Oh, *really*? the girls said. "We were kidding around with Jon," 46 recalls Laura. "It wasn't like, 'Oh my God, that's awful.' Usually, if you're in someone's room, it's because you want to be." Even though Chris was in the room, too, it's not terribly unusual to go to bed while two people are having sex in the bunk below you. What the girls didn't know was that it was Chris having sex with the girl while Gordon (whose activities with her had not included actual penetration) waited inside for them to leave so he could sneak back to his own room.

Soon Laura and Linda said good-night to Jon. As they passed John 47 Prescott's room, they saw that the sophomore resident assistant was at his desk studying. Laura was a good friend of his, so they stopped in. After some small talk, the girls half-jokingly asked him how he would let such wild stuff go on in his wing and told him about Gordon and the drunk girl.

"It's not my job to monitor people's sex lives," Prescott told them. 48 "But I'll look into it anyway, out of the goodness of my heart."

Prescott, a hotel administration and economics major from Hudson, 49 New Hampshire, went to the room and knocked. When no one answered, he opened the door and saw two figures silhouetted on a bed. (He would later learn it was Jon, having a second round with the girl.) Prescott also

---

complied (43): did what was requested

saw Chris, sitting on a couch next to the bed, watching. (Chris maintains he was simply getting dressed.) According to Prescott, Chris looked up laughing and whispered, "Get out," waving him away. After telling Chris several times to come out into the hall and being told to go away, Prescott barked, "Get out here *now*." Chris at last obeyed. "I was tense and nervous," Prescott remembers. "You don't confront° your friends like that all the time."

Prescott asked if the girl had passed out, and Chris said no. "I want that girl out of the room," Prescott said.   50

"Oh, come on," Chris replied.   51

"Is she really drunk?" Prescott asked.   52

Chris nodded and laughed, Prescott says, although Chris denies this.   53

"Do you know that what you're doing could be considered rape?" Prescott said.   54

"No, it's not," Chris answered.   55

"You guys are going to learn one of these days that someone is going to wake up the next day and think that what happened was wrong, even if she wanted to be in there," Prescott said. "I want that girl out of the room." Chris finally agreed, but said he had to talk to her first.   56

Despite his role as the enforcer and voice of reason, Prescott nonetheless thought the events on his floor were entertaining—so much so that he went to see two of his friends and told them what had happened. "Wow! No way! Unbelievable!" Prescott remembers them saying. "We were all laughing. It was funny, in a sick kind of way."   57

As Prescott and his friends went out into the hallway, Jon emerged from the room and walked toward them. When he reached the group, two of the boys said, he gave Prescott's friends high fives. Then he continued past them, slapping the air at knee level, giving low fives to other members of the imaginary team.   58

Prescott says Jon proceeded to tell the three of them in great detail what he had done with the girl and how he had gone to get Gordon and Chris. All three remember that during this conversation Jon told them he had a "train" going in his room. (Jon denies both the high fives and the train reference.) As the boys were talking, Linda and Laura returned, "not because we were worried about what had happened," Laura remembers. "We were still just hanging out." Then Joe, another freshman on the floor, joined the group. A discussion ensued between the five boys and two girls about whether the boys' behavior was wrong. "Someone said, 'Hey, a drunk girl is fair game,'" Laura recalls, "which made Linda and   59

---

confront (49): oppose

me a little defensive, obviously." One of the boys suggested that maybe Joe could "get lucky, too." Joe walked toward the door—just to see what was happening, he says.

Inside, Chris was now alone with the girl. She got dressed, and for the first time there was verbal communication: Chris told her a lot of people were in the hallway talking about them and watching the door. He carefully explained how she could avoid them. Just as Joe reached the room, the door opened and the crowd saw a girl walk out, her shirt untucked. Without looking up, she disappeared into the stairwell. [60]

To their astonishment, everyone recognized Sara, the girl who lived on the same floor. They had all simply assumed it was someone they didn't know, maybe a high-school girl. Suddenly the atmosphere in the hallway changed. Linda and Laura were outraged. "You *assholes!*" one of them screamed. "How could you do such a thing?" No one was more shocked than Jon: "You mean you *know* her?" It was at that moment that Jon and Chris heard her name for the first time. [61]

By now there were six witnesses, two of them girls who didn't seem to understand the boys' point of view. This was trouble. Chris and Jon decided to talk to Sara to forestall misunderstanding. [62]

When Giselle, Sara's roommate, heard voices calling "Sara, Sara, Sara," she thought she was dreaming. But when she looked up from her bed, she saw two boys bent over her roommate's bed, shaking Sara's shoulder. "What the hell are you doing in here?" she demanded. [63]

"We have to talk to Sara," they said. "It's very important." [64]

Giselle got up. Sara was lying on her side with a nightshirt on. "You okay?" Giselle asked, shaking her gently. Sara nodded. "Do you want to get up?" she asked. Sara shook her head: no. "I don't think she should get up," Giselle said. [65]

But they pleaded with her, so Giselle shrugged and went back to bed. A moment later, she saw Sara standing in the middle of the room, wrapping herself in a blanket. One of the boys held her left arm with his right arm. This must have been, Giselle thought later, to prevent her from falling back into bed. [66]

When the three were out in the hallway, Chris and Jon say, they all agreed on what had happened so there could be no misunderstanding later. Chris then suggested that Jon leave so he could talk to Sara more easily. Alone, they began kissing. They walked a few steps and opened the stairwell door. Then, at some time between three and four in the morning, beneath a window through which a slice of Pi Kappa Alpha was visible, near a heating vent painted the same blue as the walls around them, Chris and Sara got down on the landing and had sex again. [67]

What is most puzzling about the way the kids in Stoke reacted to   68
the incident is that for at least three days, until Sara first spoke with a
counselor, no one called it rape. Even Prescott, who had used the term
when he talked to Chris outside the room, insists that his main concern
was the *perception*° that it was rape, not whether it actually was. "These
guys were my friends. My concern was *not* for the woman in that room.
My concern was for the men. But look where it got me. Now when I see
Gordon and say hi, he just gives me a blank look."

Prescott is thin and earnest-looking, with short blond hair and an   69
angular face. Clearly, the incident has taken its toll on him, yet he talks
about it willingly. Over the weekend, he told a friend what had happened,
setting off the chain reaction of gossip that eventually led to Sara herself;
only then did she go to the police. But Prescott's motives, he freely
admits, were entirely base°. "You know why I told him?" Prescott says
today. "I wanted to astonish him."

But why didn't Prescott consider the possibility that the girl in the   70
room was raped? "I just assumed she was willing, since I didn't know
any differently," he says. "I saw her walk out of the room. Look, that's
how sex happens here. Most scoops happen after parties, and guys go to
parties to scoop."

But *three* guys? "It doesn't surprise me that much," he says. "You   71
hear stories about that kind of thing all the time. I don't expect it to
happen, but I'm not ignorant that it goes on. I'm not naive°. My fault was
in not going to see her right away, when she walked back to her room.
Then there would be no question. I keep asking myself why I didn't. I
don't know. I was like a pendulum swinging back and forth, and finally I
just had to try to look at this objectively and make a judgment." He stares
into space. "You know, I still can't make one."

Linda, who was one of the witnesses who recognized Sara when she   72
emerged from the room, is transferring to another school. Last spring she
took one look at the huge crowds at the Judicial Board hearings and
walked away. The next day she was convinced that telling her story was
the right thing to do; now she's not so sure. Fraternity members are mad
at her, and she's disillusioned° about the social life at UNH. "I guess rape
happens all the time here," she says, sitting on the bed in her dorm room,
wearing shorts and a UNH sweatshirt. "You know, at home, I'd get really

---

perception (68): view
base (69): morally low
naive (71): without the knowledge of experience
disillusioned (72): disappointed

drunk and black out and wake up at my boyfriend's house. It wouldn't matter because I was with friends. When I came to school here, people would tell me, 'Linda, don't get so drunk. You're a pretty girl. People may want to take advantage of you.'" She looks down at her hands in her lap and says softly, "I didn't believe that anyone would do something like that. But it's true, they will."

It was a brilliant September day, warm and sunny, when I at last 73 began to feel good about my old school again. President Haaland had called a special convocation to undertake the moral reexamination he had promised in the spring. Sara had transferred to another school; Jon and Chris would soon plead guilty to misdemeanor sexual assault, for which they would each serve two months in prison. The court would also compel° them to write a letter of apology to Sara. The misdemeanor charge against Gordon would be dropped altogether.

"Universities have thrived° because they are driven by a core° set 74 of values," Haaland told the crowd of three thousand. "These shared values are free inquiry, intellectual honesty, personal integrity, and respect for human dignity." Then he announced a series of concrete steps: to make the job of coordinating the sexual-assault program a full-time position; to publicize sexual assault cases; to improve lighting, continue the escort service for women, hire a full-time coordinator for the Greek system, and improve conditions in Stoke Hall. At the end, everybody sang the UNH alma mater: "New Hampshire, alma mater / All hail, all hail to thee!"

At the outdoor reception following the convocation some of the 75 demonstrators who had trapped him on the sidewalk now chatted amiably° with Dean Sanborn. "It just floored me that the administration got up there and actually said the word *rape*," said one. "Last year we couldn't even get them to say the word *woman*." The demonstrators, Sanborn told me, "deserve some credit for the change that's occurring."

I wish I could end the story there, when the sky was blue and 76 everything seemed fine again. But then I made one last trip to Durham. Rape crisis programs and well-lit pathways are important, of course, but they don't answer the question that occurred to me when I met some of this year's freshman class.

---

compel (73): force
thrived (74): grown and succeeded
core (74): central
amiably (75): in a friendly manner

Ogre, as his friends call him, is a short, compact freshman whose   77
boxers stick out from beneath his gray football shorts. On the door of his
room is a sign that says FISH DEFENSE HQ, and if you ask him about it
he'll tell you with a deadpan look that mutant radioactive fish with lungs
are attacking us all, that they've already got Peter Tosh and John F.
Kennedy. If it weren't for Ogre's regiment, consisting of Opus and
Garfield, his stuffed dolls, they'd probably have gotten him, too. Ogre is
a funny kid.

While I chatted with Ogre in his room, we were joined by a thin   78
fellow with a blond crewcut, wearing a T-shirt with BUTTHOLE
SURFERS silkscreened across three identical images of a bloated African
belly with a tiny penis below it. His eyelids drooped: our visitor was
zonked. I asked him who the Butthole Surfers were, and he explained
they were punk musicians, "not hard-core punk, but definitely influenced
by hard-core, for sure." The subject soon turned to acquaintance rape,
and the Butthole Surferite said he'd never heard of it. Ogre had. "You
know, those notices we've been getting in our mailbox about rape, with
the phony scene where she says no and he says yes," Ogre explained.
"Oh, yeah," the kid nodded.

Then Ogre summed up what he'd learned from the incident last   79
spring: "You don't shit where you sleep," he said. "You don't have sex
with someone in your dorm. It causes too many problems. You've got to
face them the next day."

Ogre had been in college only two weeks when he made those   80
remarks, so there's hope that eventually he'll grow up. Perhaps he will
even think of other metaphors° for making love. For my old school—and,
I'd guess, for far too many others—the question is, What will he do in
the meantime?

READING COMPREHENSION QUESTIONS

Vocabulary in Context

1. The word *forestall* in "By now there were six witnesses, two of
   them girls who didn't seem to understand the boys' point of view.
   This was trouble. Chris and Jon decided to talk to Sara to forestall
   misunderstanding" (paragraph 62) means
   a. delay.
   b. prevent.

---

metaphors (80): comparisons

    c. protect.

    d. predict.

Central Point and Main Ideas

2. Which sentence best expresses the central point of the selection?

    a. Two UNH students, Jon and Chris, will serve two-month prison sentences for misdemeanor sexual assault.

    b. Alcohol abuse, uncontrolled environments, and immaturity can lead to acquaintance rape, a common occurrence on college campuses.

    c. Acquaintance rape—"forced, manipulated, or coerced sexual intercourse by a 'friend' or an acquaintance"—is extremely common on college campuses.

    d. Students can greatly influence the policies and procedures on college campuses.

3. Which sentence best expresses the main idea of paragraphs 11–12?

    a. An "educational forum" turned into a shouting match.

    b. The University of New Hampshire was too upset to hold classes.

    c. After Jon, Chris, and Gordon were found not guilty of sexual assault, angry conflict broke out on campus.

    d. Several months after their actions, Jon, Chris and Gordon were found not guilty of sexual assault.

4. Which sentence best expresses the main idea of paragraph 22?

    a. The increased influence of fraternities at UNH seems to have made the drinking problem worse.

    b. In the sixties, when the author attended UNH, fraternities were not very popular.

    c. According to the chief of police of Durham, New Hampshire, bars are controlled environments.

    d. Today, UNH has fourteen fraternities with twelve hundred members.

Supporting Details

5. John Prescott, a sophomore resident assistant,

    a. was not aware of the incident involving Sara until a few days later.

    b. reported the incident with Sara to the police.

    c. knew that what Jon and Chris were doing could be considered rape.

    d. tried to speak to Sara the night of the incident.

6. According to the author, college students often get drunk
    a. to get to know others in a hurry.
    b. to overcome the fear of sex.
    c. to be like their friends.
    d. for all of the above reasons.

7. At the Pike party, according to reports, Sara
    a. stayed for a very short time.
    b. drank her beer slowly.
    c. was at times not responsive.
    d. all of the above.

Transitions

8. The relationship between the two sentences below is one of
    a. time.
    b. addition.
    c. contrast.
    d. cause and effect.

    When I returned to Durham last fall, I wasn't surprised to
    discover that some things don't change. . . . What has changed
    dramatically, however, is where the kids party. (Paragraphs 19
    and 21)

Inferences

9. By including paragraph 5 in his article, the author implies that
    a. he feels Sandler has done a poor job of documenting the
       evidence about acquaintance rape.
    b. he has focused on the UNH incident as an example of a national
       problem.
    c. on college campuses, drugs are as common as alcohol.
    d. he feels acquaintance rape should not be considered a crime
       since it is so common.

10. The author's main point in the anecdote about Ogre is that
    a. there's hope for today's freshmen, who have a refreshing sense
       of humor.
    b. today's generation of college students have dangerous taste in
       music.
    c. an attitude that can lead to acquaintance rape still exists on
       campus.
    d. new freshmen on campus have heard about the acquaintance rape
       that took place the spring before.

SUMMARIZING

Circle the letter—*a, b,* or *c*—of the passage that best completes the following summary of "Dangerous Parties."

Acquaintance rape is very common on American college campuses. The author feels the worst type of acquaintance rape is gang rape, considered by the men who participate in it to be group sex with a willing partner. That was the defense used by the UNH men who were arrested for raping a UNH woman. The men had been drunk at the time. The woman, Sara, was extremely drunk. After one man, Jon, had sex with her, he passed the word about her. A friend of his, Gordon, engaged in sexual activity with Sara that fell short of intercourse. Chris, another friend, had sex with her twice that night. Jon also had sex with her a second time.

a. The desire to drink and have sex is not new on campus. When the author attended UNH from 1976 to 1980, students drank to be sociable and to gain the courage to have sex. A state law that raised the drinking age changed university rules about alcohol. Students were no longer allowed to have kegs of beer in dorms. In a few years, the university found it was difficult to avoid selling liquor to minors at the student union pub. As a result, alcohol was no longer sold at the pub. That left students who wanted to drink with only two options. They could either shut their doors and drink in their rooms or go to fraternity parties. Because drinking was becoming more difficult, more fraternities appeared on campus. Fraternity drinking parties, open to all students for a fee, are beyond the control of campus authorities and police. Enormous amounts of beer are drunk there at weekend parties.

b. The desire to drink and to have sex were common on campus when the author attended UNH. In recent years, however, uncontrolled drinking at fraternity parties has become common there. It was at such a party that Sara had become extremely drunk. In a campus trial, Jon, Gordon, and Chris were found not guilty of sexual assault. Conflict over the verdict broke out on campus. The next fall, the school dealt with the incident differently. Jon and Chris were to plead guilty to misdemeanor sexual assault and serve two months in prison. In addition, the university would take new steps to prevent sexual assault. Unfortunately, the lesson learned by one freshman from the resulting date-rape publicity is simply that one should not have sex with women who live in one's dorm.

c. These days it is easy for students to become extremely drunk at fraternity parties. To see what such parties are like, the author had a fraternity member take him to one. There he saw about two hundred students crowded into a basement. Many more girls than guys were at the party. The students were drinking, dancing, and making out on the dance floor. It was expected that twenty kegs of beer would be drunk that night. It was a typical weekend party at UNH. On the night of the incident, Sara had gone to such a party after having had two rum and Cokes and a straight shot. That night at the party, one friend found her so drunk that she was unresponsive.

DISCUSSION QUESTIONS

1. Do you believe that it was appropriate to sentence Jon and Chris to two months in prison? How would you respond to those who would suggest that Sara is also at fault?

2. What does paragraph 61 imply about Linda's and Laura's attitudes toward what was going on in Jon's and Chris's room? What does it imply about Jon's attitude toward Sara?

3. Is it your own experience that college students do a great deal of drinking? If so, why do you think they drink so much?

4. What do you think accounted for the change in the university's attitude about the date rape incident? What, in your opinion, could be done to make students and colleges more aware of the problem of date rape—and of ways to prevent it?

Part IV

MAKING READING A HABIT

Steps to
Regular Reading

Without question, the best way to become a *better* reader is to become a *regular* reader. As stated earlier in the book, reading is like any other skill: the more you practice, the better you get. This is a point about which common sense and extensive research are in complete agreement.

Regular reading is a habit with many rewards. Research has shown that frequent reading improves vocabulary, spelling, and reading speed and comprehension, as well as grammar and writing style. All of these language and thinking abilities develop in an almost painless way for the person who becomes a habitual reader.

The question to ask, then, is "What steps can I take to become a regular reader?" This final section of the book will suggest some directions you can take. Please remember, though, that the suggestions are only words on a page. You must decide to make reading a part of your life, and you must follow through on that decision. Only then can reading become a power in your life.

1   Reading all of the selections in this text is a good place to start. Chances are you will find a number of them to be interesting.

2   Eleven of the selections in the text are based on or taken from books. Obtain and read the books that seem most interesting to you. Here are the eleven books and how to get them:

Alicia: My Story. Alicia Appleman-Jurman. Bantam Books. Available in paperback, this book can be found in almost any bookstore or library.

Gifted Hands. Ben Carson. HarperCollins. Available in paperback, this book can be found in many bookstores and libraries. *Think Big!*, a related hardcover book (HarperCollins) by the same author, can be found in some bookstores and libraries.

A Hole in the World. Richard Rhodes. Simon and Schuster. Available in paperback, this book can be found in some bookstores and in almost any library.

I Know Why the Caged Bird Sings. Maya Angelou. Bantam Books. Widely available in paperback, this book can be found in almost any bookstore or library.

Me Me Me Me Me—Not a Novel. M. E. Kerr. HarperCollins. Available in paperback as of September 1994, this book can be found at some bookstores and libraries.

Move On: Adventures in the Real World. Linda Ellerbee. Berkley Books. Available in paperback, this book can be found at some bookstores and libraries.

Ryan White: My Own Story. Ryan White and Ann Marie Cunningham. Penguin Books. Available in paperback, this book can be found in some bookstores and libraries.

The Story of My Life. Helen Keller. Signet/New American Library. Widely available in paperback, this book can be found at almost any bookstore or library.

Taking Charge of My Life. Townsend Press. Available in paperback, this nonprofit book can be obtained by sending a check for three dollars to the Townsend Press Book Center, 1038 Industrial Drive, Berlin, NJ 08009.

Watchers. Dean Koontz. Berkley Books. Widely available in paperback, this book can be found in almost any bookstore or library.

Why Me? Sammy Davis, Jr. Warner Books. Available in paperback, this book can be found in almost any bookstore or library.

3   Develop the right attitude. Recognize that a person who can read well has more potential and more power than a person who cannot.

Reading is a source of extraordinary power. Consider the experience of Ben Carson as told on pages 165–172 of this book. After he started reading two books a week, at his mother's insistence, his entire world changed. He moved from the bottom of his class to the head of his class, and he went on to become a world-famous surgeon. After Helen Keller learned the secret of language, as described on pages 233–235, the entire world opened up despite the fact that she was blind and deaf: "That living word awakened my soul, gave it light, hope, joy, set it free!" And Stacy Kelly Abbott and Grant Berry, on pages 195–198 and 215–218, describe how a commitment to reading was the key to their hopes for the future.

Increasingly in today's world, jobs involve the processing of information. More than ever, words are the tools of our trades. The better your command of words, the more success you are likely to have. And nothing will give you a command of words like regular reading.

4   Subscribe to a daily newspaper and read the sections that interest you. Remember that it is not *what* you read that matters—for example, you should not feel obliged to read the editorial section if opinion columns are not your interest. Instead, what matters is *the very fact that you read*. Your favorite sections may be the comics, or the fashion section, or sports, or movie reviews, or front-page stories. Feel perfectly free to read whatever you decide you want to read.

5   Subscribe to one or more magazines. On many college bulletin boards, you'll see displays offering a wide variety of magazines at discount rates for college students. You may want to consider a weekly news magazine, such as *Newsweek* or *Time*, or a weekly general-interest magazine such as *People*. And you will be able to choose from a wide variety of monthly magazines, some of which will suit your interests.

You may also want to look over the magazine section at any newsstand or bookstore. Most magazines contain postage-paid subscriber cards inside that you can send in to start a subscription.

Finally, you may want to visit the magazine section of your library on a regular basis to just sit and read for an hour or so.

6   Decide to create a half hour or hour of reading in your daily schedule. That time might be during your lunch hour, or late afternoon before dinner, or the half hour or so before you turn off your light at night. Find a time that is possible for you and make reading then a habit. The result will be both recreation and personal growth.

7   Read aloud to your children, which will benefit both them and you. Alternatively, have a family reading time when you and your children take turns reading. There are many books on the market that can be enjoyed by both parents and children. One outstanding choice is *Charlotte's Web*, by E. B. White—a classic story available in any bookstore or library.

The children's librarian at your local library may be a good source for books. There are also many choices in the children's section at almost any paperback bookstore. An excellent mail order source of books for children is the Chinaberry Book Service, 2780 Via Orange Way, Suite B, Spring Valley, California 91978. Recommended books are grouped onto five levels, from titles suitable for the very young to titles for young adults. Many of the books are pictured, and each book is helpfully described. To get a catalog, you can call a toll-free number: 1-800-776-2242.

8   Read books on your own. This is the most important step on the road to becoming a regular reader. Reading is at its most valuable and enjoyable when you get drawn into the special world created by a given book. You can travel in that world for hours or days, unmindful for a while of everyday concerns. In that timeless zone you will come to experience the joy of reading. You will also add depth to your life and make more sense out of the world. Too many people are addicted to smoking or drugs or television; you should try, instead, to get hooked on books.

The books to read are simply any books that interest you. They might be comic books, science fiction, adventure stories, romances, suspense or detective stories, horror novels, autobiographies, or any other type of book. To select your books, browse in a paperback bookstore or a library or reading center or any other place with a large number of books. Find something you like and begin your reading journey. If you stick to it and become a regular reader, you may find that you have done nothing less than change your life.

A List of
Interesting Books

Following are short descriptions of a number of widely popular books. Each of these books has been read and enjoyed by at least one of the editors at Townsend Press.

AUTOBIOGRAPHIES AND OTHER NONFICTION

Born Free, Joy Adamson
> A woman raises a lion cub and helps it return to the wild. *The New York Times* described this as "moving and incredible . . . with some of the most extraordinary photographs ever seen."

I Know Why the Caged Bird Sings, Maya Angelou
> The author writes with love, humor, and honesty about her childhood and what it is like to grow up black and female.

Alicia: My Story, Alicia Appleman-Jurman
> Alicia was a Jewish girl living with her family in Poland when the Germans invaded in 1941. Her utterly compelling and heartbreaking story shows some of the best and worst of which human beings are capable.

Lauren Bacall By Myself, Lauren Bacall
> A Hollywood star tells how she broke into movies, married tough guy Humphrey Bogart, and picked up the pieces of her life when he died of cancer.

Growing Up, Russell Baker
> A giant presence in his life, Russell Baker's mother also insisted that he make something of himself. In his autobiography, the prize-winning journalist shows that he did with an engrossing account of his own family and growing up.

In Cold Blood, Truman Capote

A frightening true story about the murder of a family, the book is also an examination of what made their killers tick. Many books today tell gripping stories of real-life crimes. *In Cold Blood* was the first book of this type and may still be the best.

Gifted Hands, Ben Carson, with Cecil Murphey

This is a the inspiring story of an inner-city kid with poor grades and little motivation who turned his life around. Dr. Carson is now a world-famous neurosurgeon at one of the best hospitals in the world; his book tells how he got to where he is today. In *Think Big*, a related book, Dr. Carson presents the philosophy that helped him make the most of his life.

Riding in Cars with Boys, Beverly Donofrio

The subtitle of this book is "A bad girl who makes good." Donofrio spent her teenage years riding around in cars, drinking, smoking pot, and rebelling against authority. She describes herself as one of those girls "who got pregnant in high school." Then, after a teenage marriage failed, she decided to take her son and go off to college.

The Broken Cord, Michael Dorris

The author, of Native American ancestry, adopts a Native American son and discovers that his son is a victim of fetal alcohol syndrome. Dorris then does all he can to help his son lead as good a life as possible.

Move On, Linda Ellerbee

A well-known television journalist writes about the ups and downs of her life, including her stay at the Betty Ford Center for treatment of her alcoholism.

The Diary of a Young Girl, Anne Frank

To escape the Nazi death camps, Anne Frank and her family hid for years in an attic. Her journal tells a story of love, fear, and courage.

Man's Search for Meaning, Viktor Frankl

How do people go on when they have been stripped of everything, including human dignity? In this short but moving book, the author describes his time in a concentration camp and what he learned there about survival.

Be True to Your School, Bob Greene

Bob Greene is a celebrated, popular, nationally-syndicated newspaper columnist. This book, based on a diary he kept when he was a teenager, will take you back to some of the happiness, hurt, and struggle to grow up that you experienced in high school.

Nigger, Dick Gregory

Dick Gregory, social activist, writes about the difficulties of growing up black and poor in American society.

A Walk Across America, Peter Jenkins
> The author decided to walk with his dog across America to find out for himself what his country was really about. Along the way, he spent time with a hermit mountain man, lived with a black family in North Carolina, worked in a Southern mill, and almost died on a mountaintop.

The Story of My Life, Helen Keller
> How Miss Keller, a blind and deaf girl who lived in isolation and frustration, discovered a path to learning and knowledge.

Me Me Me Me Me—Not a Novel, M. E. Kerr
> A charming, easy-to-read account of a young woman's growing up. The author provides a series of warm and witty stories that will be enjoyed by people of all ages.

Distant Replay, Jerry Kramer
> Whether you're a sports fan or not, you will be captivated by this portrait of stars of the Green Bay Packers football team, coached by Vince Lombardi, that won the first two Super Bowls. You learn just what happens to each of them in the twenty years after their great football victories.

The Autobiography of Malcolm X, Malcolm X and Alex Haley
> Malcolm X, the controversial black leader who was assassinated by one of his followers, writes about the experiences that drove him to a leadership role in the Black Muslims.

Kaffir Boy, Mark Mathabane
> A powerful description of what it's like to be black and live in a South African ghetto and experience apartheid first-hand.

Cry of the Kalahari, Mark and Delia Owens
> A husband and wife give up the comforts of academic life, sell everything they own, and go to Africa to study wildlife there and to try to save some animals from destruction. They describe their adventures with hyenas, lions, and a more dangerous predator: man.

There's Always Something, Gilda Radner
> The beloved comedienne from *Saturday Night Live* shares the trials and fortunes of her life—and describes how everything changed when she learned she had cervical cancer.

A Hole in the World, Richard Rhodes
> Little more than a year old when his mother killed herself, Rhodes has ever since been conscious of "a hole in the world" where his mother's love should have been. In this true and terrifying account of his boyhood, he describes how he managed to survive.

Down These Mean Streets, Piri Thomas

Life in a Puerto Rican ghetto is shown vividly and with understanding by one who experienced it.

A View from the Bench, Judge Joseph A. Wapner

The star of the popular TV show *The People's Court* offers a series of real-life legal tales. At the same time, he shares his insights into human nature based on his many years as a municipal and superior court judge.

FICTION

Watership Down, Richard Adams

A wonderfully entertaining adventure story about rabbits who act a great deal like people. The plot may sound unlikely, but it will keep you on the edge of your seat.

Patriot Games, Tom Clancy

In a story of thrills and suspense, a U.S. government agent helps stop an act of terrorism. The terrorists then plot revenge on the agent and his family.

The Cradle Will Fall, Mary Higgins Clark

A country prosecutor uncovers evidence that a famous doctor is killing women, not realizing that she herself is becoming his next target. One typical reviewer comment about Clark's books is that they are "a ticket to ride the roller coaster . . . once on the track, we're there until the ride is over."

Note: If you like novels with terror and suspense, many of Mary Higgins Clark's books are good choices.

And Justice for One, John Clarkson

In this adventure-thriller, a former Secret Service agent seeks revenge after his brother is almost killed and his lady friend is kidnapped. Because of corruption in the police force, the agent must take the law into his own hands. A review describes the book as "Supercharged!. . . A constant stream of action. . . . Dark, sexy, tough, and fast."

Deliverance, James Dickey

A group of men go rafting down a wild Georgia river and encounter beauty, violence, and self-knowledge.

Eye of the Needle, Ken Follett

A thriller about a Nazi spy—"The Needle"—and the woman who is the only person who can stop him.

Lord of the Flies, William Golding

Could a group of children, none older than 12, survive by themselves on a tropical island in the midst of World War Three? In this modern classic, Golding shows us that the real danger is not the war outside but "the beast" within each of us.

The Silence of the Lambs, Thomas Harris

A psychotic killer is on the loose, and the FBI must rely upon the clues provided by an evil genius to try to find him. Like some other books on this list, this was made into a movie that is *not* as good as the book.

The Old Man and the Sea, Ernest Hemingway

One of Hemingway's most popular works, this short novel details the story of an old fisherman and his battle with a giant marlin.

Flowers for Algernon, Daniel Keyes

A scientific experiment turns a retarded man into a genius. But the results are a mixture of joy and heartbreak.

The Shining, Stephen King

A haunted hotel, a little boy with extrasensory perception, and an insane father—they're all together in a horror tale of isolation and insanity. One review says, "Be prepared to be scared out of your mind. . . . Don't read this book when you are home alone. If you dare—once you get past a certain point, there's no stopping."

Note: If you like novels with terror and suspense, many of Stephen King's books are good choices.

A Separate Peace, John Knowles

Two schoolboys enjoy a close friendship until one grows jealous of the other's many talents—and tragedy results.

Watchers, Dean Koontz

An incredibly suspenseful story about two dogs that undergo lab experiments. One dog becomes a monster programmed to kill, and it seeks to track down the couple that knows its secret.

Note: If you like novels with a great deal of action and suspense, many of Dean Koontz's books are good choices.

To Kill a Mockingbird, Harper Lee

A controversial trial, involving a black man accused of raping a white woman, is the centerpiece of this story about adolescence, bigotry, and justice. One review describes the book as "A novel of great sweetness, humor, compassion, and of mystery carefully sustained."

The Natural, Bernard Malamud

An aging player makes a comeback that stuns the baseball world.

Waiting to Exhale, Terry McMillan

Four thirty-something black women all hope that Mr. Right will appear, but that doesn't stop them from living their lives. One reviewer writes that McMillan "has such a wonderful ear for story and dialogue. She gives us four women with raw, honest emotions that *breathe* off the page."

Gone with the Wind, Margaret Mitchell

The characters and places in this book—Scarlett O'Hara, Rhett Butler, Tara—have become part of our culture because they are unforgettable.

1984, George Orwell

The well-known expression "Big Brother Is Watching You" comes from this frightening novel of a time in which individuals have no control over their lives.

Early Autumn, Robert B. Parker

A boy is a victim in a bitter divorce struggle between his parents. A private eye named Spenser, who is the hero of many of Parker's books, takes the boy into the Maine woods to give the frail fifteen-year-old a crash course in survival.

A Day No Pigs Would Die, Robert Peck

A boy raises a pig that is intelligent and affectionate. Will the boy follow orders and send the animal off to be slaughtered? Read this short novel to find out.

Goodbye, Columbus, Philip Roth

The funny title story in this collection is about a poor boy, a wealthy girl, and their ill-fated love affair.

The Catcher in the Rye, J. D. Salinger

The frustrations and turmoil of being an adolescent have never been captured so well as in this book. The main character, Holden Caulfield, is honest, funny, affectionate, obnoxious, and tormented at the same time.

Of Mice and Men, John Steinbeck

Two lonely drifters, George and his simple-minded friend Lennie, dream of a place to call their own. This short novel tells how the hopes and plans of these two outsiders go terribly wrong.

The Lord of the Rings, J. R. R. Tolkien

Enter an amazing world of little creatures known as Hobbits; you, like thousands of other readers, may never want to leave.

Charlotte's Web, E. B. White

This best-loved story, for children and adults, is about a little pig named Wilbur and his best friend, a spider named Charlotte. Wilbur is being fattened in order to be killed for a holiday meal; Charlotte must come up with a plan to save him.

Limited Answer Key

An Important Note: To strengthen your reading skills, you must do more than simply find out which of your answers are right and which are wrong. You also need to figure out (with the help of this book, the teacher, or other students) *why* you missed the questions you did. By using each of your wrong answers as a learning opportunity, you will strengthen your understanding of the skills. You will also prepare yourself for the mastery tests and reading comprehension questions, for which answers are not given here.

ANSWERS TO THE PRACTICES IN PART I

1   Vocabulary in Context

Practice

1.	b	6.	a
2.	a	7.	c
3.	c	8.	c
4.	b	9.	c
5.	b	10.	b

2   Main Ideas

Practice

A.
1. 3
2. 6
3. 5
4. 1
5. 1
6. 3

B.
7. b
8. c
9. b
10. d

3   Supporting Details

Practice

A.
1. Women are less financially dependent on their husbands.
2. There is less opposition to divorce.
3. People now expect more from marriage.
4. People are more realistic.

B.
5. b
6. b
7. c
8. b
9. fourth
10. True

4   Transitions

Practice

A. 1. Also
   2. addition.
   3. because
   4. cause and effect.
   5. Next
   6. time.
   7. For example
   8. illustration.
   9. however
   10. contrast.

B. 11-13. First of all
       In addition
       But
   14-16. On the other hand
       For example
       Unlike
   17-20. often
       however
       example
       as a result

5   Inferences

Practice

A. 1. a   B. 6. I
   2. c   7. P
   3. c   8. E
   4. c   9. d
   5. b   10. b

6   Summarizing and Outlining

Wording of some answers may vary.

Practice

Summarizing
   1. b
   2-3. Everything you do is caused
       by internal or external
       motivation.
       When you do something for
       an outside reward, you are
       being externally motivated.

Outlining
   4. A
   5-8. *Serious problems of* the Head
       Start program
       1. Uneven quality of
          teaching
       2. Not enough emphasis on
          management skills
       3. Poor salaries

Acknowledgments

Abbott, Stacy Kelly. "From Nonreading to Reading." Reprinted by permission.

Akers, Sheila. "Keys to College Success." Reprinted by permission.

Angelou, Maya. "I Know Why the Caged Bird Sings," from *I Know Why the Caged Bird Sings* by Maya Angelou. Copyright © 1969 by Maya Angelou. Reprinted by permission of Random House, Inc.

Appleman-Jurman, Alicia. "Alicia: My Story," from *Alicia: My Story* by Alice A. Appleman. Copyright © 1988 by Alice A. Appleman. Used by permission of Bantam Books, a division of Bantam Doubleday Dell Publishing Group, Inc.

Barrett, Katherine. "Old Before Her Time." Copyright © 1983, Meredith Corporation. All rights reserved. Reprinted from *Ladies' Home Journal* magazine.

Barron, Donna. "American Family Life: The Changing Picture." Reprinted by permission.

Berry, Grant. "The Role of Reading in My Life." Reprinted by permission.

Burch, Jennings Michael. "A Friend on the Line." Reprinted with permission from *Reader's Digest* (February, 1992).

Carson, Ben, with Cecil Murphey. "Do It Better!" Taken from the book *Think Big* by Ben Carson. Copyright © 1992 by Benjamin Carson, M.D. Used by permission of Zondervan Publishing House.

Conroy, Theresa, and Christine M. Johnson. "A Drunken Ride, A Tragic Aftermath," from *The Philadelphia Inquirer*. Copyright © 1986, *The Philadelphia Inquirer*.

Cush, Cathie. "Dealing with Colds." Reprinted by permission.

Davis, Sammy, Jr. "Why Me?" Excerpt from *Why Me?* by Sammy Davis, Jr., and Jane and Burt Boyar. Copyright © 1989 by Sammy Davis, Jr., and Boyar Investments Ltd. Reprinted by permission of Farrar, Straus & Giroux, Inc.

DeLeon, Clark. "A Father's Story." Reprinted by permission.

Ellerbee, Linda. "Television Changed My Family Forever," from *Move On* by Linda Ellerbee. Copyright © 1991 by Linda Ellerbee. Reprinted by permission of the Putnam Publishing Group.

Jones, Rachel L. "The Price of Hate: Thoughts on Covering a KKK Rally." Reprinted with permission of the *St. Petersburg Times*.

Keegan, Paul. "Dangerous Parties." Originally published in *New England Monthly Magazine* (February, 1988). Reprinted by permission.

Keller, Helen. "Days of Discovery," from *The Story of My Life* by Helen Keller. Published by Doubleday and Company, a division of Bantam Doubleday Dell Publishing Group, Inc.

Kerr, M. E. "'Murder' He Says," from *ME ME ME ME ME—Not a Novel* by M. E. Kerr. Copyright © 1983 by M. E. Kerr. Reprinted by permission of HarperCollins.

Koontz, Dean. "Watchers." Reprinted by permission of The Putnam Publishing Group from *Watchers* by Dean Koontz. Copyright © 1987 by Nkui, Inc.

Langella, Frank. "The Monsters in My Head." Copyright © 1986 by The New York Times Company. Reprinted by permission.

Laskas, Jeanne Marie. "Mister Rogers," from *Life* (November, 1992), copyright © Time Warner, Inc. Reprinted by permission of Time Warner, Inc.

Lewis, Claude. "Good People Don't Make Headlines," from *The Philadelphia Inquirer*. Copyright © 1989, *The Philadelphia Inquirer*. Reprinted by permission.

Lopez, Steve. "A Small Victory," from *The Philadelphia Inquirer*. Copyright © 1990, *The Philadelphia Inquirer*. Reprinted by permission.

Meyer, Richard E. "A Suicide at Twelve—Why, Steve?" Reprinted by permission of the Associated Press.

Perkins, James A. "Chicken Gizzards," from *Billy the Kid, Chicken Gizzards and Other Tales* (Dawn Valley Press). Copyright © 1977 by James Ashbrook Perkins.

Piassa, Bernadete. "A Love Affair with Books." Reprinted by permission.

Prentergast, Marcia. "Winning the Job Interview Game." Reprinted by permission.

Rab, Anita. "Let's Go Shopping." Reprinted by permission.

Rhodes, Richard. "The Battle for My Body." From *A Hole in the World*. Copyright © 1990 by Richard Rhodes. Published by Simon and Schuster. Reprinted by permission of Richard Rhodes.

Robinson, Richard M. "The Strange, True Story of Dracula." Reprinted by permission.

Rooney, Andy. "Tickets to Nowhere." Reprinted by permission: Tribune Media Services.

Rowan, Roy. "Homeless Bound." From *People Weekly*, copyright © 1990 by Time, Inc. Reprinted by permission.

Ruth, Beth Johnson. "Candle in the Wind: The Ryan White Story." Reprinted by permission.

Saffron, Gail. "Hard Times for the Town of the Dead." Reprinted by permission.

Seligmann, Jean. "The Art of Flying Solo." From *Newsweek*, March 1, 1993, copyright © Newsweek, Inc. Reprinted by permission.

Smith, Jeanne R. "One Less Sucker Lives." Reprinted by permission.

"Taking Charge of My Life." From *Taking Charge of My Life*, copyright © 1993 Townsend Press, Inc. Reprinted by permission.

Verderber, Rudolph F. "Coping with Nervousness," from *Communicate!*, 7/e, copyright © 1993. Reprinted with permission of Wadsworth Publishing Company.

Wilkes, Kim. "Giving Emotional Support." Reprinted by permission.

Yoshida, Jim, with Bill Hosokawa. "Two Worlds," from *The Two Worlds of Jim Yoshida*. Copyright © 1972, John Hawkins & Associates, Inc.

Index